An American History

Third Edition

Volume I to 1877

An American History

Third Edition
Volume I to 1877

Rebecca Brooks Gruver
**Hunter College of the City University of New York
and
The Institute for Research in History, New York City**

ADDISON-WESLEY PUBLISHING COMPANY
Reading, Massachusetts ★ Menlo Park, California ★ London
Amsterdam ★ Don Mills, Ontario ★ Sydney

Sponsoring Editor: Stuart W. Johnson
Development Editor: Kathe G. Rhoades
Production Editor: Barbara H. Pendergast
Designer: Robert A. Rose
Illustrator: Kristin Kramer
Cover Design: Robert A. Rose
Cover Lithograph: The Harry T. Peters Collection,
Museum of the City of New York

Second printing, July 1981

Library of Congress Cataloging in Publication Data

Gruver, Rebecca Brooks.
  An American history.

  Includes bibliographies and index.
  CONTENTS: v. 1. To 1877.—v. 2. 1865 to present.
  1. United States—History. I. Title.
E178.1.G9   1981   973   80-22806
ISBN 0-201-05052-8 (v. 1)
ISBN 0-201-05053-6 (v. 2)

Reprinted with corrections, July 1982

TO MY PARENTS
AND
TO MY MENTOR
ARMIN RAPPAPORT

Preface

The narration of America's often complex and chaotic past is a fascinating but demanding task. The many months spent in the preparation of the third edition of *An American History* have given me renewed respect for my predecessors and colleagues who have put their hand to a similar undertaking.

Like most historians who have written such a survey, I have looked for patterns of thought and belief which have lasted or recurred throughout the tumultuous course and sometimes startling changes of direction our history has taken. As a result, this volume, like the second edition, includes references to what I believe are the most important and enduring themes of the nation's past: the desire for individual freedom and equality of opportunity and a humanitarian concern for the less fortunate in society who have not shared equally in that opportunity to create a better life for themselves. These ideals have not been expressed with equal vigor at all times, nor have they always been in harmony. Nevertheless, American history does demonstrate the uneven efforts of a diverse population to maintain and give expression to their ideals as well as to come to terms with the discrepancy between those ideals and reality.

Of course, one of the main purposes of revising any textbook is to bring it up to date. This edition includes three chapters on the dramatic and often disquieting events of the 1960s and 1970s. The political, economic, and cultural events of the administrations of Kennedy, Johnson, Nixon, and Ford have been covered thoroughly; and I have added a completely new chapter which includes an analysis of recent social and cultural trends, a description of the efforts of women and various minorities to obtain a position of equality in American life, and coverage of the domestic and foreign policies of the Carter administration to date.

In response to criticisms and suggestions from fellow historians, I have revised the narrative in numerous places, eliminated material which seemed extraneous, and enlarged the coverage of certain topics which needed greater explanation. For exam-

ple, Chapters 8 and 9 of the second edition have been combined in an effort to make the political, economic, and constitutional events of the period 1816–1828 easier to comprehend. The cultural history previously covered in those chapters has been integrated into Chapter 11 which treats American religious and cultural history before the Civil War. Because of its importance in explaining subsequent American political and economic history, I have expanded the discussion of the Progressive Era from one to two chapters. Chapter 22 covers the development of progressivism and the presidency of Theodore Roosevelt. Chapter 23 covers the administrations of Taft and Wilson. Chapter 24 on World War I has been altered slightly by including the debate over American neutrality during Wilson's first term in Chapter 23. The result, I hope, is a clearer presentation in Chapter 24 of American participation in World War I and the American debate over the Versailles Treaty and the League of Nations.

Every effort has been made to bring the text into line with the latest research in the field of American history. For example, the coverage of the history of women and minorities (particularly Indians, blacks, and Hispanics) has been enlarged and updated throughout the book. At the same time I have attempted to show how their role in the nation's past relates to the development of American society as a whole. I have expanded and revised the discussion of such controversial topics as the history of slavery, Reconstruction, and the causes of the Vietnam War. New chapter titles, introductions, and conclusions have been added where it seemed necessary to sharpen the focus of a chapter, clarify the outcome of a controversial period, or interpret a set of events. I am especially indebted to political scientists and the "new" political historians on two counts: for their discovery of the important role played by the ethno-cultural background of voters in the ever-changing course of American politics and for their finding that to date the United States has had five recognizable party systems. I have used their insights on these topics throughout the book.

The bibliographies at the end of each chapter have been brought up to date and a new bibliography accompanies the last chapter.

Finally, this edition includes some brand-new material. There are new feature articles: biographies of John Smith, Margaret Fuller, Susan B. Anthony, and Babe Ruth; and articles on some of the more numerically important ethno-cultural groups which made their way to America: the Irish and German immigrants in the early nineteenth century, and the Italian, Polish, and Jewish immigrants in the late nineteenth and early twentieth centuries. Two short articles have been added discussing the shifting interpretations of populism (Chapter 20) and the cold war (Chapter 28). A list of significant events and dates has been added at the beginning of each chapter as a special aid to students. And several portfolios of photographs have been included at appropriate places to help the student obtain a better feel for a particular period or series of events.

Supplements

The supplementary teaching aids that accompanied the second edition have been thoroughly revised for the new edition of the text. To help instructors in preparing for lectures and discussions, there is an Instructor's Manual with Test Items. A Study Guide is available for student use.

Acknowledgments

I owe a debt of gratitude to Kathe Rhoades, development editor for the third edition, for her efforts to achieve a narrative of the highest standard of accuracy, clarity, and gracefulness of expression. I also appreciate very much the diligence and good advice of Meredith Nightingale, who selected photographs and assisted in the preparation of feature articles.

Special thanks go to the following people for their aid on aspects of the work for this edition: David Smith, who served as project editor during the beginning stages of the work; Barbara Pendergast, who copyedited the final manuscript; LaWanda Cox, Professor Emeritus, Hunter College, CUNY, whose expert advice on the chapter on Reconstruction was invaluable (any errors in my discussion of that thorny topic are, of course, my own); and Jason Berger, whose thorough research in providing new material on American social history has been very useful to me in revising the whole manuscript.

In addition, I would like to thank the following people for their perceptive comments on the manuscript at various stages:

Hugh T. Atkinson, Gainesville Junior College
Francisco A. Balmaseda, San Antonio College
Delmar L. Beene, Glendale Community College
Victor Dahl, Portland State University
Marvin Downing, University of Tennessee at Martin
Melvin W. Ecke, Georgia State University
Mark Gardner, Glendale Community College
Claude H. Hall, Texas A & M
Linda Hastings
Clifford W. Haury, Piedmont Virginia Community College
Donald Higgins
Richard Hunt
Harvey H. Jackson, Clayton Junior College
William B. McCash, Middle Tennessee State University
Roger L. Nichols, University of Arizona
May O'Neal, San Antonio College
James Pohl, Southwest Texas State University
Patricia Presnall, El Paso County Community College
Martha Swain, Texas Women's University
Felix Tejera, El Paso Community College
John Trickel, Richland College
Patricia Wesson Wingo, Jacksonville State University

Finally, I wish to thank my husband, Phil Goodman, for his patience and good humor during the many months of work on this project. He has always had a way of keeping me from taking either myself or my work more seriously than I should.

New York   R.B.G.
September 1980

To the Student

Study of History

From time to time, Americans are reminded by newspaper quizzes and public-opinion polls that they have a rather limited knowledge of the events that have shaped the nation's past. Some people may not care and others may wonder what difference it makes. But most of us feel a little guilty if we are unable to recall basic information about the history of our own country.

Yet is the knowledge of factual information about the past really a good test of knowing history? Most historians believe that history is much more than a precise recording of facts and dates. While some of us may study the past because it is interesting in itself, most of us also want to know if it can tell us something useful about human experience. We want to know why people did certain things and what the results of their actions were. We want to probe the motives of individuals and groups in earlier times in an effort to comprehend their connection with subsequent history. We wonder what we might have done if we had been confronted with an identical situation.

Can a study of the past tell us anything about ourselves and the nature of our society in general? Have human beings reacted consistently to similar sets of conditions, or are there factors in the historical process that have made them respond differently at different times? What role do economic, ideological, ethnic, and cultural forces play? Is it even possible to isolate the factors that determine how the historical process unfolds? These are some of the questions historians have asked themselves as they examine the record that remains from the past. Often the answers to these questions are contradictory; seldom are they definitive. The lack of a well-defined answer as to what the past means and what it can tell us about ourselves presents historians with an enduring challenge.

Some historians feel that the very complexity of human life prevents us from ever understanding all we can about the past. Others believe that the failure to arrive at a satisfactory solution to the historical puzzle is the result of the fragmentary record that remains to be pieced together. Whereas for many past events (especially those in the recent past) there are voluminous records, for others the information is sparse.

Every good historian, then, must become part detective, part social scientist, part artist, and part interpreter. He or she must locate the documents that will be most useful in creating an accurate picture of a bygone era. Some of the most important primary, or original, sources are government records, including laws, reports, treaties, and diplomatic correspondence; newspapers; and the letters and diaries of the prominent individuals who have participated in events or who have observed them. Such records are invaluable in studying political, constitutional, and diplomatic history. Historians who choose to study the daily lives, working conditions, and political preferences of aggregate groups look to primary sources of a different kind: the masses of data that have been accumulated on the local or community life of the citizenry. We can learn much about various ethnic, racial, religious, or economic groups by examining census records, tax rolls, church records, and voting returns. In addition to primary sources, historians make use of secondary sources—books and articles researched by other historians.

Historical evidence, whether primary or secondary, must be evaluated critically. Historians must determine whether or not their sources are genuine; they must consider what biases or outside influences may have motivated the author of an original document; and they must determine the best source to use when there is conflicting evidence. In addition, they must recognize that their own perceptions shape their interpretation of events.

While scientific objectivity about past human events has been impossible to achieve, many historians have applied the theories of sociologists, economists, and political scientists to their study of the past. Most, however, have not attempted to develop scientific hypotheses about social or political occurrences, for they believe such universal laws do not take into account the variability of human experience. But like the social scientists, they look for patterns of behavior which have recurred under similar circumstances at different times and in different places.

Perhaps the best historians are those who are able to combine careful research with literary artistry; they are good storytellers who can present an engaging narrative that is based on a thoughtful analysis of the motivations behind the flow of events. When they interpret history, however, they seek to convey the complexity of human experience and to render judgments only after careful examination of various sides of an issue.

Historians, like all of us, are influenced in their thinking by the interests and outlook of their own period; consequently, historians living at different times are even more likely to disagree than are contemporaries. For example, many scholars writing about the American past during the relatively complacent period of the 1950s stressed the unifying factors in American history—the ideals that held Americans together as a people. In the turbulent 1960s, however, revisionist historians began to view the American past from a different perspective. Where their predecessors had emphasized mutuality, they stressed the themes of social conflict and violence. The search for a "usable past," as historian Carl Becker has called it, is illustrated by the interpretive controversies labeled "Interpreting American History," which are highlighted throughout this book.

Thus far I have described how historians go about their task. But how can you, the reader of this text, participate in the spirit of historical investigation? Perhaps you will not be studying original documents during the course, and you may be assigned only a few detailed studies of specific events or periods. But you can try to read the text critically. Rather than simply memorizing facts, you, like the historian, can try to isolate the causes and effects of important events, such as the settlement of New England, the Civil War, or Watergate. You might also try to define for yourself the themes that seem to recur during the course of the development of the United States.

Careers in History

Many students enjoy the study of history but question its practical usefulness as preparation for a future career. In the past, the question was easily answered for those who wanted to teach history. After obtaining a degree in the field they sought a teaching position in a high school or college. Today, however, teaching positions are difficult to find, especially at the college level, and this situation is likely to continue for some time.

Does a degree in history prepare an individual for any other kind of work? Recently, several universities have initiated programs to train students for careers in fields which make use of historical knowledge and training. One of these is employment as an historical archivist. Depositories of historical information require efficient management, and the archivist must be adept at finding, collecting, organizing, and restoring documents. In addition, he or she must be capable of directing lawyers, scholars, and journalists to the material they need.

Another career field open to historians is that of "cultural resources management," or, more simply, historical preservation. This type of career primarily involves caring for museum collections, planning exhibits, and handling public relations. It may also include research on the development of a surrounding community and the preservation of historic buildings. Historians interested in working in this field often combine their historical background with training in a related field such as archaeology, anthropology, art history, or architecture.

Finally, a growing number of historians are being employed by corporations and consulting firms and by state, local, and national government cies in policy planning and applied research. Here again training in related disciplines, such as political science, sociology, and economics, as well as statistics, is of significant value.

Of course only a few of you may decide to pursue a career in history. For the rest, the study of history can still have practical value. If you plunge in enthusiastically, you can be challenged to develop techniques for logical analysis, learn to research a subject with care, and communicate the results of your investigation with clarity and precision. Such training will help provide a background that is useful for success in a variety of careers.

VIEW OF WASHINGTON, 1851.

Contents

1
The Meeting of Two Worlds

The First New World Settlers   4
The European Background   8
Competition for America   18
Readings   22

2
England's North American Colonies

Beginnings on the Chesapeake   26
Life in the Chesapeake Bay Area   33
The Founding of New England   35
More Proprietary Grants   41
The Development of an Empire   46
INTERPRETING AMERICAN HISTORY
Mercantilism   48
Readings   50
FEATURE ESSAY
Bold Voyager
Captain John Smith and the Settlement of Jamestown   52

3
Shaping an Identity

The Southern Colonies   58
The Middle Colonies   63
The New England Colonies   66
The Frontier   69
Women in Colonial America   70
Conflicts among the Colonies   72
The Impact of Religion   75
INTERPRETING AMERICAN HISTORY
Puritanism   78
The Secular Mind   79
Readings   84

4
Prelude to Independence

Eighteenth-Century Politics   88
The Wars for Empire   90
Britain's New Imperial Policy   96
From Discord to Disunion   102
The Evolution of Colonial Unity   106
INTERPRETING AMERICAN HISTORY
The American Revolution   108
Readings   112
FEATURE ESSAY
To Live as Equals
The League of the Great Peace   114

5
The Emergence of a Nation

The Revolutionary War   120

Creating a Nation   133

The Confederation Period   137

Readings   144

FEATURE ESSAY
Written with a Sunbeam
Women in the American Revolution   146

6
Founding a New Government

The Constitutional Convention   152

Ratification   156

INTERPRETING AMERICAN HISTORY
The Founders   158

The New Government   160

The Rise of Political Parties   172

Readings   178

7
The Jeffersonians in Power

Jefferson's First Term   182

Jefferson's Second Term   190

Madison as President   195

The War of 1812   200

Readings   206

8
Nationalism and the Emergence of Sectional Strains

Nationalism Triumphant   210

The Era of Good Feelings   212

An Expanding Economy   217

Sectional Strains Resurface   224

The Slavery Issue   227

The Adams Administration   232

Readings   234

9
The Rise of Jacksonian Democracy

Jackson Takes Command   238

Jacksonian Politics   241

Sectional Controversy   246

The Bank War   251

The New Two-Party System   257

INTERPRETING AMERICAN HISTORY
Jacksonianism   258

Readings   264

10
Life in America at Mid-Century

The Growth of the West   268

Commercial Expansion   274

Agricultural Expansion   275

Early Industrial Growth   283

Readings   288

FEATURE ESSAY
Ethnic Diversity in Pre–Civil War America
The Irish and the Germans   290

11
Religion, Romanticism, and Reform

The Religious and Philosophical Background   297
The Growth of American Literature   301
The Arts   305
Reform Movements   308
Readings   318
FEATURE ESSAY
Margaret Fuller
Feminist, Romantic, and Visionary   320

12
Mid–Nineteenth-Century Expansion: Manifest Destiny

Origins of the Expansionist Movement   326
Annexation of Texas   329
Polk's Administration   333
Further Westward Expansion   335
The Mexican War   340
The Sectional Dispute Intensifies   344
Readings   348

13
The 1850s: The Gathering Storm

Pierce's Presidency   353
Buchanan's Presidency   360
The Gathering Storm   363
INTERPRETING AMERICAN HISTORY
The Causes of the Civil War   368
Lincoln Takes Command   373
Readings   376
FEATURE ESSAY
Let My People Go
The Life of Harriet Tubman   378

14
The Civil War

The Two Sides Take Shape   384
Factors in the War Effort   387
Strategy and Conduct of the War   393
The Emancipation Proclamation   399
1863–1865: The War Grinds to an End   401
Readings   408

15
Reconstructing the Union

Presidential Reconstruction Plans   412
Congressional Reconstruction Plans   417
INTERPRETING AMERICAN HISTORY
Reconstruction   425
Grant's Presidency   426
Readings   434
FEATURE ESSAY
The First Civil Rights Movement
Reconstruction and Education   436

Appendix
A–1
Further Readings   A-2
The Declaration of Independence   A-9
The Constitution of the United States   A-11
Presidential Elections   A-20
Date of Statehood   A-24
Population of the United States   A-25
Chief Justices of the United States Supreme Court   A-25
Presidents, Vice-Presidents, and Cabinet Members   A-26

Photo Credits
A-39
Index
I-1

Maps and Charts

North American Indian Tribes   6
Religious Groups—Sixteenth-Century Europe   11
Voyages of Discovery   14
Early Colonial Land Grants—1606 to 1639   28
The Thirteen Colonies—1775   46
Colonial Economy   61
Total Population—1630–1780   62
Colonial Settlement by Nationalities—1770   65
Colonial Overseas Trade   69
French and Indian War   92
North America—1713   95
North America—1763   95
Military Campaigns of the Revolution   124
North America—1783   132
Northwest Ordinance of 1787   141
Louisiana Purchase and Western
Exploration—1803 to 1819   186
War of 1812—Northern Campaigns   199
War of 1812—Southern Campaigns   202
United States—1822   216
Canals and Roads—1820 to 1850   223
Missouri Compromise—1820   230
Election of 1824   231
Election of 1828   240
Indian Land Cessions and Migrations—1820 to
1840   244

Election of 1832   255
United States—1854   270
Agriculture—1860   276
Top Price of Slaves and Price of Cotton per
Pound—1800–1860   278
Slavery and the Underground Railroad—1840 to
1860   282
Total Population—1790–1850   288
Webster-Ashburton Treaty—1842   329
Oregon Controversy—1818 to 1846   335
Trails to the Far West   336
Mexican War—1846 to 1848   342
Compromise of 1850   348
Kansas-Nebraska Act—1854   356
Election of 1860   367
The United States on the Eve of the Civil
War   375
Major Battles of the Civil War   394
Peninsular Campaigns—1862   398
Battles at Fredericksburg, Chancellorsville,
Gettysburg   403
Grant's Vicksburg Campaign   404
Sherman's Campaigns   405
Election of 1864   407
Reconstruction of the South—1865 to 1877   420
Election of 1868   426
Election of 1876   430

American Scrapbook:
The Way They Lived

1790–1830   following page   174
1840–1870   following page   334

An American History

Third Edition

Volume I to 1877

1 The Meeting of Two Worlds

Thursday, October 11, 1492: After sunset steered their original course W. and sailed twelve miles an hour till two hours after midnight, going ninety miles, which are twenty-two leagues and a half; and as the *Pinta* was the swiftest sailor, and kept ahead of the Admiral, she discovered land and made the signals which had been ordered . . .

Presently they descried people, naked, and the Admiral landed in the boat, which was armed . . . The Admiral called upon the two Captains, and the rest of the crew who landed . . . to bear witness that he before all others took possession (as in fact he did) of that island for the King and Queen his sovereigns . . .

Journal of First Voyage to America
by Christopher Columbus

Significant Events

Leif Ericson explores coasts of Labrador and Nova Scotia [1000 A.D.]

Crusades [1096–1270]

Magna Charta [1215]

Iroquois League of the Great Peace [c. 1400–1500]

Four Voyages of Christopher Columbus to New World [1492–1504]

Treaty of Tordesillas [1494]

Amerigo Vespucci explores coast of northern South America and the Caribbean [1498]

Protestant Reformation [1500s]

Vasco Núñez de Balboa discovers Pacific Ocean [1513]

Hernando Cortes conquers Mexico [1519–1521]

Ferdinand Magellan sails around the world [1521]

Francisco Pizarro conquers Peru [1530s]

English navy defeats Spanish Armada [1588]

French settlement at Quebec [1608]

Petition of Right [1628]

LANDING OF COLUMBUS IN THE NEW WORLD.

The First New World Settlers

Americans today are aware that Europeans who arrived in America during the period of Columbus found great numbers of "native" Americans already living in the New World. What is less widely known is that people had been migrating from Asia to the Americas since long before the dawn of recorded history. Estimates of the first arrivals vary from thirteen thousand to thirty-five thousand years ago.

Most experts agree that the first immigrants came across the Bering Strait, probably traveling on foot across a land bridge connecting Siberia and Alaska. According to current theories, this land bridge was submerged at the end of the last Ice Age and all overland passage came to a halt.

Some anthropologists believe that later travelers sailed to the Americas across the Pacific. One group may have come from present-day Japan to the coast of Ecuador in about 3000 B.C. Still later, some of the first Asians who sailed to the Polynesian islands may have come farther east, arriving in the Western Hemisphere between A.D. 500 and 1000.

By the fifteenth century millions of Indian peoples were living in the Americas, organized into many different political units or tribes. Some of these civilizations were among the most advanced cultures in the world.

The Aztecs and the Incas

One of the most highly developed Indian cultures was that of the Aztecs who had established a flourishing civilization of over five million people in central Mexico in the fifteenth century. Their society, highly stratified into classes, was ruled by a single leader who governed both civil and religious activities. Although he had advisers, he was treated almost like a deity.

The Aztecs possessed a system of hieroglyphic writing and a knowledge of astronomy so precise that their priests were able to predict eclipses and devise an accurate calendar. They were advanced in mathematics, pottery-making, sculpture, and architecture and developed sophisticated agricultural techniques, including irrigation and terracing. Surely these skills did much to make possible the existence of a capital city, Tenochtitlán, with a population of sixty thousand. Yet, it is strange that in spite of their achievements, neither the Aztecs nor any of the other tribes who inhabited the New World discovered the wheel.

Another advanced Indian civilization—the Incas—flourished in the area of present-day Peru. The

AZTEC DRAWING SHOWING THE LEGENDARY FOUNDING OF THE CAPITAL CITY, TENOCHTITLAN (ABOVE). ACCORDING TO AZTEC HISTORY, THEIR GOD, HUITZILOPOCHTLI, TOLD HIS PEOPLE TO WANDER UNTIL THEY CAME TO A CACTUS GROWING FROM A ROCK, UPON WHICH AN EAGLE WOULD BE PERCHED. THE DRAWINGS BELOW REPRESENT THE SUBJUGATION OF NEIGHBORING CITIES.

Incas controlled a vast empire of seven million people that extended some two thousand miles along the Pacific coast of South America. From about 200 B.C. they possessed a culture equal in complexity to any of the civilizations of Europe or Asia.

Like the Aztecs, the Incas were sophisticated in their knowledge of agriculture. They built extensive aqueducts and irrigation systems, enriched their crops with fertilizer, and originated the cultivation of many edible plants, including the white potato. They excelled at textile weaving, fashioning llama and alpaca wools into fabric that was then ornamented with designs dyed a multitude of different hues.

The government of the Incas was dominated by an emperor and his family, who controlled every aspect of life, from public health to the transportation of food from one end of the empire to the other. All land was controlled by the ruling family or by religious leaders.

To maintain their authority over conquered peoples, the Incas imposed their language, customs, and religion on the entire empire, and obliterated the historical traditions of the resentful tribes under their rule. The totalitarian character of the Inca civilization may help to explain its eventual subjugation by the Spanish *conquistadores* in the sixteenth century. Once the emperor was overthrown, administration broke down rapidly throughout the empire.

North American Indians

Of the fifteen to twenty million Indians in the Western Hemisphere at the time Columbus arrived, it is believed that only a few million were living in what is now the United States and Canada, leaving most of the land uninhabited. Although there were many important differences among these widely scattered northern tribes, a few generalizations can be made. First, they tended to be less technologically advanced than the Aztecs or the Incas. Second, their political organizations and religious practices were very different from those of their neighbors to the south. For example, most North American Indians believed that a Great Spirit pervaded the universe, and their religious practices were likely to involve healing ceremonies rather than the rites of human sacrifice and self-torture followed by some of the Central and South American tribes. Third, the

North American Indians were very self-reliant and individualistic, and they found it hard to develop the kind of intertribal cooperation necessary to protect themselves when European settlers later imperiled their way of life.

Of all the North American Indian cultures, perhaps the most advanced, according to western European standards, was that of the Southwest, including the Hopi and Zuni tribes who were Pueblo, or town-dwelling, peoples. These peace-loving farmers lived in dwellings made of stone or adobe (dried mud) that were built into cliff walls or at the top of steep plateaus and looked down on spacious streets and squares. The Pueblo groups were community-minded and divided their wealth equally among all village residents. No distinctions of possessions, work, or prestige were permitted among the members of any village.

Pueblo life was typical of life in most Indian cultures; religion was the dominant force. The men of the village devoted much of their time to rituals performed for such purposes as healing the sick, bringing rain during periods of drought, and establishing peace.

To the northeast of the Pueblo dwellers, in the great heartland of the present-day United States, lived the Plains Indians. Before the arrival of the Europeans, these tribes were primarily agricultural, growing corn, beans, and squash. Hunting was difficult, for it had to be done on foot. Horses were not native to the Americas; they were introduced by Spanish explorers in the sixteenth century.

Still farther east, along the Mississippi River, lived the Natchez, a highly advanced tribe ruled by an absolute monarch, believed by his followers to be descended from the sun. Like the Inca emperors, the king was both a religious and a political leader and had complete authority over the tribe. When he died, his wife and servants were killed so that they could continue to serve him in the afterworld. The Natchez, like other tribes east of the Mississippi, built huge burial mounds for the dead which frequently served another purpose—that of platforms for temples. The Natchez lived by farming, hunting, and fishing, and ate such unusual fare as bear ribs and root jelly. Two dishes invented by these Indians later became popular in American cooking: hominy and corn bread.

Other important tribal groups of the Southeast—the Creeks, Chickasaws, Choctaws, and

North American Indian Tribes

ILLUSTRATION OF INDIAN TOWN OF SECOTA IN VIRGINIA, 1590. SHOWN AT LEFT CENTER ARE BARK-COVERED WIGWAMS; AT UPPER LEFT, A DEER HUNT; AT BOTTOM RIGHT, CEREMONIAL DANCES; AND AT BOTTOM LEFT, THE SACRED FIRE OF CARVED LOGS. (Courtesy Stefan Lorant: *The New World*)

Cherokees—lived in communal villages and survived by farming, hunting, and fishing. With the exception of the Creek Confederacy, however, there was no intertribal cooperation. In fact, once the English began to settle on the Atlantic seaboard, they often persuaded Southeastern Indian tribes to attack other tribes which had allied themselves with rival European groups.

The Iroquois, Algonquin, and Sioux—the major tribal groups of the Northeast woodlands—had living patterns similar to those of the Southeastern tribes. The first group the English colonists encountered in North America was the Algonquins. Relatively peaceful and thinly settled along the East Coast, the Algonquins left the settlers alone. The Iroquois, on the other hand, were more warlike and had a shrewd grasp of politics. In the fifteenth or sixteenth century—possibly even earlier—five Iroquois tribes banded together into the League of the Great Peace which became the strongest political force among North American Indians. An interesting aspect of this confederation is the fact that its central governing council was chosen by the most important women of the tribal clans.

Many of the struggles that were to develop between the Eastern Indian tribes and the Europeans who began settling in America in the seventeenth century stemmed from their different concepts of private property. The Indian hunting territories were always used in common by all members of the tribe. The Indians were usually willing to share with the colonists, but when they "sold" these lands, they believed that they were only leasing hunting rights. The newcomers, however, believed that they had acquired complete possession, a concept that was unknown to the Indians. This led to many bitter misunderstandings. Another misconception that eventually created conflict concerned the degree of authority held by Indian chieftains. It was difficult for the Europeans to understand that it was the function of a tribal leader to advise his followers but that he was not empowered to control them.

The European Background

The second important wave of immigrants to the New World came from Europe, not Asia. While the surge of European exploration and colonization of the Americas which began in the fifteenth century was on one level an attempt to secure easy access to the fabled wealth of the Middle East, India, and China, in a larger sense it was the end product of a complex process of change that had been building in Europe for centuries. These changes—economic, political, and religious—were to shape the destiny of the New World.

The Economic Revolution

Before Columbus's voyages in the late fifteenth century, Europeans had little interest in colonizing far-off lands. The excitement which began in 1492 can be explained in part by economic changes that took place in Europe between the eleventh and the fifteenth centuries.

In A.D. 1000, Europe was divided into countless small duchies, principalities, and estates. The chief economic unit was the manor, a virtually self-supporting landed estate ruled by a hereditary nobility. All food and labor required to sustain the community were supplied by serfs, servants who were in permanent bondage to the soil and who were never permitted to leave the manor. In return for a guarantee of personal safety, the serfs were required to serve the lord of the manor.

The dominant role of the manor in European life began to decline slowly around the time of a series of religious wars known as the Crusades. Between 1096 and 1270, armies of Christians from western Europe attempted to recover Palestine (and especially the holy city of Jerusalem) from the control of the Turks, a militant Moslem power. The lure of the opportunity to conquer new lands encouraged the idle European nobility to join the adventure. Although the Crusades were ultimately unsuccessful, they demonstrated the growing strength of Europe and helped to increase commercial activity. From an interest in the cloth and spices to be obtained in the Muslim world, Europeans expanded their commercial horizons to include the Orient, where they traded food and metals for silks, spices, and precious gems.

Before the Crusades, goods had been exchanged through barter and the range of trade had been confined because of the cost and danger involved in transporting goods over any significant distance. During and after the Crusades long-distance trade became safer and cheaper. Money in the form of gold and silver coins also came into widespread use, providing the means for more people to buy goods without relying on the barter system. As a result, trade between the towns of southern Italy and the eastern Mediterranean was enlarged to include Venice and Genoa, as well as port cities in the western Mediterranean. From the Italian towns goods from the Mideast and the Orient were transported overland to northern and western Europe. An increase in trade aided the growth of such towns as London, Lübech, Cologne, Augsberg, and Bruges.

The Crusades indirectly encouraged the growth of towns as well as the expansion of trade. In order to raise money for the long voyage to the Holy Land, feudal knights often sold towns the right to incorporate. Townsfolk were able to buy from their ruling baron or bishop a charter granting them the right to levy taxes, enroll a militia, and name their own officials. The growth of cities in turn encouraged the expansion of commerce. Nobles, eager to buy new products, raised money by letting their serfs buy their freedom. More and more of these freed serfs moved into the towns, increasing their populations and swelling the number of people engaged in producing goods for trade. This further heightened the demand for manufactured goods and for luxury items from the eastern Mediterranean.

The Role of Merchants in Colonization The small merchant class which for centuries had traded almost exclusively within Europe now expanded significantly. As trade between towns, countries, and even continents grew, the merchant became an increasingly important figure. Emphasis slowly shifted from making goods for local consumption to producing for distant markets. This trend was accelerated during the fifteenth century, when the founding of new sea routes to the Orient and the Americas brought about a great upsurge in trade, especially in such bulk commodities as lumber, rice, tea, and sugar. Colonization of the New World, especially, made possible trade in new raw materials. Heavy industries such as shipbuilding and cannon manufacture were also stimulated by colonization. This intercontinental trade, as well as trade within Europe itself, enlarged the role of the merchant.

Another result of the expansion of overseas trade was a great influx of precious metals, notably gold and silver imported from America. By the middle of the sixteenth century, the supply of silver from Central and South America was pushing up prices and wages, thereby contributing to the growth of trade and banking. At the same time, a burgeoning of Europe's population (about twenty million in the sixteenth century) hastened the breakdown of the old system of manufacturing whereby medieval craft guilds in the hands of powerful families had exclusive control of skilled trades. This system was challenged by the development of new industries such as the production of textiles which could be carried out either in shops or in the homes of individual workers for a set wage. Workers filled orders for merchants who sold their products at ever-increasing profits to more and more customers.

These successful European merchants directly affected the development of America in at least two ways. First, the rise of the merchant class enabled some European countries to colonize the New World, for it was the merchants, not the government, who financed the first English colonies. Second, the merchants had made international trade such a vital part of the European economy that the New World provided necessary new raw materials as well as a potentially large new market.

The Rise of the National Monarchies

In the feudal period the lords of the manor had virtually absolute control over their lands and their subjects. They could wage war, collect taxes, and administer laws as they saw fit. European monarchs were actually quite dependent on the cooperation of these powerful nobles to accomplish anything of significance. In the fifteenth century, however, the rulers of western Europe were gradually able to reverse this situation. By undermining the power of the feudal nobility and maintaining order and safety over a large territory, these monarchs improved the climate for trade and won for themselves the support of the merchant class.

In Spain the throne first established royal power by uniting the nation geographically. During most of the 1400s, the country had been divided into three separate realms. King Ferdinand and Queen Isabella joined two of the kingdoms through their marriage and added the third when their army conquered the Moslem territories in the south.

Ferdinand and Isabella became powerful figures, partly because of the wealth reaching them from their possessions in the New World. Their heirs continued to control the Spanish throne and to gain many important royal prerogatives. Funds to send expeditions to the Americas came from their assertion of the right to tax. The right to maintain an army provided military strength to protect their colonies. And the right to make laws established royal authority over trade between Spain and the distant territories.

The French monarchy developed its base of power with the aid of a growing middle class. It was a natural alliance, the merchants supplying the wealth and the king offering protection for trade as well as administrative and military appointments. The lords were gradually forced to give up the power to tax their lands, until taxation became the exclusive right of the king. Nobles were willing to surrender this privilege only in exchange for their own immunity from taxation. Since the nobility and the clergy were exempt, the tax burden fell more and more on the middle class and peasantry. The tax revenues were necessary to support a royal army. As a result of growing competition among the nations of western Europe, the French king built a permanent army composed mainly of mercenaries. Soon, Spain and England as well were forced to develop their own armies of mercenaries.

The French monarchy also strengthened its control of the state by limiting the power of the Catholic church in nonreligious matters. Church authority over official appointments was ended and the large outflow of gold and silver from France to the Vatican was restricted. At the same time, the number of royal officers greatly increased. This new bureaucracy made certain that the king's will was enforced in every town, bishopric, and feudal estate throughout France.

In England, unlike France, all citizens were taxed. In return for their tax revenues, nobles and wealthy merchants gained the right to have a voice in government. The English Parliament became a strong national force, able to check royal authority through its control of taxation. Even so, English monarchs retained extensive powers. They limited the strength of the great nobles by outlawing private armies. They also brought important church appointments under their control and enriched their own treasury by confiscating church lands. Finally, they brought members of the rising middle class into their councils.

Thus, whereas the monarchs of France and Spain were becoming absolute rulers, the power of the English throne was balanced to some degree by Parliament. All three nations were growing powerful, well able to sponsor the competition for empire.

The Protestant Reformation

Competition and hostility among the evolving nation states of western Europe were intensified by the religious upheavals of the sixteenth century. Throughout the Middle Ages the Roman Catholic church had been the one unifying institution in a politically and economically fragmented Europe. However, in the 1500s much of Europe broke away from Roman Catholicism in violent disputes over religious and political issues. This upheaval, an essential part of the background for understanding the colonization of North America, began with one man's revolutionary protest against the basic doctrines of Rome.

Martin Luther   The initial instrument of the break with Rome was Martin Luther, a sixteenth-century German monk gifted with an eloquent pen and driven by powerful religious convictions. He had not intended to break with the Catholic church. But deeply troubled by the thought of his own sinfulness, he sought a way to find peace of mind. His search led him to a deep study of the Scriptures, where he found the conviction that faith alone, not outward "works" (such as the ceremony of the Mass, public prayers, and the Sacraments), enabled a person to obtain the grace of God. Those who possessed this inner grace would inevitably lead a good life. Luther's concept, known as "justification by faith," eventually brought him into open conflict with the papacy.

According to Catholic theology, the church had the power to dispense the excess grace which had been accumulated by Christ and the saints. An indulgence represented some portion of this additional grace, and indulgences were distributed by the church to individuals to reduce the time spent in purgatory before entering heaven. In theory, priests were not authorized to sell indulgences, but at this period in history recipients of an indulgence were strongly urged to make a monetary offering after its dispensation.

The selling of indulgences was abhorrent to Luther. He believed that the mere acquisition of an indulgence did not prove that a person had absolute faith in God's love. In 1517 Luther posted his famous Ninety-five Theses on the church door in Wittenberg, Germany, in which he stressed that only through inner faith do human beings find

Principal Christian churches: ▦ Roman Catholic ▤ Lutheran ▤ Calvinist or Zwinglian ▦ Anglican

Minorities: ✦ Roman Catholics □ Lutherans ⊖ Calvinists or Zwinglians △ Anabaptists and other sects

——————————— Approximate extent of the revolt from the Roman Church

Religious Groups • Sixteenth-Century Europe

God's grace. His aim was to provoke scholarly debate on the issue. Instead, he received a stern rebuke from the Pope for his questioning attitude.

As the debate intensified, Luther began publicly questioning not only the selling of indulgences but many other aspects of orthodox theology as well. Soon his opinions had spread throughout German-speaking central Europe, an area whose peasantry

and rulers alike already were resentful of the pomp and power of the Italian papacy. The essence of Luther's beliefs was that in all matters of religion, the final authority was not the Pope or a church council, but the Bible itself. Feeling that all Christians should be able to read the Scriptures and rely on their guidance alone, he translated the New Testament from Latin into his native German. To

MARTIN LUTHER PREACHING. AT RIGHT, POPES, MONKS, AND CARDINALS IN THE MOUTH OF HELL; AT LEFT, THOSE WHO HAVE BEEN SAVED.

Luther, every Christian was a priest, since in the eyes of God there were no distinctions among true believers.

John Calvin Another important Protestant leader was John Calvin. Whereas Luther stressed the concept of justification by faith, Calvin emphasized the omnipotence of God, an idea which led him to the doctrine of predestination. According to this doctrine, each individual's salvation or damnation had been foreordained by God since the dawn of creation. Although no one could be absolutely sure of the inscrutable will of God, a sign of the election to heaven could be found in the moral quality of an individual's life on earth. Those who led morally upright lives probably were among the "elect"—those chosen by God for salvation. Because of its strict moral code, this doctrine attracted only the hardiest and most uncompromising of adherents.

Calvin's politics also differed from Luther's. Whereas Luther was willing to allow local officials to administer church affairs, Calvin believed that the church should be independent of secular rule and should take the lead in purifying society. Ideally every community would be concerned only with carrying out the will of God and all activities would be conducted according to principles drawn from the Bible. Calvin put this theory into practice when he became the leader of the Swiss city of Geneva, attempting to turn it into a model of the pure Christian community.

Another aspect of Calvin's theology was its intense individualism and its respect for material success. Calvin taught that diligence in one's occupation, which often brought success, might be a sign of possessing saving grace. Calvinism thus had a strong appeal to the growing middle class of Europe, partly because it could be used to justify their worldly ambitions. And it was this middle class which invested heavily in the great colonial ventures of the sixteenth and seventeenth centuries.

Thus, Calvinism combined an unquestioning acceptance of God's will, a devotion to efforts to Christianize society, and a recognition of individual hard work as a mark of godliness. These factors made it the most dynamic force in the spread of

Protestantism in Europe and eventually in the New World.

The Reformation in England England also broke with the Catholic church, but there the rupture began as a political contest over the personal will of King Henry VIII. Henry wanted to divorce his wife, Catherine of Aragon, and marry Anne Boleyn, hoping that the new queen would give birth to a legitimate male heir to the throne. When the Pope refused permission, Henry persuaded Parliament to abolish all ties between Rome and England. Parliament then established the Church of England, with the king as its supreme authority. In the next few years, Henry VIII seized a great amount of church land, parceling much of it out to his followers. This strengthened his support among the new landed middle class, many of whom were wealthy entrepreneurs.

After a period of religious turmoil in the 1550s, Elizabeth I, the second child of Henry VIII, ascended the throne. A brilliant ruler and a Protestant, she brought England to a peak of power, wealth, glory, and national pride. It was during her reign, in 1588, that England defeated the Spanish Armada, the huge naval fleet which had been the symbol of the Spanish threat to English political independence and English Protestantism. The Elizabethan Age saw England emerge as a center of world trade and culture, producing the greatest playwright of any age, William Shakespeare.

In the area of religion, Elizabeth I was responsible for stabilizing the Church of England (the Anglican church) and giving it what is essentially its present form. The Thirty-nine Articles, approved by the queen in 1571, outlined basic Protestant doctrine, at the same time retaining many Catholic rituals. However, those Protestants who followed Calvin's theology were not satisfied with this compromise. They argued that the church had to be "purified" of all remnants of Catholicism, insisting that religious laws and rituals not founded on the Scriptures be set aside. Because of their desire to purify the church they became known as Puritans. Whereas most Puritans were willing to try to reform the Church of England from within, the Separatists, a more radical faction, believed that the church was completely beyond repair. They sought a total break with the Anglican church in order to establish their own form of worship.

The Beginnings of Exploration

At the end of the fifteenth century, the desire of the nation states of western Europe for precious metals, raw materials, and new markets was intense. During the Middle Ages exploration had been inhibited by superstitious fears about the strange creatures believed to inhabit unknown lands as well as by inadequate maps and unreliable navigational techniques. The emergence of the Renaissance in the fourteenth century did much to overcome such difficulties. This long period of rebirth in European culture was accompanied by a spirit of scientific inquiry that led to practical inventions of immense significance, such as the printing press. It was during this time that the Spanish, seeking to reach the wealth of the Orient by sailing west instead of east, led the way in the discovery, exploration, and colonization of the Americas.

The Spanish owed a large debt to Prince Henry the Navigator of Portugal for his contributions to advances in the techniques of navigation. In the first half of the fifteenth century, the Portuguese, using a fast-sailing vessel, the caravel, and the magnetic compass, had sailed along the west coast of Africa and discovered the Azores, the Madeiras, and the Canary Islands. Their goal was to break the monopoly over trade from the eastern Mediterranean to the Middle East and the Orient held by the Italian merchants. By 1488 the Portuguese sea captain Bartholomeu Dias had advanced to the southern tip of Africa, and in 1497 Vasco da Gama reached India and returned to Portugal with spices, including pepper and cinnamon. The Portuguese subsequently established trading posts along the coast of India and in the East Indies. Although the Moslem Turks dominated the eastern Mediterranean after capturing Constantinople in 1541, Portugal's control of these strategic ports had enabled the Portuguese to take over the spice trade from the Venetian and Arab traders.

The Voyages of Columbus

Christopher Columbus, the son of a poor wool weaver, was born in 1451 in Genoa, Italy. He began sailing at an early age and dreamed of the day he would lead an expedition across the Atlantic to the Orient. Since Portugal was the European country

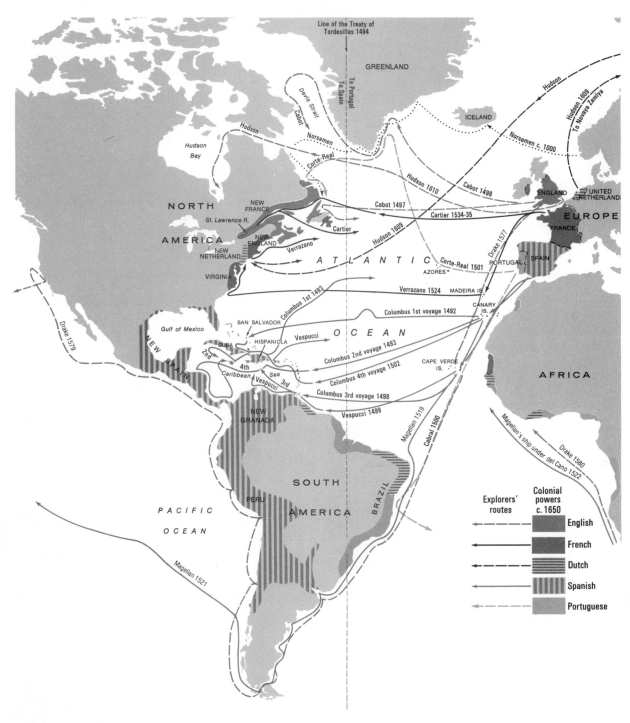

Voyages of Discovery

most interested in exploration at this time, Columbus first proposed his voyage to the king of Portugal. A committee of scholars considered the scheme and decided that Columbus had underestimated the distance he would have to travel.

Fortunately, Columbus was not willing to give up easily. He next approached Queen Isabella and King Ferdinand of Spain. After four years of arguing his case, Columbus finally received the queen's approval for a journey across the Atlantic. He was assigned three ships—the *Nina*, the *Pinta*, and the *Santa Maria*—a crew of ninety men and boys, and a budget equal to about $14,000.

Columbus set sail from Spain in August 1492. He stopped briefly at the Canary Islands and began the long Atlantic crossing early that September. After the expedition had sailed more than three thousand miles in thirty-three days, a lookout on the ship *Pinta* sighted one of the Bahamian Islands. This was the first piece of land discovered by the Spanish

in the New World. Columbus later wrote to his patrons, Isabella and Ferdinand, of his first encounters with the island people:

In order that we might win good friendship, because I knew that they were a people who could better be freed and converted to our Holy Faith by love than by force, I gave to some of them red caps and to some glass beads, which they hung on their necks, and many other things of slight value, in which they took much pleasure; they remained so much our friends that it was a marvel; and later they came swimming to the ships' boats in which we were, and brought us parrots and cotton thread in skeins and darts and many other things. . . .

Columbus was so eager to believe that he had landed in Asia that he ignored all evidence to the contrary. Every day he and his men encountered things never before seen by European travelers. His four voyages between 1492 and 1504 took him to

THIS ILLUSTRATION FROM *PICTORIAL ACCOUNT OF COLUMBUS' SECOND VOYAGE*, PUBLISHED IN 1621, IS A ROMANTICIZED IMAGE OF THE NEW WORLD AS A PARADISE OF MILK AND HONEY PEOPLED WITH FRIENDLY NATIVES. PICTURES LIKE THIS WERE PUBLISHED WITH EARLY ACCOUNTS OF NEW WORLD EXPLORATIONS.

Cuba, Haiti, many small Caribbean islands, and parts of Central and South America. In Cuba he and his men saw Indians smoking cigars called *tobacos;* on a later voyage they were amazed to see cannibals; and on another they encountered a strange Central American tribe who turned their backs when they spoke and whose diet consisted of pineapple wine and sardines. The only one of all these exotic places the he admitted might be a discovery was South America. This, he thought, was probably the Garden of Eden. But none of these extraordinary findings convinced Columbus that this New World was not the fabled Orient.

Today, the fact that many people call natives of the Americas "Indians" and refer to the Caribbean islands as the "the West Indies" is a reminder that Columbus believed he had reached the East Indies. The full extent of his error was not known until 1521, when Ferdinand Magellan, a Portuguese navigator sailing for Spain, headed an expedition which sailed around the world for the first time. Magellan himself died in the Philippines, but his crew returned with reports that accurately indicated the true size of the globe.

Other Spanish Explorations

Other explorers, attracted by the exploits of Columbus, also set sail for America and contributed to European knowledge of the New World. Amerigo Vespucci, a Florentine sailing for Spain, traveled along the north coast of South America and around the Caribbean in 1498. His glowing account of the voyage led a German geographer to publish a map of the area labeled with the Latinized form of Amerigo's name: America. Ponce de León, who sailed along the east coast of Florida in 1512, became the first European to set foot on what is now the United States. A year later Vasco Núñez de Balboa traveled through the jungles of Panama to the Pacific Ocean. Finally, from 1540 to 1542 Vásques de Coronado explored the present-day American Southwest and Hernando de Soto explored the Southeast in equally unsuccessful searches for the legendary cities of gold.

Spanish Settlements

Within a few years of Columbus's first voyage, Spanish ships were regularly crossing the Atlantic, carrying colonists to the New World and returning with cargoes of gold and silver. These expeditions were motivated by two strong impulses: religious idealism and a desire for wealth. In Queen Isabella's case, the two motives were closely related; she was a pious Catholic, and she wanted to use her new wealth to convert the inhabitants of "the Indies."

The Spanish *conquistadores*, however, as the leaders of the Spanish conquest of America were called, were more interested in land than in religious ideals. Almost every year a new territory was added to the Spanish domains, and once a region was secured, its people and riches were exploited. Within a few years the Spanish enslaved or subdued a large number of the native inhabitants of Central and South America, plundering their land for gold and forcing them to work in the mines and labor in the fields for the mother country. A form of feudalism that was still prevalent in parts of Europe at that time developed in the New World with the Indians farming for the lord of the manor four days a week and tending their own plots for two. They gradually adopted the Spanish language and the Catholic faith.

The classic example of the rapidity of the Spanish conquest was the swift subjugation of the entire Aztec empire by Hernando Cortes between 1519 and 1521. Why did the mighty Aztec empire fall so easily to a small band of Spanish adventurers? First, the conquistadores had great courage and discipline, they were mounted on horses, and they used powerful weapons. Gunpowder was unknown to the Indians. Second, Aztec legend included stories of white-skinned gods, and the Indians feared the newcomers as "men from Heaven." Third, the Aztec ruler, Montezuma, had been in power for only a short time and had little popular support among the people. Neighboring tribes previously subjugated by the Aztecs aided the Spanish. Cortes took advantage of this situation by imprisoning Montezuma and then ruling in his name.

In his conquest of the Incas in Peru in the 1530s, Francisco Pizarro followed much the same strategy as Cortes had in Mexico. After hearing rumors of dissension within the empire as well as of great wealth in the Inca capital of Cuzco, Pizarro made friendly overtures to the Inca ruler, Atahualpa. When Atahualpa visited the Spanish camp with a small group of unarmed men, Pizarro's soldiers opened fire and easily captured the ruler. The

ILLUSTRATION OF SPANISH *CONQUISTADORES* AND THEIR INDIAN BEARERS.

booty gained from Inca temples and treasuries soon exceeded all the riches taken from Mexico.

Wealth from the New World

Realizing the economic potential of the New World, Isabella and Ferdinand wanted to prevent the Portuguese from gaining a stronghold there. Although Portugal had no settlements in the Western Hemisphere at that time, it tried to claim the islands discovered by Columbus. To resolve the dispute Spain urged Pope Alexander VI to approve its exclusive possession of the newly discovered territory. In 1494 the Pope put his blessing on the Treaty of Tordesillas worked out by the two countries. The treaty divided the world by a north-south line, 370 leagues west of the Cape Verde Islands. Spain was granted all lands west of the line, which included most of the Western Hemisphere, except Brazil (which Portugal began to develop by the middle of the 1500s). On the strength of this agreement, the Spaniards extended their con-

trol northward from Mexico to present-day southern California and southward from Peru to Chile and northern Argentina.

Before the end of the sixteenth century, gold and silver from Mexico and Peru were contributing $30 million annually to the Spanish economy, which was further enriched by cattle hides and crops of tobacco and sugar. By law, one-fifth of that sum went into royal coffers, and much of the rest flowed into the European economy through trade.

The Spanish monarchs granted the conquistadores the right to draw tribute from the Indians, in the form of cheap labor. In return for this right, the conquistadores promised to protect the natives and allow Spanish missionaries to convert them to Christianity. Since the natives were considered royal subjects, they could not be enslaved legally, but it was a simple matter for the powerful conquistadores to force the Indians to work for them. When disease and overwork eventually reduced this source of cheap labor, the Spanish turned to the use of imported slave labor. Dutch and Portuguese traders began bringing African slaves to serve in Spain's colonies in the Caribbean and South America.

Spanish Colonial Government

Although several European powers were expanding their influence throughout the world at this time, Spanish America was the first important colonial possession. While the Portuguese empire consisted of trading ports in India, in the East Indies, and along the African coast, Spain sent thousands of its nationals to live in the New World. Thus the Spanish made the first European attempt to run the political affairs of a remote territory.

Spain's overriding goal was to achieve strong royal domination. In contrast to later settlements in the English-speaking colonies in North America, very little self-government was allowed. The complex hierarchy of officials originated in Spain, where the Council of the Indies was the principal body for administering colonial policy. Beneath this council were Spanish viceroys who actually ruled in the New World. The two main viceroys, based in Lima and Mexico City, were responsible for governing huge territories. The domain of these rulers, in turn, was divided into ten *audiencias* or courts of appeal. These bodies monitored the viceroys carefully, advised them, and reported to Spain on their conduct. They could also hear appeals against the viceroy's decisions. At the local level, small landed oligarchies ran the town councils and purchased their offices from the crown for life.

Competition for America

Spain's new source of wealth did not go unnoticed by the other European powers. By the sixteenth century, France, the Netherlands, and England had established strong centralized governments which were ready to join the race for overseas empires. With nationalism on the rise in western Europe, a contest for imperial power, wealth, and prestige was almost inevitable.

French Explorations and Colonization

In 1521 Magellan's crew completed its trip around the world, establishing the fact that the Americas were a huge landmass between Europe and the Orient. This discovery led geographers to imagine the existence of a Northwest Passage through the continent which would provide a shortcut to the Orient. In 1524 King Francis I of France sent an Italian navigator, Giovanni da Verrazano, to locate this passage. Verrazano sailed northward along the Atlantic coast from present-day North Carolina to Nova Scotia, but failed to find a route to Asia.

Undaunted, the king dispatched Jacques Cartier on a series of voyages from 1534 to 1541. This time the quest was for gold and diamonds. Although Cartier sailed up the St. Lawrence as far as present-day Montreal, this expedition, too, failed. In fact, the only success the French had in their search for riches during this period occurred when they raided Spanish galleons carrying gold and silver back to Europe. French ships became such a threat that Spain was forced to build a fort at St. Augustine, Florida, to guard the entrance to the Caribbean. This outpost, established in 1565, was the first European settlement in what is now the United States.

Internal religious conflicts between Catholics and Protestants delayed the next French expedition to the New World. In 1598 the Huguenots, as French Protestants were called, were granted limited toleration within the mother country, but only Roman Catholics were to be allowed to settle in any colonies that France might establish. In 1603 Samuel de Champlain led a voyage up the St. Lawrence River, and in 1608 Champlain's men built a fort at Quebec, establishing the first permanent French settlement in North America.

The French government had ambitious plans for its territories in the New World. It wanted to create a New France, an ideal feudal society with a large peasantry legally tied to the land. The duties of these peasants would be to clear the land, pay rent, and provide free labor to the landlord. They were to have no part in the lucrative fur trade.

This "ideal" system was never successfully implemented. Because labor was scarce, tenants were able to refuse most of the obligations forced upon them. The government soon found that discipline had to be considerably relaxed if the new lands were to attract settlers. By the 1680s one-third of the sparse adult male population of New France was engaged in the fur trade.

After 1660 New France came under stronger control from the French government. A royal governor was sent to organize military protection for the colony, and an official was empowered to administer justice and oversee economic development.

Dutch Exploits

Like the early French voyages, the first Dutch expeditions to the New World were aimed at finding the Northwest Passage. In 1609 the Dutch sent an Englishman, Henry Hudson, to find the westward sea route to the East. For his efforts, Hudson had a river and a large Canadian bay named after him, but he never found the Northwest Passage.

After this the Dutch settled down to more productive activities—raiding and trading. In the early seventeenth century they looted so many Spanish ships that Spain's control over the Caribbean began to wane, and the Dutch were able to occupy some of the key islands. For a while they also occupied hundreds of miles of the coast of Brazil. These outposts were convenient centers for selling the slaves they bought from Portuguese traders in Africa.

Although the Netherlands had a population of only two million in the mid-1600s, the Dutch were the most successful merchants in the world. Their trading network spread like a web over the globe. Aggressive and practical, many Dutch merchants became extremely wealthy despite the fact that their homeland had no natural resources. They were the go-betweens, buying spices, cotton, and tea in the Orient, and sugar, tobacco, and furs in America for sale in Europe. Amsterdam, the center of Dutch commerce, became the center of the world's shipping routes, and the Bank of Amsterdam made that city the financial center of Europe until the late eighteenth century.

The English Move toward Colonization

Like other Europeans, the English first came to the shores of the New World in search of a Northwest Passage. In 1497, five years after Columbus's first voyage, John Cabot sailed to the mouth of the St. Lawrence River. A few years later his son, Sebastian, explored the Hudson Bay region of Canada. But neither of these ventures produced lasting results. In the early sixteenth century Britain was economically dependent on the Belgian market at Antwerp and was not yet ready to look for new overseas markets or to challenge Spanish dominance in the Western Hemisphere. Moreover, English rulers were too preoccupied with internal problems to initiate successful attempts at overseas colonization, and during the reign of Elizabeth I far easier profits were available through raiding Spanish vessels.

In 1604, after years of conflict, England and Spain signed a peace treaty. This brought an end to English privateering and forced the English to look to other means of generating profits. It was not long before they joined the race for overseas colonies.

Struggles between King and Parliament

The idea of representative government which was later to be transplanted to England's colonies in the New World was deeply rooted in English history. In 1215 some of the great nobles and church leaders of England had drawn up the Magna Charta, a document that compelled the king to rule with their "common counsel." In 1265 members of the middle class joined with these two groups to form the first Parliament. The power of Parliament grew steadily, and in the mid-1300s it was formally divided into two houses, the hereditary House of Lords and the elected House of Commons.

By the sixteenth century monarchs of the Tudor family were relying on the approval of Parliament for most major decisions. However, the Stuart family, which came to the throne in 1603, claimed to rule by "divine right" with no parliamentary restrictions. Whenever the first of the Stuarts, James I, was unable to get the House of Commons to provide him with the tax money he wanted, he became so enraged that he dissolved the session.

The greatest power possessed by the House of Commons was its control of the government's purse strings. This power was reaffirmed in 1628 when Charles I, son of James I, accepted the Petition of Right, which asserted that "no man hereafter be compelled to make or yield any gift, loan, benev-

A VIEW OF A SESSION OF
PARLIAMENT UNDER
QUEEN ELIZABETH I.

A Heritage of Representation in Government

"12. No scutage or aid shall be imposed on our kingdom, unless by common counsel of our kingdom, except for ransoming our person, for making of our oldest son a knight, and for once marrying our eldest daughter, and for these purposes there shall not be levied more than a reasonable aid. . . .

14. And for obtaining the common counsel of the kingdom, a rent, the assessment of an aid (except in the three cases aforesaid) or of a scutage, we will cause to be summoned the archbishops, bishops, abbots, earls and greater barons severally by our letters; and we will moreover cause to be summoned generally through our sheriffs and bailiffs, all others who hold of us in chief, . . .

38. No Bailiff for the future shall, upon his own unsupported complaint, put anyone to his "law," without credible witnesses brought for this purpose.

39. No freeman shall be taken or imprisoned or disseised, or exiled or in any way destroyed, nor will we go upon him nor send upon him, except by the lawful judgment of his peers or by the law of the land.

40. To no one will we sell, to no one will we refuse or delay, right or justice."

Magna Charta, 1215

The Divine Right of Kings

"Kings are justly called Gods, for that they exercise a manner or resemblance of Divine power upon earth: For if you will consider the Attributes of God, you shall see how they agree in the person of a King. God hath power to create, or destroy, make, or unmake at his pleasure, to give life, or send death, to judge all, and to be judged nor accomptable to none; To raise low things, and to make high things low at his pleasure, and to God are both soule and body due. And the like power have Kings: They make and unmake their subjects: they have power of raising and casting downe, of life and death; judges over all their subjects, and in all causes and yet accomptable to none but God onely. . . . "

The Political Works of James I, 1609

olence, tax or such like charge, without common consent by Act of Parliament." In practice, this meant that although Parliament might be dissolved or ignored, it would eventually have to be reconvened if a monarch hoped to obtain revenues. The Petition of Right was an important forerunner of the idea that "taxation without representation is tyranny," one of the earliest slogans of the American Revolution.

Nevertheless, after signing the petition, Charles I tried to reign without Parliament. From 1629 to 1640 he not only defied the Petition of Right, but also tried to stamp out the Puritan influence in the Anglican church. When he failed to force his religious views on Scotland, he had to call on Parlia-

ment to obtain revenues for his army. Because the king was unwilling to allow Parliament to control taxation completely and to regulate the church, a parliamentary session took steps to raise its own army in May 1641. The two armies met in the English Civil War, the king was imprisoned, and, to the horror of the crowned heads of Europe, he was beheaded in 1649.

Economic and Religious Factors in Colonization

While the king and Parliament struggled for control of the purse strings in early seventeenth-century England, enterprising merchants were undeterred in their efforts to find new markets for trade and investment. By the mid-1500s the European demand for British woolens had fallen off and the merchant class which had capital available for investment began to seek alternative markets, including the establishment of colonies overseas. The crown gave legal sanction to exploration and settlement, but from the beginning the influence of private capital was predominant in the colonization of North America.

The first American colonies were financed by a new form of business organization known as the joint-stock company. These companies, like the modern corporation, pooled the capital of a number of investors who expected to make a quick profit from the venture. Since each investor bought only a small share of the company, the risk was not substantial in any one enterprise; for this reason joint-stock companies became an attractive source of investment. Backed by the joint-stock companies English immigrants brought with them to the New World the spirit of early seventeenth-century capitalism. Moreover, the fact that the joint-stock companies were self-governing aided the early establishment of a form of local self-government in the English colonies.

Economic distress as well as economic opportunities influenced English colonization. The enclo-sure of grazing land for the growing sheepherding industry ruined many small farmers and drove them into the cities. As the population of the cities swelled and unemployment rose, bands of unemployed laborers turned to begging or thievery. These homeless and discontented laborers made up a large percentage of the emigrants to the New World. Others who left England in search of new economic opportunities were the second sons of the country gentry who could not inherit their fathers' estates under English law. There were even a few nobles among the emigrants, pushed aside by the aggressive merchant class.

Many English colonists also came to the New World to escape religious persecution. Some moved to the Netherlands, which tolerated a variety of Protestant sects. But life in Holland was difficult, and in 1620 a group later known as the Pilgrims set sail for the New World. Ten years later they were followed by the Puritans who brought with them the same religious zeal which had characterized their movement since Elizabethan times. In subsequent decades other religious groups fled to North America to escape religious persecution in England and in various parts of Europe.

Readings

General Works

Bainton, Roland, *The Age of the Reformation*. New York: D. Van Nostrand, 1956.

Brebner, J. B., *The Explorers of North America, 1492–1806*. New York: Macmillan, 1933.

Cheyney, E. P., *The Dawn of a New Era*. New York: Harper & Row, 1936 (Paper: Harper Torch Books, 1962).

Chiapelli, Fredi, *et al.* (Eds.), *First Images of America: The Impact of the New World on the Old*. 2 vols. Berkeley and Los Angeles: University of California Press, 1976.

Debo, Angie, *A History of the Indians of the United States*. Norman, Okla: University of Oklahoma Press, 1970.

Driver, Harold E., *Indians of North America*. Chicago: University of Chicago Press, 1961 (Paper, 1964).

Farb, Peter, *Man's Rise to Civilization: The Cultural Ascent of the Indians of North America*. New York: E.P. Dutton, 1978.

Ferguson, Wallace K., *Europe in Transition, 1300–1520*. Boston: Houghton Mifflin, 1962.

Gibson, Charles, *Spain in America*. New York: Harper & Row, 1966.

Josephy, Alvin M., Jr., *Indian Heritage of America*. New York: Bantam Books, 1969. (Paper)

McNeill, William H., *The Rise of the West*. Chicago: University of Chicago Press, 1963.

Nowell, Charles E., *The Great Discoveries and the First Colonial Empires*. Ithaca, N.Y.: Cornell University Press, 1954.

Washburn, Wilcomb E., *The Indian in America*. New York: Harper & Row, 1975.

Wright, Louis B., *Gold, Glory & the Gospel: The Adventurous Lives & Times of the Renaissance Explorers*. New York: Atheneum Publishers, 1970.

Special Studies

Bindoff, S. T., *Tudor England*. Baltimore, Md.: Penguin, 1950.

Boxer, C. R., *The Dutch Seaborne Empire: 1600–1800*. New York: Knopf, 1965.

Bridenbaugh, Carl, *Vexed and Troubled Englishmen, 1590–1642*. New York: Oxford University Press, 1968.

Coe, Michael D., *Mexico*. New York: Praeger, 1962.

Elton, G. R., *England Under the Tudors*. New York: Barnes & Noble, 1955.

Hemming, John, *The Conquest of the Incas*. New York: Harcourt Brace Jovanovich, 1970.

Jones, Gwyn, *A History of the Vikings*. New York: Oxford University Press, 1968.

Mattingly, Garrett, *The Armada*. Boston: Houghton Mifflin, 1959 (Paper: Sentry Edition, 1962).

Morison, Samuel E., *The European Discovery of America: The Northern Voyages*. New York: Oxford University Press, 1971.

_____, *The European Discovery of America: The Southern Voyages*. New York: Oxford University Press, 1974.

Parkman, Francis, *Pioneers of France in the New World*. Boston: Little, Brown, 1900.

Powicke, F. Maurice, *The Reformation in England*. New York: Oxford University Press, 1961.

Prescott, William H., *Prescott's Histories: The Rise and Decline of the Spanish Empire*. Edited by Irwin R. Blacker. New York: Viking, 1963.

Quinn, David B., *England and the Discovery of America, 1481–1620*. New York: Knopf, 1974.

Rowse, A. L., *The England of Elizabeth*. New York: Macmillan, 1961.

Simpson, Alan, *Puritanism in Old and New England*. Chicago: University of Chicago Press, 1955 (Paper: Phoenix Books, 1961).

Weber, Max, *The Protestant Ethic and the Spirit of Capitalism*. New York: Scribner's, 1958.

Primary Sources

Diaz del Castillo, Bernal, *The Discovery and Conquest of Mexico*. Edited by Genaro Garcia. Translated by A. P. Maudslay. New York: Farrar, Straus & Cudahy, 1956 (Paper: Farrar, Straus and Giroux, 1965).

Komroff, Manuel (Ed.), *The Travels of Marco Polo*. New York: Random House, 1953.

Leon-Portilla, M., *The Broken Spears: The Aztec Account of the Conquest of Mexico*. Boston: Beacon Press, 1962.

Viereck, Philip (Ed.), *The New Land*. New York: John Day, 1967.

Biographies

Bainton, Roland, *Here I Stand*. New York: Abingdon, 1950 (Paper: New American Library, 1955).

Hackett, Francis, *The Personal History of Henry VIII*. New York: Modern Library, 1945.

Morison, S. E., *Admiral of the Ocean Sea*. Boston: Atlantic Monthly-Little, Brown, 1942.

Neale, J. E., *Queen Elizabeth*. London: Jonathan Cape, 1935 (Paper: Doubleday Anchor, 1957).

Rowse, A. L., *Sir Walter Raleigh: His Family and Private Life*. New York: Harper & Row, 1964.

Williamson, J. A., *Sir Francis Drake*. New York: Macmillan, 1962.

Historical Novels

Cather, Willa, *Shadows on the Rock*. New York: Knopf, 1931.

Forester, C. S., *To the Indies*. Boston: Little, Brown, 1940.

Hugo, Victor, *Notre Dame de Paris*. New York: Modern Library, 1941.

Kingsley, Charles, *Westward Ho!* New York: Airmont, 1968.

Scott, Walter, *Kenilworth*. New York: Airmont, 1968.

_____, *Quentin Durward*. New American Library, 1963.

Shellabarger, Samuel, *Captain from Castile*. Boston: Little, Brown, 1945.

Shute, Nevil, *An Old Captivity*. New York: Morrow, 1940.

2 England's North American Colonies

The mildness of the aire, the fertilitie of the soile, and the situation of the rivers are so propitious to the nature and use of man as no place is more convenient for pleasure, profit, and mans sustenance. . . . The waters, Isles, and shoales, are full of safe harbours for ships of warre or marchandize, for boats of all sortes, for transportation or fishing, etc. The Bay and rivers have much marchandable fish and places for Salt coats, building of ships, making of iron, etc.

Captain John Smith,
Narratives of Early Virginia

Significant Events

Jamestown, Virginia, settled by English [1607]

First meeting of House of Burgesses [1619]

Mayflower Compact [1620]

Pilgrims settle at Plymouth, Massachusetts [1620]

Virginia becomes first royal colony [1624]

Puritans begin settlement of colony of Massachusetts [1629]

Rhode Island settled by Roger Williams [1636]

Fundamental Orders of Connecticut [1639]

Confederation of New England [1643]

Maryland Toleration Act [1649]

Proprietary grant of Carolinas [1663]

England takes colony of New Amsterdam from Dutch [1664]

King Philip's War [1675]

Bacon's Rebellion [1676]

British Navigation Acts [1660–1696]

Proprietary grant of Pennsylvania to William Penn [1681]

Dominion of New England [1686–1688]

The Glorious Revolution in England [1688]

Georgia settled [1732]

THE ENGLISH ARRIVE AT ROANOKE, VIRGINIA, IN 1585.
(Courtesy Stefan Lorant: *The New World*)

At the beginning of the seventeenth century there were no English colonies anywhere in the world. This situation would soon be remedied. In 1582 the English geographer and scholar Richard Hakuylt had argued that England must enter the competition for colonies first in order to spread Christianity, and second to establish a place from which to attack the Spanish. Moreover, he had stressed that colonies could provide England with a source of raw materials and a market for the sale of its products, as well as a new start for young, ablebodied youths who were unemployed at home.

We read that the bees, when they grow to be too many in their own hive at home, are wont to be led out by their captains to swarm abroad and seek themselves a new dwelling place . . . if we would behold . . . how all our prisons are pestered and filled with able men to serve their country, which for small robberies are daily hanged up in great numbers . . . we would hasten and further . . . the deducting of some colonies of our superfluous people into those temperate and fertile parts of America. . . .*

Those who actually risked the long and hazardous ocean voyage to the New World in the seventeenth century came for a variety of reasons. Soldiers of fortune came to find wealth. Poor farmers came to improve their economic position. Religious dissenters came looking for a place where they could live and worship freely. Few of the colonists had the remotest notion of what life would be like in this distant land.

England's first attempts to establish colonies in the New World had gone badly. The efforts of explorers Sir Humphrey Gilbert and Sir Walter Raleigh in the 1580s had ended in disaster. Indeed, the last colony founded by Raleigh on Roanoke Island vanished without a trace, leaving a mystery which has never been solved.

These early failures were warnings. Colonizing the New World would prove to be a difficult and often frightening undertaking. In some cases the barest essentials of life would have to be eked out of a grudging land, and the process of establishing a stable, well-organized society would be slow. Considering the hardships the colonists would face, it is amazing that by the end of the seventeenth century a quarter of a million settlers had finally established themselves along the Atlantic seaboard.

Beginnings on the Chesapeake

In 1604 James I of England signed a peace treaty with Spain which brought his people twenty years of security. The nation prospered, and the colonization effort, abandoned since the earlier failures, began again.

The king himself had little interest in the founding of colonies, which was sponsored chiefly by merchants in quest of profits. But the king's advisors had considerable interest. In fact, many members of his Privy Council had invested in the joint-stock companies that financed the first American colonies.

In 1606 two joint-stock companies petitioned the English king for a charter to settle Virginia (the English name for the area of the Atlantic seaboard stretching from Maine to Florida). The king granted their petitions, giving the Virginia Company of

Plymouth the northern half and the Virginia Company of London the southern half.

A False Start in Maine

The Plymouth Company's activities were short-lived. After sending two ships to explore the coast, the company dispatched 120 men who landed on the coast of the present state of Maine in August 1607. They chose a place for their settlement, or "plantation," and spent the next two months building a fort and trying to establish friendly relations with the Indians. Unfortunately, the president of the plantation lacked the qualities of leadership the situation demanded, and the colonists soon began quarreling among themselves. The Indians lost respect for their new neighbors and refused to trade with them. A bitter cold winter shattered their expectations of a temperate climate, several important members of

*Richard Hakluyt, Preface from Divers Voyages touching the Discovery of America, *1582*

the expedition died, and a fire destroyed their storehouse and other buildings. The colonists packed their belongings and returned to England.

The Settlement of Jamestown

The London Company settlement met with even greater hardship but endured to become the first successful English colony. In December 1606, 140 men and four boys set sail from England. When they arrived in Virginia in May 1607, thirty-nine had died at sea and Captain John Smith, the military officer for the expedition, had been thrown in the brig for mutinous grumblings.

The goals of the Jamestown settlers were primarily commercial: to discover a passage through the mainland of North America to the fabled riches of the Orient, to trade with the Indians, and to mine gold, copper, and iron for sale in England. Largely because of their inexperience, however, the colonists were beset by troubles from the beginning. The site they chose for establishing a fort proved to be a swampy breeding ground for malaria located far from fresh water. The settlers had selected it because it appeared to be secure from marauding Indians. Yet within only days of their arrival, they were set upon; seventeen men were wounded and one boy was killed.

Almost half the Jamestown settlers were English gentlemen. Unaccustomed to physical labor and interested almost exclusively in turning a quick profit, they chose to mine the gold of Virginia rather than to plant a crop for the coming winter. "No talk, no hope, nor work," wrote Captain John Smith

A SKETCH OF THE SPREADING JAMESTOWN COLONY MADE BY A DUTCH VISITOR.

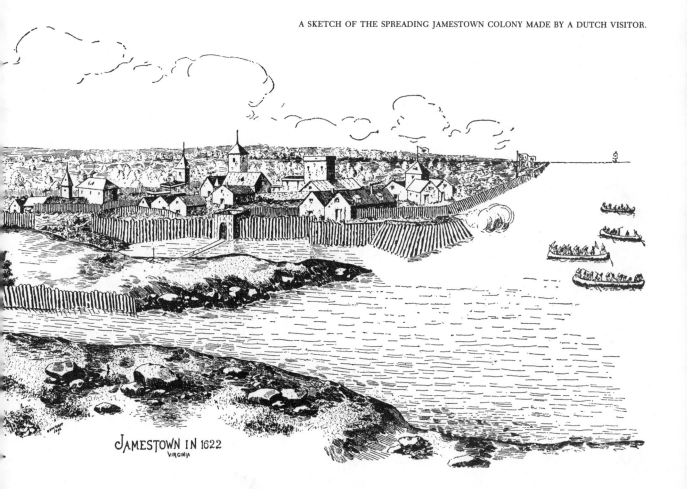

JAMESTOWN IN 1622
VIRGINIA

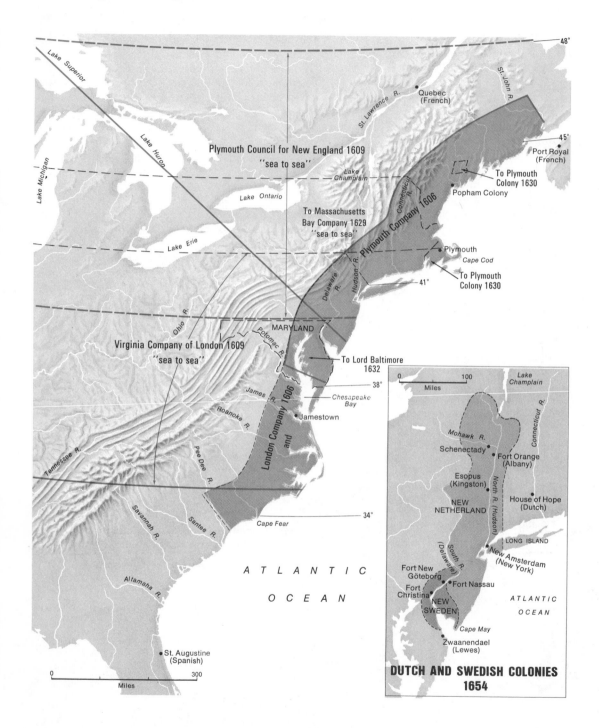

Early Colonial Land Grants • 1606 to 1639

IN HIS WRITINGS JOHN SMITH RELATED A DRAMATIC EPISODE IN WHICH THE INDIAN MAIDEN POCAHONTAS INTERCEDED FOR HIS LIFE AS HE WAS ABOUT TO BE CLUBBED TO DEATH BY HIS INDIAN CAPTORS. WHILE IT IS UNLIKELY THAT SMITH'S TALE IS FACTUAL, IT IS TRUE THAT POCHAHONTAS DID MUCH TO KEEP PEACE BETWEEN THE INDIANS AND THE JAMESTOWN COLONISTS.

in despair, "but dig gold, wash gold, refine gold, load gold." In the end Virginia's "gold" turned out to be a commonplace mineral called iron pyrite.

By the autumn of 1607, half the settlers had died, and as winter set in, more and more of them perished from disease and starvation. It was only with the help of the friendly Powhatan Indians that a few were enabled to survive. As one early settler wrote:

It pleased God, after a while, to send those people which were our mortal enemies to relieve us with victuals, as bread, corn, fish and flesh in great plenty, which was the setting up of our feeble men, otherwise we had all perished. Also, we were frequented by diverse kings in the country, bringing us store of provision to our great comfort.

Even so, in January 1608, when a ship finally arrived from England bringing supplies and 120 new settlers, there were only thirty-eight colonists left to receive them.

It is likely that without the help of the Indians through the first difficult years the Jamestown settlement might not have lasted any longer than the ill-fated plantation in Maine. The Indians not only brought the settlers food when they would have

perished without it, they also taught them many of the skills they needed to survive in their new environment, including how to clear the forests for farm land and how to grow new crops such as corn and yams. Unfortunately, the settlers did not reciprocate this kindness. When they began to appreciate the excellent quality of the Indian land, they simply appropriated it for their own use—by force if necessary. As a result, relations with the Indians began to deteriorate. Faced with the threat of a debilitating struggle with the Indians, the colonists finally came to realize that if they were to survive in the New World they must learn to become self-sufficient.

Jamestown's Early Years The winter of 1608–1609 was much better: only twelve people died and the colony began to prosper. This improvement was due to the leadership of the indomitable John Smith, who was elected president of the resident council in September 1608. Smith immediately called a halt to the search for gold and saw to it that buildings were repaired, crops planted, livestock nurtured, and slackers punished. Through his reasonably fair-minded approach to the Indians, he helped improve relations. It was even rumored that he wanted to marry the Indian princess Pocahontas and make

Virginia's "Starving Time"

"This was that time, which still to this day we called the starving time; it were too vile to say, and scarce to be believed, what we endured: but the occasion was our own, for want of providence industry and government, and not the barrenness and defect of the Country, as is generally supposed; for till then in three years, for the numbers were landed us, we had never from England provision sufficient for six months, though it seemed by the bills of loading sufficient was sent us, such a glutton is the Sea, and such good fellows the Mariners; we as little tasted of the great proportion sent us, as they of our want and miseries. . . ."

Captain John Smith,
*The Generall Historie of Virginia, 1624;
The Fourth Booke*

The Pilgrim's Trial

"But here I cannot but stay and make a pause, and stand half amazed at this poor people's present condition; and so I think will the reader too, when he well considers the same. Being thus passed the vast ocean, and a sea of troubles before in their preparation . . . they had now no friends to welcome them, nor inns to entertain or refresh their weatherbeaten bodies, no houses or much less towns to repair to, to seek for succor. . . . And for the season it was winter, and they that know the winters of that country know them to be sharp and violent, & subject to cruel & fierce storms, dangerous to travel to known places, much more to search an unknown coast. Besides, what could they see but a hideous & desolate wilderness, full of wild beasts & wild men? and what multitudes there might be of them they knew not. . . ."

William Bradford,
*Of Plymouth Plantation,
The Pilgrims in America, 1604–1646*

himself emperor of Virginia. His ambitions were not meant to be, however. Reports of his harsh rule and rumors of his "plans" reached the London Company and he was sent back to England for trial.

Although he was removed from office, Smith had demonstrated the importance of strong leadership. When the king granted the company a new charter in 1609, it called for an all-powerful administrator and reduced the council to an advisory role.

The new charter, in addition to raising much-needed revenue, included a provision to encourage emigration. Settlers could exchange seven years of unpaid labor on company lands for free passage. Those who took advantage of this opportunity were called indentured servants. Settlers who paid their own way received one share of stock in the enterprise. All agreed to work for the company until 1616, when the profits would be divided equally and every shareholder would receive a bonus of a hundred acres.

In May 1609, six hundred people left England for Jamestown. With their numbers thus increased

some fivefold, and lacking a strong leader and sufficient provisions, the colonists suffered badly through the next winter. When the interim governor, Sir Thomas Gates, finally arrived in May 1610, he was appalled to find a settlement "which appeared rather as a ruins of some ancient fortification, than that any people living might now inhabit." Only sixty settlers had survived.

This was Jamestown's "starving time." Food was so scarce that the settlers were reduced to eating dogs, cats, rats, snakes, and boiled shoes. When the colony's permanent governor finally arrived a few weeks after Gates, he managed to restore some order and to organize repairs to the town. However, he could do nothing about the colonists' terrible susceptibility to disease. In fact, he himself finally became so ill that he had to return to England in March 1611.

Yet the worst was almost over. In May 1611 Thomas Dale, a stern Puritan, was appointed governor, and it was not long before he had established discipline with a new code of harsh laws.

The House of Burgesses During Dale's stern governorship and that of his successor, life in Jamestown took a turn for the better. John Rolfe's agricultural experiments with tobacco enabled the colonists to develop a profitable export crop, and his marriage to Pocahontas, the daughter of the Powhatan chief, made possible a truce with the Indians. By 1617 Jamestown was shipping some twenty thousand pounds of tobacco to England. Another boon was the arrival of a group of ninety young women in 1620. The women, whom the company guaranteed to be "pure and spotless," came over to be the colonists' wives. The cost of one wife: 120 pounds of tobacco!

Prosperity created a demand for more economic and political freedom. In 1619 a new charter was issued. Once again the company was allowed to transport settlers in exchange for seven years of indentured servitude. Those who paid their own way were given fifty acres of land (called "headright"), plus fifty acres more for every person they brought with them, on the condition that they cultivated the land, established a habitation on it, and paid a yearly land tax (called a "quitrent").

There was also a major innovation in the charter: the colonists were given permission to elect representatives to an assembly, called the House of Burgesses. In July 1619 Virginians met in the first representative assembly of the New World. The representatives had the authority to recommend laws for the entire colony and to ratify all directives sent by the London Company. In practice, the colonists assumed the right to make laws unless they were overruled by the company. This strong provision for self-government was the work of the company treasurer, Sir Edwin Sandys. It made practical the statement in the original company charter that the settlers were to enjoy the rights of Englishmen.

Jamestown Becomes a Royal Colony Sandys had other new plans for the colony, too. Under his direction the company began to sell private plantations to small groups. These semi-independent estates had two representatives in the House of Burgesses. He also convinced the company to send tradespeople and artisans (glassblowers, ironmongers, shipbuilders) so that the colony could diversify its business interests and protect itself against a possible tobacco crop failure. In his enthusiasm, however, Sandys failed to ensure that the colony had enough food, housing, and supplies to support the more than thirty-five hundred new arrivals he had attracted. Three years later, all but about nine hundred had died of disease or starvation. To make matters worse, in March 1622, the Indians, alarmed by the encroachments on their lands, massacred some 347 settlers, including John Rolfe. The colonists responded in kind. They invited 250 Indians to a peace conference, offered them poisoned wine, and killed every one of their guests.

The colony's future looked uncertain at best. In spite of the increasing export of tobacco, the London Company still had not seen a return on its investment and was near bankruptcy. In 1623 a royal commission investigated the company's management of the colony, and in 1624 its privileges were revoked. To improve its administration, the colony was then handed over to the king and his Privy Council, thus making it the first royal colony. The king dissolved the House of Burgesses, appointed a royal governor, who was to have absolute authority, and sent him to Virginia. As it soon became apparent that he could not govern effectively alone, however, the new governor quickly appointed a council of local property holders.

The arrival of a royal governor threatened to undo all the progress the colonists had made toward self-government. But the governor and his council found that it was easier to govern with the colonists' cooperation than without it. So in 1629 the governor invited a group of former representatives to begin to function informally as a representative assembly. In 1639 the king formally recognized the law-making powers of this reorganized House of Burgesses.

While the Jamestown settlers faced severe hardship, and while the London Company's shareholders never realized the profits they had expected, the colony endured and ultimately flourished. Farming improved, children were born, and the Indian threat gradually diminished. From 1629 on, some form of representative government was functioning again in the House of Burgesses. Thus the first steps had been taken toward establishing a permanent English presence in the New World.

Maryland: A Proprietary Grant

While Virginia was organized by merchants for the sole purpose of making a profit, Maryland was settled by the Calvert family as a refuge for perse-cuted Catholics.

George Calvert, a nobleman in James I's Privy Council, was intrigued by schemes for settling the New World. During his years of service to the throne he converted to Roman Catholicism. This was an unpopular action to take in a country domi-nated by Protestants. Moreover, it severely dimin-ished his usefulness to the government because his dealings with Catholic countries such as Spain became immediately suspect. Calvert stepped down from power but remained a royal favorite. The king personally excused him from taking the Oath of Supremacy and made him a baron, with the title Lord Baltimore.

When George Calvert applied for an area to colonize, King Charles I, who had succeeded his father, granted him land on the Chesapeake Bay north of Virginia. The charter was finally fixed with the king's seal only after Calvert had died, so the colony went to his son Cecil, the second Lord Balti-more. The colony was named Maryland, in honor of the queen, Charles I's wife. In November 1633, two Jesuit priests, seventeen gentlemen and their wives and children, and about two hundred other settlers set sail on the *Ark* and the *Dove*. Leading the enter-prise was Cecil's brother, Leonard Calvert.

The two brothers were able administrators who successfully avoided the problems that had plagued the Jamestown settlement. The site they chose for their first town (St. Mary's) had an excellent harbor and plenty of fresh water, and they were careful to obtain rights to the land by trading with the friendly local Indians. The settlers planted vegetable gardens and asked the Indians to teach them how to cultivate corn. When ambitious farmers wanted to devote their fields to tobacco, a profitable export, the governor borrowed a Virginia law and insisted that they also cultivate at least two acres of corn.

A Feudal Estate The royal charter that granted the settlement of Maryland created what was basically a feudal estate. In theory, at least, the new colony was completely subject to the will of the proprietor who owned the land and was free to make laws, almost without restriction. Indeed, Lord Baltimore theo-retically had more power in his colony than the king was permitted to exercise in England. In return he had only to promise the crown one-fifth of all the gold and silver discovered in Maryland and two Indian arrowheads a year.

The economic structure of Maryland also was somewhat medieval. Relatives of proprietors re-ceived six thousand acres, gentlemen who brought five other people with them were allowed to estab-lish manors of three thousand acres, and all estates were to be worked by tenants.

Other male settlers in the colony (called free-holders) were given a hundred acres of land plus another hundred acres for a wife and each servant, and fifty acres for each child over age sixteen. Manor lords also could dispense land to freeholders. This unequal granting of land created social-class distinctions based on the size of a person's property holdings. The lords of manors (who comprised the colony's Catholic elite) enjoyed the same rights and privileges enjoyed by the nobility in England, while the freeholders lacked all such privileges. Both manor lords and freeholders had to pay the pro-prietor a quitrent.

In spite of these feudal characteristics of the colony, the medieval pattern of life never took a strong hold in Maryland, partly because of the inde-pendent nature of the people who came to settle there and partly because of the wisdom of the pro-prietor.

Representative Government The gradual emer-gence of representative government in Maryland helped to prevent the development of a firmly en-trenched feudal state. Lord Baltimore's charter had guaranteed him and his heirs control over the colony's government, with the "advice, assent, and approbation of freemen." Three years after the colony was settled, the governor convened an assembly in order to receive this assent. The mem-bers, however, wanted the right to initiate legisla-tion and balked at merely endorsing laws handed down to them.

Although Lord Baltimore at first rejected the assembly's right to draft laws of its own, he soon dis-covered that he would have to bow to the people's will if he wanted his statutes approved. Before long, the people's representatives were introducing legis-lation and rewriting most of the proprietor's propos-als. By 1650 Maryland had a strong legislature which did not hesitate to oppose the wishes of the Baltimore family. As in Virginia, Maryland's government now consisted of a governor, an appointed council of wealthy property holders, and a representative assembly consisting of two elected officials from each of the local counties.

Religious Toleration Despite the Calverts' land policies, which favored Catholics, there were more Protestants than Catholics settled in Maryland from the start. Lord Baltimore tried to maintain peace by demanding "no scandal or offense to be given to any of the Protestants," but ensuring religious toleration required stronger measures. In 1649 an official Toleration Act was passed banning all religious insults and providing that anyone who believed in Jesus Christ—whether Catholic or Protestant—would not be persecuted on religious grounds.

Life in the Chesapeake Bay Area

The settlers in the Virginia and Maryland colonies in the seventeenth century led similar lives, largely because of the geography of the area. Chesapeake Bay, fed by hundreds of rivers and creeks, was perfectly suited to farming tobacco, an export crop. Farms were never located more than a few hundred feet from water, so farmers who lived along smaller rivers and creeks could ship their tobacco in canoes to Jamestown or St. Mary's, and those who lived along the deep rivers could load their crops directly onto ocean-going vessels.

This pattern of settlement also made the area extremely difficult to administer. As one English official put it, "How is it possible to govern a people so dispersed?" In the early years this problem was magnified by the kind of people who came to settle the area. Many of Virginia's first colonists were so-called undesirables: as early as 1618 the city of London had sent a hundred homeless children, and the following year a hundred "fellons and other desperate villanes" were shipped over. By the mid-1660s, however, most of Virginia's forty thousand white settlers were English freemen, indentured servants, and apprentices.

Because labor was in very short supply, workers of African descent were brought by slave traders to the Chesapeake Bay area as early as 1619 (ironically, the same year in which representative government was instituted at Jamestown). At first the legal status of the African laborers was unclear. But because the black workers were different from whites in appearance, the English considered them inferior beings, and it was not long before their condition began to worsen. By 1670 there were some two thousand black Africans and West Indians in the Virginia colony. In the early years of settlement, however, most farms were small enough to be worked by their owners and a few indentured servants. It was not until the eighteenth century that the use of slave labor became extensive enough to support the growth of huge plantations and a well-to-do class of white property owners.

Freemen and Indentured Servants

Many people who came to America were seeking to improve their economic and social status so they did not want to work for someone else. Nevertheless, if they could not otherwise pay their passage, they were often willing to exchange a term of service for the chance to better themselves afterwards. Those who came over as indentured servants worked for whoever paid their fare: the company, the crown, or a private citizen. More than half of those who came to the colonies in the eighteenth century came as indentured servants; about one-quarter of them were women. Indentured servitude was common throughout the colonies except New England.

Under the headright system (used in Maryland as well as in Virginia), the amount of land that colonists received depended on the number of people they brought with them. The more land they received, the more help they needed cultivating it. This created a major source of employment for indentured servants. Initially the tobacco economy of Virginia and Maryland was built on the labor of gangs of indentured servants which were gradually replaced with slaves only in the late seventeenth century.

Indentured servants were not permitted to own land until they had completed their term of service. Their other rights were also limited, since they were considered to be their master's dependents. They could be bought and sold, rented out, and inherited. They could engage in trade only with their master's consent. They could sue and be sued, but they could not vote. They were subject to corporal punishment, but could petition the courts against abusive treatment. They could not marry without their master's consent.

Once their term of service was over, they were free to seek their fortune and were entitled to fifty acres of land. Their employer usually gave them a new suit of clothes and some agricultural equipment. Some who did not receive land tried to save enough money to buy their own farm; others "squatted" on unclaimed land and farmed it.

Bacon's Rebellion

By the late seventeenth century, the influx of large numbers of indentured servants had gradually increased the population of the Virginia colony. As these settlers completed their terms of service, the demand for new land on which to plant tobacco increased at the very time that wealthier and better established planters had secured control of the coastal tidewater area with its rich soil and ready access to trans-Atlantic commerce. Poorer farmers had to migrate into the interior where river transportation was remote and Indian tribes still posed a danger to one's very survival. Many of the farmers were young and rebellious, renters of land rather than owners, and spoiling for a fight with Indians they considered hostile. The emerging economic and political elite of well-to-do planters along the seaboard was fearful of these younger farmers who were challenging their own economic and political control and who were perceived as threatening the order and stability of the colony. Their fears increased as Virginia's prosperity declined under the burden of the overproduction of tobacco.

It was, however, the uneasy relations between the white settlers on the frontier and the Indian tribes which finally shattered the superficial calm of Virginia politics and led to open rebellion against the government. Settlers found that the government forts intended to protect them from Indian attack were useless since it was a simple enough matter for the Indians to skirt them. The settlers felt exposed and, in their fear, were often unable to distinguish between hostile and friendly tribes. By 1670 the frontier was fifty miles from Jamestown, far enough to have worn thin the sense of common purpose that had bound the first settlers together. One faction, composed of county leaders (especially those from the frontier), wanted the government to open up new territories for settlement and to take a more aggressive stance against the Indians. The other faction, consisting of the royal governor, Sir William Berkeley, and his followers among the wealthy planters and office holders, was enjoying a profitable monopoly of the fur trade with the Indians and did not want to jeopardize this trade by helping the frontier settlers antagonize the Indians.

In response to Indian attacks in 1676, a brash young frontier planter named Nathaniel Bacon raised an army of back-country men and led indiscriminate reprisals against peaceful as well as hostile tribes. When the governor ordered him to stop his attacks on the Indians, Bacon rallied his men and marched on Jamestown. The frightened governor and the House of Burgesses granted Bacon's request for an army with which to continue fighting the Indians. But as soon as Bacon returned to the frontier, Berkeley branded him a rebel. Furious, Bacon marched back to Jamestown and burned it to the ground. Then, suddenly, Bacon died of dysentery and the largest popular uprising before the American Revolution was over.

Was the rebellion of any significance? Bacon had had no program except to kill the Indians, and the remaining leaders of the rebellion were hanged. This put an effective end to open challenges to the colony's leadership, but the problems that had caused the uprising remained. Relations with the Indians did not improve. Moreover, the number of freemen who did not own land continued to grow, and many of them had to work for wealthier planters who controlled the best land. Popular unrest continued to expand beneath the surface of Virginia life and apprehensive planters began to turn to the use of slaves, who seemed easier to control.

This rebellion also gave expression to several grievances which had long-range significance for colonial America. Before the rebellion a new assembly had been elected by the vote of all men with property. This House of Burgesses now supported a number of laws designed to increase popular participation in colonial government and to curb the political power of the wealthy planters. While these laws did not endure, the issue of a more democratic political process had been raised in Virginia for the first time.

The Founding of New England

Religion played a relatively minor role in the settlement of the Chesapeake Bay area. Even though Maryland was founded as a refuge for persecuted Catholics, Lord Baltimore and his heirs never tried to create an exclusively Catholic settlement. In Virginia the Church of England was receiving government support by the 1640s and all non-Anglicans were required to "depart the colony with all convenience." Yet the religious establishment was never strong in Virginia. Control of church matters was in the hands of the important lay members of the church, known as the vestry.

In the founding of New England, which began over a decade before Maryland was settled, conditions were very different. Here, religion was the crucial factor.

The Plymouth Colony

The "Pilgrims," as they have since become known, were the first English settlers in New England. A group of Separatists from northern England, they had fled to Leyden in Holland in order to escape persecution by the Anglican church, which was seeking to establish absolute religious conformity.

But life in Holland was not a success for the Pilgrims. Most of them were farmers who found city life strange and unnatural. Their children were growing up speaking Dutch, and some were even drifting away from their parents' faith. The Pilgrims wanted land of their own. They wanted to preserve their customs and language, and to practice their religion freely.

Emigration to the New World seemed the answer. Before they left, however, the English king made them promise to remain loyal to him personally, and he, in return, promised to refrain from interfering in their activities as long as "they carried themselves peaceably." In 1620 the London Company of Virginia granted the Pilgrims a patent, permitting them to settle in Virginia. A group of merchants formed a joint-stock company to finance the venture and agreed to provide free passage in return for half of all the profits generated after seven years. The company's financial affairs were to be managed by officers residing both in London and in the New

World. To those who tried to dissuade the group from such a risky voyage, one leader replied:

. . . all great and honourable actions are accompanied with great difficulties and must be both enterprised and overcome with answerable courages. It was granted the dangers were great, but not desperate. The difficulties were many, but not invincible . . . It might be sundry of the things feared might never befall; others by provident care and the use of good means might in a great measure be prevented; and all of them, through the help of God, by fortitude and patience, might either be borne or overcome.

In September 1620 the *Mayflower* set sail for an area near the Hudson River with 101 passengers, 87 of them Pilgrims. Among the "strangers," as the Pilgrims called those of other faiths, was Captain Miles Standish, who helped prevent a mutiny when the settlers sighted the forbidding, rocky coast of New England instead of the warm, inviting coast of Virginia.

The landing of the *Mayflower* so far north of its destination meant that the ship was outside the legal jurisdiction of the London Company. Fearful that their patent would be useless and that the "strangers" (some of whom were regarded as undesirables) would take control, the Pilgrims drew up the famous Mayflower Compact. This document, scarcely two hundred words long, was signed by forty-one men who agreed that they were forming a "body politic" and that they would obey whatever laws the group passed. The compact was a temporary contract to be observed until the Pilgrims could obtain a patent from the rightful owners of New England, a company of aristocrats called the Council of New England.

On December 21, 1620, the Pilgrims landed at Plymouth. Never did an enterprise face more difficulties. By spring, half the settlers had died. A friendly Indian named Squanto saved the rest from starvation by teaching them how to fish and plant corn. Sometime in October 1621, they gathered to thank God for their first harvest. They had little else to cheer them. When the *Mayflower* returned to Plymouth the following November, it brought

THE PILGRIMS LANDING AT PLYMOUTH.

thirty-five more mouths to feed and no supplies at all. Six years after their arrival, the colonists had only one cow for every six people and one goat for every three. By the 1640s they still had only one plow. The region produced scarcely any useful commodities other than furs, lumber, and fish.

The London merchants soon realized they would never make a return on their investment. So, on November 15, 1626, they sold their stock to the Pilgrims. This transaction placed the tiny, impoverished community under an enormous debt that took seventeen years to repay.

Plymouth's governor, William Bradford, governed with absolute authority for more than

thirty years. As the colony gradually became self-supporting, new towns were added, and the problems of government grew increasingly complex. In 1636 the first system of laws that originated in the colonies was passed. The Great Fundamentals created a representative government in which each town elected two deputies to a unicameral (single house) legislature that sat together with the governor and the governor's assistants.

The settlers never managed to obtain a charter from the king, and their patent from the Council of New England said nothing about establishing a civil government. So in 1691, when Plymouth and its related villages were absorbed into the flourishing colony that had grown up around the city of Boston, there was little they could do about it. Throughout its history Plymouth remained devoted to the unworldly pursuit of personal piety rather than to expansion of its political power.

The Massachusetts Bay Colony

Ten years after the landing of the Pilgrims, another group of Protestant dissenters, the Puritans, crossed the Atlantic to New England. One thousand settlers, including many well-to-do merchants, arrived in a great fleet of seventeen ships, four of which carried livestock and supplies. The leader of this sizable venture was John Winthrop, an English gentleman and lawyer. Through the force of his character and administrative skills, he dominated the Massachusetts Bay Colony for many years. From the beginning of the establishment of the colony until his death he kept a *Journal*, which is one of the most important early records of the settlement.

Like the Pilgrims, these newcomers shared the Calvinist theology and they despised the "popish practices" which they felt had infected the Church of England. Their purpose in coming to the New World was to build a self-governing "community of saints." Unlike the Pilgrims, however, the Puritans remained loyal to the church, wanting only to reform it.

The Puritans possessed common sense and spiritual confidence in equal measure. They had an unshakable conviction that God would favor their migration. "We doubt not but God will be with us," one Puritan wrote, "and if God be with us, who can be against us?" They set sail in the spring so that they would be able to plant a crop before winter. When they landed at Salem, they were met by four hundred settlers who had come over in 1628 and 1629 to prepare the way. Yet even with the precautions they had taken against hunger, nearly two hundred people died from starvation the first winter. Fortunately, fresh supplies arrived in February, and by the middle of 1631 more colonists had arrived, bringing with them guns, saws, and window glass. Except for their first difficult winter, the Puritans never suffered the horrors of Jamestown or Plymouth.

From the outset the Puritans established the right to govern themselves. They received a royal charter which formed them into a joint-stock company called the Massachusetts Bay Company. The charter gave twenty-six investors the right to the land which lay approximately between Boston and what is now the state of New Hampshire. In most respects this charter resembled earlier ones, but there was one crucial difference: neither the charter nor company headquarters had to remain in England.

This was the first time that the headquarters of a joint-stock company moved to the colonies with the settlers. The Puritans took the charter and some of the investors with them to America, creating a legally independent and self-governing body unhampered by royal governors and English officials. They were free to make laws, levy taxes, establish a school system, administer justice, and, most important, follow their own religious beliefs.

Unlike Virginia and Maryland, New England was settled in towns. This was partly because the Puritans wanted to reproduce the existing order of life in England as they knew it. But they also felt safer in numbers and town living made it easier for them to practice their religion.

The Great Migration Over the next decade, between fifteen and twenty thousand more Puritans emigrated to New England while many more journeyed to English colonies in the West Indies. Known as the Great Migration, this massive exodus resulted from bitter struggles between Charles I and Parliament. The king had dissolved Parliament in 1629, crushing Puritan hopes of church and state reform. The Puritans wanted a church independent of state authority and a simplified service. The king, however, was increasingly impatient with those who would not accept the crown as the head of the church and the existing Anglican service. Puritan ministers were turned out of their churches. Puritan books were burned. Government officials who happened to be Puritans felt the weight of royal displeasure.

Political and religious oppression was accompanied by economic decline. Prices and unemployment rose. Rents for farmland were fixed by law, and disgruntled landlords (including a large number of Puritan country squires) watched their property decline in value every day. They concluded that a mighty disaster was about to befall the entire country. As John Winthrop wrote, it was better to

A MAP OF NEW ENGLAND IN 1634.

"avoid the plague when it is foreseen than to tarry till it should overtake us."

Puritan Government The Puritan leaders were determined to keep Old World vices out of the New World. They therefore designed a strong government modeled closely after their religious ideals. Theirs was not a democracy: only the virtuous were considered deserving of a voice in the colony's affairs. Since only men were allowed to participate in government in the seventeenth century, the right to vote was restricted to the male membership of the church. Church membership was not easy to attain: those who were members in good standing had had to demonstrate that they had been touched by the grace of God and that the true meaning of being a Christian had been revealed to them. Yet even after Winthrop and his aides were persuaded to extend the status of freeman (voter) to all adult male church members, the governor, the lieutenant governor, and the governor's assistants (called magistrates) still controlled the colony.

It required renewed effort on the part of the freemen to bring about real self-government in the Massachusetts Bay Colony. At first the freemen could elect only the governor's magistrates. But in 1632 they gained the right to elect the governor, too. And in 1634 the towns gained the right to elect annually two deputies each to a General Court.

As the years passed, the governor's authority became more and more restricted. Whereas originally the deputies had no power to enforce their decisions against the governor and his magistrates, in 1644, as a result of a dispute between deputies and the magistrates, the General Court was divided into two houses: an upper house consisting of the governor and the magistrates, and a lower house consisting of the deputies. The approval of each house was required before proposals could be carried out.

Although only male church members could vote for deputies of the General Court, nonfreemen could vote in their town meeting, which was the vehicle of all local government, and hold local offices such as "hog reeve," fire warden, or "fense mender." The town meeting became an important instrument for direct participation in government, and even now in many New England communities the townspeople vote directly on local issues.

Puritan Relations with the Indians

There has been a continuing debate among historians over the Puritans' relations with the Indians. Although the Puritans have long had a poor reputation in this regard, some historians now believe that the Puritans treated the native tribes with a degree of fairness. They point out that the Puritans were careful to offer the Indians something in exchange for the cultivated land they took and that they felt that Indian claims to undeveloped land were weak since the Indians used them only intermittently as game preserves. In addition, the Indians were often given the right to hunt, trap, and fish on these lands, and these rights were written into the deeds.

The Indians also are known to have participated in the Puritans' courts, sometimes even sitting on juries in cases involving other Indians. In one case, three English servants were executed by the courts for murdering an Indian.

Yet, the point must be made that the coastal tribes were weak and intertribal conflicts were common. Only the Iroquois Confederation, made up of tribes to the west of early colonial settlement, was a strong buffer against European encroachment on traditional tribal hunting grounds. By the early eighteenth century the colonists in the New England area, as in the Southern colonies, had destroyed or driven the coastal tribes into the interior in ferocious warfare.

The Pequot War was the first major struggle between New England settlers and their Indian neighbors. In 1637 Massachusetts, Connecticut, and their Indian allies all but eradicated the Pequot tribe of southern Connecticut. This war prompted the formation of the Confederation of the United Colonies of New England in 1643. The confederation, the first instance of cooperation among any of the American colonies, consisted of Massachusetts, Connecticut, New Haven, and Plymouth. Rhode Island was never allowed to join, since Massachusetts still hoped to uproot the heretics settled there.

The Pequot War was followed by almost forty years of peace between the colonists and the native Americans. Then in 1675 a Wampanoag chieftain known as King Philip initiated hostilities against settlers in Massachusetts. King Philip charged the settlers with acquiring Indian lands by devious means. There is little evidence to support his claims, however, and it seems likely that his real grievance was against the increasing number of Indians who were converting to Christianity. It is a fact that the Puritans tried to convert the native Americans and that by 1675 they had succeeded in attracting perhaps a thousand. The Puritan missionary John Eliot had even gone so far as to establish fourteen so-called praying towns, where converted Indians could live in a Christian environment.

Some five hundred colonists and at least a thousand Indians were killed in King Philip's War. Many captured warriors were sent as slaves to the West Indies. Peace returned to the area, and the New England Confederation fell into disuse.

Rhode Island

It is hard for Americans today to appreciate how seriously the Puritans regarded the smallest issues of religious doctrine. And yet, Rhode Island was founded as a result of a theological dispute.

In 1631 a stubborn young minister named Roger Williams came to the Massachusetts Bay Colony. Williams, who believed that the Church of England was beyond redemption, soon found himself at odds with the Puritan majority, who felt that reforms were possible without breaking from the church. Williams considered this position unacceptable and demanded a complete break. He also argued that the law requiring everyone to attend church brought unregenerate sinners into houses of worship, a practice for which he could find no precedent in the Bible. As far as he was concerned, only those who had been "born again" into God's love should be allowed to attend services.

Politically, young Williams was even more of a troublemaker. He felt that the king of England's claim to America was unsound. The English neither owned the land, nor had they discovered it. Properly speaking, he argued, the land belonged to the Indians, and the English should have bought it from them. In fact, the Puritans had paid the Indians whenever they took cultivated land, but they had regarded undeveloped land as free for the taking.

Williams also questioned whether the people should have to pay taxes to support ministers. In what biblical passage did the Puritans find words to justify such high-handed procedures?

Williams's outspoken criticisms of the Puritan commonwealth threatened to disrupt the colony,

and the magistrates banished him in 1635. Fleeing south with a few followers, he founded the colony of Providence, Rhode Island, which broke with the Church of England and forbade the civil government to interfere in religious matters.

Williams had long been tormented over the question of who had been redeemed. He finally came to the conclusion that only God could judge whose worship was just; therefore government should let God accept or reject individual religious practices. Thus, it was in Rhode Island that genuine religious freedom was for the first time practiced in America.

Roger Williams received a charter from the crown for his colony in 1644. It provided for a governor with assistants and an assembly based on representation from the towns. In this it resembled the Massachusetts Bay government. But there was one notable difference: here the right to vote was not limited to church members.

Anne Hutchinson Another dissenter from accepted Puritan thinking, Anne Hutchinson, was banished

THE TRIAL OF ANNE HUTCHINSON, RELIGIOUS REFORMER AND FEMINIST.

from Massachusetts at about the same time. She and her family had come to Massachusetts Bay from England in 1634. They settled in Boston and she began holding weekly prayer meetings where she discussed matters of religious doctrine. Her meetings became so popular that she soon had a large following. Contrary to the view of the Puritan leadership in Massachusetts, Hutchinson held that divine revelation was a continuing process and truths gained through revelation could supplant biblical authority. To the Puritans this was nothing short of heresy. Moreover, the male-dominated Puritan leadership was offended that a woman was speaking out on religious matters. As a result, in 1637 the General Court banished the leaders of the Hutchinsonian party and Mrs. Hutchinson herself was brought to trial. Although she gave a spirited defense, she was banished by the colony. She fled with her family to Rhode Island where she founded Portsmouth. In 1643 Anne Hutchinson and twelve members of her family were killed by Indians.

Connecticut and New Hampshire

Other Puritan colonies sprang up in other parts of New England, though not always as a result of a religious quarrel. Some congregations started new settlements because they found life in Boston or other older towns in the Massachusetts Bay Colony either too strict or too wicked.

In 1636 Thomas Hooker, a minister, led his congregation to the Connecticut Valley and established Hartford, Springfield, and two other towns.

Hooker was looking for better land and a less oppressive religious atmosphere. He modeled his colony after Massachusetts, but followed Rhode Island's lead in not restricting the right to vote to church members. In 1639 the Fundamental Orders of Connecticut, the first written constitution in the New World, was drafted. The Orders left voter qualifications up to the individual towns.

In 1638 John Davenport and Theophilus Eaton established New Haven, a strict little religious colony, south of Hartford. New Haven and the towns on the Connecticut River (including Hartford) banded together in 1662 and obtained a charter from the English government as the colony of Connecticut. Connecticut and Rhode Island retained their charters, under which they elected all their officials, throughout the colonial period.

In their search for new land, Massachusetts Bay colonists went north as well as south. In the 1640s and 1650s Massachusetts incorporated settlements in Maine and New Hampshire under its jurisdiction. In 1679, however, the British government made New Hampshire a separate royal colony.

New England's economy depended originally on farming and on unlimited trade in lumber and fur. But by the middle of the seventeenth century commerce had replaced agriculture, and fishing became a new source of wealth. The Puritan settlers never found a single commodity which could make them as wealthy as tobacco made the Virginians. But this proved to be a blessing in disguise, forcing them to diversify their economy.

More Proprietary Grants

Between 1640 and 1660 England was convulsed by a bitter civil war which grew out of a long struggle between the Parliament and the Stuart monarchy over political and religious issues. The Parliament, dominated by Puritan members, had resisted the efforts of Charles I, to stamp out Puritan reforms in the Anglican church. They also had resolutely refused to allow the king to collect taxes without their consent. The intense feelings surrounding these issues and the king's own deviousness ultimately led to his undoing. In 1649 he was beheaded.

An eleven-year period of parliamentary domination followed under the leadership of the Puritan general Oliver Cromwell. These were times of internal strife and disorder as well as conflict with both the Dutch and the Spanish. It gradually became clear that a return to stability in England would be possible only by restoring the monarchy. In 1660 Charles II was invited to assume the throne.

During this period of turmoil, Virginia, Maryland, and the New England colonies were England's tenuous claim to an empire on the North American mainland. Little attention was given to further colonization. After 1660, however, the government regained its interest in the international competition for overseas acquisition.

New York

While England was preoccupied with the civil war, a commercial rival, the Netherlands, already had laid claim to an attractive part of the North American coastline. In 1624 the Dutch established a fur-trading outpost at Albany, and in 1626 the Dutch West India Company purchased Manhattan Island. The company made little effort to increase the colony's population but made every effort to control and exploit the settlers who were already there. The only plan for colonial expansion advanced by the company called for settlement of the entire Hudson Valley with immense feudal estates called patroonships. This plan was never popular, however, and only one Dutch estate, Rensselaerswyck, was successfully established in the area. Even with the efforts of a strong administrator, such as Peter Stuyvesant, the colony remained a poorly organized series of semiautonomous villages.

By the middle of the century the Dutch and the English were involved in an intense rivalry for control of sea trade. Although the Dutch were never deeply committed to colonizing the Hudson Valley, they did want to hold onto New Amsterdam, their settlement on Manhattan Island. It was an excellent base from which to raid gold-bearing Spanish galleons and to compete with English merchant vessels for the increasingly profitable colonial trade. In addition it was desirable because it was the main entrance to the fur-trading regions of the interior.

The English recognized these advantages, too, and in 1664 Charles II bestowed the area between New England and the Chesapeake Bay settlements on his brother, the Duke of York. In April of that year, an English officer leading four ships seized the unprepared Dutch colony of ten thousand people on Manhattan without a fight. By the 1670s Great Britain's navy had reduced Dutch sea power and driven the Dutch out of North America.

From the time of its founding New Amsterdam was a cosmopolitan city. When the English took control, they found that eighteen languages were spoken in New Amsterdam, and so many religious sects prevailed that one governor wrote:

Here be not many of the Church of England; few Roman Catholics; abundance of Quakers . . . Singing Quakers, Ranting Quakers; Sabbatarians; Antisabbatarians; some Anabaptists; some independents; some Jews; in short, of all sorts and opinions there are some, and the most part of none at all. . . . The most prevailing opinion is that of the Dutch Calvinists.

New Amsterdam's sophisticated young ladies followed the latest Paris fashions and spoke several languages. The Dutch had provided a few schools, a fire patrol, and a small police force. By 1680 the colony of New York (as the English renamed it) had some thirty taverns doing a thriving business, and rents were considered outrageously high.

Yet the colony's economic and political development lagged behind that of New England. Although the English exported some grain and cattle, they were slow to exploit the advantages of their farmlands and their superb harbor at the mouth of the Hudson. Under the Dutch New Amsterdam had been ruled autocratically, and it was not until the end of the century that Great Britain finally gave the colony a representative government. Up to that time, it was ruled by a governor and council appointed by the proprietor.

New Jersey

Three other English colonies—New Jersey, Pennsylvania, and Delaware—were carved out of the land under the jurisdiction of the Duke of York. Immediately after receiving his grant, York gave the part which became New Jersey to his friends Sir George Carteret and John, Lord Berkeley. In 1676 the territory was divided in half. Lord Berkeley sold his portion to a group of Quakers; Carteret inherited a settlement of Puritans with his half. In 1702 the king of England rejoined the two areas and made the territory a royal colony, which shared New York's governor until 1738.

Pennsylvania and Delaware

Like New England, Pennsylvania was settled by religious dissenters. The proprietor of the new colony was William Penn, the son of a wealthy admiral in the British navy. As a young man Penn was expelled from Oxford University for unruly conduct and his father sent him to Europe to study. There he was attracted to Calvinist ideas. On returning to England, he studied law and then managed his father's estates in Ireland. It was at this point that he became interested in the Society of Friends, or the Quakers. His father was outraged and forced him to leave home. Shortly thereafter he wrote his famous pamphlet "The Great Cause of Liberty of Conscience."

The Quakers The Society of Friends was a Separatist group that had been founded by George Fox in 1646. Fox preached a form of Christian mysticism, claiming that every human being had a spark of divinity and could therefore communicate directly with God, without the need of the clergy, church services, or even the Bible. All a person had to do to experience God's presence was learn to detect this inner light. Fox's religion was an emotional, even an anti-intellectual one.

Such notions were offensive to Anglicans and Puritans alike. To make matters worse, the Quakers refused to pay taxes for the support of the Church of England and its clergy, and they claimed exemption from military service because they were pacifists.

Finally, even though their religious services were illegal in England, they continued to hold them anyway.

In America the Friends fared little better at first. Quakerism was illegal in Virginia, and in 1660 two Friends were lashed and then banished from that colony. In New England, they demonstrated against the Puritans by breaking bottles in churches to symbolize the emptiness of the services or by bursting noisily into a Puritan church and emphatically denouncing the minister. Such outrageous acts aroused the Puritans' fury. They reacted by fining people for reading Quaker tracts, branding, whipping, and banishing Quakers, hanging them, and even trying to sell Quaker children as slaves to sugar farmers in the West Indies.

The Founding of Pennsylvania William Penn longed for a refuge for his fellow Quakers, and in 1681 he received a royal grant for territory north of Maryland. Penn's father had once loaned the king a great sum of money which he had never repaid. Although the king seldom felt compelled to repay his debts, he used this debt as an excuse for helping his persecuted Quaker friend. Charles II may have had

WILLIAM PENN MAKES A PEACE TREATY WITH THE INDIANS.

his own best interest at heart, too. It seems that he urged Penn to settle the new territory as quickly as possible. As Penn wrote later, "The government at home was glad to be rid of us at so cheap a rate as a little parchment to be practiced in a desert three thousand miles off. . . ." In this new land Penn, like the Puritans in the New England colonies, hoped to create an ideal Christian community. And, in fact, he was so sure that Quakerism would thrive and attract believers that he made religious freedom for all who believed in God one of the cornerstones of his "holy experiment."

Because concern for humanity was an essential aspect of their faith, the Friends formed committees to help the poor, the Indians, and the slaves. The friendship they extended to the Indians resulted in seventy-five years of peace between the two groups.

In 1682 Penn drew up the Frame of Government as the basic structure for the colony's government. Penn gave himself the authority to choose the governor, but also provided for a bicameral (two-house) legislature whose members would be elected by the freemen of the colony. (All male citizens who owned a small amount of land or paid taxes were freemen.) The members of the lower house or assembly won the right to initiate legislation when Penn lost his charter for a few years (1692–1696) as a result of turmoil in British politics. When he regained his colony from the crown, Penn found that the only restriction on an otherwise all-powerful legislature was the governor's power to veto legislation. Being a wise administrator, Penn accepted this new arrangement.

The Charter of Liberties, enacted in 1701, confirmed the legislature's power. In addition to restricting the governor's authority and creating a unicameral legislature, it gave three counties their own representative assembly. These counties later became the colony of Delaware, but Pennsylvania's governor continued to administer them until the Revolution.

Penn was not only a wise legislator, but a gifted propagandist as well. He wrote promotional brochures about the advantages of the colony which were circulated throughout Europe. By 1684, fifty shiploads of settlers had come to Pennsylvania from England, Wales, Holland, Germany, and Ireland. By 1700 there were nearly eighteen thousand settlers. The production of large quantities of wheat, flour, beef, and pork helped Philadelphia to become the most prosperous commercial center in North America.

Penn himself, however, did not prosper. His tenants rebelled against paying the rents they owed him, and a dishonest agent further aggravated his financial problems. In his last years he spent a short time in debtor's prison. After he was released he suffered a stroke, and in 1718 he died.

The Carolinas

In 1663 Sir George Carteret, Lord Berkeley, and six other aristocrats received a grant to Carolina, the territory lying between the colony of Virginia and the Spanish outpost of St. Augustine in Florida. The English hoped that by colonizing the area, they could prevent the Spanish from advancing any farther into North America. They also wanted to take advantage of the colony's warm climate to grow crops they could not produce in England—silk, in particular. Carolina's proprietors hoped to populate their lands with settlers who were already in the New World. But this plan was never a great success. The Puritans were reluctant to move, since they would have to live with people who did not share their religious beliefs. Lord Berkeley persuaded a few Virginians to migrate south, but because they found no advantages to the area, few other Virginians followed their example.

Despite the proprietors' reluctance to sponsor immigrants, many of the people who settled in the Carolinas came from overseas. The first group came from Barbados and Jamaica. These West Indian islands had originally been colonized by poor English farmers, but over the years the small landholders were driven out as great sugar-growing estates were consolidated and English yeomen were replaced by African slaves. By 1666 some eight hundred white settlers from the West Indies had tried to establish themselves near Cape Fear in North Carolina. This group was soon discouraged by frequent storms and the apparently barren soil. Most of them moved on to other colonies or returned to Barbados.

The likelihood of populating the Carolinas seemed remote. In 1669, however, Sir Anthony Ashley Cooper, one of the proprietors, brought over three shiploads of colonists from England. By 1672 there were two hundred colonists in South Carolina,

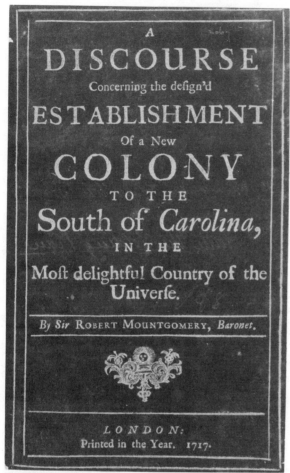

A
DISCOURSE
Concerning the defign'd
ESTABLISHMENT
Of a New
COLONY
TO THE
South of *Carolina*,
IN THE
Moſt delightful Country of the
Univerſe.

By Sir ROBERT MOUNTGOMERY, Baronet.

LONDON:
Printed in the Year. 1717.

AN ADVERTISING TRACT DESIGNED TO ENTICE ENGLISH SETTLERS TO MIGRATE TO SOUTH CAROLINA.

and in the 1680s they were joined by a small group of French Protestants and Scots.

The proprietors of Carolina had been granted broad authority. With the help of Cooper's confidential secretary, the philosopher John Locke, they drew up the Fundamental Constitutions of Carolina. Recently accepted political theories held that a just and stable society was one in which a noble leisured class was balanced by a larger class of independent freeholders. The Fundamental Constitutions therefore provided that 40 percent of the colony's land would be reserved for a hereditary nobility, and that the rest would be distributed to freeholders.

The government consisted of an appointed governor and a bicameral legislature. The upper house, representing the nobility, reserved the right to introduce legislation. Gradually, however, the Fundamental Constitutions were liberalized. As in the other colonies, the lower house fought for and slowly won more power. By the end of the century the Fundamental Constitutions were no longer used.

After 1691 the northern part of the colony became known as North Carolina and had its own governor. There never had been much to bind the two Carolinas together. Most of North Carolina's population had settled around Albemarle Sound, the colony's northernmost region. The poor, fiercely individualistic farmers who inhabited this area raised vegetables, tobacco, and livestock, and made naval stores. Economically the region was a satellite of Virginia, since most of its imports and exports moved through what today is the Norfolk area. South Carolina's population, on the other hand, was conservative, aristocratic, and cosmopolitan, and its economy gradually flourished by exporting furs and deerskins, and by producing rice and indigo on large plantations worked by slave labor. Both Carolinas were made royal colonies in the 1720s in response to the repeated complaints of settlers that their proprietors were not defending them against attacks by the Spanish and the Indians.

Georgia

In 1732, in an effort to secure British control of the Atlantic seaboard from Maine to Florida, King George II created Georgia, a new colony on the southern border of South Carolina. Although the crown intended Georgia to serve as a buffer against Spanish encroachment on English settlements, the group of English philanthropists led by General James Oglethorpe, to whom the colony was granted, had a nobler purpose: they wanted to make Georgia a refuge for debtors languishing in English prisons.

At first, Georgia's administration reflected the idealism of its trustees. Settled not by debtors, but by the "worthy poor" of England, the colony allowed no one to become extremely wealthy; farmers could own no more than five hundred acres, and slavery was prohibited, as were rum and

Royal

Proprietary

Corporate

The Thirteen Colonies • 1775

Colony	Date chartered	Settlement	Status in British Empire
Massachusetts	1629	1630	1691-Royal
New Hampshire	1621	1630	1679-Royal
Rhode Island	1644(1st Charter) 1663(2nd Charter)	1636	Remained self-governing
Connecticut	1662	1636	Remained self-governing
New York	1621(Dutch) 1664(English)	1624 1664	1685-Royal
Pennsylvania	1681	1681	Remained proprietary under Penn family
New Jersey	1665 and 1674	c. 1660s	1702-Royal
Delaware	1638(Swedes) 1655(Dutch)	c. 1624	Proprietary under Penn after 1682. Seperate assembly in 1704.
Maryland	1632	1634	Remained proprietary under Baltimore family
Virginia	1606(1st Charter) 1609(2nd Charter) 1612(3rd Charter)	1607	1624-Royal
North Carolina	1663	c. 1653	1729-Royal
South Carolina	1663	c. 1670	1729-Royal
Georgia	1732	1733	1753-Royal

brandy. However, the mixed group of Scots, Welsh, Germans, and English who came to Georgia did not accept these restrictions gracefully. In 1742, as a result of their protests, the law forbidding rum was repealed, and in 1750 slavery became legal, along with the right to dispose of land as an individual wished. The five-hundred acre limit on ownership of land was also lifted. Georgia did not prosper, however, and in 1752 the colony was turned over to the crown.

The proprietary colonies of the Carolinas and Georgia never had a strong sectional character. Unlike New England, where the English Puritan majority gave the region a distinct unity, the three southern colonies had a diverse population. Except for a few Virginians who had drifted down into North Carolina, most Carolinians came directly from England, France, or the West Indies. Georgia was populated by an even greater mixture of nationalities.

The Development of an Empire

During the first half of the seventeenth century the English government took little interest in its American colonies. The constant disputes between the monarchy and Parliament focused attention on matters close to home. Beginning in 1660, however, a period of internal stability encouraged the government to take a more forceful approach toward governing its possessions in the New World.

As just described, one aspect of this effort was the distribution of uncolonized areas of the Atlantic seaboard (and even some areas settled by the Dutch) to royal favorites. This was followed by a series of acts regulating colonial trade for the profit of England. These so-called Navigation Acts had far-reaching effects on relations between England and the New World colonies.

The Mercantilist Theory

In the sixteenth century the economic theory called mercantilism was in its heyday. Basically, the idea was that governments should regulate commerce in order to end their economic dependence on other nations. Gold and silver were considered the only true measure of wealth. Therefore, a nation's economic goal should be to increase its own supplies of precious metals in order to create a self-sufficient economy.

One of the main reasons Spain colonized the New World was to add to its supply of gold bullion. England, France, and the Netherlands colonized for the same reason, but their colonies did not yield large enough quantities of precious metals for these countries to attain self-sufficiency. They concluded that the best alternative was to export more goods than they imported, and require foreign buyers to pay in bullion.

The British government viewed the American colonies as a useful part of this system. England's native industry depended on certain raw materials that could not be grown at home. If these goods were purchased from foreign countries, England would have to export gold to pay for them. But if they could be purchased from English colonies, the gold would remain within the British Empire. And England's situation could even be improved if the colonies could be made to exchange their resources for English goods rather than bullion. British wealth would thus be returned to British coffers. Besides accumulating as much hard cash as possible, this system would protect native industry and agriculture from competition and encourage the growth of English shipping. The government influenced new manufacturers to employ any excess population and to produce goods for the overseas market.

The Navigation Acts

In 1651 Parliament passed the first of a series of Navigation Acts to put the theory of mercantilism into practice. The first Navigation Act provided that goods bought in England could be transported to the colonies only in English ships and that foreign goods could be brought to England only in English vessels or in ships from the product's country of origin. This act was aimed at the Dutch, who produced few goods themselves but whose merchant fleet was busy establishing the Dutch as leaders in world trade.

The first Navigation Act was difficult to enforce, since England did not have sufficient shipping to supply the colonies. In fact, the colonies continued trading directly with European countries. However, by the time Charles II ascended the throne in 1660, the English fleet had expanded, Dutch power in the New World was reduced, and enforcement became more effective. A second Navigation Act was passed which severely limited colonial trade with Europe. Now, all goods bound for the colonies had to be shipped in English or colonial vessels, and the master of the ship and most of the sailors had to be either English or English colonials. In addition, the colonies were forbidden to sell certain "enumerated" articles directly to the nations on the Continent. These goods, including sugar, tobacco, indigo, and cotton, had to be shipped to England or to other English colonies. European nations, therefore, had to go to England to purchase colonial goods and had to pay the additional English duties.

In 1663 still another law was passed. Now, all European goods bound for America had to be brought first to England and loaded onto English vessels for shipment to the colonies. Salt, slaves, and wine were the only exceptions.

English officials soon discovered that they had left a loophole in their regulations. The colonies could still trade freely among themselves. Colonial shippers carrying enumerated articles would simply tell the customs officials that they were headed for another colony, then they would smuggle the goods into European ports. In 1673, therefore, a new act forced American captains to pay export duties when they left port. Customs officials were stationed in all important colonial ports. A final act passed in 1696 summarized previous mercantile regulations and provided vice admiralty courts to try cases of smuggling.

The Navigation Acts were enlarged in the following decades, mainly by modifying the list of enumerated articles. This allowed England to control

INTERPRETING AMERICAN HISTORY

MERCANTILISM What effect did the strong mercantilist regulations have on colonial trade? Historians have long debated the question. In the 1830s George Bancroft, a prominent American historian, wrote a *History of the United States*. Bancroft pictured British mercantilism as a cold-blooded plan to exploit the colonies' natural resources and stunt their economies. He even argued that American resentment over the Navigation Acts was one of the principal causes of the Revolution.

Fifty years later, George L. Beer and Charles M. Andrews took quite a different tack. They contended that the Navigation Acts had done more to protect American industries and encourage American shipping than to dampen the colonial economy. True, certain minor industries had been forbidden in order to prevent competition with English industries. But this was a small price to pay for guaranteeing other markets—and occasionally even monopolies—in England. Furthermore, the acts guaranteed the colonials a part in the British Empire's lucrative sea trade with the rest of the world. Beer and Andrews also rejected the argument that the Navigation Acts had played an im-

portant role in precipitating the American Revolution, as did L. A. Harper's important study of the Navigation Acts which he wrote during the New Deal era.

In the late 1930s, the (then) Marxist historian Louis M. Hacker described the Navigation Acts as an attempt by one capitalist state to suppress another. According to Hacker, the colonies had to throw off the restrictions in order to fulfill their own capitalist destiny.

In the 1950s Oliver M. Dickerson examined seventeenth- and eighteenth-century pamphlets, newspapers, and essays, and found that the colonists rarely objected to the Navigation Acts until 1763, when the British began to exploit the colonies.

The relevant evidence is enormous and insufficient at the same time. While thousands of contemporary writings remain, shipping and trade figures are incomplete. At this time it seems unlikely that more data will be uncovered. Future interpretations will probably depend upon more sophisticated analysis of the information we already have and on the biases of the historians themselves.

---

the manufacture as well as the trade of certain colonial products. These included certain colonial textiles, rice, naval stores, copper and furs, and American-made hats. The Iron Act of 1750 made it illegal to build new iron mills for manufacturing products from iron and removed English import duties on pig and bar iron.

Enforcing the Navigation Acts In 1675 the Lords of Trade (renamed the Board of Trade in 1696), a committee of Charles II's Privy Council, was created to enforce the acts and oversee all aspects of colonial rule. One of its first actions was to send an agent to New England. This agent, Edward Randolph, was charged with investigating reports of smuggling and other evasions of the Navigation Acts. Randolph returned the antipathy the colonists felt toward him in kind and his report condemned almost every aspect of life in Massachusetts (the col-

ony with the worst record for violating British laws). He reported that French ships were entering New England ports in open violation of the Navigation Acts and that colonial merchants were cooperating with them. He made other charges, too: that public officers were neglecting to take oaths of allegiance to the king, that the Church of England was virtually nonexistent in New England, and that Massachusetts had annexed Maine and New Hampshire without royal permission and against the will of the people in those colonies.

The Dominion of New England Alarmed by Randolph's reports, the committee annulled the Massachusetts Bay Company's charter in 1684 and those of Connecticut and Rhode Island two years later. When James II succeeded his brother Charles II as king in 1685 he continued the effort to tighten control over the colonies. One of his first acts was to join

New England, New York, and New Jersey together into a single administrative district called the Dominion of New England. The Dominion was to be ruled from Boston by a royal governor.

In December 1686 Sir Edmund Andros, the first and only Dominion governor, sailed into Boston harbor. Three hours after his arrival, he antagonized the Puritans by holding an Anglican service. That was only the first of many indignities he inflicted on them. What the colonials resented most was that Andros possessed dictatorial powers. The English king had seen to it that the Dominion's constitution included no provision for a representative assembly. A council of officials appointed by the king was the only limit on the royal governor's authority. The governor and his advisers could make laws, dispense justice, and levy taxes as they saw fit.

Andros enraged the colonists by imposing a heavy duty on imported rum, brandy, and wine, levying a direct tax on real estate, and questioning the validity of all New England land titles. He rigidly enforced the Navigation Acts. Offenders were tried by judges expert in maritime law rather than by civil courts with juries.

The Andros regime was the beginning of the end of the Puritans' dominance in New England. Their rights to their land, to trial by jury, to representative government—all were in jeopardy. They were reduced to being dependent on the crown. A new crisis was brewing in British politics, however, which soon led to the overthrow of the Dominion of New England.

The Glorious Revolution

James II made two foolish mistakes which led to his abdication in 1688. First, by trying to reinstate the absolute monarchy he angered Parliament, which was determined not to lose the powers it had consolidated over the last century. Second, by indicating that he would prefer to see the Roman Catholic church become the state church he enraged the majority of his subjects, who were Protestant. James became so unpopular that a number of prominent Englishmen boldly invited Prince William of Orange, James's Dutch Protestant son-in-law, to come to England and seize the throne. The anticipated revolution turned out to be a peaceful and triumphant procession. James II fled the country,

THE DUTCH PROTESTANT WILLIAM OF ORANGE AND HIS ENGLISH WIFE MARY ASSUMED THE ENGLISH THRONE IN THE GLORIOUS REVOLUTION OF 1688. THIS BLOODLESS REVOLUTION LED TO UPHEAVALS IN THE AMERICAN COLONIES.

and Parliament crowned the foreign prince William III king. In order to maintain a link with the English succession, James's daughter Mary, who was William's wife, was crowned queen.

In exchange for the crown, William agreed to abide by a Bill of Rights drawn up by Parliament. The bill denied the king the right to suspend laws, levy taxes, or maintain a standing army without the consent of Parliament. In an effort to end religious strife, Parliament also passed the Toleration Act in 1689, permitting all Protestants to worship openly. The Glorious Revolution which brought William III to the throne established once and for all that Parliament, not the king, was the ultimate source of authority in England.

As word of the revolution spread, several colonies carried out small rebellions of their own. Massachusetts threw Governor Andros in prison. Connecticut, Plymouth, and Rhode Island began to govern themselves again. In New York, a wealthy merchant named Jacob Leisler ousted Andros's assistant and governed the colony for almost two years in the name of the new king. In 1691 New York became a royal colony.

In Maryland, John Coode led a Protestant revolt against the government in order to prevent Lord Baltimore from making Maryland a Catholic colony. Coode governed Maryland until 1691 when it became a royal colony. It was not until 1715 that the Baltimore family again gained control of Maryland.

The Colonial System

The Glorious Revolution was a turning point in America's colonial history. Although there was no central agency governing the colonies, by the end of the seventeenth century most of the colonies founded by joint-stock companies or by proprietors had come under royal jurisdiction. The English government was interested not in close political control over its empire, but in regulation of colonial commerce for England's own profit.

In 1691 Massachusetts received a new charter which enlarged its territory by adding Plymouth and Maine, but restricted the colonists' political autonomy. Massachusetts governors were now appointed by the English king, and all laws passed by the assembly would be subject to review in England. The new charter forced Massachusetts to drop the religious qualification from the right to vote, thus allowing more people to take part in the political process, and to accept religious toleration of dissenters.

This new charter strengthened the authority of the royal governors. In theory, and to some extent in practice, British monarchs retained direct control over America. The king appointed the governors as well as most of the upper houses of the colonial legislatures. In the eighteenth century, English kings vetoed one out of every twenty laws passed by colonial assemblies. The royal governors actively promoted the Anglican faith. The number of colonial goods that could be shipped to England was increased, but new restrictions prevented the colonists from trading with any other foreign country. In addition, fewer and fewer of these items could be exported from the colonies at all, not even to England where they would compete with English goods.

Despite these limitations, the new order did have some advantages. Local customs were usually observed out of respect for individual rights. Dutch shippers and other commercial rivals were no longer allowed to interfere with colonial trade, thus guaranteeing American merchants a place in Britain's thriving commercial network.

Although royal control was occasionally oppressive, in many ways it simplified regulations and promoted harmony among the colonies. And even with the British restrictions, widespread smuggling was still possible. For the time being, most colonials were willing to accept the relatively mild restrictions in order to enjoy the advantages of belonging to a mighty empire.

Readings

General Works

Andrews, Charles M., *The Colonial Period of American History*, Vols. 1–3. New Haven: Yale University Press, 1964.

Crane, V. W., *The Southern Frontier, 1670–1732*. Ann Arbor: University of Michigan Press, 1956.

Craven, Wesley F., *The Southern Colonies in the Seventeenth Century*. Baton Rouge, La.: Louisiana State University Press, 1949.

_____, *The Colonies in Transition, 1660–1713*. New York: Harper & Row, 1968 (Paper: Harper & Row).

_____, *White, Red, and Black: The Seventeenth Century Virginian*. Charlottesville, Va.: University Press of Virginia, 1968.

Langdon, George, *Pilgrim Colony: A History of New Plymouth, 1620–1691*. New Haven: Yale University Press, 1966.

Pomfret, John E., and Floyd M. Shumway, *Founding the American Colonies, 1583–1660*. New York: Harper & Row, 1970.

Simmons, R. C., *The American Colonies: From Settlement to Independence*. New York: McKay, 1976.

Vaughan, Alden T., *American Genesis: Captain John Smith and the Founding of Virginia*. Boston: Little, Brown, 1975.

Wertenbaker, T. J., *The Middle Colonies*. New York: Scribner's, 1938.

_____, *The Old South*. New York: Scribner's, 1942.

Wertenbaker, T. J., *The Puritan Oligarchy*. New York: Scribner's, 1947 (Paper, 1970).

Special Studies

Bailyn, Bernard, *The New England Merchants in the Seventeenth Century*. Cambridge: Harvard University Press, 1955 (Paper: Harper & Row Torchbook, 1964).

Battis, Emery, *Saints and Sectaries: Anne Hutchinson and the Antinomian Controversy in the Massachusetts Bay Colony*. North Carolina: University of North Carolina Press, 1962.

Demos, John, *Little Commonwealth: Family Life in Plymouth Colony*. New York: Oxford University Press, 1970.

Harper, L. A., *The English Navigation Laws*. New York: Octagon Books, 1964.

Jennings, Francis, *The Invasion of America: Indians, Colonialism, and the Cant of Conquest*. Chapel Hill, N.C.: University of North Carolina Press, 1975.

Kammen, Michael, *Colonial New York: A History*. New York: KTO Press, 1975.

Lovejoy, David S., *The Glorious Revolution in America*. New York: Harper & Row, 1972.

Morgan, Edmund S., *The Puritan Family*. New York: Harper Torchbook, 1966.

Morison, Samuel E., *Builders of the Bay Colony*. Boston: Houghton Mifflin, 1964.

———, *The Intellectual Life of Colonial New England*. New York: New York University Press, 1956 (Paper: Cornell University Press, 1960).

Smith, Abbot E., *Colonists in Bondage: White Servitude and Convict Labor in America 1607–1776*. Chapel Hill, N.C.: University of North Carolina Press, 1947.

Thompson, Roger, *Women in Stuart England and America: A Comparative Study*. London: Routledge & Kegan, 1974.

Tolles, Frederick B., *Meeting House and Counting House: The Quaker Merchants of Colonial Philadelphia 1682–1763*. Chapel Hill, N.C.: University of North Carolina Press, 1948 (Paper: W. W. Norton, 1963).

Vaughan, Alden T., *New England Frontier, Puritans and Indians 1620–1675*. Boston: Little, Brown, 1965.

Washburn, Wilcomb E., *The Governor and the Rebel: A History of Bacon's Rebellion in Virginia*. Chapel Hill, N.C.: University of North Carolina Press, 1967.

Wright, Louis B., *The First Gentlemen of Virginia*. San Marino, Calif.: The Huntington Library, 1940 (Paper: University Press of Virginia, 1964).

Primary Sources

Beverly, Robert, *The History and Present State of Virginia*, Louis B. Wright (Ed.). Charlottesville, Va.: University Press of Virginia, 1968.

Bradford, William, *Of Plymouth Plantation*, Samuel E. Morison (Ed.). New York: Knopf, 1952.

Hawke, David F., *Captain John Smith's History of Virginia*. New York: Bobbs-Merrill, 1970. (Paper)

Miller, Perry, and Thomas H. Johnson (Eds.)., *The Puritans: A Source Book of Their Writings*. New York: Harper & Row Torchbooks, 1969.

Tolles, Frederick B., and E. G. Alderfer (Eds.), *The Witness of William Penn*. New York: Macmillan, 1957.

Winthrop, John, *Winthrop's Journal*, James K. Hosmer (Ed.). New York: Scribner's, 1908.

Biographies

Barbour, Philip L., *The Three Worlds of Captain John Smith*. Boston: Houghton Mifflin, 1964.

Dunn, Mary M., *William Penn: Politics and Conscience*. Princeton, N.J.: Princeton University Press, 1967.

Morgan, Edmund S., *The Puritan Dilemma: The Story of John Winthrop*. Boston: Little, Brown, 1958.

Spalding, Phinizy, *Oglethorpe in America*. Chicago: University of Chicago Press, 1977.

Winslow, Ola E., *Master Roger Williams*. New York: Macmillan, 1957.

Historical Novels

Barth, John, *The Sot-Weed Factor*. New York: Grosset & Dunlap, 1964.

Cannon, Le Grand, Jr., *Come Home at Even*. New York: Holt, 1951.

Forbes, Esther, *Paradise*. New York: Harcourt, Brace, 1937.

Hawthorne, Nathaniel, *The Scarlet Letter*. New York: New American Library, 1970.

Johnston, Mary, *To Have and to Hold*. New York: McGraw-Hill, 1953.

Bold Voyager

CAPTAIN JOHN SMITH AND THE SETTLEMENT OF JAMESTOWN

*Here lies one conquer'd
that hath conquer'd Kings,
Subdu'd large Territories,
and done things
Which to the World
impossible would seeme,
But that the truth is
held in more esteeme.*

So begins the inscription carved on the gravestone of John Smith who was buried in St. Sepulchre's Church, London. The epithet does not exaggerate; in fact, it only hints at the scope and vitality of a life played out like a highly embellished fantasy. John Smith was a daring adventurer and a soldier of fortune who traveled over four continents, living by his wits and his sword. As an explorer and colonizer, he founded the first permanent British colony in America. Also a writer and an historian, he became an important propagandist for the New World and produced a principal history of Virginia as well as maps, promotional literature, and books on New England. Above all, John Smith personified the restless spirit, the yearning for conquest, and the thirst for change that pervaded seventeenth-century England.

John Smith was born in 1579 or 1580, the son of a tenant farmer in Willoughby, Lincolnshire. After acquiring a traditional grammar school education, he left school at the age of fifteen to become an apprentice to a prosperous merchant in Kings Lynn. However, such a sedate existence held little appeal for a youth who yearned for the excitement of the sea and the glory of the battlefield. His opportunity for adventure was close at hand, for the Elizabethan era was in full flower. This was a period described by Christopher Marlowe as an age "of wonder and delight."

During the reign of Elizabeth, England had become a powerful nation-state, and her long quest for empire had begun. Scotland and France had to be pacified, the Protestant uprising in the Low Countries needed support, and preparations had to be made to defeat the powerful Spanish

CAPTAIN JOHN SMITH.

Armada. Symbolic of the times were the daring escapades of Sir Francis Drake and other English "sea dogs" who pillaged Spanish ships and colonies in the West Indies. These seafarers returned with tales of fabulous treasures and exotic natives.

This was an era of a burgeoning new social order in which class distinctions were becoming less rigid. Position and family background had begun to yield to talent and ability. Such accelerating social changes encouraged venturesome individuals to better themselves and enabled John Smith to break away from his modest beginnings. Not long after his father's death, he joined other British volunteers in the Netherlands where Protestants were fighting for independence from the Catholic king of Spain, Philip II. There Smith learned the arts of warfare. On his return to England he became a traveling companion to the sons of Peregrine Bertie, Lord of Willoughby Manor. Although this position was short-lived, it enabled Smith to travel through Paris, Holland, and Scotland. Eventually he returned to Lincolnshire where, as he wrote in his memoirs, he "retired himselfe into a little wooddie pasture . . . His studie was *Machiavills* Art of warre, and *Marcus Aurelius;* his exercise a good horse, with his lance and Ring."

Always practical, Smith used this period of study to form his plans for further adventures. Soon he set forth for Hungary where he joined the Austrian forces in their war against the Turks. Over the next year and a half, he distinguished himself many times in battle. He was made a captain for successfully deceiving the enemy with a display of fireworks, and he killed three Turkish officers who had chal-

lenged him to single combat. However, in Rumania his army was decimated, and Smith, left for dead on the battlefield, was captured and sold as a slave, first in Constantinople and then in Tartary. With luck and cunning, Smith succeeded in killing his master and escaping. By Christmas of 1603, he had made his way to Leipzig. There the Prince of Transylvania granted him his formal discharge papers which verified his position as captain, confirmed his coat of arms, and awarded him 1500 gold ducats. With this newfound wealth and status, Smith toured Germany and Spain, finally moving on to North Africa where he took a turn as a privateer. By late 1604 he was back in England.

John Smith returned home at a time when England's interest in America was reviving. Britain had generally ignored the New World ever since 1497 when the Cabots had failed to discover a northern passage to the Orient. New expeditions were sent to America in 1602, and by 1605 explorers were returning with reports that aroused fresh interest in colonization. In 1606 leading merchants succeeded in convincing King James to charter two organizations, the Plymouth and the London Companies, to which he gave sole rights to a section of the American mainland. The colonies were to be governed by resident councils chosen by the parent corporations. It is likely that Smith followed the progress of the charters, waiting for the right moment to enlist. His chance came when Bartholomew Gosnold, a chief organizer of the London Company and a relative of the Berties, began seeking men to lead an expedition to Chesapeake Bay.

On Saturday, December 20, 1606, John Smith set sail for Virginia

aboard the *Susan Constant,* accompanied by two other vessels, *Godspeed* and *Discovery.* For four months the expedition held to its course across the rough Atlantic. By the time the three little ships reached the Canary Islands, trouble was fomenting aboard. Although details are unclear, Smith was held chiefly responsible and was taken prisoner under suspicion of concealing a mutiny. Upon landing on the muddy peninsula in the James River on May 14, the colonists opened a sealed box containing the names of the seven chosen councilors. Smith's name was included; however, because of the charges against him he was excluded from the governing body for over a month. This conflict set up a pattern of dissent which was to plague the struggling Virginia enterprise for many years.

Numerous problems beset the new colony. The danger of Indian attack, malnutrition, disease spread by the brackish water, and internal discord all threatened the survival of the settlers. At the end of eighteen months, nearly half of Jamestown's inhabitants had perished. Although Smith became seriously ill, he recovered and soon began to take charge of affairs. Under his leadership, new houses were built, the colony was successfully defended from Indian attacks and trade with local tribes was established, and explorations of Chesapeake Bay and its surroundings were begun.

During Jamestown's early period from June 1607 through December 1608, Smith's power and influence increased. He was skillful at resolving factional disputes and took on the role of principal negotiator with the Indians. In his relations with the Indians, Smith combined firmness, tolerance, and occasional cruelty. While he grudgingly came to recognize their skill, he never was able to trust them. His caution was not unjustified, for the Algonquins of the area were expanding their empire and regarded the white colony as unwelcome. In December while leading one of his expeditions into the interior, Smith was taken prisoner by a band of Indian hunters. He was brought to the camp of Powhatan, the most powerful chief in the Chesapeake area. Powhatan finally freed him, although his reasons for doing so are unclear. There are several accounts of the incident; one indicates that Smith so impressed Powhatan that he made him a subordinate chief. Only Smith's 1624 *Generall Historie* mentions the intercession of Powhatan's favorite daughter, Pocahontas.

In 1608 Smith assumed formal control of Jamestown through his election as president of the council. For almost a year his dogged perseverance and common sense gave him virtually absolute authority. He had inherited a tinderbox of factionalism and discontent. In addition to continuing tensions among the colonists and unstable relations with the Indians, there were London investors and directors who had to be assured that the venture was turning a profit. Matters were complicated when Christopher Newport, captain of the *Susan Constant*, sailed into the harbor with new orders from the London Company that Smith felt were ridiculous: Newport was directed to crown Powhatan king in the hope that this action would bring the chief under the yoke of English authority; he was also instructed to adopt a softer approach toward the Indians than Smith had taken. A ludicrous coronation followed, and English-Indian relations were undermined. In addition, although Newport brought fresh supplies, he also brought more mouths to feed, and the settlement's food supply was depleted.

During the difficult winter of 1608–1609 only Smith's diligence and prompt actions kept the colony from starving. Maintaining an uneasy peace with the Indians, Smith bullied, wheedled, and threatened Powhatan until the chief reluctantly agreed to supply the settlers with corn. As conditions worsened, some colonists simply joined the Indians. There was such a severe deterioration of morale among those remaining in Jamestown that Smith finally declared that those who did not work would not eat. Just as the colony had begun to revive in the spring, it was discovered that their storehouses of corn were infested by rats. Smith had no choice but to disperse the colony into small groups that were to live off the land. A regular system of fishing was established and crops were planted, but still dissatisfaction increased.

The situation was resolved in August 1609 when four supply ships from London reached Jamestown. Aboard were several former colonists who had been sent back to England and had remained bitter enemies of Smith. They brought word that Sir Thomas Gates, who had been appointed the new lieutenant governor by King James, had been detained but was on his way to take over leadership of the colony. Lord De La Warr would follow as governor. In the interim before the new officers arrived, there was great confusion as to who was in authority. Smith's enemies, seeing their chance, banded together, brought charges against him, and forced him out of office. In September, returning from an attempt to assist a small group that had settled up-river, Smith was seriously burned when his powder bag caught fire. Ailing and disillusioned, he left Virginia in October on a ship bound for England.

After Smith's departure, Jamestown began to disintegrate. Many of the colonists were killed by Indians; others returned to England. Again faced with starvation, the remaining settlers were forced to eat acorns and roots and even the bodies of dead comrades. Out of five hundred, only sixty were still alive when their new leaders finally arrived.

The last stage of Smith's career, from his return to England to his death in 1631, was dominated by growing frustration as his efforts to play an active part in the growth of the New World were repeatedly thwarted. He journeyed to America once again in 1614 when he mapped the New England coast and gave the area its name. A second attempt in 1615 to establish a permanent settlement in New England was blocked by storms and an attack by pirates. Ill luck intervened once more in 1617, when strong winds held his ships to the English coast for three months. Eventually the expedition had to be cancelled. By 1624 Smith had resigned himself to finding other ways of fostering English settlement of the New World.

Smith's later years were not lacking in accomplishments, for during this period he produced and published some of his most important writings. In 1612 he established himself as an expert on the early history of the Virginia

C. Smith taketh the King of Pamavnkee prisoner -1608.

hope of inviting future support and investments in America, Smith's work examined the whole English involvement in the New World, from John Cabot's discoveries in 1497 through Britain's role in Virginia, Bermuda, and New England. The books also set down Smith's vision of America's future, including the concept of prosperity and individual advancement as the key to a new social order.

Smith's final work, *Avertisements for the unexperienced Planters of New England or any where,* was penned a year before his death and appropriately capped his career as the foremost promoter of English colonization. In it he summed up his life in a concise and often touching manner. The work revealed its author's abiding concern for England's position in the world, his profound belief in the necessity of learning from experience, and his deep commitment to the prosperity of the colonies.

John Smith did not live to see his ideas take root in English colonies along the eastern coast of North America. On June 21, 1631, the indefatigable adventurer who had survived battle, slavery, imprisonment, illness, shipwrecks, and other catastrophes made out his will and died in his London bed. His life came to an end just as England was beginning to make a success of its colonizing efforts. But for a little more than half a century he had been a participant in one of the most colorful and exciting periods of European history.

colony with his *A Map of Virginia, with a Description of its Commodities, People, Government, and Religion.* The book provided the most thorough account of events in Jamestown since 1606, and the map of eastern Virginia, as well as a later map of New England, became the principal cartographic reference on British America.

Two themes appear over and over again in Smith's writings: the future greatness that could be England's if the mother country could learn to settle colonies and govern them wisely and the necessity of learning from the trials of other colonizers. Smith's idea that America was "the fittest place for an earthly Paradise" was a major concern of *The Generall Historie of Virginia, New England, and the Summer Isles,* his most ambitious and significant work.

The Generall Historie was divided into six books. While it was not a literary masterpiece and borrowed heavily from other sources, it provided the British with an epic account of their efforts to claim a continent. With the

3 Shaping an Identity

After a foreigner from any part of Europe is arrived, and become a citizen; let him devoutly listen to the voice of our great parent, which says to him, "Welcome to my shores, distressed European; bless the hour in which thou didst see my verdant fields, my fair navigable rivers, and my green mountains!—If thou wilt work, I have bread for thee; if thou wilt be honest, sober, and industrious, I have greater rewards to confer on thee—ease and independence."

St. John de Crèvecoeur, French author and diplomat
Letters from an American Farmer, 1782

Significant Events

Kingdoms of Ghana, Mali, and Songhai in Niger River Valley of Africa [700–1600]

First Africans brought to North America [1619]

Harvard College founded [1636]

Slavery legalized [1660 and after]

Half-way Covenant [1662]

Principia Mathematica by Sir Isaac Newton [1687]

Witchcraft in New England [1692–1693]

Immigration of Huguenots from France [1685 and after]

Immigration of large numbers of Germans and Scotch-Irish settlers [1700 and after]

Boston Newsletter founded [1704]

Peter Zenger case [1733]

The Great Awakening [1730s and 1740s]

A PAINTING OF A PLANTATION MANSION SURROUNDED BY THE SLAVE QUARTERS, BARNS, LAUNDRY BUILDINGS, KITCHEN, AND GRIST MILL. CROPS WERE STORED IN A WAREHOUSE ON THE WATERFRONT FROM WHICH THEY COULD EASILY BE TRANSFERRED TO OCEAN-GOING SHIPS. (The Metropolitan Museum of Art. Gift of Edgar William and Bernice Chrysler Garbisch, 1963.)

During the seventeenth and eighteenth centuries, the American colonies gradually developed their own distinct identity. By 1700 some families had been in North America for three generations, and economic and cultural patterns transplanted from Europe were slowly evolving into new, uniquely American forms.

The English settlers came to North America from a society in which social distinctions were clear. Those on the lower rungs of the ladder expected to submit to their "betters." Yet because labor was scarce, it was possible for those with ambition to rise to economic and political prominence through industry and wits, regardless of their previous social position in England. Leaders in the New World did not receive the automatic deference that members of the permanent aristocracy received in Europe, and social-class distinctions were much less rigid. In America one's place on the social scale was determined not so much by inherited wealth as by the successful acquisition of wealth. Nevertheless, a recognizable class structure was evident by the middle of the eighteenth century. About 5 percent of the free population, including royal officials, wealthy planters, merchants, lawyers, and clergy of the Anglican and Congregational churches were regarded as an upper class. Another 70 percent of the free population, yeoman farmers who owned their own land, or skilled workers and owners of small businesses living in the towns, were the eighteenth-century equivalent of a middle class. The other 25 percent were poor farmers, indentured servants, tenants on great estates, or day laborers. With some effort, many of these people were able to enter the middle class. With the important exception of blacks, who by 1775 made up about 20 percent of the total population, there was no large, oppressed lower class.

Throughout the seventeenth and eighteenth centuries, the population of the American colonies grew rapidly. An increase in the birthrate accounted for much of the growth. Non-English immigration and greater longevity were also contributing factors. Most of the large numbers of indentured servants who settled in the New World were young adults between eighteen and twenty-four years of age. The majority of the women in the colonies were of child-bearing age and they married young. In 1720 the population was about half a million; by 1775 it had jumped to about 2.5 million.

Most colonists lived on farms or in small villages, with only a small number living in the five largest seaports. By the eighteenth century all the colonial governments had eased the conditions for acquiring land, and ownership became widespread among the burgeoning population. Large landholders engaged in extensive land speculation or in renting their lands to tenants.

The individual colonies were in some ways as different from each other as they were from Europe. In order to understand the varying patterns of life in the New World, it is necessary to examine the economic and social systems of the three major colonial regions.

The Southern Colonies

During the first half of the seventeenth century, the Southern economy was maintained by yeoman farmers working their own modest landholdings. However, near the end of the century, a new aristocracy, whose position was based on control of large estates called plantations, was asserting control over the region's economic life. Less than 5 percent of new immigrants were becoming landowners. Yet, even with economic control limited to a small group of the wealthy, competition was keen and the chances for success risky.

The Plantation System

The main reason for the rise of the plantation system lay in the type of export crops grown in the South: tobacco, rice, and indigo. All three were enumerated articles which, under the requirements of the Navigation Acts, had to be shipped to England. While the privileged position of these products on the British market encouraged the colonial planters to expand production, customs duties reduced the profit that could be earned on all enumerated articles. This tended to affect small farmers the most, keeping them continually in debt.

Tobacco, popular for smoking in England, became the major export of Virginia and Maryland after America was granted a monopoly of the English market for tobacco in 1617. Production rose from twenty-five hundred pounds in 1616 to thirty million pounds in the late seventeenth century, and by the time of the Revolution, the figure had reached a hundred million. Indeed, tobacco became so abundant that supply exceeded demand, causing prices to plunge and forcing colonial planters to curtail production. In addition, the planters had to rely on an English agent, called a factor, to market their products—an arrangement which increased their expenses. This additional strain further encouraged the development of a plantation system, since only those growers who owned vast estates where huge quantities of crops could be cultivated could hope to make a profit. In fact, by the eighteenth century most planters were deeply in debt. Large landholders were able to rotate crops or to create self-sufficient plantations which would provide a living even in times of great financial stress. Small farmers, on the other hand, had no choice but to keep planting and replanting until their soil was depleted of its nutrients.

The Introduction of Slavery

As the plantation system developed, it became necessary to find an extensive and stable source of labor. Most European immigrants were unwilling to perform back-breaking work, and if forced into it through indenture, a worker could look forward to being free when the period of servitude had ended. Only on the proprietary estates in Maryland was there a tenant class of farmers bound to the land by contract for life. A few Indians were enslaved, but they proved difficult to capture in large numbers. Most were skilled warriors, familiar with the territory, and it was difficult to hunt them down. So colonial farmers began looking more and more to the importation of Africans, thinking they could hold these people in bondage permanently to meet their labor needs.

It was relatively easy for the colonists to make slaves of the Africans, since by the sixteenth century the English had come to believe that black people were inferior. The Africans' dark skin and non-Christian culture made a negative impression on British traders, and these reactions spread rapidly among the English population. This racial prejudice and the economic need for a permanent and cheap labor supply combined so that by 1700 an economy based on slavery became widespread in the Southern colonies.

The Europeans conducted the slave trade from ships or trading centers established along the west coast of Africa. Slaves were captured by other Africans, mostly leaders of coastal tribes who raided villages in the interior and exchanged their captives, many of whom had already suffered some form of slavery, for firearms, liquor, or trinkets. They were then held in corrals until a full shipload had been collected. Next they were branded, packed tightly into stifling, unsanitary holds, and dispatched on a six- to eight-week trip to the Western Hemisphere. One out of every eight slaves usually died on the voyage, and the rate of suicide was high. There are also circumstantial records of some fifty-five mutinies by blacks during the years 1699 to 1845 and references to many others.

The first cargo of Africans to appear in North America was brought to Jamestown in 1619 by Dutch traders. Although some may have been enslaved from the beginning, others were considered indentured servants and were allowed to gain their freedom. As the plantation system gradually replaced small-scale farming, however, the custom of holding slaves for life became widespread. After 1660 most of the colonies legalized slavery for blacks and by 1700 slavery was a major source of labor in the Southern colonies.

Of course, slavery was not confined to the South. Although they were never a large portion of the population in New England or the Middle colonies, slaves could be found throughout America. The population of New York City was 15 percent black. Merchants in Rhode Island played an active role in the slave trade, often bringing home to Newport blacks they were unable to sell in the South.

In general, Northern slave codes were not as severe as those of the South. Although slaves in the Northern colonies were sometimes brutally punished, they had the right to a jury trial, the right to sue, and the right to testify in court. Many were able to obtain some education and religious instruction.

TO BE SOLD, on board the Ship *Bance-Ifland*, on tuefday the 6th of *May* next, at *Afhley-Ferry*; a choice cargo of about 250 fine healthy

NEGROES,

juft arrived from the Windward & Rice Coaft. —The utmoft care has already been taken, and fhall be continued, to keep them free from the leaft danger of being infected with the SMALL-POX, no boat having been on board, and all other communication with people from *Charles-Town* prevented.

Auftin, Laurens, & Appleby.

N. B. Full one Half of the above Negroes have had the SMALL-POX in their own Country.

AN ADVERTISEMENT FOR THE SALE OF NEGRO SLAVES STRESSES THEIR FINE HEALTH, PARTICULARLY THE FACT THAT THEY ARE FREE OF SMALLPOX.

A PLAN SHOWING THE METHOD USED TO STOW SLAVES ABOARD A BRITISH SLAVE SHIP. HUNDREDS OF SLAVES COULD BE TRANSPORTED BY UTILIZING EVERY INCH OF SPACE.

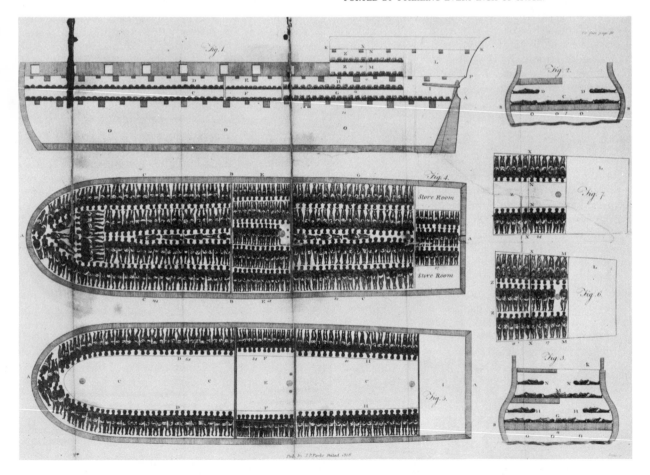

In the South slaves could not testify against whites, nor were their marriages recognized as legal. If a Southern slave died while being beaten for insubordination or trying to escape, the killing was not considered manslaughter. The only means of resistance available to Southern slaves were work slowdowns or destruction of crops and equipment.

A Slave Economy

Slavery was thought to be essential to the Southern system of large-scale staple crop production. Unlike indentured servants, slaves worked for life and could be forced to do exhausting, unhealthy work which no free person would do. On smaller farms women slaves worked in the fields and in the house, but on the plantations they were often cooks or maids.

In South Carolina and Georgia rice was cultivated exclusively by slaves because of the difficult working conditions involved. Rice was grown in low-lying coastal areas or near rivers where the fields could be flooded. Slaves were forced to work in swampy areas where they were frequently exposed to malaria. If a slave survived for only six or seven years, the owner's investment would have been repaid.

One recent explanation as to why slavery in the American South took these brutal forms is that there were no traditional institutions in the region to restrain it. European feudalism provided certain rights for laborers in the Old World, but these did not apply in America. The health and safety of blacks were of no concern to the crown, which was primarily interested in its customs revenues. Moreover, the colonial governments and churches were not strong enough to control the actions of plantation owners toward what they claimed was their legal property.

African Culture

Most Europeans have generally assumed the superiority of their own culture over the cultures of west Africa. However, the fact is that highly developed civilizations flourished in Africa as early as A.D. 700.

The great kingdoms of Ghana, Mali, and Songhai dominated life in the Niger River valley from 700 to 1600. These were complex confedera-

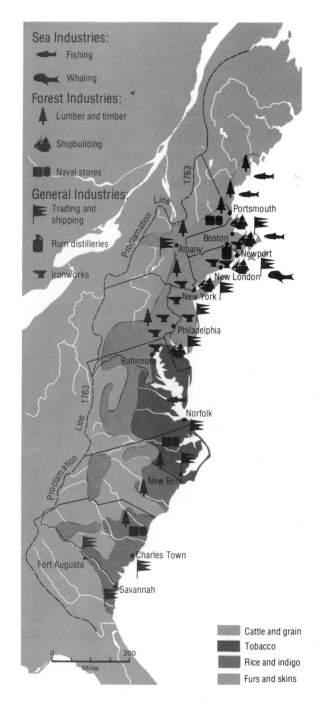

Sea Industries:
Fishing
Whaling
Forest Industries:
Lumber and timber
Shipbuilding
Naval stores
General Industries:
Trading and shipping
Rum distilleries
Ironworks

Portsmouth
Boston
Albany
Newport
New London
New York
Philadelphia
Baltimore
Norfolk
New Bern
Charles Town
Fort Augusta
Savannah

Cattle and grain
Tobacco
Rice and indigo
Furs and skins

0   200
Miles

Colonial Economy

tions of tribes governed by a king, a council of ministers, and royal representatives assigned to the tribal villages. Although the villages themselves frequently had political autonomy, the king was usually the final arbiter in matters of justice.

The social and economic life of these kingdoms, and of the smaller coastal kingdoms directly involved in the slave trade, was equally complex. Family life was of great importance. Religious practices included the worship of ancestors and nature as well as the use of magic. The Moslem faith was an important influence by the eleventh century, and Christianity was introduced by the slave traders in the sixteenth century. Based on agriculture, cattle raising, mining, and crafts, the west African economies were characterized by much commercial activity. Gold from the Niger Valley, for example, was traded with Arab merchants in the north for textiles and salt.

These civilizations produced a highly developed art. In addition to creating beautiful pottery and religious objects, the people built and decorated huge temples. Skilled artisans worked in bronze, silver, copper, and gold. At the height of west African civilization, there was a university at Timbuktu with a library containing thousands of books.

Despite the oppressive conditions of slave life, some of the black heritage survived in the New World. Because of the isolation of the black communities, Africanisms remained in the *Gullah* dialect of slaves living in the coastal islands off Georgia and South Carolina. Blacks who acquired the Christian faith merged elements of their African music with European music to produce the Negro spiritual. Much of their folklore also later became a part of American culture.

Southern Aristocracy

The elegant life-style of the minority of plantation owners set the tone of Southern life. Many of these rural aristocrats came originally from families of humble English background and made their fortunes in the 1600s.

These well-to-do planters were not gentlemen of leisure. They were directly involved in the business of managing their estates. Nevertheless, they tried to model their way of life closely after that of the English country gentry, furnishing their huge

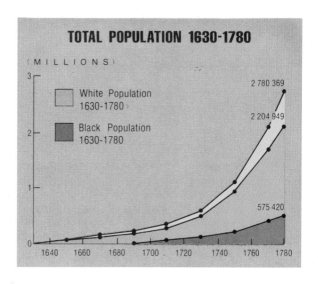

mansions with expensive English imports, copying manners and dress, even subscribing to forms of behavior dictated by English manuals.

Southern plantation owners often entertained each other on their magnificent estates. Balls frequently ran for days, and visits easily stretched into month-long stays. Hospitality was lavish, and socializing inevitably led to matchmaking. By the time of the Revolution, many of the great planters were related by marriage.

The plantation owners were the chief political leaders in Southern society. Wealth and power were based on the amount of land a person owned. In Virginia, Maryland, North Carolina, and Georgia, land ownership was a requirement for voting. In South Carolina, voters had to have either land or money. This allowed a small group of well-to-do planters to dominate electoral politics. Out of custom, the active electorate year after year chose the same representatives to the assemblies.

Politics at the local level was also dominated by the aristocracy. The governor of the colony appointed county officials such as justices of the peace, sheriffs, and judges and usually restricted his choices to members of the upper class. Subdivisions of the counties, known as parishes, were initially controlled by officials elected by members of the parish church. But by the later part of the seventeenth century, these positions had become hereditary in the wealthiest of the local families.

The only city of consequence in the South was Charleston, South Carolina. In the summer wealthy planters and their families generally left the country for a stay in this cool, seaside town. And Charleston was well prepared to cater to their tastes. Huge banquets were held at the major taverns, and traveling shows were scheduled for the summer season. Merchants, tailors, and skilled workers were on hand to show the latest English styles.

The Middle Colonies

The four Middle colonies—Delaware, New York, Pennsylvania, and New Jersey—lay between Maryland and New England. In the early years they were primarily farming areas. Corn was usually the first crop a newcomer cultivated because it was easy to grow, required little attention, provided abundant nourishment, and served as fodder for livestock. After farmers began to prosper, they generally turned to producing other cereal such as wheat, barley, and oats.

During the eighteenth century huge surpluses of wheat were shipped from Philadelphia and New York to New England and the West Indies, and meat products were exported to southern Europe. Horses were sold to New England and the American South. This intercolonial trade helped to tie the colonies together, as well as to increase specialization; each area gradually became able to market what it could produce most efficiently, because it could rely on the other colonies to supply what it lacked. By the middle of the eighteenth century, the volume of trade flowing through Philadelphia exceeded that of all the New England ports.

Land Holding

In the Middle colonies land was distributed by the headright system, which required that all the land that a person claimed had to be cleared, planted, and inhabited. As a result, most farms were modest in size, averaging between one hundred and three hundred acres. By the eighteenth century, however, land speculators began to abuse the system. Through political cronyism investors obtained estates of up to a hundred thousand acres, although the legal limit on land accumulation was only two thousand acres.

In New York these landholders sometimes resold their enormous holdings, but more often they rented out small parcels to tenant farmers. The terms of the rental often included additional obligations reminiscent of feudalism. For instance, land might be leased for ten bushels of wheat, "four fat hens," and a few days' work on the landlord's own property. The landlords also reserved all milling and mineral rights for themselves and sometimes even established private court systems on their property. These practices tended to slow immigration to the colony.

COVER OF PENNSYLVANIA *ALMANACK* FOR THE YEAR 1756.

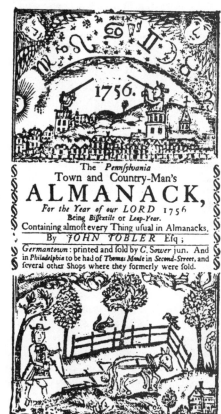

Life in Urban America

"[Philadelphia] must certainly be the object of every one's wonder and admiration. It is situated upon a tongue of land, a few miles above the confluence of the Deleware and Schuilkill; and contains about 3,000 houses, and 18 or 20,000 inhabitants. It is built north and south upon the banks of the Delaware; and is nearly two miles in length, and three quarters of one in breadth. The streets are laid out with great regularity in parallel lines, intersected by others at right angles, and are handsomely built: on each side there is a pavement of broad stones for foot passangers; and in most of them a causeway in the middle for carriages. Upon dark nights it is well lighted, and watched by a patrole: there are many fair houses and public edifices in it. . . . The city is in a very flourishing state, and inhabited by merchants, artists, tradesmen, and persons of all occupations. There is a public market held twice a week, upon Wednesday and Saturday, almost equal to that of Leadenhall; and a tolerable one every day besides. The streets are crowded with people, and the river with vessels."

Andrew Burnaby
Travels through the Middle Settlements in North America in the years 1759 and 1760.

The Small Farmer

"None of my ancestors, on either side, were either rich or great, but had the character of honesty and industry, by which they lived in credit among their neighbors, free from real want, and above the frowns of the world. . . . Meat, bread and milk was the ordinary food of all my acquaintance. I suppose the *richer sort* might make use of *those* and other luxuries, but to such people I had no access. We were accustomed to look upon, what were called *gentle folks*, as beings of a superior order. For my part, I was quite shy of *them*, and kept off at a humble distance. A *periwig*, in those days, was a distinguishing badge of *gentle folk*—and when I saw a man riding the road, near our house, with a wig on, it would so alarm my fears, and give me such a disagreeable feeling, that, I dare say, I would run off, as for my life. Such ideas of the difference between *gentle* and *simple*, were, I believe, universal among all of my rank and age. . . ."

Devereux Jarratt, Virginia minister
The Life of the Reverend Devereux Jarratt, 1794

By the eighteenth century a well-to-do landed and merchant class, comparable to that of the South, had emerged in the Middle colonies. Although merchants in New York City were frequently undercut in trade by the more enterprising traders in Philadelphia and Boston, they were nevertheless financially successful. New York merchants were usually landholders as well and shared social and political power with the landed elite of the colony. The Quaker merchants of Philadelphia controlled the political life of Pennsylvania until the 1750s but they were constantly opposed by other Quakers and Scotch-Irish Presbyterians who lived further inland.

Immigration

With the exception of a few thousand French Protestants (Huguenots) fleeing religious persecution, the population of colonial America in 1700 was composed primarily of farmers, tradespeople, and skilled workers from England and Holland. By the 1760s the population had increased to almost two million, about one-third of whom had been born abroad.

The Middle colonies, where newcomers of diverse faiths and backgrounds found religious toleration, tended to absorb most of the non-English immigrants to the New World, especially in the late

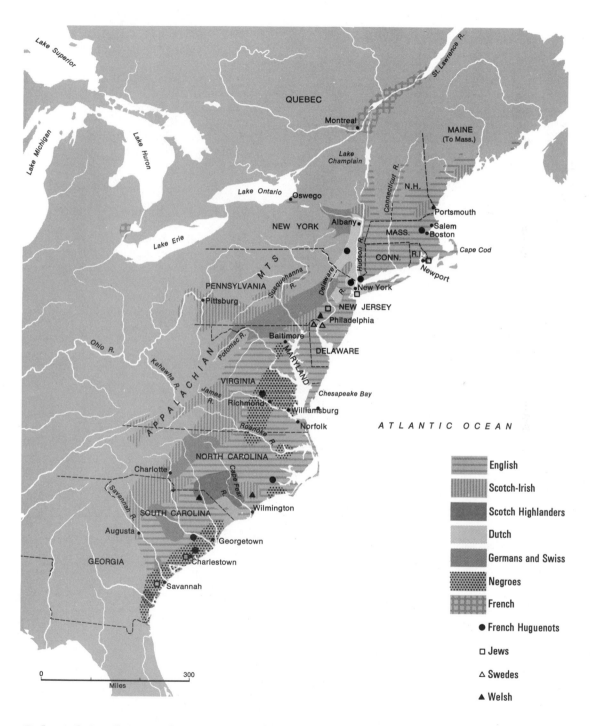

Lake Superior

Lake Michigan

Lake Huron

Lake Erie

Lake Ontario

QUEBEC

Montreal

St. Lawrence R.

Lake Champlain

MAINE
(To Mass.)

Oswego

NEW YORK

Albany

N.H.

Portsmouth

Connecticut R.

MASS.

Salem
Boston

MTS

PENNSYLVANIA

Susquehanna R.

Pittsburg

Hudson R.

CONN.

R.I.

Cape Cod

Newport

Delaware R.

New York

NEW JERSEY

Philadelphia

Baltimore

Ohio R.

Kanawha R.

Potomac R.

MARYLAND

DELAWARE

APPALACHIAN

VIRGINIA

James R.

Richmond

Williamsburg

Chesapeake Bay

ATLANTIC OCEAN

Roanoke R.

Norfolk

NORTH CAROLINA

Charlotte

Cape Fear R.

Savannah R.

SOUTH CAROLINA

Wilmington

Augusta

GEORGIA

Georgetown

Charlestown

Savannah

0   300
Miles

English	English
Scotch-Irish	Scotch-Irish
Scotch Highlanders	Scotch Highlanders
Dutch	Dutch
Germans and Swiss	Germans and Swiss
Negroes	Negroes
French	French
●	French Huguenots
□	Jews
△	Swedes
▲	Welsh

Colonial Settlement by Nationalities • 1770

seventeenth and early eighteenth centuries. The South had an ample supply of slave labor with which the immigrants did not compete, and Puritan intolerance and exclusivity tended to discourage newcomers to New England.

Impoverished by wars and crop failures on the Continent and hounded by religious persecution, thousands of Germans from the Rhineland fled to the colonies in the early eighteenth century. Almost half of these immigrants eventually settled in Pennsylvania, where they became known as the Pennsylvania Dutch (a corruption of the word *Deutsch*, meaning "German"). Pennsylvania attracted them because it offered almost complete religious freedom, a generous land policy, and soil that was very similar to that of Germany.

A few of the German immigrants were members of strict religious sects such as the Mennonites, Moravians, and Dunkards, who wished to avoid contact with the rest of the world. The vast majority, however, threw themselves into commerce and politics. Many were artisans whose skill far surpassed that of most Anglo-American settlers.

Another substantial wave of immigrants in the early 1700s came from northern Ireland. A few were of pure Irish ancestry. Most, however, were Presbyterian Scots who had moved to northern Ireland early in the seventeenth century, and who became known as the Scotch-Irish. This group left the British Isles following a series of economic and political disasters. Among these was a terrible drought which struck northern Ireland in 1714. Four years of bad

crops followed, and in 1717 landlords of Irish properties doubled and even trebled their rents. Faced with economic ruin, thousands of Scotch-Irish began to leave for America. They first headed for New England, but the Puritans gave them a cold reception. Soon, like the Germans, they moved to Pennsylvania and from there slowly pushed west to the Appalachian Mountains and into the Southern uplands, becoming America's most rugged frontier people.

Counties: Governmental Units

Except in New England, colonial farms were widely scattered and separated by vast expanses of forest. Since there were few towns in the Middle colonies, farmers conducted their civic activities through counties—larger, looser governmental units. This practice was similar to that of the Southern colonies.

About once a month, farmers rode to the county courthouse to vote, take part in drills of the local militia, or pursue legal business. Once a year those who met the property qualification elected representatives to the colonial assembly. At the county courthouse births, deaths, and marriages were registered, wills and deeds recorded, and licenses issued for various businesses. County judges had significant influence on an area's growth and development through their power to permit the building of new roads or the opening of new ferry lines.

The New England Colonies

Throughout the colonial period, New England remained predominantly Puritan in religious outlook and English in ethnic background. Despite the differences among the various Calvinist branches, the area possessed a more unified regional character than any other part of America.

Another factor promoting regional unity was the method by which unsettled land was distributed. In New England, virgin lands were granted to groups of settlers, a system which automatically organized new immigrants into towns. A group usually received a tract of land five miles square. Near the center of the tract the citizens erected a village around a town square. Here all the farmers and

their families lived in a true community, with a church and a school. The land around the village was divided into farms, pastures, and woodlands. Farms were parceled out to each family, but pastures and timberlands were held in common by the village. Such close-knit communities helped to maintain Puritan control of religious life, and assured economic and physical security through group cooperation.

The Puritans encouraged participation in local government. All adult male members of the township were eligible to vote on municipal issues, but citizen involvement went well beyond the ballot. At some time in his life, almost every New England townsman held a local public office. In fact, interest in local politics was so intense that the average New Englander tended to neglect the larger colonial issues, leaving them to the elected representatives in the colonial assembly. Merchants, lawyers, and prosperous farmers usually held these positions, and, as was the practice in the Southern colonies, the same individuals were often elected over and over again.

Family Life

A typical seventeenth-century New England household consisted of a husband and wife, their children (usually six or seven), at least one grandparent, and often servants or apprentices. It was rare for more than one couple to live under one roof, even if they were closely related. After marriage, a man was usually given land, cattle, tools, and a house, or the promise of help in building one. A bride was given movable property: furniture, clothing, or money.

The family was the center of community life—the society in microcosm. As a result, laws meted out severe punishment for disrespect to parents. Yet even in colonial New England there was a loosening of family ties and a concern that the American environment was undermining parental authority.

Although parents were sometimes able to use land-ownership to prevent their children from striking out on their own, most young adults found it fairly easy to live independently because of the abundance of free land. Often, a son was able to develop his own farm on land whose title remained in his father's name. Because labor was in short supply, parents had to look to their children for help; this, too, made it difficult to maintain firm control over them.

Crafts

Despite the efforts of New England farmers, the region could not grow enough food to meet its needs. The ground was too rocky, the growing season too short, and the amount of arable land too small. Throughout the eighteenth century, the area had neither a large staple crop nor any important mineral resources—and yet New England prospered.

New England's wealth was based on the productivity of its merchants, artisans, and fishing industry. Even small towns had need for skilled laborers such as carpenters, tailors, weavers, and blacksmiths. Some villages built their fortunes by specializing in one craft. In the 1760s, for instance,

A DEPICTION OF THE VARIOUS CRAFTS AND TRADES, INCLUDING WOODCUTTING, TAILORING, FARMING, AND SHIPPING, PRACTICED IN AND AROUND BOSTON DURING THE EARLY EIGHTEENTH CENTURY.

eighty thousand pairs of shoes a year were being manufactured in Lynn, Massachusetts. Crafts-people in New England were paid considerably higher wages than their counterparts in England, and their importance to the region's economy helped keep them relatively prosperous.

The Triangular Trade

The success of New England's manufacturing was matched by that of its commercial ventures. In the seventeenth century the Northern colonies were the indisputable masters of America's trade. Later their dominance was threatened by New York and Pennsylvania, but New England merchants always controlled a large part of colonial shipping.

To a great extent, commercial enterprise was built on what has been called the triangular trade, with Europe or Africa, the West Indies, and some American port as the three corners. The triangular trade route was necessary to convert locally abundant products into products of value to trade with England. Part of New England's contribution to the trade stemmed from its fishing industry. Great catches were dried and shipped to southern Europe and the West Indies. In the Caribbean the fish were exchanged for molasses, which would be converted into rum in New England distilleries. Next, the rum was transported to the west coast of Africa, where it was traded for slaves, ivory, or gold dust. Finally, the slaves were taken to the West Indies and sold to plantation owners. The profits were used to purchase more molasses. The triangular trade was not a neat, precise pattern. There were many criss-crossings back and forth across the ocean by large numbers of small merchants, with New England vessels often stopping off along the Atlantic coast in southern Europe or England.

New England Cities

Thriving commerce created thriving cities, and the most important city in New England was Boston. By 1722 Boston had a dozen major shipyards, forty-two principal streets, three thousand houses, and sixteen thousand citizens. Most citizens owned some property. Although the number of town-dwelling poor grew in the eighteenth century, they did not experience conditions of starvation, and their percentage of the population was small when compared to the masses of destitute people living in English cities during this period.

At the end of the seventeenth century, anyone with a little cash to invest held shares in New England's shipping ventures. This widespread ownership of mercantile wealth had created a large middle class. But as Boston's wealth increased, it became unnecessary to rely on the less affluent citizens for commercial investment, and by the time of the Revolution the control of shipping had become concentrated among a relatively small number of highly competitive entrepreneurs. Thus the distinctions that already existed within the propertied class itself tended to become more pronounced during the 1700s. Property owners were clearly differentiated between a large body of shopkeepers, artisans, and laborers on the one hand, and a much smaller group of wealthy commercial investors on the other. But labor was scarce and Boston was prosperous enough to offer a living to workers in trades and crafts of every variety. In addition to necessary occupations such as carpentry, bricklaying, and leather-tanning, the city could support the services of America's finest goldsmiths, silversmiths, and clockmakers.

Despite the strictness of Puritan morality, Boston was much like any city in England. The Puritan ban against frivolous amusements and luxuries ensured that no plays or concerts were performed in the city, but was hardly strong enough to prevent the prostitution to be found in any port city in the world. Several merchants, including the famous John Hancock, were rich enough to afford coaches, fine houses, and expensive furniture. Boston also had more than a thousand blacks in bondage during the eighteenth century. Women going shopping or men conducting business were carried about in sedan chairs or carriages, often accompanied by slaves.

In the area of fashion, the yearning for sophistication often conflicted with Puritan self-denial. In the seventeenth century, for instance, gentlemen began to wear wigs costing as much as $250. When hundreds of settlers were killed in the Indian attacks of 1676, stern preachers attributed the disaster to God's anger over the "elect" making such displays of themselves.

Even with its wealth and luxury, Boston had many problems. By the 1740s, its growth rate was falling behind that of other colonial cities. Portsmouth, Rhode Island, began to take over much of

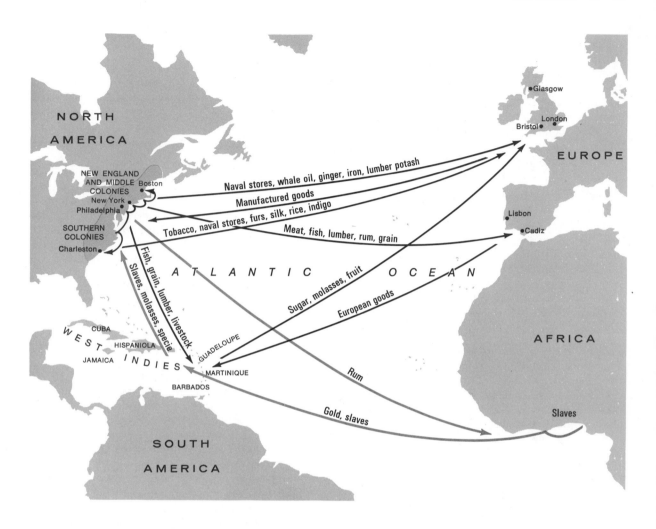

Colonial Overseas Trade

←——— Triangular trade

the shipbuilding industry, and Newport's ship-owners (who controlled half of America's slave trade) diverted a great deal of business away from Boston. Boston was also facing the kinds of social problems that are found in all cities. It became nec-essary for the city to build jails, pay doctors to visit the city's poor, and organize a public fire department. Called the Boston Fire Society, the group had twenty gentlemen members.

The Frontier

Although its five main cities—Newport, Boston, Philadelphia, New York, and Charleston—bore similarities to transplanted English communities, colonial America was unlike any place in Europe. It was different partly because of its diverse regional and ethnic mixtures, but also because of the unique demands placed on those who settled the frontier. To the colonists the word *frontier* meant the land running the length of the Atlantic seaboard just beyond the settled area along the coast. With each new generation the line of the frontier moved westward into the interior.

One famous American historian, Frederick Jackson Turner, considered the frontier the most decisive factor in the formation of the American character. In 1893, Turner wrote:

American social development has been continually beginning over again on the frontier. This perennial rebirth, this fecundity of American life, this expansion westward with its new opportunities, its continuous touch with the simplicity of primitive society, furnish the forces dominating American character. . . . Thus the advance of the frontier has meant a steady movement away from the influence of Europe, a steady growth of independence on American lines.

Today, however, many historians contend that Turner overemphasized its importance. Some stress the persistence of the English and European political and cultural heritage, while others claim that the cities contributed as much as the wilderness to the creation of a uniquely American way of living.

Yet a strong case can be made that the development of life in the New World was influenced significantly by the sheer immensity of the unexplored continent. Because frontier settlers lived isolated lives, families had to rely on themselves for practical and spiritual needs. They built their own furniture, raised most of their own food, and made most of their own clothes. Parents taught their children how to read, write, and do simple arithmetic.

The demands of frontier life also made large families advantageous. Parents frequently had ten or twelve children who supplied help with the farm work. As soon as a boy was seven years old, he would help his father in the fields. As soon as a girl was old enough to follow instructions, she attended her mother in the kitchen or at the sewing table. In addition, women often labored in the fields beside their men.

Children were rarely a permanent solution to the labor problems of a frontier family, however; the frontier offered too much free land to keep young adults at home. Newlyweds usually started their own farms, and servants were as hard to keep as grown children. Indeed, servants were in such short supply that families had to pay them three or four times the normal wages in London. Most hired help were able to save enough money to start farms of their own.

The constant movement of people into new territories tended to erode old class distinctions. Permanent differences of rank were replaced on the frontier by social distinctions based on a family's intangible qualities, including strength of will and self-control.

In addition to the social effects of the frontier, the geography of the continent influenced the way the New World was settled. Inland settlements were somewhat impractical since land travel was difficult over any great distance. The Dutch, for instance, founded Albany 150 miles up the Hudson River immediately after arriving in New York. But almost a hundred years passed before other towns were established only a few miles inland from the river or the Atlantic Coast. Roads were expensive to build and maintain. As late as 1723 Benjamin Franklin preferred to travel from Boston to Philadelphia by taking a boat down the coast to New York and up the Delaware River, rather than making the journey by road.

Women in Colonial America

For centuries Christians had looked upon the biblical account of creation as evidence of the inferiority of women. According to this account Eve was created as a helpmeet to Adam. She could not resist the enticements of Satan, and so was the first to disobey God. Because she tempted Adam and thus brought about his fall, she was relegated to a position of subservience. As was written in the book of Genesis: "In sorrow shalt thou bring forth children, and thy desire shall be subject to thine husband, and he shall rule over thee" (Genesis 3:16).

Given the long-held belief in this account of creation, it is not surprising that the chief role of women in colonial society was that of homemaker

IN THE MID-1700S A WOMAN'S PLACE WAS BELIEVED TO BE IN THE HOME. HERE COLONIAL WOMEN, GATHERED AROUND THE HEARTHSIDE, ENGAGE IN SIMPLE DOMESTIC ACTIVITIES.

and mother. Just as in the Indian cultures of North America, there was a division between the domestic labors of women and the public activity of men. For the most part, a woman's life was devoted to cooking, sewing, caring for her husband, and instilling in her children the moral and spiritual values of the community. Because women in the colonies were in short supply, they had little difficulty finding a marriage partner. Indeed, a woman who had reached the age of twenty-five and was still single was looked upon as an old maid! American men were generally faithful husbands who treated their wives with tenderness and respect.

Although the role of wife and mother afforded considerable security, it was not without many restrictions. While women living in the towns were often able to obtain a rudimentary education, had access to books and newspapers, and could visit other women, most women living in rural areas lived isolated lives punctuated with some church at-

tendance and occasional quilting bees and barbecues. Most colonial women were either pregnant or nursing much of their adult lives, a situation which caused great physical strain and contributed to rapid aging. A wife's earnings and property—if she had any—belonged technically to her husband (unless he consented to her ownership), and widows had little control over estates left by their husbands. If a woman wished to separate, her husband retained rights to the children. Divorces were granted only in the most extreme cases. The freedom of women was limited in other ways as well. For example, a woman could not marry without her father's consent, nor could she vote or sign contracts. She was even subject to corporal punishment.

In less settled areas of the colonies, where the need for labor was compelling, women often worked in the fields and even shouldered guns in emergencies. Here on the frontier women were afforded greater opportunities to develop their individual talents: they managed large farms, became seamstresses, milliners, innkeepers, and printers. Some taught in their own homes or managed stores and ran newspapers. While most of the women involved in business activities were working with their husbands or were widows carrying on the business, a few were simply enterprising individuals. Elizabeth Lucus of South Carolina was the first to grow indigo in the 1740s, a plant from which was obtained a rich purple dye which became a profitable export in the decades before the Revolution. Margaret Brent became executor of the huge estate of Governor Leonard Calvert of Maryland. In order to settle his business Brent undertook court proceedings and sold property to pay the back salaries of Maryland soldiers. Elizabeth Inman, a woman of initiative and independent spirit, was a successful Boston businesswoman who achieved financial security by selling millinery, cloth, and sewing supplies. At the same time, she helped to raise five nieces and aided other women in becoming self-supporting.

However, by the eighteenth century in more settled areas, women began to be discouraged from seeking fulfillment outside the home. The professions, medicine, and the law were normally closed to women, and while piety was considered an important feminine virtue, women were not allowed to enter the ministry. For example, when Anne Hutchinson began speaking out on matters of religious doctrine, she was considered to be not only a religious radical, but also an upstart forgetting her proper subordinate place in the social hierarchy. Only the Quakers interpreted the Scriptures so as to give women who were spiritually reborn the right to be ministers and to hold important administrative positions in the church.

Until recently many historians believed that women in colonial society enjoyed a relatively high status and some independence. Although colonial women had no political power, it has been argued that they did have considerable latitude in deciding whom to marry and how to run the household. Specifically, these historians argue, since women were in short supply, they could be particular in choosing a husband. Moreover, since they processed the food and made the clothes, no household could be adequately managed without them. Thus, women exerted influence, along with their husbands, in decisions regarding economic matters, for example. Finally, these historians contend, sex roles were somewhat relaxed in order to accommodate the frontier conditions of the seventeenth and eighteenth centuries.

Recent studies of colonial women cast doubt on this interpretation. Although women were scarce in the seventeenth century, most of them were not allowed to make their choice of a husband independently. And by the middle of the eighteenth century there was no longer a scarcity of women. Indeed by then they comprised about 50 percent of the colonial population. As to the contention that a woman's importance to the running of the home gave her great influence over it, there is evidence that unless a woman was in business, she usually was uninformed about family landholdings and income. Ignorance of economic matters surely would have hampered a woman's influence on decision making, as well as limiting the opportunities available to her. It would seem that colonial women knew and accepted their place as homemaker and that they did not, for the most part, participate in political or economic decisions. Only in the late eighteenth century is there evidence that women's educational opportunities were improving and that young women were gaining greater freedom in choosing a marriage partner.

Conflicts among the Colonies

Distance, isolation, and poor transportation tended to make each colony a distinct entity. Colonists had little sense of belonging to any larger group. Thomas Jefferson himself usually referred to "my country, Virginia," and people in New York and Pennsylvania generally felt more closely allied with England than with the other colonies. Southerners speculated on the New England character as though they were studying foreigners. In general, aristocrats of the Chesapeake country disliked the plain manners and democratic ways of New England, while John Adams of Massachusetts prided himself and his "countrymen" on their "purer English blood, less mixed with Scotch, Irish, Dutch, French, Danish, Swedish, etc., than any other."

As a result of these and other differences, there was little cooperation among the colonies: Maryland tried to undersell Virginia in the tobacco trade; and New York, New Jersey, and Pennsylvania all refused to help New England during a series of French-provoked Indian attacks in 1703. Border disputes erupted frequently. The settlers of the Carolinas and Georgia, for example, engaged in several bitter quarrels over trading rights with the Cherokees and Chickasaws.

Conflicts between Eastern and Western Regions

The sharpest disagreements were between the eastern and western regions within each colony. Although the frontier in colonial times was seldom more than a hundred miles inland, the distance was sufficient to generate hostility. People living in the western region faced different problems and had different needs from those who lived in the more settled eastern areas. While land was plentiful, population pressure for it was great and access was difficult because of mountain barriers and Indian resistance to the westward movement of settlers. Western pioneers wanted the government to spend money on new roads to make the frontier land accessible, and they demanded strong fortifications against the Indians. Easterners objected to the use of public money for these purposes. Western pioneers also resented the high prices they were forced to pay for goods and the high rates of interest on loans set by wealthy eastern merchants in such towns as Charleston, Philadelphia, New York, and Boston.

These merchants, along with a group of wealthy landowners along the Atlantic seaboard, had formed a small native-born aristocracy in British North America. Theirs was not an aristocracy based on culture and education, but one based on expertise. Its status was economically uncertain, and because it did not have the legal protections enjoyed by the aristocracy in England it did not command the undivided respect accorded its counterpart in Britain.

In many colonies these conflicts were intensified by differences in national origin. The thousands of Germans and Scotch-Irish who came to Pennsyl-

vania in the early eighteenth century pushed into the back country of Virginia in the 1730s, the Carolinas in the next two decades, and Georgia in the 1760s. Unlike the wealthier Anglicans living in Charleston or Jamestown, the newcomers were usually Presbyterians or German Pietists. Often the judges, sheriffs, and other officials of English background appointed to administer the new counties frankly despised the Germans and the Scotch-Irish. These officials were interested in serving only the interests of the governor and the eastern clique of well-to-do merchants and large plantation owners.

The political power of the older, established seaboard counties enabled them to exercise control over the provincial assemblies. They usually favored their own interests and often denied fair representation to the back country. In 1760, for example, Lancaster County in western Pennsylvania had twice the population of Bucks County in the east, but Bucks had twice as many representatives in the assembly. At the time of the Revolution, the older counties still elected two-thirds of the representative assembly.

In the decades immediately preceding the American Revolution, an observer might have predicted that a war between easterners and westerners was more likely than a united colonial effort against England. Tempers flared in frontier counties and rhetoric became heated. One frontiersman denounced the eastern ruling class as "cursed hungry Caterpillars, that will eat out the very Bowels of our Commonwealth, if they are not pulled down from their Nests in a very short time." In North Carolina a group of small farmers in the west decided to actually "pull down the Caterpillars" in order to end political corruption. In 1771 some two thousand frontiersmen banded together and engaged in a battle with the governor's militia. The Regulators, as the westerners called themselves, were defeated, but their resentment against corrupt officials, high taxes, and underrepresentation continued.

Indian Warfare

An issue that continually created conflict between east and west was the question of how to handle relations with the Indians. Westerners were eager to exploit new land, which for the most part meant land that belonged to the Indians. As a result they found themselves in frequent danger of Indian attack. Easterners, whose settled communities were located far from harm's way and who wanted to trade for Indian furs, had no wish to engage in warfare with the Indians. From about 1660 to 1760 powerful tribes kept the western colonists from penetrating too far west by controlling passage through the Appalachian Mountains. These tribes included the Iroquois in the North and the Cherokees in the South. To the north of the colonies lay New France, which also had claims to land in the Ohio Valley. The Indians maintained their power for nearly a century by playing the French and English factions off against each other. They were willing to trade with the white settlers, but not to permit encroachments into their own territories.

Nevertheless, western squatters did gradually manage to intrude upon Indian lands, driving away game that was essential to Indian survival. Deadly clashes took place almost daily. The Indians were almost always at a disadvantage in these encounters, since the colonists were more numerous and better armed. Divided into tribes, the Indians were often as preoccupied with warring on each other as in turning back the English settlers. Although at times they posed a threat to isolated frontier families, the Indians were usually too independent in outlook to band together successfully to wage war on the unwelcome whites. Colonial authorities did nothing to stop the conflict. Leaders in England and America seemed to feel that it was the price that must be paid to establish settlements and destroy French control north of the Ohio River and Spanish dominance south of Georgia.

In 1763 an uprising similar to Bacon's Rebellion in seventeenth-century Virginia took place in Pennsylvania. A band of Scotch-Irish from the western

A DEPICTION OF THE PAXTON EXPEDITION. BELOW IS A POETIC ACCOUNT OF THE INCIDENT PENNED BY A PHILADELPHIAN.

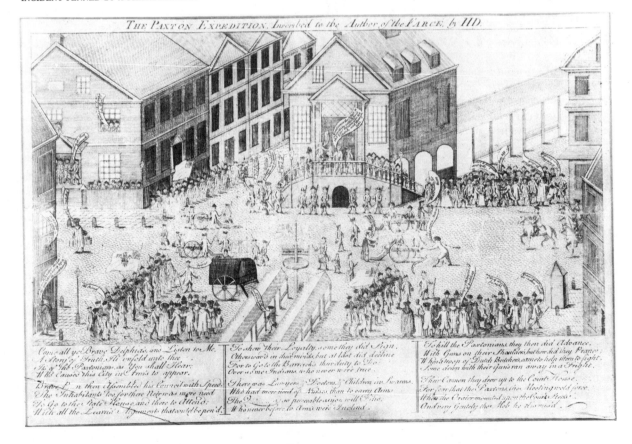

townships of Paxton and Donegal in Pennsylvania killed twenty peaceful Conestoga Indians in revenge for raids carried out by another tribe. The Paxton Boys next decided to march on the capital and force the governor to send troops against the Indians. The Quakers in Philadelphia had maintained peaceful relations with the Indians for decades. To them, Scotch-Irish fierceness seemed more of a problem than the Indians had ever been. Benjamin Franklin and four others were delegated to negotiate with the Paxton Boys. Ten miles outside the city, Franklin made peace with the mob. He was forced to promise a bounty for Indian scalps, and in private he referred to the frontiersmen as "Christian white savages."

Tensions between the seaboard and the frontier mounted throughout most of the eighteenth century, and it took a strong common cause—the Revolution—to relax them even partially.

The Impact of Religion

There were several striking facts about religion in colonial America. First, the colonies were overwhelmingly Protestant. At the time of the Revolution there were about twenty-five thousand Catholics and two thousand Jews out of a total population of about 2.5 million. Second, many colonists attended no church at all. By the middle of the eighteenth century, there were more nonchurchgoers in the colonies than in any European country, mostly because large areas of the country were too poor or too sparsely settled to support a church. In 1701, for example, the Carolinas had a population of about twelve thousand, but no ministers from the Church of England.

Anglicans and Dissenters

Although the Church of England (Anglican church) was established and supported by colonial governments from Maryland to Georgia by the middle of the eighteenth century, it was not a strong institution. In Virginia laws made attendance at Anglican services compulsory and deprived dissenters of the right to vote; nevertheless, the number of adherents to other faiths increased in the western part of the colony. In Maryland Lord Baltimore had been forced to accept the establishment of the Anglican church after the Glorious Revolution in England in order to maintain control of his overwhelmingly Protestant colony. Yet since the population in the Southern colonies was mainly rural and isolated, it was difficult for people to attend services. Many Southerners, who were not Anglicans or who seldom came to church, resented public support of the Anglican ministers.

The Anglican church was further weakened by organizational problems. An American bishop had never been appointed for the colonies, and the Bishop of London, who had authority over American Anglicans, never once crossed the Atlantic to visit his charges. Moreover, ordination to the ministry meant sailing to London, and few colonists were willing to make the trip. As a result, ministers frequently were appointed by the laity and were often not members of the clergy themselves. Since they had no contact with and therefore no loyalty to the church hierarchy in England, they evolved a form of Anglican service that was closer to the simplicity of the Puritan or Congregational churches in New England.

With the arrival of large numbers of immigrants from northern Ireland after 1700, the Presbyterian faith (a form of Calvinism) spread throughout colonial America. The Presbyterian church was especially strong along the frontier from Pennsylvania to Georgia. Like the Puritans of New England, Presbyterians stressed the need for literacy so people could study the Bible to learn of the divine will. And like their New England counterparts, they were hard-working, orderly, and thrifty. Unlike the Puritans, they gradually created a highly structured intercolonial church organization. In matters of religious doctrine, church members were expected to adhere strictly to the Calvinist principles of predestination and the sovereignty of Divine Providence as preached by an educated clergy. The government of the church was more democratic than its theology, however. Day-to-day activities of individual congregations were left to lay members. The twin characteristics of democracy and discipline implicit in this widely held faith had a profound impact on the development of American life during the colonial period.

By the eighteenth century the Baptist church had an increasing number of adherents in British North America. Roger Williams is usually considered to have been the first American Baptist, and by the 1650s his fellow believers were coming not just to Rhode Island but to the colonies of Massachusetts, New Jersey, Pennsylvania, and Delaware as well. Calvinist in doctrine, they differed from the Congregationalists in New England and the Presbyterians streaming into the Middle colonies on two important theological points. They aroused antagonism in New England especially because, unlike other Calvinists, they argued that the baptism of infants was ineffectual. They believed that a person should be baptized only after a spiritual conversion. Following Williams's lead in Rhode Island, they also demanded the complete separation of church and state. They asserted that religious belief was a matter between an individual and God; therefore, the state should have no power to interfere in matters of conscience.

OLD BOSTON TOWN HOUSE SQUARE ABOUT 1657. LAWBREAKERS IN BOSTON WERE SHAMED BY BEING PLACED IN THE STOCKS ON PUBLIC DISPLAY.

Challenges to Puritanism

The Puritan commonwealth of Massachusetts was a strong fortress in the seventeenth century. The founders of the colony had come to America partly in search of religious freedom, but once they had secured it they had no desire to extend it to others. Convinced that they had recreated a society which closely resembled the original community of Christ and his followers, the Puritans were determined to exclude all nonconformists. Seventeenth-century laws allowed whipping, branding, and executing non-Puritans under certain circumstances. In 1659 and 1660 four Quakers were put to death in Massachusetts after habitually and defiantly disobeying Puritan ordinances, including banishment and the threat of execution if they returned to the commonwealth. Yet, Puritans were not as repressive as they have sometimes been pictured. They were not opposed to liquor or sexual activity per se. God had provided wine for the purpose of pleasure, although drunkenness was another matter. Sexual enjoyment between husband and wife was completely permissible, and between those engaged to be married, at least condoned. Adultery, of course, was forbidden, yet even here the Puritans were willing to make al-

lowances for the weakness of human nature. Laws against drunkenness and fornication were enforced with patience and understanding, and the emphasis was on prevention rather than punishment despite the impression to the contrary left by Nathaniel Hawthorne's famous novel *The Scarlet Letter*.

By the middle of the seventeenth century, Puritan control of the colony's population was much reduced. While there was no open rebellion against Puritan rule, many people were now coming to the area for economic, rather than religious reasons, and attendance at the Puritan or Congregational church was becoming more and more a ritual. Few children of church members were able to prove that they had undergone a religious conversion, a personal experience of God's grace that signaled that they were among the elect. Proof of such an experience was required for church membership.

Hence, the growth of the Congregational church was threatened by a lack of younger members and a loss of control over New England society. Consequently, in 1662 the leaders of Massachusetts felt compelled to change the requirements for joining the church. They adopted the so-called Halfway Covenant, which automatically permitted the children of any church member to be baptized. The result was a "halfway" membership, entitling the recipients to have their own children baptized. Full membership was still reserved for those who had experienced a religious conversion, and only they could receive communion.

The Halfway Covenant muted dissent within the colony for a while, but in 1699 hostility toward old-line Puritanism again erupted. A group of well-to-do merchants broke away from the Boston congregation and started the Brattle Street Church. The members of the new congregation gave their emphatic approval to the Halfway Covenant. They also insisted that baptism could not be denied to any child and argued that anyone who attended and contributed to a church was entitled to help select the minister, even if that person was not a full church member. Conservatives in the community tried to stop the spread of such reform measures, but their efforts were to no avail. The Puritan churches were beginning to take on the character of the communities they served rather than standing apart as a gathering of "visible saints."

Witchcraft Trials Meanwhile, the Puritan ruling class suffered other blows that weakened its hold over the colony. The charter of 1691, which made Massachusetts a royal colony, was one blow, and the Puritans' respected position was further undermined by the hysteria and remorse generated by the infamous Salem witchcraft trials.

By the early 1690s many Puritans were certain that God had abandoned them as his chosen people. They felt that they had failed to live up to the standards of orthodox Calvinism, and they were ready to interpret all their misfortunes as signs of divine wrath. Since almost everyone still believed in witchcraft in the seventeenth century, rumors of the presence of witches in the little village of Salem, Massachusetts, were easily accepted as just such signs.

The episode began when a few young girls, overexcited by voodoo stories told to them by a West Indian woman, began shouting and twitching nervously for no apparent reason. A doctor was summoned, and he announced that the girls were under a witch's spell. Next the girls pointed out their tormentors, mostly older women against whom they may have felt some resentment. Soon a witch-hunt was launched which spread rapidly to neighboring areas, including Boston.

The trials, which began in June 1692 and continued into 1693, were not based on evidence testified to by witnesses. Instead, "spectral" evidence was used—voices or apparitions which supposedly had affected the young girls. The Puritan clergy refused to intervene, perhaps feeling that the outbreak of emotion would help strengthen their authority in the colony. In fact, many members of the clergy encouraged the people to believe in witches and demons in the period leading up to the trial. In 1689, for example, one of Boston's most eloquent and respected theologians, Cotton Mather, published a widely read tract on the subject of witchcraft. It dealt with a case in the 1680s in which the children of a Boston Puritan had, according to Mather, really been bewitched. On the other hand, the modern historian John Demos has argued that the accusers in Salem Village were "projecting" their feelings of aggression onto older, eccentric members of the village.

By September 1692, twenty "witches" had been executed and 150 suspects were in jail awaiting their fate. Gradually a few brave souls stepped forward to speak out against the executions. The governor finally lost patience when his own wife was accused of being a witch. He ordered all suspects released. Years later several of the girls who had made the original accusations confessed that they had lied. It was an embarrassing episode for the Puritan hierarchy, and it cost them much public respect.

The Great Awakening

By the early decades of the eighteenth century there was a widespread atmosphere of religious tension. Colonial society was still generally religious but the established churches—the Congregational in New England and the Anglican in the Southern colonies—had become formal institutions rather than organizations dedicated to bringing about spiritual conversion. Alarmed at this trend, ministers began a great crusade aimed at gaining new converts and re-inspiring their congregations.

As early as 1725 Theodore Frelinghusen, a Dutch Reformed minister in New Jersey, was delivering highly emotional sermons to his congregation, insisting on faith rather than reason as a means to salvation. In New England, the most outstanding thinker, writer, and preacher of this period

INTERPRETING AMERICAN HISTORY

PURITANISM Historians have disagreed about the Puritan influence on American culture. Some have said that the Puritans obstructed freedom of thought and religion; others have maintained that the Puritans established the foundations of American democracy. These viewpoints tend to reflect the personal outlooks of the historians themselves, since students of the past often frame their interpretations according to the needs of the present.

Most nineteenth-century historians idolized certain Puritan personalities. John Gorham Palfrey, a descendant of the Puritans, for example, regarded John Winthrop as a genius for his part in establishing the idea of self-government.

Yet by the twentieth century some historians had developed an anti-Puritan attitude. In the 1920s critics such as H. L. Mencken saw the narrow-mindedness of their own day as a cultural result of the Puritan outlook. Other students of this period were strongly affected by the economic and social inequities of the times. They found the roots of some of these modern ills in the Puritan past and condemned the early Puritan leaders for their oppressive control over peoples' lives.

In the 1930s, however, a group of historians began to draw a more sympathetic portrait of the Puritans, emphasizing their intellectual sophistica-tion. Samuel Eliot Morison, in particular, praised the self-discipline and energy which enabled the Puritans to carry European culture to the wilderness of America. While other colonists often degenerated into half-savagery in their struggles with the new land, he wrote, the Puritans founded Harvard College only a few years after arriving in Boston; created a public elementary school system; printed, imported, and read a great many books; and were in touch with most European scientific and artistic developments.

After World War II, when America's security seemed threatened by the cold war and subversion from within, historians such as Daniel Boorstin claimed that Puritan institutions were still strong and viable. These neoconservatives suggested that the Puritans' practical approach to problem solving was a uniquely American characteristic.

One final point of view, represented by Darrett B. Rutman, argues that Puritanism has been overemphasized. According to Rutman, the early settlers in New England were concerned with personal economic gain and did not subordinate their own interests to the schemes of the Puritan leaders. Many facets of New England thought and character were not uniquely Puritan, he claims, but merely reflected the former way of life in England.

was the Congregational minister Jonathan Edwards. In the 1730s Edwards turned to highly charged rhetoric to remind his parishioners of the suffering awaiting sinners in hell. His sermons, such as "Sinners in the Hands of an Angry God," appealed to the emotions as he urged people to surrender themselves to God's mercy and to return to the strict Calvinist doctrines of predestination and religious conversion. The most important figure in the Great Awakening, however, was an English revivalist named George Whitefield. Whitefield made his first speaking tour of the colonies in 1739 and quickly became the best-known preacher of his generation in America.

Whitefield drew such large crowds in every town he visited that the meetings were almost always held outside the church. One of his sermons outside of Philadelphia attracted ten thousand people. Aside from his great oratorical skill, Whitefield excited his audiences with his emotional intensity. Other preachers, such as Gilbert Tennant, began imitating his style, and many of them were soon able to whip their listeners into a frenzy of emotional fervor. Zealous men and women would exhibit the most extraordinary behavior at these revival meetings. As one observer noted:

Some would stand in the pulpit exhorting, some in the body of the seats, some in the pews, and some up in the gallery; and oftentimes, several of them would speak together; so that some praying, some exhorting, and testifying, some singing, some screaming, some crying, some laughing, and some scolding, made the most amazing confusion that ever was heard.

The Great Awakening had far-reaching effects, not all of them desirable. For example, revivalism produced a strong tendency toward anti-intellectualism. Traveling evangelists assured their listeners that education was not a prerequisite for salvation; many congregations fired their ministers simply for being too learned. As a result, the position of the ministry began to be undermined, since the inner spirit was considered more important than outward erudition.

In addition, the Great Awakening brought about the growth of a variety of new religious denominations. The Presbyterians split into two groups: a conservative wing and a "new side" which called for spiritual democracy. An offshoot of the Anglican church, later known as the Methodists, gained large numbers of followers in the back country. The emotional preaching of their ministers appealed to frontier settlers disenchanted with the ritualism of the Church of England. The Baptists, too, added adherents and emerged as one of the largest Protestant denominations.

The growth of dissenting churches and the fact that the religious revival spread throughout the colonies had important political consequences. As we have seen, the Anglicans in the South had political as well as religious authority. As the Church of England weakened, so, too, did respect for British authority. The growth of churches such as the Baptists and Methodists during the Great Awakening helped prepare the way for the separation of church and state that would become central to the American system of government. Equally important, as the first truly intercolonial movement, the Great Awakening helped foster the growth of cooperation and unity among the colonies, laying the basis for American nationalism.

The Secular Mind

While the ordinary people of America were experiencing a religious revival, the rich, educated, and influential minority were developing a new way of looking at the world: the philosophy of the Enlightenment. Puritan theology had seen people as essentially evil creatures dependent on the mercy of God. Eighteenth-century philosophy, on the other hand, taught that reason was the most important human faculty and that through reason life could be progressively improved.

The Enlightenment

In England the two leading figures of the Enlightenment were Sir Isaac Newton and John Locke. In 1687 Newton published his *Principia Mathematica*, in which he described his discovery of the law of gravity. Newton's discoveries had far-reaching implications. He had created a new view of the universe as an orderly place that operated according to scientific laws. To many educated people it seemed that human reason could comprehend anything. Through reason people might discover the laws relating to many areas of life, including politics, economics, and religion.

Accepting the implications of Newton's work, John Locke published his *Essay on Human Understanding* in 1690. He argued that the human mind is like a blank slate, an empty page. Thus children at birth are not filled with sinful ideas, or with any particular knowledge. Rather, all knowledge comes through the senses, from observation and experiment. Locke's radical new theory struck many colonists as a strong argument against the doctrines of original sin and predestination.

An interest in politics led Locke to write two treatises on government. According to his political theory, people are born free under the natural law of the universe and endowed with the natural rights of life, liberty, and property. But a disorganized society could prevent people from enjoying their rights, for people could be violent and selfish as well as rational. This meant that individual freedom could be jeopardized by aggressive neighbors. According to Locke, however, reason could potentially overcome this danger. By making a contract among themselves, people could protect their rights. In practical terms, this meant establishing a government based on law, a division of power, and majority rule.

Locke also believed that since government is an artificial creation, people could modify it, even by revolution if necessary. Thus his political ideas offered strong support for the right to rebel against established authority.

Another influence on Americans came from the philosophical concepts of a group of eighteenth-century Scottish thinkers. Men such as David Hume and Adam Smith believed, as did Newton, that the universe operated according to scientific laws. They, too, thought that a precise science of politics and morality could be discovered by human beings. These philosophers believed that people possessed both rationality and a strong moral sense. The combination of these two qualities could lead to the creation of a society in which human beings would live together harmoniously through mutual attraction—an attraction similar to the pull of gravity in the physical universe.

Newton's explanations of the laws of the universe and Locke's theories of political philosophy gave rise to a new view of God. In their theories God had created a grand design before retiring quietly. God did not intervene in people's lives. In this sense, God was like a watchmaker who built and wound a perfect machine, then sat back and watched it tick. The scientist and political philosopher need only study nature in order to see God's plan.

This faith, which stressed human reason over divine revelation, was called Deism. It stood in startling contrast to the beliefs fostered in the same period by the Great Awakening. The Deists pictured God as utterly indifferent to human affairs once the universe had been set in motion, whereas the revivalists saw him as a stern father, passionately concerned over the deeds of his wayward children. Yet both movements stressed religious freedom, separation of church and state, educational improvements, and reliance on experience rather than traditional authority.

In America the ideas of the Enlightenment at first appealed primarily to the social and intellectual elite of the cities. By the time of the Revolution, however, many of these ideas had filtered down to the masses. Although many people had never heard of Newton, Locke, or the Scottish philosophers, the idea that government was created to serve human needs had become a familiar one. Religious denominations such as Methodists and Quakers also

preached that people were ultimately perfectible. Some Baptists gave up the doctrine of predestination and embraced the belief that salvation could be attained through faith and righteous living. The need for scientific investigation was not strange to frontier Americans, who had learned long before about the importance of practical experimentation. Ultimately, when the English government began enacting laws that seemed unjust and tyrannical, the American people felt justified in rebelling. They did not feel that they were breaking the law. Rather, they saw themselves as conforming to the natural law of the universe, as outlined by John Locke.

Education

Since the early seventeenth century, many colonists had been concerned about education, and in the eighteenth century, the Enlightenment created a new interest in founding schools. Of the three major regions in America (New England, Middle, and Southern), New England had always given the most encouragement to education. Puritan theology required each individual to be able to read and interpret the Bible and make independent religious judgments.

Elementary education played a prominent part in New England life. In 1647 the Massachusetts assembly ordered all towns of at least fifty families to hire a reading instructor for the children to be paid out of public funds. Learning to read was compulsory, and parents who did not want to send their children to school were required to teach them at home. Some of the schools were free and some demanded a small tuition, but children of the poor could attend any school without paying.

In 1636, only six years after arriving in Massachusetts, the Puritans founded a college. It began with one house, one professor, one acre of land, and the revenues from the local ferry service. When a Bostonian named John Harvard died in 1638, leaving four hundred books and half of his money to the college, the Board of Overseers decided to name the school after him. Harvard was originally built to train new ministers, but in 1738 John Winthrop (great-grandson of the colony's early governor) began instructing students in mathematics and science. John Locke's *Essay on Human Understanding* was part of Harvard's curriculum as early as 1742.

HARVARD COLLEGE, FOUNDED IN 1636, DEMONSTRATED THE GREAT IMPORTANCE PLACED
ON EDUCATION BY THE PURITANS.

Over time the other New England colonies slowly followed Massachusetts's example. A Puritan-supported college was established in Connecticut in 1701 and permanently located at New Haven in 1716. Two years later it was named Yale College. Rhode Island College was founded in Providence in 1764 by a group of Baptists who felt the need to educate clergy for their own denomination. In 1804 it was renamed Brown University.

In the Middle colonies the level of education was slightly lower. There were no public-school systems, although there were fourteen private schools in New York by 1762. In addition, various religious denominations had founded elementary schools in Pennsylvania and New Jersey. In the religious enthusiasm of the Great Awakening, several important colleges were established by different denominations. The Quakers and the Scotch-Irish had already started church schools of their own in Penn-sylvania. The Presbyterians started the College of New Jersey (Princeton, 1746); Dutch Reformed revivalists founded Rutgers (1766); and Anglicans and Presbyterians together founded King's College (Columbia, 1754) and the College of Philadelphia (University of Pennsylvania, 1755).

The South lagged behind the other two regions in both elementary schools and colleges. The first Southern college, William and Mary, was founded at Williamsburg, Virginia, in 1693. Grammar schools did not exist in the South, and wealthy planters had to hire private tutors for their children. Women and blacks seldom received any education at all, and most backwoods farmers could neither read nor write. At the end of the seventeenth century, only 55 percent of the white men in Virginia were able to sign their own names, as opposed to at least 90 percent of the men in New England.

Historians are often tempted to picture the colonial period as one of unbroken progress. In the field of education, however, the facts belie this interpretation. Although there were more schools in the colonies in the eighteenth century than there were in the seventeenth, they had become less effective. In fact, illiteracy was on the rise in the years before the Revolution. Third- and fourth-generation Americans may have been better adapted than their parents to life in the wilderness, but fewer were able to read. Those who were in school were receiving an inferior education.

Most universities offered only the traditional courses. As in European schools, students learned Latin, Greek, Hebrew, rhetoric, and moral philosophy. Few courses prepared graduates for professional careers other than the ministry, and only 25 percent of all college graduates followed this career. If a young man wanted to go into law, he had to apprentice himself to an established lawyer and read law books on his own. Consequently, the highly specialized professional distinctions of England disappeared. Technical legal training was hardly necessary where only general legal services were needed.

The medical profession was also less specialized in America. American doctors were general practitioners, and the scarcity of trained doctors produced the need for practical medical knowledge among laypeople. Of the thirty-five hundred doctors in America on the eve of the Revolution, only two hundred held medical degrees, and these they had earned abroad.

Scientific Advances

Most of the outstanding scientists in colonial America were amateurs. While reflecting the eighteenth-century interest in natural science which resulted from knowledge of Newton's discoveries, few were connected with universities, or had even attended college. Botany and zoology were two fields in which America's early scientists excelled. The leading naturalist of the colonial period was Dr. Alexander Garden of South Carolina, for whom the gardenia is named. Garden was famous throughout Europe for his genius in classifying plants. Other well-known American botanists included John Bartram, who collected and catalogued plants from Florida to the Great Lakes, and Dr. John Mitchell of

Virginia, who discovered twenty-two new classes of plants. In 1721 the Puritan minister Cotton Mather developed the technique of inoculation against smallpox, the most deadly disease of colonial times. A storm of controversy broke out in Boston when Mather began injecting live smallpox germs into his fellow citizens, but a lowered casualty rate in the next epidemic proved the value of this practice.

America's most prominent scientific genius during the colonial period was Benjamin Franklin. Franklin, who was self-educated through extensive reading, was passionately devoted to science and convinced that the universe is governed by knowable laws. His intense curiosity about every aspect of his environment led him to many practical inventions: the Franklin stove, bifocal spectacles, the lightning rod, and the grocery store's long arm (a pole with a movable clamp for fetching objects from high shelves). His famous experiment with a kite and metal key during a thunderstorm provided the first definite proof that electricity is a force which courses freely through nature.

Development of the Arts

Some of the best writers of the colonial period were ministers, and religious literature composed the bulk of colonial reading matter. John Wise of Massachusetts wrote a rousing defense of Puritanism; the energetic Cotton Mather authored a famous treatise on witchcraft and a church history of New England; and Jonathan Edwards was also a writer of some note. The leading historian of New England was Thomas Hutchinson, whose *History of the Colony of Massachusetts* is generally considered straightforward and scrupulously fair.

New England also had a number of fine poets, including Michael Wigglesworth, whose sincere and deeply religious poetry was written as a device for teaching ordinary people. His most artistic poem describes the punishments in store for New England because of its failure to keep faith with God. Samuel Eliot Morison called Anne Bradstreet "the greatest American poetess before Emily Dickinson." Her religious poetry was an intense expression of her own emotions. Edward Taylor, minister of the First Congregational Church of Westfield, drew from his observations of community life to write a series of meditative poems to be read before administering or partaking of the Lord's Supper. Benjamin Franklin was probably the most prolific of all colonial writers. His *Poor Richard's Almanack*, a collection of pithy sayings, is still enjoyed today, as is his autobiography.

Many towns established public libraries during the prerevolutionary era. Although most of the volumes dealt with religious subjects, every collection contained works on science, history, medicine, and farming. A few individuals were able to amass impressive private libraries at a time when books were so scarce and costly that most were owned by churches and schools. Cotton Mather owned three thousand books and William Byrd II of Virginia had four thousand. Most educated people, however, seldom owned more than a hundred volumes.

America's first successful newspaper, the *Boston Newsletter*, was started in 1704. By 1763, twenty-three newspapers were being printed in the colonies. Most articles concerned news about other colonies, England, and other European nations, rather than about local affairs. In 1729 Franklin took over the *Pennsylvania Gazette* and made some lively innovations, such as the inclusion of poems, literary essays, and cartoons. These ideas were later copied by other colonial newspapers.

An important incident in the development of the press in America was the famous *Peter Zenger* case. Zenger was tried in New York in 1733 for publishing articles which the governor of the colony claimed were libelous because they criticized his conduct. Zenger was finally acquitted on the grounds that the articles were true, even though they were highly critical of the colony's executive. This case set an important precedent for the publication of controversial articles, although it was not widely accepted for many years to come. It did, however, pave the way for freedom of the press and its protection by the First Amendment to the United States Constitution.

American painters, furniture makers, and architects were dependent on English models and styles. The architect Christopher Wren designed church spires and the main building of William and Mary College in the English style. Peter Harrison designed several houses of worship including King's Chapel in Boston and the synagogue Congregation Jeshuat Israel in Newport. But one of the most famous painters of the period, John Singleton Copley, took a new, characteristically American approach to his art; he showed his subjects working.

JOHN SINGLETON COPLEY PAINTED THIS FAMOUS PORTRAIT OF ARTIST AND SILVERSMITH PAUL REVERE AROUND 1770.

When he painted the early American master engraver and silversmith Paul Revere, he showed him at his workbench wearing workclothes. An English painter would have posed him in his Sunday best to give the impression that he was really a country squire. Copley's portraits expressed an American pride in manual labor.

As we have seen, colonial America was fundamentally a hybrid culture. There were sharp regional differences, as well as important similarities. Although certain basic traditions clearly reflected the Old World heritage, other aspects were unique, born of the experience of settling a new land. In some ways, America was a mature culture well before the Revolution. It had its own political structures, religious movements, educational systems, and even booming cities. But in other ways, it was very dependent on Europe, especially England. In the decades before the Revolution, many possible futures could have been predicted for the American experiment, but few would have included a violent break with the mother country.

Readings

General Works

Boorstin, D. J., *The Americans: The Colonial Experience*. New York: Random House, 1958.

Bridenbaugh, Carl, *Myths and Realities: Societies of the Colonial South*. New Orleans: Louisiana State University Press, 1952. (Paper: Atheneum, 1963)

Cremin, Lawrence A., *American Education: The Colonial Experience, 1607–1783*. New York: Harper & Row, 1970. (Paper)

Gipson, L. H., *The British Empire Before the American Revolution*, Vols. 1–11. New York: Knopf, 1936–1965.

Hofstadter, Richard, *America at 1750: A Social History*. New York: Knopf, 1971. (Paper)

Jones, H. M., *O Strange New World: American Culture—The Formative Years*. New York: Viking, 1964.

Mead, S. E., *The Lively Experiment: The Shaping of Christianity in America*. New York: Harper & Row, 1963.

Morison, S. E. (Ed.), *The Parkman Reader*. Boston: Little, Brown, 1955.

Parrington, V. L., *The Colonial Mind. Main Currents in American Thought*, Vol. 1. New York: Harcourt Brace Jovanovich, 1927.

Rossiter, Clinton, *Seedtime of the Republic: The Origin of the American Tradition of Political Liberty*. New York: Harcourt Brace Jovanovich, 1953.

Stearns, Raymond P., *Science in the British Colonies of America*. Springfield, Ill.: University of Illinois Press, 1970.

Ver Steeg, C. L., *The Formative Years: 1607–1763*. New York: Hill & Wang, 1964.

Wright, L. B., *The Cultural Life of the American Colonies: 1607–1763*. New York: Harper & Row, 1957.

Special Studies

Bridenbaugh, Carl, *Cities in the Wilderness: The First Century of Urban Life in America, 1625–1742*. New York: Putnam's, 1964.

Bridenbaugh, Carl, and Jessica Bridenbaugh, *Rebels and Gentlemen: Philadelphia in the Age of Franklin*. New York: Oxford University Press, 1965.

Degler, C. N., *Neither Black nor White: Slavery and Race Relations in Brazil and the United States*. New York: Macmillan, 1971. (Paper)

Hansen, M. L., *Atlantic Migration, 1607–1860: A History of the Continuing Settlement of America*, A. M. Schlesinger (Ed.). Cambridge, Mass.: Harvard University Press, 1940 (Paper: Harper & Row, 1964).

Heimert, Alan E., *Religion and the American Mind: From the Great Awakening to the Revolution*. Cambridge, Mass.: Harvard University Press, 1966.

Jordan, Winthrop D., *White Over Black*. Chapel Hill, N.C.: University of North Carolina Press, 1968 (Paper, Penguin, 1969).

Klein, Herbert S., *Slavery in the Americas: A Comparative Study of Virginia and Cuba*. Chicago: University of Chicago Press, 1967. (Paper)

Smith, A. E., *Colonists in Bondage: White Servitude and Convict Labor in America, 1607–1776*. Chapel Hill, N.C.: University of North Carolina Press, 1947.

Starkey, M. L., *The Devil in Massachusetts: A Modern Inquiry into the Salem Witch Trials*. New York: Knopf, 1949 (Paper: Doubleday, 1969).

Sydnor, C. S., *Gentlemen Freeholders: Political Practices in Washington's Virginia*. Chapel Hill, N.C.: University of North Carolina Press, 1952.

Wertenbaker, Thomas J., *The Old South*. New York: Scribner's, 1942.

Wood, Peter H., *Black Majority: Negroes in Colonial South Carolina from 1670 Through the Stono Rebellion*. New York: Knopf, 1974.

Primary Sources

Bruchey, Stuart (Ed.), *The Colonial Merchant*. New York: Harcourt Brace Jovanovich, 1965.

Colden, Cadwallader, *History of the Five Indian Nations*. Ithaca, N.Y.: Cornell University Press, 1958.

Franklin, Benjamin, *Autobiography*. New York: Simon & Schuster, 1970.

Heimert, Alan E., and Perry Miller (Eds.), *Great Awakening: Documents Illustrating the Crisis and its Consequences*. New York: Bobbs-Merrill, 1967. (Paper)

Riley, E. M. (Ed.), *The Journal of John Harrower: An Indentured Servant in the Colony of Virginia, 1773–1776*. New York: Holt, Rinehart & Winston, 1964.

Sewall, Samuel, *Diary of Samuel Sewall*. New York: Putnam's, 1967.

Biographies

Crane, V. W., *Benjamin Franklin and a Rising People.* Boston: Little, Brown, 1954.

Ketcham, Ralph, *Benjamin Franklin.* New York: Simon & Schuster, 1965.

McLoughlin, William G. (Ed.), *Isaac Backus and the American Patriotic Tradition.* Boston: Little, Brown, 1967.

Marambaud, Pierre L., *William Byrd of Westover.* Virginia: University Press of Virginia, 1971.

Van Doren, C. C., *Benjamin Franklin.* New York: Viking, 1964.

Winslow, O. E., *Jonathan Edwards, 1703–1758: A Biography.* New York: Macmillan, 1940.

Historical Novels

Cooper, James F., *The Deerslayer.* New York: Macmillan, 1962.

———, *The Last of the Mohicans.* New York: Airmont, 1964.

———, *The Pathfinder.* New York: Airmont, 1964.

———, *The Pioneers.* New York: Airmont, 1964.

Johnston, Mary, *Audrey.* Boston: Houghton Mifflin, 1902.

Michener, James A., *Chesapeake.* New York: Random House, 1978.

Simms, William Gilmore, *The Yemassee.* Boston: Houghton Mifflin, 1961.

4 Prelude to Independence

Engrav'd Printed & Sold by Paul Revere Boston

If we inquire into the business of a king, we shall find that in some countries they may have none; and after sauntering away their lives without pleasure to themselves or advantage to the nation, withdraw from the scene, and leave their successors to tread the same idle round. . . . In England a king hath little more to do than to make war and give away places; which, in plain terms, is to empoverish the nation and set it together by the ears. A pretty business indeed for a man to be allowed eight hundred thousand sterling a year for, and worshipped into the bargain!

Thomas Paine, *Common Sense*, 1776

Significant Events

King William's War [1689–1697]

Queen Anne's War [1702–1713]

King George's War [1744–1748]

Albany Conference [June 1754]

French and Indian War [1756–1763]

Treaty of Paris ending French and Indian War [1763]

Sugar Act [1764]

Stamp Act [1765]

Declaratory Act [1766]

Townshend Acts [1767]

Boston Massacre [1770]

Committees of Correspondence organized [1772]

Boston Tea Party [1773]

Intolerable Acts [1774]

First Continental Congress [September 1774]

Battles of Lexington and Concord [April 1775]

Second Continental Congress [May 1775]

Battle of Bunker Hill [June 1775]

Thomas Paine's *Common Sense* [January 1776]

Declaration of Independence [July 1776]

ENGRAVING OF THE BOSTON MASSACRE BY PAUL REVERE.

The tensions in American economic, religious, and political life needed only the right combination of pressures from Britain to erupt. When that eruption came, it created not only a great revolution but ultimately a new nation. After 1760, as alienation from English policy increased, the colonists articulated the themes of individual liberty and equality of opportunity more clearly than they had before.

British imperial policy was sharply resented as a denial of political liberty and as an interference with colonial economic freedom. The most famous expression of the desire of the colonists for self-determination—the Declaration of Independence—specifically stressed this theme: the inalienable right of the colonists to liberty and equality.

Eighteenth-Century Politics

As the eighteenth century unfolded, American political life continued to diverge from that of Great Britain. In theory, the colonial governments were thirteen little replicas of the British system which consisted of an executive branch (the king) and the legislative bodies, the House of Lords (the aristocracy) and the House of Commons (the landed gentry). The position of the monarchy in England had been redefined by the Glorious Revolution of 1688. With parliamentary supremacy confirmed, the House of Commons appointed ministers who exerted more authority, and the king was forced to resort to informal political influence as a means of manipulating elections to the House of Commons. An effort was made to avoid direct confrontations, which resulted in a more stable political order. In the colonies, however, a unique and comparatively volatile political life was developing, and conflicts between the executive and legislative branches of the government were common.

England's control over the colonies depended heavily on a successful working relationship between the royal governors, who were appointed by the king, and the colonial assemblies. As long as there was cooperation, the needs of both Britain and the colonies could be met. England grew rich and powerful, and the Americans, as subjects of the British Empire, received protection which allowed them to develop their own way of life. But harmony was not easy to achieve. Although the royal governors were involved in almost all aspects of colonial life, from a practical standpoint they could not participate effectively in the colonial political process. The fact that the king had given them extensive, almost arbitrary, authority to interfere with the American legislature and judiciary aroused the ire of local factions. Colonial assemblies, elected by free-

men, increased in size as population expanded. Since American representatives were more closely tied to their constituents' wishes than were their English counterparts, the governor's influence over them, even his power to dispense patronage, gradually diminished.

The Colonial Governments

Five of the original colonies were more or less self-governing. The proprietors of Pennsylvania and Maryland appointed the governors of their colonies, and Delaware, which was under the control of the Penn family, had its own assembly after 1682. The charter colonies of Rhode Island and Connecticut elected their governors by popular vote. In the remaining eight royal colonies, the governors were the direct representatives of the king.

Every royal governor came to the New World with two important documents: his commission and his instructions. The commission was a public document that established the form of government the colony was to have: a crown-appointed governor and council and an elected assembly. The instructions were secret orders for the governor to follow in regulating trade, promoting religion, and sponsoring laws in his colony. At first, the royal governors enjoyed many of the privileges of a king. They granted land; appointed judges, justices of the peace, and many other minor officials; and served as commanders in chief of the colonial militias. But the British government gradually withdrew some of their powers of appointment and land distribution. Even the military powers of the governors were diminished, first when the colonial assemblies passed laws restricting these powers and later when British troops and commanders based in America came to outnumber the governors' colonial troops. Eventually, just as the king's powers had been limited by Parliament in the seventeenth century, so the royal governors' powers were gradually curtailed by the colonial legislatures in the eighteenth century.

In the royal colonies twelve men were usually appointed to act as the governor's council. These council members were supposedly chosen by English officials, but in practice the officials merely confirmed the governor's recommendations. Massachusetts was an exception. There, the council was elected by the assembly.

The governor's council had executive, legislative, and judicial functions. (1) It was the governor's chief advisory body. The governor could not summon the assembly, appoint judges, or issue paper money without the council's consent. (2) It was the upper house of the legislature, giving final approval to the wording of all financial legislation and having an equal vote in the passing of all other laws. (3) It acted as the highest court in each colony.

By the first half of the eighteenth century, the council was beginning to lose its power. Authorities in England began dealing directly with the governor. Laws became so complex that the council members no longer had the time or the training to serve effectively as a supreme court. Most important, the lower houses of the colonial legislatures were slowly and steadily eroding the council's lawmaking powers.

The lower house of the colonial legislature was called the assembly. Colonial assemblies modeled their parliamentary procedures after England's House of Commons. However, unlike the English system, members of the assembly were elected directly by the freemen they represented. In order to be eligible to vote, freemen had to be white, male, and at least twenty-one years old, and had to own a certain amount of land or cash. Each colony had its own requirements regarding the amount of land or cash a freeman had to possess. Because it was relatively easier for an individual to acquire land in America, the percentage of men eligible to vote in America was much larger than it was in England. Yet even though 75 percent of the adult white-male population could vote, many did not exercise this right because of the small number of candidates from which to choose.

Although the colonial assemblies were more truly representative of the colonial community than Britain's House of Commons was of its constituents, few provided equal representation by twentieth-century standards. There were two main reasons for this. First, in all but the New England colonies, a disproportionate number of representatives came from the smaller, less populated seaboard counties. Second, most representatives came from wealthy families. Eighteenth-century colonial society was firmly based on the principle of deference. People believed that men of merit (and merit was often associated with wealth, education, and social position) ought to govern and use their talents for the benefit of all. They also believed that only individuals of means would be able to resist bribes and have enough of a stake in the community to be responsible legislators.

The Question of Authority

At first the authority of most colonial assemblies extended only to Indian relations, the militia, and the local courts. But by 1720 the assemblies had won the power to propose legislation and initiate money bills. This second power was particularly important. Unless the assemblies voted funds for a military expedition or a road-building program, wars could not be fought and roads could not be constructed. Unless they designated funds for the governor's salary, the governor would not be paid.

Since the governors depended on the assemblies for their salaries, they often hesitated to veto laws passed by the assemblies. The authorities in England, however, found themselves at odds with the assemblies on more than one occasion. They viewed the assemblies as subordinate agencies of the crown, possessing no real authority of their own—a perception that conflicted seriously with that of the colonists.

The assemblies' conflicts with the English authorities created confusion since it was unclear who was really in charge of colonial affairs. The king had certain claims, since most of the colonies were *royal* colonies, and all decisions required the consent of the crown through its ministers. For its part, Parliament insisted that it had the right to control colonial affairs through the cabinet, its advisers to the crown. But the king frequently disputed their claims. Finally, there was the Board of Trade, the agency with the strongest actual control over colonial administration. By 1730 all the colonies except

Rhode Island and Connecticut were required to submit their laws to the Board of Trade for review. Since the board acted slowly, years sometimes passed before it reviewed a law.

The lines of authority and communication between England and the colonies were complex, at best. If a colony wanted to object to an imperial measure, to whom should it object? To the king? the House of Commons? a particular Cabinet member? or the Board of Trade? Although colonial politicians never could answer with certainty, several colonies had agents in London who represented their interests and helped the system to function more smoothly.

The Wars for Empire

North America was frequently the arena in which the four imperial European powers (England, France, Spain, and the Netherlands) came to blows. In the sixteenth century France and Spain fought over Florida. Spain, weakened by the defeat of the Armada in 1588, barely managed to hold onto the territory of Florida. In 1670 Spain was forced to recognize British control of the Atlantic seaboard. In the seventeenth century the English expelled the Dutch from New Amsterdam and by the 1680s they had eliminated Dutch competition for colonial trade.

Thus, by the end of the seventeenth century Spain and Holland had been effectively eliminated from the contest for North America, leaving only England and France in the struggle for domination of the continent. France held Canada and the Ohio and Mississippi Valleys, and England occupied the Atlantic seaboard. French and English colonials constantly wrangled over fishing rights off the coasts of Maine, Newfoundland, and Nova Scotia. To add to these tensions, the French allied themselves with the Algonquin and Huron Indians in Canada, while the English made agreements with the Iroquois tribes in New York.

Three French and English Wars

The competition between Britain and France for dominance in Europe spilled over into North America, creating further unrest in the colonies. Between 1689 and 1697 the first of a series of French-English conflicts spread to the New World. In America it was called King William's War. Although the major campaigns took place in Europe, a number of frontier incidents erupted along the New York–New England borders. The French took Schenectady, New York, and a few villages in New England, and the New Englanders held Port Royal in Nova Scotia for a short time. Both sides had the help of their Indian allies. The struggle, however, was indecisive, and the peace settlement restored all captured territories to their original owners.

The second French-English struggle in America broke out five years later and was called Queen Anne's War (1702–1713). A force of Abenaki Indians, goaded by their French allies, pushed through the snowbound wilderness and surprised the small, fortified village of Deerfield, Massachusetts. About 40 colonists were killed and 111 taken hostage. With the aid of British reinforcements, New Englanders marched north to recapture Port Royal in Nova Scotia. When the war ended in 1713, France surrendered Nova Scotia, Newfoundland, and Hudson's Bay to Britain, and the powerful Iroquois Indians allied themselves more closely with England.

During the next thirty years, the two powers turned to strengthening their positions in the New World. France built Fort Toulouse on the border of South Carolina and made a compact with Spain for mutual aid in case of attack. England countered by settling the new colony, Georgia, and both powers strengthened their fortifications around the Great Lakes and in upper New York.

In 1739, Britain was pushed by advocates of a more aggressive foreign policy into a bitter three-year war with Spain. The conflict was called the War of Jenkin's Ear after an incident in which Spanish crewmen, suspecting that a Captain Robert Jenkins was involved in illicit trade, boarded his vessel and cut off one of his ears. During the war, thousands of Americans died needlessly both in Florida and in a disastrous naval expedition against Spain in South America. In 1744 the conflict widened into a general European war which in-

ENGLISH SHIPS LAY SIEGE TO THE FRENCH FORT AT LOUISBOURG IN NOVA SCOTIA
DURING KING GEORGE'S WAR.

cluded France. The clash (dubbed King George's War) spread to America where it was fought mainly in the Northern colonies and lasted until 1748. Tribes allied with the French crossed the St. Lawrence River and attacked English settlements. And once again, a force from New England marched north, this time seizing Louisbourg on Cape Breton Island, a strategic French fortress that protected the mouth of the St. Lawrence. This was a serious blow, weakening French control of Canada and of the American territories beyond the Appalachian Mountains. France regained the fortress in the Peace of Aix-la-Chapelle in 1748, leaving Americans bitter over the bloody frontier fighting which seemed to have gained them nothing. The French were so worried about their future power in America that they refortified Louisbourg and began building a line of forts along the Appalachian Mountains. English colonials were looking hungrily toward the Ohio Valley, and France was determined to keep them out.

The French and Indian War

The colonists' desire for more land in the Ohio Valley sparked the next French-English confrontation in America. In 1748 the Loyal Land Company, a group of land speculators from Virginia, obtained from the crown a grant of eight-hundred thousand acres in the Ohio Valley. In 1749 the Ohio Company, another Virginia corporation, obtained a grant of two-hundred thousand acres from the Virginia government. Companies in Pennsylvania and Connecticut also had claims to the unsettled territory. When an Ohio Company fur trader set up a post at Pickawillany in Ohio, the French regarded it as an invasion of their territory. In June 1752 a French and Indian force attacked the post, wiping it out and capturing five English colonials. Then, to make certain the British stayed out, the French constructed a line of forts in western Pennsylvania.

Washington's Mission The new Lieutenant Governor of Virginia, Robert Dinwiddie, had instructions

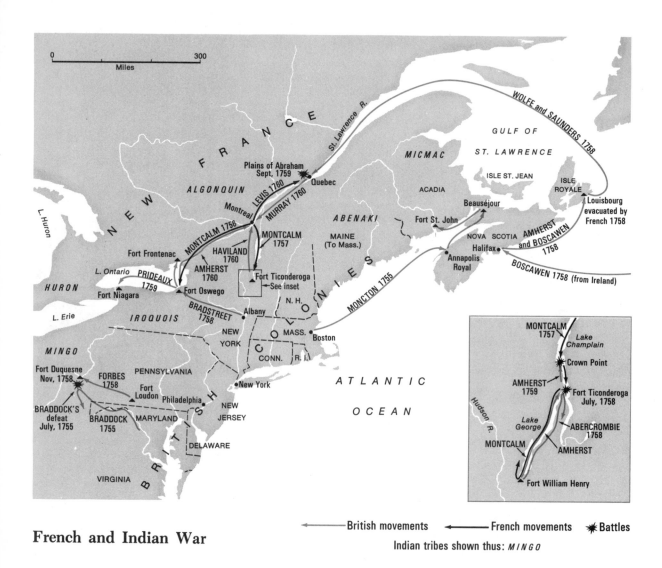

French and Indian War

← British movements ◄— French movements ✳ Battles

Indian tribes shown thus: *MINGO*

to protect the interests of the Ohio Company. Dinwiddie sent a tall, twenty-one-year-old surveyor and colonel in the Virginia militia, George Washington, to inform the French that they were trespassing on property claimed by Virginia. Washington and six other men arrived in western Pennsylvania in December 1753. They were treated with perfect French hospitality—and then rebuffed. As Washington later interpreted the situation, the French announced "it was their absolute design to take

possession of the Ohio, and by G—they would do it." In fact, the French coolly announced their intention of building yet another fort in the Ohio Valley, at the point where the Monongahela and Allegheny Rivers join to form the Ohio.

Dinwiddie, determined to beat the French to this strategic site, sent a small work detail to build a fort there. Then, in the spring of 1754, he sent Washington with a force of two hundred raw local militia to protect the work detail. It was too late;

the French had taken the forts of the Ohio and had already begun erecting their own fort (which they named Duquesne).

Washington, enthusiastic but inexperienced in military strategy, was leading his men through the mountains when he learned that the Virginians had been driven from the Ohio. That May, a group of friendly Indians helped him surprise a small band of French scouts, killing ten and taking twenty-one prisoners. A summons, addressed to the English commander, was found on the leader's body, indicating the mission might have been peaceful. When the French responded to the incident, Washington retreated and set up a rough stockade at Great Meadows (near present-day Uniontown, Pennsylvania) which he aptly named Fort Necessity. A few weeks later, five hundred French soldiers and four hundred Indians attacked the fort. After nine hours of battle, Washington and his men surrendered. The French released them after tricking Washington (who could not read French) into signing a document in which he "confessed" that he had "assassinated" the leader of the French scouts in May. This series of minor events sparked a far-reaching conflict later known in America as the French and Indian War.

Early French Victories Governor Dinwiddie appealed to England for help, and England, even though still officially at peace with France, sent General Edward Braddock and two regiments of regulars to the New World. Braddock expected to swell his ranks with American volunteers and Indian allies, but he was sharply disappointed; only eight Indians and twelve hundred colonials were willing to march with him. Furthermore, New York, Pennsylvania, and Virginia voted only paltry sums of money to finance the venture. When Braddock set off into the wilderness, he was understandably disgruntled.

As English troops forded a stream near Fort Duquesne, the French attacked. The young English officer in charge ordered a retreat, but the first wave of English soldiers turning back collided with a second wave that was rushing forward to aid them. In the resulting melee, Englishmen fired on Englishmen, while the French and their Indian allies picked them off one by one. By the end of this disastrous skirmish, Braddock was fatally wounded and had lost 976 men.

Britain now offered to accept the Allegheny Mountains as the permanent boundary between British and French colonial possessions if France would surrender control of Nova Scotia. France refused and Britain declared war.

Many Europeans had foreseen the showdown between France and England. The contest which began in North America developed into a world war, and the two powers and their allies engaged each other in Europe, India, the Caribbean, and the Philippines. In this long struggle, the crucial question was: which nation would finally control North America? English colonials greatly outnumbered French settlers. Along the Atlantic Coast, English towns, farms, and scattered industry flourished; in the French colonies around Quebec and Montreal on the St. Lawrence River, only a few soldier-settlers and fur trappers had settled. Yet the French had certain advantages: they were more familiar with the wilderness, and they had strong Indian allies, a larger, better trained army, and a line of forts in the Ohio Valley.

The first years of the war (1756–1758) went badly for the English. Because the colonists had not moved promptly to reinforce the British war effort, major British offensives were repelled, and the French captured several strategic forts. The Indians were so impressed with the French victory over Braddock that every tribe north of the Ohio River, except for those in the Iroquois Confederacy, transferred its loyalty to New France.

The Albany Congress Meanwhile, Britain began strengthening its position against the French. The first item of business was improving relations with the Iroquois Confederacy. The confederacy had complained that fur traders from New York were bypassing the Iroquois and dealing directly with other tribes under Iroquois control. They had also complained that speculators from the English colonies had invaded Iroquois lands. The British, fearing that the Iroquois might join forces with France, decided to attend to these grievances.

England ordered the colonists to meet with the Iroquois, and in June 1754 150 Iroquois leaders gathered at Albany, New York, where they were met by delegates from New Hampshire, Massachusetts, Connecticut, Rhode Island, Pennsylvania, Maryland, and New York. After much pomp and ceremony, the Indians left with wagonloads of guns,

JOIN, or DIE.

BENJAMIN FRANKLIN'S FAMOUS RENDERING OF HIS PROPOSAL TO
THE ALBANY CONGRESS CALLING FOR COLONIAL UNITY.

scarlet coats, axes, scissors, silver buttons, and other gifts. But, impressed by French victories, they departed without promising aid in the event of another war between the two European powers.

Off to a poor start, the Albany Congress failed in another effort as well. Pennsylvania's representative, Benjamin Franklin, who believed that the colonies must unite together for defense, presented the colonial delegates with a plan of union calling for a "general government . . . under which the government of each colony may retain its present constitution." Each colony in the federation would send delegates to a grand council that would handle Indian affairs, dispose of lands in the Ohio Valley, govern frontier territories, and levy taxes for an intercolonial army. The delegates took Franklin's plan back to their assemblies, and every single assembly rejected it. No colony was willing to hand over to a federation the right to levy taxes on unclaimed land in the Ohio Valley. Their rejection spared England the embarrassment of a veto, as the British believed it would have put too much power into colonial hands.

"Everyone cries, a union is necessary," Franklin wrote to a friend, "but when they come to the manner and form of the union, their weak noodles are perfectly distracted." In England, Franklin added, the proposal was "judged to have too much of the *democratic*." The first colonial attempt to join forces had come to nothing.

William Pitt Turns the Tide As the war intensified, the British were repelled in their attempts to capture Fort Niagara and Crown Point on Lake Champlain. In 1756 the French commander, the Marquis de Montcalm, captured Fort Oswego on Lake Ontario as well as nearby Fort Bull, and in 1757 he took Fort William Henry on Lake George. The war was going so badly for Britain that the Earl of Chesterfield felt moved to write: "The French are masters to do what they please in America. We are no longer a nation. I never yet saw so dreadful a project."

The tide finally turned when William Pitt, a brilliant and arrogant politician, took control of the English war effort in 1758, declaring: "I am sure that I can save the country and that no one else can." His policy was based on the belief that Britain could dominate the world once its navy controlled the sea lanes and its armies controlled North America. Pitt spared no expense in carrying out his plans. First he sent the British navy to blockade the coast of France. He then dispatched numerous English regiments and adequate supplies to America with the promise to pay the colonies whatever it cost to fight the French. He also sent new, younger commanding officers to lead the English and colonial forces.

Pitt's new armies soon gained the upper hand. In July 1758 Brigadier General James Wolfe and Major General Jeffrey Amherst took the fortress at Louisbourg, ending once and for all French control of the Atlantic fishing grounds and the mouth of the St. Lawrence. Fort Frontenac, at the other end of the St. Lawrence, fell a month later. Soon after, the French gave up Fort Duquesne, which the British renamed Fort Pitt. In the fall of 1759 the English captured Quebec. The city was protected by a high rock cliff facing the river and was generally considered safe from attack. But Wolfe discovered an undefended route up the stone precipice. One night he put his men in boats and floated them silently to the base of the path. At dawn the French saw five thousand British redcoats lined up for battle on the Plains of Abraham beside their fort. Both Wolfe and the Marquis de Montcalm died in the ensuing struggle, but the English won the day. In 1760 they took Montreal. Although the war was fought for three more years in Europe, India, and the Caribbean, in America it had come to an end.

Aftermath of the War In 1763 the Treaty of Paris ended the conflict and radically reshaped the map

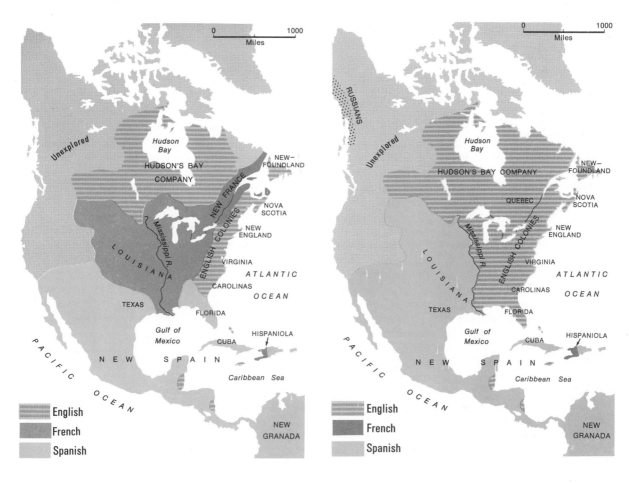

North America • 1713

North America • 1763

of America. Britain received all lands north of the Great Lakes (Canada) and all lands east of the Mississippi River, including Florida. Spain, which had fought on the side of France, lost Florida to the British. As a reward for help during the war, France gave to Spain Louisiana, the land west of the Mississippi. Of its once vast holdings in America, France retained only a few islands in the Caribbean, two islands in the St. Lawrence, and fishing rights off Newfoundland.

British money and British soldiers were responsible for victory in the French and Indian War.

Again, the colonists had to accept British troops in their midst and to suffer the arrogance of the British officers. One English officer described the poorly trained colonials as "broken innkeepers, horse jockeys, and Indian traders." Americans also chafed under a new effort to enforce the Navigation Acts and protested Britain's severe methods. Nevertheless, the English victory had been so impressive that the colonials felt a sudden surge of pride in belonging to the British Empire. In England some leaders feared that Americans might turn their thoughts to independence now that the French had been driven out of Canada, but Benjamin Franklin expressed the view of many colonials when he remarked that a union among the colonies "is not merely improbable, it is impossible," adding, "I mean without the most grievous tyranny and oppression."

Britain's New Imperial Policy

Before 1760 most Americans had accepted the way the British ran their empire. England's rule of America in the last half of the eighteenth century has been described as "salutary neglect"; that is, the British government avoided interference in colonial affairs in order to allow its North American possessions to develop naturally. While the government had never really neglected the colonies, after the French and Indian War, its leaders were determined to assert tighter control. England was laboring under a huge national debt and spending five times more to administer its overseas possessions than it had before the war. The colonies had taken on new importance as a source of revenue, and Parliament began to pay closer attention to them. Britain hoped to make Americans more directly subordinate to Parliament and to require them to share more of the costs of administering and defending the empire.

England was also beset by administrative problems. The imperial machinery for governing the colonies could no longer cope with the demands of an expanding population. Conflicting claims to the Ohio Valley had to be settled now that the territory was secured, and Canada and Florida had to be given some form of government.

In addition, English politics had become so complex that the government was almost unable to deal with new problems. George III had come to the throne in 1760 with the idea of increasing the powers of the monarchy at the expense of the powerful Whig families which had controlled English politics since the Glorious Revolution of 1688. To win support, he sometimes appointed ministers without advice from the leaders of the House of Commons and campaigned actively in British elections for candidates who agreed with his ideas. Those of his candidates who were elected to Parliament were known as the king's friends. To complicate matters, there were three important Whig factions, each with differing outlooks, but all opposed to increasing the power of the crown. One faction was led by George Grenville, the second by William Pitt, and the third called itself the Rockingham Whigs. As these three groups rose and fell from power in the House of Commons between 1763 and 1770, British policy toward the American colonies underwent many changes.

During this period of fluctuation in its internal politics, Britain instituted a series of policies designed to reorganize its inefficiently managed empire and reap the financial rewards of its victory over France. These policies turned out to be shortsighted, however. Not only were they regarded as oppressive by many Americans, but their enforcement was made more difficult by the rapid rise and fall of several ministries.

The Proclamation of 1763

British relations with the Indians, always precarious, deteriorated seriously after the war. Most of the tribes, except those in the Iroquois Confederacy, had allied themselves with the French, in the hopes that a French victory would stop the westward migration of English colonists. After the final English victories, Chief Pontiac of the Ottawa tribe made a desperate attempt to halt English expansion. In the summer of 1763 the Ottawas and their allies attacked the line of English forts and trading posts around the Great Lakes and along the Appalachian Mountains.

Pontiac's Rebellion failed, but the British government was anxious to avoid further confrontations with the Indians. It also feared that once the colonists had slipped beyond the Appalachians, outside British control, they would be impossible to govern. England therefore issued the Proclamation of 1763, prohibiting settlers from crossing the Appalachians or purchasing Indian lands. No settlers, land speculators, or fur traders were to be admitted to the new lands in the West until the Indians had been pacified and a land policy had been worked out in Parliament. Colonists who had been planning to mi-

DANIEL BOONE (1734–1820). HAVING LED A PARTY OF SETTLERS
THROUGH THE CUMBERLAND GAP INTO KENTUCKY IN 1773, BOONE
BECAME A LAND AGENT FOR THE TRANSYLVANIA COMPANY. WITH
THIRTY MEN HE CARVED OUT THE WILDERNESS ROAD AND ESTAB-
LISHED BOONSBOROUGH ON THE KENTUCKY RIVER. A FAMOUS
INDIAN FIGHTER AND EXPLORER, HE ALSO MADE IMPORTANT CON-
TRIBUTIONS AS A SURVEYOR AND COUNTY LEGISLATOR. HE DIED
IN MISSOURI IN HIS MID-EIGHTIES, HAVING SOLD MOST OF HIS
LAND TO PAY OFF DEBTS IN KENTUCKY.

grate West were advised to go to Quebec or Florida
instead.

The proclamation enraged the colonists. Some
had already migrated to Kentucky and western
Pennsylvania and into the Carolina back country.
The growing population, freed from French claims
to the area, was determined to move further westward. Dozens of land-development companies had
designs on the Ohio Valley. The Virginia farmers, in
particular, needed new farmlands, since tobacco
farming had depleted their soil, crop yields were
smaller, and erosion was eating away the topsoil.
George Washington, for one, announced that he

had no intention of conforming to the proclamation,
saying, "Any person . . . who neglects the present
opportunity of hunting out good lands, and in some
measure marking and distinguishing them for his
own (in order to keep others from settling them),
will never regain it." Washington promptly sent an
agent to protect his claims.

By 1768 opposition to Britain's frontier policy
became so fierce that the British were forced to
begin revising the restrictions. First they made a
treaty with the Cherokees that extended the western
boundary of Virginia. A treaty with the Creeks enlarged the territory of South Carolina and Georgia.
A third treaty, with the Iroquois, added land to
New York.

But these small gains did not appease the
colonists. In 1769 Daniel Boone, a woodsman and
professional scout, began exploring the land north of
the Ohio River. He had attempted to cross the
Cumberland Gap in 1773 with his own and several
other families. But the venture ended in failure after
his son James and another member of the party were
tortured and killed by Indians. Undaunted, Boone
set out again in 1775 and led the first group of settlers over the gap into the Midwest. During his lifetime, a million settlers poured across the mountains,
founding the states of Kentucky and Tennessee.

The Currency and Sugar Acts

After the war, British officials estimated that ten
thousand British troops would have to be stationed
permanently in America to protect the colonies from
Indian raids. The British public resented paying for
these troops and insisted that the Americans assume
a major part of the burden. Subsequently, in April
1764, Parliament passed the Currency Act forbidding the colonies from issuing paper money as legal
tender. English creditors were becoming increasingly uneasy over the true value of American paper
currency. At times the paper had been overissued
and had depreciated in value. As a result, English
merchants feared great losses if outstanding debts
were paid in cheaper American money. Passage of
the Currency Act meant that creditors no longer had
to accept colonial paper money in payment of debts.

The Currency Act imposed a real hardship on
the American economy. The colonies had little gold
and silver of their own, and it was against the law to

export bullion from England into America. Forbidden to issue paper money as legal tender and deprived of hard cash, the colonists found it increasingly difficult to pay for large quantities of English imports. The colonies were expected to pay their increasing debt to British merchants and to assume a large portion of the war debt with a decreasing supply of money. Moreover, the boom in commerce which occurred during the French and Indian War had collapsed after 1760, and overproduction of tobacco simultaneously drove its price down to a new low. Thus, the American economy was in chaos as Britain introduced a new imperial policy.

George Grenville, now Prime Minister of Britain, had discovered that Britain was not only paying heavily to station troops in America but also that the American customs service was costing Britain far more to operate than it was collecting in fees. Consequently, in April 1764, Parliament passed the Sugar Act, a revenue-raising measure which extended the list of enumerated articles and imposed duties on sugar, indigo, coffee, wine, and woven cloth imported into the colonies. Grenville did concede that a sixpence duty on French Caribbean molasses, essential to Yankee rum distillers, was too high and the tax was cut in half.

More important to colonial merchants were the indications that the Sugar Act would be strictly enforced. In the past, colonial shipowners had avoided the high duties by simply bribing the customs officials not to collect. The Sugar Act made smuggling more difficult by requiring shipowners to fill out lengthy documents whenever they sailed into or out of an American port. To ensure that fees would be collected, suits over payment were to be referred to an admiralty court where cases were tried by a crown-appointed judge instead of the more lenient juries composed of fellow colonists. Furthermore, defendants were to be presumed guilty until proven innocent, which was in opposition to traditional English legal practice.

The Sugar Act infuriated the colonists even more than the Currency Act. Traditionally, British duties and taxes had been designed to regulate trade by favoring exchange with England and to keep the empire's profits from trickling into foreign pockets. The Sugar Act was a different matter. It was designed specifically to raise revenue for the British government, to suppress smuggling, and to tighten imperial control.

The Stamp and Quartering Acts

The colonists were badly shaken by the Sugar Act because it was an indirect tax which coincided with a depression in economic conditions following the French and Indian War. They rebelled openly, however, when Parliament tried to impose a direct tax on them the very next year.

In March 1765 Parliament passed the Stamp Act requiring colonists to pay a tax every time they registered a legal document (such as wills and deeds). This tax also applied to newspapers, pamphlets, almanacs, and even to playing cards and sets of dice. Again, those who tried to avoid the taxes would be tried by a royal judge in an admiralty court. A few days later Parliament passed the Quartering Act, which required colonial cities to provide royal troops with living accommodations in public inns, alehouses, empty buildings, or barns and to furnish them with candles, firewood, blankets, salt, and liquor.

These new laws had an immediate impact on the colonies. The Currency Act made it difficult to do business. The Sugar Act threatened to destroy New England's rum distillers. But the Stamp Act, a direct tax, dealt the heaviest blow. Now the colonists felt deprived of their liberties as well as of their money. Most colonists believed that the Stamp Act violated their right, as English citizens, to be taxed only by their elected representatives. Clearly, it raised the question of how the colonial assemblies were related to Parliament. The colonists particularly disliked the Stamp Act because they had been given no voice in its passage into law.

The Bill of Rights, signed by William and Mary in 1689, denied the king the right to levy taxes without the consent of Parliament. The colonists had assumed that the principle of no taxation without representation extended to them, at least in legislation providing revenue for the needs of the individual colonies. Parliament, however, was jealous of the powers established by the Glorious Revolution and was not prepared to concede that a colonial legislature had as much right to legislate for its people as Parliament had to legislate for England. The colonial legislatures, it was argued, had no authority except that delegated by Parliament, and they existed only through the generosity of the mother country.

The colonial response was swift, explosive, and completely unexpected in England. Because those

BOSTONIANS GATHER TO READ THE PROVISIONS OF THE STAMP ACT, A NEW MEASURE WHICH CREATED AN UPROAR AMONG THE COLONISTS.

most immediately affected were among the most articulate groups in the colonies—lawyers, printers, and merchants—protest meetings, speeches, and pamphlets abounded. In New York, Boston, and other cities, groups calling themselves the Sons of Liberty were formed to resist the Stamp Act "to the last extremity." Made up mainly of small businessmen, artisans, and laborers, the Sons of Liberty soon engaged in open protest. In 1765 there were frequent violent eruptions; stamp collectors were bullied into resigning, and public officials who had anything to do with the stamps were harassed. Professional men and merchants who seemed inclined to go along with the law were also intimidated. In Massachusetts Lieutenant Governor Hutchinson's mansion was burned and his valuable library was destroyed. Later the Sons of Liberty organized more disciplined actions, such as writing letters to the newspapers.

The Grenville ministry tried to pacify the colonists. Grenville agreed that the colonies should be taxed only by their own representatives and maintained that every member of Parliament *was* such a representative. Even though the colonists did not actually elect any members to Parliament, Grenville maintained that they had *virtual* representation. All of the members of Parliament represented the whole empire, not merely the districts from which they were elected. Grenville's logic was not acceptable to the colonists. The members of their own colonial assemblies had to live in the colonial district they represented and they did not believe they could be fairly represented by members of Parliament in distant England. They also knew that, even if they could elect representatives to Parliament, their members would be greatly outnumbered by the English members. In addition, the colonists were painfully aware that admiralty courts were being used to deny them the traditional English right to trial by jury.

The Stamp Act Congress "One single act of Parliament set the people a'thinking in six months more than they had done in their whole lives before," wrote James Otis, the leader of the Massachusetts assembly. Suddenly colonists everywhere were questioning British policies in ways that probably would not have occurred before the Stamp Act crisis. In June 1765 Massachusetts called for the first intercolonial assembly ever summoned by the colonists themselves. This assembly, the Stamp Act Congress, representing nine colonies, met in New York City the following October.

After avowing "all due subordination" to Parliament, the representatives drafted a joint statement resolving "that the people in these colonies are not and from their local circumstances cannot be, represented in the House of Commons in Great Britain; that the only representatives of the people of these colonies are persons chosen by themselves, and that no taxes ever have been, or can be constitutionally imposed on them, but by their respective legislatures." They then petitioned the king and Parliament to repeal the Sugar and Stamp Acts and to abolish the admiralty courts.

Months before, the colonies had been so suspicious of one another that they had been unable to cooperate in even the smallest venture. Now a new spirit of unity was growing in America. Merchants in every colony agreed to stop importing British goods, in hopes that a total embargo would throw the English economy into a depression. Although the boycott never really extended far South, it was an important first step toward economic cooperation. A South Carolina representative to the Stamp Act Congress sounded a new note when he declared that "there ought to be no New England man, no

The Supremacy of Parliament
from the Declaratory Act

"Be it declared. . . . That the said colonies and plantations in *America* have been, are, and of right ought to be, subordinate unto, and dependent upon the imperial crown and parliament of *Great Britain;* and that the King's majesty, by and with the advice and consent of the lords spiritual and temporal, and commons of *Great Britain*, in parliament assembled, had, hath, and of right ought to have, full power and authority to make laws and statutes of sufficient force and validity to bind the colonies and people of *America*, subjects of the crown of *Great Britain*, in all cases whatsoever. . . ."

Declaratory Act, 1766

Samuel Adams Questions Parliament's
Right to Legislate for the Colonies

"It is an essential, unalterable right in nature, engrafted into the British constitution, as a fundamental law, and ever held sacred and irrevocable by the subjects within the realm, that what a man has honestly acquired is absolutely his own, which he may freely give, but cannot be taken from him without his consent; that the American subjects may, therefore, exclusive of any consideration of charter rights, with a decent firmness, adapted to the character of free men and subjects, assert this natural and constitutional right.

It is, moreover, their humble opinion, which they express with the greatest deference to the wisdom of the Parliament, that the Acts made there, imposing duties on the people of this province, with the sole and express purpose of raising a revenue, are infringements of their natural and constitutional rights; because, as they are not represented in the British Parliament, his Majesty's commons in Britain, by those Acts, grant their property without their consent."

Works of Samuel Adams, 1768

New Yorker known on this continent, but all of us Americans."

The Stamp Act was to go into force in November 1765, but colonial mobs so thoroughly intimidated the royal officials that no one tried to sell a single stamp. Hundreds of merchants suspended business, and when shops opened again in late December, they ignored the Stamp Act with a unanimity never before witnessed in America. To a large extent this was the work of the Sons of Liberty who had increased their agitation and had learned to focus their protests where they would have the greatest effect.

Repeal of the Stamp Act By July the king had already lost confidence in Grenville and had asked the Rockingham Whigs who opposed the Stamp Act to form a new government. Within a month, news of the American reaction reached Britain and the new government was beseiged by merchants' petitions calling for repeal of the Stamp Act. The king supported repeal in order to show his support for the Rockingham faction and prevent the return of Grenville, whom he disliked. William Pitt also supported repeal, even going so far as to say: "I rejoice that America has resisted."

In March 1766, before Parliament officially received the petition of the Stamp Act Congress, it repealed both the Stamp and the Sugar Acts. Only a one-penny duty on sugar remained. When the news reached the colonies, there was much rejoicing—even though the Americans learned that on the same day that the Stamp Act was repealed, a Declaratory Act had been passed. The Declaratory Act clearly asserted Parliament's right to "make laws and statutes of sufficient force and validity to bind the colonies and people of America . . . in all cases whatsoever." The colonists now waited to see

THE REPEAL, OR THE FUNERAL PROCESSION, OF MISS AMERIC-STAMP,
AN ENGLISH CARTOON PUBLISHED IN 1766.

whether the British government would try to enforce such a right.

The Townshend Acts

Some American political thinkers had objected to the Stamp Act on the grounds that it was a *direct* tax—that is, a tax collected on items at the time they were sold in America—and thus an infringement of colonial rights. Benjamin Franklin believed—and even informed Parliament—that the colonists objected only to direct taxes and not to indirect taxes—that is, taxes collected at ports before the goods entered the country. Seeing that colonial trade was reviving after the disruptions of the war years and the Sugar Act, Parliament concluded that the easiest way to raise revenues would be to levy a new series of indirect taxes.

The duties were proposed in June 1767 by Charles Townshend, the new chancellor of the exchequer. The Townshend Acts placed taxes on glass, lead, paints, paper, and tea—all products that under the Navigation Acts, Americans could import only from England. The duties had to be paid in gold and silver and were to be used to pay the salaries of royal officials, a method of payment intended to ensure their independence from the colonial legislatures.

Even more upsetting was the establishment of an American Board of Customs with authority to use writs of assistance (general search warrants) to look for smuggled goods. New admiralty courts were established in four major American ports, and the salaries of the customs commissioners were to be paid out of fines collected from shippers convicted in the admiralty courts. This last provision inevitably led to corruption. In addition, officials were to receive one-third of the total value of every ship and cargo caught violating British mercantile law. During this period, the British army was pulled back from western posts and concentrated in the seaports to keep order. Resistance in New York to housing these soldiers—as required by the Quartering Act—brought about the suspension of the New York legislature.

The Townshend Acts struck many people as another British attempt to interfere with colonial self-government, and Americans began to seek cooperative efforts to bring about their repeal. They knew that while they could do little to resist Parliament individually, united they posed a considerable threat.

Although Franklin had convinced Parliament that Americans objected only to direct taxes, the truth of the matter was that Americans did not want any kind of new taxes, including the indirect Townshend duties. Now the colonists had to invent a distinction between indirect taxes that were acceptable and the Townshend duties that were unacceptable. John Dickinson, a lawyer and author of *Letters from a Farmer in Pennsylvania*, devised one of the most widely accepted arguments. He maintained that it was legal for Parliament to use indirect taxation to regulate trade (as in the Navigation Acts), but not to raise revenue (which was the purpose of the Townshend Acts).

Demonstrations against the new duties were peaceful, since the organizers did not want to alienate moderates and conservatives from the repeal effort. Throughout the colonies merchants effectively boycotted the British goods listed in the acts. Colonists made their own clothes and manufactured their own paper and paint. This response was more vigorous than England had expected. Because the ill-considered Stamp Act had threatened all the colonies, it had encouraged Americans to unite in common opposition to British revenue measures. Still, the majority of both British and Americans were unaware of the full intensity of feelings as yet unreleased.

From Discord to Disunion

At the time of the Stamp Act crisis, a few influential people in each colony had begun to take a stand against British policy. These dissenters, sometimes called the radical patriots, were the first to sense that the Stamp Act had political as well as economic implications for America's future. Their activities led to widespread organized resistance. Eventually perhaps one-third to two-fifths of the moderate and conservative colonists came to support the rebels, first in their demand for redress of grievances and finally for complete independence. In a single decade the patriots engineered one of the greatest reversals of public opinion in world history, severing the colonists' loyalty to England and sowing the seeds of revolution. Although the majority of Americans probably never supported the break, a large minority did, including many influential community leaders.

In New England the battle against Parliament was led by Samuel Adams, his cousin John Adams, and James Otis. Otis, a lawyer, was an energetic speaker with a talent for highly persuasive arguments. Unfortunately his effectiveness was diminished by bouts of emotional instability, and he finally succumbed to insanity. Sam Adams, a gifted politician who had failed to make a success of any other venture, was a zealous guardian of colonial rights and a superb propagandist and organizer. He whipped the public into a fury by pouncing on every British mistake and perceived insult and, to use his own words, "improving" on them. It was he who became the driving force behind the Sons of Liberty. John Adams, a lawyer by profession, was more restrained in his approach than his cousin Sam. Nevertheless he was equally determined to promote the growing hostility toward Parliament.

There were other important patriot leaders in the South. In Virginia the fiery lawyer Patrick Henry and the wealthy planter Richard Henry Lee were outspoken in their attacks on British policy. In South Carolina Christopher Gadsden, a popular leader in the legislature, worked tirelessly for the patriot cause. Another Virginian, Thomas Jefferson, was still a young law student in 1767, but his training in political philosophy would prepare him to emerge as one of the most articulate advocates of American independence.

Trouble in Massachusetts

In 1768 the Massachusetts assembly sent a circular letter written by Sam Adams to the other colonial legislatures. The letter criticized the Townshend duties and asserted the rights of Americans as British subjects to have taxes levied only by their elected representatives. Meanwhile, people all over America were debating how much power Parliament should have over them.

The English Parliament regarded the sending of the circular letter as a threat to its authority and ordered the Massachusetts assembly to withdraw it immediately. While some of the king's advisers considered a "kind and lenient" circular letter of their own, the secretary of state instructed the royal governors to dissolve their assemblies if the dangerous document from Massachusetts was not withdrawn.

The Massachusetts assembly voted ninety-two to seventeen against withdrawing the letter, and the governor dissolved the assembly as ordered. In September 1768 two regiments of royal troops were billeted in Boston in preparation for an outbreak of violence. An unofficial Massachusetts convention met a few days later. Sam Adams tried to rouse the delegates to take strong action, but instead they issued a statement resolving that "as Englishmen they have an aversion to an unnecessary standing army, which they look upon as dangerous to their civil liberty." For the time being, British troops were received without incident, but their relations with the townspeople continued to deteriorate.

A year and a half later violence finally erupted. In March 1770 a band of unemployed laborers attacked a British sentry at the Boston customhouse. The officer on duty called for help and tried to reason with the mob, but it continued to pelt the soldiers with oyster shells and snowballs. In the confusion, someone shouted, "Fire!" The British fired. Five of the rioters were killed and six were wounded. The first man slain was Crispus Attucks, an unemployed mulatto seaman. Sam Adams and James Otis magnified this street brawl into a "massacre" for propaganda purposes, but John Adams defended the British soldiers against a murder charge, and all but two were acquitted.

By one of those strange coincidences of history, on the day of the Boston Massacre, Parliament repealed all of the Townshend duties except the one on tea. The colonial boycott of British goods had had its effect. The Townshend Acts had benefited no one: Americans had been deprived of many imports; British manufacturers had watched with dismay as American industries began to produce the

goods under embargo; and Parliament received very little revenue from the customs officers. The chancellor of the exchequer, Lord North, thought it was important to keep the tea tax, however, if only to prove that Parliament did have the right to tax the colonies. Still, for all practical purposes, England's new imperial policy was in disarray.

A Period of Peace

The Sons of Liberty tried to extend the embargo of all English goods until the tea tax was withdrawn. But most Americans were so pleased by the repeal of the other duties that colonial merchants soon began trading with England again. Thus the period from 1770 to 1773 was one of relative calm. Americans paid the small duties on tea and foreign molasses without much grumbling. Business flourished, and all but a handful of colonials seemed to lose interest in the controversy surrounding taxation.

Once the colonists stopped quarreling with England, however, they began quarreling with one another. New England Anglicans asked the Church of England to send a bishop to America, an action which infuriated non-Anglicans as well as Southern Anglicans, who wanted to continue running their own congregations. Squabbles over western lands were renewed. In the Southern colonies, tensions between settlers on the frontier and the tidewater establishment surfaced again.

Meanwhile, the patriots worked ardently to publicize every British blunder. Sam Adams utilized existing town meetings, assemblies, county courts, churches, clubs, and newspapers as vehicles for protest in his search for new ways to reach the people. In 1772 Adams formed a committee of correspondence to draw up a list of grievances, and he persuaded other Massachusetts towns to do likewise. Within three months, eight more committees had been formed, all exchanging written complaints against the English. The other New England colonies joined the growing movement, and eventually there was at least one committee in every colony except Pennsylvania.

One complaint of the committees regarded Britain's new plan for paying the governor of Massachusetts. The governor's salary had always been paid by the assembly, ensuring the colonists a certain amount of control over their royal rulers. After June 1772, however, the governor was to be paid directly by the crown. The crown soon took responsibility for paying superior court judges as well.

An even more inflammatory issue centered on an incident involving a British warship, the *Gaspee*, which had been loaned to the customs service to eliminate smuggling in New England. The ship's captain had harassed farmers and fishermen trading in the Narragansett Bay, and when the *Gaspee* ran aground in pursuit of a smuggler, local citizens boarded her at night, wounded the captain, and burned the ship.

The reaction of the British government to this outrage was surprisingly mild. However, a false rumor spread that the suspects in the *Gaspee* affair would be taken to England for trial. The right to be tried in one's own district was among the oldest principles of English justice, and the rumor so incensed the Virginia House of Burgesses that it set up correspondence committees all over the colony. By mid-1773 all of New England and South Carolina

had agreed to correspond with the committees in Virginia. An underground news system had been set up which kept alive suspicion of British policy and laid the groundwork for union.

The Boston Tea Party

The event that brought on the final crisis resulted from a grave miscalculation on England's part. For almost 175 years the British East India Company had maintained a prosperous monopoly over all trade between India and the rest of the British Empire. But in the 1770s it fell on hard times and was facing bankruptcy. High taxes in Britain and America made smuggled Dutch tea more marketable, so the company still had some seventeen million pounds of Indian tea stored in its warehouses.

Lord North believed he had a brilliant scheme for disposing of the tea and saving the East India Company. To implement his plan, he quickly

ONLOOKERS CHEER AS COLONISTS THINLY DISGUISED AS INDIANS DUMP TONS OF TEA INTO BOSTON HARBOR.

guided the Tea Act of 1773 through Parliament. The Tea Act provided that the government would withdraw its usual import duties on all tea brought *into* England. Moreover, it allowed the company to export tea directly to America without going through English or American wholesalers. This new arrangement would bring the price of East India Company tea well below the cost of Dutch tea, which Americans had been buying illegally for years.

Once again the British government underestimated American reaction to its policies. The plan pleased everyone except the colonists, who felt they were being denied freedom of choice. If Parliament could eliminate American tea wholesalers, what other colonial wholesalers would be ruined next? Then the East India Company added insult to injury by allowing only those merchants who had ignored or opposed the embargo against English goods to be its agents in America. Americans began to worry that if the Tea Act went into effect, England would start setting up other monopolies as well which would favor those merchants who could pass a loyalty test.

American opposition to the Tea Act was almost unanimous. The committees of correspondence had done their work well. In Charleston the tea was locked in public warehouses, where it remained unopened until after the Declaration of Independence. In New York and Philadelphia the tea was never even unloaded. East India Company agents were harassed in every port.

In Boston the governor was determined to land the tea, collect the duty, and proceed normally. On December 16, 1773, some thirty to sixty men, lightly disguised as Indians in war paint and feathers, boarded three British ships in the harbor. As a cheering crowd watched from the wharf, forty-five tons of tea, worth nearly £10,000, were dumped into Boston harbor.

The British government was furious. Lord North had devised the Tea Act to please the colonists, but now he realized there was no way to deal with these "haughty American republicans." The king announced: "We must master them or totally leave them to themselves and treat them as aliens."

Initial American reaction was equally critical. Most colonists thought the Boston Tea Party a shameful affair, "calculated to introduce anarchy, confusion, and bloodshed among the people." But the Boston Tea Party brought to a head the conflict

over British authority. The patriots had committed violence in an attempt to rally popular support against British rule and to see how Britain would react. They did not have long to wait.

The Intolerable Acts

To punish the Bostonians, Lord North steered the first of four measures through Parliament. The Boston Port Bill closed Boston's harbor to all shipping until the citizens compensated the East India Company for the lost tea and paid the required duty.

Boston's committee of correspondence began furiously penning letters to other committees throughout the colonies, claiming the town was facing starvation unless it bowed to British tyranny. When the news reached Virginia, Thomas Jefferson proposed that June 1 be declared a day of mourning for the "heavy calamity which threatens destruction to our civil rights, and the evils of civil war." On June 1 flags hung at half-mast, and church bells tolled in every colony. Americans who had recently denounced Boston for staging the tea party now rushed to the city's aid. Charleston sent rice. Philadelphia dispatched a thousand barrels of flour.

Meanwhile, Parliament passed three other "intolerable" acts: (1) The Massachusetts Government Act revised the Massachusetts charter. From now on, the governor's council would be appointed by the king as in the other royal colonies. The governor's powers were expanded so that he could even ban town meetings, except for the yearly session when local officers were elected. The Massachusetts Colony, which had started out as virtually self-governing, now had a governor who was appointed and paid by the king, judges who were on the royal payroll, and a council chosen by the king. (2) The Administration of Justice Act provided that any government or customs official charged with committing violence in the course of suppressing a riot or other disturbance could be tried in England. (3) A new Quartering Act authorized the housing of troops within private dwellings.

An unrelated measure, the Quebec Act, was passed at the same time. It expanded the Quebec territory south to the Ohio River and west to the Mississippi and gave the area a permanent government without a representative assembly, a form of government similar to the one it had had under

French rule. The act also established Catholicism as the official faith, to be supported by tax revenues.

Americans regarded the Quebec Act as an attempt to extend despotic rule in the colonies. Protestants objected to the recognition and support of Catholicism in a region so close to their borders, and land speculators with claims in the Ohio Valley were infuriated that those rich lands had been given to Quebec. All were disturbed that Quebec would be ruled by an autocratic governor. Although Canadians viewed the Quebec Act as an enlightened measure, the Americans regarded it as a serious threat to their struggle for self-government.

The intolerable acts brought the crisis between England and the North American colonies to the point of no return. For a century and a half Americans had regarded themselves as loyal English citizens and as recently as 1763 had expressed goodwill toward the king. Now the patriots, who were even considering a break with England, were gradually gaining the upper hand.

As far as the British were concerned, the Americans were insubordinate and ignorant of the responsibilities of empire. They had reaped the benefits of few taxes and considerable freedom, far from the bureaucratic and financial complexities of London. Now that they were richer and more populous, the time had come for them to accept taxation.

Although most Americans were willing to let Parliament make laws pertaining to imperial matters such as foreign policy and international trade, they were not willing to surrender their right as free people to participate in the formulation of internal policy. Parliament, nonetheless, stubbornly insisted on treating the colonial governments as subordinate agencies in an imperial system—agencies which it could destroy at will.

Thus assemblies had been suspended and trial by jury set aside. British troops had been stationed on American soil in peacetime. American territorial aspirations in the Ohio Valley had been frustrated. American merchants were bullied by corrupt customs officials and American overseas trade was undermined. Most insulting of all, the Declaratory Act had spelled out in no uncertain terms the right of Parliament to legislate on any matter regarding America without consulting the Americans. Parliament had finally pushed this concept to the limit in the intolerable acts. The colonies, frustrated beyond endurance, called for a meeting of an intercolonial congress in September 1774.

The Evolution of Colonial Unity

The First Continental Congress

Every colony except Georgia sent representatives to the First Continental Congress held in Carpenters' Hall in Philadelphia. The radical patriots were there in strength: Samuel and John Adams, Patrick Henry, Richard Henry Lee, and Christopher Gadsden. Among the moderates and conservatives present were George Washington, Peyton Randolph, Joseph Galloway, John Dickinson, and John Jay.

Although the delegates unanimously agreed that they should support Massachusetts against British retaliation, they held widely differing views concerning parliamentary authority over the colonies. The more radical delegates worked tirelessly to win the moderates and conservatives over to their point of view. Joseph Galloway, one of the most conservative delegates, balefully observed that Sam Adams "eats little, sleeps little, thinks much, and is most decisive and indefatigable in the pursuit of his objects."

Galloway proposed a revised system of colonial government. His plan included a grand council that would share power with Parliament on colonial matters and a president-general with the right to veto all acts of Parliament affecting the colonies. However, the radical patriots won the day, as the congress voted six to five against Galloway's plan after unanimously adopting a much more radical plan advanced by Sam Adams. Adam's plan, already adopted in his own colony of Massachusetts as the Suffolk Resolves, called on the colonies to raise troops and to suspend trade with Great Britain. To conciliate the moderates, a new petition of colonial grievances was drawn up to be sent to the British government.

Furthermore, the congress established the Continental Association charged with setting up committees at town, county, and provincial levels of

A FEW DAYS AFTER THE BATTLE OF LEXINGTON, RALPH EARL, A CONNECTICUT ARTIST, RETURNED TO THE SCENE AND MADE SKETCHES OF THE ACTION WHICH WERE LATER ENGRAVED BY HIS FRIEND AMOS DOO-LITTLE. FROM HIS ACCOUNT IT SEEMS CLEAR THAT MOST OF THE REBELS HAD TURNED TO RETREAT BEFORE THE BRITISH OPENED WITH HEAVY FIRE. AS THE OUTNUMBERED COLONIAL MILITIAMEN ARE SHOT DOWN, ONE MINUTEMAN (LOWER LEFT) SHAKES HIS FIST IN DEFIANCE AT THE REDCOATS.

government to enforce a total embargo on all British trade. The committees were also supposed to encourage frugality, publish the names of those who violated the agreement, and check all customs entries. These committees soon fell into the hands of the radical elements in each colony, who enforced the boycott rigorously and often violently during the first few months.

The Continental Association was vital to the growing revolutionary movement, not because of its effect on Britain, but because it forced moderates and conservatives to take sides. Washington, for example, supported the policy of resistance, whereas

Galloway eventually sided with Britain. America was almost ready for independence. As John Adams later wrote of the First Continental Congress and its effect, "The revolution was complete, in the minds of the people, and the Union of the colonies, before the war commenced."

Violence broke out on April 19, 1775, when General Thomas Gage, the governor of Massachusetts, was ordered to enforce the intolerable acts by force, if necessary, and to halt rebel preparations for an armed defense. Gage sent seven hundred soldiers to confiscate a supply of weapons stored at Concord by the colonial militia. When the advance guard, led by Major John Pitcairn, arrived at the town of Lexington, they found the colonial militia waiting on the village green. No one knows who fired the first shot, but when the smoke cleared, British redcoats had killed eight Americans and wounded ten.

The British hurried on to Concord and seized a few supplies (most had already been spirited away by the militia) in an encounter that cost the lives of two colonial and three British soldiers. But on the way back to Boston, they were surprised by real danger. Summoned by riders like Paul Revere, who had galloped across the countryside calling for resistance, four thousand Americans lined the Boston road and fired on the British regulars from behind rocks and trees. By the time the British limped back to Boston, 73 of their fellow soldiers had been killed

and 174 wounded. That night the colonial militia laid siege to the city.

The Second Continental Congress

From 1774 to 1775 royal control over the colonies crumbled rapidly. Most of the royal governors fled to British warships, and colonial assemblies met without authorization to raise troops and issue paper money, in preparation for the conflict they believed was inevitable. Nevertheless, caution was the keynote of rebel actions, and mob rule never took hold.

One month after the battles of Lexington and Concord, the Second Continental Congress assembled in Philadelphia. The streets of the town were

INTERPRETING AMERICAN HISTORY

THE AMERICAN REVOLUTION Throughout most of the nineteenth century, American historians took the words of the founders of the nation literally. The Revolution had been fought for life, liberty, and the pursuit of happiness, and as a blow against tyranny. The outstanding advocate of this patriotic point of view was George Bancroft, whose ten-volume *History of the United States* was published from the 1830s to the 1870s. Writing during the Civil War, Bancroft summoned up a nostalgic image of the past: a nation united, a country guided by the purity of its ideals.

By the 1890s relations with Britain had improved, and many American historians were now enthusiastic admirers of the English. George L. Beer, Charles M. Andrews, and Lawrence H. Gipson were the main exponents of this imperial school.

Beer studied Britain's mercantilist policies and concluded that, far from restricting the American economy, they had helped it prosper. Andrews and Gipson both claimed that the Navigation Acts were enlightened, liberal legislative measures. Andrews concluded, however, that the Revolution had been fought because Americans were demanding more freedom at the very time that England

was moving to tighten its imperial grip: "On the one side was the immutable, stereotyped system of the mother country, based on precedent and tradition and designed to keep things comfortably as they were; on the other, a vital dynamic organism, containing the seeds of a great nation, its forces untried, still to be proved."

In the early twentieth century a new school of historians emerged. This progressive school was deeply influenced by the growing socialist movement in America, the ideas of Marx, and the general social unrest of the period. Progressive historians viewed the revolutionary movement as a class struggle that had economic origins. Some of the flavor of their writings is reflected in the titles of their books: *An Economic Interpretation of the Constitution* by Charles A. Beard, and *The American Revolution Considered as a Social Movement* by J. Franklin Jameson.

Beard felt that the conflict between the haves and the have-nots had been as important to the revolutionary movement as the conflict between England and America. Jameson concentrated on democratic advances achieved during the Revolution: property qualifications for voting were lowered, the vast estates of Tories were confiscated and distributed to poor farmers, and lands

festooned with banners proclaiming "Liberty or Death." An impressive assembly of the colonies' most gifted men gathered at the statehouse. The president of the congress was John Hancock, Boston's richest merchant, who, according to rumor, had been one of the "Indians" at the Boston Tea Party. Among the new faces was Thomas Jefferson, who had just published *A Summary View of the Rights of British America*, in which he stated that "kings are the servants, not the proprietors of the people." Benjamin Franklin was also present, having just returned from England.

The Second Continental Congress began by forming the militia surrounding Boston into a continental army and appointing George Washington commander in chief.

Bunker Hill and *Common Sense*

Washington left to join his troops on June 23, six days after the worst battle of the Revolution had already been fought. On June 17 the patriots had seized Bunker Hill and Breed's Hill in Charlestown and were preparing to pound Boston with artillery. General Gage ordered his men to retake the hills—and they did, at a terrible cost. More than a thousand English troops fell; the patriots lost only about four hundred men. Even though the British recaptured Breed's Hill, Americans considered the so-called Battle of Bunker Hill a victory.

Meanwhile, the congress in Philadelphia attempted to deal effectively with the growing crisis. On July 5 it sent the Olive Branch Petition to George

---

that had been controlled by England were opened to the mass of Americans.

After World War II American historians tended to reflect the conservative climate in the nation. Robert E. Brown, Daniel J. Boorstin, and other neoconservatives challenged the progressives' theory that colonial America had been undemocratic. In *Middle-Class Democracy and the Revolution in Massachusetts, 1691–1780* Brown demonstrated that in Massachusetts, at least, the vast majority of men owned enough property to vote. He viewed the Revolution as a conservative movement seeking to restore the good old days before the French and Indian War. In the *Genius of American Politics* Boorstin also argued that the colonists rebelled in order to preserve the status quo. It was the English who wanted to change the existing order.

More recently, Bernard Bailyn studied the intellectual background of the Revolution. In his *Pamphlets of the American Revolution* Bailyn interpreted the Revolution as the logical outcome of a developing political theory. Bailyn read scores of colonial writers and showed the importance of those ideas that derived from English common law, Enlightenment philosophy, and New England Puritanism. American revolutionary thought held that the drive for power was a natural

but corrupting lust that government had to control. After 1763 the colonists believed that the British government was deliberately trying to deprive its subjects in England and America of their liberty. In taking up arms, Bailyn concluded, Americans were motivated by love for the rights of English citizens, which by 1776 had been expanded into the concept of universal human rights.

Recently some historians have focused their attention on the role of the common people in the Revolution. Pauline Maier has compared the traditional role of the colonial mobs to the riots that broke out in prerevolutionary crises. Mobs were not necessarily illegitimate. If they represented the whole population, then they may have reflected the common consensus aroused to uphold the law or to resist arbitrary power. Jesse Lemisch points to the evidence of increasing class stratification and reemphasizes class conflict in revolutionary America. He also criticizes Bailyn for ignoring a body of political thought which was majoritarian and democratic. While lack of available documents makes it difficult to determine the political views of the common people, more historians are examining their political actions with the purpose of establishing a connection between their lives and their political thought.

THOMAS PAINE HAD BEEN IN THE COLONIES ONLY A YEAR BEFORE PUBLISHING HIS ROUSING ESSAY *COMMON SENSE*. THE PAMPHLET PERSUADED THOUSANDS OF AMERICANS WHO HAD BEEN STRADDLING THE FENCE TO OPT FOR INDEPENDENCE.

III, denouncing Parliament and begging the king to free the colonies from incompetent management. The next day it issued a Declaration of Causes of Taking-up Arms, announcing that "the arms we have been compelled by our enemies to assume, we will, in defiance of every hazard . . . employ for the preservation of our liberties; being with one mind resolved to die Freemen rather than live Slaves." A secret committee of correspondence was created to write to America's friends abroad for support. In addition, the congress ordered an attack on Canada, appointed officials to deal with the Indians, authorized the outfitting of a navy, and urged the colonies to appoint committees of safety to direct local military operations against the English.

Despite these decisive moves, the congress hesitated to take the final step and officially declare independence. Many colonists were not sure how far they wanted to carry their fight against British rule. They were aware that some political factions in England were sympathetic to their cause. Moreover, they considered themselves citizens of England first and Americans second. English liberties were all that they had been demanding. The terrible word traitor—and the knowledge of what happened to unsuccessful traitors—weighed heavily on the minds of the delegates. Upper-class Americans feared that a revolution might drive America's native aristocracy out with the English. Once the mob was unleashed, who knew how violent it might become? Finally, no colony in the history of the modern world had ever rebelled against its mother country.

On November 9, 1775 events moved swiftly beyond the control of the moderates. The congress learned that George III had refused to read the Olive Branch Petition, had dispatched twenty thousand troops to the New World, and had declared every member of the congress a traitor. The moderates now believed that if captured they would be hanged no matter what position they took. In addition, the soldiers on their way to America were not ordinary English troops, but paid German mercenaries. The colonists believed that these Hessians would ravage the land, making no distinction between those who remained loyal to the king and those in rebellion.

The final impetus for an open break came in January 1776, when Thomas Paine, an Englishman who had been living in America for only a year, published his pamphlet *Common Sense*. Some hundred and fifty thousand copies were sold in a few months. The pamphlet called George III a "royal brute" and declared, "Of more worth is one honest man to society and in the sight of God than all the crowned ruffians who ever lived." The British government, Paine asserted, was corrupt and was corrupting America. Suddenly, the king was perceived as a tyrant and the monarchy as absurd. Though in reality George III was neither a tyrant nor a crook, Paine had presented the colonists with a forceful argument for abolishing royal rule and establishing a republican government. His ideas struck most Americans as the very essence of common sense.

The Declaration of Independence

After 1760 the colonists responded to changes in British policy with increasingly sophisticated arguments condemning them as unjust and illegal. Americans had steadily maintained that they were resisting the attempt of a powerful government to undermine the principles of political liberty set forth in the English constitution. In response to each new article of British legislation, they further refined their arguments against British interference with colonial self-government. Those who had been strongly influenced by the Great Awakening became convinced that Britain's imperial policy was an attack on a Divine plan for the spread of liberty and republicanism. Paine's passionate attack on the monarchy expressed the growing feeling that the mother country was trying to suppress self-government in the colonies and establish a tyranny.

With sentiment supporting independence growing rapidly, the Continental Congress made several decisions which laid the groundwork for a complete break with England. In March it directed American ships to raid British vessels, and the following month it opened American ports to foreign shipping. In May it asked the colonial assemblies to establish new state governments. On July 2, 1776 the congress finally adopted a resolution that had been introduced a month earlier by Richard Henry Lee. The first sentence read:

Resolved:

That these United Colonies are, and of right ought to be, free and independent states, that they are absolved from all allegiance to the British crown, and that all political connection between them and the state of Great Britain is, and ought to be, totally dissolved.

With the passage of this resolution, the Second Continental Congress became the *de facto* national government for the people of the thirteen colonies.

Early in June a committee of five men had been chosen to draw up a document justifying American independence to the world. Its members included Thomas Jefferson, Benjamin Franklin, John Adams, Robert Livingston of New York, and Roger Sherman of Connecticut. Jefferson, the chairman, was responsible for the wording of the colonies' claim to independence.

After much debate in the congress, delegates from every colony approved the document, except New York, which abstained. On the fourth of July "The Unanimous Declaration of the Thirteen United States of America" was sent to the printer. When it was read to the public four days later, a crowd tore down the king's coat of arms from the statehouse door and abandoned itself that night to demonstrations of joy.

The declaration had two parts. The first and most important section justified a people's right to rebel against a government that denied them their natural rights. Jefferson was influenced by John Locke and by leaders of the Scottish Enlightenment, such as David Hume. He paraphrased Locke's ideas in the declaration: "Men being . . . all free, equal and independent, no one can be put out of his estate and subjected to the political power of another without his consent." Jefferson had also been influenced by Locke's assertion that "absolute monarchs are but men." He commented, "I did not consider it any part of my charge to invent new ideas, but to place before mankind the common sense of the subject, in terms so plain and firm as to command their assent. It was intended to be an expression of the American mind." Most of Jefferson's contemporaries were familiar with the sentiments expressed in this first section, having read Locke or heard his ideas frequently paraphrased during the past decade.

The second part of the declaration listed the crimes the Americans accused the English king of committing against the colonies: dissolving colonial assemblies whenever they opposed the king's invasion of the colonists' rights; putting off elections of public officials; paying judges directly instead of allowing colonial assemblies to determine their salaries; and keeping "among us in times of peace standing armies, without the consent of our legislatures." It also accused the king of "cutting off our trade with all parts of the world," of "imposing taxes on us without our consent," and of many other "injuries and usurpations."

Jefferson did not mention Parliament by name in the declaration. George III was singled out as the tyrant, and he alone was held responsible for British oppression. This approach illustrated Jefferson's flair for publicizing the significance of the revolutionary movement and America's rejection of monarchy. After all, it was directed as much to the people of the world as it was to Americans. The people of Spain, France, and Prussia were not likely to understand complex references to the British parliamentary system, but they would understand accusations against a tyrannical king. In addition, Jefferson would hardly want to attack the representative branch of the British government when the goal of the Revolution was to preserve the sanctity of representative institutions.

What had begun as a colonial rebellion had culminated in a complete break with England. Once independence had been declared, two crucial questions remained: if it was necessary to preserve independence with force, could America prevail against Great Britain; and having once gained independence, could thirteen independent states create a viable new nation?

Readings

General Works

Andrews, Charles M., *The Colonial Background of the American Revolution*. New Haven: Yale University Press, 1961.

Bancroft, George, *History of the United States of America from the Discovery of the Continent*, Vols. I–VI. Chicago: University of Chicago Press, 1966.

Greene, Jack P. (Ed.), *The Reinterpretation of the American Revolution: 1763–1789*. New York: Harper & Row, 1968. (Paper).

Jensen, Merrill, *The Founding of a Nation: A History of the American Revolution, 1763–1776*. New York: Oxford University Press, 1968.

Knollenberg, Bernhard, *Origin of the American Revolution: 1759–1766*. New York: Macmillan, 1965.

Leder, Lawrence, *Liberty & Authority: Early American Political Ideology, 1689–1763*. New York: Quadrangle, 1968.

Main, Jackson T., *The Social Structure of Revolutionary America*. Princeton, N.J.: Princeton University Press, 1965. (Paper)

Miller, John C., *Origins of the American Revolution*. Boston: Little, Brown, 1943.

———, *Triumph of Freedom: 1775–1783*. Boston: Little, Brown, 1948. (Paper)

———, *Triumph of Freedom, 1775–1783*. Boston: Little, Brown, 1948.

Morgan, Edmund S., *Birth of the Republic, 1763–1789*. Chicago: University of Chicago Press, 1956.

Peckham, Howard H., *The Colonial Wars, 1689–1762*. Chicago: University of Chicago Press, 1963.

Special Studies

Bailyn, Bernard, *Ideological Origins of the American Revolution*. Cambridge: Harvard University Press, 1967.

Becker, Carl L., *The Declaration of Independence: A Study in the History of Political Ideas*. New York: Harcourt Brace Jovanovich, 1922.

Brown, Robert E., *Middle Class Democracy and the Revolution in Massachusetts, 1691–1780*. Ithaca, N.Y.: Cornell University Press, 1955.

Green, Jack P., *The Quest for Power: The Lower Houses of Assembly in the Southern Royal Colonies, 1689–1776*. Chapel Hill, N.C.: University of North Carolina Press, 1963.

Labaree, Benjamin W., *The Boston Tea Party*. Oxford: Oxford University Press, 1964.

Maier, Pauline, *From Resistance to Revolution: Colonial Radicals & the Development of American Opposition to Britain, 1765–1776*. New York: Knopf, 1972.

———, *From Resistance to Revolution: Colonial Radicals & the Development of American Opposition to Britain, 1765–1776*. New York: Random House, 1973. (Paper)

Morgan, Edmund S., and Helen M. Morgan, *The Stamp Act Crisis: Prologue to Revolution*. Chapel Hill, N.C.: University of North Carolina Press, 1953 (Paper: Collier Books, 1963).

Schlesinger, Arthur M., *The Colonial Merchants and the American Revolution*. New York: Atheneum, 1968.

Zobel, Hiller B., *Boston Massacre*. New York: Norton, 1971. (Paper, 1970)

Primary Sources

Commager, Henry S., and Richard B. Morris (Eds.), *The Spirit of Seventy-Six: The Story of the American Revolution As Told by Participants*, Vols. I–II. New York: Harper & Row, 1967.

Morgan, Edmund S., *Prologue to Revolution: Sources and Documents on the Stamp Act Crisis.* Chapel Hill, N.C.: University of North Carolina Press, 1959.

Oliver, Peter, *Peter Oliver's Origin and Progress of the American Revolution: A Tory View*, Douglas Adair (Ed.). Stanford, Calif.: Stanford University Press, 1961.

Paine, Thomas, *Common Sense and Crisis.* New York: Doubleday, 1970.

Biographies

Bailyn, Bernard, *The Ordeal of Thomas Hutchinson.* Cambridge, Mass.: Harvard University Press, 1974.

Beeman, Richard R., *Patrick Henry: A Biography.* New York: McGraw-Hill, 1974.

Chinard, Gilbert, *Honest John Adams.* Boston: Little, Brown, 1933.

Crane, Verner W., *Benjamin Franklin and a Rising People*, Oscar Handlin (Ed.). Boston: Little, Brown, 1954.

Cunliffe, Marcus, *George Washington: Man and Monument.* Boston: Little, Brown, 1958.

Forbes, Esther, *Paul Revere and the World He Lived In.* Boston: Houghton Mifflin, 1942.

Hawke, David F., *Paine.* New York: Harper & Row, 1974.

Malone, Dumas, *Jefferson and His Time: Jefferson the Virginian*, Vol. I. Boston: Little, Brown, 1948.

Miller, John C., *Sam Adams: Pioneer in Propaganda.* Boston: Little, Brown, 1936.

Historical Novels

Cannon, Legrand, Jr., *Look to the Mountain.* New York: Holt, Rinehart and Winston, 1942.

Churchill, Winston, *Richard Carvel.* New York: Macmillan, 1914.

Forbes, Esther, *Johnny Tremain.* New York: Dell, 1969.

Gordon, Caroline, *Green Centuries.* New York: Scribner's, 1941.

Roberts, Kenneth, *Arundel* (1944), *Lydia Bailey* (1947), *Northwest Passage, Oliver Wiswell* (1940), *Rabble in Arms* (1947). New York: Doubleday (Paper: Fawcett, 1970).

To Live as Equals

THE LEAGUE OF THE GREAT PEACE

When white people first crossed the great water, they came to our country like naked babies washed up on the rocks. We Indian people took pity on them. We fed them and helped them build their shelters because we saw that they would die if we did not help them. We saw that there was plenty of room for everyone on our Mother, the Earth, and we wanted life to be good for our white brothers. When we had taught the white people how to find food and shelter, we taught them about how to have good government. They were not happy being ruled by kings, so we showed them the good way our Creator, the Great Spirit, taught us to live as equals.

Iroquois leader, 1974

DEMOCRACY was not a new concept imported to America by Europeans. A number of Indian tribes practiced democracy for centuries before white people came to America. In fact, many whites enthusiastically studied Indian governments and the principles on which they were founded.

Hundreds of Indian nations existed in what is now the United States. Although every nation was unique, most shared certain cultural values. These included a respect for individual freedom, government through the consent of the governed, dedication to the welfare of the nation, respect for the variety of people and their visions, and reverence for the environment and for all living things.

Many colonials were deeply impressed with the ways of Indian people. Native Americans believed that no human being had the right to tell another what to do. For the most part,

Indian chiefs were the servants of their people and could do nothing without their support.

News of native American political and philosophical life even reached Europe, where it was of interest to Locke, Montesquieu, Rousseau, Voltaire, and other great philosophers. Of particular interest was the most powerful and highly developed native American government north of Mexico, the League of the Great Peace.

Under the League of the Great Peace (which the British called the Five Nations Confederacy), five powerful Iroquois-speaking nations with a long history of conflict renounced warfare among themselves and formed a peaceful alliance. This league of Indian nations was based on the concept of states within a state which we have

come to call federalism. Originally, it included the Mohawk, Oneida, Onondaga, Cayuga, and Seneca nations. The stronghold of the League of the Great Peace was the heart of what is now New York State. The Mohawks, or People of the Flint, occupied the Mohawk River area; the Oneidas, or Standing Stone People, were settled around Oneida Lake; the Onondagas, or People of the Hills, lived along Onondaga Creek; the Cayugas, or Great Pipe People, were settled along Cayuga Lake; and the Senecas, or People of the Great Mountain, lived along Canandaigua Lake. It is said that between fifty and sixty nations were included at one time or another in the League of the Great Peace.

It is not possible to state exactly when the Iroquois formed the League of the Great Peace. Some say it was developed in the fifteenth or sixteenth century, while others say it began several centuries earlier. At any rate, it is certain that the league began when two great statesmen, known as the Peacemaker and the Lawgiver, persuaded the five warring nations to join together under one constitution, the Great Law of Peace. The newly united Iroquois people compared themselves to one longhouse in which there were five fireplaces, but all who lived within were of one family.

This government of the League of the Great Peace was a natural extension of the political system which had been practiced by the individual Iroquois nations for centuries. Under the Iroquois system all people had a voice in the government, which operated by consensus in open council. The chiefs did not have the authority to carry out any decisions with which the people did not agree.

Women had a unique role in the Iroquois political system. Their task of bringing forth the future generations was considered to be the most impor-

SCENES ABOUT A SENECA BARK LODGE BY JESSE CORNPLANTER, SENECA ARTIST. SCENE DEPICTS TRADITIONAL IROQUOIS LIFE. WOMEN POUND CORN INTO MEAL AND PREPARE IT OVER THE FIRE. THE LODGE, OR LONGHOUSE, WAS OFTEN MUCH LONGER, OVER ONE HUNDRED FEET, AND LODGED SEVERAL FAMILIES.

tant responsibility of the nation. Because of their experience observing and carefully nurturing potential leaders from infancy, it was the women who appointed and removed chiefs. But here again, no decisions could be made without the approval of the people.

To hold the office of chief was a reward for public service. The word for chief means, among other things, "one of the nice people," "support in the Longhouse," and "he who eats last." The Great Law of Peace carefully outlined the qualifications of the chiefs of the league. It said that they were to be unselfish, immune to anger and criticism, peaceful, and of goodwill. Their minds were to be "filled with a yearning for the welfare of the people."* They were to be patient, unselfish, and receptive to good advice. The Great Law instructed that the chiefs should "look and listen for the welfare of the whole people, and always have in view not only the present, but also the coming generations, even those whose faces were yet beneath the surface of the ground—the unborn of the future Nation." The power of the chiefs was in their ability to reason, to persuade, and to maintain the respect of the people. They were usually poor, as they traditionally shared their wealth with their people.

It is not possible to begin to understand the democracy of the Iroquois without first attempting to develop

*This and all future quotes from the Great Law of Peace by permission of Akwesasne Notes, Mohawk Nation at Akwesasne via Rooseveltown, New York.

115

some insight into their traditional values. As with most other native Americans, the principle which is at the basis of Iroquois belief was respect for one another and for all other creatures, for the ways of nature, for the earth, and for the Creator. According to this tradition, when an Iroquois man took a tree for firewood, he first spoke to the trees in the forest and apologized for taking the life of one of their brothers. He then gave thanks to the trees for allowing him to take one of them to keep his people warm. Similarly, when a woman harvested the corn, beans, and squash, she gave thanks to her mother, the earth, for providing food for her people. She celebrated the spirits of the crops in dance and ceremony.

Respect was deeply spiritual and was part of every aspect of Iroquois life. It followed from respect for one's people that food, shelter, and clothing were available equally to all, since all were seen to be equally deserving. Respect permeated all activities and institutions and made possible a smoothly functioning society in which each individual was valued and agreement in council could be attained. The fundamental importance of respect was recognized in the development of the Great Law of Peace, which instructed that every session of the Grand Council begin with an expression of gratitude to the statesmen gathered in council and a statement and offering of thanks to the earth, waters, food and medicine plants, forests, animals, winds, thunder, sun, moon, and the Creator.

When the League of the Great Peace was established, individual nations continued to decide local issues. The League dealt only with matters which were crucially important to all members. These included major alliances and wars, internal disputes between member nations, sale of territory, and relations with outsiders. The League also served as an information center for the sharing of news and opinion. The Great Law of Peace stated that nations of the League were ". . . completely united and enfolded together, united into one head, one body and one mind." The long-range aim of the League was to bring peace to all the world. It was a spiritual union as well as a political one.

The Great Law called for fifty statesmen, or chiefs, to sit on the Grand Council of the League of the Great Peace. Though some nations seated more chiefs than others, there was an equal distribution of power because each nation had only one voice, and all units were equal. Operations of the government were based on agreement in council. Once a decision was reached, it was final, and all nations were bound to it.

In sessions of the Grand Council, the Mohawk and Seneca chiefs functioned together as one body, the Older Brothers, similar to the upper house of Congress, the Senate. All questions went to them first. When they discussed and unanimously passed on an issue, they reported their decision to the Oneida and Cayuga chiefs, who also functioned together as one body, the Younger Brothers, similar to the lower house of Congress, the House of Representatives. Their decision was then referred to the Onondaga chiefs for final judgment and ratification. The Onondaga confirmed the decision when the two bodies were in agreement and offered a compromise or tabled the issue when the two bodies were in disagreement. When the Onondaga disagreed with both of the two bodies, the question was again considered by the two sides and if they reached the same decision as before, the Onondaga were compelled to confirm their decision.

In 1851 Lewis Henry Morgan, noted student of the Iroquois, stated that "it would be difficult to describe any political society, in which there was less of oppression and discontent, more of individual independence and boundless freedom."

Both Thomas Jefferson and Benjamin Franklin studied the political system of the League of the Great Peace. In 1744, when a council was held between the colonies of Pennsylvania and Connecticut and the league, one of the chiefs of the league suggested that an organization patterned after the League of the Great Peace might be advisable for the American colonies. The Iroquois saw that the common speech and interests of the colonies were sufficient basis for such a union.

At the Albany Congress of 1754, where a union of the colonies was formally proposed for the first time, Benjamin Franklin said that it would be strange if the Iroquois ". . . should be capable of forming a scheme for such a union and be able to execute it in such a fashion that it has subsisted for ages and appears indissoluble; and yet that a like union should be impracticable for ten or a dozen English colo-

RAISING THE SLAIN HERO BY JESSE CORN-PLANTER. THE ANIMAL "PEOPLE" TOWARD WHOM THE SLAIN IROQUOIS HERO HAS SHOWN RESPECT AND FRIENDSHIP COME TO HIS AID AND BRING HIM BACK TO LIFE.

nies. . . ." Franklin utilized the Great Law of Peace in his contribution to the Albany Plan of Union, and the framers of the Articles of Confederation also studied it.

Our history tells us that the League of the Great Peace was at the height of its power from the time of early white settlement to the Revolution. From that point on, white expansion reduced the territories of the nations of the league, which at one time included much of the land east of the Mississippi River. While the league was at the height of its power, the English, Dutch, and French both solicited and threatened it. Many people believed that it was the league's aid to the British which decided the outcome of the French and Indian War.

Lewis Henry Morgan stated that the League of the Great Peace "never even approximated dissolution from internal disorders." Four hundred years of white influence, however, considerably weakened it. Nonetheless, the league has continued functioning in the twentieth century. On every Iroquois reservation but one, there is a Longhouse, or meeting place for League members. (There are Iroquois reservations in Ontario, Quebec, and New York.) Many Iroquois people still follow the Great Law of Peace and the councils continue to meet as they have for centuries. In order that "the strength of the union be preserved," the chiefs have maintained the wisdom of the Great Law, "to be firm so that if a tree should fall upon your joined hands, it shall not separate or weaken your hold."

5 The Emergence of a Nation

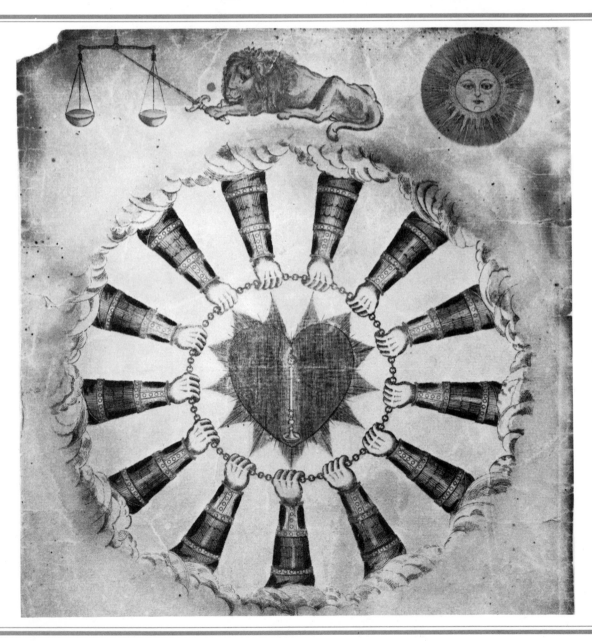

We hold these truths to be self-evident, that all men are created equal, that they are endowed by their Creator with certain unalienable rights, that among these are life, liberty, and the pursuit of happiness. That to secure these rights, governments are instituted among men, deriving their just powers from the consent of the governed; that whenever any form of government becomes destructive of these ends, it is the right of the people to alter or to abolish it. . . .

The Declaration of Independence, 1776

Significant Events

British capture (occupy) New York City [September 1776]

Washington captures Trenton and Princeton [December 1776–January 1777]

British defeated at Saratoga [October 1777]

Franco-American alliance [February 1778]

Valley Forge [Winter 1777–1778]

Savannah, Ga., taken by British [December 1778]

Charleston, S.C., taken by British [May 1780]

Articles of Confederation go into effect [March 1781]

American and French forces defeat British at Yorktown [October 1781]

Peace treaty signed with England [November 1782]

Final treaty signed [September 1783]

Land Ordinance [1785]

Shays's Rebellion [1786–1787]

Northwest Ordinance [1787]

THIS ETCHING, *AMERICAN INDEPENDENCE*, DEPICTS THE THIRTEEN AMERICAN STATES "WARM'D BY ONE HEART, UNITED IN ONE BOND."

Having proclaimed their independence, the thirteen American states were faced with an unprecedented challenge. Now they had to work together to field an army to defeat Great Britain and to form a national government strong enough to administer the country if they should succeed. Neither of these goals could have been achieved had the colonists not developed during the decades immediately preceding the break with England the feeling that being an American was somehow different from being English. Americans were part of the British Empire, but they believed that they lived better (albeit more simply) and enjoyed greater individual freedom and opportunity for economic advancement than their British counterparts. In their quest for self-fulfillment they were less bound by powerful political and religious institutions than their European contem-

poraries. Most Americans believed that people's lives could be improved through the proper application of human reason.

The French-born observer St. John de Crève-coeur, in his *Letters from An American Farmer*, described well the ebullient and supremely optimistic view of the future that was held by many Americans: "What then is the American, this new man? . . . He is an American, who, leaving behind him all his ancient prejudices and manners, receives new ones from the new mode of life he has embraced, the new government he obeys, and the new rank he holds. . . . Here individuals of all nations are melted into a new race of men, whose labours and posterity will one day cause great changes in the world."

The Revolutionary War

In embarking on the fight for independence, America faced formidable obstacles. The Continental Congress did not have the authority to pass binding legislation or to impose taxes. The new nation had no army and no navy, and its population numbered only 2.5 million people. Britain, by contrast, was a mighty power of eleven million people with the world's best navy and a well-disciplined army. Fifty thousand troops were in North America in 1778, and during the war thirty thousand German mercenaries also served with the British.

America faced not only an impressive enemy abroad, but also opposition from within. It has been estimated that between one-fifth and one-third of the population sympathized with the English, and between thirty thousand and fifty thousand of these Loyalists (or Tories) actually fought on a regular basis for the king.

British sympathizers came from all classes and all states. Tory strength was greatest in the Middle states, the Carolinas, and Georgia, and weakest in New England, Virginia, and Maryland. Office-holders under the crown, members of the Anglican clergy, and some planters and merchants remained loyal to the king. In addition, many middle- and lower-class farmers from the Middle and Southern states were Tories. Many of these farmers probably did not understand the real purpose of the Revolu-

tion. Some may have feared the colonial aristocracy more than the British government.

Whatever their reasons for siding with the English, Tories were forced by the states to take loyalty oaths, and they were imprisoned if they refused. Much Tory property was confiscated. Their freedoms restricted, about a hundred thousand Loyalists eventually left their homes. Some returned to England with the retreating British army; others fled to Canada.

In addition to those Americans who were actively opposed to the Revolution, between one-third and two-fifths remained uninterested or unmoved by the break with England, many simply refusing to take any part in the war effort at all.

Military and Financial Problems

Before the Continental Congress could establish an American government, it had to make certain there would be a nation to govern. The first order of business was to create an effective army to drive out the British.

The Battle of Bunker Hill had demonstrated that the American patriots were not as ineffective as the British liked to think. Nevertheless, the men encamped around Boston were a hastily assembled gathering of untrained volunteers, not a disciplined army. When the Continental Congress appointed George Washington commander in chief of the colonial troops, it was for the purpose of transforming these ragged units into an efficient instrument of war.

One of Washington's first tasks was to acquire a capable staff. Few Americans had professional military training. The local militias had elected their own officers, but popularity proved to be no predictor of competence. Washington therefore decided to bypass many officers and appoint his own. At the same time, however, he tactfully consulted the generals appointed by the states and gave careful consideration to their recommendations and to those of the Continental Congress.

He was fortunate to receive the aid of a few officers from abroad, such as the Polish Count Casimir Pulaski, the French Marquis de Lafayette, and the Prussian Baron Friedrich von Steuben, who was particularly helpful in drilling raw recruits.

Washington's problems were further aggravated by the fact that this was a volunteer army. The Continental Congress had no power to draft soldiers or to requisition supplies. Food, arms, and housing were supposed to be furnished by the states, but supplies were always inadequate. Most of the enlisted men were farmers and they could not afford to be away from their fields for long. Just when they were beginning to learn how to follow orders and perform their military drills, they had to return home to harvest the crops. Although some four hundred thousand Americans took up arms at one time or another during the war, Washington never had more than twenty thousand men serving under him at any one time. He could never count on keeping more than perhaps five thousand regular troops in the Continental army and had to call on the local militia for back-up help wherever he went.

Because of the chronic shortage of troops, many blacks were accepted as soldiers in the Revolutionary War. Some served in colonial militias even when their participation was prohibited by law. Enrollment in a militia usually resulted in emancipation for those who were slaves. Washington, a slaveholder, was at first reluctant to use black troops but he changed his mind after learning of a British proclamation which encouraged blacks to join the British army in return for their freedom. Eventually some five thousand blacks served in the Continental army in both integrated and all-black units.

The struggling nation suffered from financial problems throughout the war. The Continental Congress, urgently needing money to finance the rebellion, devised three methods of fund-raising: it borrowed about $8 million from American citizens through the sale of national bonds and another $8 million from foreign governments; it collected some $5.5 million from state governments; and it issued more than $240 million in paper money. America had always been short of bullion, and this paper money had little backing in gold or silver. To make matters worse, wealthy Tories fled, taking much of the existing supply with them.

Each of the individual states also issued its own paper money. Soon there were fourteen different currencies in circulation. As more and more paper notes were printed, the purchasing power of the individual currencies fell well below face value. The consequence of this was an inflationary spiral which was worsened by profiteering American entrepreneurs who kept hiking the price of war supplies.

These economic problems made serving in the army a serious financial burden for most soldiers. Officers had to pay most of their own expenses. Ordinary soldiers were paid very low salaries in nearly worthless paper money.

Strategic Advantages

Despite these military and financial problems, America had certain strategic advantages. The primary one was that Britain was located three thousand miles away, and British troops and supplies had to be shipped across the Atlantic. In addition, no single American city was so crucial to the revolutionary effort that by taking it, Britain could win the war. The English were forced to spread their forces over the entire length of the Atlantic coastline and into the interior at selected points. Most of the vast interior was inaccessible, since there were few roads. As one English officer said, the lack of roads, "absolutely prevented us this whole war from going fifteen miles from a navigable river."

Under these circumstances American patriots could prolong the war indefinitely merely by keeping symbolic resistance alive. Though ill trained, ill equipped, and few in number, the Americans had learned from the Indians the techniques of sneak attacks, ambushes in the woods, and fighting in all

A THIRTY-SIX SHILLING NOTE ISSUED BY THE
MASSACHUSETTS BAY COLONY IN 1775.

kinds of weather. They continually harassed the professional British soldiers with these guerrilla tactics, and the British, who persisted in fighting according to the formalized, open-battlefield rules of European warfare, were baffled.

The final advantage enjoyed by the Americans was that the war had little support among the English people. Although a parliamentary majority supported Lord North's policies, few British politicians had much enthusiasm for what they considered a civil war within the empire. The British commanders hesitated to engage in military tactics that were too destructive, fearing to ruin any lingering chances of reconciliation. In addition, because the British still had not paid off the debts they had accumulated during the last conflict with France, they were reluctant to accumulate more debt. And finally, powerful enemies on the Continent were eager for British humiliation. Many in England had serious doubts about the wisdom of sending their troops thousands of miles away when they might suddenly be needed to defend the homeland against French or Spanish attack.

First Conflicts with the British

Boston, the first center of political resistance, now became the first major theater of the war. After the Battle of Bunker Hill in June 1775, the American troops under Washington fortified Dorchester Heights, which overlooked the city from the south. Rather than risk another battle as bloody as that of Bunker Hill, the English commander, General William Howe, withdrew his forces, even though it meant leaving behind supplies for which ships were not available. About a thousand Tories left Boston with Howe's army. Thus abandoned, the city was occupied by Washington in March 1776.

In the South the Americans were successful during the opening months of the war. In February 1776, a thousand patriots defeated a Tory army at the Battle of Moore's Creek Bridge in North Carolina. Four months later the British tried to sail into Charleston, South Carolina, but they were unable to get past a fortress that guarded the harbor on Sullivan's Island.

In Canada, however, the Americans were less successful. Although the American general, Richard Montgomery, captured Montreal, he and his assistant, Colonel Benedict Arnold, failed to take Quebec. Arnold's troops fought bravely, but they had been greatly weakened by a long march through Maine and their numbers had been reduced by disease, hunger, and cold. After the defeat at Quebec, the thirteen states gave up the hope that Canada would join the revolutionary effort.

The British Campaign against New York City

Temporarily repulsed in Boston and the South, the British now turned their thoughts to seizing New York City in order to split the states in half and thus isolate New England. From there they hoped to defeat General Washington decisively. New York not only occupied a central position, it also had a large Loyalist population (which could be counted upon to aid the British) and an excellent port.

The British put together the largest invasion force ever seen in the eighteenth century: thirty-four thousand troops, ten thousand sailors, four hundred transport vessels, and thirty warships. General William Howe was in command of the British land forces, and his brother, Admiral Richard Howe, led the naval contingent.

Washington arrived before the British and fortified Brooklyn Heights. He thought that because these bluffs overlooked the East River and the island of Manhattan, he could use them to his advantage much as he had used Dorchester Heights to protect Boston. Washington, however, had only twenty thousand men, and he was relatively inexperienced as a commander.

General Howe arrived with his army on July 2, 1776, and camped on Staten Island. Ten days later Admiral Howe arrived with his fleet. The two leaders sent a joint letter to Washington, asking him to submit peacefully to the superior English force. Washington refused to open the letter because the address did not acknowledge his rank as general, thereby denying America's struggle for independence.

Since the sheer presence of the royal forces was not enough to awe the Continental army into submission, General Howe attacked one of Washington's divisions on Long Island. The battered American army managed to retreat to Manhattan, and Howe again offered to confer with the rebels. Congress replied by sending Benjamin Franklin, John Adams, and Edward Rutledge to speak with the British commanders.

The conference was a failure. After dining on "good claret, good bread, cold ham, tongues and mutton," Admiral Howe remarked sentimentally that "he felt for America as a brother, and, if America should fall, he should feel and lament it like the loss of a brother." To this Benjamin Franklin tartly replied: "My lord, we will do our utmost endeavours to save your lordship that mortification." The Americans made it clear that they would accept nothing less than independence.

In September, Howe attacked Washington on Manhattan and, defeated once more, the Americans fled north, finally crossing to New Jersey. Washington was so discouraged that he admitted, "I think the game is pretty near up." Nevertheless, in an effort to prevent a more massive defeat, he decided upon a new strategy: "We should on all occasions avoid a general action or put anything to the risk, unless compelled by a necessity, into which we ought never to be drawn."

Trenton and Princeton

In December 1776 General Howe drove Washington across the Delaware River into Pennsylvania. But instead of seizing the opportunity to deal the badly weakened American army a death blow, Howe suspended operations for the winter, as was the custom among those trained in formal warfare, and quartered his troops in New Jersey.

Washington, discouraged by his own defeats, became further disheartened upon learning that the British had captured Newport, Rhode Island, on December 8. In less than three months the enemy had gained control of New York City and most of New Jersey. Washington's army had dwindled to fewer than eight thousand men, and at the beginning of the new year most of them would complete their terms of service.

Washington decided on a drastic course. On a wintry Christmas night he crossed the Delaware River with his men, marched them nine miles to Trenton, and attacked the enemy in its winter camp. In forty-five minutes the Americans captured a thousand of Howe's Hessian soldiers and killed their colonel.

Buoyed by this success, Washington attacked Princeton a few days later. Using brilliant strategy, he outmaneuvered the British and drove them back to New Brunswick. Neither victory was decisive, but they helped to boost American morale.

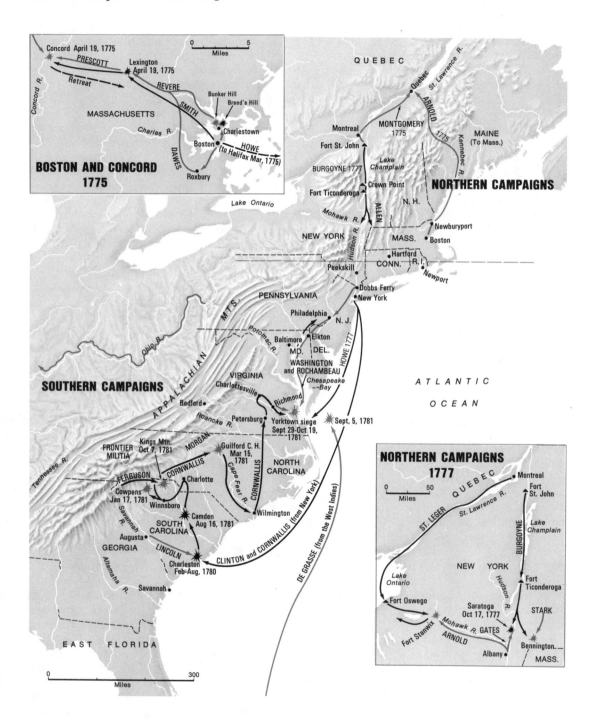

Military Campaigns of the Revolution

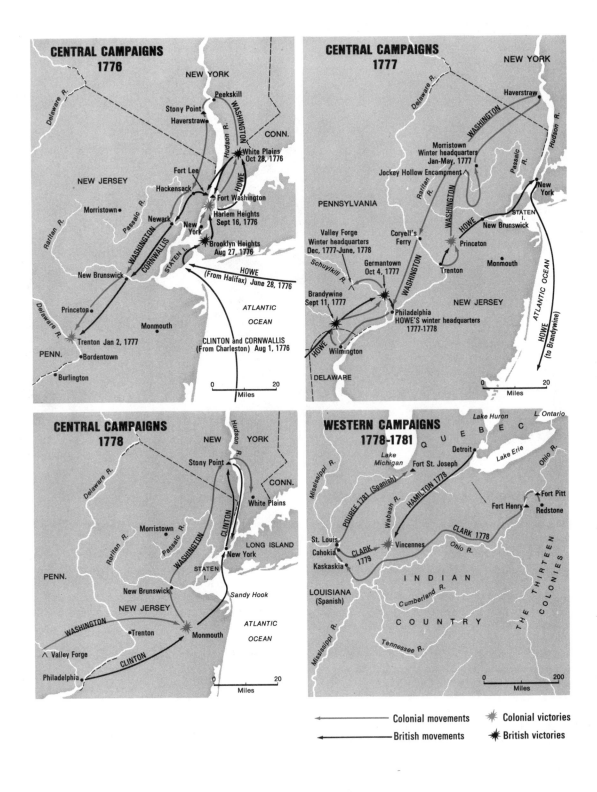

CENTRAL CAMPAIGNS 1776

NEW YORK
Peekskill
Stony Point
Haverstraw
WASHINGTON
Hudson R.
Delaware R.
CONN.
White Plains
Oct 28, 1776
HOWE
Fort Lee
NEW JERSEY
Hackensack
Fort Washington
Morristown
Harlem Heights
Sept 16, 1776
Newark
New York
Passaic R.
Raritan R.
WASHINGTON
CORNWALLIS
STATEN I.
Brooklyn Heights
Aug 27, 1776
New Brunswick
HOWE
(From Halifax) June 28, 1776
Princeton
Delaware R.
Monmouth
ATLANTIC OCEAN
Trenton Jan 2, 1777
PENN.
Bordentown
CLINTON and CORNWALLIS
(From Charleston) Aug 1, 1776
Burlington
0   20
Miles

CENTRAL CAMPAIGNS 1777

NEW YORK
Delaware R.
Haverstraw
WASHINGTON
Hudson R.
Passaic R.
Morristown
Winter headquarters
Jan-May, 1777
Jockey Hollow Encampment
New York
STATEN I.
New Brunswick
PENNSYLVANIA
Raritan R.
WASHINGTON
HOWE
Coryell's Ferry
Princeton
Monmouth
Valley Forge
Winter headquarters
Dec, 1777-June, 1778
Germantown
Oct 4, 1777
Trenton
ATLANTIC OCEAN
Schuylkill R.
Brandywine
Sept 11, 1777
WASHINGTON
Philadelphia
HOWE'S winter headquarters
1777-1778
NEW JERSEY
HOWE
(to Brandywine)
HOWE
Wilmington
DELAWARE
0   20
Miles

CENTRAL CAMPAIGNS 1778

NEW YORK
Hudson R.
Stony Point
CONN.
White Plains
Delaware R.
WASHINGTON
CLINTON
Morristown
Passaic R.
Raritan R.
LONG ISLAND
New York
New Brunswick
STATEN I.
PENN.
Sandy Hook
NEW JERSEY
WASHINGTON
Monmouth
ATLANTIC OCEAN
Trenton
Valley Forge
CLINTON
Philadelphia
0   20
Miles

WESTERN CAMPAIGNS 1778-1781

Lake Huron
L. Ontario
QUEBEC
Detroit
Lake Erie
Ohio R.
Mississippi R.
Lake Michigan
Fort St. Joseph
POUREE 1781 (Spanish)
HAMILTON 1778
Wabash R.
Fort Henry
Fort Pitt
Redstone
CLARK 1778
St. Louis
Cahokia
CLARK 1779
Vincennes
Ohio R.
Kaskaskia
INDIAN
THE THIRTEEN COLONIES
LOUISIANA
(Spanish)
Cumberland R.
COUNTRY
Mississippi R.
Tennessee R.
0   200
Miles

Colonial movements   ✳ Colonial victories
British movements   ✴ British victories

GEORGE WASHINGTON LEADS THE AMERICAN PATRIOTS IN A SURPRISE ATTACK ON TRENTON, DECEMBER 26, 1776. THE HESSIANS, ROUSED FROM SLEEP AFTER THEIR CHRISTMAS REVELRIES, COULD MUSTER LITTLE RESISTANCE.

The Summer and Fall Campaigns: 1777 A decisive American victory finally occurred during the summer and fall campaign of 1777. The British, having occupied New York City, now made plans to take the upstate town of Albany. If this plan succeeded, it would give them control of the Hudson River Valley, further isolate New England, and provide access to the back country beyond the Appalachian Mountains.

The dashing and colorful General John Burgoyne, known as "Gentleman Johnny," masterminded a three-pronged British attack on the town. From the south, General Howe would lead his forces up the Hudson River from New York City. From the west, Lieutenant-Colonel Barry St. Leger would set out from Fort Oswego on Lake Ontario. And from the north, Burgoyne himself would de-

scend from Canada and join the other two forces in Albany.

Nothing worked as planned. General Howe, playing a cat-and-mouse game with Washington in New Jersey, postponed his departure and then decided to attack Philadelphia before fulfilling his role in the Albany strategy. He severely trounced Washington at the Battle of Brandywine, then went on to capture Philadelphia. But in October Washington retaliated at Germantown, Pennsylvania, and proved his troops were ready for combat by almost defeating Howe and thus preventing him from setting out to meet Burgoyne.

St. Leger was also slow to move his forces, and when he at last left Fort Oswego and headed east toward Albany, he was battered all along the way by American troops. He had gone only a third of the way to Albany when he was attacked by Benedict Arnold at Fort Stanwix. Arnold cleverly negotiated with St. Leger's Indian allies, convincing them to desert the British. Deprived of his large supporting force, St. Leger beat a hasty retreat back to Fort Oswego.

Meanwhile, Burgoyne was moving clumsily down toward Albany. With a force of some seven thousand men, fifty-two cannons, and a huge baggage train—including thirty carts of the general's personal luggage—Burgoyne's slow-moving caravan made an easy target. In Vermont the local militia, known as the Green Mountain Boys, fell on a foraging party of seven hundred of his redcoats and wiped them out. When the reduced British army reached Saratoga, it met with American forces and fortifications of unexpected strength. Burgoyne attacked the Americans twice. Both times he was turned back and suffered heavy losses. On October 17, 1777, Burgoyne surrendered his entire army of some fifty-seven hundred men.

The American victory astounded the British. When General Howe, who had entered and occupied Philadelphia without a struggle, heard the news, he submitted his resignation. A captured British officer declared: "The courage and obstinacy with which the Americans fought were the astonishment of everyone, and we now become fully convinced they are not that contemptible enemy we had hitherto imagined them, incapable of standing a regular engagement. . . ."

Burgoyne's surrender did not seriously reduce the superiority of the British forces in numbers of troops or supplies, but it did show how difficult it would be to defeat the Americans. More important, the American victory persuaded England's longtime enemy France to make an open alliance with the new nation.

The French Alliance

The news of the defeat at Saratoga and British fear of a Franco-American alliance prompted Lord North to try to end the war. He proposed a series of concessions that would guarantee the Americans virtual home rule. If necessary, all the acts of Parliament pertaining to the colonies passed after 1763 would be repealed. The British also would pledge that the Americans would never be taxed. Parliament, however, delayed acting on the proposals un-

THIS ENGLISH CARTOON PUBLISHED IN 1777 SATIRIZES THE FLIGHT OF THE AMERICAN CONGRESS FROM PHILADELPHIA AS "THE BRITISH LION ROARS" AND "THE GERMAN EAGLE SOARS."

til the Americans had already accepted the French offer to recognize their independence.

According to popular myth, the French rushed to the aid of the Americans because they loved freedom and democracy. It is true that the idea of a republic in the New World had appeal to many French aristocrats and intellectuals, but to the French Foreign Office, the prospective alliance was a well-calculated strategy to counteract Britain's influence in the world. After the French and Indian War, Britain had become the most powerful—and the most arrogant—nation in the Western world. As Benjamin Franklin wrote, "Every nation in Europe wishes to see Britain humbled, having all in their turns been offended by her insolence. . . ."

The Continental Congress sent Silas Deane and Arthur Lee to Paris seeking French help months before independence was declared. Both agents made themselves ridiculous in the sophisticated French capital. Deane pretended to be a figure of great mystery, wrote in invisible ink, and vowed to speak only French in order to fool the English. This behavior led the French foreign minister, the Comte de Vergennes, to remark: "He must be the most silent man in France, for I defy him to say six consecutive words in French." Lee was equally eager to play the secret agent, but he inadvertently managed to hire six British spies as aides.

Such bungling was not sufficient, however, to prevent the French from secretly helping America. Vergennes's policy was influenced by a remarkably versatile Frenchman named Pierre Augustin Caron de Beaumarchais. Beaumarchais was famous as the author of two popular, and dangerously democratic, comedies: *The Barber of Seville* and *The Marriage of Figaro*. With the permission and financial backing of King Louis XVI, Beaumarchais set up a fake private concern, Roderique Hortalez et Compagnie, through which war supplies were secretly channeled into America. In the first two and one-half years of the war, fourteen ships operated by Hortalez et Compagnie sailed back and forth across the Atlantic. Ninety percent of the gunpowder the Americans used during that period came from Europe and most of it was shipped by this company.

Five months after the Declaration of Independence, Congress sent Benjamin Franklin to encourage the French to support America openly. Congress could not have made a better choice. An

AT THE AGE OF SEVENTY BENJAMIN FRANKLIN WAS SENT TO FRANCE TO NEGOTIATE AN ALLIANCE. A SKILLFUL DIPLOMAT OF GREAT PERSONAL CHARM, HE CREATED A SENSATION IN PARIS WITH HIS FUR CAP AND HOMESPUN WAYS.

experienced diplomat, Franklin was also a great showman whose experiments with electricity were known throughout the world. Knowing that the French regarded Americans as simple, homespun pioneers, Franklin doffed his wig and donned a fur cap. The cap and its wearer were the sensation of Paris. Ladies piled their hair up into "caps," the *coiffure à la Franklin*. The great man sat for dozens of portraits, and Parisians paid good money for a vantage point to watch him walking through the streets.

For all of Franklin's charm and celebrity, it was news of the American victory at Saratoga that made it possible for Vergennes to convince his reluctant colleagues and the king that France should conclude an alliance with America. The American victory had encouraged the British to attempt to bring about a reconciliation with the colonies, and France did not want this effort to succeed. Before making an alliance, however, the French government was committed first to obtain the approval of Spain. The two nations had signed a compact in 1761 agreeing to act together in all decisions that might lead to war. Although Spain had cooperated with France in

WASHINGTON AND HIS
FROSTBITTEN TROOPS AT
THEIR WINTER QUARTERS
AT VALLEY FORGE.

providing supplies to America through Rodrique Hortalez et Compagnie, the Spanish were against forming an alliance with the revolutionaries. Spain had colonies of its own in the New World and feared that the spirit of rebellion might spread from North to South America. Finally, apprehensive that America might accept the English offers of peace, France decided to act without Spain. In February 1778 the French signed two pacts with the Americans. In the first, a treaty of commerce, France officially recognized the independence of the new nation. In the second, a formal alliance, the two nations agreed to the following: both nations would fight until American independence had been won; neither France nor America would sign a peace treaty with Britain without the formal consent of the other; and each country would respect the other's American holdings "mutually from the present time and forever against all other powers."

Within two years of the French Alliance the war against Great Britain had become global. Both France and the United States wanted to obtain Spanish arms, money, and naval support for the battle against Britain. Ultimately Spain did go to war on the side of France after being promised in a 1779 treaty that France would aid in recovering Gibraltar from England. Thus although Spain never did ally itself directly with the United States, the war for independence was indirectly tied to Spanish recovery of control of the entrance to the Mediterranean. In 1780 the Continental Congress sent John Jay to Spain to attempt to secure an alliance, and he spent two and a half dreary years there cooling his heels as an unofficial envoy. Meanwhile, the Dutch also became involved. They disavowed their earlier commitments to aid the British war effort and indirectly carried on trade with the rebels by way of France. To protect their trade the Dutch also joined a European league of armed neutrality led by Russia which was opposed to Britain's highhanded methods of treating neutral shipping in wartime. Infuriated, England declared war on Holland in 1780.

Three More Years of War

International politics had thus transformed a colonial rebellion into a world war, but this change had little immediate impact in America. While the alliance was being negotiated, Washington endured his worst trial: the winter of 1777–1778 at Valley Forge. The site proved a poor choice for quartering his soldiers. Rations and supplies were short and there was little food to be found by foraging. In addition, the weather was bitterly cold. An army surgeon summarized the desperate situation in these terse words:

Poor food—hard lodging—cold weather—fatigue —nasty clothes—nasty cookery—vomit half my time—smoked out of my senses—the Devil's in't—I can't endure it. Why are we sent here to starve and freeze?

Almost two thousand of Washington's men deserted to the enemy. The local farmers sold their crops to the highest bidder, which was usually the British. General Howe probably could have wiped out Washington's dispirited force with one quick blow, but he had already submitted his resignation and refused to stir from the comfort of Philadelphia.

Despite American misfortunes in the East, an expedition led by George Rogers Clark, acting on orders from the state of Virginia, had some success in the West. Clark was never able to take Detroit, nor was he able to gain complete control of the Ohio and Illinois country even with victories at Kaskaskia and Vincennes. But he succeeded in removing British-sponsored Indian pressure from Kentucky and western Virginia.

The Battlefield Moves South   When General Henry Clinton took command from Howe in May 1778, his orders were to move the British army to New York and to devise a strategy for overrunning the South. The British believed that once they controlled the South it would be easier to protect their interests in the West Indies against the French and the Spanish. Aware that the South was a stronghold of Tory sympathizers, they also planned to use their position in the Caribbean to gain control of parts of the Southern coast and then move their army northward again as they pacified the countryside with Loyalist support. On his march to New York, however, Clinton was attacked by Washington at Monmouth Court House in New Jersey. Although Washington did not gain a clear victory, his army's good showing cheered Americans.

Monmouth was the last major battle in the North. From there the war shifted to South Carolina and Georgia. The Americans hoped to stop the transfer of British troops from New York to Savannah with the help of the French navy, but the navy was slow to arrive and it was never engaged in decisive action. In November the French sailed south to winter in the French West Indies. The British were then able to take Savannah, Georgia, and soon controlled the entire state.

A year and a half later General Clinton arrived from New York and personally conducted an attack on Charleston. After three months, in May 1780, the most important city of the South capitulated, and the rest of South Carolina surrendered later. Clinton returned North in high spirits, leaving behind eight thousand men under the command of General Charles Cornwallis.

The situation was so alarming that Congress turned to General Horatio Gates, one of the commanders at Saratoga. Against Washington's objections, Congress directed him to take charge of American operations in the South. Washington's low opinion of Gates was soon justified. On August 16, 1780, near Camden, South Carolina, Gates launched a surprise attack on the British. Unfortunately, Gates had put untrained militiamen in charge of a key area of his line, and when the British charged, these raw troops fled. Gates retreated after suffering heavy losses. Within a four-month period Britain had thus captured two sizable American armies, and the coastal areas of Georgia and South Carolina were firmly in British hands.

In the North, rations were so scarce that Washington had to cut his army down to a scant thousand men for fear that a larger force would face starvation. Then, as the final blow, he learned that Benedict Arnold, possibly the most able officer to fight on either side in the Revolution, had defected to the British.

From this low point American fortunes finally began to improve. In October 1780 frontier patriots killed the commander of a twelve-hundred-man Tory force along with many of his men at King's Mountain, North Carolina. Washington appointed his own protégé, Nathaniel Greene, to head American operations in the South. Under Greene, American forces won several hit-and-run battles against Cornwallis, the most notable occurring at Cowpens, South Carolina, in January 1781. At the Battle of Guilford Courthouse in North Carolina the following March, Greene was forced to retreat. But Cornwallis had lost so many men that he now abandoned Britain's southern strategy of pacifying the countryside and moved into Virginia instead.

The Battle of Yorktown   In the spring and summer of 1781 American troops, led by another Washington protégé—the French general, the Marquis de Lafayette—and aided by forces under the Prussian

CORNWALLIS RESIGNS HIS SWORD TO WASHINGTON.

Baron Friedrich von Steuben, harassed Cornwallis in Virginia and drove him to Yorktown on the coast. Throughout the war the British had always felt safe on the coast, relying on their vastly superior navy to provide them with supplies and a cover of cannon fire. They had learned that once they moved inland, they could win specific battles but never hold territory for long. America was simply too vast, its roads too poor, and its citizens too rebellious to be controlled through military strength alone.

In August 1781 Washington was stationed outside British-held New York City, still awaiting the French navy. When he learned that the French Admiral, the Comte de Grasse, was sailing from the West Indies with thirty ships and three thousand marines, Washington ordered Lafayette to keep

North America • 1783

English
French
Spanish
United States

Peace Negotiations

When Lord North heard about the defeat at Yorktown, he exclaimed, "Oh, God! It is all over." Britain immediately began to extend peace feelers. Washington had expected the war to continue, but Britain was experiencing serious defeats elsewhere at the hands of other enemies. Spain had captured Pensacola, Florida, in May 1781, and would soon take Minorca in the Mediterranean. France had seized several key British islands in the Caribbean. In Africa and Asia the British were suffering reversals. In addition, the British were facing serious problems at home, not the least of which was that the national debt had doubled in the last seven years. Overwhelmed by these misfortunes, Lord North resigned in March 1782, and the new ministry decided to negotiate a peace settlement with the Americans.

Because the rebellion had turned into a world war, a settlement would have to involve America, Britain, France, Spain, and Holland. Influenced by the French Foreign Office, the Continental Congress had instructed its representatives in Paris to follow the advice of their French allies on all matters. Some delegates had been bribed by the French government; others believed that the French were sincerely interested in the problems and future of the new nation. France did indeed favor an independent nation in America, but one that was weak and confined to the territory east of the Appalachians.

The American delegation in Paris included Benjamin Franklin, John Jay, and John Adams. The new British ministry under Lord Shelburne opened discussions with Franklin in April 1782. By the time Jay arrived from Madrid, it was clear that the British wanted a peace settlement but would only recognize American independence after a treaty had been negotiated. Franklin and Vergennes were willing to accept this procedure, but Jay was adamantly opposed to it. When Franklin fell ill in August, Jay carried on the negotiations alone for several weeks. Jay, after his long period of neglect as American minister to Spain, came to Paris determined to redeem his own and his country's honor. He soon learned that the French were making an undercover trip to London, and he suspected that they might be planning to deal secretly with the British. He

Cornwallis penned up in Yorktown until he arrived in Virginia.

On September 5 de Grasse attacked and crippled the British navy in Chesapeake Bay, preparing the way for an assault on Yorktown. On September 28 Washington laid seige to Yorktown with the aid of seven thousand French troops. Three weeks later Cornwallis surrendered his entire force of seven thousand men.

knew, too, that both Spain and France were determined that the new country should gain as few concessions as possible from Britain and should not be permitted to expand into the Western territories. Convinced that America's allies were now as dangerous as the British, Jay suggested to Franklin that they would be wise to ignore the advice of the Comte de Vergennes. At first Franklin was cool to the idea. But when Adams, having just negotiated a commercial treaty with the Dutch, agreed with Jay, Franklin changed his mind. Although they knew that it would be in violation of their instructions from the Continental Congress, they did not think these directives were in the national interest, and they conferred with the British in secrecy.

As a result, a preliminary treaty was signed by the Americans and the British in November 1782. It fully recognized American independence and granted generous territorial concessions. The new country received all the lands lying between the Great Lakes and the northern border of Florida, as well as all the territory between the Atlantic Coast and the Mississippi River (Florida and the Gulf Coast had been retaken by Spain during the war). The treaty also recognized the right of both nations to navigate the full length of the Mississippi River—a provision that would cause much conflict in the future, since Spain, which was not a party to the treaty, controlled the mouth of the river. The British promised to withdraw their troops from American soil as soon as possible and granted the Americans liberal fishing rights off Newfoundland.

In return, the Americans promised that the Congress would "earnestly recommend" to the states that they compensate Tories for confiscated property. They agreed, moreover, that there should be no legal barriers to payment of pre-Revolutionary War debts owed to British merchants. In reality, however, these two clauses proved very difficult to implement.

The French foreign minister was flabbergasted when he learned of the treaty and its provisions. He wrote to Franklin:

I am at a loss, sir, to explain your conduct and that of your colleagues on this occasion. . . . You are wise and discreet, sir; you perfectly understand what is due to propriety; you have all your life performed your duties. I pray you to consider how you propose to fulfill those which are due to the King?

In spite of this, relations with France were not broken, and Vergennes, off the record, communicated his admiration of American diplomatic finesse and his amazement at British generosity. The treaty also aided France in extricating itself from the alliance with Spain, the terms of which were impossible to fulfill. The formal peace document, known as the Treaty of Paris, was signed by all parties in 1783.

Creating a Nation

The American Revolution was much more than a mere victory—however stunning—on the battlefield. Having won their independence, the Americans now faced the responsibility of creating a new nation. Freed from the dominance of the Old World, they had the rare opportunity to reshape the politics and society of their country. Americans initially believed that they only wanted to put off monarchical rule, but when they began to create new governments in the individual states and then on the national level, they began to put into effect some of the ideas that had been generated during the two decades of intensive political debate prior to the Revolution.

New State Governments

The thirteen colonies were transformed into states in a remarkably peaceful and legal way. Most Americans regarded a written constitution as essential. Feeling that their governments had been based for too long on the unwritten British constitution, Americans were determined that their rights be stated and their government's functions be clearly delineated.

In forming their new state constitutions, the framers used as guides their written charters and compacts, the philosophy of the Enlightenment, the English Bill of Rights, and their own experience with self-government. Each state established itself as a republic, and in May 1776 the Continental Congress recognized the states as independent. By the end of 1777 ten states had turned their colonial charters into state constitutions. Pennsylvania had called a constitutional convention to write a new document, but in the other nine states the assemblies had simply written and approved the new constitutions themselves.

Most constitutions made important innovations in four general categories:

1. Most of the state constitutions provided a bill of rights guaranteeing protection of life, liberty, and property; the right to trial by jury; moderate bail and humane punishment; rotation in office; free elections; and freedom of speech, assembly, and religion.

2. Most states reduced the property qualifications for voters. No state, however, eliminated them entirely, and no state extended the vote to women.

3. All the new constitutions included a provision for amendment. The framers tried to make these documents flexible enough to be changed if time proved them faulty.

4. Some of the new constitutions also tried to resolve long-standing conflicts between the regions of the East Coast and the frontier. The older coastal counties had consistently denied full representation in the colonial assemblies to the western regions. As a result, several of the state constitutions provided for equal electoral districts and residential requirements for those elected to office. Pennsylvania's new constitution came close to equalizing representation from all counties, but in the Middle and Southern states the eastern counties generally remained overrepresented.

Social Reforms

The Revolution helped to relax class distinctions and to fan a surge of philosophical idealism. In keeping with this democratic impulse, most of the new constitutions enacted limited social reforms or confirmed those already in existence. Among the important mainsprings of reform were a growing movement in opposition to slavery, a republican distaste for class distinctions, and a demand for greater religious freedom. These attitudes reflected a vigorous spirit of humanitarianism that was reaching increasing numbers of Americans.

The Beginnings of an Antislavery Movement During the eighteenth century, slavery had gradually permeated American life, particularly in the South, and few had questioned its morality. During the Revolution, however, some white people struggling for their own freedom began to recognize the injustice in denying liberty to black people. In many states both the English and the Americans promised to free slaves who fought alongside them.

The Revolutionary era thus fostered the beginnings of an antislavery movement. The Continental Congress abolished the foreign slave trade in 1774. By the end of the Revolution, all the states except Georgia and South Carolina had outlawed the slave trade. Antislavery societies were active from Virginia to Massachusetts by 1792. The first article of the Massachusetts Constitution, "All men are born free and equal," inspired one slave to sue for his freedom. He won his case, automatically freeing all the other slaves in the state. By the beginning of the nineteenth century, the other Northern states had provided for the gradual abolition of slavery. In the South most whites still considered slavery a legitimate institution, and progress lagged far behind. Nevertheless, in 1782 Virginia passed a law permitting owners to free their slaves, and by 1790 ten thousand Southern slaves had been freed. Nevertheless, from this time on, the Southern position on the slavery issue would remain out of step with that of the rest of the nation.

The Status of Women In contrast to the beneficial effect of the Revolution on the political and personal situations of black people, it brought no immediate changes for American women. For men the right to vote and to participate in politics expanded during the post-revolutionary era, but women's political status remained the same: they still had no voice in determining the nation's policies. In women's personal lives, legal protection evolved very slowly. A married woman's property remained her husband's possession (although he could establish a separate estate for his wife). However, divorce, which had been virtually unheard of in the colonial period, became possible after the Revolution. Some states permitted the legislature to grant divorces; others gave this power to the courts. But even with these legal avenues available it was difficult to obtain a divorce except under extreme circumstances such as adultery, desertion, or "intolerable severity." Even so, the number of divorces increased.

The Decline of the Aristocracy Loyalists existed in all classes of society, but those who fled the country were usually members of the colonial aristocracy. Their departure significantly diminished the number of wealthy Americans. They left behind their landed estates, which were confiscated by state governments, broken into smaller units, and sold to farmers. Land redistribution was often drastic. For example, 311 people eventually obtained ownership of small farms on the former estate of the Phillips family in New York.

Token steps were taken to increase the opportunities to own land. Feudal laws were discarded, including those providing for primogeniture (by which a man's oldest son inherited all his property), entail (by which a man could keep his property intact by dictating in advance the succession of heirs to his property), and quitrents.

In addition, it became illegal for citizens to accept titles of nobility from foreign nations. Any suspected attempts to establish a native aristocracy aroused intense opposition. When officers of the Continental army formed the Society of the Cincinnati—a charitable club named after a Roman farmer who had gone to war to protect the ancient republic—they were severely criticized for creating an organization for the elite in which membership was hereditary.

The Weakening of Ties between Church and State Another effect of the Revolution was to weaken the ties between church and state. Prior to the Declaration of Independence, most of the colonies had an established church (that is, one supported with tax money). During the War, however, the Church of England no longer received state support, and its many Loyalist ministers fled to England.

Under their new constitutions the New England states continued to support an established religion, but taxpayers could specify to which of the Protestant churches their money should go. The American Methodist church was growing rapidly, with a system of circuit riders traveling to preach in rural communities. In the absence of permanent preachers, local lay groups gathered weekly to strengthen each other's faith by testimony, admonition, prayer, and joint Bible study. Membership in the Baptist churches grew, too, on a wave of revivalist fervor.

The new state constitutions guaranteed religious freedom in their bills of rights, but what they had in mind was the freedom to belong to any established church, not necessarily the freedom to belong to no church at all. For example, all states required that their elected officials take a religious oath. Virginia was the first state to abolish all such religious requirements. Its legislature adopted a statute written by Thomas Jefferson which stated that "no man shall be compelled to frequent or support any religious worship, place, or ministry whatsoever." By 1800 most states had followed Virginia in separating church and state by law. Only Massachusetts, Connecticut, and New Hampshire maintained a state-supported church into the early nineteenth century.

Creating a National Government

After the Revolution the first loyalty of most Americans was to their own state. Yet, a new sense of being American was emerging. The members of the Continental Congress, uprooted from their homes in the various colonies, left behind some of their provincial concerns and drew up the Declaration of Independence in the name of the people of the united colonies. The flag of thirteen stars and thirteen stripes, adopted in June 1777, gave the American people a visible symbol of their unity.

The war itself had done much to foster a sense of nationalism. The struggle for liberty had taken many Americans far from their home states, and facing a common enemy had made many realize that they had a common cause.

Despite this developing nationalism, many Americans were understandably wary about uniting their sovereign states and forming a national government. Having just overturned an overly assertive government, they were very reluctant to grant similar power to another central government. Besides, many people doubted that a republican form of government was practicable in a country the size of the United States. Montesquieu, one of the influential philosophers of the Enlightenment, maintained that a large territory could not be organized as a republic; it could be ruled only by a despot. Indeed, history provided few examples of successful large republics. The republics of ancient

A WOODCUT OF OLD GLORY WITH THIRTEEN STARS.

was sent to the printer. Busy trying to run a war, Congress bickered over the document for a year. Four more years passed before all the states ratified a revised version.

The Articles of Confederation A major stumbling block to the formation of the new union was the way in which states would be represented in the new legislature. As things stood, representatives to the Continental Congress were elected annually by their state legislatures, and each state had one vote in congressional decisions. Small states thus wielded the same power as large states. The large states had agreed to this arrangement only as a temporary, wartime measure. When the first draft of the Articles of Confederation proposed to make it permanent, a vehement debate erupted that lasted almost a year. The rule of one state, one vote was finally accepted when it was further stipulated that every important measure had to pass by a two-thirds majority of the states.

The controversial first draft adopted by Congress in November 1777 attempted to establish a national government that was much stronger than most members of Congress could accept. The final draft, by contrast, was so limited that the union had become barely more than a "league of friendship" among the states.

The Articles provided for a federal system of government, but left the most important powers to the states. Congress could not regulate trade or levy internal taxes. In addition, the country was to have no chief executive or national court system. A unicameral legislature would direct the league of thirteen nations. It would have the power to ask the states for revenue, regulate foreign affairs, send and receive ambassadors, make treaties, declare war and conclude peace, establish a post office, regulate the coinage, and control Indian affairs. Each state retained "its sovereignty, freedom, and independence, and every Power, Jurisdiction and right" not delegated to Congress in the Articles.

Problems of Ratification Before the Articles could go into effect, they had to ratified by all states. Ratification was a long and difficult process. The main obstacle was the question of what to do with the immense territory beyond the Appalachian Mountains. Seven states demanded vast tracts. Six of these "landed" states (Massachusetts, Connecticut, Vir-

Greece had been city-states, not large nations; and Rome had abandoned republicanism after it became an immense empire. In a large nation, the argument ran, the legislature would inevitably sit in a capital far from the electorate, thus falling out of touch with the will of the voters.

Nevertheless, most educated Americans recognized that thirteen independent states could not survive in a world dominated by such powerful nations as Britain, Spain, and France. In an effort to establish a basis for a national government, a first-draft Articles of Confederation was presented to Congress eight days after the Declaration of Independence

ginia, the Carolinas, and Georgia) based their claims on their royal charters, which had granted them the territories to the west—in fact, all the way to the Pacific Ocean. The seventh landed state, New York, argued that since New York governed the Iroquois Indians, it should also govern their lands.

The remaining six states had fixed western boundaries. They wanted Congress to take charge of the western lands, making them accessible to the citizens of all thirteen states.

Maryland, speaking for the six states with fixed boundaries, refused to ratify the Articles of Confederation until the seven landed states renounced their claims. Maryland argued that if the landed states received territories in the west, they could sell this land and use the profits to free their own citizens from paying taxes. Citizens of the landless states

would then flock to the landed states, attracted by the prospect of paying few or no taxes.

The deadlock was finally broken when New York and Virginia gave up their western claims. Patriots in Virginia, led by James Madison, preferred giving up the Ohio Valley to standing in the way of union, as long as it was agreed that new states with a republican form of government would be carved out of this territory. Eventually all the landed states surrendered their claims to the western territories on this basis.

Maryland finally ratified the Articles of Confederation on March 1, 1781. The Articles immediately went into effect, and a fledgling nation was thus born. We might add that under the circumstances, the creation of any kind of permanent centralized authority was a remarkable achievement.

The Confederation Period

During the years 1781 to 1789 the weakness of the government became evident. According to the Articles of Confederation, Congress could pass laws but had no way of putting them into effect. The states frequently ignored federal requests for funds, and Congress had no power to impose taxes or tariffs. Another difficulty was that the delegates to Congress had little opportunity to develop a national leadership because their terms were so short. A delegate was elected for only one year at a time and could not be reelected for more than three years in every six. The older leaders of Congress during the Revolution—Patrick Henry, Thomas Jefferson, Benjamin Franklin, John Adams, Samuel Adams, John Hancock—were either serving the nation in other positions or had returned to private life. Their places were taken by younger, less experienced men.

In order to pass any legislation, the Articles required a simple majority; matters of great importance—for instance, decisions concerning war and peace or appropriations—required the support of nine states. A serious obstacle to the work of the Congress was the frequent inability to raise a quorum, which consisted of nine states. During the first four months of 1784, Congress had a quorum on only three days. This difficulty continually interrupted the work of Congress, especially since there was no executive branch to provide continuity. Con-

gress created the departments of war, foreign affairs, and finance to help fill this gap. The three department heads assumed some executive responsibility, but these appointive posts were not always filled. For example, after the first secretary of war resigned in 1783, the position remained vacant for two years.

The work of Congress was handicapped by geographical problems as well. There was no permanent capital, and the delegates wandered like gypsies, from Philadelphia to Princeton, to Annapolis, to Trenton, and finally to New York.

This dismal situation prompted John Jay, now secretary for foreign affairs, to write a gloomy letter to Washington in June 1786:

Our affairs seem to lead to some crisis, some revolution—something that I cannot foresee or conjecture. I am uneasy and apprehensive . . . we are going and doing wrong, and therefore I look forward to evils and calamities, but without being able to guess at the instrument, nature, or measure of them.

Foreign Affairs

The absence of unity among the states (which continued to behave like independent countries) and the lack of authority in the central government made it extremely difficult to carry on diplomatic relations with foreign nations. The ineffective, fragmented new country was scorned abroad. A best-selling pamphlet by Lord Sheffield indicated that the initial expressions of good will in England were being replaced by condescension or arrogance. He argued:

It will not be an easy matter to bring the American states to act as a nation. They were not to be feared as such by us. . . . We might as well dread the effect of combinations among the German as among the American states.

John Adams and Thomas Jefferson—the American ministers to London and Paris, respectively—suffered daily humiliations. Adams complained that the British treated him with "dry decency and cold civility." He wrote in despair, "No step that I can take, no language I can hold will do any good, or indeed much harm." Jefferson echoed the lament: "We are the lowest and most obscure of the whole diplomatic tribe."

Problems with the English There were several areas of friction between America and Great Britain during the 1780s. None, however, was resolved during that decade, and Britain did not even send a diplomatic minister to the United States.

One problem between the two nations was caused by mutual treaty violations. Congress had pledged that British creditors would meet with "no lawful impediment" in collecting the millions of dollars owed them by individual Americans. But when English creditors tried to get their money, American debtors flatly refused. "If we are now to pay the debts due to British merchants," asked George Mason of Virginia, "what have we been fighting for all this while?"

Loyalists met with similar difficulties. The peace treaty had promised that American authorities would "recommend" that the states restore confiscated Tory property, but in practice the recommendations were not implemented. Years later Britain itself finally awarded five thousand American Tories more than three million pounds to help cover their losses.

Britain violated the treaty by refusing to turn over the forts it held on American soil along the Great Lakes. Canadian merchants had urged the British to hold onto the forts so that the Canadians might prolong their profitable fur trade with the Indians. England also feared that the Indians in the area, left to the mercy of American frontier farmers, might turn on the Canadians in revenge for the departure of the British.

The Confederation was helpless to protect the Tories or to drive the English out of American territory. The British, knowing this, announced that they would give up the forts only when Loyalist properties were restored and English merchants repaid.

Another lingering controversy developed over Vermont. In 1777 the people of Vermont, led by Ethan Allan and his Tory brother, Levi, had created their own independent government and had promised England their neutrality during the war in exchange for British diplomatic recognition. After the war, Vermont's leaders hinted that they might reunite with the mother country and attach Vermont to Canada. British intrigue with Vermont continued until 1791, when Vermont finally chose to become the fourteenth state in the American Union.

Problems with the Spanish In the peace treaty, Britain had granted America all the land north of Florida, south of the Great Lakes, and east of the Mississippi River, as well as the right to navigate the Mississippi. But Spain, which had not been a party to the treaty, claimed the areas between the Gulf of Mexico and the Tennessee River and between the Appalachian Mountains and the Mississippi River.

By 1785 some fifty thousand Americans had settled in the areas which were to become Tennessee and Kentucky. These settlers were economically dependent on access to the Mississippi River. The only economical way for them to transport their goods was by boat, down the Mississippi to the Gulf of Mexico before heading east. Spain, recognizing their need, announced in 1784 that it was closing the river to all foreigners.

Spain further harassed settlers by arming the Southwestern Indians for periodic raids on American villages. At the same time, however, Spain offered western settlers land, religious toleration, and the use of the Mississippi at low rates if they would swear allegiance to the Spanish government.

Spain's tactics did have some effect: many American settlers in the area considered breaking off ties with the ineffective Confederation government, declaring their independence, and negotiating directly with Spain for more favorable trading conditions. One American soldier of fortune, James Wilkinson, even made a notorious attempt to bring the Tennessee area under Spanish rule in exchange for trading concessions and a pension. In 1784 George Washington, after journeying hundreds of miles through the back country, reported: "The western settlers . . . stand as it were on a pivot. The touch of a feather would turn them any way."

Spain tried to drive a deeper wedge into the union of American states by encouraging conflict between the Northeast and the South and Southwest. Merchants in New England had little use for the western settlers, whom they regarded as boors and ruffians. New England was much less interested in rights to the Mississippi River than in trade with Spain.

During the Revolutionary War Spain had permitted a limited amount of trade between its empire and the Americas. Now American business was hungry for a larger share of that profitable market. Accordingly, the Spanish envoy, Don Diego de Gardoqui, made an offer to Secretary for Foreign Affairs John Jay. Americans, Gardoqui said, could expand their trade with Spain if the United States would abandon use of the Mississippi River for twenty-five years.

John Jay—and the merchants of Boston, Newport, Philadelphia, and New York—were willing to make a treaty on such a basis, believing that commerce with Spain was more in the interest of America at that time than the use of the Mississippi River. But when Jay proposed a treaty meeting Gardoqui's terms, the Southern delegates in Congress and the whole Southwest erupted in rage. "The prohibition of the navigation of the Mississippi," wrote one indignant pioneer, "has astonished the whole western country. To sell us and make us vassals of the merciless Spaniards is a grievance not to be borne." It was clear that Congress would never support such a treaty, and Jay had to abandon his talks with Gardoqui.

In 1788, Spain did finally grant Americans the right to navigate the Mississippi (although they had to pay high duties for the privilege). But settlers in the Southwest long remembered with bitterness the East Coast's scheme to exchange free passage through the Mississippi for trade concessions with Spain.

The Western Lands

Opposition to British and Spanish control of the area between the Appalachian Mountains and the Mississippi River, as well as the westward movement of Americans, finally pushed the Confederation Congress toward its most important accomplishment —the creation of a policy for orderly westward expansion. Legislation passed from 1785 to 1787 pertaining to the Old Northwest (the area above the Ohio River) was later applied to the rest of the country as settlers continued to move across the continent.

Although the vast northwestern tract of land that America received in the treaty of 1783 was rich and promising, it was inhabited almost entirely by Indian tribes, French traders, and British soldiers. None of the area's inhabitants wanted Americans to enter their wooded paradise, but by 1785 Congress was already laying plans for American settlement.

When Virginia had ceded its claims to the Old Northwest, thus making possible the ratification of the Articles of Confederation, it had stipulated that the territory "shall be formed into distinct republican states, which shall become members of the Federal Union, and have the same rights of sovereignty, freedom, and independence of the other States." Under the Land Ordinance of 1785 and the more important Northwest Ordinance of 1787, Congress set up a system under which these goals could be realized.

Land Ordinances The Land Ordinance of 1785 provided for surveying the Northwest into six-mile-square townships. Each township was to be further subdivided into thirty-six sections. Purchasers could buy at public auction no less than one section (640 acres) at a minimum price of one dollar an acre. This large quantity favored land speculators. Although in later years the minimum number of acres was lowered, in the meantime speculators bought up large tracts of land illegally at lower prices and then resold small pieces. Many farmers simply settled on a tract, hoping that when it was eventually surveyed and put up for sale, they would have the first opportunity to buy it. The Ordinance also provided that one section in each township be reserved for education, and four sections for the use of the government.

WESTERN EMIGRATION.

JOURNAL

OF

DOCTOR JEREMIAH SMIPLETON's

TOUR TO OHIO.

CONTAINING

An account of the numerous difficulties, Hair-breadth
Escapes, Mortifications and Privations, which the
Doctor and his family experienced on their
Journey from Maine, to the 'Land of Pro-
mise,' and during a residence of three years
in that highly extolled country.

BY H. TRUMBULL.

Nulli Fides Frontis.

BOSTON--PRINTED BY S. SEWALL.

"No Part of North America will require less Encouragement for the Production of Naval Stores, and raw Materials for Manufactories in Europe, and for supplying the West-India Islands with Lumber, Provisions, &c. than the Country of the Ohio; and for the following Reasons:—1st. The Lands are excellent, the Climate temperate, the Grapes, Silk-Worms and Mulberry-Trees, abound every where. Hemp, Hops, and Rye grow spontaneously in the Vallies and low Lands; Lead and Iron Ore are found in Plenty in the Hills; Salt Springs are innumerable, and no Soil is better adapted to the Culture of Tobacco, Flax and Cotton, than that of the Ohio.—2dly. The Country is well-watered by several navigable Rivers communicating with each other.—3dly. The River Ohio is, at all Seasons of the Year, navigable for large Boats, like West Country Barges, rowed by four or five Men, and from the Month of February to April large Ships may be built on the Ohio and sent to Sea, laden with Hemp, Iron, Flax, Silk, Tobacco, Cotton, Pot-Ash, Beef, Flour, Corn, Ship-Plank, &c."

"You will, on your arrival there, be obliged to sleep in a hollow tree, or build yourself a log hut, for here are no carpenters—kill and dress your own game, for heare are no butchers—clothe yourself in skins, when your stock of apparel is worn out, for here are no factories, shoemakers, tailors, hatters or tanners—and pound your own corn, for you may travel in this wild wilderness many miles, without discovering the sign of a mill—in short, nothing can be obtained here without costing more for the transportation than the original price of any article you may want. As to *society*, if you wish to converse in any human language out of your family, you must go twenty or thirty miles to your next door neighbor, with your axe instead of staff—for you must cut your way thither, for want of roads—and perhaps, after all, find him almost as hoggish as the 'swines in your pens' or the more numerous class of the inhabitants of Ohio, the wildcat, panther etc. who frequently associate with our tame animals to their sorrow, and sometimes with young children to our mourning:—and fags I'd rather be a hog-reeve in good New-England than hold any office in this back woods country, where the inhabitants walk on all fours, with the exception of a few double headed fools. Take my advice, therefore, Scruple, and put off your journey, til you think a little further on the subject.

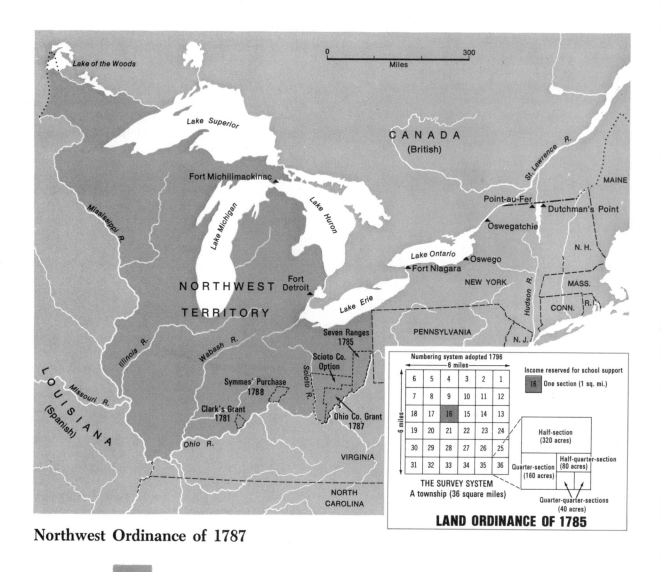

Northwest Ordinance of 1787

NORTHWEST TERRITORY

LAKE SUPERIOR · Lake of the Woods · Lake Michigan · Lake Huron · Lake Erie · Lake Ontario

Fort Michilimackinac · Fort Detroit · Fort Niagara · Oswego · Point-au-Fer · Dutchman's Point · Oswegatchie

CANADA (British) · MAINE · N.H. · MASS. · R.I. · CONN. · NEW YORK · N.J. · PENNSYLVANIA · VIRGINIA · NORTH CAROLINA

Mississippi R. · Missouri R. · Illinois R. · Wabash R. · Scioto R. · Ohio R. · St. Lawrence R. · Hudson R.

LOUISIANA (Spanish)

Seven Ranges 1785 · Scioto Co. Option · Symmes' Purchase 1788 · Clark's Grant 1781 · Ohio Co. Grant 1787

Miles 0 — 300

THE SURVEY SYSTEM
A township (36 square miles)

Numbering system adopted 1796
← 6 miles →

6	5	4	3	2	1
7	8	9	10	11	12
18	17	16	15	14	13
19	20	21	22	23	24
30	29	28	27	26	25
31	32	33	34	35	36

Income reserved for school support
16 One section (1 sq. mi.)

Half-section (320 acres)
Quarter-section (160 acres)
Half-quarter-section (80 acres)
Quarter-quarter-sections (40 acres)

LAND ORDINANCE OF 1785

Northwest Territory (acquired 1781; organized 1787) ▲ British posts after 1783

◄ TWO EARLY VIEWS OF PIONEERING IN OHIO. THE GLOWING ACCOUNT APPEARED IN A 1799 ADVERTISEMENT OFFERING OHIO LAND FOR SALE. THE SAD TALE, ON THE OTHER HAND, APPEARED IN *DOCTOR JEREMIA SIMPLETON'S TOUR TO OHIO*, AN ANTIEMIGRATION TRACT PUBLISHED IN BOSTON IN 1819. THE TRUTH PROBABLY LAY SOMEWHERE IN BETWEEN.

The Northwest Ordinance of 1787 pertained to the government of new—and usually disorderly —territories. It declared that the entire Northwest Territory was to be divided into no more than five and no fewer than three states. These states were required to provide public elementary education, to maintain religious freedom, and to be free forever from the institution of slavery. The Ordinance established three stages of government through which territories must pass in order to be eligible for statehood:

1. The first stage would consist of a governor, a secretary, and three judges, all appointed by Congress. When five thousand male inhabitants over twenty years of age had settled in the territory, the second stage of territorial government would begin.

2. Property owners with fifty acres or more could elect the lower house of a legislature of their own; the upper house, a five-member legislative council, would be appointed by Congress. The assembly would enact laws for the region, subject only to the governor's veto. Moreover, the assembly would send a nonvoting delegate to Congress.

3. When the territory had sixty thousand inhabitants, the third stage of government would begin. The territory could be admitted into the Union "on an equal footing with the original states in all respects whatever," as soon as it formed a state constitution similar to the ones in the original thirteen states.

Thus, the Ordinance of 1785 solved the problem of how to dispose of America's vast territory, and the Ordinance of 1787 established the basic procedures by which most new territories would become states. In outlining this process, the Confederation Congress ensured that American pioneers would retain their political rights as they moved west. The British empire in the New World had foundered on the question of imperial control versus home rule, but the new nation had found a way to avoid the same mistake. In establishing its policy of territorial stages the Confederation Congress followed the British system of providing an appointed governor and council, and an elected assembly. But it wisely decided against a policy of indefinite colonial status for the newly settled areas.

Economic Problems

The Confederation Congress inherited an economic situation that can be simply described in one word—terrible. The government's credit was collapsing, the army lacked food and uniforms, and the Continental dollar was almost worthless.

Foreign Trade Imbalance The war and its aftermath disrupted the balance between American and foreign trade and created a depression which badly weakened public confidence in the Confederation government.

In the first few years after the war, America imported three times as much from Britain as it exported, thus draining large amounts of American silver and gold into British coffers. Britain, operating according to the principles of the mercantile system, was simultaneously attempting to increase British exports to America and to prohibit American exports to Britain. The British permitted America to import only a few English raw materials, and these had to be transported in British ships. To make matters worse, the British prohibited the exporting of American manufactured goods to England. In addition, Britain cut America out of the lucrative trade with the British West Indies, so American merchants were forced into smuggling or doing without the trade.

This imbalance of trade virtually crippled the American shipbuilding industry. Although American merchants were desperately trying to establish new markets, this made only a slight dent in their losses. Trade with France and Holland provided some relief, and American merchants turned profits in far-off China by selling sea-otter skins they had purchased from the Pacific Northwest Indians. Another article of trade was American agricultural products that were being produced in increasing abundance after the war. By the late 1780s American exports to England and elsewhere had surpassed prewar levels.

The unfavorable balance of trade prevented the stabilization of the American economy, caused prices to drop by as much as 25 percent, caused numerous bankruptcies, and eventually undermined the currency. Most nations faced with an economic situation of this sort would set up tariffs to protect their native industries, but the Articles of Confederation had specifically denied Congress this power. Some of the states passed laws to discourage imports, but these were piecemeal measures that often backfired.

Seeing the need for a national tariff system, eleven states agreed to grant Congress that power as early as 1781. The Articles of Confederation, however, required that any amendment receive the unanimous consent of the states. The amendment was defeated by one vote, and so was a similar amendment introduced a few years later. The country's economy demanded more national direction, but the existing governmental machinery was incapable of providing it.

The lack of foreign trade further strained the domestic economy. During the war, Congress had printed large quantities of paper money to meet its operating expenses. The problem was that there was no gold in the national treasury to back the paper, and the Continental dollar had become almost worthless by 1781. Robert Morris, who became head of the newly created Department of Finance, managed to stabilize the currency by borrowing gold to back the paper money. Nevertheless, after the war Congress was saddled with a domestic debt of approximately $42 million and a foreign debt of about $12 million. Congress had to rely on the states for the needed funds, but only about one-fourth of the requested sum was honored, and the debts could not be paid. Faith in the government declined.

Each of the states had war debts of its own to meet, and some of them also needed money to repair war damage. Those states therefore continued to print paper money, but their currencies also fell sharply in purchasing power, for there was no gold in state treasuries either. To restore credit, the states began imposing heavy taxes on their citizens; and some severely restricted the issue of new paper currency.

The Postwar Depression The postwar depression affected merchants in the cities first. At this time, however, about 90 percent of the population was farmers, and they were only gradually affected by hard times. During the war and for a few years after, farmers profited by selling their produce at very high prices to both the British and the American armies. But by 1785 the British army had been withdrawn and the American army disbanded, and the state legislatures began raising taxes. During the war debtors, who were usually farmers, could pay their creditors in easily available, devalued paper money. But now they were called upon to pay their debts and high taxes on a sharply reduced income.

Nonetheless, this depression was not as damaging as some modern historians have stated. Virginia farmers were soon selling more tobacco than before the war. By 1790 the export of American farm produce had doubled over its prewar level. During these postwar years the state legislatures granted many new charters of incorporation to build turnpikes, roads, canals, and banks—projects that would employ many workers—and to support manufacturers. Banks were paying handsome dividends to their investors. Cities were growing rapidly. In fact, the depression that followed the French and Indian War may well have been worse.

Trouble in Rhode Island Although we do not want to exaggerate the severity of the postwar depression, it was very serious for many people. Throughout the country, debtor farmers were begging their state governments for relief. They had three demands: the enactment of stay laws (which would give debtors a period of grace before they had to resume paying their loans) and tender laws (which would allow them to pay their debts in produce), and the issue of more paper money (which would devalue the currency and favor those with large debts).

In 1785 and 1786 seven state governments yielded to these demands. In South Carolina, New York, and Pennsylvania, where paper money was issued with care, the new currency held its value. In other states, however, devaluation soon set in. In Georgia, for example, state dollars lost 75 percent of their value in one year. In Rhode Island a new issue of paper money prompted a minor crisis. Creditors distrusted the new notes and refused to accept them. Finally, in a move to force acceptance of the new money, the Rhode Island assembly (which was controlled by debtor farmers) passed a law fining creditors for declining payment in paper dollars. In 1786 in a test case trying the constitutionality of the law, the Rhode Island Supreme Court refused to rule on the matter. The law was subsequently repealed.

Shays's Rebellion

During the Confederation period, political leaders in most states were nervous about signs of unrest anywhere in the nation. In 1786, when a group of Massachusetts farmers rose in protest, these leaders became apprehensive that the collapse of authority was at hand.

Hard times, tight money, and heavy taxes had sent many bankrupt Massachusetts farmers to debtors' prison and caused more to lose their land. The state legislature was controlled by wealthy merchants from the Atlantic Coast. Weary of fruitlessly

AN EPISODE FROM SHAYS'S REBELLION IN 1786.

Thomas Jefferson, from his perspective in Paris, looked upon this as only "a little rebellion." But George Washington, who feared mob violence, exclaimed, "What, gracious God, is man! That there should be such inconsistency and perfidiousness in his conduct? We are fast verging to anarchy and confusion!" When Massachusetts appealed to Congress to quell the rebellion, Congress was powerless to help. Washington's horror of the Massachusetts mob was equaled only by his disgust with Congress, which he described as "a half-starved, limping government, always moving upon crutches and tottering at every step." This sort of reaction might have been expected from the conservative Washington, but the pervasiveness of this feeling is revealed by the fact that even that reliable radical, Samuel Adams, insisted bitterly that "the man who dares to rebel against the laws of the republic ought to suffer death."

petitioning an unresponsive legislature to pass stay laws and issue paper money, about a thousand farmers in the western part of the state rebelled. They were led in a haphazard way by Captain Daniel Shays, a veteran of the Revolutionary War. Shays's ragged forces shut down the civil courts where hundreds of mortgage foreclosure cases were scheduled to be heard. When the rebels menaced federal arsenals, state troops put down the disturbances. By the end of February 1787, Captain Shays had fled the state and his "army" had vanished.

Many Americans believed that the time had come to grant their central government more power. American representatives were being insulted in foreign capitals; American exporters were suffering from foreign competition and British restrictions on trade; and American settlers west of the Appalachians were threatened by the British, the Spanish, and the Indians. Finally, in 1786 the country was still suffering from a persistent economic depression and Congress was powerless to take action. Although many Americans were still fearful of a more powerful central authority, those leaders who wanted a stronger central government were more active in the pursuit of their objective and more confident that the opportunity to achieve it was now at hand.

Readings

General Works

Alden, John R., *The American Revolution, 1775–1783*. New York: Harper & Row, 1954.

Burnett, Edmund C., *The Continental Congress*. New York: Macmillan, 1941 (Paper: Norton, 1964).

Calhoon, Robert M., *Revolutionary America: An Interpretive Overview*. New York: Harcourt Brace Jovanovich, 1976.

Davis, David B., *The Problem of Slavery in an Age of Revolution, 1770–1823*. Ithaca, N.Y.: Cornell University Press, 1975.

Douglas, Elisha P., *Rebels and Democrats*. Chapel Hill: University of North Carolina Press, 1955.

Henderson, H. James, *Party Politics in the Continental Congress*. New York: McGraw-Hill, 1974.

Higginbotham, Don, *The War of American Independence*. Bloomington: Indiana University Press, 1971.

Jensen, Merrill, *The Articles of Confederation: An Interpretation of the Social-Constitutional History of the American Revolution, 1774–1781*. Madison: University of Wisconsin Press, 1940.

_____, *The New Nation*. New York: Knopf, 1950.

Main, Jackson T., *The Sovereign States, 1775–1783*. New York: Franklin Watts 1973. (Paper)

Morris, Richard B., *The American Revolution Reconsidered*. New York: Harper & Row, 1967.

Nagel, Paul C., *One Nation Indivisible: The Union in American Thought, 1776–1861*. New York: Oxford University Press, 1964.

Nash, Gary B., *The Urban Crucible. Social Change, Political Consciousness, and the Origins of the American Revolution*. Cambridge, Mass.: Harvard University Press, 1979.

Nettels, Curtis P., *The Emergence of a National Economy, 1775–1815*. New York: Holt, Rinehart & Winston, 1969.

Nye, Russel B., *The Cultural Life of the New Nation, 1776–1830*. New York: Harper & Row, 1960.

Peckham, Howard H., *The War for Independence. A Military History*. Chicago: University of Chicago Press, 1958.

Shy, John A., *A People Numerous and Armed: Reflections on the Military Struggle for American Independence*. New York: Oxford University Press, 1976.

White, Morton, *The Philosophy of the American Revolution*. New York: Oxford University Press, 1978.

Wood, Gordon S., *Creation of the American Republic, 1776–1787*. Chapel Hill: University of North Carolina Press, 1969.

Special Studies

Bemis, Samuel F., *The Diplomacy of the American Revolution (Foundations of American Diplomacy, 1775–1823)*. New York: Appleton-Century-Crofts, 1935 (Paper: Indiana University Press, 1957).

Calhoon, Robert M., *The Loyalists in Revolutionary America, 1760–1781*. New York: Harcourt Brace Jovanovich, 1973.

DePauw, Linda Grant, and Conover Hunt, *"Remember the Ladies": Women in America 1750–1815*. New York: Viking Press, 1976.

Jameson, J. Franklin, *The American Revolution Considered as a Social Movement*. Princeton, N.J.: Princeton University Press, 1926 (Paper, 1967).

MacLeod, Duncan J., *Slavery, Race, and the American Revolution*. New York: Cambridge University Press, 1974.

Main, Jackson T., *The Antifederalists: Critics of the Constitution: 1781–1788*. Chapel Hill: University of North Carolina Press, 1970.

Morris, R. B., *Peacemakers: The Great Powers and American Independence*. New York: Harper & Row. (Paper)

Nelson, William H., *The American Tory*. New York: Oxford University Press, 1962 (Paper: Beacon Press, 1964).

Starkey, Marion L., *A Little Rebellion*. New York: Knopf, 1955.

Zilversmit, Arthur, *The First Emancipation: The Abolition of Slavery in the North*. Chicago: University of Chicago Press, 1967.

Primary Sources

de Crèvecoeur, J. Hector, *Letters from an American Farmer*. New York: Dutton, 1969.

Kenyon, Cecelia M. (Ed.), *Antifederalists*. New York: Bobbs-Merrill, 1966. (Paper)

Biographies

Brant, Irving, *James Madison: Father of the Constitution, 1787–1800*, Vol. II. Indianapolis: Bobbs-Merrill, 1950.

Flexner, James T., *George Washington in the American Revolution, 1775–1783*. Boston: Little, Brown, 1968.

Mitchell, Broadus, *Alexander Hamilton*, Vol. II. New York: Macmillan, 1957.

Tyler, Moses C., *Patrick Henry*. Ithaca, N.Y.: Cornell University Press, 1962.

Historical Novels

Bellamy, Edward, *The Duke of Stockbridge: A Romance of Shays' Rebellion*. Cambridge, Mass.: Harvard University Press, 1962.

Boyd, James, *Drums*. New York: Scribner's, 1968.

Brown, Charles B., *Ormond*, Ernest Marchand (Ed.). Darien, Conn.: Hafner, 1969.

Cooper, James Fenimore, *The Spy*. New York: Oxford University Press, 1968.

Edmonds, Walter D., *Drums Along the Mohawk*. Boston: Atlantic Monthly Press–Little, Brown, 1969.

Lancaster, Bruce, *Guns of Burgoyne*. New York: Stokes, 1939.

Simms, W. Gilmore, *The Partisan: A Romance of the Revolution*. New York: AMS Press, 1969.

Written with a Sunbeam

WOMEN IN THE AMERICAN REVOLUTION

Yes, I am a rebel!
My brothers are rebels!
And our dog Trip
is a rebel, too!

With these words, Isabella Ferguson of South Carolina summed up the sentiments of colonial women who had chosen to stand against the British in the American Revolution.

Everywhere throughout the colonies, women were "making the revolution" in the 1770s. As consumers, women helped to make successful the boycott of tea, spices, fabrics, and other British imports. As spies, women traveled across British lines to warn American troops of impending attack.

As soldiers, women took up arms and contributed to American political victories. As writers, women produced political satire, debated forms of government, and reported on the growing revolution. As fundraisers, munitions manufacturers, farmers, tavern-keepers, seamstresses, doctors, morticians, and publishers, women paid the bills, made the bullets, grew the food, housed the troops, sewed the uniforms, ran the hospitals, buried the dead, and kept the presses rolling.

Who were these Founding Mothers and where is their history to be found?

Elizabeth Ellet set out to answer these questions half a century after the Revolution. Her three-volume work,

A BRITISH CARTOON SATIRIZING AMERICAN WOMEN'S SUPPORT OF THE REVOLUTIONARY EFFORT. PUBLISHED IN 1775.

Women of the American Revolution, was first published in 1850 and has become the classic work of the period. Her thoughts on the role of women in the Revolution were capsulized in her introduction:

It is almost impossible now to appreciate the vast influence of woman's patriotism upon the destinies of the infant republic . . . History can do it no justice; for history deals with the workings of the head, rather than the heart.

Yet a considerable history of women revolutionaries has survived in addition to Ellet's work. This body of knowledge is contained primarily in the private writings of women who took part in the struggle. In particular, the work of two women has been preserved almost in its entirety, while fragments of other women's lives have been retained both on paper and by oral tradition. The recent growth of interest in the history of American women is bringing this information to the attention of historians.

Despite the fact that formal education was not available to women and that they were not allowed to vote or hold office, two Massachusetts women distinguished themselves as political thinkers: Abigail Smith Adams, who took the penname of Portia, and Mercy Otis Warren, who was known to her correspondents as Philomela, and to her biographer as the First Lady of the Revolution.

Reared under similar circumstances, the two women became friends at an early age. Their friendship spanned many years, as both lived into their eighties. Their thoughtful correspondence in which each developed her own political ideas is one of the origins of the Revolutionary Committees of Correspondence.

As the twentieth-century historian Mary Sumner Benson points out in her study, *Women in Eighteenth Century America,* Abigail Adams was a person of considerable political foresight. By late 1773 she was predicting that civil war within the British Empire would be the likely outcome of the colonists' protests. Two years later she was urging separation from England and had begun to develop her ideas regarding the form of the new government.

On March 31, 1776, "Portia" wrote the letter which distinguished her as America's first suffragist, indirectly seeking the vote for her sex. She implored her husband to:

Remember the Ladies, and be more generous and favourable to them than your ancestors. Do not put such unlimited power into the hands of the Husbands. Remember all Men would be tyrants if they could. If particular care and attention is not paid to the Laidies we are determined to foment a Rebelion, and will not hold ourselves bound by any laws in which we have no voice, or Representation.

Traditionally, history fails to mention Abigail Adams's political contributions but does record her for one other distinction. She was the only woman in American history to have been both wife and mother to American presidents. John Adams, who followed Washington to the presidency, was her husband; John Quincy Adams, the nation's sixth president, was her son.

While the Adams family's place in history has been secured, Mercy Otis Warren's clan has often been ignored. However, both the Otises and the Warrens were leaders in fighting the Revolution and in forming the new government. Mercy Otis Warren herself occupied a unique role as the Revolution's foremost political satirist, dramatist, and (later) historian.

Though her plays were never performed, her reputation spread rapidly and her works were widely published. Her first play about the British appeared in the March 1772 issue of the magazine the *Massachusetts Spy.*

As the Revolution progressed, "Philomela's" work became bolder in language. Her caricatures of the Tories became increasingly transparent. In 1775 she published *The Group,* which became her most popular work, probably because its characters were immediately recognizable to the audience of the day. The members of the British government were portrayed as Brigadier Hate-All, Hum Humbug, and Crusty Crowbar.

After the new government came into being under the Constitution, Mercy Otis Warren turned to prose. Now she used her pen to attack the Federalists and to express her staunch opposition to a strong centralized government. In her opinion, such a government encouraged its officials to act like royalty. Her strong commitment to this belief caused a severe rift in her friendship with the Adamses, who were now among the leading Federalists. It was not until many years later that their friendship was renewed.

In her later years, Mercy Otis Warren completed her most significant but little recognized work, the three-part *History of the Rise, Progress and Termination of the American Revolution.* If publication had not been delayed due to the unpopularity of her political beliefs, this work would have been the first complete history of the American struggle.

Other women wore the mantle of soldier, an aspect of revolutionary activity which was almost exclusively reserved for men. Deborah Samson, a young schoolteacher from Massachusetts, outfitted herself in men's clothing, and at the age of nineteen, enlisted in the Army under the assumed name of Robert Shurtliffe. Her disguise was

MERCY WARREN.

ABIGAIL ADAMS.

so successful that she managed to serve for three years without being discovered and even spent time at West Point. Eventually a severe attack of fever forced her to see a doctor while on duty in Philadelphia. He discovered that Robert was in fact Deborah and, with her knowledge, wrote a letter to her commanding officer at West Point who gave her an honorable discharge at the age of twenty-three.

More typical was the case of Mary Ludwig Hays who, like many women, lived with her soldier-husband in camp. During the intense June heat of the Battle of Monmouth, she hauled water to the weary men who called out as she approached, "Here comes Molly with her pitcher." As the day wore on, the chant was shortened to "Molly Pitcher," and so she was known for the rest of her life.

But hauling water was not her only contribution to the battle. When her husband fell stricken at his gun, she took his place behind his cannon and fired round after round. Some historians have written that on the following day Washington commissioned her as a sergeant.

The most celebrated military heroine of all was the legendary Nancy Morgan Hart. In what may have been one of the most incredible feats of the struggle, she single-handedly captured five Tories who had come to her house demanding a meal. Thinking quickly, she got them drunk, then grabbed one of their rifles and killed one, wounded another, and trained the gun on the rest while her daughter went to get additional help.

Yet another group of women provided intelligence to American troops at critical moments. Lydia Darrah, a Philadelphia Quaker, overheard the plans of British officers who were staying at her house to attack at Whitemarsh the following morning. Later that night, she slipped out, crossed through British lines, and warned the American troops. When the British arrived the next morning, the rebel army was ready and waiting.

At the age of twenty-two, Deborah Champion rode from New London, Connecticut, to Boston, Massachusetts, with an urgent message for Washington. According to a letter which she wrote to a friend describing the adventure, she was stopped only once by the British who quickly released her, saying, "Well, you are only an old woman anyway."

Jane Thomas, an accomplished horsewoman from the South, undertook a similar journey, riding sixty miles to warn the Americans at Cedar Springs, South Carolina, of a planned British attack.

Still other women labored at equally important though rarely mentioned work. Two Rhode Island women, Dorcas Matteson and Anne Aldrich, reportedly "labored in fields, making hay, harvesting corn, hoeing potatoes and in many other ways doing the work of their absent husbands."

Like many other women who chose to contribute their wealth to the cause, Mary Draper of Dedham, Massachusetts, melted down her pewter heirlooms and made them into bullets. According to Mary Beard's history, *America Through Women's Eyes:*

Colonial women could fire guns and make munitions. "Handy Betsy the Blacksmith" was the peer of the most skilled in her work on cannon and other arms. Mrs. Proctor of Salem, who owned a tool factory at the opening of the war, was a boon to Joseph Swain placed in charge of collecting a rebel arsenal.

Esther Reed formed the Philadelphia Relief Association to raise funds for the army in 1780. Elizabeth Peck Perkins, a Boston businesswoman, subscribed $1000 to this effort.

Not that all the women involved in the Revolution were very wealthy. Other women, concerned with simply feeding and clothing their families, reacted spontaneously to injustices which affected their everyday lives.

While much has been written of the Boston Tea Party, little has been said of what might be called the Boston Coffee Party. As reported by Abigail Adams, on July 31, 1777, a group of 100 women took matters into their own hands when a Tory merchant refused to sell them coffee at a reasonable price:

. . . one of them [the women] seized him by his neck and tossed him into the cart. Upon his finding no quarter, he delivered the keys, when they tipped up the cart and discharged him, then opened the warehouse, hoisted out the coffee themselves, put into the trucks and drove off . . . A large concourse of men stood amazed, silent spectators of the whole transaction . . .

Even more women contributed to the revolutionary effort in ways which history has not recorded. Their names may be anonymous but their thoughts have often survived, as in the letter of this, now nameless, Philadelphia woman. She, as much as anyone, summarized the revolutionary spirit of the American woman:

. . . I know this—that as free I can die but once, but as a slave I shall not be worthy of life. I have the pleasure to assure you that these are the sentiments of all my sister Americans. They have sacrificed assemblies, parties of pleasure, tea drinking and finery, to that great spirit of patriotism that actuates all degrees of people throughout this extensive continent . . . You say you are no politician. Oh sir, it requires no Machiavellian head to discover this tyranny and oppression. It is written with a sunbeam.

6 Founding a New Government

[James Wilson] contended strenuously for drawing the most numerous branch of the Legislature immediately from the people. He was for raising the federal pyramid to a considerable altitude, and for that reason wished to give it as broad a basis as possible. No government could long subsist without the confidence of the people. In a republican Government this confidence was peculiarly essential. He also thought it wrong to increase the weight of the State Legislatures by making them the electors of the national Legislature. All interference between the general and local Governments should be obviated as much as possible. On examination it would be found that the opposition of States to federal measures had proceeded much more from the Officers of the States, than from the people at large.

The Records of the Federal Convention of 1787

Significant Events

Constitutional Convention [May 25, 1787–September 17, 1787]

Ratification of Constitution (eleven states ratified) [December 1787–July 1788]

Judiciary Act [1789]

Bill of Rights [1791]

First Bank of the United States [1791]

French Revolution begins [1789]

United States Neutrality Proclamation [1793]

Genêt mission [1793]

Jay's treaty [1794]

Whiskey Rebellion [1794]

Pinckney's treaty [1795]

XYZ affair [1797–1798]

Alien and Sedition Acts [1798]

Virginia and Kentucky Resolutions [1798–1799]

Convention of 1800 with France [1800]

AMOS DOOLITTLE'S ENGRAVING SHOWS GEORGE WASHINGTON AND JOHN ADAMS BEING INAUGURATED ON THE BALCONY OF FEDERAL HALL IN NEW YORK CITY.

As we saw in the preceding chapter, the American states had succeeded on the battlefield, but they had not succeeded in forming a national government that was strong enough to administer the country. This condition was a matter of concern to an increasing number of Americans. Some believed that the unrest evidenced by Shays's Rebellion was a preface to further violence and social upheaval in defiance of government authority. A persistent economic depression—that the national government seemed powerless to alleviate—served to heighten this unrest. Many Americans were coming to believe that their security could perhaps be threatened as much by a weak central government as by a strong one. Increasingly, Americans began to seek ways in which they could strengthen their national government without diminishing individual rights and opportunities. The state legislatures also were becoming a matter of concern. Many of them were dominated by men lacking previous political experience. Many influential leaders believed that these legislators were paying too little attention to the needs of the community as a whole and too much attention to special-interest groups. Moreover, many thought that the state legislatures were abusing their power by taking over executive and judi-cial functions. Advocates of a strong federal government insisted that the excesses and factionalism of the state governments be curbed.

It was becoming increasingly obvious to people who were politically experienced that an extensive governmental reorganization was overdue. The crux of the problem was the division of power between the national and state governments. A balance had to be struck between national and local power and between governmental authority and individual freedom.

In 1786 representatives from five states gathered in Annapolis, Maryland, to discuss commercial problems that were affecting the entire country. This convention brought together two staunch nationalists: James Madison of Virginia and Alexander Hamilton of New York. Together they succeeded in convincing the state governments and the Confederation Congress to endorse a national meeting of delegates from all the states. The purpose of the proposed convention would be to consider how to revise the Articles of Confederation; as Madison put it, "to render the Constitution of the Federal government adequate to the exigencies of the Union."

The Constitutional Convention

The Constitutional Convention was held in Philadelphia. During the four months between May 25 and September 17, 1787, a new constitution was created.

Of the fifty-five delegates who attended, most were well-to-do, literate, and politically experienced gentlemen. Many were college-educated, in an era when attending a university was unusual even for the wealthy. Law was the most common profession among them, and only one, William Few of Georgia, represented the average farmer. Although the average age was forty-two, five representatives were in their twenties, and many more were in their early thirties. Benjamin Franklin, at eighty-one, was by far the oldest member. Many delegates had been active in the Revolution, and over half had attended the Continental Congress and held important political positions in their states.

Four of these "Founding Fathers" had already achieved widespread recognition. The revered George Washington, highly respected as a man of wisdom and judgment, was elected president of the convention. James Madison had been working for years to strengthen the federal government; Alexander Hamilton was the group's most ardent advocate of a strong centralized government; and Benjamin Franklin was regarded as the sage of the convention.

Despite disagreements on specific issues, the delegates shared a number of basic ideas. The product of five generations of self-government, they were influenced by the Enlightenment philosophy which held that people could govern themselves if they could devise a workable balance of power. The majority of the delegates agreed that the Articles of Confederation should either be strengthened or

GEORGE WASHINGTON ADDRESSING THE CONSTITUTIONAL CONVENTION BY J. B. STEARNS.

scrapped and that a new government should be created which would have its own source of income as well as control over foreign affairs and commerce. Their goal was to create a central government strong enough to curb private interests yet protective of local autonomy and individual rights. The new government should consist of three branches—executive, legislative, and judicial—to prevent a concentration of power in the hands of one person or one group. The delegates further agreed that the states should retain some of their powers and that the central government should be directly responsible to each citizen. Whenever possible, government officeholders would be elected by popular vote to ensure that the strength of the central government would not undermine the liberty of the people.

Although the convention originally had been called to revise the existing Articles of Confederation, on May 30, urged by the Virginia delegation, the members voted to forge an entirely new constitution instead. They quickly agreed that the new government should have additional powers, includ-

ing the right to levy taxes, to regulate interstate and foreign commerce, and to raise and maintain an army and a navy. At the same time, they deprived the states of the right to coin money, make treaties, or tax imports and exports without the consent of Congress.

Although these were major issues they aroused little debate. There were some other questions, however, that led to weeks of controversy and nearly destroyed the Constitutional Convention.

Controversy and Compromise

Trouble appeared as early as the third day of the convention. Edmund Randolph presented a plan—mainly the work of James Madison—that was designed to solve the problem of representation. Instead, it almost deadlocked the convention. This "Virginia Plan" called for a national government composed of three branches—legislative, executive, and judicial—each of which would check and balance the others. The application of the principle of separation of powers did much to dispel public fear of a strengthened national government. The presently existing unicameral legislature was to be replaced by a bicameral legislature, similar to those in many of the states. The legislative branch was to be the most important arm of the government, for it would elect both the executive and the judicial departments. The legislature would consist of a lower house elected by the people and an upper house chosen by the lower house. Seats in both houses would be distributed according to each state's population.

The smaller, less populous states immediately protested this method of apportioning representatives. These states generally had no western land holdings, and thus had no room to expand. They were afraid that states with unsettled land would grow in population and eventually surpass them in representation. They therefore banded together to present an alternative plan which was introduced by William Paterson of New Jersey. This "New Jersey Plan" differed from the Virginia Plan in two basic ways. First, it essentially called for a continuation of the form of government that existed under the Confederation: a Congress consisting of one house in which each state, regardless of size, would have one vote. Second, in order to maintain the sovereignty of the states, the representatives to this new Congress would be elected by the state legislatures rather than directly by the people. In addition, the New Jersey Plan offered three specific changes in the way the government would operate: Congress would have the power to tax and to regulate trade, and the government would have an executive branch with authority placed in several individuals chosen by the Congress (a concept similar to a proposal in the Virginia Plan).

In early July, realizing that the convention was at an impasse, Benjamin Franklin arranged for the appointment of a committee to review the question of representation. Three days later it presented a plan, devised earlier by John Dickinson, which has come to be known as the Great Compromise. The Congress would be made up of two houses. In the lower house (the House of Representatives) the states would be represented according to population. In the upper house (the Senate) each state would have two representatives, regardless of its size. The compromise worked: the smaller states and the states without western land holdings—Con-

necticut, New Jersey, Delaware, Maryland, and North Carolina—were finally ready to accept a strong federal government because the protection of their interests had been ensured. Nevertheless, despite the provision for proportional representation in the lower house, nationalists in the large states still were not satisfied. Pennsylvania, Virginia, South Carolina, and Georgia, fearing that representation in the Senate by states might undermine recognition of the national authority of Congress, voted against the compromise. But the Massachusetts delegation split its vote, and the compromise just passed, five votes to four. The way was now paved for discarding the Articles of Confederation and creating a federal government with real power to act.

Now a new question arose. If representation in the lower house of Congress was to be determined by population, and if each state's share of direct federal taxes was to be figured on the basis of population, then who would be counted? Southerners wanted slaves to be counted as part of their population (although they had no intention of allowing them to vote). Northerners agreed, provided that slaves also be considered when computing each state's federal tax bill. Southerners objected to this stipulation. Once again Franklin's committee worked out a compromise: three-fifths of the slaves would be counted as both property and as human beings.

The North and South were also divided on the issue of federal regulation of commerce. The North, which derived much of its income from commerce, wanted the federal government to have the authority to make protective commercial regulations and to impose a low tariff on imports as a source of revenue. The South, on the other hand, which profited by exporting staple produce, such as tobacco and rice, feared that a government with the power to regulate commerce might legislate high export duties on such goods. The South therefore insisted that all acts regulating commerce be passed by a two-thirds majority in Congress. In addition, the South demanded assurance that Congress would not interfere with the slave trade.

Many of the Founders had mixed feelings about working to create a new nation based on freedom for white people and slavery for most blacks. But because of the firmness of their opposing views regarding the use of slave labor, the delegates again sought a compromise in order to resolve their differences. The North made several concessions: the Constitution provided that the government would never levy export taxes, that the slave trade could continue for twenty more years, and that the states would return fugitive slaves to their owners. In return, the South agreed that Congress could pass acts regulating commerce by a simple majority vote.

The New Constitution

On September 17, 1787, thirty-nine of the fifty-five delegates signed the new Constitution. It incorporated many aspects of the various state constitutions and the Virginia and New Jersey plans and introduced a few new provisions as well. The construction of the Constitution was based on the principle of the separation of powers (ensuring that the three branches would each have distinct powers and would remain independent of the others) and the system of checks and balances.

The most significant innovation was the provision for an executive, the president, with the authority to veto congressional legislation, negotiate treaties with foreign nations, appoint a number of government officials, and act as commander in chief of the army and navy. Although this office was to be a powerful one, almost all of its powers would be limited to some extent by the legislature. For example, the president's veto could be overridden by a two-thirds majority of both houses of Congress, and treaties required the approval of two-thirds of the Senate. In addition, although the president would be commander of the armed forces, only Congress could appropriate military funds and only Congress could declare war. Congress could also try the chief executive for "Treason, Bribery, or other high Crimes and Misdemeanors."

While the Constitution created a much stronger national government, it brought this new government closer to the citizenry. Voters would directly elect members to the House of Representatives, and the popularly elected legislature of each state would select its two senators. Voters would participate indirectly in the selection of the president.

Most of the delegates feared that selecting the president by popular vote might tend to result in the election of demagogues primarily concerned with pleasing crowds. Nevertheless, because nationalists wanted a strong executive, they did not want the president to have to depend on the legislature for election. As a compromise, the electoral college was devised. Each state would have as many delegates to the electoral college as it had representatives and senators in Congress. The method of choosing the electors was left up to the individual state legislatures. For example, they could be popularly elected or they could be chosen by the state legislature itself. Each elector would cast votes for two people. The candidate with the most votes would be president; the one with the second largest number of votes would be vice-president. If no two individuals received a clear majority, the election would be determined by the House of Representatives.

The specific powers given to the legislative branch of the federal government and those forbidden to the states were listed in Article I of the Constitution. They included the power to tax, to regulate interstate and foreign commerce, to coin and borrow money, to establish post offices, to raise an army and navy, and to declare war. Powers not delegated to the national government were to remain with the states. While the states had less authority to regulate commerce and could neither coin money nor impair valid contracts, they were not forbidden to levy some taxes, to maintain a police force, to establish educational policy, or to regulate working conditions.

The Constitution also provided for a federal judiciary and a procedure for implementing federal laws. Article III established a Supreme Court and stated that Congress could create "such inferior courts" as it desired. The judicial power of the United States was to cover all cases relating to the Constitution and all laws and treaties made under its authority. Article VI defined federal law as "the supreme law of the land" and required that state courts be responsible for its enforcement.

Since the Constitution was the work of many minds, the final document necessarily contained compromises and provisions which could be interpreted in various ways. Of course, no member of the convention was completely satisfied with it, yet most probably agreed with Benjamin Franklin when he said to Washington: "I consent, Sir, to this Constitution, because I expect no better, and because I am not sure that it is not the best. The opinions I have had of its errors, I sacrifice to the public good."

Ratification

The next step in the formation of the new government was ratification of the Constitution. It took months of public debate before, as it proclaimed itself, the new document became "the supreme Law of the Land."

The framers of the Constitution were realistic enough to expect opposition and did what they could to simplify the ratification process. The delegates defined ratification as approval by nine, rather than all, of the states. Rhode Island had not even sent a delegate to Philadelphia, and it was known that powerful forces in some states opposed a strong central government. The convention provided insurance against opposition from these quarters.

Because the Constitution reduced the power of the states—and therefore that of the state legislatures as well—the state legislatures would have a vested interest in its defeat. Foreseeing this, the Founders provided for approval of the Constitution not by the state legislatures, but by popularly elected conventions in every state. The Founders believed that these state ratifying conventions, chosen directly by the people, would be more likely to react favorably. Moreover, popular ratification would authenticate the Constitution's opening words: "We the people of the United States. . . ."

Federalists and Anti-Federalists

Those who championed the new Constitution called themselves "Federalists," and those who opposed the document were labeled "Anti-Federalists." Although many Federalists were wealthy and well-

TO CELEBRATE THE RATIFICATION OF THE CONSTITUTION, NEW YORKERS HELD A PARADE AND BANQUET ATTENDED BY SOME SIX THOUSAND PEOPLE. THE FLOAT PICTURED HERE HONORS ALEXANDER HAMILTON, WHO PLAYED A KEY ROLE IN OBTAINING THE STATE'S RATIFICATION. AS THE "SHIP" PASSED WASHINGTON AND HIS CABINET, IT FIRED A THIRTEEN-GUN SALUTE.

educated and many Anti-Federalists were yeoman farmers, no clear-cut geographic or economic differences can fully account for their division over ratification. In order to understand why people took different positions on the ratification issue, one must also take into consideration the economic differences between the small and large states. Support for the Constitution was strongest in the small states, which favored the provision giving them as much influence in the upper house as the larger states had. They recognized that a strong federal government could protect them from competition with the larger states. Several of the large states, on the other hand, felt they did not need either the economic support or the political protection that a strong federal government could offer.

In addition, many citizens still felt that their first loyalty was to their state government and feared that the new system would threaten the autonomy of the states. Anti-Federalists raised an outcry over the broad powers which the new Constitution gave to the federal government and seized on the document's lack of a bill of rights as clear proof that the new federal government could become tyrannical. The authority given to the executive might, some Anti-Federalists argued, enable the president to assume the powers of a king.

Under the new Constitution, both the federal government and the states would have the right to tax. Anti-Federalists, worried that the poor would be bled dry by tax collectors, claimed that the Constitution was the handiwork of the nation's wealthy, who simply hungered for personal power. As a Massachusetts farmer put it:

These lawyers, and men of learning, and moneyed men . . . expect to get into Congress themselves; they expect to be managers of this Constitution, and get the power and all the money into their own hands, and then they will swallow up all of us little folks. . . .

The Anti-Federalists also raised the old argument that a republican government could not rule a country as large as the United States. Congress would sit in a distant city, and gradually lose touch with the interests of its many constituents. So many special-interest groups would clamor for legislation favorable to themselves that the actions of Congress would please no one.

In answer to this, the Federalists stressed that the Constitution was based on a key principle which emerged from the Revolution—the sovereignty of the people. The power of the national government was not derived from the states but, like the power of the state governments themselves, was derived from the popular will. From this viewpoint, the large size of a country was a positive, not a negative factor. The people in any nation were made up of various interest groups, and in a large country it would be more difficult for them to unite and seriously threaten the well-being of the nation as a whole. The national government would speak for the best interests of the entire citizenry.

The State Conventions

In popular elections of delegates to state ratifying conventions, the Federalists had the advantage. Nearly everyone agreed that the Articles of Confederation needed some revision. The Federalists had a positive program, and it was well known that both Washington and Franklin favored ratification.

Although the Anti-Federalists mounted a strong attack against the Constitution, they had no common program and often did not even know one another. People living in the remotest areas were likely to see no need for a strong central government, but they were also likely to have a difficult time getting to a polling place. Three-quarters of those who were eligible to vote failed to do so, and those who did tended to favor the Constitution.

The Federalists believed they could count on strong support from the small states and from the Southern states, which had been wooed by several compromises. They were also aware that if any one of the large states—Massachusetts, Pennsylvania, New York, and Virginia—failed to ratify, the new government might not survive.

Concerned about the circulation of printed attacks on the Constitution, Hamilton, Madison, and Jay collaborated in writing an influential series of articles supporting the document. These articles were collected as The Federalist and were published in the New York press between October 1787 and July 1788. Considered impressive political literature, they stressed both the limitations on governmental authority that were woven into the fabric of the Constitution and the importance of the powers granted to the new government in order to make it strong at home and respected abroad.

In general, the first states to ratify were those whose experience as independent states had been the least successful. The small state of Delaware ratified first, voting unanimously for the Constitution on December 7, 1787. By June 21, 1788, Pennsylvania, New Jersey, Georgia, Connecticut, Massachusetts, Maryland, South Carolina, and New Hampshire had followed, in some cases after strenuous debate and by a narrow margin. Although the nine-state adoption requirement had been met, there was still concern about the two remaining large states, Virginia and New York. The majority in these crucial states felt that because they were economically self-sufficient, they did not need a federal government to protect their interests, and many of their delegates feared a powerful federal government.

Washington wrote that in Virginia the Anti-Federalists were using "every art that could inflame the passions or touch the interest of men." Patrick Henry, ardently loyal to Virginia, seized on the opening words of the Constitution as proof that it would undermine the states: "The question turns, sir, on that poor little thing—the expression, We the *people*, instead of the *states*, of America." Henry played on the deepest fears of the Anti-Federalists, declaring that: "Your President may easily become your king. Your Senate is so imperfectly constructed that your dearest rights may be sacrificed by what may be a small minority; and a very small minority may continue forever unchangeably this govern-

INTERPRETING AMERICAN HISTORY

THE FOUNDERS Throughout the nineteenth century American historians generally viewed the Founders as enlightened visionaries struggling against lesser-minded folk who had no comprehension of the nation's future destiny. In 1913, historian Charles Beard published *An Economic Interpretation of the Constitution of the United States* in which he claimed that the Constitution was "an economic document drawn with superb skill by men whose property interests were immediately at stake." Beard had found that most of the Founders held United States public securities and therefore stood to gain if the national credit were strengthened. He interpreted this to mean not that the Founders had worked cynically to further their own interests, but that their attitudes had been shaped by their economic concerns. Nevertheless, more than any other historian, Beard succeeded in demoting the Philadelphia delegates from their status as "demigods" (Jefferson's own word for them).

By the 1950s, after decades of acceptance, Beard's thesis came under attack. In *Charles Beard and the Constitution* (1956), Robert E. Brown criticized virtually every important statement in Beard's work. "There was absolutely no correlation between the delegates' property holdings and the way they behaved on the question of a constitution. Farmers as a class were by no means chronically debtors; many were creditors and many others were both. The supporters of Shays's Rebellion . . . were certainly not united against the Constitution."

Forrest McDonald's *We the People* (1958) was a major attempt to disprove Beard's analysis of the differences between Federalists and Anti-Federalists. McDonald claimed that there was no political difference between landed wealth (supposedly Anti-Federalist) and monied wealth (supposedly Federalist). He maintained that an individual's position on national issues was determined not by the intercolonial property interests that Beard thought were so compelling but by specific economic interests in specific places. "The states where ratification was achieved most readily were those that were convinced, for one reason or another, that they could not survive and prosper as independent entities; those holding out the longest were the ones most convinced that they could go it alone."

Jackson Turner Main, in *The Antifederalists: Critics of the Constitutions, 1781–1788* (1961) has shown, however, that Federalists as a group were wealthier than the Anti-Federalists. They tended to dominate the towns and rich agricultural areas in each state, and in some states they occupied slightly higher social positions than the Anti-Federalists.

ment, although horridly defective." The Anti-Federalists were suspicious of putting so much power into the hands of a few people. They felt it would be safer to leave the protection of liberty to the states, rather than entrusting it to a remote centralized authority.

Virginia finally ratified by a slim majority, after Governor Edmund Randolph dramatically switched his loyalties to the Constitution at the last minute, declaring: "I am a friend to the Union." Madison had assured him that a bill of rights would be enacted under the new government. Madison and Hamilton arranged for couriers to speed the news of Virginia's ratification to New York, where the Anti-Federalists had an overwhelming majority. New York was enjoying extraordinary prosperity,

and the state government's financial position was particularly strong. As a result, an upstate faction, led by Governor Clinton, opposed ratification, believing that New York State could continue to prosper without the help of a strong central government.

Some members of the New York ratification convention were probably influenced by the arguments for ratification presented in *The Federalist* essays. Others were probably swayed more by the news that nine states, and now Virginia, had ratified. In addition, the delegates from New York City, who favored ratification, vowed to take the city into the Union on its own if the convention did not ratify the document. In July 1788 New York adopted the Constitution by a narrow margin.

If there was a correlation between the Founders' interest in a strong government and their ownership of property, this may have been more a reflection of their interest in John Locke's Enlightenment philosophy than an indication of their own self-interest. According to Locke, one of the main purposes of government was the protection of property, and human freedom could be defined and measured only by the amount of protection afforded to private property by the government. The Founders went beyond Locke, for the security of property was only part of their larger dream. They envisioned a nation that offered and protected individual and political liberty as well as economic opportunity. If a stronger central government could achieve this, many Founders believed, the republic would fulfill its great destiny.

If the Founders were not moved primarily by personal eocnomic considerations, were they then acting from purely idealistic motives? Stanley Elkins and Eric McKitrick, in "The Founding Fathers: The Young Men of the Revolution" (*Political Science Quarterly* LXXVI, June 1961), examined the nine leading Federalists and nine leading Anti-Federalists and came up with some observations that throw a different light on the possible motivations of these men.

The Federalist leaders were ten to twelve years younger, on the average, than the Anti-Federalists. Most of the Federalists saw their careers

launched by the Revolution. In fact, the political futures of these younger men came to depend on the national activity. They viewed any effort to limit the scope of national concerns as a powerful personal challenge.

On the other hand, the careers of the Anti-Federalists were state-centered and rested on events preceding 1776. They apparently found it difficult to think in national terms. According to Cecelia M. Kenyon in "Men of Little Faith: The Antifederalists on the Nature of Representative Government," *William and Mary Quarterly*, 3rd Ser. XII (January 1955), "Their minds could not embrace the concept of a national interest which they themselves might share and which could transcend their own parochial concerns. Republican government that went beyond the compass of state boundaries was something they could not imagine."

In his influential book *The Creation of the American Republic, 1776–1787* (1970) Gordon S. Wood concluded that while the Constitution was a document designed to check the excessive disorder and factionalism of democratic rule, it also provided for a strong national government that rested at every point on popular support. The concept of the sovereignty of the people would prevent a strong national government from undermining individual freedom.

The two remaining states entered the Union after the new government was already in operation. North Carolina held out until November 1789. Rhode Island finally ratified in May 1790, after Congress threatened to deal with the state as a foreign power.

The New Government

Early in 1789 the states began choosing their representatives to the new Congress, which was to convene on March 4, 1789, in New York's City Hall. But travel was difficult, and another month passed before both houses had quorums. A congressman from Boston moaned: "The people will forget the new government before it is born." When the electoral college ballots were finally counted, no one was surprised at the results: Washington, who had run unopposed, was unanimously elected president. John Adams was elected vice-president.

Washington, hesitant to risk his reputation on an uncertain venture, had been considering his nomination for the past year and stated, "it brought a kind of gloom upon my mind." Eventually his concern for the welfare of his country won out, and he made a triumphal journey from his Virginia plantation, Mount Vernon, to New York City. Everywhere parades and cheering crowds greeted the revered "Father of His Country." Washington himself recognized that his new office carried awesome responsibilities. As he phrased it, "There is scarcely an action, the motive of which may not be subject to a double interpretation. There is scarcely any part of my conduct which may not hereafter be drawn into precedent."

It was the task of the first president and first Congress to establish a working government from a written document and to create a unified republic out of thirteen states with disparate and sometimes conflicting interests. From the first days of the Washington administration, there was contention over how these goals should be accomplished.

Washington as President

Stern, dignified, with a handshake like steel, Washington was a man of impeccable integrity who seemed to symbolize the aspirations of the new nation. He deliberated carefully before making any decision, and, aware that the Anti-Federalists feared that the president might become a tyrant, he took great care never to overstep his constitutional authority. For example, he took literally the stipulation that the president must make treaties with "the

WASHINGTON'S JOURNEY FROM MOUNT VERNON TO NEW YORK CITY, THE TEMPORARY CAPITAL, WAS MET BY REJOICING CITIZENS WHO FIRED CANNONS, RANG BELLS, AND STREWED FLOWERS ON THE ROADS. IN TRENTON, WHERE HIS ARMY HAD DEFEATED THE HESSIANS, HE RECEIVED A HERO'S WELCOME.

advice and consent" of the Senate. Once, when negotiations over an old boundary dispute between the Creek Indians and the state of Georgia were pending, he personally went to the Senate to ask for advice. Intimidated by Washington's presence and unprepared for his sudden request, the best the senators could do was suggest that the proposals be studied by a committee. Washington stood up angrily, exclaiming: "This defeats every purpose of my coming here," and left abruptly. The incident had several consequences. First, it became customary to seek Senate approval of treaties after, not before, they were negotiated. Second, a committee system began developing in the Senate, and last, the Senate had defined itself as a legislative body, not a council of state subordinate to the president.

Although Washington had no interest in being revered as a king, he continued to enjoy his aristocratic way of life at Mount Vernon. He traveled in a magnificent coach drawn by six cream-colored horses, and his mansion in Manhattan was staffed by twenty-one uniformed servants. His birthday was the most important event of the social season. Like the king of England in Parliament, Washington delivered his State of the Union speech to Congress personally and then insisted that the members of both houses attend him to his mansion. He regularly held receptions for dignitaries; Mrs. Washington did the same for their wives. Madison, serving as the administration leader in the House, complained that the "satellites and sycophants which surrounded him had wound up the ceremonials of the government to such a pitch of stateliness which nothing but his personal character could have supported, and which no character after him could ever maintain."

A Cabinet of Advisors The Constitution had provided for executive departments to aid the president. One of the first acts of the new Congress was to create the offices of attorney general and postmaster general. Congress also provided for the continuation of the departments created under the Articles, the departments of state (formerly called foreign affairs), war, and treasury. Because the treasury was so important, it was made directly responsible to Congress as well as to the president.

Washington asked Thomas Jefferson to head the State Department. Alexander Hamilton, his former wartime secretary, was appointed secretary of the treasury. Henry Knox continued as secretary of war, and Edmund Randolph, who was a personal friend of the president, was chosen as attorney general.

Washington's failure to obtain the Senate's advice on the matter of the Indian treaty led him to turn increasingly to the heads of his executive departments for counsel. Thus began the institution of the cabinet, which was holding regular meetings by 1793. Washington, a skilled administrator, left the work of the individual departments to those in charge while overseeing all government activities himself. He asked for the opinions of the department heads on important questions, but he never hesitated to make the final decisions and to take responsibility for them. He was industrious, prompt, systematic, and exacting.

Washington did not, however, take a leadership role in relations with the Congress. He believed that he should never propose or even appear to favor legislation while it was being debated and that he should never use his veto unless a proposed bill was, in his opinion, unconstitutional.

Because Washington took little or no initiative in guiding the Congress, Madison, Hamilton, and (later) Jefferson filled the vacuum. Madison was elected to the House and quickly became its leading member, as well as a close personal adviser to the president. Hamilton's greatest contribution was his keen understanding of the intricacies of high finance. Only thirty-two when he became secretary of the treasury, Hamilton not only advised the House on financial matters, but often drafted the bills he wanted, as well. Short and dapper, he had enormous energy and vast powers of persuasion and was so influential in the government that he was dubbed "Prime Minister." Jefferson, on the other hand, had little official contact with Congress but, nevertheless, gained considerable influence through his close friendship with Madison.

The First Congress Legislates

An important accomplishment of the First Congress was the creation of a federal judiciary. On the subject of establishing the third arm of government, the Constitution had stated: "The judicial power of the United States shall be vested in one Supreme Court, and in such inferior courts as the Congress may from time to time ordain and establish."

In September 1789 Congress passed the Judiciary Act, which set the number of Supreme Court justices at six—five associate justices and one chief justice. (Washington appointed John Jay as chief justice.) The act also set up thirteen federal district courts and three circuit courts which were to have both original and appellate jurisdiction in cases involving the United States Constitution and federal laws and treaties. The Supreme Court was specifically empowered to review decisions of the state courts and, if necessary, to nullify state laws that violated the federal Constitution or laws and treaties established under it.

The Anti-Federalists had cited the omission of a bill of rights as reason for not ratifying the new Constitution. So to honor the promises that Federalists had made regarding the protection of individual liberty, Madison proposed a bill of rights as one of the first orders of business in the new Congress. "If we can make the Constitution better in the opinion of those who are opposed to it without weakening its frame, or abridging its usefulness in the judgment of those who are attached to it," Madison said, "we act the part of wise and liberal men to make such alterations as shall produce that effect."

Madison drew up twelve amendments listing guaranteed liberties, but only ten of them were ratified. Passed by Congress on September 25, 1789, and by three-fourths of the states by 1791, the Bill of Rights was added to the Constitution as its first ten amendments. The first eight amendments guaranteed freedom of speech, religion, peaceful assembly, and the press; the right to bear arms; freedom from unreasonable search; no general search warrants; and the right to the protection of certain legal procedures known as the due process of law. The ninth and tenth amendments promised that the federal government would not assume any powers not accorded it in the Constitution and assured that all other rights belonged to the states and the people.

Hamilton's Fiscal Policy

The new national government's most pressing need was to establish a sound economic policy. The government under the Articles had not had the power to tax and had failed to support itself or to impose its authority on the country. Now a second government had been born which had been given the right to raise revenue. Would Americans submit to federal customs officers and tax collectors? Could Americans learn, as Washington wrote, "to distinguish between oppression and the necessary exercise of lawful authority"?

Washington appointed a brilliant lawyer, Alexander Hamilton, as the first secretary of the treasury. Hamilton believed that the national interest was morally superior to the private interests of individuals; therefore, it was the civic responsibility of individuals to sacrifice their personal interests for the public good. The new secretary, however, took a pessimistic view of human nature. Since humans were naturally selfish, a strong central government was necessary to channel the pursuit of self-interest toward the good of the nation as a whole. Hamilton had more faith in the upper class than in the mass of ordinary citizens, for he believed that the wealthy were less likely to act from motives of greed and self-interest or to demand policies that would be incompatible with good government. Thus he associated good government and the national interest with the interests of the rich and well-born.

Hamilton himself was not from the monied class but was a self-made man. Born out of wedlock in the British West Indies, he had used his natural charm, zeal, and intelligence to get ahead. Eventually, marriage into a prominent New York family brought him the wealth and social position he needed to advance his political career. Hamilton's fiscal policies aimed at bonding the upper class and the national government, sometimes to the exclusion of the interests of other classes. His intentions were in direct opposition to the spirit of egalitarianism that was widespread in America after the Revolution. Nevertheless, Hamilton was a man of vision who had immense confidence that given appropriate leadership the United States would become a great nation.

Hamilton believed that a sound economy was essential to an effective government. A strong national government must be able to balance its budget and pay its debts. In order to achieve these goals, he advocated expanding the commercial and manufacturing sectors and allowing the predominant agricultural interest, which comprised over 90 percent of the population, to continue developing on its

DETAIL FROM *ALEXANDER HAMILTON* BY JOHN TRUMBULL. ONLY THIRTY-TWO WHEN HE ENTERED THE CABINET, HAMILTON WAS AN EFFICIENT, HARD-BOILED POLITICAL REALIST WHO BELIEVED THE NEW GOVERNMENT WOULD NOT SURVIVE UNLESS WEALTHY CITIZENS COULD MAKE MONEY FROM THEIR INVESTMENTS IN IT.

own. Although he acknowledged the importance of agriculture to the nation, Hamilton was more interested in the economic potential of American industry. Eventually, he reasoned, all areas of the economy would become equally strong and interdependent. His economic policies were designed to please the business community and establish a tie between commercial and manufacturing interests and the government. From an economic standpoint the program was a brilliant success, but it soon alienated the agricultural sector.

The National Debt America had a foreign debt of over $11 million. The new government also owed some $42 million to citizens who either had bought government certificates of indebtedness to support the Revolutionary War or had fought in the war and received certificates instead of pay. By 1790, however, few of these certificates remained in the hands of their original owners. Their value had declined over the previous ten years, for it seemed increasingly unlikely that the government would ever redeem them. Speculators, mainly the commercial interests on the Eastern seaboard, had bought most of the certificates at a fraction of their original price.

In his *Report on Public Credit*, presented to Congress in 1790, Hamilton recommended that these certificates be called in and refunded at face value. To fund the national debt, he proposed replacing the old certificates with new interest-bearing government bonds which could be paid off slowly. The goal was to restore American credit by demonstrating the ability to pay at least a small portion of the national debt each year or to pay the interest on the debt.

Hamilton's bold plan created an uproar. His chief opponent was Madison, who objected to the scheme for two reasons. First, four-fifths of the national debt was owed to Northerners. If in order to redeem the certificates the entire country were taxed equally, a massive transfer of money from Southern to Northern pockets would result. Second, Madison vehemently objected to rewarding the speculators, some of whom had bought the certificates only recently from soldiers and citizens at a quarter of their original price.

Hamilton defended his proposal as firmly as Madison opposed it. First, he pointed out, if the government distinguished between one sort of certificate holder and another, America's credit would remain shaky. Foreign and native investors would be unlikely to trust a government that did not pay *all* its debts, no matter to whom they were owed. Second, Hamilton believed that the well-to-do speculators who owned most of the certificates (many of them members of Congress) were the only people in America who "thought continentally." The rest of the population, "the community at large," was provincial in its outlook and still felt that its first loyalty was to the states. Little support for a strong federal government could be won from them. Therefore the government should court the well-to-do, for only through their support could the new government succeed and the country expand in the areas Hamilton thought important: commerce and manufacturing.

Eventually Hamilton had his way: the entire national debt was funded. This action undeniably benefited speculators, but it also had the desired effect of restoring the national credit. Henceforth, citizens and foreign bankers were not afraid to invest in the United States.

The State Debts Hamilton's financial plans did not stop at funding the repayment of the national debt. He also called for the government to assume an additional obligation: repayment of the debt that each state had incurred during the Revolutionary War. Hamilton believed that if this plan were put into effect the states' creditors would become increasingly attached to the national government and the influence of the states would gradually wither away.

The heated controversy over assumption (as this plan was called) deadlocked Congress for nearly six months. In general, members of Congress approved of the plan if their own state still had large unpaid war-time debts, but disapproved if their state's debts had been paid off. The opposition was particularly strident in Virginia which had already paid half of its debts and felt it should not have to assist states that were less prompt in discharging their obligations.

The controversy was finally resolved in July 1790, when Hamilton agreed that states that had already paid a large part of their debts would receive partial reimbursement. More important, Hamilton made a deal with Madison and Jefferson. The two Virginians, who had opposed Hamilton's plan, now agreed to support it in return for his promise that the national capital would be moved, after a temporary stay in Philadelphia, to the banks of the Potomac River.

Jefferson later regretted this compromise. But at the time, he thought that conceding on the matter of assumption was not too high a price for placing the nation's capital in Virginia. He anticipated that the move would attract people and business to the South, make it easier for Southern legislators to get to Congress, and improve the chances that Southerners would be appointed to government positions.

First Bank of the United States Hamilton next proposed that Congress charter a national bank funded by a $10 million investment. Although some of this money would come from the government, most would come from private individuals. Most of the private investment could take the form of certifi-

cates of government indebtedness, with only a small amount of the total investment consisting of gold and silver, commodities in short supply. In Hamilton's view, if a public debt "is properly funded, and an object of established confidence, it answers most of the purposes of money." An abundance of money in the form of bank notes would stimulate commerce and capital investments in industry.

Jefferson and Madison were immediately opposed to the bill. Along with other agrarians, they were suspicious of banks in general and saw the creation of a national bank as a scheme to build up commerce and manufacturing at the expense of rural interests. Hamilton tried to play down the fact that those with wealth in money and government securities rather than land could enrich themselves further through bank investment and bank credit for financing new enterprises. Instead, he stressed that the bank's incorporation was necessary for a number of reasons: it would serve as a safe depository for government funds; it would facilitate the collection of taxes; and it could issue a uniform national currency which would be unlikely to fluctuate in value since it would be accepted by the government in payment of taxes just like coins.

Washington profoundly respected Hamilton's financial genius, but conversations with Madison led him to wonder whether the proposed bank might be unconstitutional. The president therefore decided to consult Jefferson. Jefferson cited the Tenth Amendment, which states that "all powers not delegated to the United States by the Constitution . . . are reserved to the states, or the people." He argued that establishing a central bank was clearly *not* a power delegated to the federal government. Although the last clause of Article I, Section 8 of the Constitution allowed the Congress to "make all Laws which shall be necessary and proper for carrying into Execution the foregoing Powers," Jefferson did not believe that a central bank was "necessary" in the sense of being absolutely essential to the operation of the government. He reasoned that if Congress expanded its powers without authority, the states would rise up in anger, and soon Congress would "take possession of a boundless field of power, no longer susceptible to any definition."

Hamilton replied to this argument by submitting his own *Opinion on the Constitutionality of the Bank* in February 1791. In contrast to Jefferson's

A 1799 ENGRAVING OF THE FIRST BANK OF THE UNITED STATES, ESTABLISHED TO ISSUE PAPER MONEY AND CONTROL NATIONAL CREDIT.

"strict construction," he favored a broad, or loose, construction of the Constitution. As he put it, "the powers contained in a constitution of government . . . ought to be construed liberally in advancement of the public good. . . ." Hamilton insisted that the right to set up a bank was implied in the "necessary and proper" clause. In fact, one of his reasons for creating the bank was to test the "necessary and proper" clause and to create a precedent for expanding the powers of the federal government. He argued that "a bank has a natural relation to the power of collecting taxes—to that of providing for the common defense," all of them "powers vested by the Constitution in the government." Therefore the bank was wholly in accord with the

Constitution. According to Hamilton, "necessary" did not have to mean that which was absolutely essential, only that which was convenient. Washington was convinced by this argument and signed the bank bill.

Economic Growth One of Hamilton's goals as secretary of the treasury was to encourage American manufacturers and make the United States independent of other nations. In December 1791 he submitted to Congress a *Report on Manufactures*. This document completed his basic economic policy for the new country. To protect fledgling American manufacturers, he proposed to construct a system of tariffs, subsidies, and "bounties" (or awards) favorable to new industries. Again, his proposal aroused a great deal of controversy. The South, a primarily agricultural area, opposed the plan. Southern farmers would gain nothing from the establishment of higher tariffs; they would simply have to pay higher prices for manufactured goods. Many Northern merchants, fearing that high tariffs would discourage trade, joined the Southerners in opposing the plan, and as a result, the overall plan was never implemented, although many of its suggestions were incorporated into the Tariff Act of 1792.

First Signs of Political Tension

Hamilton's fiscal policies, his admiration of the rich and distrust of the common people, and his clear preference for the North over the South earned him the political enmity of both Madison and Jefferson. Whereas Hamilton had little use for the state governments, Jefferson and Madison were convinced that an overly powerful federal government was a real threat to liberty. Jefferson and his supporters claimed that Hamilton was leading a royalist plot to overthrow republicanism in America and to replace it with a monarchy.

In return, Hamilton called Jefferson "the most intriguing man in the United States," and characterized him as "cautious and sly, wrapped up in impenetrable silence and mystery." To help him build support for his views, Hamilton enlisted the support of John Fenno, the publisher of a Philadelphia newspaper called the *Gazette of the United States.* Out of "gratitude" for many treasury-printing contracts and outright loans, Fenno praised Hamilton as the greatest American statesman next to Washington. For his part, Jefferson subsidized Philip Freneau, a well-known poet of the Revolution, by giving him an honorary paid post in the State Department. In 1791 Freneau set up a rival newspaper, the *National Gazette*, which heralded Jefferson as "the Colossus of Liberty" and attacked Hamilton and his policies. Fenno retaliated by characterizing Jefferson as an atheist and a foe of orderly government and the Constitution.

Washington tried to remain above the quarrel, although it greatly disturbed him. He disliked the developing political controversy and longed to return to the peace of his beloved Mount Vernon. But Hamilton, Jefferson, and Madison, believing that the new government would collapse without him, convinced the reluctant Washington to serve another term. He and John Adams were reelected in the fall of 1792. Although Washington persuaded Hamilton and Jefferson to maintain at least an outward show of mutual respect, their antagonism subsided only temporarily.

Foreign Policy

Jefferson and Hamilton were also in disagreement over American foreign policy. Jefferson's main goal, as secretary of state, was to establish American independence from European influence. The only real ally of the United States was France. Although Jefferson had a strong personal attachment to France, his primary interest in maintaining the alliance was strategic. France did not menace the new nation's western borders; Spain at the mouth of the Mississippi and England around the Great Lakes were continual sources of concern to Americans. Jefferson believed that France might help the United States expel these two powers. He wanted to establish American sovereignty to the banks of the Mississippi River and at the same time keep the country out of European quarrels.

Hamilton's main goal, on the other hand, was to develop the United States into a strong and wealthy nation by protecting the national credit. To this end, he convinced Congress not to pass measures (favored by Jefferson and Madison) that would have cut off all trade with the British until they had negotiated a favorable commercial treaty with the United States. Britain sold more to the United States than did any other nation, and the main source of revenue for the hard-pressed United States Treasury was the tariff on imported goods. In this case, Hamilton's foreign policy won out.

Reaction to the French Revolution Hamilton and Jefferson clashed again when events in France caused the Franco-American Alliance to become an issue. Following the French Revolution of 1789, a French republic was proclaimed in 1791. At first, Americans of every political persuasion greeted the news with enthusiasm; the ally of the American Revolution had won freedom from the yoke of royal tyranny.

But by the fall of 1792, the first, relatively moderate phase of the French Revolution had come to an end, and France, led by a radical party anxious to spread the doctrines of the Revolution throughout Europe, was at war with Austria and Prussia. The constitutional monarchy of 1791 had been overthrown by the combined forces of the radical activists (Girondists) seeking international revolution, the urban workers, and the peasantry; and the government had resorted to the guillotine to restore order. In January 1793, King Louis XVI was beheaded. A "reign of terror" had begun.

American conservatives began to fear that this wave of violent attacks on property and government authority might spread to the United States. Washington and Hamilton and their followers were horrified by the revolutionary excesses, but Jefferson, while deploring the terror, remained steadfast in his approval of the goals of the Revolution. With

exaggerated enthusiasm, he announced: "The liberty of the whole earth was depending on the issue of the contest and . . . rather than it should have failed, I would have seen half the earth devastated."

American Neutrality Alarmed at the radical turn of events in France, Great Britain formed an alliance with Holland, Prussia, and Austria (and later Spain) against what they considered to be a threat to European civilization. In February 1793 France declared war on these powers.

In America news of the declaration of international war refocused the national debate. Now Americans were concerned not with the merits of the French Revolution but with whether the United States should become involved in the conflict. One of the terms of the Franco-American Alliance

THIS FEDERALIST CARTOON EXAGGERATES JEFFERSON'S PRO-FRENCH POSITION AND WASHINGTON'S ANXIETY OVER AMERICA'S POSSIBLE INVOLVEMENT IN THE EUROPEAN CONFLICT WHICH FOLLOWED THE FRENCH REVOLUTION. WASHINGTON IN HIS FEDERAL CHARIOT ADVANCES TO MEET AN INVASION OF FRENCH REPUBLICAN "CANNIBALS." HE IS HINDERED BY CITIZEN GENÊT, ALBERT GALLATIN, AND THOMAS JEFFERSON WHO TRY TO BLOCK THE WHEELS. A DOGS LIFTS HIS LEG ON THE REPUBLICAN NEWSPAPER.

of 1778 required the United States to defend French possessions, such as the French West Indies, against the enemies of France.

Hamilton watched with horror as France's "war of all peoples against all kings" progressed. If America were drawn into the conflict, he would find himself siding with a country whose policies directly opposed everything he believed in. What was more, the war would reach into the American treasury. Hamilton argued that the Treaty of 1778 was no longer valid, since it had been made with the French monarchy and not with the government now in power, and he urged the United States to renounce the treaty, proclaim its neutrality, and refuse to receive a minister from the revolutionary government.

Jefferson strongly disagreed. Although he recognized that it would be foolhardy to enter the war against Great Britain—a course of action which the French did not even expect—he urged Washington not to declare American neutrality without first obtaining congressional support. He further argued that the United States should not renounce the Alliance of 1778 unless American security was directly endangered. The agreement had been made with the French people, not with a specific government, and it was important for America to set the precedent of living up to its international commitments.

Washington finally compromised. He proclaimed American neutrality in April 1793, but without using the word *neutrality*. Instead, he asked Americans to be "impartial." At the same time, the United States did not renounce the French Alliance, nor did it refuse to receive a new French minister to the United States. America's goals were to avoid political involvement in the European war and, as a neutral, to take advantage of trade with both sides.

Citizen Genêt Although the French had decided not to press the United States to defend the West Indian islands, they did wish to use American ports for launching attacks on British merchant ships. In April 1793 the young French minister, Edmond Genêt, arrived in Charleston, South Carolina, a stronghold of pro-French sentiment. In violation of American law, he commissioned fourteen Charleston ship captains as privateers for the French, and they captured about eighty British ships without the sanction of the United States government. Genêt then moved on to Philadelphia where he plotted an

expedition, led by Revolutionary War hero George Rogers Clark, against Louisiana.

Deeply displeased, President Washington warned Genêt to stop his illegal activities. But the Frenchman was unperturbed, for everywhere he had been met with public adoration. Encouraged by so much popular support, Genêt decided to ignore the president and appeal to public opinion.

Genêt's actions antagonized the whole administration. Washington was furious. Hamilton was convinced that unless Genêt was stopped, Federalist heads would soon be rolling in Philadelphia. Even Jefferson lost patience because he knew that although the majority of Americans might be pro-French, they certainly did not want to enter the war. Washington finally demanded the recall of the impudent Genêt to Paris. However, the government that had dispatched Genêt had been overturned by an even more radical group (the Jacobins) who declared that the diplomat's actions were "criminal maneuvers." Rather than send Genêt back to face almost certain death, Washington relented and granted him asylum in the United States.

Foreign Aggression British criticism of Genêt's actions had led the president to ask Congress for legislation to keep America out of the war.

In June 1794 Congress passed a Neutrality Act which prohibited foreign powers from recruiting soldiers in the United States and banned belligerents from engaging in warfare in American coastal waters. Unfortunately, the passage of the act came too late. Between 1793 and 1794 England and France seized some six hundred American ships in international waters. The provocation for these seizures was simple: the struggle between Britain and France provided a strong stimulus to American foreign trade, and both powers intended to disrupt American dealings with the enemy. France captured American vessels carrying goods to England, and England seized American ships sailing for France. France, whose ships had been virtually swept from the seas by the powerful British navy, hoped to obtain urgently needed supplies from American merchants, and this demand greatly stimulated American commerce.

But the British, possessors of the most powerful navy in the world, invoked the Rule of 1756, which declared that commerce prohibited in time of peace would not be allowed to neutrals in time of war. Although international law accepted the right of a nation engaged in war to prevent neutral nations from delivering "contraband" (war) goods to enemy ports, the British disagreed with the American definition of contraband. Since the Revolutionary War, the United States had insisted that only arms and ammunition should be considered contraband, while the British insisted that anything (food, for example) that might conceivably aid the French war effort was contraband and therefore subject to seizure. British warships seized some 250 American vessels trying to trade with the French West Indies and confiscated their cargoes. The British navy also impressed (forced) many American sailors into its service.

England further aroused anti-British sentiment by helping the Northwest Indians resist American encroachment on Indian lands. Although the United States had obtained the Northwest Territory in the Treaty of 1783, few American settlers had been able to enter the area. In 1791 Washington sent Arthur St. Clair to crush the Miamis of Ohio, but the Indians, encouraged by the British, routed the Americans. By February 1794 American troops under General "Mad Anthony" Wayne were prepared to enter the Northwest. The British governor of Canada had given supplies to the Indians in preparation for the fight. To make matters worse, there were still a thousand British redcoats stationed in the Northwest, and England was beginning to build a new fort in the Ohio country.

War between the United States and Great Britain became a real and immediate danger. American public opinion was inflamed over British conduct, and even Hamilton characterized England's aggressive behavior on the high seas as "atrocious." Although Jefferson had resigned as secretary of state in December 1793, his followers in Congress secured a temporary embargo on trade with England in early 1794. Hamilton, alarmed that a conflict with England would destroy his fiscal policy, persuaded the president to send a special negotiator to London to prevent outright war between the two countries. After receiving congressional approval in April, Washington sent Chief Justice John Jay to England with instructions to get the British out of the Northwest, force England to pay for American ships that had been seized, urge Britain to accept America's rights as a neutral, and negotiate a new commercial treaty with Britain.

Jay's Treaty After months of discussion, Jay and the British foreign minister, Lord Grenville, drafted the Treaty of London. During the negotiations Hamilton revealed to the British minister in America that Washington had decided not to arm American merchant ships to prevent seizure by England, as the neutrals Denmark and Sweden were doing. While some historians allege that this information weakened Jay's negotiating position, it is unlikely that it substantially affected the outcome. Although the British did not want to make concessions that would weaken their war effort against France, neither did they want to go to war with the United States.

The Treaty of London (popularly known as Jay's treaty), signed in November 1794, secured only moderate concessions from the British. They agreed to evacuate their forts in the Northwest within two years, and they granted American merchants the right to trade with the British Isles, the British East Indies, and, within strict limitations, the British West Indies. The waterways of the American continent were to be open to both countries. Finally, the British agreed to pay damages to American shipowners whose vessels had recently been seized. The precise amounts were to be determined by an arbitration commission.

These were the only concessions Jay was able to squeeze out of the English. He was unable to get their assurance that they would respect American rights as a neutral nation on the high seas or that they would give up the infuriating practice of impressment. In addition, Jay gave ground by agreeing that the United States would pay British merchants for debts contracted before the Revolutionary War. Again, arbitration boards would decide on the exact figures. When the terms of Jay's treaty were leaked out by a Republican senator, Americans responded with indignation. They nicknamed the unfortunate emissary "Sir John Jay." President Washington observed that a cry went up against the treaty "like that against a mad dog."

The article pertaining to American participation in British West Indian trade was particularly irritating. One of Jay's primary goals had been to convince the British to reopen this lucrative trade, closed to America since the Revolution. But Britain had responded with a plan hedged with restrictions that allowed United States vessels to trade only between the West Indian islands and American ports, virtually cutting American merchants off from world trade in such valuable Caribbean produce as molasses, coffee, cocoa, sugar, and cotton.

Although acceptance of the treaty seemed humiliating, rejection might have meant war with England. Stifling his pride, Washington submitted the treaty to the Senate which threw out the annoying provisions for trade with the British West Indies and, after much debate, ratified the rest in June 1795, by a bare two-thirds majority.

Whereas agreeing to the treaty was one of the most unpopular decisions of Washington's career, it was also one of the wisest. It probably kept America out of a war it could have ill afforded and would have had little hope of winning, and it opened up a ten-year period of relatively friendly relations. It allowed the country to continue making immense profits as a neutral nation trading with the two great belligerents, France and England; and it finally cleared the way for American expansion into the Ohio Valley. In August 1794 General Wayne defeated the Indians in the Battle of Fallen Timbers. As a result, the Northwest Indians ceded most of the Ohio Territory to the American government in the Treaty of Greenville (1795). The following year the British fulfilled their commitment under Jay's treaty to evacuate their posts in the territory.

Pinckney's Treaty Unpopular though it was, Jay's treaty helped prepare the groundwork for a treaty with Spain that was an unqualified success. Having broken their alliance with England, the Spanish feared a joint British-American attack against their possessions in North America—Florida and the Gulf Coast. Moreover, the Spanish government was bankrupt and knew it could no longer hope to hold back American expansion into the Mississippi Valley. Therefore Spain decided to placate the United States by signing a treaty in 1795 with Thomas Pinckney, a special American envoy to Madrid. Pinckney's treaty granted everything the United States wanted: free navigation of the Mississippi "in its whole length from its source to the ocean"; free use of the port of New Orleans for three years, after which time a new arrangement would be made; and Spanish acceptance of the thirty-first parallel as America's southern boundary. The Spanish also abandoned their claims to the disputed areas of the Southwest and even promised to discourage Indian attacks on American settlements. For its part, the United States pledged only to try to pacify the Indians in the area.

The Senate ratified Pinckney's treaty unanimously in March 1796. Now that Western farmers had access to the Mississippi, Kentucky and Tennessee, which had become states in 1792 and 1796, would be unlikely to follow through on their threat to secede from the Union and annex themselves to Spain. American sovereignty over the territory between the Appalachian Mountains and the Mississippi River had been achieved. The promise of the Treaty of 1783 had at last been fulfilled.

The Whiskey Rebellion

While Jay was negotiating in London, Washington's administration faced unrest on the domestic front.

AMERICANS RESPOND TO JAY'S TREATY BY BURNING THE UNHAPPY JAY IN EFFIGY.

Alexander Hamilton on the Whiskey Rebellion

"In compliance with your requisitions, I have the honor to submit my opinion as to the course which it will be advisable for the President to pursue, in regard to the armed opposition recently given in the four western counties of Pennsylvania to the execution of the laws of the United States laying duties upon spirits distilled within the United States, and upon stills . . .

A competent force of militia should be called forth and employed to suppress the insurrection, and support the civil authority in effectuating obedience to the laws and punishment of offenders.

It appears to me that the very existence of government demands this course, and that a duty of the highest nature urges the Chief Magistrate to pursue it. The Constitution and laws of the United States contemplate and provide for it. . . ."

Letter from Hamilton to Washington, August 1794

Thomas Jefferson on the Whiskey Rebellion

"The excise law is an infernal one. The first error was to admit it by the Constitution; the 2d, to act on that admission; the 3d and last will be, to make it the instrument of dismembering the Union, and setting us all afloat to chuse which part of it we will adhere to. The information of our militia, returned from the Westward, is uniform, that tho the people there let them pass quietly, they were objects of their laughter, not of their fear; that 1,000 men could have cut off their whole force in a thousand places of the Alleganey; that their detestation of the excise law is universal, and has now associated to it a detestation of the government; and that separation which perhaps was a very distant and problematical event, is now near, and certain, and determined in the mind of every man."

Letter from Jefferson to Madison, December 1794

Democratic Clubs, which had begun organizing while Genêt was minister to the United States, actively supported both the French Revolution and Republican candidates for Congress. The Federalists, however, soon found a way to undermine the Democrats' effectiveness and to regain some of their lost popularity.

Whiskey was an extremely important product to Western farmers. While the Mississippi was closed to American traffic, whiskey was the only form in which grain could be transported cheaply overland. It was also used instead of money in exchange for other goods.

Hamilton's excise taxes were high, as much as twenty-five cents on every dollar. Western farmers began to protest in 1792, and in 1794 rioting broke out in western Pennsylvania. Government agents were terrorized, federal court proceedings were interrupted, and the federal inspector for that area was forced to surrender to an unruly mob which burned his house. The Whiskey Rebellion was a test of the authority of the new federal government.

Would the government be able to suppress the armed uprising?

After calling for compliance with the law, Washington denounced the Democratic Clubs for their involvement in the rebellion and then called out some thirteen thousand militiamen and put Alexander Hamilton in charge. Washington was so popular that his speaking out caused an immediate dissolution of some of the clubs. However, putting Hamilton in charge was a political mistake. The secretary of the treasury, despite his ability, was loathed by Western farmers. Hamilton welcomed the opportunity to demonstrate the power of the federal government, but to his dismay, the rebels fled at the approach of such a large army. Although Hamilton later announced that the government had gained "reputation and strength" by its display of military force, only two of the few prisoners taken were accused of high treason. Washington pardoned both of them, labeling one a "simpleton," the other "insane."

The Rise of Political Parties

Political parties originated in the United States during the 1790s. Before that period there had existed factions and family cliques similar to those in British politics. Under the new American government, organizations were needed which could bring order to political life by appealing to a national electorate. Political parties were a practical innovation to help resolve problems in a pluralistic society. These new organizations channeled political differences into verbal confrontations and prevented them from threatening the Union. They also helped bind together similar interests in all parts of the country and brought issues before the public in a coherent way.

By the 1790s, political life in America was dominated on the one hand by Thomas Jefferson and his political ally, James Madison, and on the other by Alexander Hamilton. Even after Jefferson and Hamilton had resigned from the cabinet, both men continued to exert strong influence over their followers. Jefferson's supporters called themselves Republicans or Democratic Republicans. Hamilton's followers and those who supported the more moderate John Adams were known as Federalists. From now on in American history this label would refer to a political party rather than the original group who had supported ratification of the Constitution.

Jefferson's chief complaints against the Federalists arose from his antagonism toward what he believed was the purpose behind Hamilton's fiscal policies. Although the Virginian supported the federal government, he charged that the Federalists wanted to strengthen it at the expense of the states and of individual liberty. He even charged them with conspiring to convert America into a monarchy. Hamilton outlined his differences with Jefferson in a remarkably dispassionate summary:

One side appears to believe there is a serious plot to overturn the state governments, and substitute a monarchy to the present republican system. The other side firmly believes there is a serious plot to overturn the general government and elevate the separate powers of the states upon its ruins.

Jefferson, the gentleman farmer, also distrusted Hamilton's efforts to promote the interests of manufacturing and urban life instead of farming. According to Jefferson, "those who labor in the earth are the chosen people of God," whereas "the mobs of great cities" were like sores sapping "the strength of the human body." He felt that America could remain morally pure and true to its traditional virtues only so long as it remained rural.

The Jeffersonians and the Federalists also had different views concerning the potential of the human race. While acknowledging that human nature consisted of both worthy and unworthy instincts, Jefferson had more faith than the Federalists in the possibility of improvement through education and experience. Whereas the Federalists believed that "those who own the country ought to run it," Jefferson wanted eventually to extend the vote to every white male and to do away with all property qualifications (although he did believe that universal education had to precede universal suffrage).

Hamilton's leading supporters were the elite of the Revolutionary era. Having already achieved prominence, they viewed any challenge to government authority as an attack on an order of which they were a part. The Jeffersonians, on the other hand, were generally newcomers to politics who felt excluded from the inner circles of power. Perhaps it was natural that they should regard a strong national government as a means of protecting a native aristocracy and as contrary to the democratic ideals of American life. The aristocratic bias of the Federalists predisposed them to admire Great Britain and its obvious class distinctions. Correspondingly, the Jeffersonians' democratic predilections led them to admire the French Revolution and its attacks on entrenched power.

The Federalists and the Jeffersonians should not be compared to twentieth-century political parties. They were neither as highly structured, nor had they evolved to the point of having national committees or conventions. There were state and local committees, and by 1796 a Jeffersonian Republican caucus in Congress was nominating candidates. The Federalists and the Democratic Republicans were the first true parties in America in that they both followed a clearly formulated set of ideas and sought to administer the government for the benefit of distinctly national economic interests.

The Federalists generally represented the merchants, shipowners, and financiers of the Northeast, as well as the decreasing number of prosperous Northern farmers and tidewater planters in the South. Predominantly English in ancestry, Federalists usually belonged to the Congregational, Episcopal, and Quaker churches. The Jeffersonian Republicans represented many artisans and workers from the towns, as well as small independent farmers from all parts of the country. They were gradually joined by wealthy farmers as well, who were becoming increasingly alienated by Hamilton's fiscal policies. Eventually, the party developed into a broad political coalition composed largely of people of British, Scotch-Irish, and German descent who resisted centralized authority and were frequently religious dissenters (Presbyterians, Pietists, Methodists, and Baptists).

The Election of 1796

When Washington decided to step down from office in 1796, the nation experienced its first contested presidential election. Washington, unanimously chosen to office, had always considered himself above political parties. Nevertheless, because of his support of Hamilton's program, most Americans regarded him as a Federalist. Most Jeffersonians considered Washington's Farewell Address, which called for an end to partisanship in domestic affairs and warned against permanent entangling alliances in foreign relations, to be a partisan statement.

Through their congressional caucus, the Democratic Republicans put forward Jefferson as their presidential candidate. Jefferson was aided by the organizational skills of James Madison and James Monroe and by state and county committees. Hamilton's policies, the Whiskey Rebellion, and above all the unpopularity of Jay's treaty, consolidated support for Jefferson's candidacy.

On the Federalist side, their leading politicians passed over the controversial Hamilton and instead gave their support to Washington's vice-president, John Adams. Thomas Pinckney, negotiator of the popular Spanish treaty, was nominated as vice-president.

Hamilton, rejected by his own party, then tried to manipulate the vote in the electoral college in order to prevent the independent Adams from obtaining the presidency. As provided for in the Constitution, each elector voted for two candidates without having to specify his choice for president. The candidate with the most votes became president, and the candidate with the second largest number of votes became vice-president. In order to avoid a tie between their presidential and vice-presidential choices, electors favoring one party had to divert some of their second votes to another candidate. This was risky, for if too many votes were diverted, then the presidential candidate of the opposing party might win the vice-presidency. Another idiosyncracy of the system, which Hamilton hoped to capitalize on, was that if both parties wanted the same individual for vice-president, he might inadvertently receive a majority of votes and thus become president. Hamilton hoped to persuade enough Democratic Republicans to vote for Pinckney so that the combined Republican and Federalist vote would elect him president. His maneuver failed to gain the necessary support, however; Adams was narrowly elected president with seventy-one electoral votes and Jefferson was elected vice-president with sixty-eight votes. The contest revealed a weakness of the electoral college system: the presidential candidates of two opposing parties could be brought into the two highest offices of the government.

The Adams Administration

John Adams was a temperamental man of outwardly reserved appearance who often lashed out in anger at those with whom he disagreed. Yet he also possessed great personal courage and integrity and could show considerable patience during a crisis. His political philosophy was more moderate than Hamilton's and actually represented the thinking of a larger proportion of Federalist voters. Although Adams despised Hamilton for his maneuvering in the recent presidential contest, he shared his opponent's cynical view of human nature. Nevertheless, Adams believed that a government based on the principles of separation of powers and checks and balances would curb the human weaknesses characteristic of all social classes. Concerned with establishing a balanced government, he was distrustful of

STOUT JOHN ADAMS WAS A CRUSTY, HARD-WORKING NEW ENGLANDER WITH STRONG PRINCIPLES AND A HOT TEMPER. DURING THE WAR FOR INDEPENDENCE, HE HAD BEEN INFLUENTIAL IN SECURING WASHINGTON'S ELECTION AS COMMANDER-IN-CHIEF, IN DRAFTING THE DECLARATION OF INDEPENDENCE, AND IN LOBBYING IT THROUGH CONGRESS. HE WAS THE FIRST MINISTER TO ENGLAND AFTER THE REVOLUTION AND THE FIRST PRESIDENT TO LIVE IN THE WHITE HOUSE.

A VIEW OF EARLY WASHINGTON FROM THE PRESIDENT'S HOUSE.

granting excessive power to the monied group to whom Hamilton catered. Although Adams favored the expansion of commerce he, unlike Hamilton, did not approve of land speculation or the expansion of bank credit. He believed that widespread ownership of land was the basis of social stability and that a country's true wealth was based on rising land values. Like Jefferson, Adams thought the only true aristocracy was one of education and talent, not money. But unlike the Virginian, he did not believe that the future would necessarily bring progress for the mass of humanity.

In order to reassure the Democratic Republicans that the Federalists did not intend to turn the

The First, Second, and Last Scene of Mortality.   Prudence Punderson.

IN COLONIAL AMERICA UNORGANIZED LEISURE WAS
CONSIDERED UNDESIRABLE, AND YOUNG WOMEN WERE
TAUGHT ALL MANNER OF "FEMALE ARTS" TO DISCIPLINE
THEIR MINDS AND BEAUTIFY THEIR HOUSEHOLDS. PRU-
DENCE PUNDERSON'S EMBROIDERED BIOGRAPHY RE-
FLECTS THE STERN MORAL VALUES AND PRACTICAL
CONCERNS OF THE PERIOD. SHE HAS DEPICTED HERSELF
FIRST AS A LITTLE CHILD BEING ROCKED IN A CRADLE,
THEN AS A YOUNG MERCHANT'S WIFE AND HOUSEKEEPER
PREPARING HER NEEDLEWORK, FINALLY AS THE "P.P."
LYING IN THE COFFIN. (The Connecticut Historical Society)

TWO CLEVERLY CARVED AND
BRIGHTLY PAINTED WHIRLGIGS PRO-
VIDED AMUSEMENT FOR CHILDREN
IN THE AMERICAN COLONIES.
(© Sotheby Parke-Bernet. Agent: Editorial
Photocolor Archives)

▲
A COUNTRY FAIR, HELD IN PENNSYLVANIA IN 1824, GAVE LOCAL FARMERS AN OPPORTUNITY TO SOCIALIZE AND DISCUSS NEW METHODS FOR IMPROVING THEIR CROPS, TO STUDY NEW TOOLS AND MACHINERY, AND TO DISPLAY THEIR PRIZE LIVESTOCK. (The Bettmann Archive)

HEAVY WAGERING ACCOMPANIED ILLEGAL GAMECOCK MATCHES. BRED AS FIGHTERS FOR THOUSANDS OF YEARS, THE ROOSTERS RECEIVED SPECIAL MASSAGES AND EXERCISES TO TOUGHEN THEIR SKIN AND STRENGTHEN THEIR MUSCLES. AT TIMES KNIFE-EDGED GAFFS WERE ATTACHED TO THEIR NATURAL SPURS, AND CONTESTS WERE FOUGHT TO THE DEATH. (The Bettmann Archive)

Blindman's Bluff

GAMES FROM *AN AMERICAN GIRL'S BOOK*,
1831.

Robin's Alive

▲
A GROUP OF YOUNG COUNTRYFOLK HAVE DRESSED IN
THEIR BEST CLOTHES AND GATHERED TO HUSK A NEIGH-
BOR'S CORN. THE YOUNG MAN WHO HUSKS A RED EAR WINS
A KISS FROM THE LADY SITTING BY HIS SIDE.
(Culver Pictures)

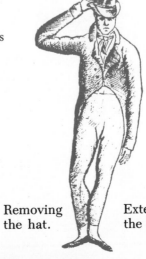

STEPS TO "ELEGANCE OF MANNERS," 1810.
(*Magazine of American History*, May 1887)

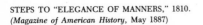

Removing
the hat.

Extending
the hand.

Bowing
slightly.

new government into a monarchy, Adams made it clear in his inaugural address that he was, and always would be, loyal to the principle of republicanism. Republican newspapers praised his "incorruptible integrity," and Jefferson hailed the "talents and integrity" of the new president. Political partisanship seemed to be on the decline.

Party factionalism was not to be so easily dispelled, however. Federalist leaders discouraged Adams from sending Madison, Jefferson's ally, as an envoy to France. Then Adams had to break with Jefferson after a letter was brought to public attention in which the vice-president seemed to criticize George Washington.

Adams inherited not only the in-fighting that had characterized the previous administration, but the cabinet as well: Secretary of the Treasury Oliver Wolcott, Secretary of War James McHenry, and Secretary of State Timothy Pickering. All three were mediocre administrators, and all three received constant instructions from Hamilton, now practicing law in New York.

To make matters worse, Adams devoted only part of his energies to the business of running the nation. His wife was ill, and he spent much of his time at home in Quincy, Massachusetts. Since he was not a politician by inclination, Adams never tried to develop a program or mobilize his congressional supporters to direct the party toward a more moderate course than it was following under Hamilton's guidance.

Conflict with France

In the meantime, France, still at war with England, began to suspect that the United States, while claiming to be neutral or even an ally, actually favored Britain. Jay's treaty, in particular, seemed to violate the spirit of the Franco-American Alliance of 1778.

The French, quite rightly, blamed this pro-British bias on the Federalists. In 1796 France tried to engineer a Federalist defeat by threatening to break off relations with America should Adams win the election. When Adams did win, the French carried out their threat. They captured several American vessels bound for England, refused to receive the American minister, C. C. Pinckney, and announced that from then on, France would follow Great Britain's example in its commercial dealings with America.

The XYZ Affair To persuade France to reverse its policy, Adams sent Pinckney, John Marshall, and Elbridge Gerry on a mission to Paris. The Americans failed completely. The French foreign minister, Talleyrand, kept the envoys waiting for several weeks, then offered a humiliating proposal through a trio of unaccredited French agents. These agents, referred to as X, Y, and Z, suggested to the Americans that a bargain could be worked out between the two nations in return for a substantial bribe, a not uncommon demand in eighteenth-century diplomatic circles. France also demanded a sizable loan and an apology from the president for remarks criticizing the French Revolution. "No, no, not a sixpence," declared Pinckney, and he and Marshall departed.

Adams decided to expose the French demands to the American public. He released the commissioners' reports, and Pinckney's relatively mild retort was quickly magnified into the overblown slogan, "Millions for defense, but not one cent for tribute!"

Some Federalists, who sympathized with Britain, seized on the news as a pretext for demanding war with France. The Jeffersonians, until now strongly pro-French, refused to believe Adams and demanded to see the commission's papers. The documents were presented, and they substantiated French guilt. Now both parties agreed to repudiate America's treaties with France, suspend trade with France, establish a navy department, and authorize American vessels to attack French warships and privateers. Washington even came out of retirement to command the army. For the next two years France and America waged an undeclared war on the high seas.

The French ruler, Napoleon, anxious to avoid a full-fledged war with the United States and aware of the improvement in Anglo-American relations following Jay's treaty, ordered Talleyrand to reverse French policy. Talleyrand therefore assured the president's son, John Quincy Adams, that an American envoy to Paris would "undoubtedly be received with the respect due to the representative of a free, independent and powerful nation."

While Hamilton's supporters continued to clamor for a declaration of war, Adams appointed a new mission to negotiate with France, and a compromise was reached in 1800. The United States was formally released from the Alliance of 1778 and, in

THIS 1799 CARTOON DEPICTS TALLEYRAND AS A MULTI-HEADED MONSTER DEMANDING MONEY FROM THE THREE-MAN AMERICAN COMMISSION. PINCKNEY RESPONDS, "CEASE BRAWLING, MONSTER! WE WILL NOT GIVE YOU SIX-PENCE."

return, agreed to drop its demands for compensation for American commercial losses. By placing patriotism ahead of popularity, Adams had spared the United States a needless war.

The Alien and Sedition Acts

On the domestic front, the furor aroused by the XYZ Affair gave the Federalists an opportunity to attempt to silence political opposition. In June and July 1798, Congress passed several laws known collectively as the Alien and Sedition Acts. The Naturalization Act increased the length of time a foreigner was required to live in America before qualifying for citizenship; it was designed to hurt the Democratic Republicans since most new immigrants joined their ranks after becoming citizens. Two Alien Acts empowered the president to expel aliens if he believed it necessary for American security.

The most controversial law was the Sedition Act, which made it illegal to instigate a conspiracy against the government and to publish or utter any "false, scandalous and malicious" criticism of the government or its top officials. Under the stern guidance of Timothy Pickering, the Federalists used the Sedition Act to silence criticism from some of Jefferson's followers. Their particular target was the increasing number of widely read Republican newspapers. For example, under the act three editors who favored Jefferson's policies were given stiff fines and jail sentences.

Madison and Jefferson responded immediately to this attack on civil liberties with the Virginia and Kentucky Resolutions. The Virginia Resolutions declared the Alien and Sedition Acts to be flagrant violations of the First Amendment guarantee of freedom of speech and press. In the Kentucky Resolutions, Jefferson proposed that a majority of the state legislatures had the right to nullify a federal law which they felt was unconstitutional. He based his argument on his belief that the Constitution was a compact among the states. The states had never given up their sovereignty, and they therefore had an "equal right" to judge the constitutionality of laws passed by the federal government.

Most state legislatures either disagreed with or ignored the Virginia and Kentucky Resolutions. Nevertheless, Jefferson's ideas on state sovereignty, as reinterpreted by a later generation, would prove a dangerous legacy for the future stability of the Union.

The Election of 1800

As the war scare waned, so did the popularity of the Federalists. Although the public respected Adams for his peaceful stand, many Americans now viewed the Federalists as warmongers. In addition, the undeclared war against France had led to new taxes and an increase in the national debt.

Federalist unity was also weakened and the enmity between Adams and Hamilton became more open. The passage of the Alien and Sedition Acts and the raising of an army for purposes of fighting the French (should it become necessary) drove moderate Federalists into an alliance with the Jeffersonians. The Federalist party declined further as wealthy farmers joined the small farmers already supporting the Democratic Republicans.

Jefferson's vigorous Democratic Republican party attracted many young, energetic politicians while the older Federalists sank back into what has been called "opulent apathy." Many leading Federalists refused to run for political office, preferring luxurious privacy to the glare of public life. Washington's death in December 1799 symbolized the passing of an era.

The presidential contest in 1800, again between Adams and Jefferson, was very close. When the electoral votes were counted, the Democratic Republicans had won, but it was not clear whether Jefferson or his running mate was to be the new president. Republican electors, voting strictly according to party loyalty, had returned as many votes for the rising New York politician Aaron Burr as

they had for Jefferson. The Constitution provided that in such cases the House of Representatives would choose between the two candidates. The Federalists controlled the votes in the House, however, and a deadlock resulted. Through thirty-five ballots neither candidate won a clear majority.

Several factors created a swing to Jefferson on the thirty-sixth ballot. Hamilton, a longtime rival of Burr, viewed the former New York senator as "the most unfit and dangerous man of the community" and did all he could to defeat him. Meanwhile, Jefferson's backers won support by giving reassurances to Federalist delegations. Maryland and Vermont then switched their votes to Jefferson, and on February 17, 1801 he was finally elected. To prevent a recurrence of these sorts of deadlocks in the electoral college, Congress drafted the Twelfth Amendment, providing for the president and vice-president to be elected by separate ballots.

In the election of 1800, the Federalists lost some forty seats in the House of Representatives, which left it with a sound Democratic Republican majority. Jefferson, the Democratic Republican candidate, had become president. The Federalists awaited with trepidation the future destruction of constitutional government.

Federalist Accomplishments

On March 4, 1801, Jefferson was sworn in at the new national capital, the crowded, half-built city of Washington on the banks of the Potomac.

The Federalist era had ended, but the party's accomplishments endured. The Federalists had strengthened the national government and rescued its finances. They had implemented the Constitution and demonstrated that large republican governments could be both stable and beneficial to the public welfare. And they had resolved the nation's remaining disputes with Great Britain, established American sovereignty to the Mississippi River, and in general maintained American neutrality in the European war.

After its defeat in 1800, the Federalist party waned as a national force. Historian Paul Goodman accounts for its decline by pointing to the newness of political parties in America. The first parties were fragile associations without deep roots, fixed loyalties, or entrenched organizations. Furthermore, their leaders did not consider themselves professional politicians, but statesmen called from their regular occupations to serve their country. They had not yet experienced the cyclical return of parties to power; their defeat seemed final. David Fisher has shown that although a younger generation of Federalists built elaborate party organizations in different states after 1800, this effort to revive the Federalist party ultimately failed to reestablish it as a national force.

Why had the once dominant Federalists lost the election of 1800? The reason most likely had to do with their aristocratic prejudices. As Noah Webster put it, "they have attempted to resist the force of current public opinion, instead of falling into the current with a view to direct it." More to the point, the Federalist outlook was out of tune with the forces shaping the future direction of the nation. Most Americans did not want a strong central government to guide their political and economic activities. The majority believed the future of the republic lay in the increasing number of opportunities open to individuals for participating in political life and for bettering themselves economically. They wanted to achieve these goals on their own or through their state legislatures. It was the Jeffersonians, not the Federalists, who sponsored these ideals.

Readings

General Works

Adair, Douglass, *Fame and the Founding Fathers*. New York: Norton, 1974.

Bowman, Albert H., *The Struggle for Neutrality: Franco-American Diplomacy During the Federalist Era*. Knoxville: University of Tennessee Press, 1974.

Buel, Richard, Jr., *Securing the Revolution: Ideology in American Politics 1789–1815*. Ithaca, N.Y.: Cornell University Press, 1972.

Chambers, William N., *Political Parties in a New Nation*. New York: Oxford University Press, 1963.

Charles, Joseph, *The Origins of the American Party System*. Williamsburg, Va.: Institute of Early American History and Culture, 1956.

Cunningham, Noble E., Jr., *The Jeffersonian Republicans*. Chapel Hill: University of North Carolina Press, 1957.

Dauer, Manning J., *The Adams Federalists*. Baltimore: Johns Hopkins Press, 1953.

Hofstadter, Richard, *The Idea of a Party System: The Rise of Legitimate Opposition in the United States, 1780–1840*. Berkeley: University of California Press, 1969.

Main, Jackson T., *Political Parties Before the Constitution*. Chapel Hill: University of North Carolina Press, 1974.

Miller, John C., *The Federalist Era 1789–1801*. New York: Harper & Row, 1960.

Nichols, Roy F., *The Invention of the American Political Parties: A Study of Political Improvisation*. New York: Free Press, 1967. (Paper, 1972)

Rutland, Robert A., *Ordeal of the Constitution*. New York: Quadrangle, 1968.

Schachner, Nathan, *The Founding Fathers*. New York: Putnam, 1954.

Special Studies

Ammon, Harry, *The Genêt Mission*. New York: Norton, 1973.

Bemis, Samuel F., *Jay's Treaty*. New Haven: Yale University Press, 1962.

———, *Pinckney's Treaty*. New Haven: Yale University Press, 1960.

Combs, Jerald A., *The Jay Treaty*. Berkeley: University of California Press, 1970.

Cooke, Jacob E. (Ed.), *Alexander Hamilton: A Profile*. New York: Hill & Wang, 1967.

DeConde, Alexander, *Entangling Alliance: Politics and Diplomacy Under George Washington*. Durham, N.C.: Duke University Press, 1958.

———, *The Quasi-War*. New York: Scribner's, 1966.

Gilbert, Felix, *The Beginnings of American Foreign Policy: To the Farewell Address*. Princeton, N.J.: Princeton University Press, 1961.

Kurtz, Stephen G., *The Presidency of John Adams*. Philadelphia: University of Pennsylvania Press, 1957.

Lycan, Gilbert, *Alexander Hamilton and American Foreign Policy*. Norman: University of Oklahoma Press, 1970.

McDonald, Forrest, *We the People: The Economic Origins of the Constitution*. Chicago: University of Chicago Press, 1958. (Paper, 1958)

Perkins, Bradford, *The First Rapprochement: England and the United States*. Berkeley: University of California Press, 1967.

Rossiter, Clinton L., *Seventeen Eighty-Seven: The Grand Convention*. New York: New American Library, 1968. (Paper)

Rutland, Robert A., *Birth of the Bill of Rights, 1776–1791*. New York: Macmillan, 1962. (Paper) Chapel Hill: University of North Carolina Press, 1955.

Smith, James Morton, *Freedom's Fetters: The Alien and Sedition Laws and American Civil Liberties*. New York: Cornell University Press, 1956. (Paper)

Stourzh, Gerald, *Alexander Hamilton and the Idea of Republican Government*. Stanford, Calif.: Stanford University Press, 1970.

Primary Sources

Commager, Henry S. (Ed.), *Selections from the Federalist*. New York: Appleton-Century-Crofts, 1949.

Biographies

Brant, Irving, *James Madison*, Vols. I–VI. Indianapolis: Bobbs-Merrill, 1970.

Flexner, James T., *Washington: The Indispensable Man*. Boston: Little, Brown, 1974.

Malone, Dumas, *Jefferson and His Time*, vols. 2 & 3. Boston: Little, Brown, 1951 and 1969.

McDonald, Forrest, *Alexander Hamilton: A Biography*. New York: Norton, 1979.

Miller, John C., *Alexander Hamilton: Portrait in Paradox*. New York: Harper Torchbooks, 1959.

Peterson, Merrill D., *Thomas Jefferson & the New Nation: A Biography*. New York: Oxford University Press, 1970.

Walters, Raymond, Jr., *Albert Gallatin*. New York: Macmillan, 1957.

7 The Jeffersonians in Power

I know, indeed, that some honest men fear that a republican government can not be strong, that this Government is not strong enough; but would the honest patriot, in the full tide of successful experiment, abandon a government which has so far kept us free and firm on the theoretic and visionary fear that this Government, the world's best hope, may by possibility want energy to preserve itself? I trust not. I believe this, on the contrary, the strongest Government on earth. I believe it the only one where every man, at the call of the law, would fly to the standard of the law, and would meet invasions of the public order as his own personal concern. Sometimes it is said that man can not be trusted with the government of himself. Can he, then, be trusted with the government of others? Or have we found angels in the forms of kings to govern him? Let history answer this question.

Thomas Jefferson,
The First Inaugural Address, 1801

Significant Events

Marbury v. *Madison* [1803]

Louisiana Purchase [1803]

Lewis and Clark Expedition [1804–1805]

Napoleon's Berlin Decree [November 1806]

Burr conspiracy [1806–1807]

British Orders in Council [1806 and 1807]

Napoleon's Milan Decree [1807]

Chesapeake affair [1807]

Embargo Act [1807]

Force Act [1809]

Nonintercourse Act [1809]

Macon's Bill No. 2 [1810]

Harrison marches against Tecumseh [1811]

United States declares war on Great Britain [June 1812]

Treaty of Ghent [December 1814]

Hartford Convention [December 1814–January 1815]

Battle of New Orleans [January 1815]

Rush-Bagot agreement [1817]

Convention with Great Britain [1818]

THE U.S.S. *CONSTITUTION* ("OLD IRONSIDES") ENGAGES AND DESTROYS THE H.M.S. *GUERRIERE* AT THE BEGINNING OF THE WAR OF 1812. (THE GRANGER COLLECTION, NEW YORK)

The election of the Jeffersonians in 1800 brought into power a party that embodied the revolutionary spirit and humanitarian ideals of the majority of the American people. With hindsight, we may say that this was one of the most significant elections in American history. The Federalists, who had controlled the young nation since the Revolution, were defeated in both the presidential and the congressional elections. Therefore the United States would enter the new century with a new leadership that represented the concepts to which most Americans were committed.

Jefferson called this election the "Revolution of 1800." The majority of voters had indicated that they did not favor a strong central government and that they were opposed to excessive federal direction of the economy. The vote represented a protest by the agricultural sector against the tremendous influence of the commercial and banking interests on national policy.

In the years to come, the Jeffersonians were to prove that, contrary to deeply held Federalist fears, they did not plan to overthrow the Constitution or the government established by it. Jefferson had an unqualified commitment to republican government. His party, a forerunner of the modern political parties, had exercised the right to dissent from official policy—to challenge it in an organized way—and it had succeeded. This became a permanent aspect of the American system of government. In an era characterized by war and repression in Europe, the majority of adult white men in America had voted in free elections for government by the party of their choice.

Jefferson's First Term

Jefferson's Philosophy Jefferson's political and social thought was a dominant influence in the party he led to power. A lawyer who was renowned for the breadth and depth of his intellectual interests—ranging from philosophy to agriculture and natural science, music, and languages—he wrote prolifically in a style that was a model of clarity and eloquence. He believed that the future direction of the republic was toward increasing political democracy, but he did not feel that everyone was equally qualified to participate in the political process. And although he was firmly committed to the advantages of majority rule, he did not believe that the majority always decided wisely and he believed that citizens should be educated before they were given the right to vote. Jefferson reflected the contradictions of his times: the man who had written in the Declaration of Independence "all men are created equal" remained a slaveholder.

Although he was a landowning member of the Virginia gentry, Jefferson believed in a natural aristocracy based on talent, education, and virtue rather than social position and wealth. He was convinced that individual and social betterment could be accomplished under conditions of individual freedom coupled with opportunity for economic advancement. Through the holding of private property (which gave an individual independence), freedom of expression (including religious freedom), the expansion of educational opportunity, and the institution of a government of limited power, individuals could fulfill their potential and the nation could grow strong.

Jefferson's democratic tendencies were expressed not only in his writings but also in his unpretentious style of living and in his egalitarian manner of dealing with others. At social functions he purposely ignored customary protocol and allowed his guests to sit wherever they wanted. At times he even served dinner himself from a dumbwaiter. Jefferson explained his behavior by saying, "The principle of society with us is the equal rights of all. . . . Nobody shall be above you, nor you above anybody, *pell mell* is our law."

Under this studied casualness, however, was a poised and refined mind. Jefferson was probably the most skilled statesman of his day. He was a man of moderation and willingness to compromise, and he made every attempt to reconcile the opposition to his presidency as he pursued his vision of the public good.

Jefferson's Inaugural Address reflected popular demands while at the same time assuring his political opponents that he would be fairminded: " . . . every difference of opinion is not a difference of principle. We are all republicans; we are all federalists," he declared, and, "the minority possess their equal rights, which equal law must protect,

ALTHOUGH ONE OF OUR MOST SOPHISTICATED AND VERSATILE PRESIDENTS, THOMAS JEFFERSON WAS OFTEN DECEPTIVELY CASUAL IN MANNER AND DRESS. IN ONE INSTANCE HE STARTLED THE MINISTER FROM GREAT BRITAIN BY RECEIVING HIM IN WELL-WORN SLIPPERS AND A COAT AND PANTALOONS THAT WERE "INDICATIVE OF UTTER SLOVENLINESS AND INDIFFERENCE TO APPEARANCES."

Old and New Policies

Jefferson believed that in 1800, as in 1776, the American people had demonstrated their virtue by overthrowing corrupt rulers. Much to the surprise of the Federalists, however, the new administration made few changes in the policies that were already established. At the urging of the new secretary of the treasury, Albert Gallatin, Jefferson retained Hamilton's entire economic program. This was unexpected because Hamilton's framework had formed the centerpiece of Federalist domestic policy and Jefferson, as secretary of state, had opposed virtually all of it. The difference now was that with the Federalists out of power Jefferson saw little danger that the system would be used as a tool of corruption. Consequently, funding of the national debt and assumption of the states' Revolutionary War debts went ahead as scheduled and the bank of the United States continued to operate until 1811, when its charter expired. Many Federalists were suspicious of this reasonable behavior, cynically attributing it to Jefferson's "immoderate thirst for popularity."

Some aspects of the Federalist legacy were changed. When the Alien Act expired in 1801, Jefferson refused to renew it; when the Sedition Act expired in the same year, Jefferson freed all citizens who had been imprisoned under it and refunded their fines. Finally, the residence requirement for citizenship, which Adams had raised to fourteen years, was returned to the original five-year period.

Jefferson believed in a policy of frugal management of the nation's economy. He and Gallatin wanted the United States to pay off the national debt as quickly as possible in order to lessen the influence of the monied class on government. By following a strict budget, Gallatin was able to shrink the national debt during Jefferson's two terms from $83 million to $57 million. All federal bonds were paid off by 1807.

Jefferson's second economic goal was for the United States to meet its expenses through revenues from tariffs, land sales, and postal services. Jefferson thought that tariff duties, the major source of income, would fall primarily on the wealthy, who could best afford to pay them. Accordingly, the Congress repealed all excise taxes, including the hated whiskey tax, and eliminated tax collectors. To cut back on federal expenses, Jefferson reduced the

and to violate would mean oppression." The new president warned the nation against entering into "entangling alliances" with European powers and emphasized his desire to limit the role of the federal government. He stated his belief that domestic concerns belong in state hands and that the function of the federal government was to keep order, preserve personal freedom, and reduce the national debt. In addition, Jefferson promised to stimulate and protect both agriculture and its "handmaid," commerce.

army from four thousand officers and enlisted men to twenty-five hundred. He also decreased the navy's annual appropriation from $3.5 million to $1 million in 1802 by selling a few oceangoing vessels and halting the construction of others. Other savings were made by reductions in the diplomatic corps, leaving American ministers in only three European cities: Madrid, Paris, and London.

These measures, the reflection of Jefferson's philosophy of economic *laissez-faire*, were intended to bring into being Jefferson's ideal state: a nation of citizens "managing their own affairs in their own way and for their own use, unembarrassed by too much regulation, unoppressed by fiscal extractions."

War on the Judiciary

When Jefferson took office, he was free to appoint members of his own party to important political positions. At first he adopted the moderate approach that Federalist officeholders would be removed only if they had been appointed after the election or if they had been found guilty of misconduct. But the continued hostility of the Federalists, along with pressure from his own party, caused Jefferson to become more partisan, and by mid-1803, almost 60 percent of the offices within the president's domain were held by Democratic Republicans.

Since Congress was also controlled by the Jeffersonians, the only remaining Federalist stronghold was the judiciary. In the final days of the Adams administration, the departing Congress had passed the Judiciary Act of 1801, instituting some badly needed reforms. The new law gave Adams a chance to make some last-minute judicial appointments (dubbed the "midnight justices"). These new federal judges were all Federalists, and they were appointed for life. Among these appointments was the naming of John Marshall of Virginia as chief justice of the Supreme Court. Born in a log cabin and raised on the frontier, Marshall was a tall, unpretentious man with a keen intellect and considerable personal magnetism. He was a staunch Federalist, favoring strong federal government, and an enemy of the new president.

In 1802 the Democratic Republicans repealed the Judiciary Act of 1801 and passed a new Judiciary Act. They believed that with the repeal of the first act the midnight justices would be automatically re-

moved from office. Abolishing Adams's appointments, however, was an act of dubious legality: the Constitution guarantees that federal judges "shall hold their offices during good behavior." Did the Constitution permit the executive and legislative branches to control the judiciary by eliminating jobs in this way? In theory, it was the function of the Supreme Court to check the executive and legislative branches, but the Court had never yet reviewed the constitutionality of any law. Did the Supreme Court have the authority to rule on the constitutionality of congressional acts? This process, known as "judicial review," was not mentioned in the Constitution. Many Americans doubted that the Supreme Court had the right to review legislation at all.

Marbury v. *Madison* In the famous case of *Marbury* v. *Madison* (1803), Chief Justice Marshall boldly set forth a rationale establishing the Court's right to declare an act of Congress unconstitutional. President Adams had signed Marbury's commission as a justice of the peace in the District of Columbia on March 2, 1801, and the Senate had confirmed him the next day. When Jefferson took office on March 4, Marbury still had not received his papers, and Secretary of State James Madison refused to deliver them. Informed that his appointment was ineffective, Marbury petitioned the Supreme Court to issue a writ of *mandamus* ordering Madison to deliver the commission to him. Marbury's request was based on a clause in the Judiciary Act of 1789 granting the Supreme Court the right to issue writs of *mandamus* as part of its "original jurisdiction" —that is, to those applying directly to the Court without going through the lower courts and the system of appeals.

Justice Marshall was in a difficult position. Issuing the writ could result in open warfare between the executive and the judicial branches. Should the writ be ignored, the Court would have no means of forcing Madison to comply. Marshall knew that if this happened, the Court would lose prestige. But failure to act would amount to an admission that the Court was afraid to challenge the president. Finally, Marshall settled on a third course. He declared that Madison (and Jefferson) were wrong in illegally withholding the commission, but that in this case the Supreme Court did not have the authority to issue the writ because the law granting it that power was unconstitutional. That law, the Judiciary Act of 1789, had defined the kinds of cases over which the Supreme Court had jurisdiction. Marshall argued that the Supreme Court's original jurisdiction under Article III of the Constitution did not mention writs of this sort. Since Congress did not have the power to delegate such authority to the Court, the clause in the Judiciary Act was therefore unconstitutional.

Thus Marbury did not receive his appointment. Although Marshall seemed to be handing a victory to Jefferson and Madison, in fact, he had established the right of the Supreme Court to invalidate federal laws that conflicted with the Constitution. This case had the effect of increasing the Court's jurisdiction by defining its power to rule on the constitutionality of legislative acts without a formal amendment to the Constitution. Although this power was never used again under Marshall, the precedent had been established.

Impeachment Jefferson, who had been cleverly outmaneuvered, soon devised another scheme to drive out the Federalist judges. On Jefferson's orders the House began impeachment proceedings against a New Hampshire district judge named John Pickering, charging him with "high crimes and misdemeanors." The Senate quickly voted to remove him from office. Pickering, however, had been delivering drunken harangues from the bench for three years and was considered almost insane. Because an insane person cannot be tried on such charges, the impeachment proceedings were of doubtful legality, even though drunk and abusive conduct obviously was not the "good behavior" required for independent tenure.

The Republicans then selected another victim for their impeachment strategy. Only one hour after Pickering was convicted, the House impeached another Federalist, Supreme Court Justice Samuel Chase. Chase was a staunch opponent of Jefferson and had once lectured a grand jury for hours on the evils of the Jefferson administration. Jefferson made every effort to remove Chase, but although the House of Representatives passed articles of impeachment, he could not obtain the two-thirds majority in the Senate needed for conviction. Chase returned triumphantly to the bench. Most Senators agreed that Chase had not maintained the dignity expected of a Supreme Court justice, but even many staunch

Jeffersonians could not be convinced that he had committed either "high crimes" or "misdemeanors."

In some ways, Chase's acquittal was fortunate. Had he been convicted, Jefferson might have been tempted to continue his war against the Federalist judges, and the courts might have lost their independence. In his anger, Jefferson had come perilously close to suppressing political opposition.

The Louisiana Purchase

The outstanding achievement of Jefferson's presidency was most likely the purchase of the Louisiana Territory, one of the most fabulous real estate bargains in history. Jefferson, an ardent expansionist, dreamed that one day the territory belonging to the United States would stretch from the Atlantic to the Pacific Coast, forming a great "empire for liberty." He envisioned a continent made up of small towns and independent farms which would comprise one great agrarian Republic. When Jefferson became president, nearly one million Americans had settled in the vast area between the Appalachian Mountains and the Mississippi River. Jefferson, to encourage further settlement of Western lands, successfully urged Congress to pass new land acts lowering the price and minimum acreage of individual farms. The prosperity of the Western farmers depended on their access to the Mississippi River and the port of New Orleans because it was far too expensive to send their produce to East Coast markets by the shorter route over the mountains. Although the Louisiana Territory, along whose eastern border the Mississippi flowed, was controlled by Spain, the Spanish, under the terms of Pinckney's treaty, had agreed to permit Americans to deposit their cargoes in New Orleans and then reload them onto ocean-going vessels. Jefferson much preferred to own New Orleans outright, but because Spain was weak and did not obstruct American commerce, he was willing to be patient.

Negotiations with France Just before Jefferson assumed office in 1800, Spain agreed to return the Louisiana Territory to France, the strongest nation in Europe. The effect of this agreement would be to place the strategic port of New Orleans under the personal control of Napoleon, who was apparently ready to try again to extend the French empire in the Western Hemisphere. Spain was willing to give up the territory only because the effort to hold it had

Louisiana Purchase and Western Exploration • 1803 to 1819

grown too costly and because France had promised to turn over Tuscany, a region of Italy, to Spain. The Spanish also believed Napoleon's assurances that French settlers would form a reliable buffer be-

tween Spain's other possessions in the New World and the aggressive Americans to the east.

Deeply concerned by rumors of the secret agreement, Jefferson instructed Robert Livingston, the American minister in France, to secure American commercial rights in New Orleans and to negotiate the purchase of West Florida. In a letter to Livingston, he wrote that there was "on the globe one single spot, the possessor of which is our natural and habitual enemy. It is New Orleans, through which the produce of three-eighths of our territory must pass to market. . . . The day that France takes possession of New Orleans we must marry ourselves to the British fleet and nation." Given Jefferson's well-known antipathy to England and his long-time advocacy of a foreign policy based on the avoidance of entangling alliances, it is clear that he regarded the possibility of French possession of the mouth of the Mississippi as a serious threat to the United States. His apprehension was reinforced when before Louisiana was formally transferred to France in 1802, the Spanish official at New Orleans suspended American citizens' right of deposit. If this action was any indication of coming French policy, the United States faced a crisis.

In the meantime, Santo Domingo, the most important island in the French West Indies, had fallen into the hands of rebellious slaves led by the "Black Napoleon," Toussaint L'Ouverture. Napoleon sent an expedition under General LeClerc to crush the revolt. The presence of French troops so near Louisiana alarmed Jefferson further. To avoid open conflict, he warned Congress of the dangers of a French occupation of New Orleans and, in a secret message, requested funds for purchase of both New Orleans and West Florida. Livingston discussed the sale with Napoleon's foreign minister but made little headway. Finally in December 1802, Jefferson appointed James Monroe as a special envoy to France to offer $10 million for New Orleans and the Floridas.

Two days before Monroe arrived in Paris, Napoleon suddenly reversed his policy and offered to

IN NAPOLEON'S HEADQUARTERS AT THE LOUVRE, THE EMPEROR SHAKES HANDS WITH THE AMERICAN ENVOYS WHO PURCHASED LOUISIANA. "I RENOUNCE LOUISIANA, THE WHOLE COLONY WITHOUT RESERVE," HE DECLARED.

sell not only New Orleans, but the entire territory of Louisiana as well! The American ministers had no time to await instructions from home and, after a brief hesitation, they agreed to accept responsibility for purchasing an area that would almost double the size of their nation.

What caused the French to make this incredible proposal? Part of the reason was that Napoleon was having second thoughts about extending the French empire in the Western Hemisphere. Le-Clerc's Caribbean expedition had ended in disaster. Yellow fever had decimated the French forces, and even though L'Ouverture was tricked into surrendering, the French were still unable to put down the rebellion.

Another factor was that since 1799 the chief goal of French diplomacy in the New World had been to prevent an alliance between America and Britain. Napoleon was a military genius, and he knew that Britain's superior navy could defeat the French in any contest over North American territory. Thus the sale of Louisiana would prevent the French from becoming contestants in a part of the world where their prospects of success were not bright, and it would also enrich the French treasury in preparation for pending campaigns in Europe. The sale of the territory also would secure for France the friendship of the United States and would prevent the Americans from joining forces with the British. In addition, it might in the long run assist the Americans in becoming Britain's maritime rival.

In the final agreement, reached on April 30, 1803, the United States, in return for the small sum of $15 million, gained millions of acres of land with vaguely defined boundaries, inhabited by a population of two hundred thousand Spanish, French, and Indians. The United States paid one-quarter of the price in cash. The remainder was obtained by borrowing without the introduction of any new internal taxes.

Most Americans rejoiced over the Louisiana Purchase. The Jeffersonians called the purchase a great diplomatic victory, and Westerners were relieved to have secured the Mississippi River. Only a few stubborn Federalists raised any objections, arguing that the president had exceeded his powers in buying the new land. Their real concern, however, was that the rural interest of this vast new re-

gion might some day overwhelm the commercial concerns of the East.

Jefferson himself had mixed feelings about the purchase. As an expansionist, he could foresee great possibilities in a landed empire stretching to the Rockies and inhabited by free farmers. Yet he was a strict constructionist in his interpretation of the Constitution, and the document did not specifically provide for the acquisition of new territory. After much agonizing, however, he decided the purchase could be justified under the Constitution's treaty-making power. In later years Jefferson defended his action in these words: "Strict observance to the written laws is doubtless one of the high duties of a good citizen, but it is not the highest. The laws of necessity, of self-preservation, of saving our country when in danger, are of a higher obligation."

Exploration of the Louisiana Territory

Jefferson was in no hurry to open the Louisiana Territory to settlement; he regarded it as Indian land to be governed by military administration. Exploration was a different matter. The vast, unknown region appealed strongly to the president's interest in natural science, and early in 1803 Congress appropriated $2500 to finance an expedition supported by Jefferson and headed by an experienced wilderness explorer, Meriwether Lewis, and an Indian fighter, William Clark (a brother of George Rogers Clark).

Jefferson issued copious instructions, directing the team to report all kinds of geographical, geological, and meteorological information and to study flora and the remains of extinct animal species. The expedition was also instructed to find a usable route to the Pacific and to study the possibilities for developing fur trade with the Indians.

Lewis and Clark left St. Louis in May 1804 with about forty-five men. They followed the Missouri River up to North Dakota where they spent the winter. In April 1805, after shipping nine boxes of specimens and curios back to the eager president, they pushed farther west. Guided by a French Canadian and his Indian wife, Sacajawea, and assisted in many ways by Clark's resourceful slave, York, the expedition passed over the Continental Divide in southwestern Montana and descended by the Columbia River to the Pacific. It reached the

A)

B)

A) MERIWETHER LEWIS, JEFFERSON'S THIRTY-TWO-YEAR-OLD PRI-
VATE SECRETARY AND AN EXPERIENCED FRONTIERSMAN, WAS
PICKED TO HEAD EXPLORATION OF THE VAST LOUISIANA TERRI-
TORY.
B) *CAPTAIN LEWIS AND CLARK HOLDING A COUNCIL WITH THE
INDIANS* APPEARED IN A SERIES OF ETCHINGS BY PATRICK GLASS,
ONE OF THE MEN TRAVELING WITH THE EXPEDITION. GLASS'S IL-
LUSTRATIONS ACCOMPANIED THE FIRST ACCOUNT OF THE EXPEDI-
TION PRINTED IN 1807.
C) CLARK'S OWN SKETCH OF A CANOE USED BY THE NORTHWEST
COAST INDIANS.

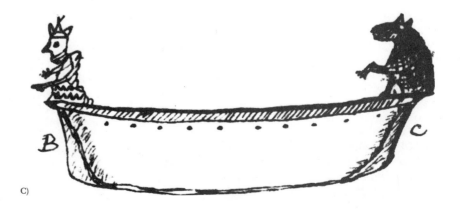

C)

ocean in November and wintered on the coast, then returned to St. Louis in September 1806. The greatest scientific achievement of the journey was a map released in 1814; full records were not published until 1904.

Other explorers charted the West as traders and new settlers slowly moved into the territory. Thomas Freeman journeyed through the Spanish-owned Southwest, and between 1805 and 1807 Lieutenant Zebulon Pike explored the upper Mississippi Valley and present-day Colorado. Pike discovered the peak named after him and eventually made his way into Spanish territory. He drew a map of the far Southwest and brought back the first detailed reports of the Rockies and the Great Plains.

By 1812 there were seventy-five thousand people in the territory adjacent to the mouth of the Mississippi River, and that year Louisiana entered the Union as the eighteenth state. Although a few fur traders pushed into the northern region, it remained virtually unsettled for many years.

The Essex Junto

The Louisiana Purchase contributed greatly to the political problems of the Federalist party. With most of the country supporting the Jeffersonians, settlers in the new territory were likely to be Democratic Republicans. Some of the more ardent Federalists even considered a plan to secede from the Union. A group known as the Essex Junto, centered in Massachusetts and headed by Senator Timothy Pickering, proposed forming a new country which was to include Newfoundland, New England, Pennsylvania, and New York. As Pickering declared, "The people of the East cannot reconcile their habits, views, and interests with those of the South and West."

The plan received little support, however, even among Federalists. When Hamilton refused to take part in the plot, Pickering turned to Aaron Burr, who had become discontented with his position as vice-president. Jefferson openly disliked and distrusted Burr, particularly after Burr refused to renounce the support of Federalists who sought to defeat Jefferson during the election of 1800. Jefferson had subsequently deprived Burr of patronage and excluded him from important decision making. Hungry for power, Burr decided to run for governor of New York in 1804. Pickering approached him during the campaign and promised Federalist support if Burr would bring New York into the "Northern Confederacy."

Burr's overwhelming defeat in the election in New York had important consequences. First, the Essex Junto collapsed. Second, Hamilton, who had played a major role in defeating the conspiracy, allowed his low opinion of Burr to appear in public print. Burr demanded a retraction from Hamilton and then formally challenged him to a duel. The two longtime rivals met with pistols in July 1804. According to some observers, Hamilton aimed his gun to miss. Burr's bullet lodged in Hamilton's spine, and within thirty hours Alexander Hamilton, the financial wizard of the new republic, was dead.

Jefferson's Second Term

Political Opponents

Jefferson won the presidential election of 1804 by a landslide, defeating weak Federalist opposition. The administration had shown that it was possible to have a federal government that was limited in its powers and frugal in its expenditures without creating economic and political disorder. There had been no lawlessness during Jefferson's first term, and internal taxes had been abolished without harm to the nation.

There were some dissidents, however, within the Jeffersonian coalition. One group, led by John Randolph of Roanoke, advocated an extreme states' rights position. Randolph had originally been a supporter of Jefferson, but by 1804 he began to fear the federal government was becoming too powerful. He resented Jefferson's leadership on the grounds that it interfered in the legislative process. When Jefferson prepared a bill that called for the use of federal money to settle fraudulent land claims, Randolph was successful in securing its defeat. He also opposed Jefferson's attempts to buy West Florida from Spain as unconstitutional. From that point, Randolph opposed the administration at every opportunity and joined with other dissatisfied Republicans in forming a short-lived third-party movement called the Quids. Randolph's drive and defiance won him some sympathy, but his influence in Congress waned, and in later years he suffered from periodic bouts of insanity.

Aaron Burr posed a different sort of threat to Jefferson. Although he was politically ruined by his unsuccessful New York campaign and by a murder indictment, Burr was still an ambitious schemer with an unstable mind. He began to entertain bizarre dreams of acquiring a Western empire.

While still vice-president, Burr approached the British minister in Washington with a reckless offer:

BURR'S LAST DAYS WERE MARKED BY UNHAPPINESS. THE SHIP ON WHICH HIS CHERISHED DAUGHTER THEODOSIA WAS TAKING AN OCEAN VOYAGE WAS LOST AT SEA, AND FOR YEARS BURR FREQUENTED THE BATTERY OVERLOOKING NEW YORK HARBOR IN THE HOPE THAT SHE WOULD MIRACULOUSLY RETURN. AT SEVENTY-SEVEN HE MARRIED HIS WEALTHY OLD MISTRESS, BETSY JUMEL, BUT SHE EVENTUALLY TURNED HIM OUT OF HER HOME AND DIVORCED HIM ON CHARGES OF ADULTERY. THE NEWSPAPERS REPORTED THAT AS HE LAY DYING HE STRUGGLED WILDLY AND CRIED, "I CAN'T DIE; I WON'T DIE!" TO WHICH HIS PHYSICIAN REPLIED, "MR. BURR, YOU ARE ALREADY DYING."

if England would supply one-half million dollars, Burr would lead the Western part of the United States in an insurrection to create a separate confederacy. Then, without waiting for a response, Burr traveled west to enlist the support of another expert at intrigue, General James Wilkinson, Jefferson's military commandant of the Louisiana Territory and a Spanish agent. The two conspirators organized a small band of soldiers on Blennerhassett Island in the Ohio River, and in December 1806 Burr led them south to join Wilkinson at New Orleans.

No one knows exactly what Burr intended to do; he may have been planning to foment a revolt in the Western states or even to take over Mexico. In any event, Wilkinson suddenly changed his mind and revealed the plot to Jefferson. Captured while trying to escape to Florida, Burr was charged with conspiracy and treason.

Burr's trial began in August 1807. Chief Justice Marshall, who conducted the proceedings, and President Jefferson both took a partisan approach. Determined to see his political rival convicted, Jefferson went so far as to instruct the government attorneys on how to organize the case and to take personal charge of assembling the evidence. Marshall was hostile toward Jefferson and clearly sympathetic to the defendant. The chief justice tried to subpoena the president, but Jefferson refused to appear on constitutional grounds.

Burr's defense was based on the fact that he was not actually on Blennerhassett Island when the force left and thus was not party to an overt act of treason. The government claimed that Burr was guilty anyway because he had instigated the plot. Marshall sided with the defense, arguing that under the Constitution "treason" included only overt *acts*, not verbal plans. A conviction would require "the testimony of two witnesses to the same overt act." The application of this narrow definition in Marshall's instructions to the jury not only forced the jury to acquit Burr, but also set an important precedent for the future of civil liberties in the United States.

International Problems

Jefferson was the first president to end the policy of appeasement which the United States government had taken toward the Barbary pirates since the

1780s. For years, corsairs from the northern coast of Africa had plundered commercial shipping vessels, forcing the American and European governments to buy immunity from the rulers of Morocco, Algiers, Tunis, and Tripoli. Consequently, the United States was forced to pay some $100,000 in bribes annually, a practice which always had infuriated Jefferson.

Jefferson reached the limit of his tolerance when the pasha of Tripoli tried to squeeze more money from the United States and chopped down the flagpole of the American consulate as a declaration of hostilities. In return, Jefferson sent the American navy to bombard Tripoli. Unfortunately, the president's budget cutting had so weakened the navy that it could not overwhelm the pirates. It did, however, manage to establish a blockade in 1805, and the pasha was obliged to make peace. Although some form of tribute was paid for another ten years, America was in a position to demand a lower price for the "protection." In addition, the war provided the inexperienced American navy under the command of Commodore Edward Preble with some useful training.

The French and British Conflict

Jefferson's second term was so controversial and trying in the area of foreign affairs that he wrote a friend: "Never did a prisoner released from his chains, feel such relief as I shall on shaking off the shackles of power."

Two weeks after arranging for the sale of Louisiana, Napoleon resumed his efforts to gain control of Europe. This new conflict, which ravaged all of Europe for the next twelve years, again stimulated American commerce and shipbuilding. Between 1803 and 1812, Americans reaped immense profits from a flourishing neutral trade. In fact, these profits were not equaled again in real value until the late 1940s.

During the first years of the European war, America was able to trade with Britain and France with little interference from the two adversaries. England and the United States were on fairly good terms, and the French navy was not strong enough to patrol the Atlantic. After 1803, however, the British began to fear a French invasion and stepped up measures to recruit seamen for their ships and to tighten the blockade around France. Earlier disagreements between the United States and Britain

over impressment, contraband, and neutral rights were renewed. In 1805 the *Essex*, an American vessel carrying cargo from Spain to Cuba by way of Salem, Massachusetts, was seized by an English frigate. This action proved to be the beginning of a campaign to capture scores of American merchant vessels on the grounds that they were trading illegally between European ports and enemy ports in the Caribbean.

The war developed into a strange stalemate. British triumphs at sea were matched by French victories on land. Unable to strike a direct military blow, both nations turned to relentless commercial warfare. In November 1806 Napoleon issued the Berlin Decree, which set up a blockade of the British Isles. Britain retaliated with the Orders in Council of 1806 and 1807, which closed the northern coast of Europe to all trade, forbade coastal trade between European ports under French control, and required all neutral vessels to obtain a British license before entering a European port. Napoleon followed in 1807 with the Milan Decree, which declared all ships with a British license subject to immediate seizure.

The United States was caught in a vise. American vessels sailing between French ports without a British license could be taken by the British. If they entered a French port with a British license, they would be seized by the French. British merchants were happy to have this opportunity to undermine America's expanding trade, which had become a threat to Britain's commercial supremacy. British men-of-war hovered off the American coast to capture goods being reshipped to European ports. The result was a virtual blockade of key ports on the Atlantic seaboard and in the Gulf of Mexico.

Americans also were infuriated by the British practice of impressment. According to British law, the navy was permitted to stop any neutral vessel, remove all English subjects, and impress them into service—a practice which the British believed was crucial to their maritime supremacy. Under this official sanction, many American ships were stopped at sea and searched for potential recruits. In truth, many British sailors, attracted by comparatively high wages and good working conditions, regularly deserted their own vessels to join American crews. British officers were not scrupulous, however, when searching for their countrymen. Swedes, Danes, and Portuguese sailors were hauled

THE BRITISH NAVY IMPRESSING AMERICAN SEAMEN.

away, and between 1793 and 1811 the British captured about ten thousand native-born Americans.

An American Embargo By 1807 the British had seized more than five hundred American ships. This interference with trade, plus the practice of impressment, caused much bitterness. Nevertheless, Jefferson continued to believe that prosperity was more important than national honor: "We have principles from which we shall never depart," he insisted. "We do not want war, and all this is very embarrassing." Negotiations in England by James Monroe and William Pinkney resulted in a treaty which Jefferson decided not to submit to the Senate because the British had not renounced impressment. He believed the protection of American citizens on the high seas was too vital to be abridged.

Then an incident in 1807 struck such a blow to American pride that war seemed almost inevitable.

The admiral of the British frigate *Leopard* violated international practice by halting the American warship *Chesapeake* and demanding the right to board to search for deserters. When Commodore James Barron refused, the *Leopard* opened fire. Three men were killed, eighteen were wounded, and the *Chesapeake* was forced to surrender. After the British seized four deserters, they allowed the crippled *Chesapeake* to return to Norfolk, Virginia.

The American people were outraged. Jefferson described the nation's mood: "Never since the battle of Lexington have I seen this country in such a state of exasperation as at present, and even that did not produce such unanimity." But although the public clamored for war, Jefferson knew that America's tiny navy was no match for British seapower. Determined nevertheless to strike back rather than submit to humiliation, he turned to a strategy of economic coercion. Jefferson had always believed such a pol-

THE *LEOPARD* TAKES THE *CHESAPEAKE*.

icy could protect the country's interests with dignity and preserve American neutrality without resorting to military action. In December 1807 Jefferson's congressional supporters passed the Embargo Act, prohibiting the export of American goods by land or by sea and permitting only coastal trade between American ports. While Jefferson was aware that the law would hurt the American economy, he hoped it would put an end to incidents that insulted the national honor. The embargo was expected to put effective pressure on Britain and France, since many nations depended on America for food and other commodities.

Some segments of the British economy were adversely affected by the embargo. Textile factories which needed American cotton were forced to shut down, leaving thousands of factory workers suddenly unemployed. Nevertheless, because 1808 was a good year for English crops, the effect of the embargo was somewhat weakened. Indeed, the embargo actually helped some English merchants by increasing the market for British goods.

As it turned out, the embargo created the greatest hardship in America itself. Exports fell from $108 million in 1807 to $22 million in 1808. Commercial wharves lost business, and the price of manufactured goods and farm products suffered a sharp decline. New England merchants, dependent on overseas commerce, again talked of seceding from the Union. And although some Yankee skippers were able to evade the embargo by smuggling goods into Canada, the United States faced a serious depression.

The president, recognizing that economic pressures could not be expected to yield immediate results, refused to revoke the unpopular law. Rather than building a bigger navy capable of enforcing American rights, he resorted to stricter trade regulations which he ineffectively tried to enforce. He obtained from Congress the Force Act of 1809, giving federal collectors almost arbitrary power over American trade. To Jefferson, the act was preferable to the more dangerous centralization of authority which he believed war would bring. Nevertheless, the Embargo Act proved unworkable because of American ingenuity in circumventing the law. Three days before Jefferson was scheduled to leave office, Congress replaced the Embargo Act with the Nonintercourse Act, which prohibited trade only with Britain and France. Had Americans had a little more patience with the embargo, it might have forced the British to repeal the Orders in Council three and a half years earlier than they actually did.

Ironically, the Embargo Act may have had one beneficial side effect. When Northern merchants were cut off from international trade, many were forced to invest their capital in manufacturing enterprises. Jefferson, who was opposed to the development of factories in the United States, had unintentionally laid the foundations for the industrialization of America.

Madison as President

By the end of his second term, Jefferson, now sixty-six years old, was eager to leave active political life. He had always disliked the speech making, the bickering, and the direct confrontations involved in politics. He also believed, as had Washington, that no president should serve more than two terms. In one of his final political acts, he personally intervened in the legislative caucus to win the next presidential nomination for his close friend, Secretary of State James Madison.

Madison easily won the election of 1808. Unfortunately, the new president did not have the political skills of his brilliant predecessor. A scholarly, conscientious man, Madison was a serious student of political philosophy. Yet despite his experience in politics, he periodically exhibited poor judgment and difficulty making decisions. He was no match for stronger, more aggressive politicians and was the first president to have cabinet choices forced on him by Congress, which had become the center of governmental power. Madison's vivacious wife, Dolley, eighteen years his junior with black hair and creamy skin, turned out to be a valuable political asset. The public and the press were interested in all her activities, and she achieved great popularity as the nation's official hostess.

The Failure of Peaceful Coercion

The biggest problem facing Madison when he took office was how to avoid war with England. The Nonintercourse Act, passed early in 1809, was beginning to have some effect on the English economy. Napoleon had sealed off most of continental Europe from trade with Britain, so British industrialists needed the American market. They began to pressure Foreign Minister George Canning to repeal the Orders in Council. Canning responded half-heart-

JAMES MADISON WAS A SMALL, BRISK MAN WHOSE SCHOLARLY AP-
PEARANCE CONCEALED A DRY SENSE OF HUMOR AND A MIS-
CHIEVOUS MANNER WITH THE LADIES. DESPITE HIS INTELLI-
GENCE AND POLITICAL EXPERIENCE, HE LACKED THE PERSONAL
CHARM AND ADMINISTRATIVE SKILLS WHICH WOULD HAVE MADE
HIM A STRONG LEADER.

DOLLEY MADISON AND HER HUSBAND BECAME ACQUAINTED
WHEN HE HELPED HER UP FROM A SLIPPERY SIDEWALK IN PHILA-
DELPHIA. THE COUNTRY'S FIRST PRETTY NATIONAL HOSTESS, SHE
WAS IMMENSELY POPULAR AND FASCINATED THE PUBLIC WITH
HER HABITS OF GAMBLING AT CARDS, ROUGING HER CHEEKS, AND
WEARING EXTRAVAGANT GOWNS AND GOLD AND SILVER SLIPPERS.

edly. Although willing to admit that Britain had no right to search American warships, he would make no apology for the attack on the *Chesapeake*.

Canning went so far as to open some European ports to American trade and to instruct the British minister in Washington, David M. Erskine, to negotiate a settlement. The sympathetic Erskine reached an agreement which provided for Britain's withdrawal of the Orders in Council with no concessions asked in return. Madison was delighted and lifted the embargo on June 10, 1809, without waiting for the agreement to be approved in London.

Unfortunately, Erskine's terms had been more lenient than Canning intended. The foreign minister was furious when he received news of the gen-

erous settlement. He immediately repudiated it, summoned Erskine back to London, and replaced him with a disagreeable man who abhorred Americans.

Politically embarrassed by the haste with which he had lifted the embargo, Madison was forced to restore nonintercourse. In the interim, however, tons of American produce had been unloaded in England, bringing relief after a long period of hardship. With its warehouses stocked with food and cotton, England was in a good position to drive a hard bargain.

On May 1, 1810, the United States instituted another weak economic policy. Macon's Bill No. 2 attempted to restore trade by playing off Britain and

War Hawks in Congress

"An honorable peace is attainable only by an efficient war. My plan would be to call out the ample resources of the country, give them a judicious direction, prosecute the war with the utmost vigor, strike wherever we can reach the enemy, at sea or on land, and negotiate the terms of a peace at Quebec or Halifax. We are told that England is a proud and lofty nation that disdaining to wait for danger, meets it half-way. Haughty as she is, we once triumphed over her, and if we do not listen to the councils of timidity and despair we shall again prevail. . . ."

Henry Clay, Annals of Congress
January 1813

New England Doves

"The war cannot be carried on by the Militia. A regular army will be enlisted with the utmost difficulty; besides money cannot be raised by Loans; and if Taxes be collected, the popularity of the Party according to Mr. Jefferson's former opinion, must be destroyed. I infer that the war will drag on heavily; that it will become very, and extensively, unpopular; that the dread of French connexion will greatly increase the mass of discontent; that the Congressional Elections will show the perilous unanimity of the Northern States agt. the war, and if England have a wise ministry, we must soon return to Peace."

Rufus King, Letter to C. Gore

France. If France would agree to respect America's neutral rights, the United States would suspend trade with Britain. If Britain would repeal its Orders in Council, America would suspend trade with France.

Napoleon immediately saw a chance to manipulate the new law to his advantage. He announced that France would repeal its commercial restrictions, then hedged the promise with qualifying clauses which rendered it virtually meaningless. Madison was tricked by Napoleon's offer and asked England for a similar concession. When the British refused, Congress again moved to prohibit trade with England, and Madison severed diplomatic relations by recalling the American minister. Meanwhile, Napoleon was not fulfilling his pledge. On the very day he made his offer, France raised the tariffs on American goods and seized all American ships in French ports. Outmaneuvered by the Europeans, Madison had accomplished nothing.

Relations with Britain deteriorated further in May 1811. A chance encounter between the American frigate *President* and the British warship *Little Belt* led to a battle off the coast of Virginia in which the British ship was blasted out of the water killing nine crewmen. The American public was exultant, seeing in the incident revenge for the *Chesapeake* affair. The atmosphere in both countries was becoming increasingly hostile.

The War Hawks

When Congress met in November 1811, most of the representatives who had opposed war with Britain had been replaced by a new group. Sensitive to questions of American honor, these newly elected representatives were furious at England's arrogant behavior toward the United States. The leaders of the war faction, popularly known as the "War Hawks," were a small band of youthful Democratic Republicans from the Southern and Western states. They were dominated by the new Speaker of the House, thirty-four-year-old Henry Clay of Kentucky. These angry young men had little interest in the question of states' rights and were quite willing to delegate more power to the federal government, particularly in wartime. They tended to be intensely nationalistic and eager for territorial expansion. Believing that only through war could America assert its power and redress insupportable indignities, they clamored for revenge on England.

By late spring of 1812 both the president and Secretary of State James Monroe had become more receptive to the aggressive demands of the War Hawks. Ultimately there was no split within the Republican party when the vote for war was taken. Even many of Jefferson's followers in New England advocated armed resistance. Although the Federalists were in the minority, they were even more cohesive on the issue than the Jeffersonians, for they feared the power the federal government might assume during wartime. When votes were cast in June 1812, not a single Federalist broke ranks to support going to war against Britain.

Those who favored the conflict were motivated by a strong desire to vindicate the nation's honor and to protect America's republican form of government. They argued that France was no longer interfering with American commerce. As Henry Clay put it: "As to France we have no complaint . . . but of the past. Of England we have to complain in all tenses." However, America had been in a serious depression since 1808. The attacks on American shipping had resulted in a downturn in the economy of the West and South, and prices for hemp, cotton, and tobacco had fallen steadily. Farmers blamed these conditions on commercial restrictions set by England.

New Englanders also needed a free flow of trade with Europe, but people of this region had a lingering emotional attachment to Britain which influenced their view on the war issue. New England was still the stronghold of Federalism. Politically and culturally its conservative citizenry strongly sympathized with the British in their struggle with the French. They believed a war with England would be a blow against the tradition of parliamentary government and a triumph for Napoleon, who held all of Europe in his autocratic grip.

Westward Expansion

Maritime problems were not the only factors contributing to the war movement. Americans were eager to expand their territory westward, and settlers and speculators rushed to the most fertile areas, often displacing the Indians who occupied the land.

GENERAL WILLIAM HENRY HARRISON AND TECUMSEH.

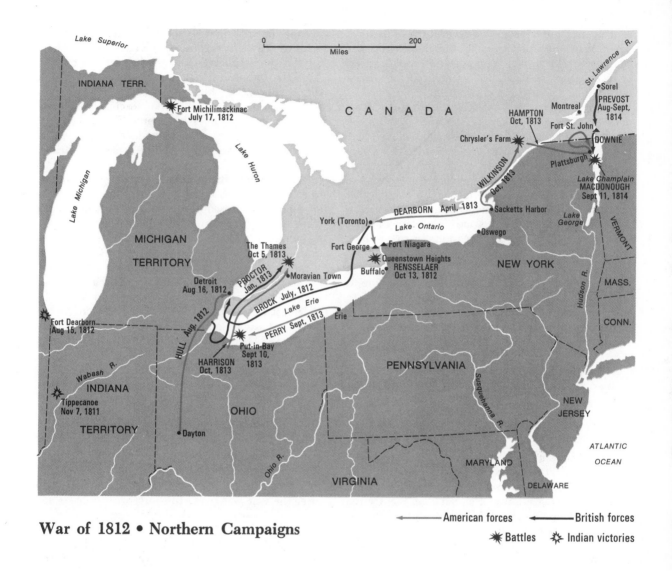

War of 1812 • Northern Campaigns

American forces ⟵   British forces ⟵

✷ Battles   ✷ Indian victories

Despite his expressed concern for the welfare of the Indian tribes, Jefferson had done little as president to protect their rights. Instead, Indians had been cajoled into ceding lands under treaties they usually did not fully understand.

Madison expressed the belief of many citizens that British officials in Canada were aiding Indian reprisals by supplying tribes with weapons and paying a bounty for American scalps. In fact, Canadians encouraged the Indians to make peace. A strong Indian force would make them less vulnerable should war break out between the United States and Great Britain. Most Indian attacks were actually prompted by American plundering of their tribal hunting grounds.

Tecumseh General William Henry Harrison, governor of the Indiana Territory, considered Indians "wretched savages" and mere obstructions to American "civilization." Through deceptive treaty arrangements he had deprived several tribes of their lands. When Shawnee chief Tecumseh and his half-brother Tenskwatawa, known as the Prophet, tried to reverse this trend, Harrison prepared for an all-out battle.

Tecumseh was a compelling orator and a man of bold insight and imagination. Traveling from the Great Lakes to the Gulf of Mexico, he preached that Indians should live separately from the white people, safe from their power, their corrupting laws, and their liquor. By 1806 he had organized the tribes east of the Mississippi into a confederacy. So great was Tecumseh's influence that even Harrison was obliged to admit: "He is one of those uncommon geniuses which spring up occasionally to produce revolutions and overturn the established order of things."

In November 1811, General Harrison came to Indiana to wipe out Tecumseh's camp. Hoping to drive the whites away, Tenskwatawa led an attack against them; however, Harrison managed to repel the Indians and destroy the camp on Tippecanoe Creek. Although the battle was indecisive, it threw Tecumseh's confederacy into disarray and alarmed many Americans. To them the incident was another instance of British incitement of the Indians and yet another reason for going to war. Moreover, they viewed the conflict as an opportunity not only to drive the Indians farther west, but also to strike at the British bases which supposedly supplied them. Some War Hawks even hoped to annex Canada and the Floridas (still held by Spain, England's ally). They believed that once Canada became part of America, the continent would be free of the British forever.

Eventually, Britain made a few vague attempts to win American friendship. Two of the four deserters who had been captured aboard the *Chesapeake* were returned to American soil. An editorial in a Baltimore newspaper was typical of American reaction: "Presented at such a time," it read, "the reparation was like restoring a hair after fracturing the skull." Ironically, on June 16, 1812, a new British ministry decided to suspend the Orders in Council. But it was too late. In his message to Congress on June 1, Madison had asked for a declaration of war. On June 18, 1812, before news that the hated orders were to be suspended had arrived in Washington, Congress made the declaration final.

The War of 1812

The United States was so poorly prepared and deeply divided that the War of 1812 almost ended in disaster. Having allowed the Bank of the United States to expire in early 1811, the government then had no central agency to handle the complexities of issuing war bonds. Moreover, with the bank gone, the confidence of many investors in the government's ability to redeem the issued bonds diminished. As a result, only half of $11 million in bonds offered for sale were bought. Congress had equal difficulty raising money from other sources. It finally doubled tariffs and introduced new excise taxes, but these were widely evaded.

The inadequacy of the army and navy was an even more serious problem. To reduce the national debt, Jefferson and Secretary of the Treasury Gallatin had trimmed America's armed forces to a bare minimum, a policy that Madison was pursuing as late as the fall of 1811. Several months after the war started, Congress finally authorized the construction of new forty-four gun frigates and seventy-four gun ships, but none were ready to sail until after the war was over. In short, with only sixteen seaworthy warships, the United States was taking on the world's most powerful navy.

But the War Hawks were not particularly concerned about the strength of the navy. They planned to defeat Britain on land by capturing Canada, a feat which they believed could be easily achieved. They expected little resistance from the Canadians, believing that England would be reluctant to withdraw troops from the struggle against Napoleon in order to protect the northern territory.

Unfortunately, while on paper America had an army of thirty-five thousand men, in actuality this force usually consisted of just under seven thousand poorly trained soldiers. The strongest American land forces were the state militias, which together comprised about seven hundred thousand men. Many enlistees refused to serve outside their state

QUEEN CHARLOTTE AND JOHNNY BULL GOT THEIR DOSE OF PERRY, A CARTOON CELEBRATING PERRY'S NAVAL VICTORY ON LAKE ERIE.

boundaries, however, and the strongest units were in New England—a region which strongly opposed the war.

The Canadian Campaign

To the disappointment of expansionists, Canada refused to become part of the United States. The Canadian army of five thousand professional soldiers was well trained, and all three American invasions turned into fiascoes. The United States should have directed an attack on the centrally located town of Montreal in order to sever British forces on the Great Lakes from the rest of Canada. Instead, three separate, poorly planned invasions were undertaken in the lake area for the purpose of elimi-

nating Indian attacks on Ohio. In the first attempt, Revolutionary War hero William Hull was surrounded near Detroit by a small British force backed by Tecumseh and several hundred Indians. Paralyzed by fear and indecision, Hull surrendered without firing a shot. A second invading force, which attempted to cross the Niagara River, met defeat when the New York militia refused to cross its state boundary. As the New Yorkers watched from safety, their countrymen were mowed down by the Canadians. General Henry Dearborn led the final campaign into Canada and moved along Lake Champlain toward Montreal. However, Dearborn's militiamen also balked at the boundary line, and eventually the general was forced to march back to Plattsburgh, having accomplished nothing. Thus ended the American offensive of 1812.

In 1813, however, America's performance was partially vindicated by Captain Oliver Hazard Perry's brilliant victory on Lake Erie. In ships he had designed and built, Perry defeated a British squadron and secured American control of the Great Lakes. General Harrison gained a second American victory in October at the Battle of the Thames in southern Ontario. With a troop of Kentucky militiamen, Harrison routed a British force and their Indian allies led by Tecumseh, who was then serving as a Brigadier General in the British army. Tecumseh died mysteriously in the battle, and the remnant of the Indian confederacy was demolished. Despite these triumphs, the goal of conquering Canada remained beyond reach.

The Naval War

Although described by the *London Evening Star* as a "few fir-built frigates, manned by a handful of bastards and outlaws," the small American fleet scored a series of dazzling triumphs in the first few months of the war. American frigates, while few in number, were larger, faster, and better armed than their British counterparts. Two months after the war began, Captain Isaac Hull of the U.S.S. *Constitution* gunned the H.M.S. *Guerrière* into submission in the middle of the Atlantic. In October 1812 Stephen Decatur, who had fought skillfully in the war against the Barbary pirates, pitted the U.S.S. *United States* against the H.M.S. *Macedonian*. Decatur's ship emerged victorious and hauled the battered enemy vessel as a prize into New London, Connecticut. Soon the *Constitution* (nicknamed "Old Ironsides") was in action again off the coast of Brazil where it put the British frigate *Java* out of action.

In spite of these glorious episodes, the American navy was too small to seriously affect the outcome of the war. By 1813 most American men-of-war were bottled up in their home ports by the Royal Navy, and British squadrons roamed at will up and down the American coast. Although American privateers harassed British commerce, the English blockade nearly succeeded in destroying American shipping. Since the United States still had few roads most shipments of goods were made along coastal waterways, and interstate trade suffered as well.

This economic impact was exactly what the New England Federalists had feared. In the peak year of 1807 American imports and exports had totaled one-quarter of a billion dollars. By 1814 they had declined to one-tenth of that figure. Federalists regarded President Madison as a greater enemy than the British king, and the governors of Massachusetts and Connecticut refused to send their state militias to the aid of the national government. The Democratic Republicans temporarily lost ground throughout New England, and the states in that region subscribed to only a tiny fraction of the government's war bonds.

The British Attack

With the defeat of Napoleon in April 1814 the European war was finally brought to an end. Now the British were able to devote their full attention to chastising their troublesome former colonies. Some of England's best troops were shipped to American

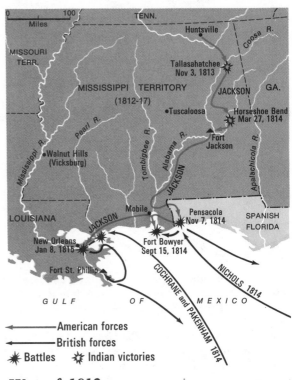

American forces
British forces
✳ Battles ✴ Indian victories

War of 1812 Southern Campaigns

and Canadian shores. With these reinforcements, the British proceeded to follow through on a three-prong plan of attack. A major land force gathered in Canada in preparation for a march down from Montreal, while a second army sailed from Jamaica to New Orleans in an attempt to close off the West. Meanwhile, a third, smaller unit made a diversionary strike in the Chesapeake Bay area. In August 1814 the redcoats invaded Washington, burning the Capitol, the White House, and other public buildings. The rout inflicted one of the worst psychological blows experienced by Americans during wartime, and Madison himself was forced to flee the city.

The first major British offensive was launched at Niagara in July 1814. General Jacob Brown and his subordinate Winfield Scott quickly turned it back by taking Fort Erie and outfighting the British at Lundy's Lane. Two months later the British, under Sir George Prevost, attempted to capture Lake Champlain, thereby threatening to detach New England from the rest of the Union. In September, however, Prevost paused at Plattsburgh, New York, to await the outcome of a brutal confrontation between British and American warships on Lake Champlain. When the American fleet won a decisive victory, Prevost was forced to retreat into Canada. This was the last battle fought before a treaty brought the war to a close.

Because transatlantic and transcontinental communications were so slow, the most spectacular American victory of the war was actually fought after the peace treaty had been signed. In March 1814 General Andrew Jackson, a natural military genius from Tennessee, defeated the Creek Indians at the Battle of Horseshoe Bend in Alabama. As a result, the Indians ceded twenty-three million acres of land to the United States government. Jackson went on to capture and destroy Pensacola in Spanish Florida, rendering it useless as a possible enemy base. Then he marched his army of sailors, local pirates, and militiamen (one unit of which was made up of free blacks) to New Orleans where he awaited the British troops.

Having arrived from Jamaica, the British secretly approached New Orleans through the maze of swamps that opened into the Gulf of Mexico. On January 8, 1815, between six thousand and eight thousand seasoned British troops under Sir Edward Pakenham advanced against Jackson and his men,

who had barricaded themselves behind earthen parapets and cotton bales. Jackson was outnumbered, but he used brilliant tactics in the placement of his artillery and formed his men behind the earthworks in three ranks. As one line fired, it moved back to let another take its place. The result was a continuous barrage of rifle fire. In less than one-half hour the Americans inflicted some twenty-six hundred casualties on the British, including Pakenham, but lost only some thirteen men themselves. Badly crippled, the British army was forced to retreat in haste. The Battle of New Orleans made Andrew Jackson (called Old Hickory by his men because of his toughness) the most popular American hero since George Washington.

The Hartford Convention

The war years first benefited then undermined the Federalist party. Although the Federalists did not run a candidate for president in 1812, early military disasters suffered by American forces enabled the Federalists to elect a number of their candidates to Congress and to many state and local offices in New England. Although Madison was reelected president, Federalist support of his Republican opponent, DeWitt Clinton from New York, cost the president votes in the electoral college.

The prosperous New England states remained opposed to the war throughout its duration. Massachusetts and Rhode Island were seldom blockaded, and merchants in those states continued to trade with the British whenever possible. As late as 1813 New England was selling one million bushels of grain per year to British armies.

In December 1814 the Massachusetts legislature called for a convention of the New England states to meet in Hartford, Connecticut, to protest the war. At the convention, the moderate Federalists outnumbered the extremists, and they succeeded in toning down its decisions. They debated for three weeks whether to secede or make a separate peace with England, and finally proposed a number of constitutional amendments designed to restore the dominance of New England and its commercial interests. Their recommendations included a proposal to repeal the Three-fifths Compromise concerning the enumeration of slaves and the apportioning of representatives according to the number of free peo-

ANDREW JACKSON AT THE BATTLE OF NEW ORLEANS. HIS TENNESSEE AND KENTUCKY RIFLEMEN AND HIS PIRATE-TRAINED CANNONEERS DECIMATED THE SCARLET ROWS OF BRITISH SOLDIERS ADVANCING FROM THE BEACH.

ple in each state. They also proposed to reduce the power of the federal government by limiting embargoes to sixty days and by requiring a two-thirds majority in Congress to declare war, restrict foreign trade, or admit new states.

Unfortunately for the Hartford convention these proposals were poorly timed. When their delegation arrived in Washington, the war was over. Jackson had scored his great triumph at New Orleans, and a peace treaty had just been signed. Madison paid no attention to the malcontents in New England, whom the public regarded with ridicule and a suspicion of traitorous intent. The discredited Federalist party never recovered from the effects of this convention.

Peace and Postwar Diplomacy

The War of 1812 is generally viewed as a second war for independence, which finally secured favorable international recognition for the United States. Unlike most wars, peace negotiations began soon after the outbreak of hostilities. The first attempt took place in June 1812, only one week after the war began. A second effort was made the following fall, when the Czar of Russia offered to mediate between America and Britain. Madison was optimistic, about this, but the English distrusted Russian motives and diplomatic motions never materialized.

By August 1814 Britain and the United States had settled down to direct negotiations in Ghent,

Belgium. The British representatives were men of little stature who were controlled by the British foreign minister, Lord Castlereagh. Initially, they were uncooperative, for they expected the 1814 offensive to turn the tide in England's favor. The American delegation was made up of some of the most respected politicians in the country, including John Quincy Adams, Albert Gallatin, and Henry Clay.

Signed in December 1814, the Treaty of Ghent did little more than return to the *status quo ante bellum*, or prewar conditions. Such issues as neutral rights, impressment, national boundaries, fisheries, and compensation for shipping losses were not even mentioned in the treaty. "Nothing was adjusted, nothing was settled," said negotiator John Quincy Adams, "nothing in substance but an indefinite suspension of hostilities." The real losers were the Indians. After suffering heavy casualties, they no longer had any promise of British firearms or supplies. In effect, they were left to the mercy of the land-hungry American people.

Although British industrialists were pleased with the outcome, British shippers, the landed gentry, and the English press were not. In America, on the other hand, peace was greeted with total jubilation. Suddenly the ineptness, the lack of public support, and the nasty infighting were all forgotten. Holidays were proclaimed, and cheering patriots embraced each other in a mood of spirited celebration. Many Americans had feared that once Napoleon had been defeated, the British would turn vengefully on the United States. However, the American victory at the Great Lakes had caused the British to reconsider their stand. Without control of the Great Lakes their demands for territorial concessions were weak, and they eventually agreed to settle for the prewar status quo. "Not one inch of territory ceded or lost" was the slogan of the hour. Madison submitted the treaty to the Senate, which ratified it unanimously the next day.

Effects of the War

As soon as the War of 1812 ended, most Americans turned their attention to domestic concerns. Tecumseh's Indian confederacy had been crushed, opening the area east of the Mississippi to settlement. American manufacturing had been forced to develop, so the country was now more self-suffi-

cient. The most widespread effect of the war was probably the rebirth of pride in the United States. Since the war in Europe had ended almost simultaneously, the country was no longer divided in its foreign sympathies. Gallatin wrote: "The war has renewed and reinstated the national feelings and character which the Revolution had given. . . . The people . . . are more Americans; they feel and act more as a nation." Americans forgot the humiliating moments of the war and made heroes of Andrew Jackson, William Henry Harrison, and Oliver Hazard Perry. The country had suffered very little financially. Most important, the people felt that they had "licked the British twice." Psychologically, it was a glorious victory. American territory remained intact and the country's economic independence was assured.

Although a great deal of ill feeling remained between the people of England and the United States, the governments of the two countries reached agreement on several important issues in the years immediately following the war. In the Rush-Bagot agreement of 1817 each nation promised to demilitarize its side of the Great Lakes. In 1818 a convention successfully established the northern boundary of the Louisiana Territory at the forty-ninth parallel, between Lake of the Woods and the Rockies, provided a ten-year joint occupation of the Oregon Territory, extended an earlier agreement banning discriminatory duties on each other's goods, and reopened the Newfoundland fisheries to Americans. These agreements signaled a new era of rationality on both sides.

Conclusion

Once they had gained political control, the Jeffersonians learned what all newly elected parties learn: that it is not always easy to implement one's philosophy. During Jefferson's first term, by exerting strong presidential leadership, some reductions in federal spending and federal power were achieved. Yet the president did not even try to abolish the first Bank of the United States, the strongest agency of federal power. In fact, during the Republican administrations the crises in international politics—especially during the war years—actually led to the enlargement of the national debt and the role of the national government in directing the nation's affairs.

Nevertheless, despite struggles within the Republican coalition over the growing divergence between Jeffersonian principles and Jeffersonian politics, the Republicans nurtured the growth of a more democratic policy in the nation. During their years of ascendency the United States also achieved successes in its foreign policy: the Louisiana Purchase doubled American territory and gave substance to Jefferson's dream of an "empire for liberty"; and although poorly prepared for the War of 1812, the government ultimately did redeem American honor. Thus, in 1815 most Americans had supreme faith in the future of their republic.

Readings

General Works

Adams, Henry, *History of the United States During the Administration of Jefferson and Madison.* Englewood Cliffs, N.J.: Prentice-Hall, 1963.

Borden, Morton, *Parties and Politics in the Early Republic, 1789–1815.* New York: Crowell, 1967.

Cunningham, Noble E., Jr., *The Jeffersonian Republicans in Power.* Chapel Hill: University of North Carolina Press, 1963.

Fischer, David H., *The Revolution of American Conservatism.* New York: Harper & Row, 1965.

Horsman, Reginald, *The Frontier in the Formative Years, 1783–1815.* Albuquerque: University of New Mexico Press, 1973. (Paper)

Johnstone, Robert M., Jr., *Jefferson and the Presidency: Leadership in the Young Republic.* Ithaca, N.Y.: Cornell University Press, 1978.

McDonald, Forrest, *The Presidency of Thomas Jefferson.* Lawrence, Kans.: Regents Press, 1976.

Peterson, Merrill D., *The Jefferson Image in the American Mind.* New York: Oxford University Press, 1960.

Smelser, Marshall, *The Democratic Republic, 1800–1815.* New York: Harper & Row, 1968.

Wiltse, Charles M., *The Jeffersonian Tradition in American Democracy.* Chapel Hill: University of North Carolina Press, 1935.

Wiltse, Charles M., *The New Nation: 1800–1845.* New York: Hill and Wang, 1961.

Young, James B., *The Washington Community: 1800–1802.* New York: Columbia University Press, 1966.

Special Studies

Banner, James M., Jr., *To the Hartford Convention.* New York: Knopf, 1970.

Brown, Roger H., *The Republic in Peril: 1812.* New York: Columbia University Press, 1964.

Burt, A. L., *The United States, Great Britain and British North America.* New Haven, Conn.: Yale University Press, 1940.

Coles, Harry L., *The War of 1812.* Chicago: University of Chicago, 1965.

Commager, Henry S., *Thomas Jefferson, Nationalism and the Enlightenment.* New York: George Braziller, 1974.

Ellis, Richard E., *The Jeffersonian Crisis: Courts & Politics in the Young Republic.* New York: Oxford University Press, 1971.

Horsman, Reginald, *The Causes of the War of 1812.* New York: Octagon, 1970.

Levy, Leonard W., *Jefferson & Civil Liberties: The Darker Side.* New York: Quadrangle, 1973. (Paper)

Miller, John C., *The Wolf by the Ears: Thomas Jefferson and Slavery.* New York: Free Press, 1977.

Perkins, Bradford, *Prologue to War.* Berkeley: University of California Press, 1963.

Pratt, Julius W., *Expansionists of 1812.* Gloucester, Mass.: Peter Smith, 1957.

Risjord, Norman K., *The Old Republicans: Southern Conservatism in the Age of Jefferson.* New York: Columbia University Press, 1965.

Sisson, Daniel, *The American Revolution of 1800.* New York: Knopf, 1974.

Primary Sources

DeVoto, Bernard (Ed.), *The Journals of Lewis and Clark.* Boston: Houghton Mifflin, 1953.

Koch, Adrienne, and William Peden (Eds.), *The Life and Selected Writings of Thomas Jefferson.* New York: Random House, 1944.

Padover, Saul (Ed.), *The Complete Madison.* New York: Harper and Brothers, 1953.

Biographies

Bedini, Silvio, *The Life of Benjamin Banneker*. New York: Charles Scribner & Sons, 1973. (Paper)

Brant, Irving, *James Madison*, vols. 4 and 5. Indianapolis, Ind.: Bobbs-Merrill, 1956 and 1961.

Dangerfield, George, *Chancellor Robert R. Livingston of New York, 1746–1813*. New York: Harcourt, Brace & World, 1960.

Ketcham, Ralph, *James Madison: A Biography*. New York: Macmillan, 1971.

Lomask, Milton, *Aaron Burr: The Years from Princeton to Vice President, 1756–1805*. New York: Farrar, Straus & Giroux, 1979.

Malone, Dumas, *Jefferson and His Time*, vols. 4 and 5. Boston: Little, Brown, 1974.

Tucker, Glenn, *Tecumseh: Vision of Glory*. Indianapolis, Ind.: Bobbs-Merrill, 1956.

Schachner, Nathan, *Aaron Burr: A Biography*. Cranbury, N.J.: A. S. Barnes, 1961.

Historical Novels

Roberts, Kenneth L., *Captain Caution*. New York: Fawcett World, 1970. (Paper)

Vidal, Gore, *Burr*. New York: Bantam Books, 1974. New York: Random House, 1973. (Paper)

8 Nationalism and the Emergence of Sectional Strains

Mr. Chairman, our confederacy comprehends within its vast limits great diversity of interests—agricultural, planting, farming, commercial, navigating, fishing, manufacturing. No one of these interests is felt in the same degree, and cherished with the same solicitude, throughout all parts of the Union. Some of them are peculiar to particular sections of our common country. But all these great interests are confided to the protection of one government—to the fate of one ship; and a most gallant ship it is, with a noble crew. If we prosper, and are happy, protection must be extended to all: it is due to all.

Henry Clay

Significant Events

Cumberland or National Road [1811]

Protective tariff [1816]

Second Bank of the United States [1816]

Era of Good Feelings [1816–1819]

McCulloch v. *Maryland* [1819]

Adams-Onís treaty [1819]

Economic panic [1819]

Missouri Compromise [1820]

American recognition of Latin American republics [1822]

Monroe Doctrine [1823]

Gibbons v. *Ogden* [1824]

Erie Canal opens [1825]

Tariff of Abominations [1828]

LOCKS ON THE ERIE CANAL.

Following the War of 1812 the United States entered a short period of national self-congratulation. Freed from preoccupation with the activities of foreign countries, the American people looked forward to a new era of unlimited possibilities. Although they were provoked by the attitude of foreign visitors who often described Americans as materialistic and unrefined, they basked in the accounts of those visitors who praised the generosity and energy of America's people and who were impressed by the widespread economic opportunity and the general lack of class distinctions seen in the young nation.

In fulfillment of the public's expectations, the period immediately following the war was one of national prosperity. The nation was energized by rapid economic development as commerce revived and manufacturing methods and transportation improved. The burgeoning population—which was doubling every generation—contributed to eco-nomic growth and pushed the frontier farther west. By 1820 Indiana, Mississippi, Illinois, and Alabama had all become states.

The successful conclusion of the long dispute with England also gave a powerful boost to feelings of political nationalism. A new sense of confidence in the government's ability to achieve national goals led many Republican politicians to abandon Jefferson's ideals in all but rhetoric. The policies they began to pursue actually resembled Hamilton's program for expanded government involvement in the economy. These policies were often referred to as Neo-Federalist.

This outburst of nationalism soon subsided. With prolonged peace and a thriving economy people turned their attention to local matters. Moreover, by 1820 the sectional differences that had been buried by preoccupation with national concerns once again resurfaced.

Nationalism Triumphant

By the end of the War of 1812 the political climate in the United States was going through a profound transition. By this time, even though the Federalist party existed in only a few areas, its influence was not on the wane; indeed, its principles were being adopted by large numbers of the opposition. Whereas the Jeffersonians had originally championed states' rights, a strict construction of the Constitution, and the agrarian way of life, Madison now pointed the party toward new goals and greater government participation.

An important aspect of America's growing national pride was the desire on the part of a number of politicians to achieve an integrated economy at home and an expansion of trade abroad. Toward this end, Madison supported internal improvements, efforts to increase domestic production, and an independent American commercial policy. It was during his administration that Henry Clay, the brilliant Speaker of the House, began to develop a program known as the American System, which was aimed at binding the nation together through economic interdependence.

The American System

Henry Clay The architect of the American System, Henry Clay, was the most intelligent and flam-boyant Western leader to emerge in the 1820s. Gray-eyed, lean, and handsome, Clay was a persuasive and hypnotic orator. Little of his magic in debate can be gleaned from the written records of his speeches, for they do not show "the strange posturings and glidings, the punctuating pinches of snuff, the pointed finger, the unforgettable smile, and all the music of that wonderful voice."

Clay was born in Virginia, but at age twenty he moved to Kentucky, where he practiced law. Elected to Congress from Kentucky in 1810, Clay served as Speaker of the House from 1811 to 1820, and again from 1823 to 1825. During his first term as speaker he was a leader of the War Hawks, who advocated war with Britain. The architect of the Missouri Compromise of 1820, he later played a key role in achieving a compromise during the Nullification Crisis of 1833. His skill at working out acceptable compromise solutions to difficult issues earned him the title the "Great Compromiser." At the end of his career he initiated one more great achievement, the Compromise of 1850.

Clay's American System, which he had formulated completely by the early 1820s, was intended to benefit all parts of the country. Roads and canals would improve transportation between East and West. Tariffs would protect manufacturers in the East. Northeastern industries would consume

THE ELOQUENT STATESMAN HENRY CLAY POSSESSED A SUBSTANTIAL EGO, STRONG POLITICAL AMBITIONS, AND A SINCERE DEVOTION TO THE UNION. HE PLAYED AS HARD AS HE WORKED, ENJOYING FINE KENTUCKY WHISKEY, HORSE RACING, AND LATE-NIGHT CARD GAMES FOR HIGH STAKES.

Southern cotton; Southern cotton growers and Northern city dwellers would consume Western farm produce. Western farmers would purchase Northern manufactured goods, and the national bank would make all these economic exchanges run smoothly. The most clearly articulated aspects of the American System dealt with protective tariffs, the second national bank, and federal support of internal improvements.

Protective Tariffs After the War of 1812, British manufacturers began flooding American markets with the surpluses they had been accumulating since the war began. These cheaply produced goods easily outsold American commodities and threatened to destroy America's infant industries. Manufacturers, particularly in New England, felt the need for tariff protection. Other parts of the country also had something to gain from protectionist measures. In

the Carolinas and New England cotton mills were suffering from English competition. In western Pennsylvania iron smelters had to compete with Scottish and Swedish iron. In Kentucky manufacturers of hemp bags were outdistanced by Russian hemp merchants and the Scottish bagging industry. In New York grain farmers, no longer permitted to sell to England, demanded sole rights to the American market. In Vermont and Ohio wool growers sought measures to protect them from English wool merchants.

In response to these needs Congress passed the rather mild Tariff of 1816, which maintained the wartime rates of about 20 to 25 percent on imported goods. The vote in the House of Representatives revealed the diversity of the economic interests in the country. New England, which had the most to gain, voted for the tariff, though New England's shipping interests voted against the measure, fearing that higher duties would diminish foreign trade and thus reduce profits. The South, with almost no manufacturing, voted against the bill, although some Southern representatives supported the measure as a patriotic gesture. John C. Calhoun of South Carolina, for example, believed that if there were to be another war with England the American army and navy would need American manufactures. Moreover, a few Southerners expected that their region would experience its own manufacturing boom in the near future. Only the Middle Atlantic and Western states gave the measure their wholehearted support. They were convinced that the tariff would create markets in the North and South for their produce and livestock.

Revival of the National Bank Five years after the first Bank of the United States had expired, some 250 state and private banks had been chartered. Since there was no national bank and therefore no national currency, these banks issued their own paper money. Few state-chartered banks had adequate reserves of gold and silver with which to back their paper money. These various paper currencies were frequently not negotiable in neighboring areas and, worse still, were seldom able to command their face value.

The absence of a national bank caused other problems, too. The federal government no longer had a place to deposit its funds or a reliable system for transferring money. Nor did it have a financial institution through which to sell government bonds to raise needed revenue.

To solve these problems, Congress chartered the second Bank of the United States in 1816. The new bank's structure was similar to its predecessor's, except for an increase in its capital from $10 million to $35 million. As before, the federal government provided one-fifth of its capital, and five of its twenty-five directors were appointed by the president and approved by the Senate.

A National Program for Improvements The recognition of the need for internal improvements dated from Jefferson's administration. Secretary of the Treasury Gallatin had advocated federal expenditures for building roads and canals, and for improving harbor facilities. When Ohio entered the Union in 1803, it was promised that a road would be built at government expense connecting the state with Eastern cities. While construction did not begin until 1811, twenty miles of the Cumberland, or National Road, stretched westward from Baltimore by 1815. It finally reached Ohio in the 1830s.

The nation had a pressing need for extensive improvements in interstate transportation. American commerce traveled a circuitous route to market. Western goods going east traveled on barges down the Mississippi and then on ships around Florida and up the Atlantic coast. Eastern goods traveled west in wagons across poorly built roads, many only dirt paths. Leading politicians in Washington had long recognized the need for such internal improvements as a national highway and canal system, if only for military transport. In 1817 John C. Calhoun had told a congressional committee:

Whatever impedes the intercourse of the extremes with this, the centre of the republic, weakens the union. . . . Let us, then, bind the republic together with a perfect system of roads and canals. Let us conquer space.

Clay's American System included a bill which would raise revenue from the sale of Western lands to be distributed to the states for financing internal improvements. There was much resistance to be overcome before Clay's ideas could be implemented. New England was opposed to a national system of roads; the region already had good roads, and merchants feared that an improved interstate system might divert trade to Philadelphia, Baltimore, or New York. The South felt it had little to gain from the establishment of trade routes between the North and the West. Nevertheless, after much debate, a transportation bill passed both houses of Congress. To the surprise of many people, however, President Madison vetoed the bill. Although he agreed with the need for national roads, he felt that the Constitution should first be amended to permit Congress to legislate in this area.

When another transportation bill was introduced in the 1820s, President Monroe also opposed it on constitutional grounds. Henry Clay exclaimed in irritation: "A new world has come into being since the Constitution was adopted. Are the narrow, limited necessities of the old thirteen states, of indeed, parts only of the old thirteen states, as they existed at the formation of the present Constitution forever to remain the rule of interpretations?"

Clay's protests had little effect on the reluctant federal government. In fact, federally sponsored internal improvements, with the exception of the Cumberland Road, were never put into effect in his time.

The Era of Good Feelings

From 1816 to 1819 the United States enjoyed a period of political harmony. Pride in the quality of American accomplishments and faith in the American way of life were widespread. Americans believed that their political institutions were superior to all others and that their country offered unbounded economic opportunity.

In 1816, at Madison's insistence, the Jeffersonians nominated James Monroe as their presiden-

tial candidate. William H. Crawford of Georgia was actually a more popular choice, but Monroe won out and easily defeated his opponent, Rufus King, the last Federalist ever nominated for the presidency. Monroe had been a respected public servant for many years. While he had neither Jefferson's idealism and range of interests, nor Madison's fine, theoretical mind, he had fought under Washington during the Revolution, had served twice as governor of Virginia, and was later elected to the Senate. A stately, dignified man with old-fashioned manners and dress, Monroe also had served as a diplomat in Paris, Madrid, and London, and had been a member of Madison's cabinet as secretary of state and secretary of war.

Monroe's was not an innovative presidency as far as domestic policy was concerned. In fact, most of his policies were inherited from the Madison administration. President Monroe accepted the bank, the tariff, and the need for internal improvements, though he did not expand on the American System.

For a time Monroe was able to ride the wave of good feeling pervading the country. He began his first term with a goodwill tour of New England, formerly the center of Federalist opposition. Greeted everywhere by cheering crowds, he addressed the Massachusetts legislature with these words: "I indulge a strong hope that our principal dangers and difficulties have passed, and that the character of our deliberations and the course of the government itself, will become more harmonious and happy than it has heretofore been." A Federalist newspaper published an article about the new administration entitled "Era of Good Feelings." The slogan caught on. It seemed an apt expression of the domestic harmony and prosperity of the postwar period.

Constitutional Nationalism under John Marshall

The wave of postwar nationalism that swept over the United States had a strong proponent in the Supreme Court: Chief Justice John Marshall, who served from 1801 to 1835. Throughout this period most Supreme Court decisions were a direct result of his intellectual influence. Indeed, his thinking so completely dominated the Court that in more than thirty-four years he was part of the minority opinion in only eight cases. Not always an impartial judge, he sometimes decided a case before hearing the arguments.

Although Marshall was an unpretentious man with simple tastes, he entertained a lifelong suspicion of putting too much power in the hands of the masses. Most of his decisions reflected his defense of a strong central government and vested property rights, and he was consistently sympathetic to the business interests. His decisions were the legal counterpart to Clay's American System.

The Marshall Court handed down major decisions in cases involving monopolies in interstate commerce, state taxation of a federal bank, and contractual obligations under state laws. Each of these decisions set lasting precedents. When Marshall retired, he had shepherded the Supreme Court through five administrations. He had seen the country progress from a loosely knit collection of states into a unified nation. He had played a significant role in this process by delivering judgments that set Congress and the Supreme Court above the state legislatures and state courts.

Marshall's court established the right of judicial review in the 1803 case of *Marbury* v. *Madison* (discussed in Chapter 7), asserting the right of the Supreme Court to decide whether a law passed by Congress and signed by the president was constitutional. Marshall was a nationalist, however, and he wanted to enhance the prestige of Congress, not undermine it.

In keeping with the chief justice's nationalist outlook the Marshall Court declared state laws unconstitutional on thirteen occasions and also overruled the decisions of state courts. In *Cohens* v. *Virginia* (1821), for example, the Supreme Court held that it had the right to review the decisions of state courts when questions of national powers were involved.

In several important cases Marshall upheld the supremacy of the national government when fulfilling functions provided for by the Constitution. In *Gibbons* v. *Ogden* (1824) the Court held that a state could regulate commerce and navigation within its own boundaries but that these same activities carried across state lines were subject to regulation by Congress. This decision had a liberating effect on the nation's economy.

The *McCulloch* v. *Maryland* decision (1819) also strengthened the federal government's authority and demonstrated Marshall's concern for providing a favorable climate for business. The case arose when the state of Maryland sought to tax the Baltimore branch of the Bank of the United States. The Constitution does not specifically grant Congress the right to charter a bank. Marshall, however, following the line of reasoning originally put forth by Alexander Hamilton, maintained that such authority was implied in the Constitution. He further asserted that states did not have the power to "retard, impede, burden, or in any manner control" the operations of constitutional laws passed by Congress. "Let the end be legitimate," Marshall wrote, "let it be within the scope of the Constitution, and all means which are appropriate, which are plainly adapted to that end, which are not prohibited, but consistent with the letter and spirit of the Constitution, are constitutional." This broad interpretation of the powers of Congress extended its authority into finance. By defending the national bank against state regulation, Marshall again aided the business community: the bank could now continue to make business loans, provide business with a safe place for investment, and help maintain a reliable national currency.

Three other significant decisions aided the business community by establishing the inviolability of contracts. The first one was the case of *Fletcher* v. *Peck* (1810), in which the Court struck down a Georgia state law on grounds that it violated a

IN A SERIES OF MOMENTOUS RULINGS, CHIEF JUSTICE JOHN MARSHALL ASSERTED THE SUPREMACY AND UNITY OF THE FEDERAL GOVERNMENT.

private contract. The case of *Dartmouth College* v. *Woodward* ten years later defined charters as contracts that could be altered only with the consent of both parties. It also determined that licensed corporations could not be regulated by states except under restrictions written into the original charter. Finally, in *Sturges* v. *Crowninshield* the Court declared unconstitutional a New York law that relieved debtors of their obligations. In rendering this decision, Marshall cited a constitutional provision that forbade all legislation which impaired contractual obligations.

Reactions to Marshall's Decisions The long-range effects of Marshall's rulings were as follows: to establish the right of judicial review, an important factor in balancing power among the three branches of the federal government; to extend congressional authority over interstate commerce; to set the Supreme Court and Congress above state legislatures and state courts; to affirm the sanctity of contracts; and to ally the Court with a broad and flexible interpretation of the Constitution.

Leaders such as Jefferson, suspicious of concentrating power in the federal government at the expense of states' rights, were alarmed by Marshall's decisions. Jefferson declared: "The Constitution is a mere thing of wax in the hands of the judiciary, which they may twist and shape into any form they please." Even so, the use of the Constitution which Marshall had envisioned—as a buttress and protection for the business community—was not fully realized until after the Civil War. And Marshall's vision of a strong central government capable of regulating the economy on behalf of the national welfare did not become acceptable to a majority of Americans until the twentieth century.

A Nationalistic Foreign Policy

American foreign policy in the postwar era also reflected the optimistic nationalism of the country. The United States aggressively settled territorial disputes with Spain that had existed since the purchase of Louisiana; and despite a decline in domestic nationalism, announced the Monroe Doctrine, which was among other things a strong statement of American independence from European politics.

Efforts to Acquire Florida Jefferson had thought that the Louisiana Purchase included West Florida, and he claimed East Florida as compensation for Spanish interference with American commerce. In 1805 and 1806 he tried to persuade Napoleon to force Spain to sell the Floridas to the United States. Congress even appropriated $2 million in secret funds to start the negotiations. Napoleon, however, would not agree.

Americans had had their eyes on East and West Florida ever since the Louisiana Purchase. In part this was because they were hungry for new land. In addition, the Floridas would link the Atlantic Coast to New Orleans and provide new river transportation to the Gulf of Mexico. Finally, many Americans feared that if the United States did not, Britain might buy the Floridas from Spain and use the territory as a strategic base against the United States. In 1810 following an uprising by a group of American settlers, President Madison illegally took possession of a portion of West Florida.

Now Americans began to eye East Florida. Spanish forces were so preoccupied with armed revolt in Spain's Latin American colonies that Florida was left unguarded. Certain elements in America had already rushed into this vacuum: white renegades, escaped American slaves, and hostile Indians who used Florida as a base from which to raid Georgia outposts.

During the War of 1812 General George Matthews, a former Georgia governor acting as Madison's special agent and supported by United States navy gunboats, led a revolution of American settlers in East Florida. Matthews occupied East Florida and claimed it for the United States. Madison disavowed his actions and returned East Florida to Spain when the war ended.

The new president, James Monroe, wanted to secure the rest of Florida and to establish the as yet uncertain western boundaries of the Louisiana Purchase. He was anxious to settle American territorial problems with Spain. The United States had already instituted some trade with Spain's rebellious Latin American colonies and Henry Clay was particularly eager to expand this trade as part of his American System. In addition, Americans regarded the Latin rebellions as attempts to break the yoke of tyranny; they wanted to be the first to recognize the new independent nations. If the United States extended recognition before negotiations with Spain were undertaken, however, the talks would almost certainly be undermined and the nation might even find itself at war. Therefore, Secretary of State John Quincy Adams began negotiating the territorial and boundary issues with the Spanish Minister, Luis de Onís, in December 1817.

In the midst of the negotiations Monroe unintentionally created an incident which provoked the Spanish. He authorized Andrew Jackson, the commander of American troops patrolling the Florida-Georgia border, to cross the American border into East Florida, if necessary, to chastise marauding Indians. Jackson interpreted his orders liberally, to say the least. He crossed the border and seized a Spanish military outpost, then executed two British subjects he suspected of inciting the Indians to attack American settlers, and proceeded within a matter of weeks to capture every Spanish fort in East Florida except St. Augustine. In the process he deposed the Spanish governor, replaced him with an American, and declared the revenue laws of the United States to be in force. The British were outraged by Jackson's executions of English subjects, but their government did not protest the incident since England was working to improve trade relations with the United States.

Jackson's critics in Congress, led by the Speaker Henry Clay, initiated an investigation of his conduct. But every resolution to condemn the popular general was defeated, and the American public erupted in long victory celebrations when Jackson was finally cleared.

Spain demanded an apology, but the American secretary of state saw an opportunity to press the offensive. He accused the Spanish of being unable to govern Florida. He asserted that if Spain could not restrain the Indians from making raids into United States territory, it should immediately cede the territory to the United States. Adams also demanded that the Louisiana Territory include the territory of Texas and a western boundary line stretching to the Pacific. After months of hard bargaining, the Spanish finally agreed to all the American demands, except for the territory of Texas. Spain ceded East and West Florida, accepted the Rocky Mountains as the western boundary of Louisiana, and the forty-second parallel as the northern boundary of Spanish North American claims west of the Rockies. This last provision excluded Spain from any further claim to the Oregon Territory.

The Adams-Onís, or Transcontinental treaty, drawn up in February 1819, gave the United States undisputed control of the territory to the Rocky Mountains and a window on the Pacific by virtue of joint control of the Oregon Territory with Great Britain. These remarkable gains cost the United States a mere $5 million worth of American claims against the Spanish government.

The United States quickly ratified the treaty, but a revolution in Spain delayed ratification by the Spanish until 1821. The following year President

Monroe recognized the independence of Spain's Latin American colonies.

The Monroe Doctrine

Even though the United States had declared that it recognized the freedom of Spain's Latin American colonies, the possibility remained that Spain might try to recover possession of them. The question be-

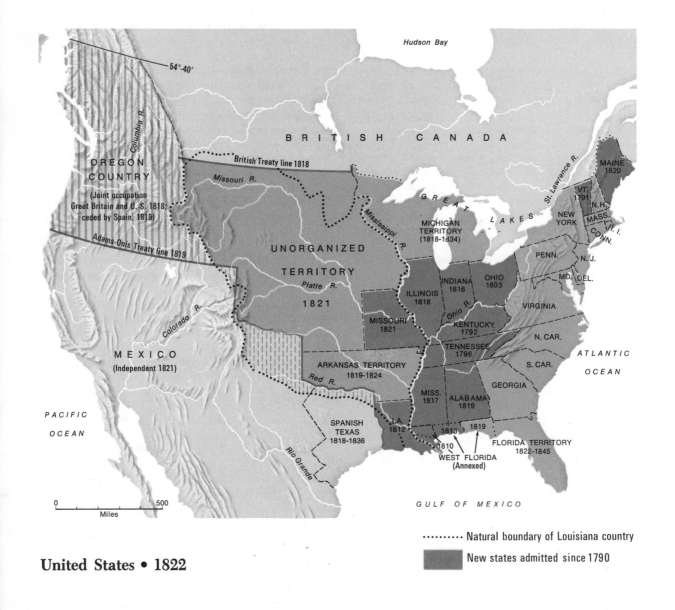

United States • 1822

·········· Natural boundary of Louisiana country

New states admitted since 1790

came a matter of immediate concern in the fall of 1823 when a dispatch from the American minister to Great Britain, Richard Rush, indicated that British Foreign Secretary George Canning was interested in issuing a joint statement with the United States guaranteeing the independence of the new Latin American countries. Britain's motivation stemmed from a concern about the Holy Alliance, a coalition of the monarchs of Russia, France, Prussia, and Austria established in 1815. Canning believed that if these antidemocratic European powers intervened in the Western Hemisphere to help restore to the Spanish their Latin American lands, France would stand to regain influence and Great Britain would be excluded from the profitable Latin American trade. By October, however, the British had lost interest in a joint statement and were, in fact, busy securing France's promise not to intervene on the side of Spain in Latin America.

Even without knowing that the English had changed their minds, however, Secretary of State John Quincy Adams persuaded the president to abandon the idea of a joint declaration and to make an independent statement instead. Whether the timing of the statement was closely connected to Adams's desire for the presidency is unclear. But it is clear that he saw that Russian attempts to settle the Alaska panhandle might renew European efforts to colonize North America and limit American expansion and political dominance on the continent. Adams also was astute enough to see that America was safe in making an independent statement because the power of the British fleet would support it.

The president enunciated the policy known as the Monroe Doctrine in a message to Congress delivered on December 2, 1823. It was a general statement which committed the nation to no specific action and has been subject to a variety of interpretations. The basic points of the doctrine were that the Western Hemisphere was no longer open to colonization or military intervention by the European powers and that the United States would not intervene in the affairs of Europe. It thus recognized the existence of spheres of influence in the world and implicitly claimed the Western Hemisphere as the area of American dominance. In addition, the doctrine represented America's belief in the superiority of its own political system as well as a determination to prevent the autocratic powers of Europe from interfering with its national destiny or with that of any other country in the hemisphere. Following the tradition of isolation begun during the early years of the republic, the doctrine was directed against no nation in particular but against all those not in the Western Hemisphere.

The Monroe Doctrine drew little international attention when it was first expounded. The French had abandoned their rather vague plans to help Spain in Latin America nearly two months before Monroe issued his now-famous statement, because England had disapproved of the project. The new Latin American republics regarded the Monroe Doctrine with indifference once they realized that the United States had no intention of making specific commitments to Latin America. America was too small and too weak to back its foreign policy statements with action. Nevertheless, the Monroe Doctrine did clearly assert the principle of America for the Americans.

An Expanding Economy

Early Industrialization

The war years not only rekindled American nationalism but paved the way for the development of native industry as well. Alexander Hamilton had once noted that there existed "in the genius of the people of this country, a peculiar aptitude for mechanical improvements." Hamilton's observation was soon borne out. The disruption of American trade by both the French and the British navies after 1805 led many entrepreneurs to invest their capital in the development of domestic industry. There were also a number of minor inventions and mechanical improvements that led to major changes in American manufacturing after 1815.

Improved waterwheels, leather transmission belts, and metal gears made machines more durable and more efficient. The rolling mill eliminated the need to hammer out sheet metal by hand. A new process for refining pig iron facilitated a switch from coal to the cheaper charcoal. The perfection of the cylinder process for making paper led to the mech-

A CARPENTER'S CLOTHIER SHOP IN WHICH SAMUEL SLATER'S SPINNING MACHINES WERE INSTALLED. (Smithsonian Institution)

anization of that industry. A new method of canning food in airtight containers conserved perishable foods for transportation from the country to the city. Eli Whitney, best known as the inventor of the cotton gin, devised a way of manufacturing rifles using machinery with interchangeable parts—a significant advance toward the assembly-line method of production.

The Development of the Factory Following the War of 1812, most workers continued to labor in their homes or in small shops. By 1823 most of the country's one-half million urban laborers were still engaged in household manufacturing, making everything from shoes and hats to cigars, pencils, and barrels. Few people worked full-time at these occupations, however; most domestic manufacturing was a sideline engaged in by farmers, shopkeepers, lawyers, doctors, and others, and their products were usually sold only to the immediate neighborhood. Occasionally, however, domestic manufacturers would sell to a national market. For example, merchants in the Northeast bought shoe leather wholesale and distributed it to cobblers who worked in their homes. The finished shoes were then collected, inspected, and stored in a central warehouse from which they were then shipped all over the United States.

During these years manufacturers increasingly began to realize that production would be cheaper and more efficient if labor and resources were consolidated in a factory setting. As early as the 1780s an Englishman, Richard Arkwright, had devised a rudimentary assembly line for producing cotton fabric that was less expensive and more durable than hand-spun cotton. Americans were eager to copy Arkwright's factory system, but the English government tried to prevent the export of textile machines and did not permit skilled textile workers to travel abroad or to emigrate. Nonetheless, in 1791 a young Englishman named Samuel Slater slipped out of Britain, came to America, and reconstructed the cotton-spinning machines from memory for the Pawtucket, Rhode Island, firm of Almy & Brown. Slater's work marked the beginning of the factory system.

During the Napoleonic wars Americans established several hundred mills for spinning cotton thread, but most of them were forced out of business by British competition in the years before the Tariff of 1816 helped to protect native industry. One manufacturer, however, Francis Cabot Lowell of

Massachusetts, recognized in the growing home market for cotton cloth and the abundant domestic supply of raw materials an opportunity to challenge British supremacy in textiles. Lowell joined with several other merchants to form the Boston Manufacturing Company, and in 1814 they built a cotton mill in Waltham, Massachusetts. Under one roof, raw cotton was unbaled, corded, and spun by efficient power looms designed by Lowell himself. The finished cloth was then dyed and printed. This factory was the first wholly integrated cotton-manufacturing plant in the world.

The venture was a great success, and it was not long before the output of the Waltham plant could not keep up with the demand. Lowell and his colleagues began to develop plans to establish an expansive textile community along the Merrimack River. Although Lowell died before his ambitious design could be realized, his partners, who incorporated as the Boston Associates, raised the needed capital to begin the project. Mills were established at Lowell, Massachusetts, and farm girls were hired to provide the necessary labor. The Lowell mills proved very successful, and by the 1830s Lowell had become the leading industrial city in New England. The Boston Associates invested their profits in additional mills as well as in banks, insurance companies, and other enterprises.

The Rise of the Corporation The Lowell venture was the first successful enterprise in America to make use of a new legal entity: the corporation. By the 1820s the corporation, which made it possible to finance large factories, was the nation's principal economic institution.

The corporation had not played a significant part in the New World since English joint-stock companies had financed the early settlements, but its advantages were becoming increasingly obvious. The corporation was attractive to business because issuing stock to many investors simplified the matter of acquiring capital. It was attractive to investors because they were not legally responsible for the corporation's debts; they risked only the depreciation or loss of their original investment. The corporate form made it possible for people to pool their resources to raise large amounts of capital. In addition, stocks could be bought and sold without disturbing the financial structure of the business.

Although corporations were relieved of certain kinds of internal red tape, they were governed by external regulations. Throughout the early 1800s incorporation required obtaining a special charter from the state legislature. There were so many petitions for incorporation and the procedure for acquiring a charter was so complicated that for a long time most businesses remained unincorporated. By the 1830s, however, general incorporation laws, which could be issued to any corporation without specific legislative action in every case, simplified and improved the incorporation procedure.

A number of states also introduced tax concessions to aid new businesses. New York, for example, passed a law in 1817 that exempted textile mills from taxation; Ohio extended tax benefits in 1823 to textile, iron, and glass companies.

The Dominance of Cotton

The technological innovations that fostered the rise of manufacturing also changed the nation's agriculture. In particular, the application of new machinery to cotton production in the South had far-reaching economic and political effects in pre–Civil War America.

The invention of the cotton gin made cotton the leading cash crop in the South and in the nation. The idea for the gin originated with Mrs. Catharine Greene of Savannah, Georgia, the widow of Revolutionary War General Nathanael Greene, who commissioned Eli Whitney to build one for her in 1793. Before the invention of the gin only long-staple cotton could be grown profitably, because its black seeds could easily be removed by hand. This variety, however, would grow only in a warm, humid climate. The hardier, short-staple variety could flourish in greater varieties of soil and weather, provided the growing season was sufficiently long. Its green seeds, however, were extremely hard to remove; one person working all day could clean only about one pound.

The cotton gin made it quick, efficient, and easy to clean both varieties of cotton. One small machine could clean fifty pounds of cotton a day, and soon huge, horse-driven gins were cleaning thousands of pounds a week. By the 1820s the South was producing three-quarters of the world's supply of cotton.

Equally significant to the growth of the cotton industry was the opening up of new Western territories. The profitable raising of cotton required rich black topsoil, and the soil of the Southern coastal states had been exhausted by nearly two centuries of tobacco planting. Once the West was cleared for farming, cotton production rose from eighty million pounds per year in 1810 to nearly five hundred million pounds per year in the 1830s.

Cotton had a major impact on the economy of the period. Most American cotton was exported to England and the Continent. Northern merchants benefited by arranging the sale and transportation of the crop. And since Southern planters used every inch of land to grow it, they helped enrich the Western farmers from whom they purchased large quantities of foodstuffs and work animals.

A) ELI WHITNEY'S ORIGINAL, HAND-CRANKED MODEL OF THE COTTON GIN. (Smithsonian Institution)
B) A LARGE VERSION OF THE COTTON GIN.

A)

B)

Waterways and Overland Transportation

When Western farmers were able to grow surplus produce, they had difficulty finding markets for it. Farm products could be floated down the Mississippi on rafts and flatboats, but with spring floods and summer droughts, this was a risky business. Carrying produce upriver was even more difficult. Thus, although the Mississippi River network made it possible for the West to sell to the East, there was no equivalent system enabling the East to sell to the West. Eastern products had to come overland, so roads were needed.

Turnpikes In the days before explosives and modern machinery, building a road through a mountain range or leveling uneven ground was a slow, laborious, and expensive operation. In spite of such difficulties, the Lancaster Turnpike, an excellent road complete with drainage ditches, firm foundations, and a gravel surface, was built in 1794 to connect Lancaster, Pennsylvania, with Philadelphia. By 1825 private companies in the Northeast and Middle Atlantic states had built some ten thousand miles of turnpike roads. There were also a few highways, built at federal- or state-government expense, serving the West: the National Road, which connected Maryland with Illinois by the 1840s; the Wilderness Road, which crossed on a diagonal from the northern boundary of Virginia through the Cumberland Gap into Kentucky; and the Natchez Trace, which lay between Nashville, Tennessee, and Natchez, Mississippi.

These projects were so expensive (the sixty-two mile-long Lancaster Turnpike cost $465,000) that the turnpike owners were forced to charge high tolls. Therefore, although some of the roads provided excellent routes for migrating pioneers, they were too expensive to use for transporting goods. The cost of transporting a ton of oats from Buffalo to New York, for example, was twelve times greater than the value of the cargo. This discouraged traffic to such an extent that by the 1830s, thousands of miles of turnpike had to be abandoned or handed over to the states.

Steamboats The expense of hauling goods overland and the lack of a federally financed road system focused increasing attention on waterways.

(Courtesy, American Antiquarian Society)

Engineers in the 1790s had been experimenting with the steam engine in water transportation. But it remained for Robert Fulton, a young American artist and engineer, to make steam navigation commercially successful. Fulton devised a workable means of combining all the essential elements: the engine, the paddlewheels, and the steam boiler.

Fulton entered into partnership with Robert R. Livingston, who had obtained a monopoly for steam navigation on New York state waters, and in 1807 he made his famous voyage up the Hudson River in the *Clermont*. Four years later, another Fulton steamboat, the *New Orleans*, sailed down the Mississippi from Pittsburgh to its namesake city.

By 1830 some two hundred steam-powered vessels were sailing freely through the waterways of the West. Since the steamboat could travel upriver, it turned the major waterways into two-way highways. Frequent steamboat travel along the Mississippi reduced transportation costs and established regular trading routes between the East and West.

It was in the West that the steamboat made its greatest contribution to the development of the American economy. Steamboats could move much faster than flatboats. Shipping on light keelboats poled by strong men was slow and the rates were high—before 1820 as much as $5.00 for every one hundred pounds. By 1820 the rate for steamboat transport was $2.00, and by 1842 the rate was only twenty-five cents per one hundred pounds. Steamboats also offered a pleasurable way to travel. Luxury passenger vessels, their comfortable cabins

decorated with carpets and mirrors, offered an attractive alternative to road travel.

The Canal Boom   Before 1816 canal construction had been extremely modest. Canals were costly to build and the work could take years. In 1817, when construction began on the Erie Canal, there was only one canal in the nation that was almost thirty miles long and there were only one hundred miles of canal altogether. The Erie Canal marked the beginning of a boom in canal building.

The canal was the brainchild of the people of New York state, who wanted a direct route between Albany and Buffalo. New Yorkers believed that construction of an easy route would facilitate the

THE GRAND SALOON OF THE PALACE STEAMER DREW. OPULENT ACCOMMODATIONS WERE AVAILABLE TO PASSENGERS BOARDING THE LUXURY STEAMBOATS THAT PROVIDED DAILY SERVICE ALONG THE HUDSON RIVER.

Legend:
- Roads
- Canals
- Navigable rivers

0 ——— 300
Miles

Canals and Roads • 1820 to 1850

growth of cities in the Mohawk Valley, and promote the emergence of New York City as the major American seaport. The federal government refused to provide financial assistance for the project, so the people of New York raised the money by borrowing in England. The canal, completed in 1825 and 363 miles in length, had a profound effect on the growth of the state of New York, the movement westward, and the economy of the nation as a whole. Tolls paid off the original investment in the first nine years of operation and were soon bringing $3 million a year into the state treasury. Freight rates from Buffalo to Albany were reduced from $100 to $15 a ton, and the trip was shortened from twenty to eight days. The state experienced rapid industrial growth, new cities sprang up, and New York City soon became a major trade center for Western livestock and grain, as well as the country's leading seaboard city. Most of the goods sent from Europe to the western United States now passed through New York rather than New Orleans.

The Erie Canal enabled thousands of settlers to pour into the area south of the Great Lakes. It also inspired many other canal-building projects that helped to bind the nation together. New York state opened a second canal, between Lake Champlain and the Hudson River, in 1823. New England promoters sponsored a series of short canals connecting Worcester and Northampton, Massachusetts, to the coast. In 1828 a canal running from northeastern Pennsylvania, across New Jersey and New York, to the Hudson River began carrying Pennsylvania coal in barges to the Eastern seaboard. Pennsylvania built a route that was part canal and part railroad across the Allegheny Mountains from Philadelphia to Pittsburgh. However, this system, with its 177 locks and stretches of railroad in between, proved too cumbersome and slow to be a great success.

West of the Allegheny Mountains canal building also met with great popular support. By 1837 Ohio had 750 miles of canals. Indiana constructed the 450-mile Wabash and Erie Canal. By 1840 there were some thirty-three hundred miles of canal in the United States, most of them in the East and the West.

A network of canals was creating a bond between the East and the West. Only the Southern states, with their excellent natural river system, did not feel the need to invest heavily in public roads and canals.

Sectional Strains Resurface

The Era of Good Feelings lasted only a few short years. By 1820 the outburst of nationalism was subsiding, and the sectional differences that had prevailed since colonial times resurfaced.

President Monroe desired to end partisan politics, which he looked upon as contrary to republican principles and contrary to the national interest. In an effort to promote national good will, he was careful to avoid making any disparaging remarks in public about the few remaining Federalists, and he cultivated personal friendships with individual members of that party. The president underestimated the intensity of sectional differences in the country, however, and mistakenly viewed the divisiveness they caused as a practical problem capable of solution through compromise. Yet because there was only one viable political party, Monroe was reelected in 1820 with only one dissenting vote in the electoral college. By the early 1820s the Federalist party had died out.

Sectional Differences after 1812

The War of 1812 set in motion certain processes which would exaggerate the growing differences among the various regions. The development of manufacturing in the Northeast ultimately brought New England's factories into competition with Britain's, and the North began to agitate for high tariffs which would restrict foreign imports and facilitate economic self-sufficiency in the region.

The South remained a specialized agricultural economy in the colonial tradition, exporting its crops to Europe in exchange for manufactured commodities. Southerners knew that they could not rely on Northern mills to consume all the cotton they produced. The region's major customers were, and would continue to be, the English textile factories of Lancashire. The economic interests of the North and the South were therefore in opposition. While the North had everything to gain from high tariffs, the vast majority of Southerners believed that high protective tariffs would hurt their economy because they would have to pay higher prices for imported goods. Only a few Southerners backed the tariff as a shield for the development of industry in their own section. Most Southerners also opposed the tariff for an additional reason: they viewed it as a tax on their section to provide money for the building of roads and canals in the North and West. With their marvelous river system they did not need these internal improvements to carry staples to their seaports. Without industry, most Southerners also saw no need for the complex credit operations provided by a national banking system.

The South, which before 1812 had been equal to the North in size, wealth, population, and political influence, gradually began to develop a sense of regional self-consciousness as the North expanded in manufacturing and population. Southerners began to view their region as a society apart and took refuge in the doctrine of states' rights to protect their minority position and the institution of slavery.

The West was also a significant factor in the American economic equation. Before 1812 most settlers west of the Appalachian Mountains were Southerners. Most had migrated from Virginia and North Carolina to Kentucky and Tennessee. Thus the early West was basically an extension of the old South. After the war, however, many Northerners joined small farmers from the South to settle the Illinois and Indiana Territories. These territories soon comprised one quarter of the nation's population and had a strong influence on national politics.

Conflicts of interest, particularly over the issue of slavery, divided the Western territories much as the North and South were divided on Clay's American System. Yet the Western region as a whole still displayed a political cohesiveness on specifically Western issues. Regardless of their origins or views on slavery, all Westerners wanted better roads linking them to the East, protection against hostile Indians, and cheap farmland.

The Panic of 1819

The Era of Good Feelings came to an abrupt end with a nationwide economic panic in 1819. Even the limited efforts taken by the federal government to alleviate distress served instead to intensify the differences in sectional economic interests.

Between 1816 and 1819 Europeans, starved by the Napoleonic wars and suffering from two bad harvests, had bought unprecedented quantities of American corn, beef, pork, flour, cotton, and tobacco. Britain's textile manufacturers had purchased American cotton at extremely high prices to provide clothing, which had been scarce during the war years.

But by 1818 the situation in Europe was improving. Abundant harvests replenished European wheat, and cheap cotton from India began replacing expensive American cotton in Britain's textile factories. Although these developments were healthy for Europe, they had an adverse effect on the American economy. The prosperity of the postwar years was followed by the country's first nationwide depression, the Panic of 1819.

Several factors led to this contraction of the American economy. Overproduction of cotton in the United States caused a drop in cotton prices. At the same time, the amount of precious metals on the world market declined when mining in Mexico and Peru was disrupted during the Latin American revolts against Spain. This, in turn, led to a severe decline in world prices, which compounded the difficulty of selling American cotton at a profit.

Unaware of international economic conditions, Americans had been speculating wildly in Western lands. Moreover, Western farmers, eager to buy farm equipment and additional land, had become heavily indebted to the Bank of the United States. In 1818 almost two and a half million acres were sold and in 1819 over five million acres were sold. But by 1820 land sales declined to a little over a million acres and in 1821 only about three-quarters of a million acres were sold despite the liberal land law of 1820. The bank, particularly its Western branches, had pursued a generous policy in making loans on mortgages, renewing notes repeatedly, and issuing new loans without ensuring that they could be repaid. When Europe's demand for American cotton and wheat declined, farmers in the South and West had trouble paying for agricultural equipment and meeting their mortgage payments.

To make matters worse, the Bank of the United States was terribly mismanaged. It issued great quantities of paper money without having adequate supplies of gold and silver on hand to back it up. Then, to curtail the inflated economy, it began calling in loans and pressuring state banks to redeem their notes in specie. After making the mistake of lending too much money too easily, the bank became too restrictive at a time when money was scarce.

In the depression that ensued, the Bank of the United States became known as "the Monster." One after another, state banks closed their doors. Prices fell drastically. Almost one-third of the population of Pittsburgh abandoned the city; its textile, glass, and iron manufacturers closed shop. In Cincinnati the national bank suddenly became the unwilling owner of hotels, stables, and stores when debtors defaulted on their loan payments.

Because the Jeffersonians believed that the federal government had little responsibility for the country's economic problems federal action to alleviate the crisis was minimal. Sectional tensions and disagreements over economic policy prevented wide support for any specific measures. As a result, all that Congress was able to do was increase the tariff and reduce the price of land.

Land Policy Public attitudes toward government land policy reflected the diversity of sectional interests in the country. The federal government owned millions of acres in the West. Westerners wanted to be able to buy this land as cheaply as possible, whereas Northerners and Southerners regarded it as a public asset which should be sold for large sums to ease the nation's tax burdens. Northern industrialists also feared that if land were cheap, many factory workers would abandon their jobs and head west and that those who stayed behind would be able to command steep wages as factory owners competed for their services. The cotton planters of South Carolina and Georgia also feared that cheap Western land would create a rival cotton-growing area.

Despite these pressures, demands by farmers for cheaper land encouraged the government to formulate a more liberal land policy. The Land Act of 1800 specified that land could be sold in lots of no less than 320 acres at no less than $2.00 per acre. In 1804 the minimum lot size was reduced to 160 acres, and the price was reduced to $1.64 per acre. The Land Act of 1820, passed in an effort to ease the plight of farmers after the Panic of 1819, reduced the minimum lot size to 80 acres and the minimum price to $1.25 per acre. The installment plan, which had led to so many foreclosures during the panic, was abolished, and buyers now had to pay imme-

diately and in cash. Land was offered at a government auction and went to the highest bidder. Much of it, especially the more fertile areas, went for a great deal more than the minimum price. The following year a Relief Act supplemented the Land Act by allowing those who had bought more land on credit than they could pay for to turn back a portion of the land in lieu of further payments.

Protective Tariff Debated The Tariff of 1816 had taxed certain itemized imports at about 25 percent of their value. Now Northern manufacturers, hit by the Panic of 1819, wanted to increase these duties. At the same time, the panic was hurting Southern cotton growers as much as it was Northern manufacturers. The price of cotton had dropped drastically, and the industrial growth that some Southerners had anticipated was not taking place. Southerners, therefore, had no reason to support a higher tariff, and their votes in Congress defeated both a proposed tariff in 1820 and a bill to provide money for the National Road in 1822. The South's stand on these two issues alienated Northern manufacturers and Western farmers who believed that the depression would end only if the government would provide tariffs to protect American industry and federally sponsored transportation systems to connect the West to the East.

In 1824 the attempt to raise the tariff was finally successful, though the bill barely scraped through the Congress because of pressure from competing interests in the country. American wool growers, for example, wanted a high duty on imported wool, but woolen manufacturers proposed an increased duty only on imported woolen fabrics. The net effect of the tariff was to boost duties to between 30 and 36 percent of the value of certain imported goods.

By the mid-1820s prosperity returned to the United States. But the panic had left deep scars, especially with regard to the Bank of the United States. Large numbers of Americans blamed paper money for the inflationary cycle that had culminated in panic and depression. Although industry soon recovered, a depression in the agricultural sector continued for several years. It was aggravated in the Southern coastal states by soil depletion and declining production.

Lingering resentment against the bank was strengthened when Congress investigated certain financial irregularities and then took no action to chastise or control the national bank. Western settlers viewed the national bank as the darling of Eastern financiers, which added to their distrust of Eastern business interests. Yet a new economic interdependence was growing between the Northern states and such Western states as Ohio, Indiana, and Illinois. For a time the new West continued to support positions taken by Southern politicians. Ultimately, however, economic ties with the North destroyed this alliance.

The Slavery Issue

Nowhere did sectional differences become more bitter than over the issue of slavery. Never economically important to the North, slavery had been abolished in all states north of Maryland and Delaware by 1804. Slavery had also been legally excluded from the Northwest Territory. In the South, however, the institution became even more important to the economy after the introduction of the cotton gin and after settlement of new lands made cotton a profitable crop.

Slave labor was easily adapted to cotton farming. Tobacco required careful planting and delicate pruning, but cotton could be managed by unskilled workers of any age. The cotton plant, which could be cultivated most of the year, grew only waist high, allowing a single overseer to keep track of many slaves at once. Slave labor became particularly profitable on large plantations which needed a constant supply of labor.

As provided in the Constitution, the federal government had outlawed the foreign slave trade in January 1808. Nevertheless, thousands of Africans continued to be smuggled into America to meet the demand for more laborers. The sale of slaves also became a major source of profit in the upper South. States such as Virginia, Maryland, and Kentucky, whose diminishing cotton production did not require extensive slave labor, became slave traders for the cotton kingdom. Licensed traders bought slaves at auctions and sent them to the Deep South. In the forty years before the Civil War 742,000 blacks were transported from the upper South to the cotton-growing states.

The Missouri Compromise

Slavery and its expansion had not been an issue in national politics since the debates over ratification of the Constitution. Slavery was tolerated as the South's "peculiar institution."

When Louisiana became a state in 1812, the rest of the Louisiana Purchase was organized into the Missouri Territory. By 1820 this territory had a population of sixty-six thousand, ten thousand of whom were slaves. When Alabama entered the Union in 1819, an exact balance of eleven free states and eleven slaveholding states was achieved in the Senate. That part of the Missouri Territory west of Illinois between the Mississippi and the Missouri rivers had petitioned Congress for admission to the Union as early as 1817. Admitting a new state to the Union had always been a routine matter, but Missouri's application created a furor that occupied Congress from 1819 to 1821 and aggravated the nation's increasingly sectionalist attitude toward slavery.

The Northwest Ordinance of 1787 had prohibited slavery in the Northwest Territory and had set a precedent against extending slavery into territories outside the South. Now, however, Missouri's request led Southerners to work aggressively to extend slavery beyond the area of containment that had been tacitly, and in part legally (according to the precedent of the Northwest Ordinance), agreed upon since the Revolution.

Many Northerners opposed the Missouri petition for statehood because it would allow the expansion of slavery. The Northern states had abolished slavery within their boundaries, and they felt the practice of apportioning representatives to Congress on the basis of three-fifths of the slave population was unfair to the North. Also, the creation of a new slave state west of the Mississippi River would give the South, which was outnumbered by the Northern states in the House, an advantage in the Senate. Finally, even though abolitionist societies were now gaining support and had moral objections to the admission of another slave state, most Northerners simply wanted the territories reserved for white settlers.

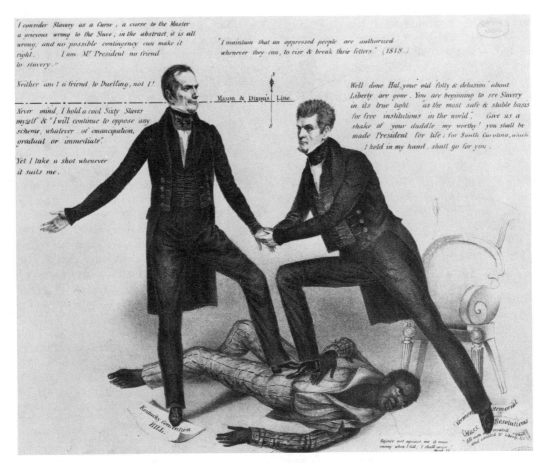

SENATE CHAMBER U.S.A. CONCLUSION OF CLAY'S SPEECH IN DEFENSE OF SLAVERY.

For their part, Southerners argued that it was their right to take property into lands that they had paid for as much as Northerners had. They were fearful that if slavery were prohibited in Missouri, it would also be prohibited in the rest of the territories in the Louisiana Purchase. Some Southerners also realized that it would not be long before they would be outnumbered in the government, and they sought to preserve what influence they had.

In February 1819 James Tallmadge, Jr., a New York representative who believed that slavery was a moral evil, made the following proposal concerning Missouri:

That the further introduction of slavery or invol-untary servitude be prohibited except for the punishment of crimes whereof the party shall have been duly convicted: and that all children born within the said State after the admission thereof into the Union shall be free, but may be held to service until the age of twenty-five years.

The Tallmadge Amendment passed the House of Representatives by a small majority, but was de-feated in the Senate. A few Northern senators joined the Southern bloc in voting against it because they felt that the government did not have the constitu-tional right to meddle in the internal affairs of a state.

When the next Congress met in December 1819, statehood for Missouri was proposed again. Now, however, the issue was complicated by the fact that the District of Maine, having separated itself from Massachusetts, was also applying for statehood. Speaker of the House Henry Clay proposed a compromise: Missouri would enter the Union as a slave state and Maine as a free state. To prevent similar conflicts in the future, another provision was added: slavery was to be "forever prohibited" in all other parts of the Louisiana Purchase north of the 36° 30′ line. The compromise was enacted, leaving Arkansas and Oklahoma as the only two territorial areas open to the expansion of slavery. In accepting the compromise, the South was tacitly agreeing that the national government could exclude slavery from unorganized territories, an admission that meant Missouri might eventually be surrounded by free states.

In 1820 Maine was duly admitted as a state, and Missouri was authorized to write a constitution.

When it was presented for congressional approval, Missouri's constitution contained a clause forbidding the state legislature from freeing slaves without the consent of their owners, and a clause forbidding free blacks or mulattoes from other states from entering Missouri "under any pretext whatever." The latter clause clearly violated the federal Constitution's provision that "the Citizens of each State shall be entitled to all Privileges and Immunities of Citizens in the several States." Missouri's constitution was accepted, however, with a proviso that no law passed in Missouri should ever discriminate against the citizens of other states. Even though Missouri's constitution was already in clear violation of the federal Constitution, the territory was admitted as a state in 1821.

Attacking the Expansion of Slavery

"Sir, extend your view across the Mississippi, over your newly acquired territory; . . . Look down the long vista of futurity. . . . Behold this extended empire, inhabited by the hardy sons of American freemen—knowing their rights, and inheriting the will to protect them—owners of the soil on which they live, and interested in the institutions which they labor to defend—. . . . Compared to yours, the Governments of Europe dwindle into insignificance, and the whole world is without a parallel. But, sir, reverse this scene; people this fair dominion with the slaves of your planters; extend slavery—this bane of man, this abomination of heaven—over your extended empire, and you prepare its dissolution. . . . The envious contrast between your happiness and their misery, between your liberty and their slavery, must constantly prompt them to accomplish your destruction. Your enemies will learn the source and the cause of your weakness. . . . With this defect, your Government must crumble to pieces, and your people become the scoff of the world. . . ."

James Tallmadge,
United States Congress,
Debates and Proceedings,
February 15, 1819

Defending the Expansion of Slavery

"The real question is, what disposition shall we make of those slaves who are already in the country? Shall they be perpetually confined on this side of the Mississippi, or shall we spread them over a much larger surface by permitting them to be carried beyond that river? . . . Now, sir, in relation to the physical force of the country, if ever the time shall come when we shall be engaged in war, and they should be excited to insurrection, it is obvious that there must be an immense subduction from the efficiency of the slave-holding section of our country; its actual efficiency would consist only, or nearly so, in the excess of the white beyond the black population; by spreading them over a more extended surface, you secure these advantages; first, by diminishing the proportion which the slaves bear in point of numbers to the whites, you diminish their motives to insurrection. Secondly, that if that event ever should occur, it would obviously be much more easily and certainly suppressed, because. . . . they would have a much smaller relative proportion of physical force."

Philip P. Barbour,
United States Congress,
Debates and Proceedings,
February 16, 1819

The Missouri Compromise made slavery a national issue and polarized the country even further. Defensive as a result of the Missouri debates, Southerners began proclaiming slavery a positive good. Charles Pinckney of South Carolina insisted: "Every slave has a comfortable house, is well fed, clothed, and taken care of; he has his family about him, and in sickness has the same medical aid as his master, and has a sure and comfortable retreat from old age. . . . During his whole life he is free from care, that canker of the human heart."

Two years after the Missouri debates a freedman, Denmark Vesey, taking his authority from the Bible and the Declaration of Independence,

planned a massive uprising in Charleston. The plot was discovered and the conspirators hanged, but Southerners linked the revolt to the emotions created by the debates on the admission of Missouri. As a result, white South Carolinians tightened the reins even more for slaves and free blacks. Freedmen were prohibited from entering the state, since they might foment further uprisings; and black churches were closed, since it was assumed that they provided a convenient meeting place for conspirators.

The compromise also affected the treatment of free blacks. In much of the North they already were denied the franchise and prevented from testifying in court cases involving whites. Moreover, they were

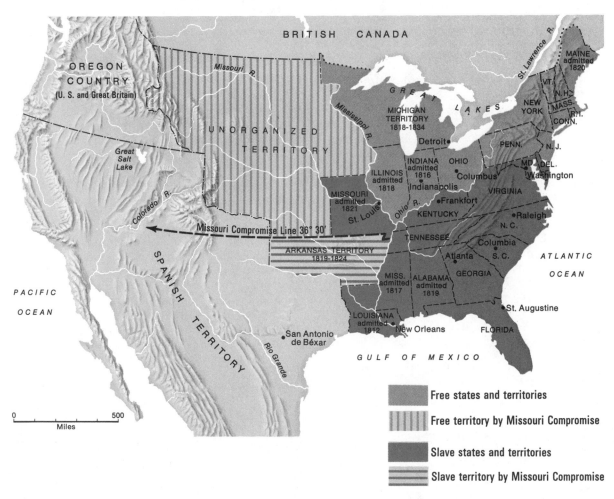

Missouri Compromise • 1820

generally excluded from jury duty and from becoming judges. Denial of such rights virtually assured unfair legal treatment of blacks. The Missouri Compromise focused increased attention on black people at a time when few Northerners believed in racial equality. In 1821, for instance, the Supreme Court of New Jersey—a state which had legally abolished slavery in 1804—proclaimed that "black men are *prima facie* slaves." This ruling severely retarded the elimination of slavery in that state by requiring that in court cases in which slaveholders claimed fugitive slaves as their property, the burden of proof was on the blacks to bring evidence that they were free. Other states now limited or denied free blacks equal opportunities for education and economic advancement.

The question of slavery, conveniently buried for three decades, was being debated at a time when the South was more than ever dedicated to preserving the institution. Jefferson wrote John Quincy Adams that the dispute, "like a fire bell in the night, awakened and filled me with terror." Adams responded: "I take it for granted that the present question is a mere preamble—the title page to a great tragic volume."

The Election of 1824

The election of 1824 showed clearly how political alliances were being drawn along sectional lines. The candidacy of William H. Crawford, Monroe's secretary of the treasury and one of the most prominent politicians from the South, was supported by a number of congressional leaders as well as the president. He was nominated by a congressional caucus as the official presidential candidate of the Jeffersonian party and represented the "Old Republicans" who resisted the American System and advocated a return to the pure Jeffersonian principles of states' rights and limited government. But there were some other prominent politicians, including John Quincy Adams, Henry Clay, and Andrew Jackson, who considered the caucus system undemocratic and whose supporters encouraged them to run. The party, already weakened by the Panic of 1819 and the Missouri controversy, never recovered from this disastrous splintering. The caucus system for nominating candidates also was dead, and the candidates sought endorsements from mass meetings and various state legislatures.

John Quincy Adams The best-known Northern political figure, John Quincy Adams, was the son of the second president. The younger Adams, an able diplomat, had served on the commission that forged the Treaty of Ghent, and as Monroe's secretary of state had negotiated the brilliant Adams-Onis treaty with Spain.

Adams's strict upbringing imbued him with the lifelong habit of examining his own character flaws as well as everyone else's. By the time he ran for the presidency, he was a bald, stout man with a tense and compulsive attitude toward work. His highly developed moral sense made him often harsh and dogmatic. Introspective by nature, he recorded his

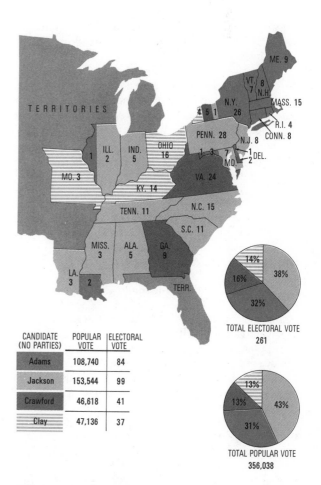

CANDIDATE (NO PARTIES)	POPULAR VOTE	ELECTORAL VOTE
Adams	108,740	84
Jackson	153,544	99
Crawford	46,618	41
Clay	47,136	37

Election of 1824

thoughts in a voluminous diary which was, "next to the Holy Scriptures," his most valuable book.

Adams was an ardent nationalist who subscribed enthusiastically to Henry Clay's concept of controlled expansion and rational planning on the federal level. Although he believed in a democratic suffrage, he felt that the federal government and its policies could best be managed by an intellectual elite. He also believed that the most reliable supporters of nationalism were the nation's merchant and manufacturing interests.

The Emergence of Jackson

Adams was not popular outside New England, and Southerners particularly disliked the prospect of having another Yankee elected to the presidency. Clay's supporters were concentrated mostly in the West, so he, too, was unable to generate broad enthusiasm.

Andrew Jackson, the hero of the Battle of New Orleans, emerged quite unexpectedly as a serious presidential contender and succeeded in building a national following where his rivals had failed. In part, he appealed to the nation's patriotic memories, but he also appealed to a rapidly growing electorate that was as disillusioned with the caucus system as he was. Jackson was regarded as pure and unspoiled because he was not part of the political establishment.

Although Jackson received the highest popular vote and also led in the electoral college, he had received a plurality, not a majority. According to the Constitution the decision now had to be made by the House of Representatives with each state casting one vote. According to the Twelfth Amendment to the Constitution, the House was to choose from the three leading candidates, which meant that Clay, who had placed fourth, was automatically eliminated. Crawford, who had placed third, had become seriously ill and was no longer regarded as a serious contender.

Thus the choice was between Jackson and Adams, with the three state votes that Clay controlled being the decisive factor. Clay feared Jackson's rise to political power. He also recognized that Adams was much more likely to support the American System than was Jackson, whose political views never had been clearly stated. Therefore, ignoring the fact that his own state of Kentucky had instructed him to vote for Jackson, Clay met secretly with Adams and then announced that he would support him. He also persuaded several other representatives to follow his example, and when the votes were counted, Adams emerged the winner.

The Adams Administration

One of President Adams's first acts was to appoint Clay secretary of state. Jackson, furious, accused Clay and Adams of having made a corrupt bargain, complaining: "So you see the Judas of the West has closed the contract and will receive the thirty pieces of silver. His end will be the same." Clay's decision to support Adams was justified in terms of national policy, but his acceptance of an appointment in the new administration was a serious political blunder.

The dissolution of the Jeffersonian Republican party, the persistent name-calling by the Jacksonians, and the failure of his later foreign negotiations damaged Adams's prestige and efforts to assert presidential leadership. In his first annual address to Congress, Adams was greeted with scorn, even though most of his proposals were remarkably far-sighted. As a nationalist, he was out of step with

popular sentiment in the country, and the congressional elections of 1826 put a new Jacksonian coalition of Adams's enemies, renamed the Democratic Republicans, in control of both houses of Congress. Thereafter, every move the president made was blocked by a hostile legislature.

Adams and the American System

Adams was determined to extend the American System. In fact, to the dismay of his cabinet, his recommendations for federally sponsored improvements went beyond even Clay's earlier proposals. Adams, however, ignored their warnings and proceeded with his "perilous experiment" of bold recommendations to Congress. He suggested that Congress finance expeditions to explore the Far

West, establish a uniform standard of weights and measures, found a national university, and build an astronomical observatory. He urged general laws "promoting the improvement of agriculture, commerce, and manufactures, the cultivation and encouragement of the mechanic and of the elegant arts, the advancement of literature, and the progress of the sciences, ornamental and profound. . . ."

These recommendations seemed farfetched and absurd to a nation internally divided and basically devoted to the concept of a federal government with limited power. When he urged Congress not to be "palsied by the will of our constituents," his enemies accused him of holding American democracy in contempt and attempting to rule like a European monarch. The president was ridiculed and only fragments of his grand design were ever realized: $2.5 million was appropriated for the maintenance of the National Road, and an additional sum of roughly $2 million was allocated to support private canal companies.

The Tariff of Abominations

The most controversial article of legislation passed during the Adams administration was the Tariff of 1828, a piecemeal collection of provisions representing the demands of different special-interest groups.

Manufacturers in the Northeast wanted higher duties on foreign factory-made goods. Senator Thomas Hart Benton of Missouri, an influential Western politician, demanded duties on fur and lead. Levi Woodbury of New Hampshire asked for a duty on manufactured silk to protect his state's silk mills. Similarly, the hemp raisers in Kentucky, the wool growers of New York, and other regional interest groups all called for their own protective tariffs.

Supported by a majority of Western and Northern votes, the tariff was passed. Southerners called it the "Tariff of Abominations." New England merchants, who formerly advocated free trade, retrenched and instructed Senator Daniel Webster, a persuasive orator whose views reflected their own and who was directing administration forces in the Senate, to vote for the bill. Senator Martin Van Buren, who supported Andrew Jackson and opposed a higher tariff in theory, arranged for Old Hickory's Northern backers to vote for the tariff in the belief that it would add Western and Northern voters to the Democratic Republican

THE FIRST PHOTO OF AN AMERICAN PRESIDENT, JOHN QUINCY ADAMS, TAKEN IN 1843. DURING THE 1820s WHEN THE WHITE HOUSE OPENED ON THE POTOMAC RIVER, THE PORTLY PRESIDENT WOULD SLIP OUT BETWEEN 4:00 AND 6:00 A.M FOR A BRIEF SWIM. AFTER DRYING HIMSELF WITH NAPKINS AND DONNING HIS CLOTHES, ADAMS RETURNED TO HIS STUDY TO READ THE BIBLE AND THE DAILY NEWS BEFORE HIS NINE O'CLOCK BREAKFAST. (The Metropolitan Museum of Art, Gift of I. N. Phelps Stokes, Edward S. Hawes, Alice Mary Hawes, Marion Augusta Hawes, 1937)

party. This regional alignment echoed the regional response to the Tariff of 1824. The ever-rising tariff was now as high as 60 percent on some items. The South, increasingly opposed to a high tariff, was frustrated once again.

International Problems

Adams had shown great diplomatic skill as Monroe's secretary of state. But as president, he suffered defeat and humiliation. In 1825 Simon Bolivar, the liberator of much of South America, called for a Pan-American Congress. Adams, wanting to send two delegates, asked Congress for approval and received a conflicting and hostile response. Many isolationists were opposed to participating in any international gathering. Southerners, in particular, disapproved of the convention, fearing that Latin Americans who opposed slavery might try to discuss the presence of slavery in the United States. On the other hand, Northern commercial interests thought that contacts with South American countries would be economically beneficial. After four months of debate, Congress gave its reluctant approval. It came too late, however, and the conference was held without the United States.

Adams also was frustrated over negotiations to gain access to the British West Indian trade. The British had excluded American shipping from the West Indies since the 1780s. Finally, in 1820, Congress had retaliated by refusing to allow the British to ship any West Indian goods to the United States; and in 1825 Britain offered to lift some of its restric-

tions in return for an end to discrimination against British shipping. Adams instructed his minister in London to agree to a reciprocal end to trade restrictions, but at this point the British reversed their position and once again blocked American trade with the islands. Adams, unwilling to press the question further without support from a reluctant Congress, once again closed the nation's ports to British West Indian shipping.

The puritanical, soul-searching Adams had been a failure as president. His strong nationalism was out of tune with the times. His belief that an educated elite should shape the destiny of the nation repelled the ordinary citizen. His unwillingness to engage in partisan politics made it difficult to build up a constituency that could be depended on to support his policies. Even so, Adams returned to government service as a representative from Massachusetts and remained in the House until his death in 1848, accomplishing enough good that even his enemies came to hold him in high regard.

Readings

General Works

Abernethy, Thomas P., *The South in the New Nation*. Baton Rouge: Louisiana State University Press, 1961.

Arieli, Yehoshua, *Individualism and Nationalism in American Ideology*. Cambridge, Mass.: Harvard University Press, 1964.

Billington, Ray A., *Westward Expansion*. New York: Macmillan, 1967.

Burlingame, Roger, *The March of the Iron Men*. New York: Grosset & Dunlap, 1960.

Dangerfield, George, *The Awakening of American Nationalism, 1815–1828*. New York: Harper & Row, 1965.

_____, *The Era of Good Feelings*. New York: Harcourt, Brace & World, 1962.

Dorfman, Joseph, *The Economic Mind in American Civilization*, Vols. I–V. New York: Viking, 1946–1959.

Eaton, Clement, *The Growth of Southern Civilization*. New York: Harper & Row, 1961.

_____, *The Mind of the Old South*. Baton Rouge.: Louisiana State University Press, 1964.

Hofstadter, Richard, *The Idea of a Party System: The Rise of Legitimate Opposition in the United States, 1780–1840*. Berkeley: University of California Press, 1969.

Horsman, Reginald, *The Frontier in the Formative Years, 1783–1815*. Albuquerque: University of New Mexico Press, 1970.

Nagel, Paul C., *One Nation Indivisible: The Union in American Thought, 1776–1861*. New York: Oxford University Press, 1964.

North, Douglass C., *The Economic Growth of the United States, 1790–1860*. Englewood Cliffs, N.J.: Prentice-Hall, 1961.

Rosenberg, Nathan, *Technology and American Economic Growth*. White Plains, N.Y.: M. E. Sharpe, 1972.

Taylor, George R., *The Transportation Revolution*. New York: Harper & Row, 1968.

Wish, Harvey, *Society and Thought in Early America*. Vols. I–II. 2d ed. New York: David McKay, 1962.

Wright, Louis B., *Culture on the Moving Frontier*. Bloomington: Indiana University Press, 1955.

Special Studies

Commons, John R., *et al.*, *History of Labor in the United States*, Vols. I–IV. New York: Macmillan, 1918–1935.

Curti, Merle, *The Roots of American Loyalty*. New York: Columbia University Press, 1946.

Faulkner, R. K., *The Jurisprudence of John Marshall*. Princeton, N.J.: Princeton University Press, 1968.

Goodrich, Carter, *Government Promotion of Canals and Railroads, 1800–1890*. New York: Columbia University Press, 1960.

Gray, Lewis C., *History of Agriculture in the Southern United States to 1860*, Vols. I–II. New York: Kelley, 1969.

Haines, Charles G., *The Role of the Supreme Court in American Government and Politics, 1789–1835*. Berkeley: University of California Press, 1944.

Havighurst, Walter, *Voices on the River: The Story of the Mississippi Water Ways*. New York: Macmillan, 1964.

Livermore, Shaw, Jr., *The Twilight of Federalism*. Princeton, N.J.: Princeton University Press, 1962.

May, Ernest R., *The Making of the Monroe Doctrine*. Cambridge, Mass.: Harvard University Press, 1975.

Miller, Nathan, *The Enterprise of a Free People*. Ithaca, N.Y.: Cornell University Press, 1962.

Moore, Glover, *The Missouri Controversy*. Lexington: University of Kentucky Press, 1953.

Perkins, Bradford, *Castlereagh and Adams*. Berkeley: University of California Press, 1964.

Perkins, Dexter, *A History of the Monroe Doctrine*. Boston: Little, Brown, 1963.

Rothband, Murray N., *The Panic of 1819*. New York: Columbia University Press, 1962.

Shaw, Ronald E., *Erie Water West: A History of the Erie Canal, 1792–1854*. Lexington: University Press of Kentucky, 1966.

Turner, Frederick J., *Rise of the New West*. New York: Collier, 1962.

Wade, Richard C., *The Urban Frontier*. Chicago: University of Chicago Press, 1959.

Warren, Charles, *The Supreme Court in United States History*, Vols. I–III. Boston: Little, Brown, 1923.

Weisberger, Bernard A., *They Gathered at the River*. Boston: Little, Brown, 1958.

Whitaker, Arthur P., *The United States and the Independence of Latin America, 1800–1830*. New York: Norton, 1964.

Primary Sources

Benton, Thomas H., *Thirty Years View*, Vols. I–II. New York: Greenwood Press, 1968.

Nevins, Allan (Ed.), *The Diary of John Quincy Adams*. New York: Ungar, 1929.

Van Buren, Martin, *Autobiography*. J. C. Fitzpatrick, ed. New York: Kelley, 1969.

Biographies

Ammon, Harry, *James Monroe: The Quest for National Identity*. New York: McGraw-Hill, 1971.

Baker, Leonard, *John Marshall: A Life in Law*. New York: Macmillan, 1974.

Bemis, Samuel F., *John Quincy Adams and the Union*. New York: Knopf, 1956.

Beveridge, Albert J., *The Life of John Marshall*, Vols. I–IV. Boston: Houghton Mifflin, 1916–1919.

Chambers, William N., *Old Bullion Benton*. Boston: Little, Brown, 1956.

Current, Richard N., *Daniel Webster and the Rise of National Conservatism*. Boston: Little, Brown, 1955.

_____, *John C. Calhoun*. New York: Washington Square Press, 1966.

Dalzell, Robert F., *Daniel Webster & the Trial of American Nationalism, 1843–1852*. Boston: Houghton Mifflin, 1973.

Eaton, Clement, *Henry Clay and the Art of American Politics*. Boston: Little, Brown, 1957.

Green, Constance M. L., *Eli Whitney and the Birth of American Technology*. Boston: Little, Brown, 1956.

Huff, Archie Vernon, Jr., *Langdon Cheves of South Carolina*. Columbia: University of South Carolina Press, 1977.

Nevins, Allan, and Jeannette Mirsky, *The World of Eli Whitney*. New York: Macmillan, 1962.

Remini, Robert V., *Martin Van Buren and the Making of the Democratic Party*. New York: Columbia University Press, 1959.

Wiltse, Charles M., *John C. Calhoun: Nationalist*. Indianapolis, Ind.: Bobbs-Merrill, 1944.

Fiction

Melville, Herman, *Moby Dick*. New York: Modern Library, 1950.

Twain, Mark, *Life on the Mississippi*. New York: Signet New American Library, 1961.

9 The Rise of Jacksonian Democracy

But the experience of the world goes to prove that there is a tendency to monopoly wherever power is reposed in the hands of a minority. Nothing is more likely to be true than that twenty wise men will unite in opinions in opposition to a hundred fools; but nothing is more certain than that, if placed in situations to control all the interests of their less gifted neighbors . . . , fifteen or sixteen of them would pervert their philosophy to selfishness. This was at least our political creed, and we therefore admitted a vast majority of the community to a right of voting. Since the hour of the Revolution, the habits, opinions, laws and I may say principles of the Americans are getting daily to be more democratic.

James Fenimore Cooper
Notions of the Americans

Significant Events

South Carolina Exposition and Protest [1828]

Law for Indian removal [1830]

Maysville Road Veto [1830]

Cherokee Nation v. *Georgia* [1831]

Anti-Masonic party holds first national convention [1831]

South Carolina Ordinance of Nullification [1832]

Jackson's veto of recharter of Bank of the United States [1832]

Compromise Tariff [1833]

Specie Circular [1836]

Economic panic [1837]

Charles River Bridge v. *Warren Bridge* [1837]

Independent Treasury Act [1840]

GENERAL JACKSON, PRESIDENT-ELECT, ON HIS WAY TO WASHINGTON, DRAWN BY HOWARD PILE.

By the time Andrew Jackson was elected President of the United States, the majority of his countrymen had come to believe not only that all men were created equal but that they should all have the same opportunities for advancement. It was this emphasis on the equality of opportunity that was the most important difference between Jeffersonian and Jacksonian democracy. The Jeffersonians believed that political leaders emerged inevitably from a natural aristocracy based on talent, education, and virtue. The Jacksonians, on the other hand, believed that careers in politics should be open to all men, no matter how simple their origins. The career of Jackson himself was the prime example of this outlook. Jackson, a man of humble beginnings and little formal education, rose to the nation's highest office. His success demonstrated to ordinary men throughout the nation that political ambition was no longer the birthright of the upper classes. Jackson enjoyed tremendous support as the hero of the common people, and he and his followers insisted that his election proved that social status and education were unnecessary for political leadership.

Nevertheless, in spite of the personal achievement of President Andrew Jackson, the Jacksonian era did not advance political democracy quite so much as some historians have claimed. Individuals had risen from humble origins to wealth and power from the earliest colonial times. Political power continued to come not so much to the common man as to shrewd and ambitious politicians who had mastered the arts of flattery.

Jackson Takes Command

The Democratization of Politics

The trend toward the democratization of American politics had been underway since the Revolutionary period. As the spirit of egalitarianism became increasingly widespread many states either reduced or dropped the property qualifications for voting. By the early 1800s farmers in newly settled frontier areas, reformers, small businesspeople, and artisans in Eastern cities all were demanding the right to vote. Opposition to the trend was limited to extreme conservatives who feared the consequences of extending political influence to an unstable, propertyless electorate. New Western states entered the union with white manhood suffrage, and Eastern states that had retained some restrictions on the right to vote removed them. By the 1850s all adult white men in the nation could vote. There was no state, however, in which women were allowed to vote, and only New England (with the exception of Connecticut) granted free black men the franchise.

Even though the vote was being extended to larger numbers of white men, the social and economic structure of the country did not change significantly as a result. In fact, there may have been less social mobility during the Jacksonian period than before. As in the past, men of talent and ambition could achieve success, but most of those who became wealthy started with wealth. There were still stark contrasts between the luxurious homes of the rich and the humble dwellings of the working classes. Pauperism was on the rise. Most city-dwellers continued to face long hours of work, frequent unemployment, and payment in depreciated currency. Most small farmers were still trapped in lives characterized by frugality, monotony, and lack of leisure time.

Although political leaders of the 1820s debated such issues as the tariff, the national bank, and the sale of public lands, most accepted the institution of slavery and were unconcerned with the problems of working people. Reform movements to aid the enslaved, the poor, and the weak were led largely by people outside the mainstream of American politics.

Yet the liberalization of the suffrage did have important effects. It created demands for certain political changes. On the state level, many offices, including that of governor, became elective; and on the national level, by 1832 presidential electors were chosen directly by the voters in all states except South Carolina, and party nominating conventions replaced the secret congressional caucus which had named presidential candidates since Jefferson's time.

During the 1820s the vote came to be seen as a tool for influencing not merely elections, but government policies as well. The Panic of 1819 and the depression which followed caused many Americans to take a new interest in national economic policy. Small businesspeople, unskilled workers, and large-scale farmers discovered that tariffs, banking laws, and legislation concerning internal improvements could all be affected by using their vote. At the same time, inexpensive party newspapers proliferated, and political affairs received more publicity than ever before. The result was that by the 1820s many more people began voting in national elections. In 1824, 28 percent of eligible voters went to the polls; by 1828 the number had risen to 56 percent. While this increase might have been due in part to Jackson's personal appeal as a candidate, an increase to 78 percent by 1840 suggests that voting was becoming more and more common no matter who was running.

Office-seekers responded to this increased participation by openly and actively wooing voters. Political candidates staged parades and rallies, held barbecues, and lavished great quantities of hard cider on their constituents. Their speeches often played on popular fears and prejudices, and they tried to advocate policies that would be uncontroversial enough to attract a large number of votes. Although the politicians of this era tended to be well-to-do, seldom were they members of the old aristocratic families. Men of inherited wealth had been put off by the increasing vulgarity of politics.

Jackson: The People's Candidate

Andrew Jackson's background was well suited to the freewheeling political climate of the times. Born in the backwoods of South Carolina, he had lost his family and fought in the Revolutionary War by the time he was fourteen. He spent much of his youth brawling and carousing. Although he was a poor speller, he learned to write clearly and became a self-taught lawyer. Jackson's venturesome nature attracted him to the West, and he moved to the Tennessee Territory, where he practiced law, married, and formed friendships with influential people. He became a well-to-do cotton planter, land speculator, and slaveowner. When Tennessee became a state Jackson held various political positions and eventually became general of the Tennessee militia. After his victory against the Creek Indians in the Battle of Horseshoe Bend in the War of 1812 he was made a general in the United States Army. His tremendous success in the Battle of New Orleans made him a great popular hero and was an important fac-

tor in his becoming a presidential candidate in the election of 1824.

Jackson's campaign in the 1824 election was based on his record as a military hero, an Indian fighter, and a symbol of the democratic forces of the West. His understanding of national issues, however, was unimpressive. Although he was intelligent, he had received little formal education, and his enemies considered him common and vulgar. Although he had the look of a frontiersman, "Old Hickory" was a natural gentleman with chivalrous manners and a sharply-honed sense of honor. His

AT SIXTY-TWO, ANDREW JACKSON WAS A TALL, LEAN, IMPOSING FIGURE. AFTER HIS ELECTION HE TRAVELED TO WASHINGTON, TIRED AND IN POOR HEALTH. HE WAS STILL MOURNING THE DEATH OF HIS WIFE, WHO HE BELIEVED HAD BEEN HOUNDED TO HER GRAVE BY THE MALICIOUS FALSEHOODS SPREAD BY HIS POLITICAL OPPONENTS.

judgment, though based on instinct, was usually sound. Over six feet tall, with proud military bearing, an impressive shock of white hair, and a hot temper, the frontier general was intensely patriotic and had an unshakable faith in the American common people. His iron will was matched by an iron constitution, as witnessed by his ability to withstand a persistent siege of illnesses that plagued him throughout his years in the White House.

The Election of 1828

Sizing up the national political situation after the election of 1824, Senator Martin Van Buren of New York recognized that the formless group of politicians calling themselves Republicans had no cohesive national program. Van Buren, who had risen to prominence in New York politics by leading a faction devoted to the idea that political parties should function as agents of the people, concluded that formation of a cohesive national party was imperative. Such a party, as the representative of the popular will, would work to implement policies to benefit the country as a whole. Van Buren conceived a plan to create a new political coalition which he hoped could survive the country's growing sectional dispute over slavery as well as achieve the ouster of such neo-Federalist politicians as Clay, Webster, and Adams.

Van Buren was motivated in part by personal ambition, but he also wanted to reinstate in national politics the Jeffersonian principle of limited and decentralized government, an outlook popular south of the Mason-Dixon line. He hoped to form a coalition between the people of the South and the small farmers of the North, based on their support of the Jeffersonian principles of egalitarianism and states' rights. Van Buren planned to unite these groups behind the candidacy of the popular General Jackson.

By 1827 Van Buren had succeeded in regrouping the political forces in the country. The political alignments now were composed of the Democratic–Republicans led by Jackson and the National Republicans led by Adams and Clay. Along with Van Buren himself, those who backed Jackson's candidacy were all masters of the new party politics: Thomas Hart Benton of Missouri, John H. Eaton of Tennessee, and John C. Calhoun of South Carolina.

In the congressional elections of 1826 Adams lost his majority to Jackson's followers. The new majority spent the entire preelection year attacking Adams's conduct of the presidency and his personal life. They also blamed him for the Tariff of Abominations of 1828, a measure which infuriated the South.

Jackson, who believed he had been robbed of the election of 1824, spent the intervening years trying to arouse popular support for his candidacy in 1828. Although his earlier career had seldom shown him to be a devoted champion of democracy, he almost instinctively associated himself with that position after 1824. He also declared that he favored

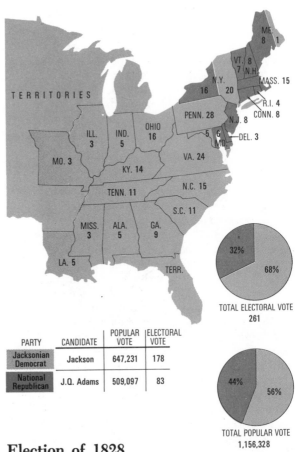

PARTY	CANDIDATE	POPULAR VOTE	ELECTORAL VOTE
Jacksonian Democrat	Jackson	647,231	178
National Republican	J.Q. Adams	509,097	83

TOTAL ELECTORAL VOTE
261

TOTAL POPULAR VOTE
1,156,328

Election of 1828

a federal government with limited powers as well as a strict interpretation of the Constitution, a position which appealed to many Americans.

The campaign of 1828 was a hostile personal clash between the supporters of Jackson and the supporters of the incumbent president. Jacksonians were furious over the political bargain between Adams and Clay that had resulted in Adams's election in 1824. They touted Jackson as the candidate of reform whose hickory broom would sweep clean the "corruption" of the previous administration. Mud-slinging, misrepresentation, and name-calling escalated on both sides. Jackson was accused of being a "drunk," a "tyrant," and a "gambler." His ailing wife, Rachel, was attacked as a "convicted adulteress" (her divorce from a previous husband was discovered not to have been legally final when she married Jackson). Adams, on the other hand, was accused of paying for private possessions with public money, of supplying the Russian Czar with a young American mistress, and of pandering to private interests in the administration of public lands. The accusations on both sides descended to the lowest levels the country had yet seen in a political campaign.

Without the benefit of debate on the real issues facing the country, and aroused by the emotional appeals of the Democratic-Republican party managers, the majority of the voters backed Jackson. Jackson defeated Adams with 56 percent of the popular vote and 178 electoral votes to Adams's 83—a decisive victory but by no means a landslide. The Jacksonians also gained control of both houses of Congress.

Jacksonian Politics

On March 4, 1829, the day of Jackson's inauguration, ten thousand visitors jammed into Washington. After taking the oath of office, Jackson pushed through the mob, mounted his horse, and rode to the White House. The crowd followed on horseback, on foot, and in wagons. Well-wishers surged into the White House and interrupted the official reception. They climbed up on delicate chairs, muddied valuable rugs, shouted, overturned furniture, broke glassware, and even pressed the new president helplessly against the wall. Jackson had to make an escape through a rear window.

The unplanned celebration evoked a variety of reactions. Some political observers expressed fear of the coming rule by "King Mob." Others saw the festivities as symbolic of the victory of the common people.

The Spoils System

As a reform president Jackson immediately set out to bring new faces into the government. There had not

THOMAS NAST'S CARTOON SATIRIZES JACKSON'S USE OF THE SPOILS SYSTEM. REPUBLICANS, WHO HAD DOMINATED THE NATIONAL GOVERNMENT FOR SOME TIME, CLAIMED THAT JACKSON'S POLITICAL APPOINTMENTS WERE "PROSCRIPTION" AND A NEW "REIGN OF TERROR."

been a real turnover in the civil service for many years. Although there always had been a small number of replacements in political appointments, the concept of relative permanence of tenure in office had kept many men in public service until they had grown old, inept, and sometimes corrupt. Jackson was easily persuaded that they should be replaced. The Democratic call for reform paved the way for a redistribution of political offices to Jacksonians.

The practice of rewarding party workers who had proved their loyalty with public offices had a long tradition in New York and other Northern states. Now Jackson's lieutenants decided to put this system to use on a national level by rewarding loyal supporters and financial contributors with offices in order to build up the party. Under Jackson's administration more and more of these political appointees came to view their jobs as a prosperous livelihood rather than as a public trust. The system itself gained the appropriate designation the "spoils system" after a remark in 1832 by Senator William L. Marcy of New York that " . . . to the victor belong the spoils of the enemy."

Under Jackson's administration the spoils system was greatly expanded at the federal level. On the one hand, Jackson tended to play down the importance of training and experience for political office, feeling that the duties involved were essentially simple and that any intelligent person could readily assume them. As a result, many offices came to be held by inefficient, incompetent, or dishonest men whose primary interest was to become rich. On the other hand, the president also appointed wealthy, experienced, and socially prominent men to high government positions.

Jackson liked to say that appointive offices should be rotated, both to prevent corruption and to increase opportunities for wider participation in government by the common people. He believed that holding the same office for a long time bred indifference and that this was far worse than any of the problems that might arise from periodic rotation. In practice, Jackson was not especially immoderate in his use of the spoils system. He did not fire experts in the departments of the army and navy. Nor did he dismiss judges or high-ranking diplomats. In fact, he replaced only about 250 presidential appointees out of 612 and only about nine hundred of the more than ten thousand officeholders on the government payroll. Nevertheless, under his administration the spoils systems secured a firm grip on American politics that continued for more than half a century.

A Strong Executive

During the presidential campaign Jackson's opponents had portrayed him as a simple soldier being manipulated by greedy politicians. His behavior in office, however, left little doubt that he was his own master. Although Jackson had his speeches written for him and sought advice from personal friends and campaign backers in his unofficial "Kitchen Cabinet," he ultimately made his own decisions.

Whereas earlier presidents had accepted the idea that there should be an equal balance among the three branches of government, Jackson felt that the executive branch should be ascendent. The president alone, he maintained, was elected by the whole country and it was he who should be their spokesman.

Jackson had no hesitation about using his presidential authority to veto congressional legislation. All of his predecessors together had vetoed only nine bills, in every case on the grounds that the bill in question was unconstitutional. Jackson alone vetoed twelve bills. In some cases he acted out of personal disapproval rather than on constitutional grounds; in other cases he thought the bills would have granted powers to the federal government that had already been delegated to the states. Jackson was also the first president to employ the "pocket veto"—the practice of leaving a bill unsigned until Congress adjourned, thereby automatically preventing it from becoming law.

As president Jackson intended to make policy rather than merely to carry out the laws enacted by Congress. In the name of the people he put pressure on Congress, and on several occasions he ignored the rulings of the Supreme Court. Jackson's determination to play a powerful role as president ended an era of strong congressional leadership and contributed directly to the modern concept of the presidency. Not surprisingly, he aroused strong opposition among his enemies. Congressional leaders, such as Clay and Webster, deeply resented his assertion of executive power and argued that he should leave final decisions about policy and legislation to the legislative branch.

Foreign Affairs under Jackson

In foreign affairs Andrew Jackson was stubborn and extravagantly patriotic. These qualities often caused him to take unnecessary risks to achieve petty victories, but they also helped him resolve several long-standing diplomatic problems. In addition, his strongly nationalistic foreign policy helped to strengthen loyalty and cohesion within the Democratic party.

Ever since the Revolution the United States had been trying to persuade the British to reopen West Indian trade to American shipping. Jackson, negotiating with patience and tact, finally succeeded. Though he privately threatened to respond "with the promptness and energy due our national character" if Britain continued to delay settlement, he made a concession to which the British finally responded; he granted British ships the same access to American ports that ships of all other countries enjoyed, and he repealed retaliatory duties. The British government then opened its West Indian islands to direct trade with the United States, but subject to such duties as it might decide to impose.

Using a tougher approach, the president also succeeded in forcing foreign countries to settle damage claims from the Napoleonic wars. France, for example, had agreed in 1831 to pay American claims against ships and cargoes damaged or destroyed in the wars. In 1833 the United States presented France a bill for $1 million for the first payment, but the French Chamber of Deputies had neglected to provide the funds. Jackson was furious. He sent a message to Congress calling for "a law authorizing reprisals upon French property." When Congress refused to act on his request, believing it might lead to war, Jackson broke off diplomatic relations with France and ordered the navy readied. Insulted, the French sent a fleet to the West Indies.

Jackson remained adamant, however, and in 1835 France voted the money to pay the claims. French payments soon began flowing into the American treasury.

Indian Removal

On the domestic scene Jackson's policies reflected the rising political power of the West. The American population was growing rapidly, with an influx of new immigrants contributing to the burgeoning native population. Most of the territories east of the Mississippi had achieved statehood, and American farmers were hungry for the fertile land owned by the numerous Indian tribes.

By the end of the War of 1812 the power of the Indian tribes in the area between the Appalachian Mountains and the Mississippi River had been broken. Traditionally the government had dealt with the tribes as independent nations, but this seemed increasingly irrelevant in the face of the weakness of the Indian position. Despite the legal fiction that the tribes were independent, the United States had always maintained its right to take Indian lands if paid for, a claim which meant that the federal government had final authority over the purchase of Indian lands. Although the government had committed itself to protecting the rights of the tribes to their lands it had neither the will nor the power to carry out such a policy. The belief was widespread among Americans that Indian and white societies could not exist peacefully together.

By the mid-1820s President Monroe was aware that the Southern tribes could not long remain on their traditional lands, which were some of the most fertile in the South. Pressure for their removal was too strong. The president therefore advocated a solution earlier proposed by Jefferson: to move the Southern Indians to the Great Plains, primarily to an area known today as Oklahoma.

When Jackson became chief executive, he continued to follow this policy. As a Westerner, an expansionist, and a renowned Indian fighter, he argued that Indians were unhappy living among white people and that removal was the only way to protect them from extermination by white settlers. "Doubtless it will be painful to leave the graves of their fathers," Jackson acknowledged, but it was only necessary to "open the eyes of those children of the forest to their true condition" to make them recognize the "humanity and justice" of their removal. In addition, he advocated the breakup of the tribes so that each Indian would either have to move west or take up land within one of the existing states and farm it as any white person would.

To implement the policy, Jackson ordered all federal protection withdrawn from the tribes, and in 1830 Congress passed a law enabling the president to negotiate treaties with the Indians for their removal westward. Removal was to be carried out by drawing a line west of the Mississippi River, from the Wisconsin Territory in the north to the western borders of Missouri and Arkansas in the south. Land west of this line was pledged to the Indians "forever." At the same time numerous white land speculators and farmers moved into the vacuum and by means of fraud and threats took over the vast majority of the tribal lands at a great profit.

The Cherokees of Georgia took legal action to fight for their lands. Long-time farmers, they had adopted many of the white people's ways, raising cattle and building roads, houses, churches, and schools. Convinced that literacy was the key to their survival, they had developed a written language, printed Bibles, and published a weekly newspaper. In 1827 they drafted a constitution and formed a Cherokee nation within the state of Georgia. The United States formally recognized the Cherokee nation, but Georgia did not, charging that the tribe had violated Article 4, Section 3 of the Constitution forbidding the creation of a new state within the

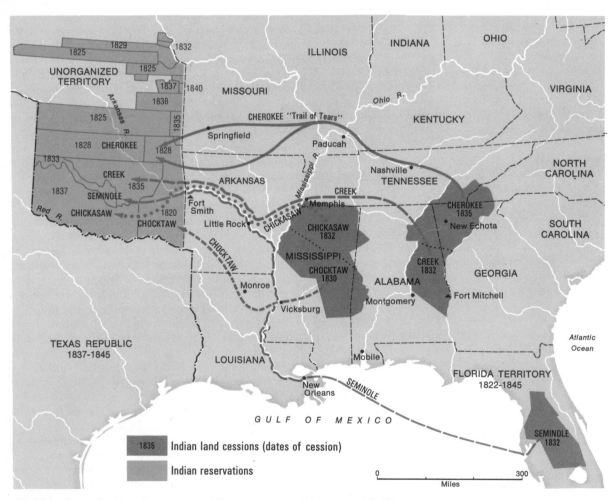

Indian Land Cessions and Migrations • 1820 to 1840

jurisdiction of an existing state. Besides, gold had been discovered on Cherokee land and Georgians already were mining it. In 1828 Georgia passed a law nullifying all Cherokee laws and claiming Cherokee lands.

Friends of the Cherokees appealed to the Supreme Court to restrain Georgia from enforcing its laws over the Indians. In *Cherokee Nation* v. *Georgia* (1831) the Court ruled that Indians were "domestic dependent nations" under United States sovereignty and that they had a right to the land they occupied until title to it had been transferred to the federal government. The following year, in *Worcester* v. *Georgia*, the Court held that the Cherokee nation was a distinct political community wherein Georgia law had no force and which Georgia citizens could not enter without consent. With the tacit approval of the White House, Georgia defied the Supreme Court rulings. In 1838 the Cherokees were finally put in stockades and then marched west at gunpoint.

Other tribes were given "evacuation treaties" and token payment for their lands and then were forced to move west to land that was rarely as fer-

ROBERT LINDNEUX DEPICTED THE SUFFERING OF THE INDIANS ON THEIR FORCED MIGRATION WEST IN *THE TRAIL OF TEARS*. (Woolaroc Museum, Bartlesville, Oklahoma)

tile as that from which they were driven, and that was already inhabited by hostile tribes. The migrations themselves were poorly planned and caused great suffering. Indians from the South, for instance, thinly dressed and without moccasins, were forced to move west in December. They crossed the Mississippi in subfreezing weather and many died from cold, hunger, or disease.

Alexis de Tocqueville, author of *Democracy in America*, watched as a group of Choctaw Indians began crossing the Mississippi River at Memphis. "Never will that solemn spectacle fade from my remembrance," he wrote. "No cry, no sob, was heard among the assembled crowd; all was silent. Their calamities were of ancient date, and they knew them to be irremediable." Later historians have called the western migration, in which about four thousand died, the "Trail of Tears."

The forced migration of the 1830s continued for more than ten years and involved over a hundred thousand Indians. Only a few tribes resisted and these were treated severely. In 1832 about one thousand Sac and Fox Indians led by Black Hawk moved back across the Mississippi River to their native Illinois, hoping to find a hospitable place to plant corn for their starving people. Their attempted resis-

tance, referred to as the Black Hawk War, was quickly crushed by militia and regular army troops.

In the vast Florida Everglades, however, the Seminoles were able to wage a more effective, though equally futile struggle. Led by the young warrior Osceola and supported by a great number of runaway slaves, the Seminoles held off the United States Army from 1835 to 1842. Their rebellion cost the United States about $40 million and two thousand lives. Most of the Seminoles were wiped out or sent to Oklahoma, but the breaking point came with the capture of Osceola himself when he was treacherously seized during a peace conference in 1837.

In spite of the suffering it caused the Indians, President Jackson looked on his policy of removal as benevolent. A few humanitarian critics in the Northeast expressed outrage at the treatment accorded the Indians, but such criticism was not widespread. In Jackson's view the Indians were now on their own land and could live without fear of white encroachment. The federal government would protect them in their new homes. In fact, however, within ten years white settlers began moving into the territory of the Great Plains, again threatening the very survival of the Indians.

Sectional Controversy

Internal Improvements

From the beginning of his presidency, Jackson faced the problem of holding together the several factions that had elected him. One of the early issues that caused shifts in party affiliations concerned internal improvements. Democrats in the West firmly supported federal financing of roads and canals. Democrats in the South, New York, and Pennsylvania were adamantly opposed. New York and Pennsylvania had financed their own internal improvements and were not enthusiastic about supporting Western competition. No matter what action he took, the president was sure to antagonize some elements of his party.

Jackson revealed his position in 1830, when he vetoed a bill authorizing federal funding for a sixty-mile road to be built from Maysville to Lexington, Kentucky. Jackson said that he opposed as unconsti-

tutional the use of federal money for internal improvements within a state. He was not opposed if the project was national in scope, although he did hint that all public programs at federal expense might be unconstitutional.

The Maysville Road veto was a shrewd political move aimed at pleasing the majority of voters. Jackson had evaluated the public mind accurately: most people agreed with him that federal funds should be saved to pay off the public debt. His veto showed the administration's regard for economy and a strict construction of the Constitution. In addition, it was a clever slap at Jackson's rival for Western affection, Henry Clay, accomplished without alienating large numbers of voters.

The Maysville Road veto did not completely stop the use of federal funds for internal improvements. Jackson himself actually endorsed an average of $1.3 million per year in internal-improvement bills, including some that allocated federal funds for local projects. But he had made his point: his party stood for limiting the use of federal money in financing internal improvements within a state.

Public Lands

Westerners believed that the government should encourage the settlement of lands in the public domain by selling it cheaply. The alternative, which had been Adams's policy, was to keep land prices high in order to bring as much money as possible into the federal treasury.

Senator Thomas Hart Benton, a colorful politician devoted to the interests of the farmer, suggested that the government gradually lower the price of poor public land from a dollar and a quarter an acre (instituted in 1820) to fifty cents an acre, and give away free to settlers whatever land remained unsold. This plan was called graduation. Another plan, called preemption, would give squatters already settled illegally on 160-acre sections of public land the first opportunity to buy when the government offered the land for sale.

These two plans, which Jackson favored, placed more importance on opening up the country to settlement than on raising revenue for the treasury. Jackson believed that settlers should be able to buy small tracts for little more than it cost to survey and clear away Indian titles. He also felt that each new state should be given the public lands that lay within its borders. In 1832 he told Congress that "the public lands shall cease as soon as practicable to be a source of revenue."

Moderate though these plans were, they greatly displeased Easterners, who viewed westward migration as a severe drain on their sources of labor. They feared that those who stayed behind would demand higher wages for their scarce services. Completely opposed to graduation and preemption, Easterners proposed legislation known as the Foot Resolution to halt for a period of time the survey and sale of new lands in the West.

In 1832 Clay suggested a compromise. Instead of giving public lands to individual Western states, the land would be sold: one-eighth of the proceeds could go to the Western states, and the remaining revenue could be distributed among all the states. Congress passed Clay's bill in 1833, but Jackson vetoed it.

Opposition to Protective Tariffs

The South was generally opposed to the distribution of surplus revenue out of fear that it would so deplete the federal treasury that higher tariffs would be needed to obtain the funds necessary to meet government expenses. In fact, the most divisive sectional controversy of Jackson's administration arose over the protective tariff. Because the tariff raised the price of everything they bought but protected nothing they sold, Southerners felt that they were being required to pay too large a share of federal taxes. As the tariff increased, Southerners began to feel more and more ill treated. The loudest protests came from South Carolina.

South Carolina's plantation aristocracy was already uneasy over race relations and feared that a powerful federal government might try to interfere with the institution of slavery. This was particularly alarming to them because the state's slave population outnumbered its white citizens. White South Carolinians therefore were especially protective of their state's right to define its own institutions and way of life without federal interference.

Uneasiness over slavery was a long-standing condition, but the acute economic difficulties experienced by South Carolinians in the 1820s increased their fear of federal authority. The days when South Carolinian planters could make huge fortunes cultivating rice and cotton had ended with the Panic of 1819. Cotton prices had dropped in the depression and had fallen even lower as planters in the new states of Alabama and Mississippi increased the world's supply of cotton. South Carolina's worn-out fields produced small yields, and the state's population stagnated as ambitious farmers migrated west in search of better land. Unwilling to attribute their misery to soil exhaustion and competition from newer states, South Carolinians blamed the tariff.

By the 1820s people all over the South were gathering at public meetings to protest the tariff. When Jackson first took office, he had endorsed import duties on "all products that may be found essential to our national independence." Now, to please his Southern supporters, he asked Congress for a revenue tariff that would give only "temporary and, generally, incidental protection," a position more in line with traditional Jeffersonian laissez-faire economics. The president's reversal encouraged South Carolina's legislature to assume (incorrectly) that he would tolerate direct state action against the high import duties.

Calhoun's Dilemma   Southern opposition to protective tariffs posed a dilemma for Vice-President John C. Calhoun, South Carolina's leading politician. A graduate of Yale, Calhoun had a logical and precise mind that was always dazzling in argument, though not always adapted to practical politics. A Calvinist who had converted to Unitarianism, he combined the rigor of his first religion with the rationality of his second.

His career reflected the changing political climate in his native state. Elected to Congress in 1811, Calhoun persuaded the state to participate in the postwar nationalism of the Era of Good Feelings. South Carolina, the dominant state of the Southern cotton kingdom, actually supported a moderately protective tariff, sacrificing its own interests to strengthen the nation's economy. In 1817 Calhoun became secretary of war under President Monroe. Believing that America needed to become stronger and more unified in the event of a future war, Calhoun called for a well-trained army, a large navy, and a federally supported, unified system of roads and canals. His support of a moderate tariff and the national bank was also based on the idea of making the United States more self-sufficient. "Our true system is to look to the country," stated Calhoun, "and to support such measures and such men, without regard to sections, as are best calculated to advance the general interest."

But his disinterested nationalism did not last. As long as South Carolina had led all other states in cotton production, it had been able to endure generously the inconvenience of a protective tariff. After the Panic of 1819, however, the state was less prosperous and the newly settled states of the lower South were becoming dangerously competitive. By the 1820s Calhoun had to find a way to modify his views to satisfy his Southern constituency without at the same time offending Northern friends whose support he needed to further his ambition for the presidency.

Calhoun's Doctrine of the Concurrent Majority   In 1828 the South Carolina legislature published anonymously a tract by Calhoun (the *South Carolina Exposition and Protest*) in which the theory of states' rights was presented in its most

JOHN C. CALHOUN WAS A LESS PASSIONATE ORATOR THAN DANIEL WEBSTER, BUT HE WAS LEARNED AND MORE LOGICAL IN HIS ARGUMENTS.

sophisticated form. Calhoun argued (as Jefferson had in the Kentucky Resolutions of 1798) that the states had not surrendered their sovereignty when they ratified the Constitution. They had merely formed a "compact" creating a federal government to serve as their "agent" for executing the powers provided in the compact. The agent had limited powers, and these were determined not by the Supreme Court, but by the sovereign states.

A sovereign state had the right to determine through a convention whether an act of Congress was unconstitutional. If the decision was in the affirmative, the convention would declare the act null and void within the state and the decision would be binding on the citizens of the state. It would also be binding on the national government unless the federal Constitution were then amended to give the federal government the power to pass such a law. In effect, this meant that a nullifying state's interpretation of the Constitution would prevail unless three-fourths of the rest of the states disagreed. By this procedure the rights of the minority South would receive the greatest protection against the will of the numerical majority of the nation. Calhoun believed that in practice his theory would produce a "concurrent majority" by which the ability of any state to block a piece of legislation would permit the passage of only those laws agreeable to a majority in all sections of the country.

While Calhoun's ideas were built on his desire to maintain the federal union, he also believed that a state could exercise its sovereign right to withdraw from the Union if its citizens felt the threat to their well-being were grave enough. Unlike Jefferson, however, Calhoun was not arguing for the protection of liberty, but for the protection of the Southern planter class whose interests were supported by the use of slave labor.

In 1830 Calhoun's doctrine underwent a full-scale review in the Senate when a debate over the Foot Resolution on public land policy expanded into an examination of the nature of the federal union. Calhoun, vice-president and presiding officer of the Senate, listened as Robert Hayne of South Carolina brilliantly explained and defended nullification, recited the South's grievances, and appealed to the West to adopt the doctrine as a means of preventing enforcement of policies that would limit the sale of public lands.

Daniel Webster, a great orator and staunch defender of the national government, responded in the most eloquent speech of his career. He denied that the federal government was an agent of the states. "It is," he said, "the people's constitution, the people's government, made for the people, made by the people, and answerable to the people." If a state felt that it had not been justly treated, it could seek action in the courts, at the polls, or in the amending process. Otherwise, any disturbance of federal sovereignty by a state would be considered treasonable and could lead to civil war. Webster closed his speech with the phrase: "Liberty and Union, now and forever, one and inseparable!"

Jackson Splits with Calhoun Although the Democrats tended to favor states' rights and a low tariff, Jackson would not tolerate an attack on the legitimate use of federal power specifically provided for in the Constitution. He made his position clear at a Democratic party banquet celebrating Jefferson's birthday shortly after the Webster-Hayne debate. Calhoun and his followers proposed toast after toast, each subtly implying a connection between nullification and Democratic party principles. Jackson sat silently through twenty-three toasts. Then, called upon to give a toast, he rose, raised his glass, and, looking straight at Calhoun, declared, "Our Federal Union—It must be preserved."

Calhoun, his political alliance with Jackson already in jeopardy, brought his personal relations with the president to the breaking point with his countertoast, delivered in a halting voice: "The Union—next to our liberty, the most dear! May we all remember that it can only be preserved by respecting the rights of the states and distributing equally the benefits and burdens of the Union."

The rift between the president and vice-president was encouraged by the crafty secretary of state, Van Buren, who hoped to take Calhoun's place as Jackson's presidential heir. Van Buren exploited an incident of "petticoat politics" in order to win Jackson's favor. The incident involved a social clash created by administration wives when Secretary of War John Eaton married Peggy O'Neale Timberlake, the beautiful, bold, but morally suspect daughter of a tavernkeeper. Mrs. Calhoun refused to receive the "hussy," and her stand was quickly imitated by the wives of other cabinet members. Always gallant and still haunted by the memory of slander against his own wife before her death, Jackson was outraged by the incident. He called a special meeting of the cabinet, refuted the charges made against Peggy Eaton by cabinet wives, and pronounced her "as chaste as a virgin." When cabinet members refused to intercede with their wives, Jackson, acting upon a scheme suggested by Van Buren, dismissed his entire cabinet and appointed a new one. The reorganization forced Calhoun's friends out of the administration and elevated Van Buren to the position of Jackson's most trusted advisor.

The break with Calhoun became final when William H. Crawford, an old political enemy of Calhoun's, let it be known that in 1818, when he was secretary of war, Calhoun had criticized Jackson's invasion of Florida. Calhoun defended himself with a long, explanatory letter, but Jackson immediately rejected it as "full evidence of the duplicity

A SATIRIC CARTOON OF THE CABINET MEETING CALLED TO DISCUSS THE REPUTATION OF PEGGY EATON. EATON, WHO DID NOT ATTEND THE REAL MEETING, IS DEPICTED AS A BALLET DANCER. WHILE VAN BUREN EYES HER THROUGH HIS LORGNETTE, THE FURIOUS JACKSON DECLARES: "SHE IS AS CHASTE AS A VIRGIN!"

and insincerity of the man." Shunted aside as a national leader, Calhoun now devoted all his attention to being the chief defender of the South.

The South Carolina Showdown Meanwhile, the nullification controversy simmered, and South Carolina waited for Congress to reduce the Tariff of Abominations. In 1832 Congress passed a new tariff bill, which reduced rates to their 1824 levels. South Carolina, however, still considered them intolerably high.

The South Carolina legislature called for a convention to draw up an Ordinance of Nullification. The delegates declared the tariffs of 1828 and 1832 null and void and forbade the collection of federal duties within the state. Furthermore, the state legislature voted funds to raise a volunteer army to defend the state from "invasion."

Interpreting South Carolina's actions as open defiance, Jackson quickly reinforced the federal army and navy; he hoped that a show of force would result in a peaceful political solution. On December 10, he issued an official proclamation declaring nullification "incompatible with the existence of the Union, contradicted expressly by the letter of the Constitution, unauthorized by its spirit, inconsistent with every principle on which it is founded, and destructive of the great object for which it was formed." Nullification was treasonous; nullifiers were to be punished by force.

Jackson asked Congress to pass a force bill giving him the authority to use the army and navy, if necessary, to collect customs duties. At the same time, in an effort to restore harmony, he called for a new tariff bill that would significantly lower duties.

It was obvious that a military confrontation would be virtually suicidal for South Carolina, and the rest of the South, while generally in sympathy with that state's point of view on the tariff, refused to support nullification as a constitutional remedy.

The problem was that conceding defeat would incur a loss of prestige and would be the ruin of the state's political leaders. The state and Calhoun were saved by the intervention of the "Great Pacificator," Henry Clay, who devised a compromise that would gradually lower tariff rates over a ten-year period to no higher than 20 percent.

The compromise tariff bill was passed, ironically, on the same day as the force bill. Jackson signed both measures, confident that national harmony would now be restored. Although he had not effected a permanent solution, he nevertheless was able to reduce national tensions on a crucial issue and avoid a military confrontation.

The South Carolina convention repealed its Ordinance of Nullification, but nullified the force bill to show its defiance. Calhoun and his followers continued to work for nullification by building Southern solidarity until a united Southern front might effectively resist federal political and military power. Calhoun's faction also worked more closely with Clay for the next few years in an effort to embarrass Jackson whenever possible.

The Bank War

During the Panic of 1819 Jackson himself had come close to financial ruin as a result of the tight lending policy of the Bank of the United States. Moreover, he had seen many Western farmers destroyed when the bank foreclosed on their property. He had opposed the Bank of the United States before he became president and continued to criticize it steadily during his first term. Jackson's stand on the bank became the primary and most popular issue of his reelection campaign, and his second term was dominated by his obsession to destroy the "moneyed monster."

Jackson was supported in his eagerness to destroy the bank by a coalition of agrarian-minded Southerners, ambitious Westerners, and Eastern intellectuals and workingmen. Some resented any central bank with the power to control state banks. Others distrusted all banks and regarded the Bank of the United States as the prime offender and a natural target for reform. All feared the power and monopolistic privilege of the bank, with its enormous sums controlled by a few rich and powerful people and little regulation from the Congress or the chief executive.

The "Monster" Institution

In 1823 the able but autocratic Nicholas Biddle had become the president of the Second Bank of the United States. Under his direction the bank became a conservative and responsibly administered business enterprise. Biddle was an astute economist who recognized that the bank and its twenty-nine branches had the potential to regulate the growing American economy. Under his careful direction, the bank bought and sold government bonds, advanced loans to businesses, and issued bank notes that gave the country a sound and uniform paper currency. The government accepted the notes of the Bank of the United States in payment for all obligations to it. The bank also restrained state banks from reckless lending policies by forcing them to back their own paper notes with gold and silver and to repay loans from the national bank on demand. This control over the supply and exchange of money gave the national bank tremendous influence. And since Biddle knew much more about banking than did his board of directors, the power of the bank lay entirely in his hands.

Biddle's careful regulation protected the state banks and the nation's economy as well as the bank itself, but the institution still met with considerable opposition. A distrust of paper money and bankers still lingered from the days of Adams and Jefferson. Jackson was among those who wanted all transactions to be made in gold and silver. Many working people agreed. Resentment of the institution's immense power was increased by the fact that it also acquired much of the coin that had been in the state banks.

The business community was divided in its opinion of the bank. The more stable and traditional banks and businesses, such as the old merchant firms, wanted sound money and a conservative credit policy and supported the institution. But newer, less well-established banks and businesses

Attacking the Constitutionality of the National Bank

"It is maintained by the advocates of the bank that its constitutionality in all its features ought to be considered as settled by precedent and by the decision of the Supreme Court. To this conclusion I can not assent. Mere precedent is a dangerous source of authority, and should not be regarded as deciding questions of constitutional power except where the acquiescence of the people and the States can be considered as well settled. . . .

If the opinion of the Supreme Court covered the whole ground of this act, it ought not to control the coordinate authorities of this Government. . . . The opinion of the judges has no more authority over Congress than the opinion of Congress has over the judges, and on that point the President is independent of both. The authority of the Supreme Court must not, therefore, be permitted to control the Congress or the Executive when acting in their legislative capacities, but to have only such influence as the force of their reasoning may deserve."

Andrew Jackson, July 10, 1832

Defending the Constitutionality of the National Bank

"I now proceed, Sir, to a few remarks upon the President's constitutional objections to the Bank; and I cannot forbear to say, in regard to them, that he appears to me to have assumed very extraordinary grounds of reasoning.

Hitherto it has been thought that the final decision of constitutional questions belonged to the supreme judicial tribunal. The very nature of free government, it has been supposed, enjoins this; and our Constitution, moreover, has been understood so to provide, clearly and expressly. . . .

The President is as much bound by the law as any private citizen, and can no more contest its validity than any private citizen. He may refuse to obey the law, and so may a private citizen but both do it at their own peril, and neither of them can settle the question of its validity. The President may *say* a law is unconstitutional, but he is not the judge. The judiciary alone possess this unquestionable and hitherto unquestioned right. . . ."

Daniel Webster, July 11, 1832

wanted a more inflated paper money and easier credit (the practical effect of which would be to place more paper money in circulation). Because the national bank controlled the amount of money available to state banks, new businesses found it difficult to borrow. They resented the Bank of the United States because they considered its credit policies too conservative. Some business and government officials also condemned the bank as a monopoly that held federal funds without being subject to federal controls. States' rights and working-class groups opposed the bank because it was not provided for in the Constitution. New Yorkers were particularly hostile to the bank, for it diverted the financial plum of customs revenues from the port of New York to the bank's head office in Philadelphia.

Jacksonians also suspected the bank of supporting their political rivals and accused the bank of corrupting high officials. In fact, Biddle did win the friendships of politicians and the assurance of favor-

able press by means of generous loans. To cite one example, Daniel Webster not only borrowed heavily but, as legal counsel to the bank, was also on its payroll.

Aware of Jackson's opposition to the bank, Biddle assured the president that the bank's financial position was sound and agreed to accept some restrictions on the bank's power. But knowing that Jackson remained hostile, Biddle worked with two of Jackson's political enemies, Clay and Webster, to get the bank rechartered before the election of 1832, even though the charter would not expire until 1836.

Believing that the bank was popular and that its recharter would put Jackson in an embarrassing position, Clay assured Biddle that the bank bill would be passed. Clay thought that if the president signed the bill, his Western followers would view him as a hypocrite. If he vetoed it, he would alienate the bank's many supporters and provide the

SET TO BETWEEN OLD HICKORY AND BULLY NICK SHOWS JACKSON SQUARING OFF
AGAINST NICHOLAS BIDDLE, PRESIDENT OF THE BANK OF THE UNITED STATES.

National Republicans with a strong issue for the 1832 campaign.

The Bank Veto In July 1832 the bill rechartering the bank, with some restrictions on its powers, passed both houses and was sent to the White House for the president's signature. Possessing a keener perception of public opinion than his opponents, Jackson promptly vetoed the bill, and issued a statement pitting the poor against the rich:

There are no necessary evils in the government. Its evils exist only in its abuses. If it would confine itself to equal protection, and, as Heaven does its rains, shower its favors alike on the high and low, the rich and the poor, it would be an unqualified blessing. In the act before me . . . there seems to be a wide and unnecessary departure from these just principles. . . .

Jackson's veto message, intended to win massive support throughout the country, is the first instance in American history of a president taking his appeal directly to the people. Because his message was directed to the general public, it largely ignored the complex economic questions involved in the issue and concentrated on those points most likely to arouse emotion. Jackson attacked the bank as a monopoly with a stranglehold over the nation's economic development which undermined the principle of equal opportunity. He charged that since the Constitution had not specifically provided for a national bank, the bank was unconstitutional. Finally, he claimed that the existence of the bank was an invasion of the rights of the states and that it favored the economic development of the East at the expense of the West.

The president's message was a masterpiece of political propaganda. He clearly saw the bank's political weaknesses and exploited them for party advantage. While the bank was a powerful institution, it was not, in fact, a monopoly; it made only 20 percent of the country's bank loans and issued only 20 percent of the paper money. Jackson's stand on behalf of economic equality and against special privileges for any institution had the intended effect of strengthening his reputation as the champion of the common people. In addition, even though the Supreme Court had ruled in *McCulloch* v. *Maryland* (1819) that the bank was constitutional, many

people, including the president, did not accept the validity of that ruling. Jackson's message was a dramatic appeal to American prejudices and to states' rights, and it constituted a manifesto of what has since come to be termed Jacksonian democracy.

Jackson's opponents, more comfortable with the old style of politics which left decision making to those in public office, were offended and alarmed by this new tactic, and they accused the president of inciting class conflict with this style of politics. Clay and Webster made a counterattack in the Senate, but their reasoned economic arguments, directed to a handful of national leaders, were no match for the president's popular appeal.

The Election of 1832

The campaign of 1832 produced a third party: the Anti-Masons, led by William Wirt, a well-known Baltimore lawyer. Its role, one that has since become typical of third parties, was to focus attention on a single issue. The Anti-Masons wanted to arouse Americans against secret societies, especially Freemasonry.

The new party had begun to take shape in 1826 after the disappearance of a New York bricklayer named William Morgan. Morgan had planned to publish a book that supposedly revealed the secrets of his Masonic Lodge. Rumors began circulating that Morgan had been murdered by the Masons, reviving old prejudices against secret societies. Because a large number of political leaders and judges were Masons, many people began to suspect that Masonic secrecy might be covering up a widespread aristocratic conspiracy against democratic principles. The impression spread despite the fact that the popular Andrew Jackson was himself a Mason.

The movement against the Masons grew large enough to destroy Freemasonry in much of New England and the Northwest. Rising young politicians such as William H. Seward and Thaddeus Stevens skillfully forged the movement into an anti-Jackson party, more extreme in its attitudes than the National Republicans. In September 1831 the Anti-Masonic party held a national nominating convention in Baltimore, the first national political convention of its kind. It set the precedent, followed to this day, for nominating presidential and vice-presi-

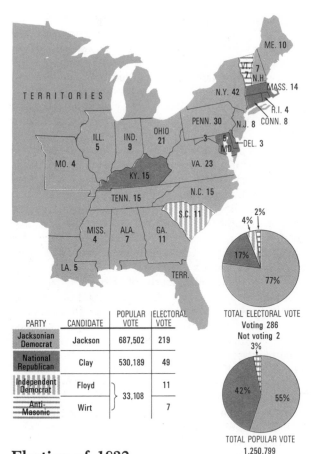

PARTY	CANDIDATE	POPULAR VOTE	ELECTORAL VOTE
Jacksonian Democrat	Jackson	687,502	219
National Republican	Clay	530,189	49
Independent Democrat	Floyd	33,108	11
Anti-Masonic	Wirt		7

TOTAL ELECTORAL VOTE
Voting 286
Not voting 2
3%

TOTAL POPULAR VOTE
1,250,799

Election of 1832

Another new political movement active in the late 1820s and early 1830s was the Workingmen's party. Consisting of semi-independent groups in a number of American urban centers, it was committed to helping skilled craftsmen obtain better working conditions through strikes, enactment of a ten-hour working day, and an end to monopolies. The party also called for a more equitable tax system and public education. Although the Workingmen's party lasted only about five years and was independent of the two major parties, its members did support some of Jackson's policies, especially the war on the bank.

The 1832 contest was a bitter campaign in which the parties attacked each other in cartoons, pamphlets, and speeches. Jackson was at the peak of his popularity, while the opposition was weakened because the votes that went to Wirt merely drained support away from Clay.

Jackson won by the comfortable majority of 219 to 49 in the electoral college. His party also picked up more seats in Congress. The reelected president viewed his strong victory as a mandate to fight and destroy the Bank of the United States.

Death of the Bank

Since the bank's charter had four years to run, Jackson feared that Clay and Biddle were using the time to spread money and influence among the members of Congress in an effort to overturn his veto. Convinced that he must "cripple the bank" in order to "deprive the conspirators of the aid which they expect from its money and power," Jackson and his advisors devised a plan that would render the bank virtually impotent. Much of the bank's power derived from its favored position as fiscal agent for the government. The administration could eliminate that power simply by making no further federal deposits in the bank and opening new accounts elsewhere.

Legally such a policy could be carried out only by the secretary of the treasury. When the incumbent secretary refused to give the order, the president replaced him. When his replacement also delayed, Jackson removed him as well and appointed Roger B. Taney, a close friend who had encouraged the president to veto the bank bill.

Under Taney the government opened accounts with a group of state banks, made no new deposits

dential candidates. The convention nominated William Wirt, who accepted because he believed his candidacy would be endorsed by the equally anti-Jackson National Republicans, thus bringing about a new and stronger anti-Jackson coalition.

But the National Republicans nominated Clay instead. They also adopted the country's first party platform, which attacked Jackson for misuse of patronage and demanded the recharter of the national bank. The Democrats, as the Jacksonians were now called, nominated Jackson as a matter of course, and a platform seemed unnecessary.

in the Bank of the United States, and drew on its existing deposits to pay government bills. The federal reserves in the Bank of the United States dwindled rapidly, while those in the state, or "pet," banks, chosen for their political affiliations, rose.

The Senate, already angry at Jackson's extravagant use of executive authority, now launched a harsh attack on him. Many Senators believed that he needed the Senate's approval to remove an officeholder who had been appointed with the Senate's consent. In December 1833 Clay pushed through resolutions censuring Jackson for replacing a second secretary of the treasury and diverting new federal bank deposits without Senate approval. In addition, the Senate rejected Taney's appointment. Jackson fought back by declaring that, as chief executive, he inherently had the authority to dismiss officeholders who refused to carry out his policies, a position later upheld by the Supreme Court. In 1837 the censure resolutions were stricken from the official records.

Biddle, meanwhile, did not intend to let the bank die. As federal withdrawals began to run into the millions, Biddle decided to call in loans made to the state banks and to raise considerably the interest rates for borrowing money. By thus creating a credit shortage, he hoped to produce a business panic so widespread that the resulting depression would turn public sentiment against Jackson. Biddle believed that this would force the president to return the deposits to the Bank of the United States and to call for its recharter. "Nothing but the evidence of suffering . . . will produce any effect," he asserted.

The suffering did indeed occur. During the winter of 1833–1834, interest rates almost tripled, businesses collapsed, and unemployment rose rapidly. Soon even business leaders who sympathized with Biddle were urging him to give in. He did finally reverse himself and began to grant credit at reasonable rates. The panic subsided, but it had failed to help the bank and had shown, in fact, how dangerously powerful the institution had become.

The bank's federal charter expired in 1836 although the bank itself died a slow death, continuing to operate for some years under a Pennsylvania state charter. Jackson had won the war, but his victory had mostly negative effects. With the national bank's restraining influence removed, the state banks began to lend vast sums regardless of their gold and silver reserves. Prices rose, and with them

the nation's economic optimism. Expansion soon began to get out of hand. Throughout the West, for example, land speculation reached a feverish pitch. The government put the vast public lands on the market at the same time that credit loosened up and interest rates declined. Many Western farmers mortgaged their own property to buy more government lands and then mortgaged these to buy still more property.

The government itself contributed to the spiral by depositing money from land sales in pet banks that eagerly lent it out again. The land boom produced a demand for internal improvements, and much of the borrowed money went into reckless canal, turnpike, and railroad projects financed privately and by the states. Senator Benton predicted that this "bloat in the paper system" would bring on another depression.

Foreseeing the truth of Benton's warning, Jackson issued a Specie Circular in 1836, ordering all federal land offices to accept only gold and silver in payment for public lands. This sharply curtailed Western land sales, but it did not curb inflation. Demand was simply diverted from land to the purchase of foreign goods. The result was a tremendous increase in tariff receipts which swelled the treasury surplus. Clay once again introduced his plan to distribute this revenue, and in 1836 a bill to distribute all surplus funds to the states as a loan gained Jackson's approval.

It would have been better if the federal government had held onto its revenues instead of using them to fuel the already overheated economy. The Specie Circular, with its implication that boom times were coming to an end, may have reduced public confidence. But the real crisis of confidence came from the international market. Overspending by Americans as well as crop failures caused the balance of trade to turn against the United States. In 1837 Americans were suddenly hit with a sharp contraction of credit from abroad, together with a rapid fall in the price of cotton on the world market. Foreigners withdrew investments and demanded the immediate settlement of accounts in hard money which American banks could not meet. The precarious American economy simply could not withstand the strain.

In the resulting Panic of 1837, prices plunged. Speculators who could not sell their lands abandoned them to the banks that held their mortgages. But the foreclosed property could not make up for the banks' losses on loans. By the time Jackson left office in the spring of 1837, many banks had been forced to close their doors. The United States sank into a depression from which it would not recover for seven turbulent years.

The New Two-Party System

By the early 1830s a new political party system had emerged in the United States. In 1820 the remnants of the Federalist party had been too weak even to run a candidate against Monroe. Left without a viable opposition, by 1824 the Republicans had fragmented into two groups: those who wished to return to the Jeffersonian principles of states' rights and limited government and those who advocated stronger governmental support for the nation's economic development. The first group, called the Democratic-Republicans, was led by Jackson. The second group, called the National Republicans, was led by Neo-Federalists such as Clay and Webster. Their opposing visions of how America should develop led to a realignment of political groups and the formation of a new political party system.

By Jackson's second term in office this new two-party system was active in every state except South Carolina. Jackson's Democratic-Republicans were called simply Democrats. The National Republicans called themselves Whigs, a label they borrowed from English history in symbolic protest against the "reign" of "King Andrew." Their point was that President Jackson was ignoring Congress and imposing an arbitrary rule. In an era when sectional disputes were brewing, the political parties provided a unifying national bond.

Although important ideological differences existed between the two coalitions, professional party leaders devoted most of their energies to organizing their followers and competing for office. For the first time, party conflicts were intense and party loyalty was prized. Party leaders attempted to instill this loyalty by educating their followers on the issues and by appointing faithful party men to local and state patronage jobs.

The division between the Democrats and the Whigs was more than ideological. They also were separated, to a certain extent, by class and economic interests and by ethnic and religious differences. The Whigs preferred to direct their appeals toward a small circle of business and political leaders. The Democrats, on the other hand, campaigned for the votes of the new mass electorate.

JACKSON'S OPPONENTS CARICATURED HIM AS KING ANDREW THE FIRST, A POWER-HUNGRY MONARCH GRINDING THE CONSTITUTION UNDERFOOT DURING HIS "REIGN."

BORN TO COMMAND.

OF VETO MEMORY.

HAD I BEEN CONSULTED.

KING ANDREW THE FIRST.

INTERPRETING AMERICAN HISTORY

JACKSONIANISM Historians have viewed the Jacksonian era and Jackson himself in varying ways. Throughout the nineteenth century most important historians admired the outlook of the Whigs. Authors such as James Parton and William G. Sumner criticized Jackson as spiteful, coarse, illiterate, and despotic. They pointed out that the Jacksonians had used the spoils system to permit the vulgar and uneducated to hold important government positions while people of worth were excluded from public office. Late-nineteenth-century historians saw the debasement of political life in their own times as a direct result of Jacksonian politics.

But in 1890 Frederick Jackson Turner began a new school of interpretation that valued the American frontier and its democratic legacy. At the turn of the century, a revival of faith in democratic reform created a new respect for the Jacksonians' emphasis on popular control of government. This idea dominated the interpretation of the Jacksonian period for several decades. It was evident in Claude Bowers's *Party Battles of the Jacksonian Period* (1922), in Marquis James's popular biography of Jackson (1933–1937), and in Arthur Schlesinger, Jr.'s, *Age of Jackson* (1945). At the same time, other critics maintained the older, more critical view of the Jacksonians as wily politicians mainly concerned with obtaining the spoils of office. T. P. Abernethy, in *From Frontier Plan-*

tation in Tennessee (1932) and Charles M. Wiltse's biography of Calhoun (1944–1951), are examples.

Arthur Schlesinger, Jr., like Turner, stressed the importance of the growth of democracy in American life, but he questioned that its roots were in the West. In his *Age of Jackson*, Schlesinger claimed that Jacksonian democracy was "a problem not of sections but of classes." He pointed out that Jacksonianism reflected above all the wish of urban workers as well as farmers "to restrain the power of the business community."

Richard Hofstadter's *American Political Tradition* (1948) and Bray Hammond's work on early American banking (1950s) have challenged Schlesinger's emphasis on class conflict and have denied that Jackson's party opposed business interests. They argued that many rising entrepreneurs were drawn to the Jacksonian movement because it attacked the monopolistic power held by the wealthy few. Far from restraining business, they argue, Jackson's party aimed at and obtained the liberation of business enterprise. Hofstadter's and Hammond's work, while disagreeing with Schlesinger's, continued the trend of deemphasizing the role of the frontier and agrarian forces in shaping American democracy. Their new emphasis on urban factors in part reflects the influence of the urban environment on the outlook of twentieth-century historians.

The Democratic Coalition

The foundations of the Democratic philosophy were a professed concern for the welfare of the average citizen and a distrust of big business and commercial interests which the Democrats claimed were attempting to control the country. Although this was not an antibusiness party, the Democrats dreamed of restoring a mythical American past which was agrarian and egalitarian in nature. Dominated by Jackson's personality, the Democratic party reflected his beliefs in equality of economic opportunity for the individual, states' rights (unless a state was attempting to violate a law Congress had the

specific power to pass), universal white male suffrage, the ability of ordinary people to conduct the affairs of government, and a strong presidency acting in the name of the people.

The Democrats embraced a diverse coalition of small farmers from both the North and the South, native-born urban workers, middle-class businesspeople who were hurt by the tariff, state bankers who disliked the restrictive policies of the Bank of the United States, and moderately well-to-do slaveholders. Ultra-conservative planters and extreme states' rights advocates left the party. Business and professional people in the Democratic coalition found it difficult to accept Jackson's idealization of

In the later 1950s historians such as Marvin Meyers and John Ward turned their attention to the intellectual and psychological aspects of the Jacksonian movement. In so doing they in part returned to Turner's theme of the frontier influence on Jacksonian democracy. Meyers described the movement as an effort to preserve the virtues of the simple, agrarian republic the Jeffersonians bequeathed to the Jacksonians. Uneasy with rapid industrialization, the Jacksonians struck out at the national bank as the symbol of the corporate money power. Yet their destruction of the bank served only to hasten the development of an unregulated capitalist economy.

In the early 1960s historian Lee Benson in *The Concept of Jacksonian Democracy* questioned whether the label "Jacksonian democracy" is appropriate. Benson does not believe that there was a well-organized political reform group centered on Jackson. The Jacksonians' emphasis on states' rights, strong executive leadership, and limited government power was not necessarily the same thing as a commitment to expand democracy. The struggle between the parties of this period was over means, not ends, with both coalitions interested mainly in obtaining jobs, not in debating issues. He also stressed the importance of ethnic and cultural ties in determining voter allegiance.

In recent years historians have tended to rein-force Benson's emphasis on the political opportunism of the Jacksonian movement. Richard P. McCormick's *Second American Party System* (1966) underlines the fact that Jacksonian politics was characterized by demagoguery and a cult of personality rather than by principles. He also shows that poor voters were not especially drawn to the Jacksonians.

Other revisionist interpretations can be found in the following books. Jean A. Wilburn's *Biddle's Bank: The Crucial Years* (1967) clearly demonstrates that the second bank was popular in the country at large and even with many state bankers. Robert V. Rimini's *Election of Andrew Jackson* (1963) describes the pragmatism of the men who organized Jackson's election victory. Finally, Glyndon Van Deusen, in his biographies of Clay and other important Whigs, as well as *The Jacksonian Era, 1828–1848* (1963), has done much to show the importance of Whig thought as a forerunner of the trend toward government planning in the twentieth century. He also portrays Jackson as more interested in executive power than in reform. Both Edward Pessen in *Jacksonian America: Society, Personality, and Politics* (1969) and Douglas T. Miller in *The Birth of Modern America (1820–1850)* (1970) maintain that economic and social inequality were widespread during the Age of Jackson.

agrarian society (Jackson believed that agricultural interests were "superior in importance" to any others and that farmers were the "best part" of the population), but they supported the president out of a sense of personal loyalty and a conviction that his popularity would make available to them many political opportunities. In fact, a shortlived movement known as Locofocoism* emerged in the New York Democratic party in the mid-1830s as a protest against its control by bankers and merchants. Led by artisans and mechanics, the Locofocos were hard-money men who opposed banks and corporations as antagonistic to the egalitarian principles of the party. The Democrats also attracted the influx of early nineteenth-century Catholic immigrants such as the Irish, many Germans, and French-Canadians who were attracted to the party because of its egalitarian outlook and whose cultural and religious differences alienated them from the Protestant Whigs. In addition, the party received the support of freethinkers who opposed all laws to regulate social conduct or to reform society. Basically a party

---

*The Locofocos received this name from an incident in which they used matches, or locofocos, to light candles at a meeting where the party's leaders had put out the lights.

of white farmers and workingmen, its championing of political and economic equality did not extend to free blacks and it gave no support to the causes of women's rights, or temperance reform.

The Whig Coalition

The Whig party, which had emerged by 1834, encompassed a variety of state and local coalitions opposed to Jackson. The Whigs generally included former National Republicans, such as wealthy Southern planters and well-to-do Northern farmers; large, well-established business, commercial, banking, and professional people who supported the economic policies included in the American System; and workers whose jobs were protected by the tariff and who feared the competition of a large influx of immigrants. While the Democrats received the backing of many urban laborers, the poorer working class wards in Boston and Philadelphia, and as well other towns and cities in the New England and Middle Atlantic states, consistently supported the Whigs. Even in New York City, which was a Democratic stronghold, the vote by the laboring poor for the Jacksonians was usually less than that of the rest of the city's population. The party also included Anti-Masons (whose party was absorbed by the Whigs by 1834), a scattering of Northern abolitionists, free blacks who had the franchise, British and Scottish Protestant immigrants, and Democrats who had become disillusioned with Jackson. Generally of New England stock, the Whigs were concentrated in the Presbyterian, Unitarian, and Congregational religious denominations.

Although there were many conflicts over policy within the party, most Whigs generally supported Clay's American System—a comprehensive program of federally sponsored internal improvements, high protective tariffs, a national bank, and a strong Congress—and they demanded respect for the rights of Indians and free blacks. The Whigs sought to secure the prosperity of the people as a whole through an economic policy which would develop every section of the country. They were willing to appropriate government funds to build roads, canals, and schools, and supported policies intended to promote the welfare of the poor. In short, the Whigs sought government action to advance equality of opportunity and to produce an economically self-sufficient nation. Furthermore, they had a strong sense that the harmony of society was as important as individual self-fulfillment.

The Whigs' political style differed from one part of the country to another. In New England and the West the reformers in the party frequently brought to their campaigns a moralistic, evangelical flavor. There, they were the party of temperance and respect for the Sabbath. In the South, on the other hand, they were so hungry for office that they concentrated on building an effective organization and sidestepped the explosive issue of slavery. This necessity for differing sectional strategies was symptomatic of a chronic weakness within the party. The reform element, which grew stronger in the 1840s and 1850s, could not accept the compromises that were necessary in a national party made up of diverse interests, and by the mid-1850s the party split apart.

The Election of 1836

Clay and Webster managed the Whigs' 1836 campaign. Recognizing that the party had no leader who could successfully oppose the Democrats, they chose popular candidates to run in each section of the country, with no national nominating convention and no party platform. These "favorite sons," it was hoped, would draw local votes away from Jackson's hand-picked successor, Van Buren, and prevent him from winning a majority in the electoral college. The election would thus be forced into the House of Representatives. Daniel Webster ran for the Whigs in New England, Hugh Lawson White of Tennessee ran in the South, and General William Henry Harrison of Ohio, who had defeated the great Shawnee chief Tecumseh in the Battle of Tippecanoe, ran in the Northwest.

The strategy failed. Martin Van Buren, who had pledged to follow the policies of his predecessor, was elected with 170 electoral votes to 124 for his opponents combined. He had only a slight popular majority, however, since he was not well liked in the South. The House was dominated by a combination of Whigs and Southern Democrats opposed to the new president.

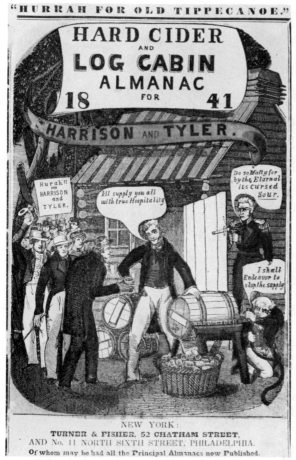

"HURRAH FOR OLD TIPPECANOE."

HARD CIDER
AND
LOG CABIN
ALMANAC
18 FOR 41
HARRISON AND TYLER.

Hurrah for HARRISON and TYLER.

I'll supply you all with true Hospitality.

Do so Matty for by the Eternal its cursed Sour.

I shall Endeavor to stop the supply

HARD CIDER

NEW YORK:
TURNER & FISHER, 52 CHATHAM STREET,
AND No. 11 NORTH SIXTH STREET, PHILADELPHIA.
Of whom may be had all the Principal Almanacs now Published.

THIS CARTOON CHARACTERIZES THE PRESIDENTIAL CAMPAIGNS
OF HARRISON AND VAN BUREN. HARRISON WAS ELECTED ON HIS
LOG-CABIN AND HARD-CIDER PLATFORM.

Van Buren's Troubled Presidency

Martin Van Buren was described, unfairly, by one of his contemporaries as a "first-rate second-rate man." Intelligent and well educated, he became a member of the New York State legislature by the time he was thirty and won a seat in the United States Senate at the age of thirty-eight. Van Buren was an able administrator, an astute politician, and a man of principle, as was demonstrated by his outspoken opposition to the expansion of slavery. In spite of his qualifications, Van Buren lacked the dynamism of his predecessor and never attracted a wide following. Moreover, it was his misfortune that his presidency coincided with the Panic of 1837 and the depression that followed. Van Buren was not responsible for the decline in the economy, and he opposed government intervention as the means of solving the crisis. "The less government interferes with private pursuits the better for general prosperity," he said. A true laissez-faire Jacksonian, Van Buren's chief interest was to keep the federal treasury from going in the red. This, he thought, would maintain confidence in the economy and therefore encourage a revival of business.

Because Van Buren believed that the government should keep out of banking, he proposed an independent treasury system. All ties between the federal government and any other banks were to be severed. Vaults were to be constructed in various cities to collect and expend government funds strictly in gold and silver. The country's banking business would be carried out by state-regulated private banks.

Naturally, this scheme aroused the opposition of the Whigs. Clay and Webster charged that it would sabotage the existing banking structure. Its effect, they argued, would be to keep gold and silver out of banks that desperately needed it to back their loans, thus curtailing credit.

Those who had lost their lifetime savings in a state bank favored Van Buren's proposal, for it reinforced their own suspicion of banks. Congress, however, did not pass the Independent Treasury Act until 1840, when Van Buren's term in the White House was virtually at an end.

The "Hard-Cider" Election of 1840

Van Buren, his image tarnished by the economic panic, was renominated for the presidency by the Democrats in 1840. Given the country's woeful circumstances, the Whigs scented victory, referring derisively to the Democratic incumbent as "Martin Van Ruin." Drawing upon the lessons learned in Jackson's campaign, they nominated for president General William Henry Harrison, who had no political enemies and no particular association with any issues. John Tyler of Virginia was selected

DUBBED THE "FLYING DUTCHMAN," THE "RED FOX
OF KINDERHOOK," THE "LITTLE MAGICIAN," AND
THE "AMERICAN TALLEYRAND," MARTIN VAN BUREN
WAS ONE OF THE DEMOCRATIC PARTY'S WILIEST
POLITICIANS. HIS OPPONENTS CLAIMED HE WAS SO
VAIN THAT HE HAD WORN OUT A PATCH OF CARPET
BEFORE THE MIRROR HANGING IN HIS STUDY.

as his running mate. Tyler had been a Democrat but switched to the Whigs when Jackson denounced nullification and attacked the Bank of the United States. Whig leaders hoped his presence on the ticket would cut into Democratic strength in the South.

The issues of the day were the depression and the independent treasury, but the campaign was based mostly on personalities and ballyhoo. The Whigs, now rivaling the Democrats at their own political game, put forward the educated Harrison, whose father had been one of the signers of the Declaration of Independence, as a rough-hewn frontiersman truly fit to represent the people. Van Buren, the son of a tavernkeeper, they denounced as a highfalutin dandy, an aristocrat who wore corsets

and ate French food from imported gold plates. The Whig's campaign theme—hard cider and log cabins—originated as an insult to Harrison from a Democratic newspaper editor. He had satirized Harrison (who owned a lovely mansion named the "Log Cabin") as a poor old farmer content to sit on the porch of his log cabin with a barrel of hard cider nearby. But the Whigs soon turned the insult to their advantage, spreading the myth of Harrison as a man of the people raised in a log cabin. Traveling from town to town, the Whigs chanted such slogans as "With Tip and Tyler We'll Bust Van's Biler," and sang:

Tippecanoe and Tyler too.
And with them we'll beat little

Van, Van, Van,
Oh! Van is a used-up man.

Seventy-eight percent of the electorate turned out to vote in 1840, compared with 56 percent in 1828. Probably voting mostly against hard times, they swept Harrison into office. The electoral college vote was a resounding 234 to 60. The Democrats had been beaten at their own game.

Though concerned with trivial and demagogic issues, the election was of major significance in the history of American democracy. From 1840 on, all political parties in America would use democratic strategies in their appeal to voters.

The Supreme Court under Taney

Although the Whigs now controlled Congress and were in nominal control of the White House, the Jacksonians still controlled the Supreme Court. Jackson had named seven of the nine justices, including Chief Justice Roger B. Taney, appointed when Chief Justice Marshall died in 1835. The nomination of Taney, a states' rights agrarian, had been bitterly contested in the Senate. Webster and other nationalists feared that the Taney Court would be overly strict in its interpretation of the Constitution and that it would reverse earlier court decisions.

In fact, the main body of the Marshall Court decisions survived almost intact, although the Taney Court tended to be less nationalistic and to give the states more power to regulate corporations. For example, in *Charles River Bridge* v. *Warren Bridge* (1837) the state had chartered one company to build and operate a toll bridge over the Charles River and then chartered a second company to build another, toll-free bridge over the same river. Although the second bridge would compete directly with the first, the Taney Court upheld the state's action. Sharing Jackson's distrust of special corporate charters, the Court asserted that the rights of corporations were less important than those of the community, and that "the happiness and well-being of every citizen depends on their faithful preservation."

Although Taney did not let his sympathy for states' rights undermine Marshall's precedents, he did make distinctions between those areas of government under federal law and those under state law. A true Jacksonian, Taney wrote in one opinion:

The object and end of all government is to promote the happiness and prosperity of the community by which it is established, and it can never be assumed that the government intended to diminish its power of accomplishing the end for which it was created.

Here was a lesson in Jacksonian democracy.

The Legacy of Jacksonian Democracy

The policies of the Jacksonian Democrats were often innovative, usually opportunistic, and sometimes paradoxical. By using the presidency as an office for policymaking rather than for the purpose of carrying out laws passed by Congress, Jackson helped shape the modern concept of presidential leadership. He and his supporters introduced rotation in office and employed the spoils system on a scale never before seen in national politics. Jackson's successors unhesitatingly followed his precedent. The opportunism evident in the spoils system also was reflected in Jackson's way of interpreting the Constitution. When it suited his purpose, as in the Maysville Road veto, he vigorously defended a narrow reading of the document. He disregarded previous Supreme Court decisions on the constitutionality of the bank, on the status of the Indian tribes, and on treaties, when they conflicted with his personal wishes.

There was a paradox in Jackson's simultaneous support of nationalism and states' rights. He dramatically rebutted South Carolina's challenge to national sovereignty in the nullification controversy but upheld the rights of the states in planning internal improvements and in seizing Indian lands. The Jacksonians fostered the ideal of a capitalist economy based on equality of opportunity without government interference or planning. These views led the president to attack the bank as a monopoly and the cause of money inflation. Regardless of the truth or falsity of these charges, they left an enduring legacy of distrust of banks and wealthy commercial interests among segments of the American population.

Above all, the Jacksonian Democrats had mastered the art of democratic politics. Their ingenuity in oversimplifying issues and catering to popular emotions kept their party in power, except for brief interruptions, until the Civil War.

Readings

General Works

Benson, Lee, *The Concept of Jacksonian Democracy: New York as a Test Case*. Princeton, N.J.: Princeton University Press, 1961.

Hammond, Bray, *Banks and Politics in America*. Princeton, N.J.: Princeton University Press, 1957.

McCormick, Richard P., *The Second American Party System: Its Formation in the Jacksonian Era*. Chapel Hill: University of North Carolina Press, 1966.

Miller, Douglas T., *The Birth of Modern America, 1820–1850*. Indianapolis, Ind.: Pegasus, 1970.

Nash, Roderick, *Wilderness and the American Mind*. New Haven, Conn.: Yale University Press, 1973.

Pessen, Edward, *Jacksonian America: Society, Personality, & Politics*. Homewood, Ill.: Dorsey Press, rev. ed. 1978.

Remini, Robert V., *The Revolutionary Age of Andrew Jackson*. New York: Harper & Row, 1976.

Schlesinger, Arthur M., Jr., *The Age of Jackson*. Boston: Little, Brown, 1945.

Somkin, Rowland, *Unquiet Eagle: Memory and Desire in the Idea of American Freedom, 1815–1860*. Ithaca, N.Y.: Cornell University Press, 1967.

Syrett, Harold C., *Andrew Jackson: His Contribution to the American Tradition*. Indianapolis, Ind.: Bobbs-Merrill, 1953.

Temin, Peter, *The Jacksonian Economy*. New York: Norton, 1969. (Paper)

Van Duesen, Glyndon G., *The Jacksonian Era*. New York: Harper & Row, 1959.

White, Leonard D., *The Jacksonians*. New York: Macmillan, 1954.

Williamson, Chilton, *American Suffrage: From Property to Democracy*. Princeton, N.J.: Princeton University Press, 1960.

Special Studies

Aronson, Sidney H., *Status and Kinship in the Higher Civil Service*. Cambridge, Mass.: Harvard University Press, 1964.

Foreman, Grant, *Indian Removal: The Emigration of the Five Civilized Tribes*. Norman: University of Oklahoma Press, 1969.

Freehling, William W., *Prelude to Civil War*. New York: Harper & Row, 1966.

Hugins, Walter, *Jacksonian Democracy and the Working Class*. Stanford, Calif.: Stanford University Press, 1960.

Meyers, Marvin, *The Jacksonian Persuasion*. Stanford, Calif.: Stanford University Press, 1957.

Miller, Douglas T., *Jacksonian Aristocracy: Class and Democracy in New York, 1830–1860*. New York: Oxford University Press, 1967.

Remini, Robert V., *Andrew Jackson and the Bank War*. New York: Norton, 1968. (Paper)

Rogin, Michael Paul, *Fathers and Children: Andrew Jackson and the Subjugation of the American Indian*. New York: Knopf, 1975.

Satz, Ronald N., *American Indian Policy in the Jacksonian Era*. Lincoln: University of Nebraska Press, 1975.

Ward, John W., *Andrew Jackson: Symbol for an Age*. New York: Oxford University Press, 1955.

Primary Sources

Benton, Thomas H., *Thirty Years' View*, Vols. I–II. New York: Greenwood, 1968.

Cooper, James F., *The American Democrat*. Baltimore: Penguin Books, 1962.

Grund, Francis J., *Aristocracy in America*. New York: Harper Torchbooks, 1959.

Nevins, Allan (Ed.), *America Through British Eyes*. New York: Oxford University Press, 1948.

Tocqueville, Alexis de, *Democracy in America*, Philip Bradley, ed. New York: Vintage Books, 1945.

Trollope, Frances, *Domestic Manners of the Americans*, Donald Smalley, ed. New York: Vintage Books, 1960.

Van Buren, M., and John C. Fitzpatrick (Eds.), *The Autobiography of Martin Van Buren*, New York: Plenum, 1969.

Biographies

Coit, Margaret L., *John C. Calhoun: American Portrait*. Boston, Houghton Mifflin, 1950.

Curtis, James C., *Andrew Jackson and the Search for Vindication*. Lubbock, Tex.: Little, 1976.

Goven, Thomas P., *Nicholas Biddle: Nationalist and Public Banker*. Chicago: University of Chicago Press, 1959.

Remini, Robert V., *Andrew Jackson and the Course of American Empire, 1767–1821*. New York: Harper & Row, 1977.

Swisher, Carl B., *Roger B. Taney*. New York: Macmillan, 1935.

Wiltse, Charles M., *John C. Calhoun: Nullifier*, Vol. II. Indianapolis, Ind.: Bobbs-Merrill, 1949.

Fiction

Adams, Samuel H., *The Gorgeous Hussy*. Boston: Houghton Mifflin, 1934.

Gerson, Noel B., *Old Hickory*. New York: Doubleday, 1964.

10 Life in America at Mid-Century

GLORY TO GOD IN THE HIGHEST. ON EARTH PEACE. GOOD WILL TOWARD MEN.

LIBERTY AND UNION NOW AND FOR EVER

ONE AND INSEPARABLE

What indomitable enterprise marks the character of our people! What immense forests have disappeared, and given place to cultivated towns, thriving villages, and wealthy cities! Agriculture, and manufactures, and commerce, and schools, and public buildings, and houses of public worship; all these testify to our matchless enterprise. The rapidity of our progress throws all Eastern countries into the shade. We build steamboats for the Sultan of Turkey, and railroads for the Autocrat of Russia; and our enterprises extend to the icebergs of the poles—to India, China, and Japan.

Orin Fowler

Significant Events

African slave trade outlawed [1808]

Land Act [1820]

Nat Turner's Rebellion [1831]

First telegraph lines [1840s]

Preemption Act [1841]

Commonwealth v. *Hunt* [1842]

Treaty of Wanghia with China [1844]

Commodore Perry opens trade with Japan [1854]

THE PROGRESS OF THE CENTURY, A LITHOGRAPH BY CURRIER AND IVES.

From 1820 to 1860 the United States experienced sudden, rapid geographical, agricultural, industrial, and urban growth. Individuals and businesses were unhampered by high taxes or government controls and often reaped large profits. Backed by hard work and shrewd investments, the potential of the American economy seemed boundless.

During this same period, economic inequality increased as well. The decades preceding the Civil War were characterized by the development of large farms, plantations, and factories producing for a mass market. By the time of the Civil War, 5 percent of the nation's families owned more than half the nation's wealth. This disparity in land and income distribution was most apparent in urban areas which were crowded with unskilled and transient workers. The era also witnessed a decline in small farms and home manufacturing. As a result, skilled workers were less in demand. Unskilled workers who could not compete effectively—particularly women, free blacks, and recently arrived immigrants—reaped the smallest share of the country's economic rewards.

Nonetheless, to most observers the manifestations of inequality in American life seemed to reflect a temporary situation, one which could be overcome with persistent effort. On the whole Americans were a restless, mobile, and optimistic people, and the living conditions of the majority were slowly improving.

The Growth of the West

Impact of Expansion on the Indians

The settlement of the West paralleled the declining power of the Indians. White settlers had no interest in preserving the native Americans' way of life. Their purpose was to occupy and exploit the Western territory, and their main contact with the Indians, other than trade, involved open conflict over possession of land. Skirmishes with neighboring tribes soon led most settlers to view the Indians as bloodthirsty savages. Only those settlers living in relative security some distance from the frontier eventually called for justice toward Southern and Western tribes.

Under federal treaties assigning native Americans to reservation land which the white settlers considered least desirable, the Indians were to receive payment for lands they relinquished as well as annual government support. No white person was to enter Indian country without a license. But the momentum of the westward movement undermined the efforts to protect the tribes. Because traders often insisted that the Indians pay their debts before being compensated for their land, many tribes received next to nothing for the massive territories they gave up. Moreover, after 1854 the Government Land Office began selling Indian lands in spite of the law.

In addition to their geographical confinement west of the Mississippi River, Indians suffered in other ways. New settlers relentlessly slaughtered the buffalo, chief food of many Western tribes, and brought native Americans into contact with smallpox, tuberculosis, and whiskey. Missionaries who tried to convert some tribes to Christianity and teach them new skills undermined native institutions and often created bitter internal factionalism.

The Movement West

Since the founding of Jamestown in 1607, an irregular flow of settlers had crossed the American continent. With no laws to restrict physical movement, people took advantage of the opportunity to improve their material circumstances by appropriating the country's landed wealth. During the seventeenth century, fur trappers extended the frontier to the Fall Line, the highest navigable point of the rivers that flowed to the Atlantic Ocean. These frontier settlers traded guns to the Indians, unintentionally supplying them with the means to resist further white encroachment. But eventually the Indian nations were weakened by military defeats and government removal programs, and the natural barrier of the Allegheny Mountains was overcome by the construction of steamboats and canals. By the middle of the nineteenth century the claims of foreign governments to Western lands had been settled. These developments, coupled with an increasing hunger for better land, created waves of

SETTLERS TRAVELING WEST ACROSS THE GREAT PLAINS.

settlers who by 1800 had pushed the frontier to the Mississippi River and by the 1840s had broken through to the West Coast. Whereas in 1810 only one-seventh of the country's white Americans lived west of the Appalachians, by 1870 over one-half the country's population had crossed these mountains.

Before the Civil War, the United States was primarily a land of farmers. Between 1820 and 1860, a great expansion of farming into Western and Southwestern lands was made possible by cheap land prices and the demands of the Eastern economy for farm produce such as corn, wheat, hogs, and cattle for domestic consumption and shipment abroad. Cotton growers, seeking to profit from the increased international demand for their crop, flocked to the rich soil of the Cotton Belt states, Alabama and Mississippi.

Thinking that land on which trees did not grow was infertile, most frontier settlers skirted the productive grasslands of Indiana and Illinois. Initially,

the region which later became Oklahoma and Kansas appeared so unsuitable that it was set aside for Indian tribes that were being relocated from their lands in the South. Only after the rise in world grain prices during the 1840s and the development of railroad links with the East did pioneers begin to plow the dense prairie sod. Many Southerners, too poor to own slaves, then moved into the free states of Indiana and Illinois. Settlement of the Far West came even later. By 1845 only a few hundred Americans had made the long trek to California, but after the discovery of gold in 1848 the population exploded.

An 1837 manual, *A New Guide for Emigrants to the West,* described the waves of immigration into lands explored by adventurers:

Generally, in all the western settlements, three classes, like the waves of the ocean, have rolled on after the other. First comes the pioneer, who de-

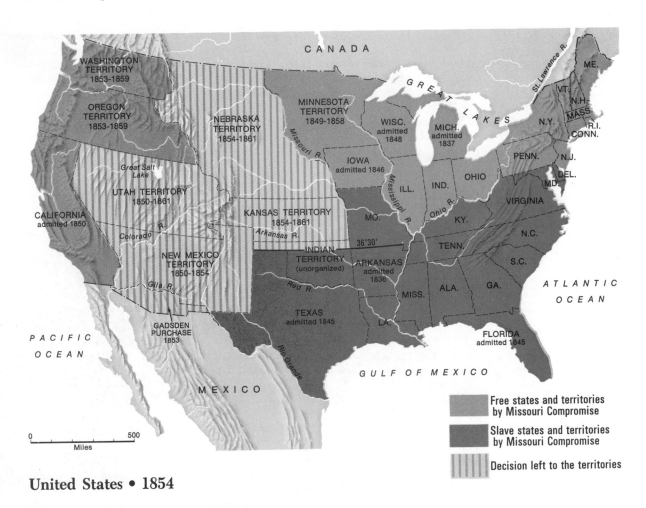

CANADA

WASHINGTON
TERRITORY
1853-1859

OREGON
TERRITORY
1853-1859

CALIFORNIA
admitted 1850

Great Salt
Lake

UTAH TERRITORY
1850-1861

Colorado R.

Gila R.

NEW MEXICO
TERRITORY
1850-1854

GADSDEN
PURCHASE
1853

PACIFIC

OCEAN

MEXICO

MINNESOTA
TERRITORY
1849-1858

NEBRASKA
TERRITORY
1854-1861

Missouri R.

KANSAS TERRITORY
1854-1861

Arkansas R.

INDIAN
TERRITORY
(unorganized)

Red R.

TEXAS
admitted 1845

Rio Grande

WISC.
admitted
1848

MICH.
admitted
1837

IOWA
admitted 1846

ILL.   IND.

MO.

Mississippi R.

Ohio R.

KY.

36°30'

ARKANSAS
admitted
1836

MISS.   ALA.

LA.

TENN.

GA.

GREAT LAKES

St. Lawrence R.

ME.

VT.
N.H.
MASS.

N.Y.

R.I.
CONN.

PENN.   N.J.

OHIO

DEL.
MD.

VIRGINIA

N.C.

S.C.

ATLANTIC

OCEAN

FLORIDA
admitted 1845

GULF OF MEXICO

0   500
Miles

Free states and territories
by Missouri Compromise

Slave states and territories
by Missouri Compromise

Decision left to the territories

United States • 1854

pends for the subsistence of his family chiefly
upon the natural growth of vegetation, called the
"range," and the proceeds of hunting. His imple-
ments of agriculture are rude, chiefly of his own
make, and his efforts directed mainly to a crop
of corn, and a "truck patch." It is quite immate-
rial whether he ever becomes the owner of the
soil.

The next class of emigrants purchase the lands,
add field to field, clear out the roads, throw rough
bridges over the streams, put up hewn log houses,
with glass windows, and brick or stone chimneys,
occasionally plant orchards, build mills, school

houses, court houses, etc., and exhibit the picture
and forms of plain, frugal, civilized life.

Another wave rolls on. The men of enterprise
and capital come. The "settler" is ready to sell out
and take advantage of the rise of property—push
farther into the interior, and become, himself, a
man of capital and enterprise in turn. The small villages rise to spacious towns or cities; substantial edifices of brick, extensive fields, orchards, gardens,
colleges and churches are seen. Broadcloths, silks,
leghorns, crapes, and all the refinements, luxuries,
elegances, frivolities and fashions are in vogue. Thus
wave after wave is rolling westward. . . .

Land Speculation

Such accounts generally glossed over the less pleasant realities of Western settlement. Blessed with seemingly endless natural resources, farmers cut down forests, overused and abandoned the soil, and destroyed grasslands and fur-bearing animals without thought for the future.

Laissez-faire government policies enabled the state banks to extend credit lavishly, thus lowering the price of land, so that by 1820 an eighty-acre farm could be purchased for a mere $100. There was no limit to how much land an individual could buy, and the government sometimes gave large tracts to railroads, canal companies, and state governments. With land so cheap and credit so readily available, Americans of all backgrounds became land speculators. In one case, a group of New York bankers with ties to the Jackson administration bought one-third of a million acres, spanning eight states and territories. Less wealthy speculators bought land at government auctions, then put it up for sale at higher prices and exorbitant interest rates.

Small farmers with limited financial resources wanted to purchase fewer than eighty acres of land, the minimum requirement under the Land Law of 1820. In addition, they wanted squatters' rights —the right to settle on a piece of government land with the hope of acquiring ownership. By 1832 the government had reduced the minimum to forty acres, and farmers won another victory in 1841 when the Preemption Act gave squatters the legal right to settle on unsurveyed land and to buy it for $1.25 an acre before it went on sale at public auction.

·Land speculators, especially absentee owners, were often irresponsible about the impact of their investment on the surrounding community. By not improving their land, they bore less of the local tax burden than settlers who did make improvements, and they were often slow in paying taxes for community services, thus inhibiting development. Speculators also brought pressure to locate internal improvements such as railroads and canals near their land in order to increase its value. As a result, railroads, county seats, state capitols, and public institutions frequently were built in unsuitable locations.

Many small farmers overextended themselves and could not afford to cultivate their lands or to pay real estate taxes. Consequently, mortgages on their farms were foreclosed, saddling banks and larger landowners with unmarketable land. In order to keep such properties income producing, creditors often convinced the indebted landowners to stay on as tenant farmers. Tenancy thus became a common feature of Western frontier settlement.

Life on the Frontier

Encouraged by reports of cheap land and endless opportunities, vast numbers of Americans uprooted themselves and their families and began the hazardous journey west in search of a better life. Life on the frontier was backbreaking and often perilous. Speculators' propaganda glossed over the poor quality of some of the land and the drudgery and loneliness of life in undeveloped areas. Isolated from their neighbors by miles of open space, settlers were forced to become self-reliant or perish. Pioneers often lived in spare cabins or erected smoky, vermin-ridden sod houses on the treeless prairies and burned buffalo dung for fuel. Corn and salt pork were the common staples of their diet, clothes were homemade, and water often had to be hauled for miles. Because trained doctors were scarce, disease took a heavy toll.

The veneer of civilization was extremely thin on the frontier. Disputes often erupted into violence, and aggressive behavior was more often restrained by social codes than by formal law enforcement, for frontier justice was crude. Frequently, private citizens had to defend their own reputations and property. As a result, Western settlers tended to develop the qualities of individualism, independence, and resourcefulness.

The West had the reputation of being a "land of opportunity" where individuals could rise as high on the social and economic ladder as their ambition and talent would take them. However, studies of settlement patterns somewhat belie the myth of Western mobility. When new Southern lands were opened to settlement, planters with slaves tended to monopolize the best land, forcing small farmers either to take the poorest lands or to move farther west; thus class lines were recreated in the image of the Old South. In the northern frontier regions, small farmers and poor families had to compete with land speculators and estate-builders. Inflation and speculation forced many into tenancy.

DURING THE MID-NINETEENTH CENTURY SOME EASTERNERS, CONCERNED ABOUT THEIR DIMINISHING WORK FORCE, PRODUCED PROPAGANDA TO DISCOURAGE MIDWESTERN SETTLEMENT. *MAJOR WALTER WILKEY'S UNHAPPY RETURN TO NEW ENGLAND FROM A TWELVE-MONTHS' MISERABLE HALF-STARVED RESIDENCE IN ILLINOIS* WAS CREATED IN 1839 FOR THIS VERY PURPOSE.

Despite these difficulties, many frontier settlers managed to improve their standard of living. Some switched from self-sufficient farming to commercial agriculture. Improved systems of transportation made it profitable for them to grow money crops for sale on the Eastern seaboard and in Europe. As more neighbors moved in, as schools and churches were built, as transportation improved, and as Eastern manufactured goods became cheaper, the hardships of frontier life eased. Thus, Western expansion created important urban centers west of the Appalachians which consumed industrial products from the East as well as produce from an expanding agricultural base.

Early Railroads

Before the advent of railroads, canal building had stimulated phenomenal growth in some regions. But the Panic of 1837 halted the national craze for canal building when several states, which had overcommitted themselves to domestic and foreign investors, finally had to repudiate their debts. As a result, public sentiment against state ownership of transportation facilities ran high, and future canal building was undertaken by private individuals and corporations. The public was more receptive to the construction of railroads, because they were to be built and run by private enterprise.

After a thirteen-mile segment of one of the first American lines, the Baltimore and Ohio, opened in 1830, many Eastern regions supported the building of local railroads in an effort to compete with New York for trade with the interior. Railroad building increased in the thirty years before the Civil War. As small, independent lines were consolidated, they joined previously unconnected parts of the country. Lines were eventually laid eastward from Chicago to meet the Eastern trunk lines and westward into Iowa and Missouri. By 1860 over thirty thousand miles of track linked many of the great cities east of the Mississippi and north of the Ohio.

Most of these early railroads were built by state-chartered private companies which were granted the right of eminent domain (the right of the government to appropriate private property for public use), monopoly status, and freedom from taxation. These early builders were more interested in monopolizing trade districts than in establishing coordinated railroad systems. Companies received financial assistance from private investors and state, county, and municipal governments in the form of loans and heavy stock investment. By the 1860s the federal government was making large grants of public land to private companies for the construction of railroads.

State and local financial support of railroad building placed a heavy burden on taxpayers, and the advantages of railroads were not immediately apparent to their passengers. At first, schedules were irregular, breakdowns were commonplace, and passengers in open cars were showered with sparks from the primitive wood-burning locomotives. Safety and efficiency were soon increased by the use of solid roadbeds and iron "T" rails and by the substitution of coal for wood as fuel. The design of the locomotives and cars was improved, sleeping cars were added to passenger trains, and the construction of telegraph lines in the 1840s made it easier to supervise railroad operations by quickly relaying messages. As more refinements were introduced, railroads became the ideal solution to the growing country's transportation needs. Trains were relatively fast, they could be built through rough terrain to service the most remote markets, and they were dependable in winter when water in

INLAND ROUTE

FOR NORTHERN AND SOUTHERN TRAVELLING.

The RICHMOND, FREDERICKSBURG AND POTOMAC RAIL ROAD COMPANY, in connection with the other Rail Road and Steamboat Companies on the route, have adopted the following Schedule, by which the daily Mail is now carried.

Leave	(NORTHWARD DIRECTION.)	Arrive at
Blakely, N. C. .... at 5 o'clock, P. M.	Petersburg, ... at 10 o'clock, P. M.
Petersburg, ... " 12 " A. M.	Richmond, ... " 4 " A. M.
Richmond, ... " 4½ " A. M.	Washington, ... " 6 " P. M.
Washington, ... " 7½ " P. M.	Baltimore, ... " 10 " P. M.
Baltimore, ... " 6 " A. M.	New York, ... " 11 " P. M.

Leave	(SOUTHWARD DIRECTION.)	Arrive at
New York, ... at 4 o'clock P. M.	Baltimore, ... at 3 o'clock, P. M.
" 5	Washington .... " 8 " P. M.

the canals often froze. In addition to drawing together the agriculture of the West and the industry of the East, railroads, with their need for metal rails, stimulated the iron industry.

The South was not as active as other regions in building railroads, although Southern states did contribute approximately one-quarter of the nation's total expenditure on them. Southerners continued to rely primarily on the Mississippi River and its tributaries to carry their goods to market. As a result, their share of the nation's trade declined sharply at the very time when the industrial Northeast and agricultural Northwest were becoming more interdependent. Increased economic ties between these two regions promoted closer social and cultural connections and contributed to the formation of strong political ties and pride in the nation's economic development.

Commercial Expansion

In the decades before the Civil War Americans greatly increased their trading activities. Two important inventions played a vital role in the expansion of domestic and foreign trade. America's first clipper ship, the *Rainbow*, was launched in 1845, and soon clipper ships were setting speed records that helped the United States gain a prominent share of the international carrying trade. These fast ships also forged a vital link between the Atlantic and Pacific oceans by cutting travel time around Cape Horn in South America almost in half. On May 1, 1844, the first message was sent over the first telegraph line between Baltimore and Washington. By 1850 thousands of miles of line had been installed across the United States, and in 1858 a transatlantic cable was buried under the ocean. At last the United States was only seconds away from Europe.

The Growth of Foreign Trade

Ten years after the Panic of 1837, internal economic recovery and a series of favorable foreign developments gave a tremendous boost to overseas trade. In 1846 Britain repealed the Corn Laws, which had protected its domestic agriculture, thereby opening up a large market for American wheat. That same year America lowered its protective tariff, thereby attracting more European manufactured goods to the United States. From 1840 to 1860, the combined value of American exports and imports tripled.

During this period imports of manufactured goods still led exports of raw materials. Textiles and iron products were the chief imports, and cotton was the major export. American whalers sailed the world's oceans, making the country the leading exporter of whalebone and whale oil. Gold gained immediate importance as an export after its discovery in California in 1848.

America's leading foreign supplier and best customer throughout the antebellum period was Great Britain. However, during this same period, the United States made trade inroads in other parts of the world as well. Early nineteenth-century American merchant ships traded in the Philippines, India, and Java. By the 1840s the United States had signed a trade agreement with Siam. In 1842, following their victory in the Opium War, the British forced China to open certain ports to foreign trade. Two years later the United States sent Caleb Cushing, its first trade commissioner, to China to negotiate for similar privileges. The Treaty of Wanghia, signed in 1844, opened five ports to American trade, secured specific customs duties favorable to the United States, and granted the United States extraterritoriality, the right of legal jurisdiction over its own nationals in the trading ports. China, however, resented the concessions it had been forced to make and tried to evade the terms of the treaty. Subsequently, in 1858 Britain and France, with America's tacit support, sent gunboats to enforce the treaty commitments.

While America had hitchhiked on the imperialist policies of Britain and France in China, it took a more direct approach toward Japan, a nation that had been isolated from the rest of the world for two centuries. In 1853 the United States government sent Commodore Matthew C. Perry, backed by a fleet of steam warships, to open up trade with Japan and to reach an agreement over the protection of shipwrecked sailors. After preliminary discussions, Perry presented Japanese officials with letters containing American demands and an array of Western

A JAPANESE RENDERING OF COMMODORE PERRY.

gadgetry from President Pierce. He informed them that they would be given one year to consider the proposals. When Perry returned the following year with an even larger fleet, he found the Japanese officials willing to receive him.

While Perry was able to secure the opening of two small ports, he obtained no binding agreement to open trade between Japan and the United States. Subsequently, the United States Department of State sent diplomat Townsend Harris to Japan as its first American Consul. Harris's charm and diplomatic skills were more effective than Perry's warships. He convinced the Japanese that the United States had no territorial ambitions in the Pacific and even obtained further commercial concessions in 1858. In 1860 the first Japanese mission visited the United States.

The Growth of Domestic Trade

The vitality of America's international trade helped spur domestic commerce, for imports and exports were deposited at port cities, creating business for home carriers. The domestic economy was helped by population increases and regional specialization as well. As various areas began to specialize in distinct commodities, they experienced a growing need to exchange goods. These exchanges were further stimulated by the gold being mined in California, which produced a stable monetary base, and by the invention of the telegraph, which promoted speedier transactions. As the amount of money in circulation increased, the pace of domestic economic activity quickened.

The country's railroad network and excellent system of waterways were great assets to the increasing domestic traffic. Coastal vessels carried Southern cotton to New York and New England. Steamboats hauled both freight and passengers along the Mississippi River and controlled the flow of goods from farm to market until the elaborate network of canals began diverting much of the business to the Great Lakes.

Agricultural Expansion

During the 1840s and 1850s many farmers left the rocky soil of New England and the worn-out farms of the old South for the rich land which lay further west. At this time, an effort was made to modify the practice of overusing and then abandoning land. Because agriculture was so important to the nation's

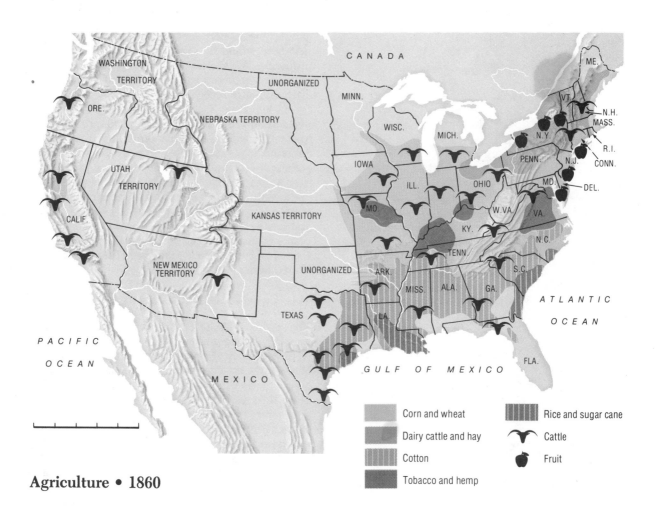

Agriculture • 1860

Corn and wheat

Dairy cattle and hay

Cotton

Tobacco and hemp

Rice and sugar cane

Cattle

Fruit

economy, agricultural reformers developed and promoted new methods for utilizing and preserving the land. Jesse Buel of New York advocated crop rotation and the use of fertilizers, promising that "by draining, manuring, ploughing, harrowing, hoeing . . . we may preserve, unimpaired, the natural fertility of our soils."

Marl, an earth rich in calcium, was first used in Virginia to counteract the acidity of fields depleted by the planting of tobacco. Later it was introduced into other areas where it was used to increase harvests of corn and wheat.

Corn was the predominant cash crop in the North. In the South, corn production was actually greater than cotton output, although it was not nearly the cash crop cotton was. Production in the Corn Belt (which reached from Pennsylvania to Iowa) increased 40 percent in the 1850s. Wheat production for domestic and international consumption also soared before the Civil War.

Mechanization of Farming

In 1800 farmers relied on wooden plows and harrows pulled by horses or oxen and a few simple hand tools. The largest area a farm family could cultivate was a little over one acre a day, and most of what they grew, they ate.

Though farmers tended to resist change, many recognized that mechanization was essential if agriculture were to develop into a commercial enterprise. Therefore, interest arose in 1830 when John Deere, an Illinois blacksmith, invented a steel plow light enough for a single person to guide behind a team and capable of cutting clean, deep furrows. By 1858 Deere was turning out thirteen thousand steel plows a year.

Cyrus McCormick of Virginia and Obed Hussey of Ohio built reapers which greatly reduced the labor of harvesting. With one of their steel-toothed, horse-drawn machines, one person could do the work of five people with scythes. By 1858 McCormick was manufacturing five hundred reapers a month and still could not keep up with the demand.

Further mechanization occurred in the 1850s. The invention of mechanical threshers, cultivators, hayrakes, and mowers reduced the need for field hands in the chronically labor-short country. But mechanization, while reducing the human labor necessary for farming, also increased the costs of farming. Whereas in 1800 the average farmer rarely spent more than $20 on tools, by 1857 farmers with one hundred acres of land needed some $600 worth of machinery. The heavy cost of mechanization diminished opportunities for farm laborers and tenant farmers to climb the economic ladder and made farmers more dependent on credit agencies and banks.

Farmers were forced to grow larger crops on more land in order to pay for the machinery and to specialize in a few crops in order to minimize the number of machines they needed. By the 1850s large-scale agriculture geared to specialized markets was firmly established as far west as Illinois and Wisconsin.

Farmers in the Northeast turned increasingly to dairy farming and to raising fruits and vegetables for nearby markets. In New York City, Boston, and Philadelphia, they initially had a distinct price advantage over distant competitors. Fruit and vegetable sales were boosted when an Englishman invented the tin can, thereby introducing a means for packaging and preserving fresh produce.

The South, including the newly settled states of Alabama and Mississippi, specialized in growing cotton. By mid-century the South was producing an astounding 60 percent of the world's cotton.

Southern cotton was important to Northern development as well, as it promoted the growth of New York City as an export center and caused an enormous expansion of the Northern textile industry.

Specialization occurred in other regions, as well: tobacco grown for export in Virginia, Kentucky, Tennessee, and Missouri; rice in the Carolinas and Georgia; sugarcane in Louisiana; and hemp in Kentucky. Most other Southern crops were raised for home consumption, with the large planters concentrating on producing a cash crop for the commercial market.

As transportation links improved, the West quickly became the dominant producer of staple food crops and livestock. By 1850, Illinois, Indiana, Iowa, and Texas had taken the lead from the Northeastern states as the principal cattle-raising areas, and Western cities such as Cincinnati and Chicago began to specialize in meat packing and flour milling.

The Growth of Slavery

As cotton, rice, and sugar production soared in the South, the demand for slave labor increased. After the African slave trade was outlawed in 1808 as permitted by the Constitution, planters in the lower South bought their slaves from the upper South. This change created a dramatic shift in the distribution of the slave population. Eventually most slaves lived in the Deep South, and by 1860 slaves outnumbered whites in three states, although in none of these did the proportion of slaves exceed 60 percent.

Despite the abolition of the African slave trade, the total number of slaves in the country grew from 857,000 at the turn of the century to almost four million by the beginning of the Civil War. Part of this increase was due to the illegal smuggling of slaves from Africa, but most was due to natural reproduction within the slave population. By the early nineteenth century, slavery had influenced every aspect of Southern life.

Slave Ownership and Class Structure Although most Southern farmers wanted to own slaves, only about one-quarter of them actually owned any. The Southern white class structure was based on the number of slaves that a person owned. At the top of

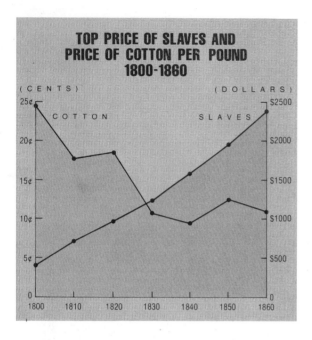

TOP PRICE OF SLAVES AND
PRICE OF COTTON PER POUND
1800-1860

The institution of slavery created a self-conscious aristocracy which dominated the economic, social, and political life of the South. Planters, who lived and entertained lavishly, set the tone for the unwritten social code that often superceded the written laws of the land. According to its apologists, the Southern code was the most effective instrument for self-government because, being based on personal honor, it left the master-slave relation to the master's conscience. That conscience, more exacting than any legal code, was supposedly characterized by generosity, warmth, and charity, as distinguished from the Northern conscience which, according to Southerners, was characterized by a concern for monetary value.

Most of the slaves lived on the plantations, for it was plantation crops that earned the bulk of Southern capital. Many also worked on small farms, however, performing a variety of tasks much like hired hands. Approximately 12 percent of the slaves on the plantations and 25 percent of the slaves in the cities were skilled workers. They were employed in nearly every trade and craft and were represented in tobacco processing, in coal mining, in textile factories, at the iron works, and among train engineers. The variety of slave-filled occupations indicates that slaves could compete effectively with free white labor.

While most historians agree that slave labor was profitable, there were some drawbacks to a slave-dependent economy. Slaves were more expensive than hired labor and required constant control. In addition, the work force could not be adjusted to meet business fluctuations. Slave labor restricted the Southern economy to a few crops, preventing the rapid diversification which was taking place in the North. It also impeded the introduction of new machinery. Nevertheless, the economic rewards were generally viewed as worth the expense, and the income of the section as a whole was not inferior to that of the Middle West.

The Organization of Slave Labor On Southern farms most slaves worked as field hands organized under either the gang system or the task system. The cultivation of cotton, a sturdy crop not easily damaged by unskilled labor, lent itself well to the gang system, in which a single overseer supervised as many as forty slaves of both sexes and varying ages. At planting time five waves of hands moved through

the hierarchy was the planter class who owned estates that were between eight hundred and one thousand acres in size (at least) and that required the labor of between twenty and thirty slaves to work. Most landowners aspired to become planters, but the planter class included only 12 percent of all slaveholders, or approximately twenty-five thousand individuals. Below the planter class was the gentry, who usually owned between ten and twenty slaves. Next came the farmers, who kept fewer than ten slaves and often worked in the fields with them. This group comprised almost three-fourths of all slaveholders. The remaining three-quarters of the Southern white population, mostly small farmers who owned between eighty and a hundred and sixty acres of land, had no slaves at all. There existed a large group of tradespeople and small farmers who strongly supported the institution of slavery because it gave them a sense of racial superiority and because they harbored a desire to own a slave or two one day themselves. Yet, on the other hand, many small farmers despised both the planter class and their slaves. Finally, at the bottom of the social and economic hierarchy were the poor whites, labeled by the classes above as "hillbillies," "crackers," or "clay-eaters."

THE FOLLOWING EXCERPT FROM *HARPER'S MAGAZINE* PRESENTS A ROMANTICIZED VERSION OF COTTON PICKING IN THE SOUTH:

The season of cotton picking commences in the latter part of July, and continues without intermission to the Christmas holidays. The work is not heavy, but becomes tedious from its sameness. The field hands are each supplied with a basket and bag. The basket is left at the head of the "cotton-rows"; the bag is suspended from the "picker's" neck by a strap, and is used to hold the cotton as it is taken from the boll. When the bag is filled it is emptied into the basket, and this routine is continued through the day. Each hand picks from two hundred and fifty to three hundred pounds of "seed cotton" each day, though some negroes of extraordinary ability go beyond this amount.

If the weather be very fine, the cotton is carried from the field direct to the packing-house; but generally it is first spread out on scaffolds, where it is left to dry, and picked clean of any "trash" that may be perceived mixed up with the cotton. Among the most characteristic scenes of plantation life is the returning of the hands at nightfall from the field, with their well-filled baskets of cotton upon their heads. Falling unconsciously "into line," the stoutest leading the way, they move along in the dim twilight of a winter day, with the quietness of spirits rather than human beings.

the fields like an assembly line. The first wave plowed the soil, the second wave harrowed dirt lumps, the third wave drilled holes for seeds, the fourth wave dropped the seeds, and the last wave covered the holes. At harvest time gangs were forced to compete. Each slave was assigned a weight of cotton he or she would be expected to pick. Under some masters, a slave who failed might be whipped, and a slave who succeeded might receive an increased assignment. Other planters offered positive rewards to encourage greater effort. Under the gang system

slaves usually worked from dawn to dusk with a short rest at mid-day.

Under the task system, used in the cultivation of tobacco, rice, and sugar, slaves were taught how to care for and harvest the plants. Each slave was assigned a specific amount of work, which was an incentive for working hard, because once the daily task was completed, the slave had the rest of the day off.

Field slaves received a weekly food allowance, generally salt pork or bacon and corn, and often slept on a narrow plank in a dark cabin with a stick of wood for a pillow and some burlap for a blanket. Since skilled workers and artisans brought higher prices than field hands, they received better treatment from their owners.

The foreman, or "driver," was the plantation superintendent's right-hand man and commanded the highest price of all plantation slaves. He called the hands to work, laid out their specific chores, and checked individual quotas at the end of the day. The driver's food rations and clothing were better than those of the other field hands, and he was occasionally awarded a bottle of rum.

Some slaves were allowed to hire themselves out to other masters or were rented either by their owners or by commercial agencies. Such rentals, five times more common than sales, were commonly used for temporary harvest help or for jobs such as railroad construction or work in the textile mills beside white laborers. Hired slaves generally received better food and clothing than did field hands and sometimes received a weekly allowance. But their owners also received a percentage of their wages.

The slaves who may have fared best in the agricultural regions of the South were the domestics —butlers, gardeners, cooks, housemaids, personal maids, and coachmen. Their work was lighter, and their food, clothing, and housing were considerably better than that of field hands. Some were even taught to read and write (although education was against the Southern slave codes), and maids and valets often accompanied their owners on travels.

While state laws considered slaves property that could be bought and sold, these same laws, in fact, recognized their humanity by depriving them of the legal right to make contracts (and therefore to marry), to own property, or to testify in court. But because planters wanted to profit from using slave labor, it was generally practical for them to maintain a minimal standard of health among their slaves and to treat them as well as was necessary to minimize the risk of rebellion.

Free Blacks Although some quarter million blacks were legally free, those who remained in the South fared little better than slaves. Laws forbade them to migrate freely to other Southern states, and if caught without their freedom certificates, they could be claimed as slaves. They could not vote, tes-

tify against whites, or serve on juries. They were subject to curfews and largely prevented from assembling without the presence of a white person. Some Southern cities even barred them from the skilled trades. Free blacks who migrated north were treated little better. There they faced the racial prejudice of whites and competition from immigrants for jobs. Public transportation, schools, prisons, hospitals, and even cemeteries were segregated. White mobs in Northern cities sometimes killed blacks and destroyed their property. Illinois and Indiana passed laws regulating the behavior of free blacks, and by the end of the antebellum period, Illinois, Indiana, and Oregon had forbidden them from entering their states. Between 1807 and 1837 five of the Northern states which had allowed blacks to vote disfranchised them. Finally, the federal government excluded blacks from the army and from most government jobs.

Despite job discrimination, free blacks in the North found work as fruit and produce vendors, barbers, stevedores, brick masons, wood sawyers, cooks, house servants, and managers of small stores serving black customers. Still, in even the most menial jobs, such as bootblacking, they were often replaced by white immigrants. In spite of this, a few free blacks were successful. Among them were Benjamin Banneker, a city surveyor who helped draw up plans for Washington, D.C., and John Russworm, an editor in New York who established America's first black newspaper, *Freedom's Journal*, in 1827. But such instances of success were rare.

The Extent of Exploitation: The Historical Debate The inhumanity of slavery, especially in a society that preached the ideal of individual opportunity, has been debated since slaves were first brought to America. In 1838 Calhoun told Congress: "We see it [slavery] now in its true light, and regard it as the most safe and stable basis for free institutions in the world." Calhoun's statement was strongly contradicted by the nineteenth-century New England historian Richard Hildreth, whose visit to the South left him convinced that slavery "is a far more deadly and disastrous thing, more fatal to all the hopes, the sentiments, the rights of humanity, than almost any other system of servitude which has existed in any other community."

Slaves, too, reported the dehumanizing nature of the system. Frederick Douglass, who fled from slavery in Maryland in 1838, described the life as one of "perpetual toil; no marriage; no husband, no wife, ignorance, brutality, licentiousness; whips, scourges, chains, auctions, jails and separations; an embodiment of all the woes the imagination can conceive."

The extent of brutality in the slave system has been the focus of much controversy among historians. John Blassingame stresses that whippings were common on plantations, and Kenneth Stampp maintains that cruelty was endemic to all slaveholding communities, especially in regions close to the frontier. Moreover, the standard of living of most slaves was at the subsistence level. Yet historians generally agree that although fear of physical punishment was used to force slaves to work harder, most masters were not sadistic, if only because brutal whippings diminished a slave's value. Some owners even offered positive incentives for hard work: holidays, extra food, cash, or land for the slave's exclusive use. Robert W. Fogel and Stanley L. Engerman argue that despite the undeniable hardships of slavery, slaves were not deprived of adequate rations.

Another disputed issue concerns the extent of disruption of family life caused by the slave system. Since slaves could not make contracts, their marriages were not legally binding under state law. Blassingame believes that at least one-third of all slave families were broken up. Yet despite the frequent breakup of marriages and families by sale and despite the absence of legal protection, new research by Herbert G. Gutman indicates that a pattern of lasting family ties developed among Afro-Americans. A majority of slaves married, raised families, and lived together until death. Most children grew up in two-parent families, and when family members were separated, other slaves assumed responsibility for the children. Moreover, children tended to view their parents favorably, in spite of separations, in appreciation of their skill and courage.

The Black Response to Slavery Several historians have studied black personality, religion, language, music, and society within the slave environment. Eugene Genovese has shown that despite its severe limitations, slave society did provide a variety of experiences. There was an interdependent relationship between master and slave with rights and obligations on both sides. Although it was not a relationship between equals, both sides understood the terms. Genovese maintains that a black culture developed within the slave system, and Lawrence Levine recently substantiated the theory that many features of Afro-American culture were remnants of the slaves' African heritage. The fusion of aspects of the Euro-Christian and African cultures transformed this heritage into a new perspective which helped blacks survive within a hostile environment. For example, by combining African folk beliefs with biblical stories, such as the liberation of the children of Israel or the persecution of Jesus, blacks created a religion which embodied their own hope for eventual deliverance from oppression.

Blacks responded to the slave system in various ways. A small number of slaves may have accommodated to their situation by assuming a docile and helpless role. While some slaves competed with one another for their master's recognition, others in the slave elite—house servants, foremen, and skilled artisans—often identified with the master class. Many slaves coped with the harsh realities of their condition by exploiting conflicts between masters and overseers, engaging in sabotage, stealing, or running away. Records indicate that a high proportion of runaways were privileged house slaves, suggesting that their childlike behavior may have been adopted consciously only to be cast off at will. These slaves, who lived closest to white society, were never able to become part of it. Many tried to buy their freedom, to little avail. Those who ran away were tracked with bloodhounds and, if caught, were severely beaten and branded as troublemakers.

Perhaps the most successful method of escape from slavery was the "Underground Railroad." This was the popular name given to a group of abolitionists operating in the upper South who helped runaway slaves. Three thousand of the railroad's "conductors" (those who helped slaves flee to the North or Canada) were escaped slaves or blacks who had been born free in the North.

Although there were few slave revolts, there was widespread fear of them in the South, especially after a rebellion led by Nat Turner. Turner was a Virginia slave and Baptist preacher who believed his plans were divinely inspired. On an August evening in 1831, he and a band of eight slaves killed Turner's master and his family. The group then pushed through the countryside gathering additional recruits along the way until they numbered seventy. Within forty-eight hours Turner's renegade band had seized and murdered sixty people. The terrified local white population mobilized volunteer reprisal forces and called out the state militia. In the aftermath, over a hundred slaves were put to death. Turner himself was caught two months later, briefly imprisoned, and executed.

Though panic over insurrections occurred many times between 1831 and 1860, Turner's rebellion was the last major organized slave revolt. Determined to maintain their way of life, Southerners imposed such strict controls over slave behavior that open revolts had very little chance of success. Throughout the South, night patrols, supported by money which fearful whites poured into town and county police departments, maintained a constant alert.

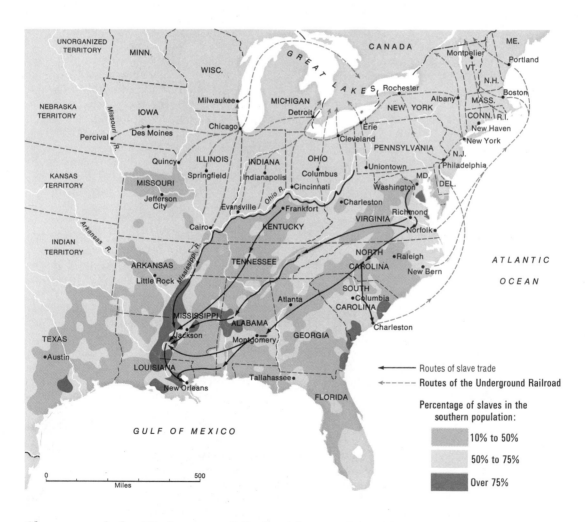

Slavery and the Underground Railroad • 1840 to 1860

Nat Turner's Plans for Rebellion

"On the 12th of May, 1828, I heard a loud noise in the heavens, and the Spirit instantly appeared to me and said the Serpent was loosened, and Christ had laid down the yoke he had borne for the sins of men, and that I should take it on and fight against the Serpent, for the time was fast approaching when the first should be last and the last should be first. . . . And by signs in the heavens that it would make known to me when I should commence the great work—and until the first sign appeared, I should conceal it from the knowledge of men—And on the appearance of the sign, (the eclipse of the sun last February) I should arise and prepare myself, and slay my enemies with their own weapons."

The Confessions of Nat Turner, 1831

Description of Nat Turner

"He is a complete fanatic, or plays his part most admirably. On other subjects he possesses an uncommon share of intelligence with a mind capable of attaining any thing; but warped and perverted by the influence of early impressions. . . . I shall not attempt to describe the effect of his narrative, as told and commented on by himself, in the condemned hole of the prison. The calm, deliberate composure with which he spoke of his late deeds and intentions, the expression of his fiend-like face when excited by enthusiasm, still bearing the stains of the blood of helpless innocence about him; clothed with rags and covered with chains; yet daring to raise his manacled hands to heaven, with a spirit soaring above the attributes of man; I looked on him my blood curdled in my veins."

Comments by Thomas R. Gray included in *The Confessions of Nat Turner*, 1831

Early Industrial Growth

During the pre-Civil War period, the foundations for the country's developing industrial economy were laid. Industrialization was spurred by technological developments that utilized the nation's massive deposits of coal, salt, oil, copper, lead, zinc, sulfur, limestone, and iron ore. Lumber and water were plentiful sources of power. Industrial development occurred at an uneven rate and tended to be concentrated in a small number of states. The South and the West lagged behind the North, and despite some technological advances, primitive techniques and distribution problems restricted production in certain areas. The country as a whole continued to use more water than steam, even though rich Pennsylvania coal fields provided a relatively cheap source of heat for smelting and steam power. In addition, many firms chose to remain small and unincorporated and continued to employ a small number of workers.

Nevertheless, the country continued to devise new techniques for converting its vast natural resources into usable forms. Before the Civil War, a process was developed to turn iron ore into steel, a durable, malleable, and inexpensive structural metal. In 1844, Charles Goodyear patented a method for "vulcanizing" rubber which made it strong, elastic, and nonsticky even under extreme temperatures, and by 1850 the rubber industry was turning out heavy rubber overshoes and knee-length boots.

The increased demand for improved methods of transportation and mechanization fanned the growth of American industry. Between 1840 and 1860 the production of pig iron tripled to meet the needs of railroad builders and farm-machinery producers. The oil industry made huge profits selling to new markets created by the kerosene lamp and the rapidly developing internal combustion engine.

During this period, mass-production methods which increased manufacturing capability were introduced. A system of manufacturing, which consisted of assembly lines, standardized operating procedures for laborers, and the use of machine tools and machines with interchangeable, precision-made parts, permitted factories to make more efficient use of people and materials. Yankee ingenuity responded to the relentless search for improved methods of production, and improvements in one area triggered expansion in another. When Isaac Singer began mass producing his sewing machine in 1851, he stimulated the growth of the garment industry.

Industrial expansion was also bolstered by the generous flow of capital into new enterprises and by the emergence of business initiative and leadership. The industrial entrepreneur and corporate form of business organization were becoming established features of American life. A powerful business community became the moving force in the development of the country's natural resources, as business interests gained control of the railroad, oil-refining, banking, meat-packing, and farm-machinery industries. By 1857 one billion dollars in private capital had been invested in the railroads, and another billion had been channeled into various manufacturing enterprises.

Government on all levels recognized the needs of the expanding business community and either directly or indirectly encouraged private enterprise. After the creation of the independent treasury for the deposit of federal funds, state banks handled all private transactions. Although some states abolished banking entirely, others, such as New York and the New England states, set up well-managed banking systems which supplied the financial support needed by new business enterprises. Both federal and state governments made land grants to the railroads. Liberal government land grants to timber and mineral interests made possible the creation of monopolies over these natural resources. While the tariffs of 1833 and 1842 were lower than those of the 1820s, they were still high enough to protect American industry from foreign competition. Only when the tariff was lowered in 1846 and again in 1857 did the manufacturing interests protest vigorously.

While government assisted developing industries, it made no effort to regulate business practices or prohibit the trend toward monopolies. To prevent labor demands from hampering their activities, companies sometimes brought unions to trial or used strikebreakers to quell boycotts and strikes.

Sectional Aspects of Industrialization

America's industrial development was concentrated in New England and the Middle Atlantic states. In New England the manufacture of cotton cloth led the Eastern industries. Iron and steel industries were centered along rivers which supplied water power for the first large-scale factories.

Although Southerners made some investments in Northern manufacturing, Southern society remained essentially agrarian. As a result, the South became increasingly dependent on Northern textile mills, Northern transportation, and Northern brokers and bankers. Only 15 percent of manufactured goods produced in the United States came from the South and Southwest, and Southern investments continued to be made primarily in cotton growing and slaves.

In the Northwest, factories sprang up to process timber into wood products, and by 1860 the country's lumber production was equal in value to its cotton-textile production. Western cattle raising supported the meat-packing and leather-tanning industries. Grain was milled into flour, meal, hard liquor, and beer by a growing number of Western mills and distilleries. The development of industry in the Northwest gradually brought this section's economic and political interests closer to those of the Northeast.

Urban Growth

The development of transportation and the rapid expansion of industry resulted in a dramatic increase in urban living before the Civil War. While city dwellers comprised only 8 percent of the population in 1820, they constituted over 20 percent by 1860. There was an almost tenfold increase in the number of new towns during the same period, and most older cities in the Northeast grew dramatically. During the early 1800s New York and Philadelphia had populations of more than ninety thousand; by 1830 their populations had risen to more than a hundred fifty thousand, and the population of New York had jumped to over eight hundred thousand. Even Boston, which lacked a navigable river connecting it to the West, more than tripled in size between 1820 and 1860. Chicago in the Middle West went from a small village of forty-five hundred in in a 1840 to a metropolis of well over a hundred thousand in 1860. In the South only the port city of New Orleans showed comparable growth, while in the newly settled Far West, San Francisco experienced a boom during the 1850s.

American cities became a study in contrasts. In 1800 Philadelphia was probably the most progressive city in America with well-planned, brightly lit streets, a good water supply, and handsome homes and public buildings. But after the industrial revolution disrupted the city's economic stability, Philadelphia became a collection of neighborhoods segregated by class. The coexistence of luxurious residences and dingy, overcrowded tenements was a common phenomenon during this period. New York may have had reason to boast of being a literary and intellectual center, but it had slums worse than those of London. While wealthy old Dutch families lived in stately yellow brick houses, beggar children scavenged among the New York streets.

Public services in the urban centers were limited. No city had an adequate sewerage system, and daily wastes were piled high on the sidewalks. In the absence of adequate sanitation facilities, pigs were allowed to forage through the garbage which littered public avenues. In Kansas City, the odor from wandering hogs was so foul that English writer Oscar Wilde complained, "They made granite eyes weep." In addition, thousands of horses pulling wagons, streetcars, and buggies deposited tons of manure each day. Wastes ran into nearby rivers, often the same source from which the public drew their water, and several major cities suffered epidemics of yellow fever.

Disease, poverty, and overcrowding caused a severe strain on fire and police protection. Street crime was a major urban problem. Muggings and murders were common; consequently, people walking the streets at night carried pistols. Large cities averaged one fire a night, and there were only

TYPE FOUNDRY AROUND 1840.

volunteer fire companies or firefighters hired by insurance firms to battle the flames.

In the early 1800s the major public services of Eastern cities were carried out on a private or voluntary basis. As the cities grew, however, their municipal governments became more important and took control of police, fire, and public-health services. Political machines emerged to fill the gap left by voluntary service groups supported by the wealthy.

The American Worker

Labor had always been scarce in America. In 1800 90 percent of Americans still lived and worked on farms, and those who worked in the cities were skilled artisans, not factory workers. However, a sizable class of wage earners began to form in response to the demands of new industries. Its members came first from the farms of the East and later from Europe.

The new industrial machinery required fewer specialized skills and less physical strength. By the early 1820s half the workers in the cotton-textile factories were children under sixteen, and by mid-century, twice as many females as males worked in the cotton mills. Many employers claimed that factory work gave young girls an opportunity to escape the boredom of farm life, to save for a trousseau, to meet new people, or to help educate a younger brother.

Some companies transported whole families from the farm to the factory. Parents and children as young as four or five worked side by side tending looms in the textile factories. Under the "Family System," they lived in factory towns provided by their employers and had little contact with the outside world. Although later generations frowned on child labor, antebellum apologists argued that it helped maintain family solidarity and provided a reasonable standard of living for the people involved.

The Boston Associates enlisted unmarried women in their late teens and early twenties to work in their Lowell, Massachusetts, mills. The "Lowell girls" enjoyed better wages and working conditions than did their English counterparts. They were well dressed and healthy, lived in relatively pleasant boarding houses, attended lectures, organized sewing circles, and edited their own literary periodicals.

On the whole, however, American workers labored long hours for low pay. Unskilled workers made only a dollar a day, and skilled workers from one to two dollars. Mill hands worked twelve to fifteen hours a day. Even the relatively favorable working conditions in the Lowell mills began to deteriorate when their management was turned over to hired professionals. In their eagerness to increase profits, these new managers lowered wages and enforced strict regimentation. For example, the girls were required to rise at 4:30 A.M. and begin work precisely at 5:00, were allowed only two thirty-minute breaks for meals, and were expected to attend church regularly. Not surprisingly, turnover was high.

Industrialization gradually modified the behavior of American workers to fit the demands of machine-oriented production. The American custom of taking time off for celebrations, hunting, and harvesting was vigorously suppressed. In Philadelphia tardy and absent workers were fined, and workers were forbidden to "carry into the factory nuts, fruits, etc., books or paper."

By 1840 employers shifted from daily wages to piece-rate payments in order to increase production. Skilled workers witnessed the degeneration of their trades as the crafting of a product by a single person gave way to the division of tasks.

The Labor Movement

Deteriorating working and living conditions blighted Eastern factory towns. Although workers were legally free, the drudgery of their lives was a form of bondage. Those who left the farms seeking to raise their standard of living endured bleak days of repetitive work for wages that barely met the cost of renting rooms, much less supporting a family. Even worse off than the mill hands were the unskilled laborers who worked in construction gangs on railroads, turnpikes, and canals.

Unable to improve their lives in the East, many factory workers and artisans moved west to look for new opportunities. An estimated one-third of the Midwestern farmers of the antebellum period had earned money for their land by working as skilled laborers in the East.

The workers who remained behind began to join together in an effort to improve their lot. In 1834 a thousand Lowell girls went on strike to pro-

THE SHOEMAKERS' STRIKE IN LYNN, MASSACHUSETTS. EIGHT HUNDRED WOMEN OPERATIVES STRUCK IN MARCH 1860.

test a 15-percent wage cut. According to a Boston newspaper, one of the protest leaders made a "flaming" speech from a stump about "the rights of women and the inequities of the 'monied aristocracy' which produced a powerful effect on her auditors, and they determined to 'have their way, if they died for it.' " But striking was regarded as a crime, and the poorly organized workers had no precedents for such protests. The leaders of the strike were fired, and the rest of the young women returned to work at reduced wages.

During this period other workers also tried to use strikes to force employers to meet their demands. Between 1831 and 1840 there were 114 strikes in Pennsylvania alone. Although the workers involved were threatened with criminal prosecution and the calling out of state troops, they believed there was no other way to press for higher wages and improved working conditions.

Eventually, skilled workers in various trades formed the country's first labor unions in order to protect their dwindling income and the loss of status caused by mass production. These early efforts to organize were opposed by both management and government. Labor unions were regarded as illegal conspiracies whose very existence menaced both employers and nonunion workers.

In 1842 the Massachusetts Supreme Court in *Commonwealth* v. *Hunt* ruled that labor unions were not illegal unless they were planning a conspiracy. Now, unions finally had official sanction. Although lasting organizations did not develop until after the Civil War, during the boom years 1834 to 1837, trade-union membership rose from twenty-six thousand to three hundred thousand.

The Panic of 1837 dealt a staggering blow to the trade-union movement. Some craft unions—independent, skilled artisans who employed journeymen and apprentices—such as the printers union, weathered the worst years, but most crafts were unable to compete with rising mass-production techniques. These crafts, together with their unions, gradually disappeared. Then, during the 1840s, labor organizations in other trades began to revive along with the economy. By the mid-1850s most skilled workers had tried with varying success to organize unions. But unskilled workers had no unions at all. Labor's greatest demand, in addition to increased wages, was the reduction of the work day to ten hours. While most strikes were broken, by 1855 seven states had passed laws ensuring a ten-hour day.

Immigrant Labor Waves of immigrants swelled the growing population of America before the Civil War. Between 1815 and 1820, 100,000 newcomers came to the United States, 500,000 arrived in the 1830s, 1,500,000 in the 1840s, and over 2,500,000 in the 1850s. Driven by unemployment, religious persecution, and hunger, they came primarily from Northern and Western Europe: Scandinavia, Germany, Great Britain, and Ireland. Steamships carrying American cotton and lumber to Europe converted unoccupied space into rough passenger quarters on their return trips. Food was bad, and quarters were cramped, stuffy, and unsanitary. Outbreaks of disease were common. During a crossing of the steamship *Lark*, for example, 158 out of 440 steerage passengers died of typhus. Nevertheless, promises of new jobs kept immigrants coming, for there was a great demand for cheap labor on farms and in factories.

The influx of immigrants before the Civil War contributed significantly to the rapid growth of the American economy. Workers from England and Wales labored in the coal mines of Pennsylvania and the lead mines of Missouri and Wisconsin. The Irish, driven from their homeland by the famine which followed the Irish potato blight, tended to settle near the Eastern seaports. Usually destitute and unskilled, they eagerly accepted jobs building the nation's railroads and digging its canals. Their desperate need for work—however deplorable the

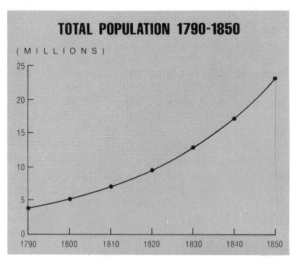

TOTAL POPULATION 1790-1850

(MILLIONS)

wages and working conditions—made them afraid to form unions, since by organizing they would displease their employers. Because the Irish demanded fewer comforts and would stay with a job for several years, they were swiftly absorbed into Northeastern factories where they worked long hours for little pay. Gradually mill owners replaced farm girls with Irish immigrants, until by 1860 the Irish accounted for over half the labor force in the New England mills.

Although the Scandinavians, Germans, Dutch, Czechs, and Finns who moved into the interior of the country were not as readily exploited as other immigrant groups, they also faced serious hardships. Life on the American frontier differed radically from life in European villages, and the newcomers were unfamiliar with the types of crops to plant. In addition, American farmers lived long distances from their neighbors, and the loneliness and isolation experienced by the immigrants took a heavy toll on their families. Yet the newcomers managed to prosper by virtue of hard work, whether as skilled craftspeople in the towns or as farmers developing their own land.

But despite their hopes, their hard work, and their contribution to American growth, the immigrants were often exploited and unhappy. Their depressed wages were hardly sufficient to live on, and many lived in dire poverty in the slums of large Eastern cities. They were ideal prospects for greedy landlords who badly overcrowded their tenements. Sanitary conditions were deplorable and the mortality rate was high.

Prejudice against immigrants was widespread. The Irish were especially disliked by native-born American Protestants for their Catholicism, which for the first time was becoming an influential religion in America. The newcomers were even blamed for their poverty and wretched living conditions, and for the spread of disease.

Conclusion

In the antebellum period American society was based on the assumption that the pursuit of individual freedom and equal economic opportunity would improve the state of society as a whole. Indeed, the tremendous untapped wealth in land and natural resources did lead to rapid expansion of the American economy and to prosperity for a large number of citizens. Nevertheless, many farmers and workers, including immigrants recently arrived from Europe, led difficult lives with little or no economic gain. Indian tribes were uprooted and relocated to new territory as a result of a growing hunger for land. Women continued to be regarded as second-class citizens, and millions of black people were trapped in a life of brutality and bondage. It would have been strange, indeed, had widespread efforts not arisen to bring American life into greater conformity with American ideals.

Readings

General Works

Billington, Ray A., *America's Frontier Heritage*. New York: Holt, Rinehart & Winston, 1966.

_____, *Westward Expansion*. New York: Macmillan, 1967.

Bruchey, Stuart, *Growth of the Modern American Economy*. New York: Harper & Row, 1975.

Clark, Thomas D., *Frontier America*. New York: Scribner's, 1969.

Davis, David B., *The Problem of Slavery in Western Culture*. New York: Cornell University Press, 1966. (Paper)

Easterlin, Richard A., *Population, Labor Force, and Long Swings in Economic Growth: The American Experience*. New York: National Bureau of Economic Research, 1968. (Distributed by Columbia University Press)

Eaton, Clement, *The Growth of Southern Civilization*. New York: Harper & Row, 1961.

———, *A History of the Old South*. New York: Macmillan, 1966.

Gates, Paul W., *The Farmer's Age: Agriculture 1815–1860*. New York: Holt, Rinehart & Winston, 1960.

Genovese, Eugene, *The Political Economy of Slavery*. New York: Pantheon, 1965. (Paper: Random).

Kraus, Michael (Ed.), *Immigration, The American Mosaic*. New York: Anvil Books. Imprint of Van Nostrand Reinhold, 1966.

North, Douglass C., *The Economic Growth of the United States*. New York: Norton, 1966.

Pessen, Edward, *Riches, Class, and Power before the Civil War*. New York: Heath, 1973.

Riegel, Robert E., and Robert G. Athearn, *America Moves West*. New York: Holt, Rinehart & Winston, 1970.

Rohrbough, Malcolm J., *The Trans-Appalachian Frontier: People, Societies, and Institutions, 1775–1850*. New York: Oxford University Press, 1978.

Special Studies
Blassingame, John W., *The Slave Community: Plantation Life in the Antebellum South*. New York: Oxford University Press, 1972.

Danhof, Clarence H., *Change in Agriculture in the Northern United States, 1820–1870*. Cambridge, Mass.: Harvard University Press, 1969.

Degler, Carl N., *Neither Black nor White: Slavery & Race Relations in Brazil & the U.S. New York:* Macmillan, 1971. (Paper)

Dick, Everett, *The Dixie Frontier*. New York: Knopf, 1948.

Elkins, Stanley M., *Slavery*. Chicago: University of Chicago Press, 1968.

Fogel, Robert W., and Stanley Engerman, *Time on the Cross*. Boston: Little, Brown, 1974.

Genovese, Eugene, *Roll, Jordon, Roll: The World the Slaves Made*. New York: Pantheon, 1974.

———, *World the Slaveholders Made*. New York: Pantheon, 1969.

Gutman, Herbert G., *The Black Family in Slavery and Freedom, 1750–1925*. New York: Pantheon, 1976.

———, *Work, Culture and Society in Industrializing America: Essays in America's Working Class and Social History*. New York: Random, 1976.

Jones, Maldwyn A., *American Immigration*. Chicago: University of Chicago Press, 1960.

Levine, Lawrence W., *Black Culture and Black Consciousness: Afro-American Folk Thought from Slavery to Freedom*. New York: Oxford University Press, 1977.

Owsley, Frank L., *Plain Folk of the Old South*. Baton Rouge: Louisiana State University Press, 1949.

Stampp, Kenneth M., *The Peculiar Institution*. New York: Knopf, 1956.

Sweet, Leonard I., *Black Images of America, 1784–1870*. New York: Norton, 1976.

Wade, Richard C., *The Urban Frontier*. Chicago: University of Chicago Press, 1959.

Ware, Norman J., *The Industrial Worker, 1840–1860*. Boston: Houghton Mifflin, 1924.

Warner, Sam Bass, Jr., *The Urban Wilderness: A History of the American City*. New York: Harper & Row, 1972.

Wright, Gavin, *The Political Economy of the Cotton South: Households, Markets and Wealth in the 19th Century*. New York: Norton, 1978.

Primary Sources
Fishel, Leslie H., Jr., and Benjamin Quarles, *The Black American: A Documentary History*. Glenview, Ill.: Scott, Foresman, 1970. (Paper)

Goodrich, Carter (Ed.), *The Government and the Economy, 1783–1861*. Indianapolis Ind: Bobbs-Merrill, 1966.

Olmsted, Frederick L., *The Cotton Kingdom*. Arthur M. Schlesinger (Ed.). New York: Knopf, 1953.

Wish, Harvey (Ed.), *Slavery in the South*. New York: Farrar, Straus & Giroux, 1964.

Biographies
Green, Constance M., *Eli Whitney and the Birth of American Technology*. Boston: Little, Brown, 1956.

Lane, Wheaton J., *Commodore Vanderbilt*. New York: Knopf, 1942.

Ortiz, Victoria, *The Sojourner Truth*. Philadelphia: Lippincott, 1974.

Fiction
Bontemps, Arna, *Black Thunder*. Boston: Beacon Press, 1968. (Paper)

Ethnic Diversity in Pre-Civil War America

THE IRISH AND THE GERMANS

BETWEEN 1650 and 1850 the fabric of European society was transformed by a dramatic rise in population and by changing economic and social conditions. The problem of integrating all these additional people into society was complicated by the technological innovations of the Industrial Revolution. As skilled artisans found their status and livelihood threatened by new factories, machines, and production methods, traditional patterns of life gradually disintegrated. In the country, farms dwindled in size as they were repeatedly subdivided between the increasing number of heirs in each new generation. Eventually many peasant families were unable to produce an adequate livelihood from their tiny plots of land. Across the sea lay America, a land of vast resources and endless opportunities. To many Europeans, driven to desperation by crop failures and debts, emigration offered the only hope for building a better life in a new country.

In the decades preceding the Civil War, more than four million of America's total population of 31.5 million were foreign-born. The immigrants who flocked to the United States during this period faced a long and hazardous ocean voyage. Steamers, which sped trans-Atlantic crossings in the 1840s, catered to wealthy passengers and valuable cargo, while the smaller wooden sailing ships offered low rates to attract poor immigrants. Each family was assigned to a bunk be-

low deck where they cooked on communal stoves and prepared their own remedies for seasickness and the contagious diseases that spread rapidly through the cramped, poorly ventilated quarters.

Roughly half of the newcomers settled in metropolitan areas, particularly New York, Boston, Chicago, Cincinnati, Milwaukee, and San Francisco. Harbor cities, such as New York and New Orleans, were inundated by the destitute and the helpless, for most travelers arrived with few resources to carry them beyond the port of entry. In 1855 Castle Garden, a huge building which had been built as a fort and later converted to a luxury theater, was turned into a receiving center. This facility, located in lower Manhattan, could accommodate up to two thousand passengers at a time. There food could be purchased, water was available for drinking and bathing, and a space could be found on a bench or the floor for a bit of sleep.

Usually the newcomers met a mixed response. Alternatively resented, admired, discriminated against, and relied upon, their eccentricities as individuals became stereotypes for their national group. The experience of the Irish and Germans, the two largest immigrant groups to arrive in America during the nineteenth century, offers a profile of the ethnic diversity that characterized the social development of the young nation.

Ireland in the 1800s was crowded with masses of impoverished tenant farmers. Although the majority of

peasants were Catholic, the small class of absentee landlords and political rulers were generally Protestant. In 1845 the great potato blight brought famine to the land. For many the only escape from religious persecution and crushing poverty lay in emigration.

Many of the Irish arrived in America weakened by their long voyage and lacking funds to begin life again as farmers. As a result, they were forced to settle in the Eastern seaports where they had landed. For the most part, they were unskilled, and before them lay a harsh adjustment to ceaseless labor and poverty in Boston and New York. Fortunately, industrialization in American cities was creating many jobs which required only brawn and the will to work. Before long Irish laborers had formed the backbone of the construction gangs which built the great canal systems, laid thousands of miles of rail, built street, sewerage, and lighting systems, and erected residential and public structures. Others became porters, tailors, and machine workers in the numerous factories. Because the pay was so low and the working hours so long, families needed more than one breadwinner to sustain them. As a result, Irish women went to work as servants, seamstresses, and washerwomen, and children were urged to earn their keep as soon as they were able.

Life for the Irish trapped in crowded city tenements was often hard and short. Some adults escaped their hopeless situation by turning to heavy drinking; youths engaged in crime and vice. The majority of Irish, however, found consolation in their cultural resources and religious institutions. In a nation dominated by Protestants —many deeply suspicious of Catholicism—the Catholic church had a significant influence on the life of the Irish immigrant. Through participation in parish activities individuals found both

social solidarity and emotional support. The neighborhood priest, who maintained a close personal relationship with his parishioners, governed most of the community's activities, and a parochial education for children was all but mandatory. In fact, some parents chose to keep their children uneducated rather than expose them to the secular influence of public schools.

The frustration of laborers desperate for work sometimes erupted in senseless acts of violence. However, local agencies gradually succeeded in channeling this rowdy energy into local politics. From manual labor the Irish moved into civil service positions, working as firefighters, police officers, and officials in departments of public works. Since dependence on the public payroll led to a direct interest in municipal government, political participation eventually became a key factor in Irish assimilation into American society. In fact, for many Irish loyalty to the Democratic party was the secular equivalent of their commitment to the Catholic church. As they mastered the art of patronage, they attained high administrative posts and won important elective offices, jobs which brought self-respect and status within the community. At the peak of their political power, Irish politicians controlled the centers of local government, as in the case of Tammany Hall during the 1820s.

The increasing visibility and power of the formerly unobtrusive Catholic community was a threat to many Protestants. Latent anti-Catholic feelings became overt, resulting not only in riots but in day-to-day discrimination in jobs and housing. Bigots blamed the immigrants for their squalid neighborhoods and rough manners and regarded them as undesirable citizens. Nineteenth-century reform movements were another source of friction between Irish and Protes-

GERMAN EMIGRANTS ARRIVE AT CASTLE GARDEN,
NEW YORK, 1879.

tant Americans. The Irish tended to view causes such as women's suffrage and temperance as Protestant-inspired and therefore insupportable. In their turn, Protestants often labeled as "Irish" or "Catholic" habits such as drinking, which they judged most urgently in need of reform. In addition, the Irish opposed abolition, for they feared that freed blacks would compete for jobs, thereby ensuring their own economic bondage.

As social problems fed religious disputes, the Irish became more resistant to reform and more insulated within their own communities. Never-

theless, despite the many factors contributing to their alienation, most Irish-Americans felt an ardent patriotism for their adopted country. This intense loyalty was clearly demonstrated during the Civil War when thousands of Irish volunteered for service on the side of the Union.

From the early to the mid-1800s Germany was a vaguely defined geographical area between the North Sea and Poland containing a politically, socially, and culturally diverse population. As in the rest of Europe, the population rose dramatically, and an influx of cheap manufactured goods

destroyed the livelihood of skilled artisans. Peasants lost their lands to large landholders, and in mid-century famine devastated Central Europe. As a result, thousands of people migrated to the cities or undertook the long voyage across the Atlantic.

The early "German" immigrants, drawn to America by the prospect of rich farmland, were a less homogeneous group than the Irish. Among them were Dutch and Swiss; Lutherans, Catholics, and Jews; farmers, artisans, and city folk. By the 1860s these newcomers constituted nearly one-third of the immigrant population. Wherever they settled they soon acquired a reputation for industry, thrift, and dependability. Other traits—their libertarian philosophies and cosmopolitan outlook—often conflicted with the narrower perspective of native-born Americans. For example, the German custom of observing the Sabbath by congregating in beer gardens for spirited discussions and song outraged the sterner Protestants.

Avoiding the open prairies and the uncivilized frontier, German peasants preferred to cluster in heavily wooded areas or to restore old farms in established communities. Nationalists among them were eager that their language and culture be preserved, for they dreamed of creating a free Germany in the New World. During the 1830s the Giessener Gesellschaft established a colony near St. Louis, and the Philadelphia German Settlement Society founded the town of Hermann on the southern bank of the Missouri River. Other settlements sprang up in Richmond, Louisville, Nashville, and Charleston. Eventually thousands migrated to southwest Texas, and by 1900 one-third of that state was German-speaking.

In the cities German-American artisans set up small shops as butchers, grocers, or bakers. Other entrepreneurs opened successful brokerage houses and banks. Some of these ventures evolved into large enterprises: Ferdinand Schumacher introduced Americans to cereal made from rolled oats, and Claus Spreckels made a fortune from his sugar refinery in San Francisco. The majority of tradespeople, however, joined the swelling ranks of the moderately prosperous middle class.

German-Americans led a varied and active social life. To maintain their cultural heritage they formed literary societies, singing clubs, musical organizations, and theater groups. By the 1850s German newspapers had become the most influential foreign-language press in the nation, encompassing 133 publications. The *Turnverein* was a group of gymnastic clubs which became instrumental in fostering political liberalism within the United States. Even more radical were the Freethinkers who proposed humanitarian and political reforms including revision of the Constitution and specific legislative devices such as initiative, referendum, and recall.

The majority of German immigrants, however, were politically and religiously conservative. Many from northern and eastern Germany were Lutheran; another large segment from Bavaria and southern Germany were Catholic. In general their governing religious organizations encouraged them to remain nonpolitical and to confine their energies to religious issues.

Many German private schools were established under Lutheran auspices. Unlike the Irish parochial schools, these institutions were less oriented toward religious instruction and more concerned with the preservation of German culture and the German language. Later generations of Germans concentrated on having the German language and curriculum taught in the public schools of their communities. These pedagogical innovations can be seen today—in vocational-training programs, physical education, and the kindergarten.

Efforts to consolidate a German-American political community in the United States were unsuccessful. Because of the varied outlooks and interests within the overall group, Germans never achieved the political clout wielded by the Irish. Nevertheless, the humanistic concerns of German-Americans were clearly expressed in their political life. In particular, German opposition to slavery became an important factor in American politics during the pre–Civil War years. German activists opposed the expansion of slavery into the territories and contributed significantly to Lincoln's election in 1860. When war broke out, Germans enlisted in surprisingly high numbers and fought with distinction at Bull Run, Shiloh, Chancellorsville, and Gettysburg.

Despite the initial hardships encountered by the Irish, the Germans, and other immigrant groups, they saw in America the hope of establishing a way of life better than the one they had left behind. To masses of Europeans, uprooted from their homelands by hunger and poverty, the opportunities offered for economic advancement and for religious and political freedom seemed prizes well worth the struggle.

11 Religion, Romanticism, and Reform

The old and moth-eaten systems of Europe have had their day, and that evening of their existence which is nigh at hand will be the token of a glorious dawn for the down-trodden people. *Here* we have planted the standard of freedom, and here we will test the capacities of men for self-government. We will see whether the law of happiness and preservation upon each individual, acting directly upon himself, be not a safer dependence than musty charters and time-worn prerogatives of tyrants. Doctrines that even now are scarcely breathed, innovations which the most fearless hardly dare propose openly, systems of policy that men would speak of at the present day in the low tones of fear . . . will, in course of time, see the light here and meet the sanction of popular favor and go into practical play. Nor let us fear that this may result in harm. All that we enjoy of freedom was in the beginning but an experiment.

Walt Whitman, *Brooklyn Daily Eagle*

Significant Events

Model community at New Harmony, Indiana [1825]

Temperance movement organized (American Temperance Union) [1826]

American Peace Society [1828]

William Lloyd Garrison publishes *The Liberator* [1831]

New England Anti-Slavery Society [1832]

American Anti-Slavery Society [1833]

Gag Rule [1836–1844]

Elijah P. Lovejoy murdered [1837]

Mount Holyoke College established [1837]

Brook Farm [1841]

Women's Rights Convention: Seneca Falls, N.Y. [1848]

DURING THE 1840s LYCEUM LECTURES BECAME A POPULAR FORM OF ADULT EDUCATION. THIS LECTURER IS EXPLAINING THE SCIENCE OF METEOROLOGY TO AN ADULT AUDIENCE IN NEW YORK CITY.

The great political and economic changes that characterized American life in the forty years preceding the Civil War were accompanied by tremendous social and intellectual ferment. Alexis de Tocqueville, a young Frenchman who visited the United States between 1831 and 1832, witnessed many of the trends himself and wrote about them with an accuracy and insight which have never been surpassed. His enduring work, *Democracy in America*, still serves as a valuable introduction to a study of the American character.

Tocqueville believed that the emphasis on equality had become *the* dominant influence in America by the 1830s. Although he recognized that individual liberty had always been an important American ideal, he argued that the desire for equality, or "the sovereignty of the people" as he called it, was the most vital force in shaping the American way of life:

In America, the principle of the sovereignty of the people is not either barren or concealed, as it is with some other nations; it is recognized by the customs and proclaimed by the laws; it spreads freely, and arrives without impediment at its most remote consequences. If there be a country in the world where the doctrine of the sovereignty of the people can be fairly appreciated, where it can be studied in its application to the affairs of society, and where its dangers and advantages may be judged, that country is assuredly America.

Tocqueville also pointed to the potential danger of the American love of equality, claiming that an excessive emphasis on egalitarianism could lead to a "tyranny of the majority." As he put it, ". . . every citizen, being assimilated to all the rest, is *lost in the crowd*, and nothing stands conspicuous but the great and imposing image of the people at large." In other words, although the desire for equality seemed to be linked with freedom, it could eventually lead to an enslavement of individuals to the opinions of the majority. Thus Tocqueville believed that the future greatness of America depended on its ability to strike the proper balance between freedom and equality. The sovereignty of the people would have to be matched by the development and preservation of personal liberty.

In addition to warning of the dangers of egalitarianism, Tocqueville observed many ways in which the ideal was influencing American life. For instance, he concluded that equality of opportunity had helped make the American people pragmatic and had given them an intense love of wealth and material comfort. "They will habitually prefer the useful to the beautiful, and they will require that the beautiful should be useful," he wrote. He also noted a growing preference for commerce and industry over agriculture and realized that the abundance of natural wealth had made the United States a middle-class country. He viewed the country's economic and social life as a unique phenomenon, characterized more by fluidity than by rigid stratification.

Tocqueville noted two other American qualities which came together in the first half of the nineteenth century to produce a powerful spirit of reform: the tendency to create organizations for civic improvement and the belief in human perfectibility. He wrote that,

. . . as castes disappear and the classes of society approximate, . . . as ancient opinions are dissipated, and others take their place—the image of an ideal but always fugitive perfection presents itself to the human mind. Continual changes are then every instant occurring under the observation of every man . . .

Although Tocqueville did not comment directly on the reform movements that were beginning to take shape, he did describe the two most important factors that characterized those efforts. He understood the theoretical ideals which motivated American reformers as well as their efforts to further their goals through collective action.

Tocqueville also perceived that a democratic and pragmatic people could still be attracted to art and literature:

As soon as the multitude begin to take an interest in the labors of the mind, it finds out that to excel in some of them is a powerful means of acquiring fame, power, or wealth. The restless ambition which equality begets instantly takes this direction, as it does all others. The number of those who cultivate science, letters, and the arts, becomes immense.

As we will see, the tremendous volume of American literary and artistic production during this period testifies to the accuracy of Tocqueville's observation. Finally, in the area of religion, Tocqueville believed that a democratic country would emphasize the substance of beliefs more than external observances. In no other country, he judged, did the Christian religion have "a greater influence over the souls of men." The intellectual and religious developments of the pre–Civil War era tend to bear out this basic assumption.

The Religious and Philosophical Background

Like the period of the Great Awakening in the early eighteenth century, the pre–Civil War era was a time of tremendous religious ferment in America. Some of the changes were disruptive; such orthodox doctrines as Puritanism were rejected by many people. On the other hand, the same religious currents that undermined some established churches often led to the creation of new religious movements.

The Second Great Awakening

The Revolutionary era had led to a decline in church membership. In an effort to restore religious enthusiasm, a number of New England ministers began a revival movement which spread rapidly throughout the country in the 1790s. Its appeal was especially strong in the South and the West, where it had a major impact on frontier life.

These revival meetings were scenes of emotional preaching and mass conversions. A typical gathering began on a Thursday and lasted until the following Tuesday. In 1801, in Cane Ridge, Kentucky, forty ministers preached for a week to thousands of "sinners." At one point, more than a hundred people passed out from exhaustion following outbursts of evangelical frenzy. Sometimes recalcitrant reprobates, moved by the evangelical spirit of a camp meeting, would even change their ways. The Reverend David Rice reported, "drunkards, profane swearers, liars, quarrelsome persons, etc., are remarkably reformed. . . . Some neighborhoods,

METHODIST CAMP MEETING.

noted for their vicious and profligate manners are now as much noted for their piety and good order."

By the 1820s the South and West were in the throes of yet another outburst of revivalism which lasted almost until the Civil War. Like the Puritans, evangelical groups such as the Baptists and Methodists believed in a literal heaven and hell and emphasized the Bible as an infallible record of divine revelation. Unlike the Puritans, however, whose doctrine stressed that salvation was predestined, the evangelical churches taught that salvation could be gained through conversion and moral behavior. They preached the egalitarian concept that people could be spiritually reborn by accepting Christ's atonement for the sins of humanity. Acceptance of Christ as their savior would enable them to receive God's mercy and forgiveness. Converted to a new and better life, they would inevitably desire to share this gift with others.

American revivalist ministers, such as Charles G. Finney and Peter Cartwright, combined an interest in saving souls with a conviction that Christians must help make society better. The idea that not only the individual but society itself could be transformed was a unifying theme in a nation of religious diversity. It was the religious counterpart of the optimistic belief of the Jacksonians that it was America's destiny to create a truly egalitarian society.

The Second Great Awakening had a marked effect on the life of frontier towns. When evangelists moved on, they usually left behind established churches which became the cultural centers of the Western towns, serving as information clearing centers and meetinghouses. The desire of church members to foster Christian education led them to organize and support the growth of religious colleges. This activity set a valuable precedent for the development of higher education in nineteenth-century America.

The emphasis of the revival movement on the moral and spiritual importance of reform had much appeal for many Northerners as well. Wealthy reformers sought to improve the lot of the urban poor. Working-class people were attracted to the idea of self-improvement through temperance, and the fast-growing Methodist church was particularly effective in converting them by emphasizing the importance of family and community responsibility.

In the South the spirit of reform that accompanied revivalism was more subdued. In order to keep their members, many of whom were slaveholders, the churches gradually retreated from any criticism of the institution of slavery. Confident that evangelical religion offered no threat to their way of life, and that religious training would make their slaves more obedient and docile, Southern planters encouraged their slaves to convert.

In addition to strengthening the Methodists, the Baptists, and the social reformers, the strong tide of religious ferment led to the creation of several new religious movements. One of them, the Disciples of Christ, or Christian church, was organized for the purpose of restoring Christian unity through simple faith in the Gospels. By the 1850s the church claimed a hundred thousand converts. Another important group was founded on a belief in the Second Coming of Christ. The movement began in the 1830s, when William Miller, a Baptist minister from Vermont, predicted the exact day in 1844 on which the Second Coming, or Advent, would occur. As the judgment day approached, Miller's disciples sold their belongings and assembled on hilltops to await the coming of the Lord. When the prophecy failed to materialize, many of the faithful gave up the idea entirely, and the group nearly dissolved. However, a core of believers justified the "Great Disappointment" and in 1846 organized a formal denomination known as the Seventh Day Adventist Church.

Mormonism

The Mormon religion, or Church of Jesus Christ of Latter-Day Saints, was founded by Joseph Smith in an area of western New York State inhabited by many poor people and known as the "Burned Over District." Influenced by the early nineteenth-century revival movement which had centered in this area, Smith reported in 1827 that he had been led by angels to a place where "there was a book deposited written upon gold plates." With the aid of Divine Providence, Smith said, he translated the tablets which were published in 1830 as the *Book of Mormon.* Written in the style of the Old Testament, the book is a mystical interpretation of the origins of the American Indians and the role to be played in their conversion by the spiritual descendants of the "good" tribes—the "latter-day saints." That same year Smith organized his church, assuming complete control as God's "prophet."

The Mormon outlook appealed to many people who had not prospered in the early nineteenth century. Most converts were poor and without much education. Alienated from an individualist and capitalist society, they longed for a sense of security and a cause to which they could devote their energies. Acceptance of the revelation that established the church's doctrines and organization gave unswerving purpose to their lives.

The Mormons' communal economic life and their belief in the unity of church and state aroused the opposition of their individualist neighbors. Clearly unwelcome, they moved first to Ohio, then to Missouri. In 1839, they made another journey, this time to Illinois, where they established the town of Nauvoo. As their numbers grew, so did their political power in a state equally divided between Whigs and Democrats. In the early 1840s Smith reported receiving a revelation approving the practice of polygamy, and he took several wives. As many other Mormon men began to follow Smith's example, the antagonism of their neighbors increased, finally exploding in 1844 in a wave of violence which reached its peak when Smith ordered an opposition newspaper destroyed for challenging his authority. Smith was arrested by the Illinois government, but before he could be brought to trial he was dragged from the jail by an anti-Mormon mob and brutally murdered. In order to preserve their way of life, most of the Mormons migrated into almost uninhabited Mexican territory in the Far West.

Unitarianism

In yet another religious upheaval in New England, many Congregationalists began to leave their church and follow a new belief: Unitarianism. Unitarianism was particularly attractive because it stressed the basic goodness of human beings and defined God as a merciful, benign being. Deeply influenced by the philosophy of the Enlightenment, Unitarians emphasized the value of human reason. They preached toleration of other faiths, urged individuals to come to their own interpretations of the Scriptures, rejected the doctrine of the Trinity, and asserted that salvation was available to everyone. Unitarianism tended to appeal to a small, well-educated group, but an offshoot of the movement, called Universalism, attracted other segments of the

New England population. Based on the belief that it was God's purpose to save every human being from sin, Universalism gradually spread throughout the North in the pre–Civil War period. Thus the pessimistic world view of Puritanism, which had held many Americans in its grip for so long, was first weakened by the Enlightenment and then undermined by Unitarianism and Universalism.

Transcendentalism

The transcendentalist movement, which began in New England in 1836, had its roots in two opposing modes of thought: American Unitarianism and European romanticism. Romanticism had emerged in the late eighteenth century as a rejection of the Enlightenment philosophy that reason could solve all human problems. Disillusioned by the violent excesses of the French Revolution and its aftermath, romanticists dismissed reason as a value, adopting instead the idea that instinct, or intuition, was the true guide to experience. Whereas the Enlightenment thinkers had cultivated the normal, the rational, the ordered, and the familiar, romanticists searched out the bizarre, the emotional, and the exotic. The Enlightenment had stressed the universality of human characteristics; romanticism emphasized the uniqueness of each individual. Romanticists also extolled untamed nature and the "natural" person. Less intellectual and more likely to follow instinct, the natural person was considered more in touch with the essentials of life than the city dweller or the overrefined aristocrat. This democratic aspect of romantic thought appealed to Americans.

Influenced by romantic thought, transcendentalism was not so much a religion as a philosophical system. As noted, most people associated with this school of thought came from New England, a surprising number had attended Harvard University, and some had served as Unitarian ministers. Starting as an informal discussion club, the group met and exchanged ideas in and around Concord, Massachusetts, for several years.

The transcendentalists were seeking a living religion, one that did not depend on a specific theological creed. They rejected the Unitarian faith as "corpse-cold," uninspiring, too dependent on human reason, and too neglectful of the human spirit.

In their search for ultimate reality, the transcendentalists argued against some aspects of the Enlightenment theories of John Locke. Locke had claimed that ideas do not arise spontaneously in the mind, but that they come about through sense impressions received from the external world. The transcendentalists contended that ordinary experience could never be a guide to absolute truth. They believed that real knowledge could be gained only by intuition, the process of looking within oneself.

In order to find reality, one had to rise above, or transcend, the level of knowledge obtained through reason. They urged people to place more trust in intuition than in reason. For the transcendentalists, an almost mystical perception of God, or the "Over-Soul," was the most important goal in life. This led them to celebrate nature, which they believed to be a direct expression of God.

Like the revivalists, the transcendentalists sought an emotional acceptance of God's power. But unlike most revivalists, they were intensely intellectual and had a great respect for formal learning. Since they stressed progress through the process of individual inspiration, most transcendentalists shared Tocqueville's fear of a stifling conformity to which the egalitarian spirit of America could eventually lead. They also disliked the trends toward industrialism and materialism. Many transcendentalists were prominent social activists, supporting and often working in the various reform groups of the period. Several of them made important contributions to the development of American literature in the mid-nineteenth century.

Ralph Waldo Emerson

Emerson (1803–1882), the leading transcendentalist and the most famous American writer and thinker of his day, was descended from a long line of New England ministers. He graduated from Harvard in 1821 and soon became a Unitarian minister himself. After several years in the ministry, he found that he disliked many of the mundane duties of his profession and that the rational theology of Unitarianism was no longer satisfying to him. Because of his need to be free of the confinements of organized religion, he resigned as pastor of the Second Church of Boston in 1831. Next, he set out on the first of three trips to Europe, where he met many of the leading intellectuals. After returning to America, Emerson settled in Concord, Massachusetts, and began to earn his living as an essayist and lecturer.

His first book, *Nature*, was published in 1836. Calling for a new independent American philosophy, this work marked the beginning of the transcendental movement. "There are new lands, new men, new thoughts," he wrote. "Let us demand our own works and laws and worship." In 1840, led by Emerson and the literary critic Margaret Fuller, the members of the Transcendental Club began to issue a publication called *The Dial*. Through this magazine they hoped to inspire many writers with the idea of an American national literature.

Emerson's frequent lectures served as the basis for several books of essays. Never systematic, his philosophy consists of brilliant flashes of insight. One of his most basic ideas is the importance of self-knowledge. Like many Americans of his time, he was intensely individualistic. In one of his most famous essays, entitled "Self Reliance," he wrote, "Nothing is at last sacred but the integrity of your own mind." Like the revivalists, Emerson believed in the continual necessity of self-improvement.

RALPH WALDO EMERSON.

Smith Attacks American Culture

"In the four quarters of the globe, who reads an American book? or goes to an American play? or looks at an American picture or statue? What does the world yet owe to American physicians or surgeons? What new substances have their chemists discovered? or what old ones have they analyzed? What new constellations have been discovered by the telescopes of Americans?—what have they done in the mathematics? Who drinks out of American glasses? or eats from American plates? or wears American coats or gowns? or sleeps in American blankets?—Finally, under which of the old tyrannical governments of Europe is every sixth man a Slave, whom his fellow-creatures may buy and sell and torture?"

Sydney Smith,
Edinburgh Review, 1820

Ingersoll Defends Cultural Advances

"The American mind has been called more to political, scientific, and mechanical, than to literary exertion. . . . In the literature of imagination, our standard is considerably below that of England, France, Germany and perhaps Italy. . . . In the literature of fact, of education, of politics, and of perhaps even science, European pre-eminence is by no means so decided. The American schools, the church, the state, the bar, the medical profession, are, all but the last, largely, and all of them adequately, supplied by their own literature. Respectable histories are extant by American authors. . . . In biography, without equal means, have we not done as much since we began as our English masters? In the literature as well as the learning of the sciences, botany, mineralogy, metallurgy, entomology, ornithology, astronomy, and navigation, there is no reason to be ashamed of our proficiency. . . ."

Charles Jared Ingersoll,
*A Discourse Concerning the Influence
of America on the Mind*, 1823

Another attitude which Emerson embodied was the American belief in equality. Though he was not an admirer of General Jackson, Emerson was nevertheless in tune with the democratic outlook of the era. In fact, much of his work was really an intellectual form of democratic theory. He believed that all people were not only equal, but that they were also part of one great spiritual mind, the Over-Soul: "There is one mind common to all individual men. Every man is an inlet to the same and to all of the same. . . . Who hath access to this universal mind is a party to all that is or can be done, for this is the only and sovereign agent."

The Growth of American Literature

In the early years of the republic writers often believed they had a moral and social obligation to try to produce a nationalistic literature. In the late 1700s playwrights such as Royall Tyler and William Dunlop had paid homage to the superior morals and manners of the new republic. The poetry of Philip Freneau and William Cullen Bryant drew inspiration from American scenes and experiences. Phillis Wheatley, an African slave who was educated by her Boston owners, celebrated the events of the Revolution in her couplets. The Hartford Wits, a coterie of Yale graduates, vied with each other to create an American epic to equal Vergil's *Aeneid*, but their attempts "merely imitated the rhapsodic effusions of debased eighteenth-century European epic poetry." In the early nineteenth century James Fenimore Cooper's *Leatherstocking Tales* depicted highly romanticized confrontations between Indians and settlers. And the Southern writer William Gilmore Simms glorified the frontier in such novels as *The Yemassee*. Yet, as one critic observed, "Despite all these efforts to create a truly distinctive literature, it was apparent . . . that Americans had not gotten off their literary knees to Europe."

By the early nineteenth century European romanticism also was beginning to influence the American imagination. The United States was changing dramatically during this period as a result of immigration and urbanization, and many Americans were bewildered by what was happening. Romantic literature could calm some of the anxieties without really challenging the American concept of progress. A good example of this type of writing is Washington Irving's "Rip Van Winkle," a tale about a man who falls asleep for twenty years, then wakes up to find everything changed. Another important literary theme was the contrast between American and European life. Although the European past was often portrayed positively, many plays and books used the contemporary high culture of the Continent as an object of derision. By contrast, the simple virtues of the American yeoman could then be emphasized favorably.

The immediate pre–Civil War era saw the first flowering of a distinctively American literature. Between 1850 and 1855 the following masterpieces were published: Nathaniel Hawthorne's *The Scarlet Letter* and *The House of Seven Gables*, Herman Melville's *Moby Dick*, Henry David Thoreau's *Walden*, and Walt Whitman's *Leaves of Grass*. As one modern critic has written: "You may search all the rest of American literature without being able to collect a group of books equal to these in imaginative quality."

Henry David Thoreau

Born in Concord, Massachusetts, Thoreau (1817–1862) was a close friend and former student of Emerson. After graduating from Harvard, Thoreau tried in vain to carry on his family's pencil-making business. He also taught school for a while in Concord, but resigned when the directors insisted that he dispense corporal punishment. In September 1839 he and his brother took a two-week river journey, which became the subject of Thoreau's first book, *A Week on the Concord and Merrimack Rivers.*

Thoreau went to stay with the Emerson family and served as their handyman for two years. He also associated with the Transcendental Club, which was active in Concord during this period. In March 1845 he built a small cabin at Walden Pond on the Emersons' property, a mile and a half from the center of Concord. For two years he used the area as a retreat from civilization. During this period he also spent a night in jail for refusing to pay a poll tax in protest against slavery and the Mexican War. He justified this protest in an essay called "On Civil Disobedience," which has become one of the most famous works ever written on the subject of nonviolent resistance.

Thoreau's masterpiece, *Walden*, appeared in 1854. The book is a condensation of most of the journals he kept throughout his life, summing up his individualistic philosophy and his observations of nature. As a modern critic has written: "The lesson he had taught himself, and which he tried to teach others, was summed up in the one word 'simplify.' That meant simplify the outward circumstances of your life, simplify your needs and your ambitions; learn to delight in the simple pleasures which the world of Nature affords. It meant also, scorn public opinion, refuse to accept the common definitions of success, refuse to be moved by the judgment of others." In *Walden* Thoreau also wrote of his objections to certain changes in the American way of life. He was especially opposed to the encroachment of the new industrial and urban forms of civilization. After the publication of *Walden* Thoreau devoted himself to lecturing in support of the antislavery movement and to continuing his explorations into natural history.

Thoreau's life was indeed as simple as the virtues he preached. As Emerson said in his moving portrait of his younger friend: "He was bred to no profession; he never married; he lived alone; he never went to church; he never voted; he refused to pay a tax to the state; he ate no flesh, he drank no wine, he never knew the use of tobacco; and though a naturalist, he used neither trap nor gun. He chose, wisely no doubt for himself, to be the bachelor of thought and Nature."

Thoreau has become famous in the twentieth century for his defense of individual nonconformity. He stated clearly and poetically his belief that it is more important to obey one's conscience than to obey the laws of the land. He also stressed that one must be willing to bear the responsibility for one's actions, especially for actions contrary to accepted norms and laws. In his love of nature and his ability to see the natural world as an expression of God, Thoreau was a romanticist. When Thoreau was on his deathbed, a friend asked him if he had made his peace with God. Thoreau responded, "I am not aware that we ever quarreled."

Walt Whitman

Walt Whitman (1819–1892) was America's first great national poet. Born in Long Island, Whitman left school when he was thirteen. In 1832 he began his long association with the newspaper business, working first as a printer's devil for the *Long Island Patriot.* By 1846 he had become editor of the *Brooklyn Eagle,* but his efforts on behalf of various social reform movements eventually led to his dismissal.

Whitman's life changed dramatically in 1848, when he began to write his masterpiece, *Leaves of Grass.* The first edition appeared in 1855, transforming him from a traveling journalist into a major poet. In the preface he set forth his artistic ideals, asserting that a poet must be in harmony with the common people of the time. This belief in the artistic value of everyday life made the subject matter of his poems unique, even shocking. Whitman's themes of individualism, physical freedom, and democracy were based on "common idioms, manners, the earth, the rude visage of animals and trees, and what is vulgar," as he himself remarked. The style of his poetry, especially its handling of sex with frankness, was also unconventional. Instead of the normal repetitious rhythms which people expected, Whitman's verse was plain and unornamented.

By 1860 *Leaves of Grass* had grown to 456 pages, with 122 new poems. Whitman continued to add to the volume for the rest of his life. It went through nine editions altogether, the last one appearing in 1892, the year of Whitman's death.

Nathaniel Hawthorne

In a sense, Emerson, Whitman, and Thoreau were all optimists. Each of them was critical of certain aspects of American culture—its conformity, its inequalities, and its materialism. But because of their belief in the essential goodness of all human beings, they felt that American life could be progressively improved. Writing at the same time, however, were three literary figures who did not hold such a positive view of life. Nathaniel Hawthorne, Herman Melville, and Edgar Allan Poe were romantic

NATHANIEL HAWTHORNE.

writers in that they ardently studied nature, valued instinct more than intellect, and were fond of exotic places and times long past. But they were also part of the older Puritan tradition, seeing evil as an active, inescapable force in human affairs. As artists, they were basically haunted by the notions of sin, vice, and pride.

Hawthorne (1804–1864) was born in Salem, Massachusetts, the son of a local shipmaster. After four years at Bowdoin College, Hawthorne retired to Salem, where he lived a lonely, secluded existence. Like his Puritan ancestors, Hawthorne was obsessed with the subject of sinfulness. Although he did not attend church, he spent much of his time brooding over religious concepts and filling his notebooks with short stories of evil impulses and the mysteries of sin.

Many critics recognized Hawthorne's mastery of prose, but the skepticism and sense of hopelessness in his work went against the popular outlook. For instance, his masterpiece, *The Scarlet Letter*, is the story of a Puritan woman who commits adultery with a minister. After giving birth to an illegitimate child, the adultress is forced by the members of the community to wear the letter *A* sewn to her dress. At the end of his tormented life, the minister finally confesses his part in the sinful situation by opening his shirt to reveal an identical letter *A* branded into his flesh by God. Hawthorne's preoccupation with this kind of tragic subject offended many Americans caught up in the prevailing optimism of the mid-nineteenth century.

Hawthorne was also drawn to the problem of the exceptional individual, the artist, within a democratic, mass society. Like Tocqueville, he was extremely concerned by the level of mediocrity which egalitarianism seemed to impose. But he also saw that an artist had to be able to establish close, human relationships with others. Even though some amount of solitude was required in order to be an artist, he considered withdrawal as an aristocratic, European attitude. This was the paradox he faced in seeking to affirm American values. To Hawthorne, human fulfillment meant resolving the contradiction, and his explorations of the issue took on a deeply religious tone.

Herman Melville

One of Hawthorne's few close friends was the novelist and poet Herman Melville (1819–1891). After working as a bank clerk and a schoolteacher in Albany, New York, Melville shipped out to sea as a cabin boy in 1837. Shortly after his return, he went off again on a series of South Sea voyages, including an eighteen-month trip on the whaler *Acushnet*. In 1842 he jumped ship in the Marquesas Islands, spending an idyllic month with friendly natives before sailing to Tahiti on an Australian ship. He finally returned to Albany after serving in the United States Navy.

Melville now began writing, using his voyages as material for his first two books, *Typee* and *Omoo*, published in 1846 and 1847. *Mardi, Redburn,* and *White-Jacket* were further stories of adventure at sea, but Melville reached his full artistic stature with the publication of *Moby Dick* in 1851.

Considered by many as one of the finest novels ever written, *Moby Dick* has been interpreted in many ways. On one level it is a superb adventure story with a wealth of detailed information about whaling. But it is also a penetrating psychological study of human obsession and a serious exploration of the human need to find meaning in the universe. The book's plot concerns a Yankee skipper, Ahab, who lost a leg in a struggle with a great white whale named Moby Dick. Driven by a desire for revenge, Ahab forces his crew to pursue Moby Dick from one end of the Pacific to the other. In the end the whale attacks the ship, and Ahab and all but one of the crew members are killed. According to some modern critics, the story represents Melville's belief that the world is as morally colorless as the white whale. Melville seems to be saying that human beings cannot tolerate such meaninglessness, however, and Ahab is both heroic and insane in attempting to conquer Moby Dick as the embodiment of evil.

Edgar Allan Poe

Born in Boston, Poe (1809–1849) was orphaned at the age of three and raised by a wealthy tobacco merchant. In 1826 he enrolled at the University of Virginia, where he drank and gambled so heavily that his adoptive father disowned him. Although his literary brilliance was soon apparent in "Tamerlane and Other Poems" (1827), gambling debts and alcoholism were already shaping the pattern of his life. Despite his great talent, Poe was never able to earn more than $300 a year as a journalist, critic, editor, and writer.

In 1836 Poe married his cousin, and they moved to New York in search of broader literary horizons. Still troubled by gambling and drinking, however, he went from one position to another, writing prolifically in order to support himself. In 1845 his wife died of tuberculosis, and Poe's private life became even more chaotic. In addition to his heavy drinking he had periods of mental instability.

In spite of his personal tragedies, Poe created a truly impressive body of work. His literary criticism is highly original, and his fine short stories include some of the first detective stories ever written. As a poet his bizarre symbolism and his experiments in pure sound had a great influence on the French symbolist movement. Like Hawthorne and Melville, Poe never accepted the American belief that human nature was perfectible. He wrote in one letter: "I have no faith in human perfectibility. I think that human exertion will have no appreciable effect upon humanity. Man is now only more active—not more happy, nor more wise—than he was six thousand years ago."

The Arts

While American literature was in full flower, American art was not far behind. Americans of the mid-nineteenth century began to take an active interest in their own society, and this was reflected in painting, sculpture, architecture, and music as well as in literature.

American Painting

In the 1820s neoclassicism, an outgrowth of the Enlightenment emphasis on reason, was the ruling style in American painting. Neoclassical art, which began in France, ignored the unusual and emotional aspects of a scene, stressing instead the rational and the ideal. Rather than showing real people, neoclassical painting showed idealized human beings, freed of any special individuality. The style was used primarily to praise such American virtues as the opportunity for upward mobility. Portraits of the merchant elite, for example, used classical backdrops and poses drawn from Greek art to give dignity to the subjects.

By the mid-1840s, however, a new mood emerged. Just as religion and literature reacted against the Enlightenment's emphasis on rationality, the visual arts now turned away from neoclassical values. "Picturesqueness" became the most desired quality in painting, and artists depicted simple, natural scenes. Themes were drawn from natural landscapes and the American frontier, reflecting the prevailing mood of romantic nationalism.

The attitude of the American clergy toward art also underwent a significant change at this time. Whereas traditionally the clergy had viewed art as frivolous, they now saw an opportunity to use it as an ally in their effort to reform society. In order to uplift the tastes of the masses, ministers urged an identification of art with religion. Landscape art made one aware of nature, and many ministers felt that nature was the "interpreter of God." Thus, insofar as art developed an awareness of nature, it was considered worthwhile.

This trend was reinforced by the fact that many American artists of this period were inspired by the British Pre-Raphaelites, who believed that the artist had a duty to uplift the masses. The Pre-Raphaelite school had a romantic view of the visual arts; its purpose was to democratize art. In the words of one artist, its goals were, "to make Art popular, not by making it low, but by opening its principles to the comprehension of all kinds in the proportion of their intelligence and moral development. . . ." In order to obtain truthfulness, the artist had to paint directly from nature.

The Hudson River School Thomas Cole (1801–1848), founder of the Hudson River School of landscape painting, emigrated to America from England at the age of seventeen. In 1825 he began painting landscapes, attempting to capture a sense of the vast American wilderness. By the time he established his own studio in New York in 1827, he was the acknowledged leader of a group of American romantic painters who drew their inspiration from the countryside along the Hudson River.

Cole was infused with a love of nature typical of romanticism. His works are distinguished by their wonderfully luminous quality, capturing the feel of light and air at a specific moment in time. Nevertheless, Cole had mixed feelings about the natural world. Sometimes he felt that whatever was natural was good and that contemplation of a landscape could lead a person to a religious experience. But other times he assumed the old Puritan view, feeling that nature was frightening, sinful, diseased, and unbearably lonely.

When Cole died, Asher Durand (1796–1886) took his place as America's greatest living painter. Durand had none of Cole's ambivalence about the absolute goodness of nature. Convinced that God was in every mountain stream, he regarded landscape as the perfect form of moral art. Durand promoted a purely Emersonian view of the natural world, marked by optimism over what could be learned from artistic images drawn directly from nature.

Overall there were about a dozen painters who were considered part of the Hudson River School. Although the members of the group differed widely in style, training, and even subject matter, they shared a strong view of the importance of humanity's relationship to the natural world. In many ways the Hudson River School expressed in visual images what the transcendentalists were saying with words—that nature is full of meaning and that Americans should develop a deeper appreciation for the vast wilderness of their own country.

Genre Painters The new interest painters were showing in American subjects was not confined to landscapes or to the natural beauty of the country. During this period there were several important painters who drew their inspiration from scenes of

the everyday life of the people of America. One of the most famous of these genre artists, as this type of painting is called, was William Sidney Mount (1807–1868), a self-taught artist whose most popular canvases portrayed black people in their daily activities on Mount's native Long Island. Traveling around in a horse-drawn studio, Mount attempted to make his paintings seem like actual scenes from life. He had a great respect for all human beings and represented their actions with simplicity and directness.

Another well-known genre artist of the pre–Civil War period was George Caleb Bingham (1811–1879). Concentrating on styles of life along the Mississippi River, Bingham's paintings show men playing cards, making music, dancing, or fishing off boats or docks. He also created many can-

SHOOTING FOR THE BEEF BY GEORGE CALEB BINGHAM. THE ARTIST, WHO WAS RAISED IN THE BACKWOODS OF MISSOURI, AT ONE TIME PAINTED $20 PORTRAITS BUT LATER BECAME FAMOUS FOR HIS DEPICTIONS OF EVERYDAY LIFE ON THE FRONTIER.

GEORGE CATLIN TRAVELED ACROSS THE WESTERN PLAINS PAINT-ING SCENES OF THE AMERICAN INDIANS' WAY OF LIFE. (Smithsonian Institution)

vases capturing moments in the political life of Missouri, such as stump speakers and election-day scenes.

Another group of mid-nineteenth century painters turned to the West for subjects. One of these was George Catlin (1796–1872). Driven by the romantic belief that "a state of primitive wilderness and rudeness" was a sure guide to ideal beauty, Catlin traveled across the Great Plains, painting hundreds of portraits of the Indians he met and lived with. He worked at such great speed that in 1832, for example, he managed to cover fifteen hundred miles and paint 135 canvases in just eighty-six days. In addition to portraits, he painted scenes of warriors enduring ritual tortures or hunting buffalo and medicine men dancing in splendid plumage.

Catlin referred to the Indians as a "truly lofty and noble race," and he genuinely lamented the white people's destruction of the native American way of life. Acting on his convictions, he attempted to raise money and gain sympathy for the Indians by touring Europe with his paintings and a troupe of braves who performed war dances for the awed spectators.

Sculpture, Architecture, and Music

Achievements in American sculpture, architecture, and music came late and were more modest. Most nineteenth-century American architects emulated the models of the French school of fine arts; Hiram Powers's *The Greek Slave* was typical of American sculptors' dependence on the classical tradition of Greece and Rome. The most notable composer in the United States before the Civil War came out of the slightly vulgar realm of the minstrel show. Stephen Foster, a dreamer and outcast who destroyed himself with alcohol, wrote more than two hundred songs, including tunes like "Camptown Races" and "Oh! Susanna" that have formed the bedrock of American popular music. It was not until the beginning of the twentieth century, however, that truly American styles of sculpture, architecture, and "classical" music began to emerge.

Reform Movements

"It may be said, without much exaggeration, that everything is done now by Societies," wrote the Unitarian minister William Ellery Channing. "You can scarcely name an object for which some institution has not been formed." From the 1820s until the outbreak of the Civil War, a host of humanitarian reform movements flourished, particularly in the Northeast. For those who sought to correct the evils of society, the main issues of concern included schools, prisons, mental hospitals, factory conditions, alcoholism, war, the status of women, and—above all else—slavery.

This wide-ranging spirit of reform was a social response to the same intellectual currents that were shaping religion and influencing the arts during the period—evangelicalism, Unitarianism, and transcendentalism. The revival movement intensified the national mood of self-examination, leading to a general desire to root out the ills of society. Many Presbyterians, Baptists, and Congregationalists responded enthusiastically to the call to transform society through the purification of individual character. The Unitarian emphasis on the basic goodness of human beings also matched the optimism of the era, encouraging men and women to believe that the possibilities were limitless for those with a righteous cause. Finally, transcendentalism provided a basis for linking religion and an ethical life. Considered as a whole, the reform movements of the pre–Civil War period were essentially moral crusades aimed at bringing the secular experience of human beings into harmony with God's will.

Led mostly by ministers and members of the evangelical churches, the goal of missionary reformers was to reduce such social evils as drunkenness and immorality. The American Bible Society and the American Sunday School Union were instrumental in the growth of the peace and prison-reform movements. Despite Herculean efforts, however, these reformers failed to gain legislative support for the two plans that were dearest to their hearts: laws to enforce the Sabbath as a day of rest and to curb the sale of liquor. Most Americans regarded such regulations as an invasion of individual freedom, and many store owners saw them as an economic threat.

The early missionary reformers not only failed in their immediate goals, but they gradually were replaced by reformers who took a broader view. The aim of the missionary reformers had been to control social problems, not to shake the foundations of society. Their theology was based on a belief in the perfectibility of humanity through moral transformation. Growing out of this belief, a new phase of reform emerged in the 1830s which stressed that an orderly society could be established only by freeing human beings from oppressive institutions. Abolitionists and temperance reformers adopted this approach. One outcome of this search for human perfectibility was the experiment in establishing model communities.

Model Communities

Industrialization had a noticeably detrimental effect on the living conditions of most American working people. As a result, some reformers wanted to reorganize society into self-sufficient communal units. The reformers hoped that their model communities would have a gradual and deeply curative effect on the country as a whole.

The most famous nonreligious experimental community was New Harmony in Indiana. Organized in the 1820s by Robert Owen, a successful Scottish industrialist and social philosopher, New Harmony was planned as a socialist venture. Property was cooperatively owned by all members of the village, and the community was governed by a democratically elected assembly. Work was limited to an eight-hour day, and a variety of extra activities was provided to interest the inhabitants. Most of the people who came to New Harmony, however, were too individualistic to adjust to communal living. Moreover, Owen wanted to run the community himself, based on his own ideals. He was firmly opposed to organized religion, marriage, and the holding of private property. As a result of his radical approach, the project soon broke down and was abandoned after a few years.

Another utopian experiment involved a group of forty communities set up in the 1840s based on principles established by the French socialist Charles Fourier. Unlike Owen, Fourier proposed that each community (called a phalanx) should be organized as a business unit. Profits from all the enterprises were to be divided between dividends to the stockholders and salaries and cash rewards for the members. Each member was allowed to choose his or her occupation; for the sake of variety, people were to change jobs *eight* times a day. As with Owen's project, each community in the phalanx movement was to be a self-sufficient unit, operating outside the rest of society.

Brook Farm was founded in 1841 to provide a center for the application of transcendentalist views. At one time or another, many of New England's leading intellectuals lived at Brook Farm, which was located only ten miles outside of Boston. The goal of its chief sponsor, George Ripley, was to combine the life of the thinker and worker, to develop the complete individual. Activities at Brook Farm included manual labor, manufacturing, several progressive schools, and stimulating conversation in the evenings. In 1845, however, it was converted into a Fourierist phalanx, and a year later a disastrous fire completely destroyed the farm building. The community was forced to disband as an economic failure.

Ultimately, all the other Fourierist communities failed, although not always for economic reasons. Exactly why they disbanded is a matter of conjecture, for many of them actually were not in debt at all. One reason was probably that many of the farmers on these communities were city-bred intellectuals, ill-prepared for rural life.

On the other hand, several experimental communities based on religious principles flourished during this period. One community, the Perfectionist settlement of John Humphrey Noyes at Oneida, New York, lasted until the 1880s. Members of this sect believed in complete release from sin through faith in God, faith healing, and a complex system of marriage in which all men and women in the community were each other's husbands and wives. At-

tempting to create the Kingdom of Heaven on earth through communal living, the members devoted themselves to logging, farming, and the manufacture of fur traps and silver plate. In spite of internal success, popular antagonism to the community's marital practices ultimately forced its abandonment.

Of all the religious communities, the largest and most successful were founded by the Shakers. Led by Mother Ann Lee, the Shakers established more than a dozen economically self-supporting communities, some of which survived well into the twentieth century. These Shaker villages grew because they offered a fulfilling life to people who had undergone the emotional transformation of revivalism and yet had no other way to express their profound change in feelings. A major aspect of Shaker belief was celibacy, and this practice helps to account for the eventual extinction of the sect. Nevertheless, more than any other group, it was the Shakers who demonstrated that utopian communities could be both socially and economically viable.

Educational Reform

The modernizing spirit of the pre–Civil War years gradually influenced American educational philosophy. Before the 1820s most Americans had not considered free public education a responsibility of the state, and even in the decades following many traditionalists continued to insist that education should not be at public expense. By the 1830s, however, educational reformers began to demand state-supported primary education.

The goal of the educational reformers was threefold: to make the United States a land of greater equality, to protect the stability of the republic, and to Americanize new immigrants. The popularity of McGuffey's *Readers* stemmed from the fact that they stressed the very qualities that the reformers believed were needed to achieve these goals: promptness, honesty, dependability, and persistence in completing a task. Reformers such as Horace Mann were aware of the growing tendency for one class in society to possess all the wealth and education, while the rest remained in poverty and ignorance. They perceived this as a threat to a truly democratic society. As Mann asserted, "If we do not prepare children to become good citizens, if we do not enrich their minds with knowledge . . . then

THE TITLE PAGE OF McGUFFEY'S *SECOND ECLECTIC READER*. THE ELEMENTARY READERS CONTAINED STORIES AND POEMS THAT STRESSED HONESTY AND MORALITY. THE MORE ADVANCED *READERS* CONTAINED MASTERPIECES OF LITERATURE AND FAMOUS SPEECHES.

equal educational opportunity for workers to combat a decline in their economic and social conditions. At the same time, however, a large number of the children of working-class families either did not go to school or left as soon as they were old enough to contribute to the family income. Many Roman Catholics (especially the Irish) also resisted sending their children to a public school system whose values they perceived as basically Protestant (although there was no official religious instruction). To preserve their identity as a separate group and to assure continued allegience to Catholic theology, Roman Catholics decided to create their own school system.

Nevertheless, with the exception of the South, by the 1850s most states had accepted Mann's position that education should be tax-supported. Several states passed laws requiring local communities to open public primary schools, and tax-supported public high schools also began to be built across the country. In addition, the system of state universities was gaining some ground. Funded by government land grants, seventeen state universities had been opened by 1860. Despite this great progress, however, education was not compulsory, nor were educational opportunities available equally to all segments of society. For example, either no provision or only limited provision was made for the education of black children in the North. Similarly, before the 1850s, most colleges did not admit women students, and women who aspired to higher education generally attended female seminaries.

Adult education The upsurge of interest in education benefited adults as well as children. Since publishing was a thriving industry well before the Civil War, many books, newspapers, and periodicals were available to the general public. Many of the books sold in America appealed to the strong instinct for self-improvement: readers could buy how-to-do-it manuals on every subject from raising chickens to carving tombstones. Moreover, newspapers, once relatively expensive, were now being sold for only a penny a copy. This enabled the evergrowing num-

our republic must go down to destruction, as others have gone before it." In 1837 the Commonwealth of Massachusetts established the first board of education. As first secretary of the board, Mann was responsible for lengthening the school term in Massachusetts, organizing a state association of teachers, and increasing teachers' salaries. Later he also helped create the first teacher-training college in America.

Demands for the expansion of educational opportunity met with mixed reactions. The well-to-do often supported the building of schools in order to transmit American values to new immigrants. They believed such training would help preserve the family and moral standards during a time of great economic change. Many workingmen's associations in towns throughout the country also supported the ideas of the reformers. They stressed the need for

ber of readers to keep informed on such subjects as domestic politics and innovations in the arts and sciences.

Adult education was furthered in a somewhat more formal manner by the lyceum movement, which started in Massachusetts in 1826 under the influence of Josiah Holbrook. A nationally organized system of public lectures on important topics of the period, the lyceum movement brought famous thinkers and writers to large audiences in hundreds of small communities across the country. Leaders of the various reform movements were also frequent lyceum speakers.

Prisons and Mental Hospitals

Many pre–Civil War humanitarians turned their attention to improving the American prison system. In essence this was a struggle to change the emphasis from punishing the guilty to reforming the weak. Recognizing that colonial criminal codes had been exceedingly harsh, most states amended their criminal codes in an attempt to create more humane laws. By the 1840s nine states had abolished imprisonment for debt, some states had provided for the separation of young offenders from hardened criminals in prisons, and a number of reform schools for youthful offenders had been established. A few states even did away with capital punishment. Sentences which previously had been so severe that juries were reluctant to convict anyone were brought into line.

But because legal measures failed to reduce crime, the idea developed that the roots of criminal behavior might lie in the breakdown of traditional family life and discipline. Consequently, penologists began shifting their focus away from the legal system toward a study of the criminal's background and the prison environment. Gradually people came to see the penitentiary as a place where the criminal could be removed from social disorder, kept in a controlled environment, and, hopefully, rehabilitated. The prison-reform movement, then, was based on the idea that the source of corruption was usually external rather than inherent in the human mind.

Some of the prison reforms of this period seem very harsh by the standards of today. The Auburn System, introduced into a New York prison, consisted of solitary confinement by night and absolute silence during meals and work by day. Reformers believed that this procedure would lead convicts to reflect at length on their wrongdoings. Pennsylvania went so far as to subject its prisoners to total isolation around the clock. Strangely enough, many visiting European penologists hailed this system as the most enlightened approach they had ever seen.

The construction of publicly supported institutions for the insane came out of the same impulse as prison reform. Between 1830 and 1860 many asylums were built, on the theory that mentally deficient behavior was caused by the environment and rehabilitation could be achieved by removing disturbed people from a disordered atmosphere. A Boston schoolmistress named Dorothea Dix was the leading crusader for improved conditions for the mentally ill. For almost fifty years she toured the country, speaking on behalf of better treatment for the insane and helping to convince most states to open public asylums.

Although the new special institutions for criminals and the insane did create improved environments for rehabilitation, they were highly restrictive. They completely isolated the inmates without really attempting to prepare them for an eventual return to society.

The Temperance Movement

The temperance movement paralleled the beginnings of industrialism and probably commanded more attention than any cause other than the abolition of slavery. While drinking was especially heavy among the working class and new immigrants, it was by no means limited to them. The clergy of several churches, especially the Methodist, denounced drunkenness as contributing to poverty, crime, and mental illness. Early nineteenth-century statistics did connect crime with drunkenness, but temperance advocates were concerned, too, about the detrimental influence of alcohol on workers' productivity.

Led by Dr. Justin Edwards, the issue developed into a movement in its own right after 1826 when the American Temperance Union was organized. To publicize their cause, temperance workers distributed tracts that illustrated the harmful effects of alcohol. Soon many local temperance societies were formed, and in 1833 the union became a national organization. Requiring a pledge of total abstinence from liquor, it attracted more than a million members within a year. The union also served as a training ground for work in other areas of reform.

A battle soon developed among temperance reformers over whether to continue to demand total abstinence or to permit the use of alcohol in moderation. While this conflict finally split the movement apart, those who wanted total abstinence revived the crusade in the 1840s under the guidance of the reformer Neal Dow. His efforts secured the passage in 1851 of a law to prohibit the manufacture and sale of liquor in his own state of Maine, and within a few years twelve other states in the North had passed similar statutes.

The Peace Movement

Although it did not have as wide an appeal as the crusade against liquor, the peace movement attracted many reformers. One American religious denomination, the Quakers, had long held that wars were evil and that conscientious people should not participate in them. Moreover, many of the revivalist sects of the early nineteenth century began to argue that killing was absolutely inconsistent with the teachings of Christ. By 1819 more than a dozen local peace societies had been created, and in 1828 a Maine merchant named William Ladd established the American Peace Society to coordinate activities by the local chapters. Unfortunately, the Civil War and its aftermath sidetracked most pacifist efforts, and the early peace movement all but evaporated.

The Women's Rights Movement

The rhetoric of the American Revolution did little to change the status of women in early nineteenth-century America. Indeed, as the young republic became more urbanized and industrialized, the roles of men and women became more clearly defined and separated both physically and psychologically. Men played crucial roles in the dynamic and productive economy; women ran the home and pre-

THE AGE OF IRON, OR MAN AS HE EXPECTS TO BE IS A SATIRICAL COMMENT ON THE WOMEN'S RIGHTS MOVEMENT.

served and transmitted cultural values to the upcoming generation.

While many young men gained at least some education by the end of the colonial period, illiteracy among women was widespread. Even those who advocated higher education for women emphasized that the value of education for women lay in helping them become better mothers. By the early nineteenth century, areas such as medicine and law, which had been open to women to a limited degree in the eighteenth century, now required professional training. Middle-class women, who might have aspired to these occupations, were effectively excluded from them because they were denied admission to the new medical and law schools. Women were barred from most institutions of higher education, on the theory that they were too frail to study certain subjects or that too much knowledge would make them unsuitable for marriage. Only in the professions of teaching and librarianship, where there was a desperate shortage, were women admitted after taking normal-school training.

The lives of middle-class women became increasingly distant from the lives of poor women. Working-class women were forced for economic reasons to leave their homes and take jobs in the factories. Even though these jobs were low paying they did offer women some advancement in income as well as opportunities to get out of the home usually denied women in easier economic circumstances.

Yet women of all classes were restricted by numerous inequities carried over from colonial times. Many state legal codes permitted husbands to beat their wives "with a reasonable instrument." Every cent a wife earned was legally her husband's. In divorce cases, which were on the increase, husbands were far more likely to be awarded custody of the children than were wives. Although married women could make contracts, they could not make wills or hold property in their own names unless their husbands established a separate estate for them. Except that they could legally hold property, single women enjoyed as few civil rights as married women. They were not allowed to speak before mixed audiences or deliver sermons, much less vote or hold public office.

In an effort to secure woman's acceptance of her subordinate status, there was a concerted effort by a number of male writers to idealize her role as wife and mother. Women were portrayed as being intuitive, pure, pious, domestic, and morally superior to men. As one historian described it: the "primary accountability for the moral welfare of society" was given to women; "the administrative and intellectual reigns of organized religion and politics" were under the control of men.

In a society based on the concept of egalitarianism, intelligent women were frustrated by such prescriptions, and many sought ways to involve themselves in a larger range of activities. The revival movement of the 1820s and 1830s enabled women to participate in social action by working in voluntary evangelical associations. Women were permitted to speak out at most revival meetings, and many women even started their own female benevolent societies. It was the antislavery movement, however, which gave women their most important outlet for political action and organization. Their participation in this far-reaching movement set the stage for their own call for emancipation. Two of the pioneer female abolitionists were Sarah and Angelina Grimké, the first women to win the right to speak on the evils of slavery at mixed public gatherings. In response to attacks on their participation, they answered that if a great moral reformation of American society was to occur, women had to take a part in it on an equal footing with men. In the words of Angelina Grimké, "What can woman do for the slave when she herself is under the feet of man and shamed into silence?" The accuracy of Grimké's words was brought home to two other antislavery activists, Lucretia Mott and Elizabeth Cady Stanton, who traveled to London in 1840 to attend the World Anti-Slavery Convention, only to be excluded from the proceedings because they were women.

It was a logical step for women outraged by the debasement of black people to perceive the close resemblance to their own subordinate position in society. Using the Declaration of Independence as the standard from which to attack slavery, they began applying its principles to their own position. With Lucretia Mott, Mrs. Stanton organized the first Women's Rights Convention at Seneca Falls, New York in 1848. The women who attended adopted the goal of equality with men and pressed their demand for the right to vote. Although this "inalienable right to elective franchise" was not gained until the twentieth century, other conventions were held during the 1850s, and more and more reformers, including some men, joined the movement. The temperance leader, Susan B. Anthony, formed a lifelong partnership with Stanton to further the cause of women's rights.

The pre–Civil War period did see several significant victories for the principle of sexual equality. Massive petition campaigns, for instance, forced a number of states to pass legislation recognizing the right of married women to hold property. Mississippi passed such an act in 1839, and sixteen other states followed by 1850. Teaching positions in elementary schools, which in some places had been open only to men, became available everywhere to women. A religious college, Oberlin, opened its doors to women in 1833 and thus became the first coeducational institution. In 1837 a women's college, Mount Holyoke, was established by Mary Lyon. By the 1850s Antioch College and the University of Iowa were accepting young women as students. While Elizabeth Blackwell had to overcome almost insurmountable obstacles to become the country's first woman doctor, in 1850 the Women's Medical College of Pennsylvania was founded, thus explicitly recognizing for the first time the right of women to prepare for a career in medicine. Finally, a few women were licensed to preach. As one historian has stated, a "silent revolution" was taking place.

The Abolitionist Movement

The continuing use of slave labor in a country supposedly devoted to individual freedom was the most explosive issue of the pre–Civil War period. By 1804 all Northern states had arranged for an immediate or gradual abolition of slavery. By 1808 Congress had banned the importation of slaves into the United States, and optimistic opponents of slavery imagined that the institution would soon die out. However, as the world cotton market expanded, slavery grew in importance. As the use of slave labor became economically more significant in the South, it became more repellent to Northern reform leaders.

The abolitionist movement which emerged in the 1830s was based on the idea that the use of slave labor was immoral. Furthermore, abolitionists believed that it was their mission to bring slaveowners to redemption for their immorality and cruelty. Because of the moralistic thrust of the movement, it had much in common with revivalism. It used many of the techniques developed by revivalists, such as highly emotional lectures, mass distribution of tracts and petitions, and an ongoing series of meetings to publicize the cause. Religious impulses provided the intellectual foundation for much of the antislavery movement. Established Protestant churches formed auxiliary organizations which became centers for abolitionist activity. Religious fervor also motivated some of the major antislavery tracts, including *Uncle Tom's Cabin*, which the book's author, Harriet Beecher Stowe, declared had been written by God. On the other hand, religious arguments were used by defenders of slavery as well. Southern theologians cited biblical texts which they claimed proved black inferiority, including Moses' acceptance of servitude, and St. Paul's advice to be obedient toward one's master. In this way the controversy created schisms within such established churches as the Baptists, Methodists, and Presbyterians.

FREDERICK DOUGLASS.

Many free blacks throughout the country worked diligently to undermine the institution of slavery. Although in the South they could do little to protest their conditions, in the North blacks established benevolent societies, mutual-aid associations, and secret fraternal orders designed to aid members of their community. Blacks also formed their own Methodist and Baptist churches in reaction to discrimination in the white-dominated churches. Free Northern blacks and former slaves were primarily responsible for the Underground Railroad. Harriet Tubman risked her life by venturing into the South on countless occasions to help more than three hundred slaves to freedom. After his own escape from slavery in 1838, Frederick Douglass became an active participant in the Underground Railroad in Rochester, New York. In addition, "personal liberty" laws passed by Northern states in the 1850s barred local officials from assisting in the capture of fugitive slaves, thereby greatly aiding the Underground Railroad. Black-run vigilance committees were organized in the 1830s to help clothe, feed, and shelter fugitives from the South.

Anti-Slavery Crusaders However, the crusade against slavery received its most powerful impetus when William Lloyd Garrison began to publish his newspaper, *The Liberator*, in 1831. Garrison, a young reformer active in the temperance and peace movements, was unswerving in his belief that slavery must be abolished. In the first issue of his controversial publication Garrison gave notice of his fierce determination: "I am in earnest—I will not equivocate—I will not excuse—I will not retreat a single inch—and I WILL BE HEARD."

Calling for immediate freedom for all blacks, he was opposed to the idea of gradual emancipation as well as to a widely discussed plan for the state governments to compensate slaveowners for freeing their slaves. Since he was also a pacifist, Garrison did not recommend armed coercion against the South. His only weapon was moral persuasion, through which he hoped to lead Southerners to repentance. To this end he founded the New England Anti-Slavery Society in 1832 and helped organize the American Anti-Slavery Society a year later.

Garrison was one of the most radical of the abolitionist leaders. Because the Constitution specifically recognized the legality of slavery, he considered the entire federal government to be as immoral as any slaveowner. He called the Constitution "a covenant with death and an agreement with hell" and publicly burned a copy of it. As the abolitionist movement grew, Garrison's extremism and his inability to compromise diminished his influence outside of New England.

With the organization of the American Anti-Slavery Society, several other leaders began to emerge. The most prominent abolitionist in the West was Theodore Dwight Weld, whose book *American Slavery As It Is* (1839) was an important indictment of the system. Weld began his career as an evangelist, preaching in favor of temperance and eventually abolition. He had been converted by the famous evangelist Charles G. Finney and soon began using revivalist techniques himself in the crusade against slavery. Weld was a powerful speaker whose eloquence and organizational abilities helped carry the abolitionist movement to the small-town and farming population of the Midwest. Weld stressed that human beings are capable of making a choice between good and evil. Slavery was evil, he argued, because it denied individuals control of their own destiny; therefore the goal of the abolitionist movement must be to free those held in bondage.

The period following the establishment of the Anti-Slavery Society saw a number of violent incidents by property owners against abolitionist speakers and free blacks. These riots were usually well planned by men prominent in community affairs, including professional leaders and politicians. Local police offered little protection to abolitionists, who were repeatedly accused of seeking to integrate the races. Garrison was threatened by mobs several times, but the most violent expression of antiabolitionist resentment was the shooting of Reverend Elijah P. Lovejoy in 1837. Lovejoy, the editor of an antislavery newspaper in Alton, Illinois, was shot and killed by a rioting mob. Abolitionists mourned him as a martyr to the cause of human dignity and freedom of the press.

Although they were initially unpopular as agitators who were threatening vast economic investments and an established pattern of race relations, the abolitionists gradually gained support among the small-town and farming populations of the Northern states after the middle of the 1830s. A flood of literature arguing the immorality of human bondage helped convince many people that slavery should be abolished. The issue was further dramatized by the martyrdom of Lovejoy as well as by the hostile reception in Congress to a flood of petitions to end the slave trade in the District of Columbia. Southern members of Congress were so outraged that they persuaded Congress to pass the Gag Rule in 1836, providing that none of the petitions should be read to the members. John Quincy Adams, now serving in the House of Representatives, was a strong defender of free speech and an opponent of slavery expansion. He led the fight against the rule until it was repealed in 1844. In the minds of many Northerners the antislavery crusade was now not only a moral issue but a matter of protection of civil rights.

A New Direction From the beginning, however, the abolitionists were seriously divided among themselves. One cause of dissension was the participation of women and blacks in the movement. Radicals such as Garrison supported the women's demands for equal rights and the opportunity to speak out against slavery in public. A few other leaders were willing to recommend certain blacks as antislavery lecturers. Most abolitionists, however, believed that women speakers would ruin any chance for a widespread public appeal. Many felt that black lecturers would precipitate feelings of racial prejudice and possibly even mob violence. To advance their cause, many abolitionists believed they had to move cautiously.

The issue of working through the political process to undermine the institution of slavery gradually ultimately led to a major split in the abolitionist movement. Garrison and the radicals opposed involvement in politics, since political action would be a slow process requiring compromise. Garrison argued that the national and state governments were the chief instruments of force to preserve slavery. His differences with more moderate abolitionists, who wished to pressure the government for action against slavery, reached the breaking point at the annual meeting of the Anti-Slavery Society in 1840, and most of the moderates left the organization at that time. Some of them went on to form the Liberty party, which polled seven thousand votes in the presidential election of 1840. Garrison's supporters ridiculed these meager results, claiming that

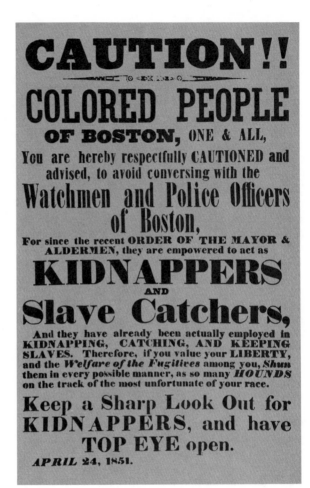

CAUTION!!

COLORED PEOPLE

OF BOSTON, ONE & ALL,

You are hereby respectfully CAUTIONED and advised, to avoid conversing with the

Watchmen and Police Officers of Boston,

For since the recent ORDER OF THE MAYOR & ALDERMEN, they are empowered to act as

KIDNAPPERS

AND

Slave Catchers,

And they have already been actually employed in KIDNAPPING, CATCHING, AND KEEPING SLAVES. Therefore, if you value your LIBERTY, and the *Welfare of the Fugitives* among you, *Shun* them in every possible manner, as so many *HOUNDS* on the track of the most unfortunate of your race.

Keep a Sharp Look Out for KIDNAPPERS, and have TOP EYE open.

APRIL 24, 1851.

the moderates had sold out their moral principles in vain. Four years later, however, Liberty party candidate James G. Birney was able to increase the total to sixty-two thousand votes.

Soon, abolitionism gained even wider appeal as it became associated with the question of westward expansion. Northerners who had not originally been sympathetic to the abolitionist cause began to fear for the future of the Western territories. They believed that if slavery was allowed to expand westward, free workers would be forced to compete with slave labor. No longer an abstract moral question, slavery was becoming a tangible economic issue in the North. These concerns were reflected in the slogan of the Free Soil party, political successor of the

Liberty party: "Free Soil, Free Speech, Free Labor, and Free Men." In 1848 the party, which promised to keep slavery out of the territories, nominated ex-president Martin Van Buren who received almost three hundred thousand votes. Moreover, there was now a small but formidable group of political abolitionists sitting in Congress who opposed the expansion of slavery into the Western territories. This group included Senators Charles Sumner of Massachusetts, Salmon P. Chase of Ohio, and William H. Seward of New York, and Congressmen Joshua R. Giddings of Ohio and George P. Julian of Indiana.

The Southern Defense of Slavery Before the rise of abolitionism, there was an attempt, fostered mainly by Southern whites, to find a solution to racial tensions by transporting free blacks to Africa. In 1817 the American Colonization Society was formed, and under its auspices the black republic of Liberia was established in West Africa. The movement, however, proved unsuccessful. Northern reformers began to suspect that the society, composed mainly of Southerners, was simply looking for a way to rid the United States of free blacks, who represented a threat to slavery. Most blacks refused to leave the country, feeling that America was now their home and that they should receive their full rights as citizens. Between 1821 and 1867 fewer than fifteen thousand blacks out of a total black population of approximately 4.4 million (slave and free combined) left the United States to settle in Liberia.

By the late 1830s, however, many Southerners began to take the offensive in support of slavery. Led by John C. Calhoun, they now described the institution as a "positive good." In a famous statement made in 1837 Calhoun said:

I hold that the present state of civilization, where two races of different origin, and distinguished by color, and other physical differences, as well as intellectual, are brought together, the relation now existing in the slaveholding States between the two is, instead of an evil, a good—a positive good . . . . I hold then, that there never has yet existed a wealthy and civilized society in which one portion of the community did not, in point of fact, live on the labor of the other . . . . I may say with truth that in few countries is so much left to the share of the laborer, and so little exacted from him, or where there is more kind attention paid to him in sickness or infirmities of age.

Many of the most commonly advanced proslavery arguments are expressed in Calhoun's statement. In essence, the champions of slavery contended that every advanced society needed slaves, that all great civilizations had depended on the use of an inferior class of people to do the menial work.

In a strong attack on the evils of the Northern industrial system, apologists for slavery also claimed that Southern slaves enjoyed much more security and comfort than did Northern industrial workers, the "wage slaves" of the factory system. Another argument was that slaves were a form of private property and that no outsider had a right to interfere with someone else's possessions. Finally, many people believed that slavery was justified by references in the Bible and in the works of ancient Greek and Roman philosophers. Some people even claimed that blacks were destined to servitude on the grounds that they were anthropologically inferior to whites.

Supporters of slavery portrayed the condition of the blacks in the rosiest of terms. George Fitzhugh, a Virginia lawyer and sociologist, attacked the individualistic and egalitarian society of the North as selfish and exploitive. He wrote in 1854 that a Southern farm by contrast, "is the beau ideal of Communism: it is a joint concern, in which the slave consumes more than the master, of the coarse products, and is far happier, because . . . he is always sure of a support."

In truth, slave life became increasingly intolerable as the Southern masters became more and more anxious about revolts and abolitionism. Slaves were forbidden by law to read or write in most Southern states. Punishments became harsher, living and working conditions more deplorable, and controls tighter as slaveowners feared for the future of the institution of slavery.

The status of free blacks always posed a threat to Southern racial stereotypes and to the control of slaves. As a result, the movement of free blacks was more tightly restricted, and free blacks were prohibited from contacts with slaves, placed under surveillance, and limited in their opportunities for employment. By the 1830s slaveowners who wished to free their slaves were under severe social pressure not to do so.

Ironically, as the debate on the morality of slavery intensified, the civil liberties of Southerners in general became more tightly restricted. Most

Southern states made it illegal for postmasters to accept abolitionist literature. Southern education excluded all mention of abolitionist ideas. Books were banned or censored, liberal teachers were fired, and reform for any cause whatsoever was grounds for suspicion. As the South fought to save slavery, it became the bastion of reaction.

Conclusion

The spirit of reform in early nineteenth-century America had far-reaching consequences. Out of the humanitarian desire to transform society through moral regeneration, the causes of equality for women and freedom for blacks were brought forcefully before the American public. In the decades before the Civil War the antislavery movement, dealing with the most crucial issue of the period, became connected with the issues of civil liberties and the control of the Western frontier. Thus abolitionism, which began as the moral crusade of a few reformers, became the preoccupation of millions of Americans. It was the intimate connection between westward expansion and the future of slavery that was the primary cause of political and moral tension in the United States during the 1840s and 1850s.

Readings

General Works

Boorstin, Daniel, *The Americans: The National Experience*. New York: Random, 1965.

Davis, David B. (Ed.), *Ante-Bellum Reform*. New York: Harper & Row, 1967.

Douglas, Ann, *The Feminization of American Culture*. New York: Avon, 1977.

Eaton, Clement, *The Mind of the Old South*. Baton Rouge: Louisiana State University Press, 1964.

Griffin, Clyde S., *The Ferment of Reform, 1830–1860*. New York: Thomas Y. Crowell, 1968. (Paper)

Jones, Howard M., *Revolution and Romanticism*. Cambridge, Mass.: Harvard University Press, 1974.

Larkin, Oliver W., *Art and Life in America*. New York: Holt, Rinehart & Winston, 1960.

Levin, David, *History as Romantic Art*. Stanford, Calif.: Stanford University Press, 1959.

Marty, Martin E., *Righteous Empire: The Protestant Experience in America*. New York: Dial, 1970. (Paper)

Matthiessen, F. O., *American Renaissance*. London: Oxford University Press, 1941.

Parrington, Vernon L., *Main Currents in American Thought*, Vols. I–III. New York: Harcourt, Brace, 1927–1930.

Wright, Louis B., *Culture on the Moving Frontier*. Bloomington, Ind.: Indiana University Press, 1955.

Special Studies

Bartlett, Irving H., *The American Mind in the Mid-Nineteenth Century*. New York: Thomas Y. Crowell, 1967.

Bestor, Arthur J., Jr., *Backwoods Utopias*. Philadelphia: University of Pennsylvania Press, 1950.

Brooks, Van Wyck, *The Flowering of New England*. Cleveland: World, 1936.

Cash, W. J., *The Mind of the South*. New York: Knopf, 1941.

Duberman, Martin (Ed.), *The Antislavery Vanguard*. Princeton, N.J.: Princeton University Press, 1965.

DuBois, Ellen Carol, *Feminism and Suffrage: The Emergence of an Independent Women's Movement in America, 1848–1869*. Ithaca, N.Y.: Cornell University Press, 1978.

Dumond, Dwight L., *Antislavery*. Ann Arbor: University of Michigan Press, 1961.

Filler, Louis, *The Crusade Against Slavery*. New York: Harper, 1960.

Flexner, Eleanor, *Century of Struggle: The Women's Rights Movement in the United States*. Cambridge, Mass.: Harvard University Press, 1959.

Fredrickson, George M., *Black Image in the White Mind: The Debate on Afro-American Character and Destiny, 1817–1914*. New York: Harper & Row, 1972. (Paper)

Jenkins, Williams, *Pro-Slavery Thought in the Old South*. Chapel Hill: University of North Carolina Press, 1935.

Kraditor, Aileen, *Means and Ends in American Abolitionism: Garrison and His Critics on Strategy and Tactics, 1834–1850*. New York: Pantheon, 1969.

McKelvey, Blake, *American Prisons: A Study in American Social History Prior to 1915*. Montclair, N.J.: Patterson Smith, 1977.

O'Neill, William L., *The Woman Movement: Feminism in the United States and England*. New York: Watts, 1971.

Perry, Lewis, *Radical Abolitionism: Anarchy and the Government of God in Antislavery Thought*. Ithaca, N.Y.: Cornell University Press, 1973.

Quarles, Benjamin, *Black Abolitionists*. New York: Oxford University Press, 1969. (Paper)

Rothman, David, *The Discovery of the Asylum: Social Order and Disorder in the New Republic*. Boston: Little, Brown, 1971. (Paper)

Smith, Timothy L., *Revivalism and Social Reform in Mid-Nineteenth Century America*. New York: Abingdon Press, 1957.

Sorin, Gerald, *Abolitionism: A New Perspective*. New York: Praeger, 1972.

Tyler, Alice F., *Freedom's Ferment*. Minneapolis: University of Minnesota Press, 1944 (Paper: Harper Torchbooks).

Walters, Ronald G., *The Antislavery Appeal: American Abolitionism after 1830*. Baltimore, Md.: Johns Hopkins, 1976.

_____*American Reformers, 1815–1860*. New York: Hill and Wang, 1978.

Wiecek, William M., *The Sources of Anti-slavery Constitutionalism in America, 1760–1848*. Ithaca, N.Y.: Cornell Univeristy Press, 1977.

Primary Sources

Commager, Henry S., *The Age of Reform 1830–1860*. Princeton, N.J.: Van Nostrand, 1960.

Kraditor, Aileen S. (Ed.), *Up From the Pedestal: Selected Writings in the History of American Feminism*. New York: Times Books, 1968.

McKitrick, Eric L. (Ed.), *Slavery Defended*. Englewood Cliffs, N.J.: Prentice-Hall, 1963.

Miller, Perry (Ed.), *Margaret Fuller: American Romantic*. Garden City, N.Y.: Doubleday Anchor, 1963.

Thomas, John L., *Slavery Attacked*. Englewood Cliffs, N.J.: Prentice-Hall, 1965.

Tocqueville, Alexis de, *Democracy in America*, Vols. I–II. Phillip Bradley (Ed.). New York: Viking, 1945.

Biographies

Arvin, Newton, *Herman Melville*. New York: William Sloane, 1950.

Banner, Lois W., *Elizabeth Cady Stanton, A Radical for Women's Rights*. Boston: Little, Brown, 1979.

Krutch, Joseph W., *Henry David Thoreau*. New York: William Sloane, 1948.

Marshall, H. E., *Dorothea Dix: Forgotten Samaritan*. Chapel Hill: University of North Carolina Press, 1937.

Merrill, Walter M., *Against Wind and Tide: A Biography of William Lloyd Garrison*. Cambridge, Mass.: Harvard University Press, 1963.

Nye, Russel B., *William Lloyd Garrison and the Humanitarian Reformers*. Boston: Little, Brown, 1955.

Rusk, Ralph L., *The Life of Ralph Waldo Emerson*. New York: Scribner's, 1949.

Schor, Joel, *Henry Highland Garnet: A Voice of Black Radicalism in the Nineteenth Century*. Westport, Conn.: Greenwood, 1977.

Thomas, John L., *The Liberator: William Lloyd Garrison*. Boston: Little, Brown, 1963.

Margaret Fuller

FEMINIST, ROMANTIC, AND VISIONARY

If Boston lawyer Timothy Fuller could have foreseen where his educational plans for his daughter, Margaret, would lead, he might have thought twice about drilling her in Latin when she was still a toddler. But Fuller wanted his daughter to have the education he would have given a son. Like many scholarly men of the early 1800s he never questioned the "whither" or "whether" of learning, and he was a stern taskmaster. Under his tutelage Margaret Fuller studied history, mathematics, philosophy, and the Bible, and by the age of seven she was familiar with the classics in French, Spanish, German, and Greek.

Margaret Fuller was an apt and eager student, but she paid a high price for her exceptional education. The rigors of her studies led to severe headaches and nervous afflictions, which plagued her throughout her life. Because she did not attend public school,

she had few playmates, and her mother was busy with the younger children. Fuller became a lonely and introspective little girl. In her memoirs she describes terrible nightmares filled with "spectral illusions" and loathsome colossal faces. Small wonder she walked in her sleep.

A problem with her vision finally ended Fuller's concentrated studies with her father, and at fourteen she was sent to the Misses Prescott's private school for girls in Groton, Massachusetts. It was not an easy adjustment, for Fuller was tall and overweight and openly contemptuous of second-rate intellects. Eventually her classmates tired of the novelty of her eccentricities and her feverish attempts at lively conversation. Alienated by her pride and intelligence, they joined forces in a cruel parody of her habit of rouging her cheeks before attending evening meals. Although Fuller appeared forgiving, she became a furtive troublemaker who created school-wide dissension by spreading false rumors.

Margaret Fuller finished her education at a private coeducational school in Cambridgeport. There she was admired and emulated by the younger girls and found she could hold

MARGARET FULLER.

her own in spirited discussions with the boys. Among her classmates were Oliver Wendell Holmes, who would later become a Supreme Court justice, and Richard Henry Dana, who developed into a noted writer. Her friends included such outstanding scholars as John Quincy Adams and Ralph Waldo Emerson, and their regard for her helped establish her reputation as a woman of charm, wit, and keen intelligence. The latter point was not lost on her: she once commented that she had not found in America any intellect comparable to her own.

A friendly faculty wife took an interest in Fuller's social development. With her guidance the young woman learned to dress tastefully, to arrange her hair more simply, and to refine her rather abrupt manner. Although never conventionally pretty, she often held the center of attention with her high spirits and forthright observations.

When Margaret Fuller was twenty-three she was suddenly removed from the excitement of Cambridge social and intellectual circles. Her father, disappointed in his political ambitions, moved the entire family to a farm in Groton. Thus, while her male classmates went on to the university, Margaret Fuller tutored her younger brothers and sister and helped with the household duties. Nevertheless, whenever she had the chance she immersed herself in her studies and her reading. One day, annoyed by an article in the *North American Review*, she sent an anonymous rebuttal to Boston's leading newspaper. Her comments appeared in a full column. This was her first published piece, and her writing ambitions were fired.

Soon after, as Fuller was planning a trip to Europe, her father died of cholera. Because Timothy Fuller had made no will, his nearest *male* relative, Abraham Fuller, was left in charge of the family. Uncle Abraham

did not believe in education for women, and he and his niece clashed over the education of her younger sister Ellen. Only after a terrible row did Margaret Fuller convince him to allow Ellen to finish school.

It fell to Fuller to take charge in other ways, as well. Because her father had been less affluent than he had appeared, she needed a job to help support the family. At the suggestion of her friend Ralph Waldo Emerson she accepted a position teaching Latin and French at Bronson Alcott's experimental Temple School in Rhode Island. As a teacher, Miss Fuller enthusiastically shared her knowledge with the children and engaged them in open discussions of the Gospel. Her students were devoted to her. However, her discussion groups were so free and her views so liberal that when they were published they aroused public indignation. Parents began withdrawing their children from the school.

During this period, Fuller's connections with Emerson, Alcott, and the Peabody sisters gave her entree to the Symposium Club, the monthly gathering of the transcendentalists. Club members were united in their desire to develop a uniquely American culture. To disseminate their ideas, they began publishing a transcendentalist magazine, *The Dial*, in 1840. When Emerson declined the editorship, Fuller was appointed to the position. A woman editor was unheard of at that time. The transcendentalists, however, had a tradition of departing from convention, and, quite simply, Margaret Fuller was the best mind for the job.

In the spring of 1839, Fuller's mother sold the farm and moved the family to the suburbs of Boston. Closer to the city once again, the young intellectual seized the opportunity to organize a discussion group for intelligent women of the area. She firmly believed that women needed to challenge their

intellects through discussion of matters other than domestic crises. Soon the bookshop of Elizabeth Peabody, a Temple School colleague, became the center of a weekly series of "conversations." The group provided Fuller with a steady income and a forum for sharing her progressive views. For several years she led stimulating debates on topics ranging from the fine arts to the influence of women on their society.

Severe, persistent headaches led to Fuller's resignation from *The Dial* in 1842. Eager for a vacation, she decided to accompany a distant cousin and his sister on a trip out West. The little company set out from Chicago in a large wagon and traveled over the plains, spending nights in taverns and isolated homes. Fuller was touched by the hardships endured by women on the frontier and in the Indian camps. From her notes of the journey grew *Summer on the Lakes* (1843), an overly erudite travelogue. Because of her reputation as a scholar, Miss Fuller was granted reading and research privileges in the library of Harvard University. This was the first time a woman had entered Harvard's hallowed halls, and it opened the first crack in the university's resistance to admitting women students.

The limitations imposed on women's intellectual pursuits by nineteenth-century American society were a source of deep frustration to Margaret Fuller. The attempt to expand educational and vocational opportunities for women gradually became her life's passion. Although she had no clear strategy mapped out, she entered the battle with two awesome weapons: her tongue and her pen. In 1843 she dashed off a long essay, "The Great Lawsuit: Man versus Men; Woman versus Women." Two years later an expanded version titled *Woman in the Nineteenth Century* was issued in book form. The volume created a stir in

A ROMANTICIZED PORTRAIT OF THE OSSOLI FAMILY DURING THE HURRICANE THAT TOOK THEIR LIVES.

Europe as well as in America, and the comparison it drew between the position of women and that of slaves received mixed reactions. Although her prose seems ponderous to the modern reader, Margaret Fuller's message was simple: "Inward and outward freedom for Woman as much as for Man shall be acknowledged as a *right*, not yielded as a concession."

Fuller's work and reputation caught the attention of Horace Greeley, editor of *The New York Tribune,* and in 1845 she accepted a position as literary critic for this newspaper. In addition to writing commentary on the fine arts, she wrote articles dealing with the hard lot of prostitutes,

women prisoners, and the insane. Her work aroused strong public interest. Before long, she had become a celebrity, invited to numerous social gatherings where she was courted as an intellectual. Today Margaret Fuller is regarded, along with Edgar Allen Poe, as one of the best critics of her generation and as one who performed an immeasurable service to the *Tribune* in the standard of excellence she set.

When she was thirty-five, Margaret Fuller fell in love for the first time. The object of her affection was James Nathan, a gentle businessman who aspired to becoming a writer. Although the couple freely expressed their passion in letters, Margaret was

inexperienced, and the brief romance remained only "an affair of the heart." They agreed to continue their correspondence when Nathan finally decided to travel abroad and keep a journal of his adventures. In 1846 Fuller accepted an invitation to tour Europe as the guest of friends. Greeley had agreed to accept any articles she wrote which might be of interest to the *Tribune's* readers. It was during this trip that Fuller received an announcement of Nathan's forthcoming marriage. Bitter and disillusioned, she requested the return of her letters, but he refused.

In London Fuller developed a friendship with the well-known writer

Thomas Carlyle. At a gathering at Carlyle's home, she was introduced to Giuseppe Mazzini, an exiled Italian Republican, and through him became caught up in the political struggle in Italy. Eventually she moved to Rome to observe events firsthand. Her subsequent articles for the *Tribune* were written to arouse American sympathy for the Italian revolution.

While living in Italy Fuller met Giovanni Angelo Ossoli, a tall, dark, impoverished aristocrat who was active in the Roman Revolutionary party. Each day Ossoli came to show her more of the sights in his beautiful city. They were an odd match: ten years younger than Margaret, Ossoli had no career except that of nobleman, and his education was limited. The pair eventually became secret lovers. When Fuller learned she was pregnant, she and Ossoli decided to marry. However, they had little money, they could not be married in the Catholic church, and civil marriages were not permitted in Rome. As a result Margaret fled to the mountains to avoid scandal. There, at age thirty-eight, attended only by Ossoli and a midwife, she gave birth to a son, Angelino.

As soon as she was able, Margaret Fuller returned to Rome. The Pope had asked foreign countries for assistance against the revolutionaries, and the city was under bombardment. While Ossoli fought with the defense forces, Fuller helped tend the wounded in the hospitals. The resistance was short-lived, however, and French troops soon occupied the city. The two lovers then joined their little son in Rieti where they were finally married in a private ceremony.

Their money almost gone, Margaret Fuller decided she could best support her family by returning to America; she and Ossoli hoped to write an account of the revolution which would provide them with a living. They booked passage on the *Elizabeth*, a sturdy freighter bound for New York. In addition to the Ossoli family, the ship was carrying two other passengers, as well as a cargo of oil, marble, silk, and old paintings. On July 19, 1850, the ship reached the New Jersey coast, and Margaret Fuller selected a pretty, hand-embroidered smock for her son to wear when they landed the next day. But during the night a storm arose. By midnight it had become a hurricane which wrenched the *Elizabeth* from its course and flung the ship against a sandbar off Fire Island. The 150 tons of marble in the hold crashed through the ship's bottom as monstrous waves pounded the decks above. From the forecastle where they had taken refuge, the passengers could see people on the distant shore, waiting to recover lost valuables. No help came, and all lifeboats were lost. A few succeeded in swimming to safety by holding onto wooden planks, but the Ossolis insisted on remaining together. By midafternoon, the rising tide destroyed their last hopes of rescue. A sailor, clasping little Angelino, leaped into the water; later the two bodies were washed up on the beach. Behind them a giant swell obliterated the ship and swept all on deck overboard. The bodies of Margaret and Giovanni Ossoli and the manuscript of her cherished history of the revolution were never recovered.

Two years later, a two-volume *Memoirs of Margaret Fuller Ossoli* was compiled by her friends and admirers. Although the effort was a well-meant testament to a brilliant and vivacious woman, many parts of Fuller's journals and letters were deleted or rewritten. Unfortunately, most of the originals have been lost. Thus, the remnants of Margaret Fuller's personal papers leave an incomplete record of the woman who dazzled an era with her insight, her passion, and her intellect.

12 Mid-Nineteenth-Century Expansion: Manifest Destiny

Why, were other reasoning wanting, in favor of now elevating this question of the reception of Texas into the Union, out of the lower region of our past party dissensions, up to its proper level of a high and broad nationality, it surely is to be found, found abundantly, in the manner in which other nations have undertaken to intrude themselves into it, between us and the proper parties to the case, in a spirit of hostile interference against us, for the avowed object of thwarting our policy and hampering our power, limiting our greatness and checking the fulfilment of our manifest destiny to overspread the continent allotted by Providence for the free development of our yearly multiplying millions. . . .

John L. O'Sullivan, journalist and editor

Significant Events

Spain establishes Santa Fe, New Mexico [1609]

First Spanish mission in Texas (San Antonio) [1718]

Franciscan mission established in California [1769]

Mexican independence from Spain [1821]

Texas declares independence from Mexico [1836]

Webster-Ashburton treaty [1842]

Texas becomes a state in Union [1845]

Oregon Treaty [1846]

Mexican War [1846–1848]

Treaty of Guadalupe Hidalgo [1848]

DURING THE 1860s SOME FIFTEEN MILLION BUFFALO ROAMED THE GREAT PLAINS. IN LESS THAN TWENTY YEARS, THESE VAST HERDS HAD BEEN REDUCED TO A FEW THOUSAND SURVIVORS, PUSHED TO THE BRINK OF EXTINCTION BY WHITE HUNTERS WHO SLAUGHTERED THEM WITH LITTLE PRETENSE OF FRUGALITY OR SPORTSMANSHIP.

From the beginning of the colonial period Americans had been constantly moving westward, even when forbidden by the British government. The Louisiana Purchase, the War of 1812, and the Adams-Onís Treaty of 1819 were all manifestations of the country's expansionist tendencies. Even the Monroe Doctrine can be seen as an attempt to prevent European interference in what was considered an area meant to be controlled by the United States. For thirty years after the doctrine was announced in 1823, American foreign policy was concerned almost exclusively with the Western Hemisphere. In particular, the United States was vitally interested in acquiring all the land between the Louisiana Purchase and the Pacific Ocean.

The movement to push the country's boundaries to the Pacific peaked during the 1840s. In a period of ten years the United States:

- Acquired seven thousand square miles of territory on the border between Maine and Canada;

- Annexed the Republic of Texas;
- Settled the Oregon boundary dispute with England; and
- Fought a war with Mexico, which resulted in the acquisition of almost half of Mexico's land.

This aggressive wave of expansion was dignified by the term "manifest destiny," which described the belief that the United States was destined to possess all of North America to the Pacific Ocean. The phrase first appeared in 1845 when John L. O'Sullivan, editor of the magazine *Democratic Review*, wrote that it was "our manifest destiny to overspread the continent allotted by Providence for . . . our yearly multiplying millions." Because it gave America's expansionist drive a tone of lofty inevitability, the phrase quickly became part of the American vocabulary. To most people it signified the spread of republican government, religious freedom, opportunities for trade, and free land.

Origins of the Expansionist Movement

Westward expansion became an American preoccupation because it satisfied so many needs. Southerners promoted expansion because they hoped it would lead to the creation of new slave states. Already outnumbered in the House of Representatives, the South believed it was vital for the region to maintain equality in the Senate. As long as the South was not outnumbered in the Senate it could prevent any bill that was against its particular interests from becoming a law. Conversely, the Northern states wanted to add new free states. By increasing free-state influence in the Congress, Southern opposition to Northern business interests could be overcome.

Westward expansion was more than a race for political leverage, however. The impulse behind manifest destiny was also prompted by a hunger for new agricultural lands. The movement was intensified by the phenomenal growth of the population. As immigrants moved into the older regions of the country in great numbers between 1830 and 1860, many people coveted the border lands of Texas, California, and Oregon.

As Americans began to settle new parts of the continent, the promise of increased commerce further reinforced the trend. Planters, textile manufacturers, and merchants dreamed of an ever-expanding market for cotton products. The superb natural harbors at Puget Sound, San Diego, and San Francisco tempted shippers. With such harbors as terminals for a planned transcontinental railroad, merchants also saw America's Pacific Coast as a stepping stone for extensive trade with the Orient.

Fear of European rivalry was another important impetus for expansion. The British already had a colony in Oregon, and many people believed that another European foothold on the continent would threaten America's mission to spread the institutions of democracy. Many Americans believed that in addition to competing with the United States commercially, foreign countries might try to establish colonies on the Pacific Coast. These misgivings made Americans eager to ensure the country's safety by expanding its borders.

The expansionist movement was at once idealistic and opportunistic. It derived in part from an optimistic, if arrogant, certainty that the American system of government was superior to all others and that Americans had the right, even the responsibility, to spread their institutions across the continent. Many Americans rationalized that by extending their boundaries, they were providing a haven for the oppressed masses of Europe. Ironically, in their efforts to provide space for their own political and economic development, Americans disregarded the claims of such peoples as the Indians who already were living in the area west of the Mississippi and the Mexicans who had considered the territory south of Oregon in the Far West as part of Mexico since becoming independent of Spain in 1821.

Tyler Becomes President

The 1840s, which developed into a decade of explosive expansionism, began quietly with the assumption of power by the Whigs under William Henry Harrison. When Harrison took office in the winter of 1841, the leaders of his own party felt that he would be a puppet president. But no one was sure whose puppet he would be: Henry Clay's or Daniel Webster's. After the election Clay, who remained in the Senate, and Webster, who was now secretary of state, became rivals for influence in the White House. While they squabbled, Harrison was besieged by Whig officeseekers looking for the same patronage they had condemned under the Democrats.

As events would have it, neither Clay nor Webster gained the ascendency. Barely into his term, Harrison contracted pneumonia and died one month after his inauguration. John Tyler became president, the first vice-president to reach the office because of the death of his predecessor.

Tyler, a devoted advocate of states' rights and supported mostly by the South, clashed almost immediately with Clay and the Whig majority in Congress. As a result he accomplished little during almost four years in office.

Tyler fought every effort of Clay to put his American System into effect. He vetoed bills on internal improvements. In addition, while he did accept repeal of the independent treasury, he vetoed two of Clay's plans to establish a third Bank of the United States. The result was an end to any kind of national banking policy.

When Clay introduced a bill in 1841 to distribute the revenues from the sale of public lands among the states to pay for internal improvements, he had to agree that land sales would cease if the tariff went up. Tyler accepted this legislation but vetoed a tariff bill the following year which provided for an increase in duties without repealing distribution. The Whigs then had to give up distribution of the federal surplus in order to get the protective tariff they wanted on manufactures. The Tariff Act of 1842 raised duties to about the level of the 1832 act.

The Whig leaders were furious with Tyler and with the exception of Secretary of State Webster the entire cabinet resigned in protest. Clay called the Whig representatives into caucus and they drew up a statement denouncing the president and reading him out of the party. Left with only lukewarm support from the Southern Democrats, Tyler became, in effect, a president without a party. Though honest and conscientious, he was virtually powerless without the backing of the cabinet and Congress.

The Maine Boundary Dispute

Expansion began modestly in 1842 when Webster, who had remained in the cabinet because he was in the midst of negotiations with England, succeeded in working out a settlement defining the long disputed border between Maine and Canada. Known as the Webster-Ashburton treaty, it helped set the tone for manifest destiny by planting the American flag in a part of the continent claimed by another country.

Several incidents along the border in the years prior to 1842 provided the background for the treaty. In 1837 a group of Americans had supported a minor Canadian insurrection, hoping it would lead to American annexation of Canada. The British suppressed the revolt easily, but Americans living near the border continued to support the rebels. One night angry Canadian officials crossed the Niagara River and set fire to an American vessel, the *Caroline*, which had been carrying supplies for the rebels. American newspapers carried inflammatory illustrations of the incident, showing the ship plunging over the falls carrying the terrified crew to their deaths. Although this was a gross distortion—the ship did not go over the falls and only one American was killed—it caused an instant uproar along the border from Vermont to Michigan. Thousands of American lumbermen banded together and pledged to destroy British power in North America.

At this point the excitement did not extend to officials in London or Washington. But in 1840 a Canadian was indicted for murder by the state of

New York after he boasted of playing a role in the raid on the *Caroline*. The British, who had had a number of conflicts with the United States in the intervening years, warned that execution of the Canadian could mean war. Fortunately the prisoner established an iron-clad alibi and was acquitted, thus diffusing the tension. In 1842 the *Caroline* incident was settled by a mutual agreement. The British expressed regret for the raid and the Americans did not demand indemnity for the ship.

A second near clash occurred in 1839. The British, as a strategic precaution, planned to build a railroad whose route would take it through the Aroostook River Valley, an area claimed by Maine as well as Canada. The territory had come under dispute as a result of the Treaty of Paris, which had described the Canadian-American border in terms so imprecise that the exact line could not be determined. The Maine militia refused to permit this "foreign intrusion," and a number of skirmishes took place in the area between lumbermen from Canada and Maine. In 1842, in an effort to settle the dispute, the British sent Lord Ashburton, an amiable financier who was married to an American. After long weeks of discussion with Secretary of State Webster, the two men at last reached a compromise on the boundary issue. In the Webster-Ashburton treaty, of the twelve thousand square miles

DISTORTED, INFLAMMATORY REPORTS OF THE BURNING OF THE REBEL SUPPLY SHIP *CAROLINE* AROUSED STRONG ANTI-BRITISH SENTIMENT IN AMERICA. THIS ILLUSTRATION ERRONEOUSLY DEPICTS "THE AMERICAN STEAM PACKET *CAROLINE* DESCENDING THE GREAT FALLS OF NIAGARA, AFTER BEING SET ON FIRE BY THE BRITISH, DEC. 29TH, 1837."

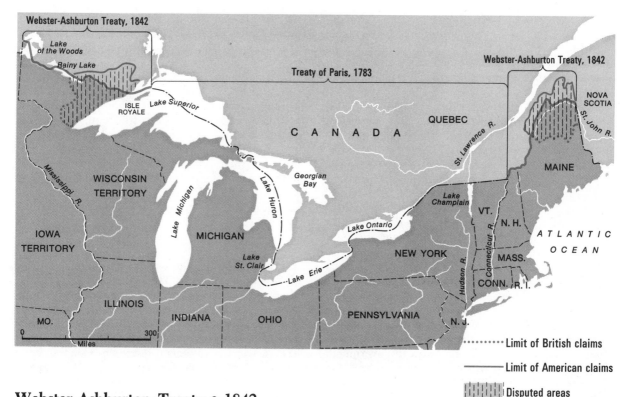

Webster-Ashburton Treaty • 1842

of disputed territory, the United States conceded five thousand square miles, but retained the remaining seven thousand as part of Maine. In addition, the British received a right of way for construction of a strategic railroad from New Brunswick to Quebec and Montreal.

Americans, especially Maine lumbermen, resented giving up territory to the British. To justify the concessions in the treaty Webster came up with an outdated map which indicated that the British were actually entitled to the entire territory. Even so, Maine and Massachusetts refused to accept the terms of the agreement until each was paid $150,000. Likewise, the British negotiators overcame sentiment in their country against the treaty by producing a map that showed that all the disputed land rightfully belonged to the United States! Ironically, it has since come to light that the United States had a legitimate claim to the entire territory. The Americans nevertheless did receive an added benefit: the boundary drawn in the northern Minnesota area gave the United States possession of the Mesabi Range where valuable deposits of iron ore were discovered years later.

Annexation of Texas

The Settlement of Texas

Early in the nineteenth century the Spanish-held territory of Texas was sparsely inhabited. The Spanish had founded San Antonio in 1718 and through-out the eighteenth century they had established missions in Texas to convert the Indians and had maintained a few army garrisons. By 1800 about thirty-five hundred Mexicans had emigrated to Texas where they farmed, grew cotton, and raised sheep and cattle. Spain, however, never demonstrated a serious interest in populating the territory, and the withdrawal of Spanish troops early in the nineteenth century encouraged Indian attacks on Mexican settlers and led to the abandonment of many missions.

Settlement of Texas began in earnest in 1823, two years after Mexico became independent of Spain. Seeking to encourage immigration, the Republic of Mexico gave grants of land to *empresarios*, or land agents, who brought in settlers from the United States. Mexico had several reasons for wanting to attract the foreigners: development of natural resources, increased tax revenues, and the establishment of a buffer against Indian raids and American land hunger were among the most important.

The first of these grants went to Stephen F. Austin who agreed to bring in three hundred American families as permanent settlers. These families were to adopt the established Mexican faith, Roman Catholicism; they were to be of good moral character; and they were to swear allegiance to the Republic of Mexico. Austin's success in settling acceptable American immigrants led the Mexican government in 1825 to open its doors to any Americans of high moral character who would pledge their loyalty to Mexico and forswear the Protestant faith. As a result, thousands of Americans streamed into Texas attracted by reports of rich land for farming. By 1835, of a population of some thirty thousand in Texas, twenty-five thousand were Americans.

Almost from the start, the newcomers clashed with their Mexican neighbors and the Mexican government. To a great extent the underlying cause was cultural. The Mexican authorities were alarmed by the growing number of American settlers and their independent ways. In large areas of the province there were so many Americans that English was the only language spoken. The settlers, many of whom were Protestants, resented the Mexican ban on practicing their religion. Slaveholders were angered by laws passed in 1830 forbidding slavery, and farmers resented the government's failure to provide adequate marketing facilities for agricultural produce.

In 1830 Mexico sought to limit these problems by banning further immigration from the United States. The new law did not stop them from coming, however. Settlers fought with Mexican troops, settled illegally, and began to demand some privileges of self-government.

An insurrection became inevitable when General Antonio Lopez de Santa Anna became dictator of Mexico in 1835. He had come to power with the support of the American settlers who had thought he was a democrat and would grant them local self-rule, but his first act as dictator was to abolish the Mexican constitution of 1824. Though seriously provoked, a majority of settlers still remained loyal to Mexico. Santa Anna refused to grant them local self-government, however, and in March 1836 Texans declared their independence from Mexico. They immediately sought support from the United States and named the colorful Sam Houston, a shrewd and skillful leader, as commander in chief of their army.

Texas Fights for Independence

The war that ensued lasted six months and consisted of two major battles. The first took place shortly after several companies of Texas volunteers captured the small town of San Antonio. A force of only 145 men, including both American and Mexican Texans under the command of Colonel W. B. Travis, was left to defend the town. General Santa Anna crossed the Rio Grande and marched on San Antonio, where Travis herded his men into an old walled mission called the Alamo. There, for thirteen days, the Texans held off four thousand Mexican troops. Then, on March 6, 1836, four days after the Provisional Government had proclaimed Texas independent of Mexico, Santa Anna began an all-out assault on the mission. Every defender was killed, including the legendary Davy Crockett and Jim Bowie. Although the defense of the Alamo was a foolhardy military tactic, it created one of the most dramatic legends of bravery in American history.

Two weeks after the Alamo, a force of 350 Texans was massacred in cold blood after their capture at Goliad. Aware that Santa Anna would give no quarter, Sam Houston retreated eastward to gather and train reinforcements. In April near San Jacinto, Houston and a force of some 800 men rushed Santa Anna's camp shouting, "Remember the Alamo!" In eighteen minutes of furious hand-to-hand fighting, 630 Mexicans were killed and 700, including Santa Anna, taken prisoner. Texan casualties totaled only nine dead and thirty-four wounded. Santa Anna soon agreed to sign a treaty recognizing the Republic of Texas and fixing the southern and western boundary, which had former-

"THE FALL OF THE ALAMO" FROM *DAVY CROCKETT'S ALMANACK.*

ly been at the Nueces River, at the Rio Grande, a change that gave Texas a great deal of new territory. Although Mexico refused to accept the treaty, the new republic immediately sent an envoy to Washington asking for annexation to the United States.

Believing that the rebels had fought a war for democracy, hundreds of adventurers poured into Texas to settle and join its army. Although President Jackson did nothing to stop American citizens from offering support, the American government remained officially uncommitted, as it was bound to do under its neutrality laws. Sensitive to the delicacy of the situation, Jackson would not take any action beyond formally recognizing the Lone Star Republic, and he postponed doing this until his last day in office in 1837.

Jackson's caution was based primarily on the thorny question of the expansion of slavery. Although the recent admissions of Arkansas and Michigan had given the Union thirteen free and thirteen slave states, Florida was the only slave territory left, and the free territories of Wisconsin, Iowa, and Minnesota would soon be demanding state-hood. The annexation of Texas could help counterbalance this Northern advantage, adding Southern votes in the Senate and the electoral college.

Many Northerners viewed the annexation of Texas as a Southern plot to extend slavery. Abolitionism was gaining political influence by this time, and some Northern members of Congress openly denounced slavery and its extension into new territories.

In an attempt to influence Northern attitudes, Sam Houston predicted that Texas would become an enormous market for manufactured goods. When this strategy did not work, Houston declared that Texas should simply find "some other friend" to protect it. With this in mind, he approached the English to explore the idea of creating an enormous southwestern country that would stretch to the Pacific and rival the United States in size and strength. The British were very interested. A new American nation would serve as a buffer against expansion of the United States, would become another large market for British goods, and might become an alternative source of cotton. Although the United States government was concerned over this possible threat

ther westward expansion, it was
it moved to ensure that the inde-
of Texas would not become an
Eng— ate.

The Election of 1844

By 1844 the country was caught up in the drive to push westward. Fever to add Texas to the Union ran high, but Mexico threatened war if the United States moved to annex the territory. As a result, the leading Whig presidential candidate, Henry Clay, and the Democratic favorite, Martin Van Buren, tried to keep the issue out of the campaign. In separate public statements each claimed to oppose annexation without the consent of Mexico.

More in touch with the mood of the country, expansionist delegates at the Democratic convention blocked Van Buren's nomination and instead named James K. Polk, a former governor of Tennessee, an ardent expansionist, and the first "dark horse" candidate. The Democrats based their campaign strategy on a party platform linking the annexation of a slave-holding Texas to a demand for the free territory of Oregon. "The re-occupation of Oregon and the re-annexation of Texas," said the platform, "at the earliest practicable period are great American measures, which this convention recommends to the cordial support of the Democracy of the Union." By using the words *re-occupation* and *re-annexation*, the Democrats attempted to make the proposed acquisitions seem legal, even though the consent of neither Mexico nor England had been obtained.

The campaign itself was one of slogans and personalities instead of rational debate of the issues facing the country. Clay was willing to support annexation only if it could be accomplished without bringing on a war. He also suggested that the disputed Oregon border, which the United States shared with England, might one day be drawn at the forty-ninth parallel. In answer, Western Democrats called for "all of Oregon or none."

It was a close contest. Although Polk won the vote in the electoral college by 170 votes to 105, he had only a small margin of the popular vote. Clay's loss of New York, where he had to compete not only with Polk but with the abolitionist Liberty party as well, cost him the election.

Texas Joins the Union

During its eight years of independence, the Republic of Texas attracted a great number of immigrants, including a steady flow of Americans as well as substantial numbers of Germans, Dutch, and French. After the Panic of 1837 thousands of slaveholders seeking to rebuild their fortunes moved into Texas with their slaves, thereby increasing the slave population tremendously. Texas won recognition from France, Britain, Belgium, and Holland, and the republic established a thriving trade with Britain, providing cotton for English textile mills.

During this period the American government remained indifferent to Texas's goal of annexation, and Texans were forced to defend their precarious independence against difficult odds. Texas government finances were in disarray, with expenditures far outweighing revenues and currency inflating rapidly. Even more ominous, periodic raids by the Mexican army were becoming more frequent; vastly outnumbered, the Texas army was easily repelled in its efforts to strike back. As Mexico became more aggressive, President Tyler grew increasingly concerned that Texas might indeed seek to ensure its safety by becoming a British protectorate. In October 1843 his secretary of state, Abel P. Upshur, made Texas a proposal of annexation. But before completing his negotiations, Upshur was killed in a freak accident aboard an American warship.

Although aware that Whig leaders in Congress would be opposed to the addition of a new slave state, Tyler selected John C. Calhoun, the leading advocate of slavery expansion, to replace Upshur in the State Department. In April 1844 Calhoun signed a treaty of annexation with Texas, but immediately undermined its chances for passage in Congress by asserting that the reason the United States should admit Texas was to protect the institution of slavery. Antislavery senators were enraged and killed the treaty in June. The election of Polk on an expansionist platform spurred Tyler to renew his efforts to acquire Texas. He decided that if the required two-thirds majority of the Senate would not approve a treaty, Texas could be invited to join the Union by a joint resolution, which needed only a simple majority in both houses of Congress. Thus Tyler offered a resolution which gave Texas control over its public lands, allowed the area to be divided into no more than five states, and protected slavery by including

Texas in the provisions of the Missouri Compromise. The measure was passed in the House of Representatives by a comfortable margin, but squeaked through the Senate by only two votes. Tyler signed the resolution on March 1, 1845, and in July a Texas national convention voted unanimously for annexation. By the end of the year Texas was admitted to the Union as the twenty-eighth state.

Polk's Administration

No president had yet entered the White House with so clearly defined a program as James K. Polk. A hardworking president, Polk was determined to facilitate the growth of American trade. His policies helped to spread American influence all over the globe. A related objective was further westward expansion. Convinced of the importance to American trade of controlling the Pacific Coast, Polk set out to resolve the Oregon boundary dispute and to acquire California from Mexico.

In domestic policy the Polk administration clearly reflected Jacksonian ideals and the growing power of the South in the Democratic party. Polk was a Tennessee planter and slaveowner. He did not want to extend slavery, but otherwise his opinions on the subject supported the Southern viewpoint. If slavery was abolished, he felt, "the dissolution of the Union . . . must speedily follow."

On the question of protective tariffs Polk believed that lower tariffs would encourage an expansion of American trade. One of his most impressive achievements was the Walker Tariff of 1846 which, by reducing the protective tariff, lowered the barriers against European imports and facilitated the growth and expansion of America's foreign trade. In the late 1840s large American surpluses of cotton and wheat were sold abroad for sizable profits. Trade treaties were established with Latin American countries, England, and France.

Finally, Polk followed in the tradition of the Democratic party by vetoing internal-improvement bills, a policy which annoyed many Westerners. On the other hand, Westerners and Southerners were pleased by the reinstitution of Van Buren's independent treasury, which the Whigs had killed in their efforts to set up a new national banking system during Tyler's administration.

All of these internal measures were accomplished in four years. Polk had indicated from the beginning that he was not a candidate for renomination. This stand, combined with his failing health due largely to overwork, limited his presidency to one term, and three months after leaving office he died.

The Oregon Controversy

When Polk took office, Tyler had already accomplished half of the Democratic party's 1844 expansionist platform by beginning the procedures for annexing Texas. The new president therefore set out to accomplish the second half: the annexation of Oregon. The problem was how to achieve the campaign promise "all of Oregon or none," for the United States had never previously claimed the entire Oregon Territory. In his Inaugural Address Polk spoke of the "right of the United States to that portion of our territory which lies beyond the Rocky Mountains," also claiming: "Our title to the country of Oregon is clear and unquestionable, and already are our people preparing to perfect that title by occupying it with their wives and children."

Until the 1840s England and the United States had occupied Oregon jointly, although the British were much more firmly established. Whereas the United States had shown little interest in the Northwest, England had built the area around Vancouver into a profitable fur-trading center. Through the years the two countries had never been able to agree on a dividing line which would give each of them a portion of the territory. The United States had suggested the forty-ninth parallel, a direct westward extension of America's northern border. The British, however, wanted to maintain control of the fur trade in northwest Oregon and the natural harbor of Puget Sound. Thus England was willing to agree on the forty-ninth parallel only as far west as the Columbia River.

In the early 1840s there were only a sprinkling of Americans in the territory. Gradually, however, more Americans became infected with "Oregon fever." Methodist, Presbyterian, and Catholic mis-

TRAVELERS ON THEIR WAY TO OREGON OFTEN STOPPED BRIEFLY AT INDEPENDENCE ROCK NEAR THE SWEETWATER RIVER IN WYOMING. HUNDREDS LEFT A RECORD OF THEIR PASSING BY SCRATCHING THEIR NAMES ON THE SURFACE OF THE MASSIVE LANDMARK.

HENRY WARRE SKETCHED THIS VIEW OF OREGON CITY IN 1845 WHEN THE TOWN HAD A POPULATION OF ABOUT SIX HUNDRED WHITE SETTLERS. BETWEEN 1849 AND 1852 IT BECAME THE CAPITAL OF THE OREGON TERRITORY.

sionaries were among the earliest settlers, having flocked to Oregon in the 1830s. Their letters and reports praised the area's rich soil and fine climate, and the Eastern newspapers spread the word. Soon Americans were convinced that Oregon's Willamette Valley was a virtual Garden of Eden. In search of new lands in the West, hundreds of courageous people often aided by friendly Indians set off on the difficult two-thousand-mile journey along the famed Oregon Trail. By 1846 some five thousand Americans had settled south of the Columbia River. The British, now badly outnumbered, quickly began to favor a peaceful settlement of the dispute.

THE WAY THEY LIVED: 1840–1870

American Scrapbook

JOHN JACOB ASTOR, RUMORED TO BE THE WORLD'S RICHEST MAN, BUILT PARK ROW IN NEW YORK CITY WHERE AN IMPRESSIVE ARRAY OF SHOPS DISPLAYED NEW, READY-MADE PRODUCTS. (Museum of the City of New York)

ABOVE: WINSLOW HOMER PAINTED THIS WATERCOLOR
OF SKATING IN NEW YORK'S CENTRAL PARK AROUND
1860. (The St. Louis Art Museum)

◄ IN SPANISH-SPEAKING CALIFORNIA, THE *VAQUEROS*
WERE EXTREMELY PROUD OF THEIR HORSEMANSHIP.
TO TEST THEIR RIDING AND ROPING SKILLS, THEY
SOMETIMES HUNTED DOWN GRIZZLIES WHICH PREYED
UPON RANCH CATTLE. AFTER BEING TAKEN CAPTIVE,
THE HUGE BEARS WERE EITHER KILLED OR MATCHED
IN FIGHTS WITH WILD BULLS. (California Historical Society)

OPPOSITE ABOVE AND RIGHT: ADVERTISEMENTS
HERALDING THE LATEST IN MEN'S AND WOMEN'S
FASHIONS WERE EAGERLY RECEIVED BY AMERICA'S
WELL-TO-DO, WHO THEN HAD THE EUROPEAN STYLES
COPIED BY THEIR OWN TAILORS AND SEAMSTRESSES.
(Culver Pictures)

LADY MOSCOW, ROCKET, AND BROWN DICK TROT FOR A PURSE STAKE OF $2,000. FOR MANY YEARS HORSE RACING WAS THE MOST POPULAR SPECTATOR SPORT IN AMERICA. (The Harry T. Peters Collection, Museum of the City of New York)

A GENTEEL OUTING AT AN ICE CREAM PARLOR. (The Bettmann Archive)

The Oregon Treaty

Polk was publicly committed to securing all of Oregon. But privately he was ready to compromise on the boundary for a number of reasons. Few Americans were willing to fight to acquire all of the Oregon Territory. Moreover, merchants wanted a port on the Pacific Coast for American ships, but the Puget Sound area at the forty-ninth parallel seemed sufficient. In addition, once Texas had joined the Union, many Southerners lost interest in securing the whole of Oregon and favored compromise. Finally, the annexation of Texas meant that California might soon follow. This possibility convinced many who desired a Pacific harbor that America's manifest destiny lay farther south, in California. Therefore, in July 1845 Polk informed the British minister in Washington that the United States would accept the forty-ninth parallel as the dividing line in Oregon.

The British minister, however, seemed not to be interested at first. Without consulting his government, he turned down the American offer. A crisis was now in the making as angry American expansionists shouted the slogan "fifty-four forty or fight" to indicate that the United States should take all of the Oregon Territory. But England, like the United States, did not want to go to war over Oregon. Great Britain did not consider the distant territory vital to the crown's interests. Already most of Oregon's settlers were Americans, and the fur trade had declined so that it was no longer of major importance. Equally important, at this point in the nineteenth century England was more interested in free trade than in territorial acquisitions. Consequently the British now suggested that Oregon be divided at the forty-ninth parallel, thus turning Polk's original proposal into their own. Publicly, Polk blustered that the offer should be rejected, but he instructed his cabinet to send it to the Senate for advice. With the decision in the hands of Congress, Polk was confident that he could have the compromise agree-

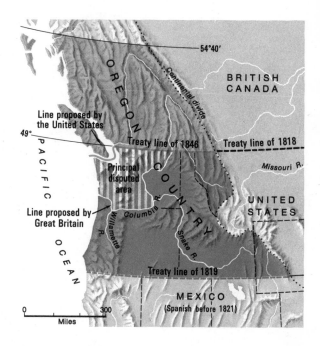

Oregon Controversy 1818 to 1846

ment he wanted, yet appear politically uncompromised.

In June 1846 the Senate advised acceptance of the compromise by forty-one votes to fourteen. This wide margin of victory reflected disapproval of the extremist views of American expansionist policy. Under the terms of the treaty, the Louisiana boundary line was extended westward to the coast, giving the United States control of the Columbia River Valley and the Puget Sound area. Vancouver Island was left to the British. The compromise had settled a long-standing dispute in a manner that was agreeable to both countries.

Further Westward Expansion

Although the main focal points of American expansionist interest as late as 1844 were Texas and Oregon, most Americans wanted to acquire all of the trans-Mississippi region to the Pacific Ocean. Not only did this idea fit with the motives behind manifest destiny, but the United States also could point to

Trails to the Far West

the growing number of American settlers in territory supposedly under Mexican control: the areas of New Mexico, Utah, and California.

The Settlement of New Mexico

By the late sixteenth century the Spanish began pushing the boundary of their colony in Mexico northward into present-day New Mexico. As a result of fantastic tales of wealthy Indian societies in the area, the Spanish encouraged Catholic missionaries, soldiers, and Mexican-Indians to begin migrating into this borderland. The first stage of settlement included the search for gold and efforts to conquer aggressive local Indian tribes; later missionaries set about to convert the Indians. A Dominican mission was established in Santa Fe in 1609 and by 1680 more than twenty-five other missions, encompassing almost a hundred villages and seventy-five thousand Indians, dotted the landscape. *Presidios* (military posts) were built nearby to protect the missions, and artisans and merchants were attracted by the prospect of profitable trade. However, many of the Indian tribes in New Mexico resented the intrusion of foreigners in their lands and made frequent raids on their villages, capturing Santa Fe in 1680.

Because of the danger of Indian attacks, the territory grew slowly throughout the eighteenth century (about eight thousand Mexicans had settled there by 1800), and settlers usually lived in fortress-like dwellings located close to the *presidios*. From friendly Indians the Mexicans learned how to cultivate corn, beans, and squash as well as how to grow cotton and fruit. In addition they learned the Indian methods of irrigation and sheepherding. Although there was a small, well-to-do landowning class, most of the territory's residents remained poor subsistence farmers.

The economy gradually began to improve after 1821 when a Missouri trader named William Beckness marked out the eight-hundred-mile trail from Missouri to Santa Fe. Thereafter, every spring for almost twenty-five years an armed caravan of American merchants drove to the outpost with wagon-loads of hardware and cotton cloth to trade for silver bullion, furs, and mules. Before long wealthy sheep ranchers and American and Mexican traders and artisans came to dominate the territory's economic life.

The Mormons in Utah

After the murder of Joseph Smith, the Mormons, under the leadership of Brigham Young, decided to move outside the United States in order to save their movement. A gifted speaker and talented administrator, Young set out to lead his people into "the midst of the Rocky Mountains . . . where we can . . . build a city in a day and have a government of our own." Soon, in one of the most remarkable westward migrations in American history, Young organized several thousand Mormons and journeyed with them into the Utah territory during the Mexican War. In July 1847 they reached the Great Salt Lake basin, and within a year five thousand Mormons had settled. In a span of only ten years their methods of irrigation had transformed the forbidding landscape into a prosperous farming area.

The Mormon community functioned as a vast cooperative. They created the "State of Deseret," a theocracy with its own money and its own army. The population increased rapidly, both because of polygamy (Young himself had twenty wives and fathered fifty-six children) and because of the settlement's missionary efforts to attract European immigrants. With shrewdness and a firm system of justice, the Mormons created the most successful communitarian project America has ever known.

In spite of their efforts, the Mormons were unable to remain apart from the rest of the United States. In 1850, as a result of the war with Mexico, their remote region came under Union jurisdiction and Young was named territorial governor. In fact, they gave up little of their independence, driving out federal judges who ruled against Young's decisions and finally provoking the federal government to such a degree that in 1857 troops were sent to support its authority. The dispute was resolved quickly, however, and the government of Utah remained independent. The Mormons' insistence on continuing to practice polygamy in violation of antipolygamy statutes prevented Utah from becoming a state until 1896.

The Settlement of California

The Spanish began to colonize California in the late eighteenth century in an effort to keep out European rivals. Under the leadership of Father Junipero Serra, a string of twenty-one Franciscan missions

IN JULY 1847 BRIGHAM YOUNG LED SEVERAL THOUSAND MORMON FOLLOWERS TO THE GREAT SALT LAKE IN THE UTAH TERRITORY.

began to be established after 1769. The missions were self-contained economic units. With labor supplied by vast numbers of local Indians, the Franciscan friars raised cattle and sheep and cultivated vineyards. To protect the province the Spanish established a series of garrisons (*presidios*) at San Diego, Santa Barbara, Monterey, and San Francisco. By 1820 the population of California consisted of perhaps three thousand *Californios*—descendants of the original Spanish settlers—and many thousands of Indians.

In 1821 when Mexico gained independence from Spain, California came under Mexican jurisdiction. In order to encourage population growth, the Mexican government in 1824 passed an act granting any Mexican citizen the right to acquire at minimal cost large tracts of land for ranching. It was not long before Mexican settlers began to covet the fertile church lands as well, and in 1833 these lands—which had been held in trust for the Indians—were secularized and made available for grants. The Indians, who received no compensation for their land, were left to their own devices. Their

numbers long since reduced by European diseases, many of those remaining became cowboys on the vast, widely scattered ranches, where they were exploited as their forebears had been as a cheap source of labor.

The *Californios*, who had long been an independent, self-governing people with a strong ethnic identity, chafed under Mexican rule. When the Mexican government attempted to limit self-rule in California, it encountered a long series of rebellions, beginning in 1828. Although the territory declared its independence in 1834, the Mexican government continued efforts to subdue California for almost a decade.

Americans first came into contact with California when New England whaling and trading ships stopped at various Pacific ports to purchase supplies or sell their products. In the 1830s some American merchants began to settle among the *Californios* in order to secure various trade agreements. Many of these men married into *Californio* families and began to take an active role in the political and economic life of the province. Within a short time

American farmers began to hear tales of lush California lands which could be had for almost nothing. And it was common knowledge that Mexico could not maintain effective control over its rebellious territory. Americans quickly saw in California another opportunity to satisfy their appetite for expansion.

American immigrants began arriving in 1841. Because they considered Mexicans inferior and had no wish to mingle with them, the first wave of Americans settled in the Sacramento Valley, far from the coastal Mexican settlements. Other groups of settlers established themselves in the valleys near San Francisco, so that by 1845 California had become home to several hundred Americans. Like the American settlers in Texas, they began agitating for annexation of California to the United States.

In 1845 Thomas Larkin, the American consul in Monterey and a member of California's governing class, sent word to President Polk that influential *Californios* and even many Mexican leaders seemed to favor annexation. Polk was delighted at the news, for it suggested that California might be acquired without bloodshed. Polk's enthusiastic response directed Larkin to do all he could to sway *Californio* opinion to the American view. But before Polk's message could be delivered in April 1846, Captain John C. Frémont, who was supposed to be on a scientific exploring expedition for the American government, but who was in fact accompanied by a large number of well-armed Mountain Men, fomented trouble with the Mexican authorities and encouraged Americans in the Sacramento Valley who were close to open revolt. In June 1846 a group of these agitators, acting on their own, proclaimed California a republic and raised the Bear Flag as its symbol. Frémont, learning that the United States had declared war on Mexico, now become involved actively; he led a group of the rebels to Monterey and joined forces with Americans who were already in control there.

THE AMERICAN FLAG GOING UP OVER THE OLD CUSTOM HOUSE AT MONTEREY, CALIFORNIA, ON JULY 7, 1846.

The Mexican War

Although California was not a major issue in the presidential election of 1844, the public soon began coupling it with the annexation of Oregon. By the following summer there was widespread talk about a great nation extending from the Atlantic to the Pacific, talk matched by the expansionist ambitions of the new president. American commercial interests were aware that California could provide several ports on the Pacific, as well as a logical terminus for the projected transcontinental railroad. Polk also desperately wanted to acquire California before it fell to England or France.

Given the American desire for California, war with Mexico was a distinct possibility. Many Americans believed that Britain and France were encouraging Mexico to resist further expansion by the United States, and there were rumors that the two European powers were willing to recognize an independent California if it would promise not to let itself be annexed. Thus in his first annual message to Congress, Polk declared that the United States would not permit European countries to establish colonies in North America or keep an independent territory from coming into the Union. "The people of *this continent* alone have the right to determine their own destiny," Polk said. The message was actually an expansion of the Monroe Doctrine, and it soon came to be known as the Polk Corollary.

Despite the agitation over California, hostilities between Mexico and the United States actually began over the boundary of Texas. Under the treaty forced on Santa Anna, Texans had fixed the border at the Rio Grande. Mexico, however, still insisted that it was at the Nueces, a river 150 miles farther north. Early in 1845, when Texas was invited into the Union, Mexico broke off diplomatic relations with the United States and moved troops into the area of the Rio Grande. For a time Polk had been

---

War with Mexico: Right or Wrong?

"But now, after reiterated menaces, Mexico has passed the boundary of the United States, has invaded our territory, and shed American blood upon the American soil. She has proclaimed that hostilities have commenced, and that the two nations are now at war.

As war exists, and, notwithstanding all our efforts to avoid it, exists by the act of Mexico herself, we are called upon by every consideration of duty and patriotism to vindicate with decision the honor, the rights, and the interests of our country."

President James K. Polk
May 1846

War with Mexico: Right or Wrong?

"It is a singular fact that if any one should declare the President sent the army into the midst of a settlement of Mexican people who had never submitted, by consent or by force, to the authority of Texas or of the United States, and that there and thereby the first blood of the war was shed, there is not one word in all the President has said which would either admit or deny the declaration. This strange omission it does seem to me could not have occurred but by design. . . . I have sometimes seen a good lawyer, struggling for his client's neck in a desperate case, employing every artifice to work round, befog, and cover up with many words some point arising in the case which he dared not admit and yet could not deny. Party bias may help to make it appear so, but with all the allowance I can make for such bias, it still does appear to me that just such, and from just such necessity, is the President's struggle in this case. . . ."

Abraham Lincoln
January 1848

trying to get Texas to seize the disputed territory between the two rivers. But the government of Texas would not act, and in the fall of 1845 Polk sent American troops under General Zachary Taylor into the disputed area.

In December the president also sent diplomat John Slidell to negotiate directly with the Mexican government. Slidell was to insist on the Rio Grande as the southern boundary of Texas and offer as much as $30 million for all of New Mexico and California. Given the rumors of American intentions to carve up their country and the instability of Mexican governments, it is not surprising that the Mexican government refused even to receive Slidell. An offer to purchase California coming so soon after the loss of Texas was considered a serious affront. Moreover, the Mexican government believed its large army could defeat the United States.

When Polk learned of Slidell's treatment, he ordered Taylor to advance to the Rio Grande. In late March 1846 Taylor was ready to send his army into action. On April 24 a Mexican force crossed the river and attacked one of his mounted patrols. All of the Americans were killed or captured. A state of war existed "notwithstanding all our efforts to avoid it," Polk announced to Congress on May 11. Actually, the president's actions had set the stage for war, and he had even been preparing a war message before the attack. Now he simply revised the address to blame Mexico directly for the hostilities. Both houses quickly voted for war, and the president issued a declaration on May 13, 1846.

The Conduct of the War

In opting for war, the United States embarked on a reckless policy when a little more patience might have brought an agreement with Mexico. Most people believed that the nation's mission to extend American territory across the continent was inevitable. Why, then, use force to accomplish it?

Polk's war plan had two major components. First, he wanted to take possession of California and New Mexico. Second, by clearing the Mexican army out of Texas and taking Mexico City, he hoped to compel the Mexican government to make peace on American terms. However, the idea of war was not universally popular. Many Northern Whigs and abolitionists refused to support the conflict, viewing it as a conspiracy of Southern slaveowners.

They were willing to repel a Mexican invasion of Texas, but were not in favor of undertaking an aggressive war to seize California.

California and New Mexico were easily taken by American forces. In June 1846 an expedition led by Colonel Stephen W. Kearny captured Santa Fe without firing a shot. Kearny announced that New Mexico was now annexed by the United States and then moved right on to California, much of which was already in the hands of the Americans. All that was left for Kearny was to put down some scattered resistance in southern California. Thus by January 1847 New Mexico and California were American possessions, and the first of Polk's goals had been achieved.

The most difficult part of Polk's plan, however, was the campaign against Mexico itself. It meant sending an army south through hundreds of miles of rough country before reaching the capital city. In September 1846 in the first step toward reaching this goal, General Taylor led his forces against the city of Monterrey in northern Mexico. After a three-day battle the Mexicans were surrounded and offered to surrender. Instead, Taylor granted them the right to withdraw and pledged not to advance farther into Mexico for two months. During this armistice the fiery Santa Anna returned from exile and marched north with an army to engage Taylor at Buena Vista, south of Monterrey. No match for Taylor's army, the Mexican general's poorly trained and hungry troops were driven out of northern Mexico in February 1847, ending the war in that region.

Polk resented Taylor's tactics of delay and wanted to replace him with a general who was also a loyal Democrat. Taylor, nicknamed "Old Rough and Ready," was a popular general who rarely wore a proper uniform and looked distinctly unmilitary. He was also a Whig who was being mentioned as a prominent candidate for the presidency. Seeking to ensure against this possibility, Polk turned to General Winfield Scott who, though also a Whig, had a reputation for being a strict disciplinarian and an able military leader.

Polk's judgment was correct when he chose General Scott to lead the major campaign of the war, the assault on Mexico City. Scott decided to invade Mexico by sea, at the Gulf Coast, and march from there straight to the capital. The first step was to land his army near Veracruz, where the Americans established their beachhead. Soon they laid

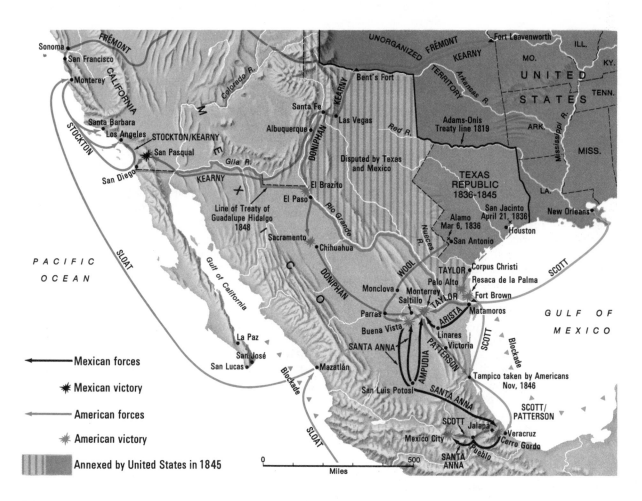

Mexican War • 1846 to 1848

siege to the city and captured it in less than three weeks. From Veracruz Scott marched inland to complete the invasion, one of the most daring and best managed in American military annals. Since Mexico's government and economy had been gravely weakened by the conflict, Scott and a small army were able to advance 260 miles through enemy territory without losing a battle.

At the edge of Mexico City, Santa Anna fought back desperately, but Scott hammered him into defeat in several hard battles. On September 14, six months after landing at Veracruz, Scott and the American army defeated the Mexican defenders and occupied the enemy capital. Santa Anna's weak government collapsed, and a new peace party, threatened on all sides by other political factions, came to power.

The Peace Settlement

Nicholas Trist, the chief clerk of the State Department, accompanied Scott's army from Veracruz. He was instructed to offer terms similar to those Slidell had carried to Mexico earlier, but negotiations pro-

"OLD ROUGH AND READY" ZACHARY TAYLOR. HIS MEN LOVED HIS ECCENTRIC HABIT OF WEARING A BATTERED STRAW HAT AND BLUE-CHECKED COAT INTO BATTLE. THE TOBACCO-CHEWING GENERAL WAS USUALLY IN THE CENTER OF THE FIGHTING. WHEN BULLETS CUT THROUGH HIS SHIRT AND COAT LINING AT THE BATTLE OF BUENA VISTA, HE RODE UP TO HIS ARTILLERY CREW AND CASUALLY ORDERED, "DOUBLE-SHOT YOUR GUNS AND GIVE 'EM HELL."

ceeded slowly and Polk ordered Trist home to receive instructions on additional demands to be made. Trist, however, believed that Mexico would not be willing to concede any more than the huge territorial concessions already being asked. Moreover, he feared that any further demands could lead to a guerrilla war, which would be to America's disadvantage. Therefore he decided to ignore the summons from Polk, and on February 2, 1948, he signed the Treaty of Guadalupe Hidalgo. Under this treaty the United States received California and the New Mexico Territory, and the Rio Grande was defined as the southern and western border of Texas—all for just $15 million. Although Trist had done well, Polk, furious that his emissary had acted against orders, fired him.

Trist's action was insubordinate, but courageous. It occurred at a time when opinion in the country was divided on the merits and possible continuance of the war. On one side, a number of expansionists were calling for all of Mexico. Such sentiment was strongest in the East, where commercial interests were already savoring the great profits to be generated from a complete takeover. The belief that slavery would not flourish in Mexico also brought some Westerners, who were against the expansion of slavery, to the cause. Furthermore, many Americans had become convinced that the United States was obligated to absorb the whole country and rule it—for the benefit of Americans, for the well-being of Mexicans, and for the advancement of world civilization.

Arguing against further expansion were many Whigs and Northern Democrats who had always opposed the invasion of Mexico. They disliked the expense of the conflict and still feared the expansion of slavery. At the same time, many Southern Democrats were also against continuing the war, because they did not believe that Mexico would be useful for agriculture. Finally, since the House of Representatives was controlled by the Whigs after 1846, Polk knew that they would resist further funding of the war. He decided to submit the treaty to the Senate, and it passed easily.

The Legacy of the War

What were the results of the Mexican War? On the positive side, the United States gained over five hundred thousand square miles of territory which, together with Oregon, completed American continental expansion in the 1840s. In addition, Americans secured outlets for trade all along the Pacific Coast and acquired valuable natural resources. Compared to later wars, the costs to the United States in lives and money were small (about thirteen thousand Americans died). The costs to Mexico and to Mexican-American relations were considerably higher. Mexico lost some fifty thousand men and over half its territory. This loss, coupled with the prejudice displayed by Americans against the Mexican people, embittered Mexicans against their aggressive North American neighbor and left a long-term legacy of mistrust.

Perhaps the most dramatic consequence of the war for the United States was the intensification of the sectional conflict over the expansion of slavery. Of course, this problem had arisen before the end of the Mexican War. In 1847 David Wilmot, a Democrat from Pennsylvania, attached an amendment called the Wilmot Proviso to an appropriation bill. According to this amendment, the funds authorized by the bill would be denied unless "neither slavery nor involuntary servitude shall ever exist" in territory acquired from Mexico. The House voted for the amendment, but the Senate turned it down. Wilmot, however, persistently attached it to other bills in Congress, and the idea was vigorously debated throughout the country. The Wilmot Proviso helped polarize opinion on the question of extending slavery in the years before the Civil War.

The Sectional Dispute Intensifies

By 1848 the issue of the expansion of slavery into new territories was agitating the whole country. Early in the year Congress voted to ban slavery from Oregon, but because cotton did not grow in Oregon and because the Oregon territory was north of 36°30′, the Missouri Compromise line of 1820, this legislation was not a real test of the nation's acceptance of antislavery laws. The election campaign of 1848 could have provided a forum for discussing the issue, but the political leaders refused to debate it.

The Election of 1848

The Democratic candidate, Senator Lewis Cass of Michigan, was an expansionist who tried to placate the South by espousing the new doctrine of popular sovereignty. Cass, an opponent of the Wilmot Proviso, believed that the people in each territory should decide for themselves whether or not to permit slavery. Unfortunately, he never stated whether the issue should be decided before or after slaves were brought into a territory already occupied by settlers without slaves.

The Whigs hoped to placate the South on the slavery issue while keeping slavery out of the new territories. To direct attention away from the slavery issue, they nominated the popular military hero General Zachary Taylor. Taylor, completely lacking in political sophistication, refused to give his opinion on any current subject, except to say that if elected he would govern without catering to the politicians. One of his campaign comments was: "I am a Whig, but not an ultra Whig."

Both Democrats and Whigs ignored the rabid antislavery factions in their parties, which were determined to make the expansion of slavery an issue in order to keep the new territories for free, hard-working white people. Leading the antislavery struggle within the Democratic party was a group known as the "Barnburners," who called for a "burning of the barn" of the Democratic party in order to get rid of the proslavery "rats." In the Whig party the Northern "Conscience Whigs" refused to compromise with the "Cotton Whigs," some of whom were New England cotton-mill owners who traded with the South. Eventually, the antislavery elements in the two major parties bolted and combined to form the Free-Soil party. Martin Van Buren, now an antislavery Democrat, was nominated as their presidential candidate.

The electorate responded with little enthusiasm. Neither of the major candidates appealed to party workers, and Van Buren lacked a national party machine to support his efforts. Influential national leaders found themselves backing one candidate or the other mostly for negative reasons. For example, Horace Greeley, editor of the New York *Tribune*, supported Van Buren only because he thought that Cass was a "pot-bellied, mutton-headed cucumber." Although Taylor, the Whig candidate, won the election, the Free-Soilers were a very important factor because they split the Democratic vote in New York enough to give the state to Taylor. In Ohio and Indiana they divided the Whig vote, giving those states to Cass. Although Van Buren and most of his supporters returned to the Democratic party, the small band of Free-Soilers held the balance in the House of Representatives. They had shown that a party based on a single important issue could significantly influence political events and that the subject of the expansion of slavery could not be shunted aside. Their emergence set the stage for a realignment of the political parties in the next decade.

THE MODERN COLOSSUS, OR EIGHTH WONDER OF THE WORLD. THIS 1848 LITHOGRAPH DEPICTS VAN BUREN, EX-PRESIDENT AND FREE-SOIL PARTY CANDIDATE, TRYING TO BRIDGE THE GAP BETWEEN THE WHIGS' ANTI-ABOLITION PLATFORM AND THE DEMOCRATS' PLATFORM IN THE 1848 ELECTION.

The Debate over the New Territories

The slavery issue receded for a while in 1848, when news spread that gold had been discovered in California. Americans were joined by goldminers from all over the world in a mad rush to get at the riches in California. Within a year the population of California had grown from ten thousand to a hundred thousand. San Francisco alone grew from a squalid village to a city of twenty thousand inhabitants within a matter of months.

As a result of this rapid growth, the government of California began to urge that California be granted statehood without first going through the territorial process. This issue, and the organization of the rest of the territory acquired from Mexico, became the major concerns of the newly elected president.

Many Northerners supported the doctrine of the Wilmot Proviso, and a number of states submitted petitions to Congress opposing the expansion of slavery into the new territories. Others supported the doctrine known as popular sovereignty.

Enraged by both doctrines, Southern members of Congress formed a bloc to oppose admitting any free state until Southern grievances against the North had been resolved. First, they wanted to be able to take their slaves anywhere, since they considered them to be property protected by the Constitution. They also wanted to settle the fugitive slave issue. The fugitive slave law of 1793 had given slaveowners the right to seize a runaway slave and obtain from a state or federal judge the authority to return the slave to the plantation. For years Northern officials had refused to enforce the statute and, to make matters worse, Northern legislatures had passed "personal liberty" laws that effectively prevented using state officials to recapture slaves. Southerners felt that Northern recalcitrance had cost them hundreds of thousands of dollars in valuable property, and they began agitating for a stricter fugitive slave law.

For its part, the North had a number of grievances against the South. Northerners resented the fact that the slave trade had been allowed to continue in the District of Columbia, the seat of the nation's democratic institutions. They also were disturbed that Texas was insisting on drawing its western boundary along the Rio Grande all the way into the present-day Colorado Rockies because this would mean that slavery would be extended into a large area that under Mexican law had been free. Finally, angered by Southern opposition to protective tariffs and internal improvements, they viewed the South as retarding modernization while being tied to an immoral labor system.

Westerners, too, were concerned about the spread of slavery, primarily because it implied the possible transfer of jobs held by free white men to slave labor. Finally, some people in all parts of the country wanted to postpone the slavery issue by extending the line drawn by the Missouri Compromise to the Pacific Coast.

The president soon resolved part of the dispute about the status of the territories by deciding that California should skip the territorial stages, because then, as a state, it could decide the slavery issue for itself. It was his opinion that New Mexico should follow a similar course.

Southerners were horrified by the president's decision, for a free California would destroy the balance in the Senate between free and slave states. Furthermore, if all the new lands were permitted to enter the Union as free states, the South would be surrounded by hostile states capable of destroying its way of life. Thus Taylor's move played directly into the hands of Southern extremists, who began to threaten secession as early as 1850.

Clay's Compromise Package

The complex slavery issue was the topic of heated congressional debate. Dozens of different bills were proposed, but the prospect of a reasonable solution seemed remote, particularly when Free-Soilers formed an unlikely alliance with radical proslavery elements to defeat any efforts at compromise. The issue became so explosive that legislators on opposite sides of the question almost came to blows.

Of all the leaders who understood the implications of the mounting crisis, the most perceptive was the aging Henry Clay. Clay believed that the Union was close to dissolution and that if California were admitted as a free state, the South was entitled to some concessions. After consulting with his old Whig rival, Daniel Webster, Clay offered the Senate a number of proposals designed to satisfy both North and South. The principal measures were as follows.

First, the North should give up the Wilmot Proviso, and in return the South should not demand formal approval of its right to take slaves into the new territories. The governments of the regions involved should decide for themselves whether or not to permit slavery. Second, the western border of Texas should be adjusted to exclude eastern New Mexico. In return, the United States government would assume the portion of the public debt contracted by Texas prior to annexation. Third, the slave trade would be outlawed in the District of Columbia, and slavery would not be permitted in the District unless approved by the white citizens of the District of Columbia and Maryland. Fourth, Congress would not interfere with the interstate slave trade. Fifth, the North should accept the enactment of a stricter fugitive slave law.

Clay's compromise proposals initiated a Senate debate which extended over a period of seven months. This was the last time that the great triumverate—Clay, Webster, and Calhoun—would appear in the Senate together. Clay and Webster made their last great speeches of their lives in defense of a compromise to save the Union. Calhoun, in an attempt to keep the country together, called for a constitutional amendment that would "restore to the South, in substance, the power she possessed of protecting herself before the equilibrium between the two sections was destroyed. . . ." He amplified his belief in the need for government by a "concurrent majority" which would allow each state to have a veto over federal legislation. While he and other Southern leaders bitterly denounced the North for its attacks on slavery and called for opening up all the new territories to slaveholders, Northern antislavery politicians, such as William H. Seward of

OPENING MOMENTS OF THE GREAT DEBATE WHICH LED TO THE COMPROMISE OF 1850: SEVENTY-TWO-YEAR-OLD HENRY CLAY REGAINS SOME OF HIS OLD FIRE AND CHARM AS HE TAKES THE SENATE FLOOR. DANIEL WEBSTER SITS TWO ROWS TO THE LEFT WITH HIS HEAD RESTING ON HIS HAND. IN THE BACKGROUND TO THE RIGHT STANDS THE AGING JOHN C. CALHOUN, GRIM FOE OF THE PROPOSED COMPROMISE.

New York, attacked the Clay compromise as immoral. Invoking "a higher law than the Constitution," he urged the Congress to forbid the expansion of slavery beyond its present boundaries.

As the debate dragged on, Clay, weak and exhausted, passed the torch of leadership to the Democratic Senator from Illinois, Stephen A. Douglas. Douglas—bull-necked, short of stature, and possessing a booming voice—fought hard to end the slavery crisis. He realized that the compromise would not be accepted as a package, but that it might have a fighting chance if broken into separate bills, since each separate proposal had a group of supporters sufficient to ensure its passage. President Taylor, however, stubbornly refused to consider any proposal that conflicted with his own. Then, in July 1850, Taylor died suddenly of a stomach disorder and Vice-President Millard Fillmore succeeded him. A political moderate, Fillmore favored the compro-

mise and the deadlock between Congress and the White House was broken.

The Compromise of 1850

Under the compromise finally passed, California entered the Union as a free state in 1850. Texas received $10 million in return for giving up all claims to the New Mexico Territory. Utah and New Mexico were formed as new territories, with the slavery question left open for their own voters to decide. The slave trade was outlawed in the nation's capital, but slavery itself was allowed to continue there. A most fateful measure was the Fugitive Slave Law, which promised strong federal action to end the practice of aiding runaway slaves.

Thus despite the turmoil that arose from America's expansion to the Pacific, the Compromise of 1850 enabled the Union to remain intact. It did

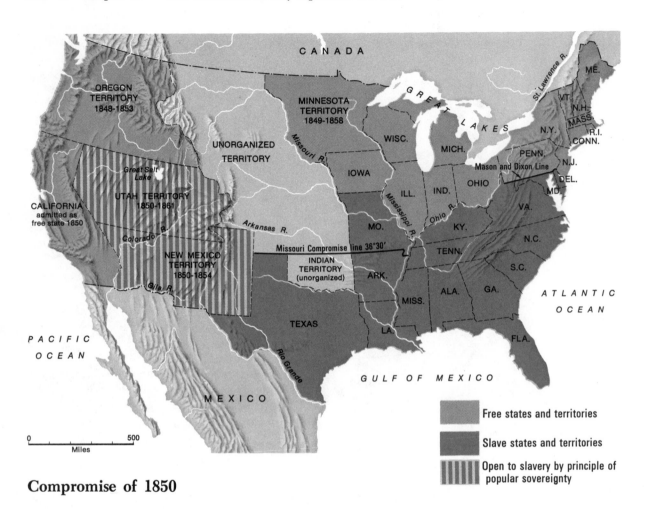

Free states and territories

Slave states and territories

Open to slavery by principle of popular sovereignty

Compromise of 1850

not, however, end the feelings of hostility that had developed on both sides. Some time had been bought, but the crucial issues had not been resolved. Manifest destiny had embodied the nation's most enduring political and economic ideals—the expansion of individual liberty, free government, and equality of opportunity—but it had also shown that there were great differences of opinion about what those ideals really meant. Americans seriously disagreed over how to organize new territories once they were acquired. Those who wanted slavery introduced into the territories believed that the country's ideals applied only to the white population. But the conscience of the antislavery reformers was gradually having an effect on a large portion of Northern public opinion. Moral aversion to slavery had become a great force in American life, along with economic and political opposition to the expansion of slavery.

Readings

General Works

Billington, Ray A., *The Far Western Frontier*. New York: Harper, 1965.

Billington, Ray A., *Westward Expansion*. New York: Macmillan, 1974.

Burns, Edward M., *The American Idea of Mission: Concepts of National Purpose and Destiny*. Westport, Conn.: Greenwood, 1973.

Campbell, Charles S., *From Revolution Rapprochement: The United States and Great Britain, 1783–1900*. New York: Wiley, 1974.

Goetzmann, William H., *When the Eagle Screamed: The Romantic Horizon in American Diplomacy, 1800–1860*. New York: Wiley, 1966.

Graebner, Norman A., *Empire on the Pacific*. New York: Ronald Press, 1955.

Graebner, Norman (Ed.), *Manifest Destiny*. Indianapolis, Ind.: Bobbs-Merrill, 1968.

Lavender, David S., *Westward Vision: The Story of the Oregon Trail*. New York: McGraw-Hill, 1963.

Merk, Frederick, *Manifest Destiny and Mission in American History*. New York: Knopf, 1963.

Parkman, Francis, *The Oregon Trail*. New York: Holt, Rinehart & Winston, 1931.

Weinberg, Albert K., *Manifest Destiny*. Baltimore, Md.: The Johns Hopkins University Press, 1935.

Special Studies

Allen, Harry C., *Great Britain and the United States*. London: Odhams Press, 1954.

Brack, Gene, *Mexico Views Manifest Destiny, 1821–1846*. Albuquerque: University of New Mexico Press, 1975.

Cleland, Robert G., *This Reckless Breed of Men*. New York: Knopf, 1950.

DeVoto, Bernard, *The Year of Decision: 1846*. Boston: Little, Brown, 1943.

Gunderson, Robert G., *The Log-Cabin Campaign*. Lexington: University of Kentucky Press, 1957.

Jones, Howard, *The Webster-Ashburton Treaty: A Study in Anglo-American Relations, 1783–1843*. Chapel Hill: University of North Carolina Press, 1977.

Jones, Wilbur D., *The American Problem in British Diplomacy, 1841–1861*. Athens: University of Georgia Press, 1974.

McDonald, Archie P., *The Mexican War: Crisis for American Democracy*. Lexington, Mass.: D. C. Heath, 1969.

Merk, Frederick, *The Monroe Doctrine and American Expansionism, 1843–1849*. New York: Knopf, 1966.

Morgan, Robert J., *A Whig Embattled*. Lincoln: University of Nebraska Press, 1954.

Pletcher, David M., *The Diplomacy of Annexation: Texas, Oregon and the Mexican War*. Columbia: University of Missouri Press, 1973.

Ruiz, Ramón E. (Ed.), *Mexican War: Was it Manifest Destiny?* New York: Holt, Rinehart & Winston, 1963.

Schroeder, John H., *Mr. Polk's War: American Opposition and Dissent, 1846–1848*. Madison: University of Wisconsin Press, 1973.

Seager, Robert, *And Tyler Too!* New York: McGraw-Hill, 1963.

Silbey, Joel H., *The Shrine of Party: Congressional Voting Behavior, 1841–1852*. Pittsburgh, Pa.: University of Pittsburgh Press, 1967.

Siegel, Stanley, *A Political History of the Texas Republic*. Austin: University of Texas Press, 1956.

Singletary, Otis A., *The Mexican War*. Chicago: University of Chicago Press, 1960.

Stegner, Wallace, *The Gathering of Zion: The Story of the Mormon Trail*. New York: McGraw-Hill, 1964.

Weems, John E., *To Conquer a Peace: The War Between the United States and Mexico*. New York: Doubleday, 1974.

Primary Source

Nevins, Allan (Ed.), *Polk: The Diary of a President*. London: Longmans, Green, 1929.

Biographies

Bartlett, Irving H., *Daniel Webster*. New York: Norton, 1978.

Hamilton, Holman, *Zachary Taylor*, Vols. I–II. Indianapolis, Ind.: Bobbs-Merrill, 1941–1957.

Hill, Donna, *Joseph Smith: The First Mormon*. Garden City, N.Y.: Doubleday, 1977.

James, Marquis, *The Raven*. Indianapolis, Ind.: Bobbs-Merrill, 1929.

Morgan, Dale L., *Jedediah Smith and the Opening of the West*. Indianapolis, Ind.: Bobbs-Merrill, 1953.

Nevins, Allan, *Frémont: Pathmarker of the West*, Vols. I–II. New York: Frederick Unger, 1955.

Nibley, Preston, *Brigham Young, the Man and His Work*. Salt Lake City, Utah: Deseret Books, 1936.

Sellers, Charles, *James K. Polk*, Vols. I–II. Princeton, N.J.: Princeton University Press, 1957–1966.

13 The 1850s: The Gathering Storm

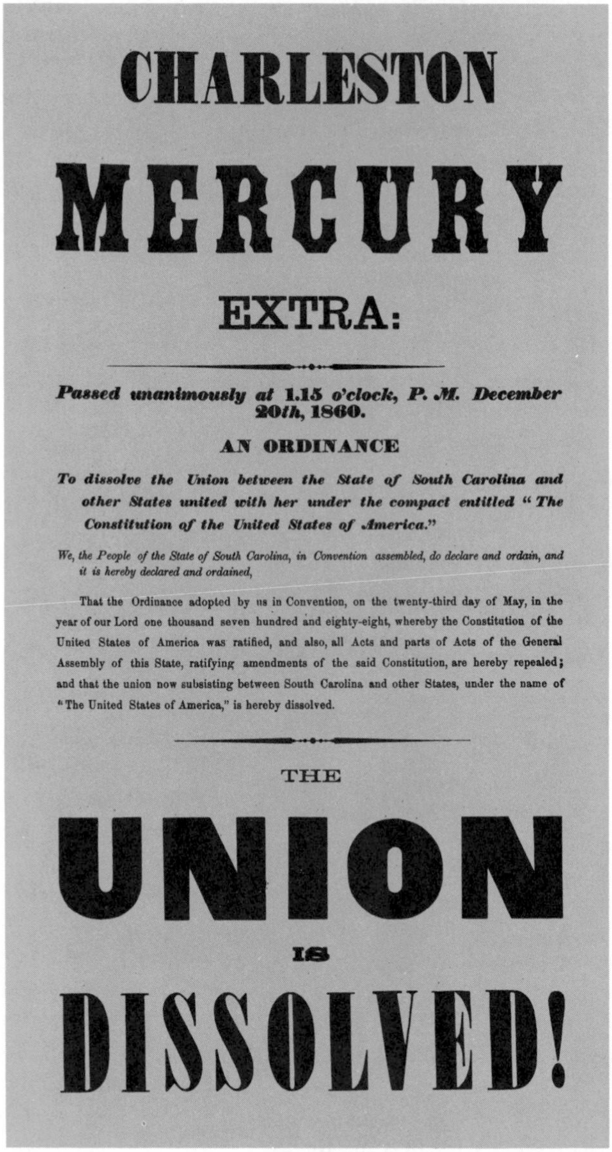

CHARLESTON

MERCURY

EXTRA:

Passed unanimously at 1.15 o'clock, P. M. December 20th, 1860.

AN ORDINANCE

To dissolve the Union between the State of South Carolina and other States united with her under the compact entitled "The Constitution of the United States of America."

We, the People of the State of South Carolina, in Convention assembled, do declare and ordain, and it is hereby declared and ordained,

That the Ordinance adopted by us in Convention, on the twenty-third day of May, in the year of our Lord one thousand seven hundred and eighty-eight, whereby the Constitution of the United States of America was ratified, and also, all Acts and parts of Acts of the General Assembly of this State, ratifying amendments of the said Constitution, are hereby repealed; and that the union now subsisting between South Carolina and other States, under the name of "The United States of America," is hereby dissolved.

THE

UNION

IS

DISSOLVED!

I believe this government cannot endure, permanently half slave and half free. I do not expect the Union to be dissolved—I do not expect the house to fall—but I do expect it will cease to be divided. It will become all one thing, or all the other. Either the opponents of slavery will arrest the further spread of it, and place it where the public mind shall rest in the belief that it is in the course of ultimate extinction; or its advocates will push it forward, till it shall become alike lawful in all the States, old as well as new—North as well as South.

Abraham Lincoln, 1858

Significant Events

Clayton-Bulwer treaty [1850]

Uncle Tom's Cabin by Harriet Beecher Stowe [1852]

American, or Know-Nothing, party formed [1852]

Gadsden Purchase [1853]

Kansas-Nebraska Act [1854]

Republican party formed [1854]

Ostend Manifesto [1854]

Brooks attacks Sumner in Senate [1856]

Dred Scott v. *Sanford* [1857]

Economic panic [1857]

Lincoln-Douglas debates [1858]

John Brown's Raid on Harpers Ferry [1859]

Seven states of lower South secede [December 20, 1860–February 1, 1861]

Fort Sumter surrenders [April 13, 1861]

Virginia, Arkansas, Tennessee, and North Carolina secede [April 17–June 8, 1861]

AN 1860 POSTER HAILING THE SECESSION OF SOUTH CAROLINA FROM THE UNION.

By 1850 sectional rivalry between the North and the South had reached almost a boiling point. Crucial questions between the sections remained unresolved: what was to be the future of slavery in the United States? what were the rights of political minorities under a democratic government? how were national policies to be devised that would benefit both agricultural and industrial interests? Not only was the political party system unresponsive to the needs that gave rise to these questions, it also proved to be incapable of alleviating the emotional and economic apprehensions of many native-born workers concerning the enormous influx of Catholic immigrants from Ireland and Germany. At a time when a strong political party system might have helped hold the nation together, the system splintered: by the end of the decade another party realignment had occurred.

Even some of the terms of the Compromise of 1850 remained in dispute. First of all, Southerners objected to the admission of California as a free state. In addition, even though slavery had been declared permissible in Utah and New Mexico, because antislavery settlers formed an overwhelming majority, slaveowners were afraid to move with their slaves into these territories. Furthermore, many Southerners believed that the federal government should protect slaveholders, even if they were in the minority, in any territory until it reached the stage of seeking entrance to the Union. Then slaveholders would feel more inclined to populate unsettled areas in the West. Southerners were disturbed that the Compromise of 1850 contained no such provision and feared that they would soon be greatly outnumbered by free states.

In the North events in the early 1850s heightened the controversy over slavery. Extreme abolitionists sought to keep their crusade alive by preventing enforcement of the new Fugitive Slave Law. In 1850 Vermont became the first of several Northern states to enact a "personal liberty law" to impede its enforcement. In these Northeastern states fugitives began receiving legal support and jury trials, and state and local law officers were forbidden to detain them. Every time a slave was returned to his or her owner more Northerners became enraged by the brutal institution.

The publication in 1852 of Harriet Beecher Stowe's *Uncle Tom's Cabin* added to the furor surrounding the issue of slavery. The daughter of a New England clergyman, Mrs. Stowe was careful to attack the moral evil of slavery rather than the Southerners who perpetuated it. In fact, Simon Legree, the novel's cruel overseer, was a Northerner. The novel sold three hundred thousand copies within a year and three million copies before the Civil War. Its melodramatic appeal, particularly as dramatized on stages across the country, turned thousands against the institution of slavery.

Moreover, Northern population and industry were growing. The entire coastal trade was in Northern hands. The completion of railroad lines linking the Northwest to the more settled areas of the country was daily creating closer political and economic ties between the Northeast and the Northwest. With fewer rail lines the South, in financial matters, had become a virtual colony of the North, and Southerners saw no end to Northern demands for higher tariffs, federal support of internal improvements, and free public lands for yeoman farmers.

POSTER ADVERTISING THE CONTROVERSIAL NOVEL *UNCLE TOM'S CABIN.*

Finally, most inopportunely, the American political party system, which had survived since its emergence in the Jacksonian era, began to break down. The American, or Know-Nothing, party, formed in the early 1850s, appealed to the prejudices of native-born Americans who resented the influx of Catholic immigrants from Ireland and Germany. At first as much a secret society as a political party, the Know-Nothings derived their name from the fact that candidates were instructed to keep their inflammatory views secret and to answer when questioned about such controversial matters that they "knew nothing." A powerfully disruptive force in the politics of the early 1850s, the American party attracted members from both Whig and Democratic parties: native-born working people who feared that competition from cheap foreign labor would threaten them economically, and Southerners who feared the population advantage which increased immigration gave the North. In short, the American party attracted those who were dissatisfied with the unresponsiveness of the prevailing party structure. By 1855 it controlled most of New England and had strength in other parts of the country as well.

Pierce's Presidency

The Election of 1852

While slavery divided the country on moral grounds, it also undermined the institutions that held the country together. The effect was most clearly seen in the divisions within the political parties.

The Democrats embraced several factions in an uneasy alliance: the small farmers of the West who were against the expansion of slavery; many planters and most small farmers in the South who defended its expansion; Eastern merchants whose business was mainly in the South; and many skilled and unskilled workers in Northern towns who were not abolitionists but who were against slavery. The Democrats had pledged to support the Compromise of 1850 and to oppose all attempts to open the question of slavery to debate again. Since the party included so many factions, however, it had difficulty selecting a presidential candidate for the election of 1852. Eventually Governor Franklin Pierce of New Hampshire, charming but irresolute, was chosen because he was considered unobjectionable to the South.

The party that had sponsored white male suffrage was now dominated by Southern slaveholders. The 1836 Democratic national convention had adopted a rule that made it necessary for a candidate to obtain the support of two-thirds of the delegates to win the nomination for the presidency. Southern delegates used this rule to block the selection of anyone they did not want. The irony of this situation was not lost on Northern antislavery Democrats.

The Northern Whigs bitterly opposed the Fugitive Slave Law and saw to it that General Winfield Scott received the nomination, instead of the pliable incumbent, President Fillmore. But the Whig platform agreed reluctantly to "acquiesce in" the Compromise of 1850. The Democrats swept the election, with Pierce carrying twenty-seven states to Scott's four. There were several reasons for this. One factor was the support given the Democrats by Southern whites. Equally important was the fact that antislavery sentiment seemed everywhere to be on the decline. Most Northerners felt that pursuing the slavery issue would threaten the Union; therefore they voted for the party that had promised to oppose all efforts to open the slavery issue to further debate.

The loss of the election was fatal to the Whigs. Southerners abandoned the party, fearing that a strong central government controlled by Northern antislavery politicians would destroy their way of life. The great Unionists in the party, Webster and Clay, had held the rival factions together in an alliance to preserve the nation, but they both died in 1852.

An Expansionist Foreign Policy

In matters of foreign policy President Pierce planned to continue the expansionist program of his predecessor, James K. Polk. For most Northerners, however, territorial expansion under a president they considered the pawn of Southern proslavery forces inevitably raised the specter of the expansion of slavery. In the past, most Americans had heartily endorsed the acquisition of new territory, but now the ever-present issue of slavery affected almost every consideration of foreign as well as domestic policy.

Efforts to Acquire Cuba Outside of the United States, Cuba, with its valuable sugar plantations, was one of the last strongholds of slavery in the Western Hemisphere. Southerners wanted to secure possession of the island in order to gain another slave state, a prospect which alarmed Northerners.

Despite the slavery issue, the acquisition of Cuba would have been of strategic advantage to the nation. It would have ensured the safety of American commerce in the Gulf of Mexico and of a proposed interoceanic canal through Central America. As long as Cuba remained in foreign hands, the island could be used as a base for attacking the United States. As early as 1848 President Polk had offered Spain $100 million for Cuba, but the Spanish, whose empire in the New World was already greatly diminished, rejected the offer.

President Pierce made the acquisition of Cuba one of his prime objectives. He appointed a Louisiana senator, Pierre Soulé, as his minister to Spain and informed him that the acquisition of Cuba was the goal of his mission.

Early in 1854, an American ship, the *Black Warrior*, was seized in Havana for violating Spanish customs laws. Pierce sought to use this incident as an excuse to declare war. Soulé was instructed to obtain an indemnity of $300,000 and an apology from the Spanish government. Acting on his own authority, Soulé presented this demand with a forty-eight-hour deadline. When Spain refused to comply, Soulé threatened war. Recognizing that the American envoy had exceeded his instructions, the Spanish foreign minister ignored Soulé's ultimatum and settled the matter directly with the ship's owners and with Pierce's secretary of state, William L. Marcy. As the New York *Herald* commented about Soulé: "We wanted an Ambassador there, we have sent a matador."

After this diplomatic blunder, Soulé was reassigned to confer with the American ministers in London and Paris. The task was to assess how the European powers would respond if America should invade Cuba. Misunderstanding their instructions, the ministers sent Secretary Marcy a confidential dispatch from Ostend, Belgium, in October 1854, recommending that the United States offer Spain $120 million for Cuba. If the offer was rejected, they wrote, the United States, "by every law, human and divine, shall be justified in wresting" Cuba from Spain "if we possess the power."

When this recommendation, known as the Ostend Manifesto, was made public in the United States, Southerners greeted it with enthusiasm. But Northern Free-Soilers branded it as a plot to add another slave state to the Union, leading President Pierce to repudiate it. For the time being, Cuba remained in the hands of Spain.

Central America During the California gold rush, many seekers of wealth had crossed the isthmus of Central America on their way to the West Coast. After this, the United States seriously considered constructing a canal through Central America to shorten the sea voyage from coast to coast. Although several American diplomats viewed the tiny republic of Nicaragua as the best site, Great Britain objected to American plans. The dispute was finally settled by the Clayton-Bulwer treaty of 1850, which provided that any canal built by either country would be open to ships of all nations and would remain unfortified even in time of war. Furthermore, the United States and Britain promised not to attempt to gain political control of Central America. American expansionists regarded the treaty as a diplomatic defeat, but it did prevent a showdown with a powerful adversary and established the principle of a neutral, unfortified canal.

Ignoring their government's pledge, some American entrepreneurs persisted in interfering in the region's economic and political affairs. A group of investors formed the Panama Railway Company and began to operate a railroad line across the isthmus of Panama in 1855. At the same time, railroad promoter Commodore Cornelius Vanderbilt subsidized a scheme to seize control of Nicaragua. In 1855 an adventurer named William Walker proclaimed himself president, apparently planning to make himself dictator of all of Central America and open the area to slavery. The Democrats expressed approval of Walker's government in their 1856 platform. Involved in a controversy with Vanderbilt, however, Walker lost his supplies and was ousted by

THE "OSTEND DOCTRINE," OR PRACTICAL DEMOCRATS CARRYING OUT THE PRINCIPLE. IN THIS 1854 CARTOON JAMES BUCHANAN, UNITED STATES MINISTER TO GREAT BRITAIN, IS BEING ROBBED BY A GROUP OF RUFFIANS WHO JUSTIFY THEIR ACTIONS BY QUOTING THE "OSTEND MANIFESTO."

the neighboring republics. When Walker attempted to return to power in 1860, British naval officials arrested him and turned him over to authorities in Honduras who executed him.

The Gadsden Purchase Despite Pierce's expansionist ambitions, the United States acquired only a few thousand acres of additional territory during his administration. An 1853 survey of possible routes for an intercontinental railroad found that the shortest southern route lay across Mexican territory south of the Gila River. To make possible the construction of the railroads, Pierce's secretary of war, Jefferson

Davis, proposed the annexation of territory extending from lower California into northwestern Mexico. Suspicious that this really was a Southern effort to extend slavery, Northerners reduced the size of the area to be purchased. James Gadsden, the American minister to Mexico, was sent to negotiate a treaty and in 1853 he purchased forty-five thousand square miles of the southern Arizona desert for $10 million. Quickly approved by the United States Senate, the treaty, which Gadsden had extorted by threats of force, was very unpopular in Mexico. It proved disappointing to Southerners as well, for the following year Congress seemed disinclined to support the building of only a southern transcontinental railroad.

The Kansas-Nebraska Act

The Pierce administration was soon embroiled in a domestic controversy that shattered the superficial calm created by the Compromise of 1850. In 1830 the areas west of Missouri and Iowa (known as the Nebraska Country) had been set aside as a permanent Indian reserve. By the 1850s, however, land hunger, fed by plans to run the projected transcontinental railroad through the area, prompted the government to revise its policy.

In 1854, the chairman of the Committee on the Territories, Stephen A. Douglas, whose success in securing passage of the Compromise of 1850 had earned him a position of prominence in the Democratic party, submitted a bill to the Senate proposing to organize the Nebraska Country into territories and eventually into states. Although Douglas's motives for introducing the bill were not completely clear, he was an ardent expansionist who wanted to open the territories west of the Mississippi River for settlement. He also wanted to obtain from the South backing for his presidential ambitions as well as support for building a transcontinental railroad from Chicago to the Pacific Coast. He hoped the pro-

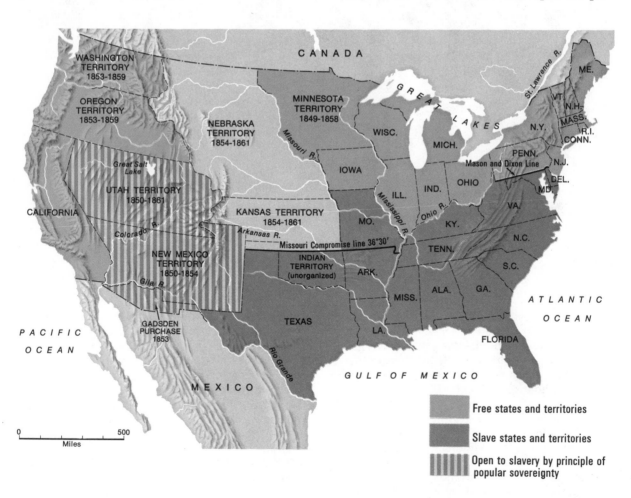

Kansas-Nebraska Act • 1854

posed line would supercede an alternative Southern plan to follow the shorter route from New Orleans through Texas and southern Arizona. This ambition to promote the economic development of Chicago and the Midwest by building a transcontinental railroad led Douglas to introduce a bill which raised once again the explosive issue of the expansion of slavery into new territories.

By the terms of the Missouri Compromise of 1820, the entire Nebraska Country was closed to slavery. But Douglas, advocating popular sovereignty, suggested that the people of Nebraska, like those of Utah and New Mexico, be allowed to decide the issue for themselves. Douglas believed that since most of Nebraska was too far north for cotton growing, it was unlikely to become a slaveholding area anyway, and he suggested self-determination in hopes of ensuring Southern support for his proposal.

Before formal debate began, Southern members of Congress brought pressure on Douglas to make three changes in the bill. Douglas's original bill empowered Congress to reject a proslavery constitution, even if the people of the territory voted to legalize slavery under their state constitution. The revised bill removed that power from Congress. Second, Douglas's bill contradicted but did not repudiate the Missouri Compromise. The revised bill explicitly stated that the compromise was henceforth "inoperative and void," an important psychological victory for the South. Third, the revised bill specifically divided the Nebraska Country into two territories: the larger Nebraska to the north, and Kansas to the south. This made it more likely that Kansas, which lay immediately to the west of the slave state of Missouri, would itself become a slave state.

Douglas made these changes in his bill simply to speed its passage through Congress. Though he viewed slavery as an outdated, inefficient institution, he had no deep feelings about the issue; in fact, he was fond of saying, "I don't care whether slavery is voted up or down." He expected the bill to generate some controversy, but thought it would please most people: his constituents in Chicago, because they would be at the eastern terminus of the proposed transcontinental railroad to be built through the territory; Westerners, because they would now have free access to lands formerly reserved for the Indians; Southerners, because the principle of popular sovereignty could extend slavery to parts of the Louisiana Purchase formerly closed to it under the Missouri Compromise; and the nation as a whole, because a new sectional controversy would be avoided and the Union preserved.

Unfortunately, Douglas failed to gauge the depth of Northern opposition to the expansion of slavery. The Northern states were enraged over the prospect of the destruction of the Missouri Compromise and the idea of leaving the vital question of slavery in the hands of a few settlers. Northern churches called upon their members to resist passage of the bill, and Northern newspapers reported that public opinion was united in resolute opposition.

Congressional debate lasted four months, but despite Northern efforts, Southerners and their sympathizers were successful. On March 3, 1854, the Kansas-Nebraska bill passed in the Southern-dominated Senate by thirty-seven votes to fourteen; two and a half months later the more sharply divided House passed it by a margin of only three votes.

Political Realignments

The new act had a profound effect on American politics. It reopened old wounds temporarily patched by the Compromise of 1850. In addition, it created serious divisions within the Democratic party; only seven of the forty-two Northern Democrats who voted for the Kansas-Nebraska Act were reelected. Finally, it undermined Douglas's position of leadership. After the passage of the bill he was mobbed by abolitionists in his home state of Illinois and ruefully claimed he could have traveled from Chicago to Boston by the light of his burning effigies.

The reaction to the Kansas-Nebraska Act also sparked the formation of a powerful new political coalition of antislavery reformers and Free-Soilers who wanted the territories preserved for free white farmers. The Republican party, as they called themselves in an effort to associate the movement with Jefferson, quickly became the country's second major political party. By the end of the summer of 1854, the Republicans had united most Northern Whigs, many Northern Democrats, former Free-Soilers, evangelicals, abolitionists, temperance advocates, and some Know-Nothings who opposed slavery. Republican strength was centered in New England and the area below the Great Lakes where New England emigrants had settled.

Despite their variety of opinions on other issues, the Republicans were solidly united against the Kansas-Nebraska Act, which they viewed as a symbol of the South's determination to spread its institutions throughout the nation. For their part, Southerners were afraid that Republicans were seeking to gain control of the federal government in order to keep Southern slaveowners out of the territories. They were right: Republican orators constantly emphasized that it was the labor of free people, who worked hard and saved their money, that was responsible for economic progress. Because of slavery, they argued, the South accorded no dignity to manual labor and was economically stagnant. Republican determination to prevent the further spread of slavery into the territories was only the first step toward the goal of destroying it altogether. While most Republicans believed in the superiority of the white race and entertained doubts as to the capability of blacks, the distinctiveness of the party lay in its belief that the institution of slavery was morally offensive and that ultimately it must be eliminated.

The Struggle for Kansas

With the passage of the Kansas-Nebraska Act, the rush to settle Kansas was begun. Northern abolitionists, determined to make the territory a free state, financed the migration of antislavery Free-Soil settlers to Kansas. At the same time, proponents of slavery from Missouri, Alabama, Georgia, and South Carolina also moved into the region.

When Kansas held its first territorial election in 1855, there were only about three thousand registered voters, most of them from the North. However, some three thousand proslavery Missourians crossed the border and cast ballots illegally. Andrew H. Reeder, appointed governor of Kansas by President Pierce, tried to disqualify eight of the thirty-one members of the territorial legislature on the grounds that they had been elected irregularly. Southern members of Congress put pressure on Pierce to veto this move since the disqualified legislators were all proslavery. Pierce acceded to their demands and refused to support Reeder. The illegally elected Kansas legislators thus remained in office. The legislature then asked the president to remove Reeder from office. Pierce complied, naming William Shannon of Ohio as the new governor.

JOHN BROWN AT HARPERS FERRY (see p. 366).

Soon the proslavery Kansas legislature passed a series of laws designed to drive Free-Soilers out of the territory: anyone caught harboring a fugitive, or even speaking out against slavery, was subject to a fine and a prison term. The Free-Soil faction responded by framing a state constitution that made slavery illegal in Kansas, creating a territorial government of their own, and sending Andrew Reeder to Washington as their territorial delegate. Kansas now had two legislatures representing two antagonistic factions. Pierce might have been able to mollify both sides if he had called for new, carefully monitored elections, but he hesitated, and the territory was plunged into violence.

"Bleeding Kansas" In May 1856 fighting erupted in Kansas, ultimately claiming two hundred lives. In one episode, a proslavery band raided the town of Lawrence and arrested several Free-Soil leaders. John Brown, a fanatical abolitionist, led a counterattack into enemy territory and murdered five proslavery settlers. In an effort to control the explosive Kansas territory, federal troops were sent and the conflict gradually subsided. Although no more blood was shed, tension over the slavery question in "Bleeding Kansas" intensified as a result of emotional propaganda spread by both sides.

Few of the Kansas Free-Soilers were true abolitionists. Most opposed slavery not because they considered it morally wrong, but because they feared that cheap slave labor would pose an economic threat to them. When Kansas finally became a state in 1861, its constitution forbade slavery but also excluded free blacks. Abolitionists in New York and New England, however, were not concerned with the economic side of the issue in 1856. They thought of Kansas as a battleground where divinely inspired abolitionists were fighting to crush the satanic forces of slavery.

The Brooks-Sumner Affair

Violence over the slavery question surfaced even in Congress. With feelings on both sides running high, legislators armed themselves with knives and pistols, which they carried with them into the chambers. The day after the raid on the town of Lawrence, Charles Sumner of Massachusetts delivered a bitter, sarcastic speech arguing for a free Kansas and criticizing proslavery advocates, among them Senator Andrew P. Butler of South Carolina. Anxious to defend his uncle's honor, Butler's enraged nephew, Congressman Preston Brooks, attacked Senator Sumner in the Senate, crying: "Mr. Sumner, I have read your speech against South Carolina, and have read it carefully, deliberately and dispassionately, in which you have libelled my State and slandered my white-haired old relative, Senator Butler, who is absent, and I have come to punish you for it." Brooks struck Sumner many times with his cane until he was unconscious. Although not permanently impaired physically, Sumner suffered such severe emotional damage that he remained out of politics for more than three years. News of the attack was sped over telegraph lines to all parts of the country. Outraged Northerners protested furiously, and Northern newspaper cartoons depicted a noble Sumner, quill in hand, falling before the merciless onslaught of "Bully" Brooks. But in the South, Brooks was cheered for his "chivalrous" action. The nation itself was moving closer to a violent eruption.

A NORTHERN CARTOON DEPICTING BROOKS'S ATTACK ON SUMNER IN THE SENATE CHAMBERS. SOUTHERN SENATORS IN THE BACKGROUND LOOK ON WITH AMUSEMENT.

Buchanan's Presidency

The Election of 1856

The continuing controversy over slavery, the violence in Kansas, and the disputes over Pierce's expansionist, pro-Southern foreign policy dominated the election campaign of 1856.

The Democrats, with their strong Southern contingent, cautiously endorsed the Fugitive Slave Act and the Kansas-Nebraska Act and supported the use of popular sovereignty to determine the status of slavery in new territories. However, because their two most eminent defenders of popular sovereignty, Pierce and Douglas, were unpopular with the Northern wing of the party, they nominated for president the politically uncontroversial James Buchanan, who had spent the last few troubled years as the American minister to Great Britain.

The new Republican party unanimously nominated the dynamic John C. Frémont, whose primary distinction rested on his fame as a explorer and his participation in California's revolt against Mexico. Like Andrew Jackson, William Henry Harrison, and Zachary Taylor, Frémont was drawn into politics as a war hero respected more for his victories than for his political views.

In an emotion-charged convention, the Republican party platform firmly opposed the Kansas-Nebraska Act and supported a federally financed program of internal improvements. Both of these positions were opposed by Southerners. Taking these two positions established still more clearly the fact that the Republicans were a Northern-based party whose appeal was only to that section.

In its platform for 1856, the American, or Know-Nothing, party emphasized its opposition to foreign immigration. Like the Democrats, however, its members were split on the issue of slavery. Ultimately the Northern wing of the party endorsed Frémont and swung over to the Republican party. The Southern wing nominated former president Millard Fillmore, who was also endorsed by the few surviving Whigs.

Buchanan scored an impressive victory in the electoral college, winning 174–114; in the popular vote he carried every Southern state except Maryland, but only five Northern states. Even though the Democratic party was a national organization, it was obvious that it owed its victory to the South.

Just as clearly, the Republicans were an exclusively Northern party. If they had won a few more popular votes in two more large Northern states, such as Pennsylvania and Illinois, Frémont would have been president. Considering that this party was a recent phenomenon, it had made a remarkably good showing in the election.

James Buchanan

James Buchanan had been in government service for forty-three years and his long public career had been favorably regarded. A lawyer, he was experienced in constitutional law, which he revered first as a Federalist and later as a conservative mainstay of the Democratic party. His most important appointments were as minister to Russia under Jackson, as secretary of state under Polk, and as minister to England under Pierce. Buchanan was sixty-six, the first bachelor and only Pennsylvanian to be president. His career in public service had been so long and varied that many people expected him to steer the ship of state expertly out of troubled waters. Unfortunately, Buchanan, like Pierce, was inclined to vacillate and to accept the views of his Southern advisers. Although he believed slavery to be morally wrong, he felt that the Constitution required its protection in states where it was already established.

The *Dred Scott* Decision

Two days after Buchanan's inauguration, the Supreme Court announced a controversial decision in the case of Dred Scott, a black man seeking freedom from slavery. Scott's owner, Dr. John Emerson of St. Louis, Missouri, was an army surgeon who had been stationed for two years in Illinois and for two years at Fort Snelling in the Wisconsin Territory—areas where slavery was prohibited. Through these changes of residence, Emerson had been accompanied by Scott. After Emerson died, ownership of Scott passed to Emerson's daughter. Emerson's widow, acting as executor of her husband's estate, left Scott in St. Louis where an agent hired him out at five dollars a month. In 1846 Henry T. Blow, an abolitionist, persuaded Scott to go to court and sue for his freedom, based on his four-year residence in areas where slavery was prohibited. The

DRED SCOTT, WHO WAS FREED BY HIS OWNER AFTER THE SUPREME COURT'S RULING, FOUND EMPLOYMENT AS A HOTEL PORTER IN ST. LOUIS ONLY TO DIE OF TUBERCULOSIS THE FOLLOWING YEAR.

aging Scott, who feared that he would be sold away from his family because his services were not in great demand, brought suit in the lower Missouri court and was quickly awarded his freedom. The Missouri Supreme Court, however, reversed the decision.

In the meantime, Mrs. Emerson remarried and her brother, John A. Sanford of New York, became executor of the Emerson estate. Because Sanford lived in another state, Scott's appeal could now be brought to the federal courts, which had jurisdiction over all interstate matters. The Supreme Court, in a six-to-three decision, ruled against Scott. Although there were several opinions given for the majority, five justices concurred in the complex, labored argument set forth by Chief Justice Taney. Justice Taney ruled that Scott was not entitled to the rights of a citizen and that therefore he had no right to come

---

Dred Scott v. Sanford

"The question then arises, whether the provisions of the Constitution, in relation to the personal rights and privileges to which the citizen of a State should be entitled, embraced the negro African race, at that time in this country, or who might afterwards be imported, who had then or should afterwards be made free in any State; and to put it in the power of a single State to make him a citizen of the United States, and endue him with the full rights of citizenship in every other State without their consent. Does the Constitution of the United States act upon him whenever he shall be made free under the laws of a State, and raised there to the rank of a citizen in every other State and in its own courts?

The court think the affirmative of these propositions cannot be maintained. . . ."

Chief Justice Taney, 1857

Dred Scott v. Sanford

"I can find nothing in the Constitution which . . . deprives of their citizenship any class of persons who were citizens of the United States at the time of its adoption, or who should be native-born citizens of any State after its adoption; nor any power enabling Congress to disfranchise persons born on the soil of any State, and entitled to citizenship of such State by its constitution and laws. And my opinion, is, that, under the Constitution of the United States, every free person born on the soil of a State, who is a citizen of that State by force of its constitution or laws, is also a citizen of the United States. . . .

I dissent, therefore, from that part of the opinion of the majority of the court, in which it is held that a person of African descent cannot be a citizen of the United States. . . ."

Justice Curtis, 1857

before the Court. He declared further that free blacks were not citizens. On the question of slavery in the territories, the Court, which was composed primarily of pro-Southern jurists, proceeded to lay down broad principles, the effect of which was to negate both the Missouri Compromise and the Compromise of 1850. In a majority opinion, the justices declared that the Missouri Compromise was unconstitutional. They argued that neither Congress nor the territorial legislatures had the right to outlaw slavery because the Fifth Amendment expressly guaranteed the protection of personal property, and a slave was considered property. Moreover, the Court flatly contradicted Douglas's doctrine of popular sovereignty. Whereas Douglas had assured the people of Kansas that they had the right to ban slavery from their territory if they chose to do so, the Court now ruled that only a state, not a territory, could make such a decision.

Two justices wrote dissenting opinions, arguing that free blacks were indeed citizens of the United States and that Congress was constitutionally empowered to exclude slavery from the territories, since the constitutional right to create territories obviously included the right to govern them.

Southerners rejoiced over their victory. The highest tribunal of the land had forbidden Congress to interfere with what now had to be regarded as a purely local issue. Outraged Northern Free-Soilers denounced the decision, claiming that slavery could now be extended into the Minnesota Territory and even Oregon. Abolitionists jeered at the irony of the Court's defending slavery in the name of the Bill of Rights. An editorial in the Chicago *Tribune* suggested that the only remedy left for restricting the spread of slavery was either to amend the Constitution or to alter the membership of the Supreme Court:

That bench full of Southern lawyers which gentlemen of a political temperament call "august tribunal" is that last entrenchment behind which despotism is sheltered, and until a national convention amends the Constitution so as to defend it against the usurpations of that body, or until the Court itself is reconstructed by the dropping off of a few of its members and the appointment of better men in their places, we have little to hope for by congressional action in the way of restricting slavery.

The Crisis over Kansas

Before the Dred Scott decision, Buchanan had secretly encouraged the Court to deprive Congress and the territorial legislatures of the authority to ban slavery. After the decision, in an effort to appease even further the Southern wing of the party, he tried to bring Kansas into the Union as a slave state, in spite of the fact that most Kansans were Free-Soilers. Since the previous territorial governor had resigned, Buchanan appointed Robert J. Walker to the position. Walker, an able administrator, quickly recognized that most Kansans wanted to prohibit slavery from their state. Accordingly, even though he was a native of the slave state of Mississippi, Walker worked to help the citizens of Kansas turn their preference into law.

By 1857 Kansas had enough settlers to apply for statehood on a popular-sovereignty basis. However, the minority proslavery faction rapidly organized a convention in the town of Lecompton and drafted a proslavery state constitution. The Lecompton Constitution was presented to the voters in such a way that they did not really have the chance to vote on the issue at all. The antislavery faction, infuriated by the unfair dealings of the proslavery group, refused to vote, and the document was ratified by the proslavery faction. Walker then went to Washington to urge the president to reject the Lecompton Constitution and to convene a new, fairly elected convention in Kansas, but Buchanan, now completely under the influence of his Southern-dominated cabinet and apprehensive over threats of Southern secession if the constitution were not accepted, refused to do this. In this decision Buchanan was not only ignoring Walker, he was also ignoring a deluge of letters that poured in from all over the North opposing the constitution.

Douglas, who had supported the Dred Scott decision in the hope that it would bring an end to the increasing sectional conflict, now broke with the president on the grounds that the Lecompton Constitution betrayed popular sovereignty. Convinced that the Southern Democrats were out to destroy the Union, Douglas gave an impassioned speech on the floor of the Senate arguing that Kansas must be allowed to vote freely on the Lecompton Constitution and that the result of the vote must be binding. Buchanan nevertheless submitted the document to Congress. It passed in the Senate, but in the House,

Republicans and "Douglas Democrats" blocked its passage. The two houses next proposed a compromise measure, the English bill, which provided that if a new referendum in Kansas accepted the Lecompton Constitution, Kansas would immediately be admitted to the Union and would receive a federal grant of about four million acres of land. If the constitution was rejected, statehood and the land grant would be delayed until the territory had about ninety thousand inhabitants. This would mean a wait of perhaps two years. The English bill passed both houses, even though Douglas himself and many Republicans opposed it.

Soon, a fairly elected legislature took office in Kansas. In a referendum on the Lecompton Constitution on January 4, 1858, the document was overwhelmingly rejected. Despite the decisive victory of the majority of Free-Soilers, Buchanan stubbornly persisted in regarding the Lecompton Constitution as a legitimate document. Congress called for another referendum, promising immediate admission to the Union and a large grant of federal lands if the document was approved. But on August 2, 1858, Kansas again rejected the Lecompton Constitution, preferring to retain its territorial status and postpone seeking admission. When Kansas finally entered the Union two and a half years later, in 1861, it did so as a free state.

Buchanan's stubbornness had not only alienated the North, but also further split the Democratic party. His rejection of Douglas's cherished theory of popular sovereignty permanently estranged Douglas and his followers. Now the party was divided into Southern Democrats, who backed the president, and "Douglas Democrats," who supported the senator from Illinois.

The Panic of 1857

In 1857 sectional strains were intensified by a downturn in the economy. When the panic came, more than five thousand businesses failed within a year, and unemployment became widespread.

Because of the country's preoccupation with slavery and territorial expansion, other factors which were undermining the economy had been neglected. Frenzied speculation in land and the rapid expansion of new railroad lines even into thinly settled areas where there was little demand for service had created economic problems. At the same time, the Crimean War had created a temporary demand for surplus American grain and meat. But when the war ended in 1856, food prices fell drastically, and many farmers began defaulting on their mortgages. Finally, the discovery of gold had inflated the currency. The result of these events was a depression which was experienced most severely in the North.

The South was relatively unaffected, since world demand for cotton remained high. Exultant Southerners, smarting under Northern attacks on their way of life, pointed to their economic invulnerability as proof of the superiority of their slave-based cotton economy. Northerners, failing to understand the true causes of the panic, blamed it on the low Tariff of 1857, which had been pushed through Congress by the South. The Republican party, incurring further Southern wrath, demanded a higher protective tariff for Northern industry.

The Gathering Storm

Abraham Lincoln

The question of the expansion of slavery was again the key issue in the congressional elections of 1858. The most dramatic debate on the subject took place in Illinois, where Stephen A. Douglas was running for reelection. Although senators were elected by the state legislatures at this time, a popular election was generally held so that the people could indicate their preference.

The Republicans nominated Abraham Lincoln to oppose Douglas. Lincoln, the son of an uneducated frontier farmer, was born in Kentucky in 1809. When he was seven, the family moved to Indiana, and they finally settled in southern Illinois in 1830. Lincoln received almost no formal schooling, but educated himself by reading widely, finally choosing the law as his profession. Physically ungainly, he once described himself thus: "It may be said I am, in height, six feet four inches, nearly; lean in flesh, weighing an average one hundred and eighty pounds; dark complexion, with coarse black hair and gray eyes. No other marks or brands recollected." His character was complex, combining an earthy sense of humor with a strong tendency toward melancholy. Open-hearted, idealistic, and compassionate, he possessed an exquisite sensitivity to life's hardships. At the same time he was shrewd and ambitious to lead.

As a youth he practiced public speaking, and he had barely reached adulthood when he became caught up in the excitement of politics. Although his family had been Democrats, he was attracted to Clay's American System. He also supported the franchise for women and was a temperance advocate. With these views it was natural for him to become a Whig. Lincoln won his first political post as a Whig member of the Illinois state legislature in 1834 at the age of twenty-three. His colleagues soon selected him for a position of leadership. In 1846 he was elected to the House of Representatives where he served for one term during the Mexican War. Two years after the passage of Kansas-Nebraska Act, Lincoln joined the new Republican party. His national reputation was made when he was nominated by his party to run against Douglas for the Senate in 1858. To capitalize on his position as the underdog, he challenged Douglas to a series of debates which were to be held in various towns throughout Illinois. The contest between the two men soon attracted national interest, and their remarks were reported in newspapers across the land.

The Lincoln-Douglas Debates

The two candidates debated seven times, covering a range of topics. Each time, however, they directed their attention primarily to the question of the extension of slavery into the territories. In order to frighten moderates away from the Republican side, Douglas tried to make it seem that Lincoln was an abolitionist who believed that blacks were the equals of whites, while he, on the other hand, did not hesitate to declare the inferiority of blacks. Actually, Lincoln took a moderate position, maintaining that he did not favor the destruction of accepted social conventions: "I am not, nor ever have been, in favor of bringing about in any way the social and political equality of the white and black races." Lincoln did, however, strongly condemn the institution of slavery as "a moral, social, and political wrong," and he declared that black people should have all the natural rights outlined in the

STEPHEN A. DOUGLAS, NICKNAMED THE "LITTLE GIANT," PROJECTED AN IMAGE OF ENERGY AND SUCCESS. HE DRESSED IN THE MOST CURRENT FASHION, PREFERRING FLASHY VESTS AND SUITS OF FINE BROADCLOTH. A MASTER OF SPREAD-EAGLE ORATORY, HE WAS FREQUENTLY IN MOTION AND USED FLAMBOYANT GESTURES AND BLUSTERY BUT SHREWD ARGUMENTS TO WIN HIS POINT.

ABRAHAM LINCOLN, WHO HAD ACQUIRED A REPUTATION AS "HONEST ABE," CHOSE TO APPEAR AS A FAIR-MINDED AND DIGNIFIED MAN OF THE PEOPLE. HE WORE SLIGHTLY WORN, RUMPLED CLOTHES, AND HIS SPEAKING STYLE WAS SINCERE AND SUBDUED.

Declaration of Independence: th... life, liberty, and the pursuit of happ...

On the question of the extensio... Douglas insisted on the doctrine of popu... eignty whereas Lincoln maintained that the ...n-sion of slavery must be stopped lest it become so divisive an issue as to result in a civil war. In a speech in Peoria Lincoln explained why slavery should be kept out of the territories: "We want them for homes of free white people. This they cannot be, to any considerable extent, if slavery is planted within them." The territories were "places for poor people to go to, and better their condition." If slavery was permitted, poor people would have to compete with slave labor or even become slaves themselves. Moreover, if so patent an evil as slavery could be restricted, Lincoln felt, it might even die a "natural death."

The crucial moment in the debates came in Freeport, Illinois, when Lincoln asked Douglas to reconcile his doctrine of popular sovereignty with the Supreme Court's recent Dred Scott decision. Lincoln knew that no matter what Douglas said, he would offend some supporters. If he rejected popular sovereignty, the Free-Soilers in Illinois would denounce him. If he rejected the Dred Scott decision, he would lose Southern support. With strong presidential ambitions, Douglas certainly did not wish to offend proslavery sentiment or alienate the Southern politicians who were in control of the Democratic party. Douglas's solution to this dilemma was his "Freeport Doctrine," which modified the Supreme Court decision by claiming that the people of a territory had the lawful means to introduce slavery or exclude it. He reasoned that slavery could not exist without the support of local police regulations, established by the local legislatures. If the people were opposed to slavery, they could elect representatives who would pass laws that would effectively prevent it. This concept displeased many Northerners because it glossed over the moral aspects of the slavery issue. It also horrified many Southerners, who were already alienated by Douglas's opposition to the Lecompton Constitution, because it suggested a loophole whereby a territory could exclude slavery.

In the popular election that followed, the Republicans won the popular vote; but because of an unfair apportionment of seats the Democrats controlled the state legislature, and returned Douglas to his seat in the Senate. Lincoln had driven an effective wedge between Douglas and the Southern Democrats, however, hastening the breakup of the Democratic party. He also had won prominence throughout the North as a sane, articulate, and moderate defender of Republican ideals.

The Raid on Harpers Ferry

As the presidential elections of 1860 drew closer, the hostility between North and South increased. John Brown's raid on a federal arsenal at Harpers Ferry, Virginia, exemplified the tension that would soon lead to a breakdown of the Union.

Brown, the abolitionist who had killed five supporters of slavery in Kansas in 1856, had shifted the focus of his activities to the upper South. His plan was to rally an army of slaves who would help him force the white South to its knees. Financed by a few Northern abolitionists, Brown and a small band of followers took over the federal arsenal at Harpers Ferry on the night of October 16, 1859, captured two local plantation owners, and recruited about ten of their slaves. Brown expected that other slaves would rush to join his mission, but instead outraged local townsmen arrived and were soon joined by a detachment of federal troops sent to retake the arsenal. In the ensuing confrontation, ten of Brown's men died and Brown and five others were captured. Brown was tried in Virginia court, convicted of treason, and sentenced to be hanged.

The incident at Harpers Ferry further intensified the already inflamed emotional climate surrounding the slavery issue. Most Southerners were furious that Northern abolitionists had financed Brown, and they feared that the raid might spark a general slave insurrection throughout the South. Southerners assumed that all Northerners supported Brown's exploits when in fact the majority of Northern moderates, including Lincoln, condemned his violent tactics. Yet Brown's behavior during the trial was so dignified and eloquent that he became a martyr for freedom. After his execution, Brown became "more alive than ever." With the elevation of this "fanatic" to heroic stature Southern antipathy toward the North hardened further and the threat of secession became more real. One North Carolinian wrote: "I have always been a fervid Union man [but now] I am willing to take the chances of every probable evil that may arise from disunion, sooner than submit to Northern insolence and Northern outrage."

The Election of 1860

The nation approached the presidential election of 1860 with grave apprehension. The North feared that the South had become more rigid than ever in its defense of slavery, for the conflict over the fate of Kansas, the Dred Scott decision, and John Brown's raid had done much to fire Southern pride and anger. The South feared that the North had gained a pronounced political advantage with the admission of the free states of California, Minnesota, and Oregon.

The central issue of the election, once again, was the fate of slavery in the territories. The Republicans were clearly opposed to the expansion of slavery. The Democrats were split: the Southern wing advocated federal protection of slavery in all territories; the Northern wing, led by Douglas, wanted the issue to be resolved by popular sovereignty.

The Political Conventions   At the Democratic convention in Charleston, held in April 1860, Southern extremists, unhappy with Douglas's Freeport Doctrine, demanded a plank stating that it was the duty of the national government to protect the rights and property of persons in the territories.

Douglas could not accept the plank that refuted the doctrine of popular sovereignty. His position was, "We cannot recede from this doctrine without personal dishonor, and so help us God, we will never abandon this principle." Douglas was supported by a majority of the delegates, and although they were willing to accept most Southern demands in hopes of maintaining party harmony, they nevertheless endorsed popular sovereignty.

Delegates from eight Southern states walked out in protest. Douglas needed the support of two-thirds of the delegates to win the nomination, and he did not receive it. Since no compromise could be reached, the convention disbanded. When a new convention met on June 18 in Baltimore the same delegates withdrew again, but this time they were replaced by new Southern delegates who favored Douglas, an indication that there still remained a number of Southern Democrats who were opposed to a breakup of the party. The official convention nominated Douglas; the Southern Democrats met

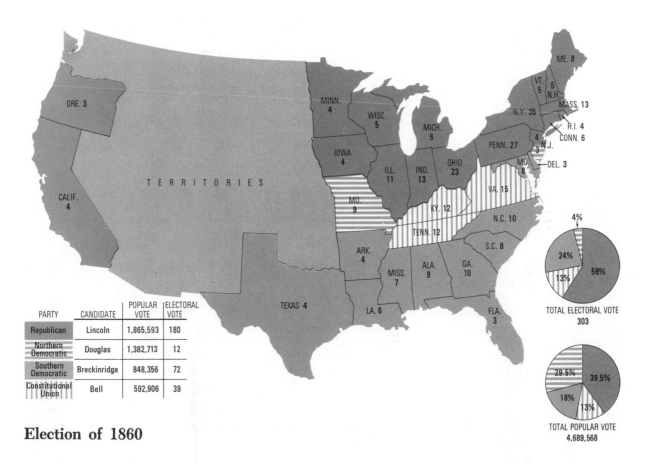

PARTY	CANDIDATE	POPULAR VOTE	ELECTORAL VOTE
Republican	Lincoln	1,865,593	180
Northern Democratic	Douglas	1,382,713	12
Southern Democratic	Breckinridge	848,356	72
Constitutional Union	Bell	592,906	39

TOTAL ELECTORAL VOTE
303

TOTAL POPULAR VOTE
4,689,568

Election of 1860

independently and nominated Vice-President John C. Breckinridge of Kentucky. The platform of the Southern wing called for a federal code to protect and expand slavery in the territories and for the annexation of Cuba. Thus the Democratic party was now fatally split.

Fearful that the division in the Democratic party posed a serious threat to the Union, a new political coalition quickly organized the Constitutional Union party. Made up of former Whigs and dissident Know-Nothings and Democrats, the new party nominated John Bell of Tennessee and campaigned on one issue: "It is both the part of patriotism and of duty to recognize no political principle other than the Constitution of the country, the union of the states, and the enforcement of the laws." Since it took no stand on the issue of slavery expansion, the party's appeal was limited. It won votes primarily in the border states along the Mason-Dixon Line, which

had the most to lose in the event of a civil war and which still retained a large reservoir of Unionist sentiment.

The Republicans gathered in Chicago on May 16. The atmosphere was one of jubilation. With the dissolution of the Democratic coalition, a Republican victory seemed within easy reach. The leading contender for the nomination was William H. Seward of New York, a dominant figure in the party from its inception. There was strong opposition to his candidacy, however, because his views on slavery were considered too radical (he had spoken boldly of a coming "irrepressible conflict" between the North and South) and because his attitude toward the new immigrants was too friendly to please the former Know-Nothings. Only Lincoln among all the contenders was without important political enemies. The promise of appointments for all of Lincoln's convention opponents helped to se-

INTERPRETING AMERICAN HISTORY

THE CAUSES OF THE CIVIL WAR

Was the Civil War inevitable? If so, what forces brought it about? Was slavery the decisive issue? How important were opposing economic interests? Could war have been avoided if the nation's leaders had acted more wisely during the 1850s?

Immediately after the war, Northern historians, many of whom had participated in the struggle or had lost relatives on the battlefield, argued that the South had plotted the destruction of the Union in order to preserve the evil institution of slavery. Henry Wilson, in his three-volume *History of the Rise and Fall of the Slave Power in America* (1872–1877), maintained that the North had fought a crusade against an absolute moral wrong. Postwar Southern historians, however, denied the importance of slavery as a cause of the war, blaming the overbearing and unconstitutional actions of the Republican party in 1860 and 1861. Others, such as former president Buchanan, felt that extremists were at fault. Had Northern abolitionists and Southern advocates of slavery been more temperate, war might have been avoided.

By the 1890s a new generation began to look at the Civil War from some distance, viewing the conflict in terms of economic nationalism. Historians such as James Ford Rhodes argued that sectionalism and slavery had hampered American growth. The war had abolished both those evils and permitted the United States to become a unified nation and a first-rate industrial power. Slavery and the South had been at fault, Rhodes wrote, but individual slaveowners were merely victims of impersonal economic forces. Southerners, not personally to blame, deserved sympathy more than censure. The Civil War had been an "irresponsible conflict" between two economic systems: the industrial wage system of the North and the agricultural slave system of the South.

Rhodes had an obvious Northern bias, but contemporary Southern historians agreed that the war had been waged between two different ways of life and two economies. Buoyed by a return to prosperity in the South, they also regarded the Civil War favorably. Southern historians of the period viewed slavery and secession not as moral wrongs, but as obstacles to economic progress in the South.

The complacency and optimism of the nationalist school was sharply challenged in the early decades of the twentieth century. Perhaps the greatest work of this period was Charles and Mary Beard's *The Rise of American Civilization*, published in 1927. Like the nationalist historians, the Beards believed that economic forces had caused the Civil War, but they did not see the results in so positive a light. Rather, they viewed the war as a "social cataclysm in which the capitalists, laborers, and farmers of the North and West drove from power in the national government the planting aristocracy of the South." Furthermore, in the postwar era a small band of Northern capitalists had ruthlessly exploited the great mass of American workers. The Beards, eager to curb the power of big business in their own day, regarded the post–Civil War period as the era during which great social and economic inequities began to develop in American life. Their arguments, which stressed the underlying economic causes of the conflict, emerged again in the 1970s in Ludwell H. Johnson's *Division and Reunion: America 1848–77* (1978).

In the 1930s a small group of American Marxist historians presented their perspective on the Civil War. Unlike the Beards, they did not deplore the outcome of the conflict. In classical Marxist theory, every economy must progress from feudalism to capitalism and then to socialism. Since the Civil War had brought an end to a slave economy, regarded by the Beards as a form of feudalism, and strengthened capitalism, the conflict was regarded as an important step toward a socialist economy in the United States. As one Marxist, James Allen, put it: "The destruction of the slave power was the basis for real national unity and the further development of capitalism, which would produce conditions most favorable for the growth of the labor movement."

During the depression, two other schools of interpretation arose. One was a movement of

Southern nationalists who blamed the conflict on the North. Typical of these was Frank L. Owsley, who attacked pre–Civil War Northerners for their abrasive approach to politics and their lack of understanding of the essence of national unity. Owsley refused to see slavery as a moral issue. In his view, it had been merely a system of discipline necessary for social control.

The second school of thought was the revisionist movement. Profoundly disillusioned over the outcome of World War I, the revisionists regarded all wars as pointless. Whereas the nationalists had emphasized economic causes, and the Marxists had viewed the Civil War as an inevitable outburst of violence in the progress toward socialism, the revisionists thought that it might easily have been averted if the country's leaders had been more skillful during the 1850s. Historians such as Avery Craven and James G. Randall insisted that the war had been a "repressible conflict" caused by a "Blundering Generation." Craven also emphasized the irrationality of the leaders as a cause of the war and charged that Americans had

permitted their shortsighted politicians, their overzealous editors, and their pious reformers to emotionalize real and potential differences and to conjure up distorted impressions of those who dwelt in other parts of the nation. . . . Opponents became devils in human form. Good men had no choice but to kill and be killed.

The revisionist position was in essence a more sophisticated restatement of Buchanan's thesis that the war had been caused by extremists on both sides.

After World War II, historians such as Allan Nevins and Arthur M. Schlesinger, Jr., returned to the theory that the Civil War was fought over the moral issue of slavery and that the North was justified in prosecuting a war against the institution. Schlesinger also rejected what he characterized as the easy optimism of the revisionists concerning the basic rationality of human nature. Schlesinger wrote that having just ended a war against the Nazis:

the experience of the twentieth century has made it clear that we gravely overrated man's capacity to solve the problems of existence within the terms of history. . . . Man generally is entangled in insoluble problems; history is consequently a tragedy in which we are all involved, whose keynote is anxiety and frustration, not progress and fulfillment.

The revisionists had contended that slavery would have eventually disappeared without the Civil War, since it was an "outmoded" institution. Given the emotional attachment of the South to slavery, Schlesinger cast grave doubt on the validity of their arguments.

The civil rights movement of the 1950s and 1960s caused historians to reexamine the position of blacks in American society and to set the institution of slavery and the Civil War within this context. Allan Nevins in The Emergence of Lincoln (1950) hypothesized that a "major root of the conflict was the problem of slavery with its complementary problem of race-adjustment. . . . It was a war over slavery and the future position of the Negro." However, this did not mean that the North was fighting for the equality of the races; there was too much evidence that Northerners as well as Southerners considered blacks to be inferior.

Other historians such as Kenneth M. Stampp, in The Causes of the Civil War (1959), have also placed the Civil War within the history of race relations in the United States. They have shown that although the war brought emancipation, it made little impact on racism. David Brion Davis's The Problem of Slavery in Western Culture (1967) shows the depth of the roots of belief in slavery, and Winthrop Jordan's massive study, White Over Black: American Attitudes Toward the Negro, 1550–1812 (1968) noted the long duration and the pervasiveness of the rejection of blacks by white Americans. Leon Litwack's North of Slavery: The Negro in the Free States, 1790–1860 (1964) con-

(Continued on next page.)

INTERPRETING AMERICAN HISTORY (Cont.)

cluded that complete segregation, formalized discrimination, and belief in black inferiority prevailed throughout the states that fought for the Union in the Civil War.

Thus most historians tend to agree that the North did not hate slavery enough to go to war because of it and certainly was not fighting for racial equality. The use of slave labor in a form of agrarian capitalism also makes it unlikely that the conflict between an industrial society and an agrarian society in itself caused the war. The definitive explanation of the conflict still eludes students of American history.

Yet slavery played an important part in every aspect of the sectional conflict. According to historian David M. Potter:

Economically, it was an immensely powerful property interest, somewhat inimical to the interests of free farming, because the independent farmer could not compete with the slave. Socially, it was the keystone of a static society of social hierarchy which challenged the dynamic, mobile, and egalitarian modes of life and labor that prevailed in the free states. Ideologically, it was a negation of the basic American principles of freedom and equality.

cure a third-ballot nomination greeted by thunderous cheers. A compromise candidate, Lincoln was ardent enough in his moral opposition to slavery to satisfy abolitionists in the Northeast while remaining moderate enough on the issue to win the confidence of former Whigs and other delegates from the Midwest.

The Republican platform took a position on slavery that directly refuted the Dred Scott decision. They based this on the guarantee of personal liberty in the Fifth Amendment. The Republicans also tried to make their party acceptable to a broader spectrum of the electorate by endorsing the immediate entrance of Kansas into the Union (to appeal to Free-Soilers), a protective tariff (to appeal to Eastern manufacturers and factory workers), a homestead law that would provide free land for settlers (to attract the votes of Western farmers), internal improvements and a transcontinental railroad (to win the allegiance of Californians and the business community), and a plank attacking any abridgement of the right of citizenship (to win votes from recent immigrants).

The Campaign The campaign was spirited. Orators led by Seward and Salmon P. Chase of Ohio toured the country on behalf of the Republican ticket, and Douglas spoke for the Northern Democrats.

The tremendous enthusiasm of the Republicans prevented them from taking seriously Southern threats to secede should Lincoln win.

The contest was a peculiar one; in reality, it was two contests. In the South, the contest was between Breckinridge and Bell; in the North, it was between Lincoln and Douglas. Breckinridge won the South. Lincoln won fewer than two thousand Southern votes; in many Southern states his name did not even appear on the ballot.

In the North, Lincoln carried every free state but New Jersey, and by winning the populous states of the North and Northwest, he was assured a majority in the electoral college. Yet the race between Lincoln and Douglas was extremely close in some Northern states. Lincoln's victory in the electoral college was decisive; he amassed 180 electoral votes to 123 for all his opponents combined. In the popular vote, however, his total was only 40 percent. Almost one million more votes were cast for his opponents than for Lincoln. Douglas alone received over 1.3 million votes.

Although Lincoln was not elected by a popular majority, he had a strong Free-Soil mandate. By casting ballots for Douglas and Lincoln, more than two-thirds of the country's voters had expressed their determination to control the expansion of slavery. Lincoln and Douglas together had received 69 percent of the total vote. A minority, sectional party had come to power.

The South Secedes

The election of Lincoln brought public emotions in the fifteen slave states to the boiling point. Southern reaction to the Republican victory was summarized by an editorial that appeared in the New Orleans *Daily Crescent*:

They have robbed us of our property . . . they have set at naught the decrees of the Supreme Court, they have invaded our States and killed our citizens, they have declared their unalterable determination to exclude us altogether from the Territories, they have nullified the laws of Congress, and finally they have capped the mighty pyramid of unfraternal enormities by electing Abraham Lincoln . . . on a platform and by a system which indicates nothing but the subjugation of the South and the complete ruin of her social, political, and industrial institutions.

For years Southerners had threatened secession. Most Southerners considered the Union a voluntary association of states and believed that states could separate from the rest of the nation whenever they chose to do so. In moving toward secession, white Southerners believed that they were preserving a way of life that provided them with individual freedom and economic opportunity. Many deeply feared that the restriction of slavery would destroy the economic and cultural foundations of their society.

Although many Southerners continued to be Unionists after Lincoln's election, the secessionists were better organized. South Carolina had long been the center of Southern separatism. As soon as the election returns were counted, its state legislature called for a convention to bring about the state's secession from the Union. The aging President Buchanan, though committed to the Union, was hesitant to take strong action. While he believed that states did not have the right to secede, he could find no constitutional authority for coercing them to remain in the Union. Furthermore, the nation had a tiny standing army of only fifteen thousand men, many of whom were stationed in the West to control the Indians. In light of the government's weak position, both legal and military, he believed that the correct course of action was to exhaust every possible peaceful measure. While the convention was meeting in South Carolina, Buchanan sent a message to Congress in which he blamed the abolitionists for the current crisis and urged Congress to nullify the "personal liberty" laws; at the same time he pleaded with the South to exercise restraint.

Nevertheless, on December 20, 1860, the South Carolina convention voted unanimously to withdraw from the United States. Despite the opposition of Southern Unionists, within six weeks six more states within the Deep South followed South Carolina's lead. Mississippi, Florida, Alabama, Georgia, Louisiana, and Texas had all withdrawn from the Union by February 1.

Yet the separatist urge in the seceding states was not nearly as unanimous as the statistics might indicate. Before secession a group of moderates had worked to preserve the Union. They pointed out that Lincoln had promised not to advocate abolition where slavery already existed. They also underlined the fact that Southern Democrats still controlled the Senate and the Supreme Court. The small farmers in northern Georgia and Alabama who did not own slaves also had tried to persuade the rich plantation owners from the southern parts of their states to wait until a slave-state convention had presented its demands to the North. Eventually the moderates saw that their cause was hopeless and most decided to cast their lot with the secessionists.

Meanwhile, Buchanan had asked Congress to frame compromise measures to halt Southern secession. The most significant were produced by a Senate committee headed by John J. Crittenden of Kentucky. The recommendations included passing a series of amendments that would guarantee the permanence of slavery in the states where it already existed, strengthen the Fugitive Slave Law, prevent interference with the interstate slave trade, and most important, reestablish the Missouri Compromise line.

Despite support throughout the country, few Northern and Southern leaders endorsed the Crittenden Compromise. Moreover, when Lincoln was approached for his approval, he rejected the plan, pledging never to compromise in his determination to prevent slavery from expanding into new territories. He also feared that the compromise would encourage the South to embark on expansion into Mexico, Central America, and Cuba.

LITTLE BO-PEEP AND HER FOOLISH SHEEP.

"Little Bo-peep, she lost her sheep, | Let 'em alone, and they'll all come home,
And didn't know where to find 'em; | With their tails hanging down behind 'em."

IN THIS 1861 CARTOON LITTLE BO-PEEP, DRESSED IN STARS AND STRIPES, LAMENTS THE INEFFECTUALITY OF HER SHEEPDOG, "OLD BUCK" (PRESIDENT BUCHANAN) WHILE HER BLACK SHEEP, TWO OF WHICH ARE NAMED GEORGIA AND SOUTH CAROLINA, STAMPEDE TOWARD THE WOODS WHERE THE EUROPEAN WOLVES AWAIT.

Why did the spirit of compromise, which had always prevailed in past national controversies, fail this time? Although hope for reconciliation was still widespread, the great national leaders who had initiated successful compromises in the past were gone. Men like Clay, Webster, and Calhoun had now been replaced by new leaders in both sections who were less willing to compromise. Also, hostility between the sections was far more intense than ever before. Lincoln's position was crucial. He insisted that any compromise would have to exclude the further expansion of slavery, and yet there was no chance that the South would ever accept any such scheme. Moreover, even as compromises were being proposed, sectional interests were undercutting their prospects for adoption. Finally, events had progressed so rapidly that by the time compromises were set forth, the precedent for secession had been set seven times.

Buchanan, still in office, stiffened his opposition to the separatist movement. When secessionists resigned from his cabinet, he replaced them with reliable Unionists. In his last message to Congress, he emphasized his duty as president to collect federal revenues and protect federal properties in the South. South Carolina flouted Buchanan's authority by demanding that the president relinquish Fort Sumter in the harbor of Charleston to state authorities. Buchanan refused and, still acting with restraint, sent an unarmed merchant ship, *The Star of the West*, with supplies to reinforce the fort which was defended by a small garrison. In addition he ordered the garrison commander, Major Robert Anderson, to hold possession of the fort and defend it, but to take no direct action to initiate hostilities. When the ship entered Charleston harbor, fire from shore batteries forced it to return to New York. The South had fired on a United States vessel, and most Americans, North and South, bewildered by the event, waited to see what course Lincoln would pursue.

Lincoln Takes Command

On March 4, 1861, when Lincoln gave his long-awaited Inaugural Address, he inherited the first stages of dissolution of the Union. The Confederate States of America had formed a new government in Montgomery, Alabama, and had chosen Jefferson Davis of Mississippi as its provisional president. A new Southern Congress was drafting a constitution, and a new flag, the Stars and Bars, was being designed.

Secessionists viewed their new nation with confidence. Northern insults would be silenced. Tension created by conflicts over the fate of slavery in the territories would be broken. Southerners would no longer be required to pay high tariffs on manufactured goods. Secession would allow the South to end its dependency on Northern manufacturing and to develop its own balanced, self-sufficient economy. The world market for cotton remained profitable and sound. Adventurers backed by the Confederacy would soon bring Cuba, Mexico, and Central America into the Southern confederation. Most Southerners were also convinced that the North would not go to war over secession.

Lincoln took a firm but cautious stance. He entreated the states of the Confederacy to return to the Union, reassuring the South that he had no intention of trying to abolish slavery where it already existed and promising to support the Fugitive Slave Law. But he emphatically denied the right of any state to secede from the Union: "I hold that, in contemplation of universal law and of the Constitution, the Union of these States is perpetual. . . . No State, upon its own mere motion, can lawfully get out of the Union." He pledged to protect federal property, collect federal revenues, and maintain federal services.

The new president insisted further that he would not initiate hostilities:

In your hands, my dissatisfied fellow-countrymen, and not in mine, is the momentous issue of civil war. The government will not assail you. You can have no conflict without being yourselves the aggressors. You have no oath registered in Heaven to destroy the Government, while I shall have the most solemn one to "preserve, protect and defend it."

In a final eloquent passage Lincoln appealed to the patriotic memories of Southerners:

I am loath to close. We are not enemies, but friends. We must not be enemies. Though passion may have strained, it must not break, our bonds of affection. The mystic chords of memory, stretching from every battlefield and patriot grave of every living heart and hearthstone all over this broad land, will yet swell the chorus of the Union, when again touched, as surely they will be, by the better angels of our nature.

Fort Sumter: The War Begins

The day after his inauguration, Lincoln received a letter from Major Anderson warning that Fort Sumter could be held only if the president dispatched twenty thousand additional men, a large naval force, and ample provisions.

For six weeks the president hesitated. He was determined to keep Fort Sumter, but he believed that there was still enough Union sentiment in the South to settle the matter without the use of force. As weeks passed, however, the press and then the people of the North began to express impatience. By the time Lincoln decided to act, Northern public opinion, which earlier had opposed forceful action, was ready to support strong moves to save the Union.

Lincoln realized that the Confederacy would consider an armed naval expedition to Fort Sumter an act of war. Yet if Fort Sumter were allowed to fall into Confederate hands, Lincoln would appear to be recognizing the independence of the seceding states. Lincoln sought advice from his cabinet and

INTERIOR OF FORT SUMTER DURING CONFEDERATE SHELLING.

military staff, and most of them agreed with General Winfield Scott that it would be dangerous to resupply the fort with provisions, which were about to run out, or with reinforcements. Only Secretary of the Treasury Salmon P. Chase and Postmaster General Montgomery Blair favored aiding Major Anderson. Secretary of State Seward urged caution out of fear that an attempt to provision the fort would cause the border states to secede.

Lincoln, however, felt he could not simply abandon the fort. He decided to send relief to Fort Sumter but, moving cautiously, he chose to send only food in unarmed ships. "If such attempt be not resisted," Lincoln wrote the governor of South Carolina, "no effort to throw in men, arms or ammunition will be made without further notice, or in case of an attack upon the Fort." Thus Lincoln, sensing that a conflict could not be averted, forced the Confederacy to take the next step. If the South attacked a peaceful expedition bringing food to a beleaguered fort, then the Confederacy would be responsible for firing the first shot of a civil conflict. Yet the president was determined to save the Union even if it meant war.

The governor of South Carolina, Francis W. Pickens, forwarded Lincoln's message to Jefferson

Davis in Montgomery. The president of the Confederacy immediately ordered General Pierre G. T. Beauregard to request that Major Anderson evacuate Fort Sumter by 4:00 A.M. on April 12, 1861. When Anderson delayed, saying he would leave the fort in three days unless ordered to do otherwise, Beauregard opened fire. The shelling began at 4:30 A.M. and continued for the next forty hours, until Anderson finally surrendered on April 13. Lincoln's unarmed flotilla then approached the fort and, with Confederate permission, carried away Anderson's troops. The war had begun.

Many Americans still doubted that a real war would follow. Some abolitionists recommended that

Lincoln permit the Confederate states to depart the Union in peace. Many merchants in the North also hoped to avoid war, since they feared that armed conflict would interrupt commerce, reduce the value of government securities, and interfere with the collection of debts owed by Southerners. Many Southerners were convinced that Northerners were too obsessed with making money to allow their economy to be disrupted by war.

Yet despite initial Northern hesitation, the desire to keep the nation together was strong. The North was divided on the question of fighting over the slavery issue, but not over fighting to preserve the Union. While continued use of the Mississippi

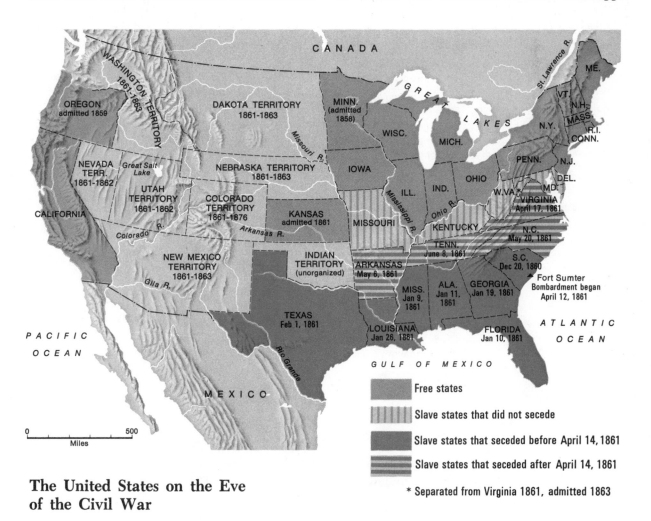

The United States on the Eve of the Civil War

Free states

Slave states that did not secede

Slave states that seceded before April 14, 1861

Slave states that seceded after April 14, 1861

* Separated from Virginia 1861, admitted 1863

River and unhampered access to Southern markets for Northern agricultural and manufactured goods played a part in the decision, there were other powerful ideas shaping pro-Union sentiment in the North. Some abolitionists saw the war as a means of destroying slavery. Most important, Northerners generally believed that the United States had a special mission to maintain an enduring democratic society.

Readings

General Works

Berwanger, Eugene, *The Frontier Against Slavery*. Urbana: University of Illinois Press, 1967.

Craven, Avery O., *Civil War in the Making*. Baton Rouge: Louisiana State University Press, 1959.

_____, *The Growth of Southern Nationalism, 1848–1861*. Baton Rouge: Louisiana State University Press, 1953.

Donald, David H., *Liberty and Union*. Lexington, Mass.: Heath, 1978.

Dumond, Dwight L., *Anti-Slavery Origins of the Civil War*. Ann Arbor: University of Michigan Press, 1959.

Holt, Michael F., *The Political Crisis of the 1850s*. New York: Wiley, 1978.

Johnson, Ludwell H., *Division and Reunion: America 1848–1860*. New York: Wiley, 1978.

Nevins, Allan, *The Emergence of Lincoln*, Vols. I–II. New York: Scribner's, 1950.

_____, *Ordeal of the Union*, Vol. II. New York: Scribner's, 1947.

Nichols, Roy F., *The Disruption of American Democracy*. New York: Macmillan, 1948.

Potter, David, *The Impending Crisis, 1848–61* (Completed and edited by Don E. Fehrenbacher). New York: Harper & Row, 1976.

_____, *South and the Sectional Conflict*. Baton Rouge: Louisiana State University Press, 1968. (Paper)

Sewell, Richard H., *Ballots for Freedom: Antislavery Politics in the United States, 1837–1860*. New York: Oxford University Press, 1976.

Silbey, Joel (Ed.), *Transformation of American Politics, 1840–1860*. Englewood Cliffs, N.J.: Prentice-Hall, 1967.

Special Studies

Borritt, G. S., *Lincoln and the Economics of the American Dream*. Memphis, Tenn.: Memphis State University Press, 1978.

Current, Richard N., *Lincoln and the First Shot*. Philadelphia: Lippincott, 1964.

Fehrenbacher, Don E., *Prelude to Greatness, Lincoln in the 1850s*. Stanford, California: Stanford University Press, 1962.

_____, *The Dred Scott Case: Its Significance in American Law and Politics*. New York: Oxford University Press, 1978.

Foner, Eric, *Free Soil, Free Labor, Free Men: The Ideology of the Republican Party Before the Civil War*. New York: Oxford University Press, 1970.

Formisano, Ronald P., *Birth of Mass Political Parties in Michigan, 1827–1861*. Princeton, N.J.: Princeton University Press, 1971.

Hopkins, Vincent, *Dred Scott's Case*. New York: Atheneum, 1967.

Jaffa, Harry V., *Crisis of the House Divided: An Interpretation of the Issues in the Lincoln-Douglas Debates*. Garden City, N.Y.: Doubleday, 1959.

Luthin, Reinhold H., *The First Lincoln Campaign*. Cambridge, Mass.: Harvard University Press, 1944.

Malin, James C., *John Brown and the Legend of Fifty-Six*. New York: Haskell, 1970.

_____, *The Nebraska Question, 1852–1854*. Gloucester, Mass.: Peter Smith, 1968.

Oates, Stephen B., *Our Fiery Trial: Abraham Lincoln, John Brown, and the Civil War Era*. Amherst: University of Massachusetts Press, 1979.

Phillips, Ulrich B., *The Course of the South to Secession*. New York: Hill & Wang, 1964.

Potter, David M., *Lincoln and His Party in the Secession Crisis*. New Haven, Conn.: Yale University Press, 1942.

Stampp, Kenneth M., *And the War Came: The North and the Secession Crisis, 1860–1861*. Baton Rouge: Louisiana State University Press, 1960.

Primary Sources

Angle, Paul M. (Ed.), *Created Equal: The Complete Lincoln-Douglas Debates of 1858*. Chicago: University of Chicago Press, 1958.

Johannsen, Robert W. (Ed.), *The Letters of Stephen A. Douglas*. Urbana: University of Illinois Press, 1961.

Biographies

Capers, Gerald M., *Stephen A. Douglas, Defender of the Union*. Boston: Little, Brown, 1959.

Donald, David, *Charles Sumner and the Coming of the Civil War*. New York: Knopf, 1960.

Johannsen, Robert W., *Stephen A. Douglas*. New York: Oxford University Press, 1973.

Klein, Philip S., *President James Buchanan*. University Park: Pennsylvania State University Press, 1962.

Oates, Stephen B., *With Malice Toward None*. New York: Harper & Row, 1977.

Swisher, Carl B., *Roger B. Taney*. New York: Macmillan, 1935.

Thomas, Benjamin P., *Abraham Lincoln*. New York: Knopf, 1952.

Fiction

Allis, Marguerite, *The Rising Storm*. New York: Putnam's, 1955.

Nelson, Truman, *The Sin of the Prophet*. Boston: Little, Brown, 1952.

Seifert, Shirley, *Senator's Lady*. Philadelphia: Lippincott, 1967.

Stowe, Harriet Beecher, *Uncle Tom's Cabin*. New York: Macmillan, 1962.

*Dere's two things I've got a
right to, and dese are, Death or
Liberty—one or tother
I mean to have.*

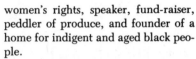

Let My People Go

THE LIFE OF HARRIET TUBMAN

AN extraordinary series of events wove the fabric of Harriet Tubman's life. Born a slave, she escaped to the North as a young woman, only to return nineteen times on the dangerous mission of freeing her family and hundreds of other enslaved blacks. Over the course of her long life she was a laborer, domestic, "conductor" on the Underground Railroad, abolitionist organizer, farmer, soldier, nurse, baker, psychic, visionary, religionist, reconstructionist, advocate of women's rights, speaker, fund-raiser, peddler of produce, and founder of a home for indigent and aged black people.

Harriet Tubman was born in Maryland around 1820—as nearly as she could remember. Her days of hard labor, whippings, and beatings began at the age of five. Tubman's duties included working as a field hand, doing housework, cleaning wheat, husking corn, cutting wood, hauling logs, driving oxen, plowing, and carrying heavy burdens. She preferred hard labor over housework, for at least she could breathe freely outdoors. Her feats of strength were famous and her master exhibited her as a spectacle of muscu-

HARRIET TUBMAN.

lar power. She worked from dawn until dusk and often into the night as well, receiving no wages whatsoever for her labors.

When she was about fifteen, Harriet Tubman received a shock which affected her for the rest of her life. One evening one of the slaves with whom Tubman was laboring suddenly put down his work and headed for town. The overseer noticed that he was missing and angrily marched off to find him. Fearing trouble, Tubman followed the overseer, who found the slave in a store and demanded that he submit to a whipping. When the slave would not cooperate, the overseer ordered Tubman to grab him. She refused, and the slave made a break for the door. The overseer seized a two-pound counterweight and hurled it after the fleeing slave. The weight hit Tubman, bashing in her skull. She fell to the floor unconscious.

For many months, Harriet Tubman wavered dangerously between life and death. She had been a rebel before this incident, but during her long illness, her bitter opposition to slavery grew. She also became deeply religious and spent much of her time in prayer. "Pears like I prayed all de time," she said. At long last, and very slowly, she recovered, but she remained the victim of a strange affliction for the rest of her life. A number of times each day, no matter what she was doing, Harriet Tubman would, suddenly and without warning, fall into a deep sleep. Her slumber would last for several minutes and it was impossible to awaken her. This malady was with her for the rest of her life.

Tubman's master died when she was a young woman. One day soon after his passing, she received a warning that she would be taken that night to be sold into a chain gang in the Deep South, a fate all slaves dreaded. So Tubman knew that she had to escape that evening. She dare not tell her mother or anyone else, for she knew that if she did, a commotion would be raised and escape would be impossible. But she had to say good-by somehow, so she strolled through the slave quarters singing this song:

When dat ar ole chariot comes,
I'm gwine to lebe you;
I'm boun' for de promised land,
I'm gwine to lebe you.

Harriet Tubman did not know where she was going when she set out alone that night in 1849, but she was determined to follow the North Star until it led her to freedom. She traveled by night, on foot, through fields and forests and across streams and marshes. She slept during the daytime, usually in the open but sometimes aided to shelter by sympathetic blacks and Quakers. At last she reached Pennsylvania and freedom.

Her initial reaction was one of ecstasy. "There was such a glory ober eberyting; de sun came like gold through the trees, and ober the fields, and I felt like I was in Heaben." Later, however, she felt like she was arriving home after twenty-five years in prison, with no house, family, or friends to welcome her. "I was a stranger in a strange land," she said. It was then that she decided to bring her family to the North and make a home for them there.

Tubman moved to Philadelphia, where she worked as a domestic in hotels and clubhouses. But even with her new freedom, she never forgot those she left behind in slavery. "I have heard their groans and sighs, and seen their tears," she said, "and I would give every drop of blood in my veins to free them." She saved all her money and, whenever she had enough, she made the dangerous journey back to her home to free members of her family and other slaves.

In her work freeing slaves, Harriet Tubman became known as a "conductor" on the Underground Railroad. The Underground Railroad was a secret and unlawful system for the freeing of slaves, a series of land and sea routes to the North which were linked together by "stations" where fugitives could find aid from sympathizers. Hundreds of blacks risked their lives as conductors during the 1850s, the period when Tubman was active. In all, some seventy-five thousand slaves reached the North via the Underground Railroad.

After the Fugitive Slave Law was passed in 1850, it became necessary to conduct slaves all the way to Canada. For Tubman, this meant a journey of some five hundred miles across Maryland, Delaware, Pennsylvania, New Jersey, and New York to Ontario Province in Canada. The dangers increased. Runaways were causing a decrease in the market value of slaves, so proslavery uniformed police, government authorities, and citizen vigilantes doubled their efforts to hunt down Harriet Tubman and her groups of fugitive slaves. Forty thousand dollars was offered for her capture.

In addition to the danger, there was the hardship of the long journey, which was conducted mostly at night, on foot and in all kinds of weather. Also, there were "perils among false brethren." Despite all this, none of the fugitives Harriet Tubman conducted to the North was ever lost, killed, or captured. She succeeded in bringing out her parents and all but one of her ten brothers and sisters, in addition to the hundreds of other slaves she led to

TWENTY-EIGHT FUGITIVES ESCAPING FROM THE EASTERN SHORE OF MARYLAND.

freedom and the thousands of fugitives she inspired. Tubman became known as the "Moses" of her people. The old spiritual took on a new meaning:

Go down, Moses
    Way down in Egypt's land
Tell ole Pharaoh
    To let my people go!

Tubman said that her strange sleeping spells played an important role in her work. During these spells she felt her soul leave her body and travel to lands and people which she would later experience in her journeys. She received messages from God, who, she said, guided her every movement. As she put it, "t'wasn't me, 'twas *de Lord!* I always *tole* him, 'I trust to you. I don't know where to go or what to do, but I expect you to lead me,' an' he always did." During one of her slum-

bers, Tubman received a message that she must go at once and free three of her brothers. She arrived in Maryland on Christmas Eve, and learned that her brothers were to be sold into slave gangs on Christmas Day. She rescued them just in time. On another occasion, she received a similar message about her parents. She arrived a few days before her father was to be tried for aiding in the escape of a fugitive. Tubman "removed his trial to a higher court," as she humorously put it, and rushed him and her mother to Canada. Another of Tubman's psychic experiences is particularly noteworthy. On October 16, 1859, Tubman announced to her friends that she felt that some tragedy had suddenly befallen her friend and ally, John Brown. It turned out that the attack on Harper's Ferry occurred that day. It was only because of a flare-up of her head injury that

Tubman herself was not with Brown for that historic event.

When the Civil War broke out, Tubman joined the Union forces. She was a spy, scout, commando, and guerrilla warrior. She was also an extraordinary nurse. With her knowledge of herbal medicine, she cured black and white soldiers of dysentery, fevers, and various other diseases.

Rather than draw army rations, Tubman returned to her small cabin late every night after a long, hard day and made fifty pies, a large amount of gingerbread, and two casks of root beer. These she sold to support herself and her aged parents in the North.

On the Combahee River in South Carolina Harriet Tubman accomplished one of the great exploits of the Civil War. This effort resulted in freedom for nearly eight hundred slaves, and may be the only time in American history that a woman planned and led a military campaign.

After four years of war service, Tubman returned to the North to join her parents in their home on a modest farm which Tubman had purchased for them in Auburn, New York. On the train home, Tubman was brutally thrown into a baggage car by a conductor and three assistants, all white, who refused to recognize her army pass. To them, it was inconceivable that a woman, especially a black woman, could legally hold such a pass. Tubman's arm was nearly torn off and she was physically and spiritually wounded for life by this incident.

Tubman spent the rest of her busy days in poverty. She took care of her

parents, fed and housed the needy and sick, worked as a domestic, supported two schools for blacks in the South, raised funds, made speeches, peddled produce, worked with the women's suffrage movement, was active in the development of the African Methodist

Episcopal Church, established a home for the black indigent and aged, and did temperance work.

Tubman fought for years to obtain a pension for her involvement in the Civil War, but it was not until she was nearly eighty years old that the government finally awarded her a pension of twenty dollars a month for her Civil War effort.

In 1913, at the age of ninety-three, Harriet Tubman died with the same spirit, energy, and strength which had characterized her life. Who else but Tubman would conduct her own farewell services? In her last moments, she led the friends and ministers gathered at her bedside in the singing of her favorite spirituals.

LIBERTY LINE.
NEW ARRANGEMENT---NIGHT AND DAY.

The improved and splendid Locomotives, Clarkson and Lundy, with their trains fitted up in the best style of accommodation for passengers, will run their regular trips during the present season, between the borders of the Patriarchal Dominion and Libertyville, Upper Canada. Gentlemen and Ladies, who may wish to improve their health or circumstances, by a northern tour, are respectfully invited to give us their patronage.

SEATS FREE, *irrespective of color.*

Necessary Clothing furnished gratuitously to such as have *"fallen among thieves."*

"Hide the outcasts—let the oppressed go free."—*Bible.*

☞For seats apply at any of the trap doors, or to the conductor of the train.

J. CROSS, *Proprietor.*

N. B. For the special benefit of Pro-Slavery Police Officers, an extra heavy wagon for Texas, will be furnished, whenever it may be necessary, in which they will be forwarded as dead freight, to the "Valley of Rascals," always at the risk of the owners.

☞Extra Overcoats provided for such of them as are afflicted with protracted *chilly-phobia.*

14 The Civil War

After passing General Lee and his staff, I rode on through the woods in the direction in which I had left Longstreet. I soon began to meet many wounded men returning from the front; many of them asked in piteous tones the way to a doctor or an ambulance. The farther I got, the greater became the number of the wounded. At last I came to a perfect stream of them flocking through the woods in numbers as great as the crowd in Oxford Street in the middle of the day. Some were walking alone on crutches composed of two rifles, others supported by men less badly wounded than themselves, and others were carried on stretchers by the ambulance corps. . . .

Arthur J. L. Fremantle

Significant Events

Confederate Constitution [March 11, 1861]

First Battle of Bull Run [July 1861]

Trent affair [November 1861]

Battle between *Monitor* and *Merrimack* [March 8, 1862]

Battle of Shiloh [April 6–7, 1862]

Second Confiscation Act [July 1862]

Second Battle of Bull Run [September 1862]

Battle of Antietam [September 17, 1862]

Emancipation Proclamation [January 1863]

National Bank Act [1863]

Battle of Chancellorsville [May 1863]

Battle of Gettysburg [July 1–3, 1863]

Battle of Vicksburg [June–July 1863]

Sherman's march through Georgia [August–December 1864]

Grant occupies Richmond [April 1865]

Lee surrenders to Grant at Appomattox Court House [April 9, 1865]

YANKEE VOLUNTEERS MARCHING INTO DIXIE, 1862.

During the Civil War the positions taken by both the North and the South revealed in many ways the differences between the professed ideals of Americans and their actual practices. In 1776, the two regions had fought together to secure the rights proclaimed in the Declaration of Independence. Now the South was fighting to preserve a system which contradicted the ideals expressed in that same Declaration. Southerners feared that an increasingly powerful national government under Republican control would undermine the unique social and economic system that had developed in the South. At the same time most Northerners believed that the preservation of the Union was the central issue leading to the war. During the summer of 1862, Lincoln wrote to Horace Greeley:

I would save the Union. I would save it the shortest way under the Constitution. . . . If there be those who would not save the Union, unless they could at the same time save Slavery, I do not agree with them. My paramount object in this struggle is to save the Union, and is not either to save or destroy Slavery.

Even in the North, in spite of the influence of the abolitionists, the moral issue of slavery was not the primary cause of war. Furthermore, during the course of the war President Lincoln bypassed federal laws and suppressed civil liberties in order to achieve his overriding goal, the preservation of the Union.

Hoping to bring the conflict to a quick resolution, Lincoln issued a call to arms immediately after the attack on Fort Sumter. Seventy-five thousand state militia were asked to serve for ninety days to "put down" the rebellion. Northern Unionists responded at once, supporting the president's action as a proper response to an illegal attempt to secede from an unbreakable Union. Southerners, however, regarded Lincoln's action as an intolerable provocation. On May 6 the Confederate Congress declared a state of war, and the initial Confederate call for a hundred thousand volunteers was met with great enthusiasm.

Contrary to Lincoln's hopes, the nation's internal disagreement was not to be easily resolved. Many who answered the call were to become casualties in one of the bloodiest of all American wars. By 1865, 620,000 soldiers had lost their lives.

The Two Sides Take Shape

The Confederate Government

The Southern states that had seceded before the firing on Fort Sumter did not intend to exist separately. Acknowledging their dependence on one another, they sent delegates to a convention in Montgomery, Alabama, in February 1861 to form a government for a new Southern republic.

The document devised at this meeting was patterned after the United States Constitution, but it incorporated some crucial differences. Most significantly, the new government was organized as a confederation of sovereign states, not a federation of united ones. The central government of the South was given no authority to impose tariffs, finance internal improvements, interfere with the government of the states, or control slavery. While it could acquire new territories, it was forbidden to interfere with slavery in these areas. This states' rights philosophy greatly handicapped the Southern mobilization effort during the war.

Under the Confederate Constitution, the structure of the government was similar to that of the United States except that the president was to serve only one term of six years. This provision undermined what little political leverage the first and only Confederate president was to have with the Confederate Congress. Delegates at the convention named Jefferson Davis of Mississippi provisional president and Alexander H. Stephens of Georgia provisional vice-president. Confederate voters confirmed these choices in their first election.

Whereas Lincoln's task was to preserve a nation, Davis's was to create one. A native of Kentucky, Jefferson Davis had served as Franklin Pierce's secretary of war and later made a reputation as a spokesman for Southern interests in the Senate. Although intelligent and hardworking, Davis also was arrogant and inflexible, which did not enhance his popularity with the public. He was unable to foster loyalty even among those working closest to him and could never bind them into a

JEFFERSON DAVIS, ARROGANT BUT INTENSELY DEVOTED PRESIDENT OF THE CONFEDERACY.

succeed, and his pessimism increased during the course of the war.

The Confederate president's official advisers were of no more help to him than was his vice-president. Throughout the war, Davis's cabinet squabbled and shifted its position on the issues with irritating regularity. Some members were unsuited for their jobs, largely because they had initially been chosen not on merit but on a geographical basis and because of their ardent support of the Confederacy. Perhaps the ablest among them was Judah P. Benjamin, who served as attorney general, then as secretary of war, and finally as secretary of state. Benjamin tried to make the Confederacy face its financial, economic, and diplomatic shortcomings, but all he received for his effort was a ceaseless stream of criticism from Southern newspapers and legislatures.

Throughout the war years Davis faced insurmountable obstacles. Unionism remained strong in the upper South, and in some of the poor, mountainous regions some of the population supported or joined the Union army. Moreover, political antagonism to Davis's presidency grew as the war continued. By 1863, Davis experienced increasing difficulty obtaining support for his policies in Congress, and by 1865 he had completely lost control of the legislature.

Lincoln as War Leader

As a war leader Lincoln proved to be far superior to Davis. Although both men determined military policy, Lincoln did so only because he could find no generals capable of formulating overall strategy. Lincoln understood the relationship between economic strength and the mobilization of military power and, unlike Davis, he was tolerant and flexible, valuable qualities for a minority president with a weak, poorly trained army and an empty treasury. He had to appease many officeholders and was willing to suffer criticism and false flattery in order to achieve the results he wanted. It was said of him, "He had a genius for giving men enough rope to hang themselves."

Convinced of the rightness of the cause, Lincoln acted boldly to preserve the Union. To bring the war to a satisfactory conclusion he stretched executive power to new limits. Because Congress was not in session from April through July

smoothly functioning government organization. Opinionated and reluctant to delegate authority, Davis meddled constantly in other officials' responsibilities, played favorites, and often replaced appointees out of whim. He also considered himself a military expert, when, in fact, his military judgment was highly erratic. As a result, he refused advice from his able commanders. For the first two years of the war he was committed to a defensive strategy which failed, and when he began to pursue military victories aggressively, it was too late. Nevertheless, he was totally devoted to the South and worked unceasingly to help the Confederacy succeed.

Vice-President Stephens was fanatical on the issue of states' rights, yet he opposed the draft and other wartime measures necessary for achieving a Confederate victory. He detested President Davis and found it difficult to work with him. Stephens was never convinced that the Confederacy would

1861, Lincoln, acting on his own as commander in chief, proclaimed a maritime blockade of the South. Then on May 3, he issued a call for forty regiments of three-year volunteers to supplement the state militia he had called out before. He further usurped congressional power by ordering $2 million for military expenditures, although the Constitution states: "No money shall be drawn from the Treasury, but in consequence of appropriations made by law." By these actions he expanded executive power further than any president before him, leading many on his own side to call him a despot, tyrant, and dictator. Ultimately, however, Congress sanctioned Lincoln's actions.

Lincoln's willingness to disregard the constitutionally protected personal rights of citizens aroused even more opposition. With his approval, the federal government examined private mail and telegrams, and military commanders were given the power to make summary arrests without warrants and to suspend the writ of habeas corpus in cases of "extreme necessity." In 1862 Lincoln issued a presidential proclamation announcing that anyone who discouraged enlistments, resisted the draft, or committed other disloyal acts would be tried by a military court-martial. At least fifteen thousand Americans were imprisoned under this order. Many remained in jail until the end of the war without ever knowing who their accusers were or what charges had been brought against them. In addition, several newspapers were temporarily forced to suspend publication because the administration accused them of making statements disloyal to the Union.

Disunity in the Union

Despite their objections to Lincoln's extension of executive authority, the majority of Northern Democrats supported the Union cause. The Democratic leader Stephen A. Douglas died in 1861, but under the leadership of Horatio Seymour and others, the party set aside factional differences in hopes of regaining power in the next election. Ironically, the surprising strength of the Democratic party, even without its Southern wing, had the effect of uniting antagonistic factions in the Republican party, thus strengthening Lincoln's leadership.

There was a small faction in the Northern Democratic party, however, whose sympathies lay with the South. The "Peace Democrats," or "Cop-

perheads," as they were called by Unionists (after the poisonous snake), wanted a negotiated peace with the Confederacy and opposed all war measures, especially those linked to proposals to abolish slavery. They encouraged Northerners to fight for the South and actively tried to prevent Union enlistments.

When one of the leading Copperheads, former Ohio congressman C. L. Vallandigham, publicly demanded that the war be brought to an end, he was arrested, tried in a military court, and sent behind Confederate lines. But Vallandigham fled to Canada and eventually returned to Ohio where he led peace demonstrations before the 1864 elections.

Although Lincoln's insistence on the preservation of the Union initially won the support of most Republicans, the Radicals, or abolitionist wing, regarded the termination of slavery as the real object of the conflict. In their view, the South not only had to be conquered but also remade. The Radicals, led by Thaddeus Stevens of Pennsylvania, had considerable strength in both houses of Congress, and they applied continual pressure on the president, who needed their support for reelection.

The Radical Republicans wanted to take control of military policy and to formulate a plan for the emancipation of the slaves. To this end they created the Congressional Committee on the Conduct of the War, whose representatives cross-examined military commanders about battle strategies and even challenged Lincoln's choice of military leaders.

AN ANTI-COPPERHEAD CARTOON PRINTED IN THE NORTH IN 1863 DEPICTS THE UNION DEFENDING HERSELF AGAINST POLITICAL REPTILES WHICH WEAR THE HATS OF MIDWESTERN DEMOCRATIC CONGRESSMEN.

General McClellan, a Democrat, was the chief target of their complaint that the prosecution of the war was insufficiently vigorous. The Radicals also pushed through Congress the Confiscation Act of 1862, providing for presidential seizure of all property (including slaves) used in furthering the insurrection. The Radicals hated to term slaves "property," and the Act had little effect. Nevertheless, its passage showed that Northern feeling against slavery was hardening. The Radical Republicans often behaved abusively, but their committee's reports uncovered scandals and inefficiency in the military, and their idealism had a powerful effect on Northern public opinion.

The Undecided Border States

One of Lincoln's most urgent concerns was to keep the border states within the Union. His official statement that the North was fighting to preserve the Union rather than to free the slaves was partly intended to prevent the border states from seceding. In spite of this, some of them decided that they could not fight against the South.

Shortly after Lincoln called for troops in April, Virginia, North Carolina, Tennessee, and Arkansas joined the Confederacy. Of all the slave states, only Delaware was openly loyal to the Union. The populace of Kentucky, Maryland, Missouri, and western Virginia remained divided. The combined white population of these states, together with that of Delaware, was more than half the total of the Confederacy. These states, however, initially refused to furnish troops for the Union army.

Kentucky finally chose to stay with the Union when Lincoln assured its pro-Union citizens that the government would make no attack on slavery. Lincoln supported Kentucky's efforts to resist secession with arms. Maryland also decided to stay in the Union after Lincoln sent a force to arrest secessionist leaders. Maryland's pro-Union governor even sent troops to the Union army, although they were to be used only for the defense of Washington and not for fighting in the South.

Lincoln capitalized on the resentment of mountain whites toward Eastern plantation interests by ordering troops into western Virginia. The presence of these soldiers encouraged anti-Confederate feelings, and in November 1861 the western counties split away to form the new state of West Virginia, which was admitted into the Union in 1863.

Missouri did not give in so easily. When the state's pro-Southern governor tried to use the state militia to seize a federal arsenal near St. Louis, federal troops attacked them and forced them to surrender. As the victors marched away, they clashed with St. Louis civilians in a riot in which many citizens were killed. The guerrilla warfare in Missouri which followed lasted for almost three years before federal troops achieved a firm victory. The governor and his supporters subsequently proclaimed an independent Missouri government, which seceded and operated as a government in exile in Texas. Ultimately about thirty thousand Missourians fought for the South, but more than three times that number served in the Union army.

The border states were very important to the war effort. With Maryland in the Union, Washington, D.C., was more secure, and the presence of Kentucky and Missouri protected transportation on the Ohio and Mississippi Rivers.

Factors in the War Effort

The South fully expected to win its independence, but its confidence rested on three miscalculations. First, Southerners failed to recognize that the Civil War was the first "modern" or industrialized war. By viewing it as a test of courage in combat, they overlooked the crucial factors of firepower, transport, food, supplies, and logistics. Second, Southern leaders believed that cotton was so important to English and French textile manufacturers that they would force their governments to enter the war on the Confederate side. Third, Southern leaders decided to pursue a defensive strategy which would force the Union army to fight the war in the South. By making the North appear to be the aggressor, Confederate leaders hoped to elicit support from Northern sympathizers. In addition, the North would require more men and equipment and longer lines of communication in order to defeat the Confederacy.

Comparative Resources

The Civil War was the first war in which railroads were used extensively to transport personnel and supplies, and the North's superior network of railways gave the Union a distinct advantage. The South had less than half as many miles of track, consisting of short lines, with major gaps between vital points. In addition, the track gauge was less uniform in the South, which prevented the interchange of railroad cars on different lines. When railroad equipment broke down in the South, it could not be replaced because train manufacturers were in the North. As the war dragged on, Rebel troops suffered severely from the Confederacy's inability to transport supplies, clothing, and ammunition.

The North had a distinct advantage in total human and economic resources as well. In 1860 its population was almost twenty-one million, while that of the South was nine million, 3.5 million of whom were slaves. Although many slaves fled to Northern lines, there were no slave revolts, and a substantial number of blacks continued to labor in the fields and factories. Others were assigned to military work details necessary for carrying on the war. Their participation freed a large number of Southern whites for service in the Confederate army.

Although the North was basically agricultural, it had nearly 110,000 manufacturing concerns which employed 1.3 million workers and turned out products valued in excess of $1.5 billion annually. The North actually produced seventeen times as much cotton and woolen goods, twenty times as much pig iron, and thirty-two times as many firearms as the South. The South's industrial growth had been stunted by its attachment to the export of cotton. About 20,000 Southern manufacturing concerns employing 110,000 workers produced only some $155 million worth of goods annually. Although the economic potential of the North was not realized immediately, by 1863 Northern factories, farms, and transportation systems were closely geared to the war effort. As the war dragged on over a period of years, this economic superiority and population advantage became crucial to the Northern victory.

The South initially imposed a cotton embargo in hopes of forcing countries dependent on raw cotton to enter the war on its side. As a result, the Confederacy was unable to exchange its cotton for foreign manufactured goods. The North, which controlled the navy and merchant marine, then cut the South's lifeline to Europe by establishing a blockade of Southern ports. Gradually the resources of the Confederacy were consumed by war, and there was no way to acquire vitally needed supplies. Throughout the war, the South lacked adequate food, uniforms, locomotives, rails, and ammunition. Although a small manufacturing establishment developed and a few blockade runners and speculators made fortunes, the majority of the population suffered serious deprivation.

In desperation, Southerners were compelled to turn most of their possessions into war material. Church bells were cast into cannons, carpets were made into clothes, and newspapers were printed on the back of wallpaper. Unfortunately, the South's defensive military strategy left its railroads and crops exposed, and many Southerners had to flee for their lives as the Union army approached.

On the Northern home front, the war acted as a stimulus to production in agriculture and certain industries. Although the overall rate of industrialization may have decreased during the war years, industries producing material for the war effort such as iron, steel, railroad equipment, petroleum, coal and lumber, woolens, boots, shoes, and prepared foods all met the demands placed on them. With increased production it became necessary to remodel old factories and to build new and larger ones. Although wages rose 43 percent, prices rose more, reducing real wages to two-thirds of their 1861 level.

At the same time, the economic boom in the North encouraged profiteering contractors and suppliers who overcharged the government and often delivered inferior goods. Sudden wealth was conspicuously displayed, and the ethical conduct of business and commercial leaders during the Civil War was more questionable than during any previous period in the nation's history.

Patriotic women, on either side of the conflict, provided an often overlooked resource. When men left their homes to fight, women frequently took

THIS FEED WON'T DO, A CARTOON OF 1861, COMMENTS ON THE CONFEDERACY'S FINANCIAL TROUBLES.

over heavy farm work or the management of the plantations. Some were hired by government departments as clerks and copyists at relatively high wages. Others worked in factories and arsenals for wages that were unfairly low where they were accused of being a distraction to their male colleagues and of behaving in a scandalously unladylike way. Many brave women, such as Clara Barton, defied public opinion to serve in the war zones. After harassing the Lincoln administration into employing female nurses, the indomitable Dorothea Dix organized a capable group of volunteers to assist both field staff and general hospitals.

Financing the War

Both the Confederate and the Union governments exerted an increasingly strong impact on their economies during the war. With no treasury and only a small amount of capital, the South had seri-

ous difficulty paying for its war needs. To make matters worse, the Confederacy was disappointed in its expectations of obtaining loans from Europe. Since its banking facilities were inadequate and its population was hostile to taxation, the Confederacy was forced to issue paper currency to help defray the cost of the war. But without adequate gold backing, the value of the $1.5 billion issue of Confederate currency dropped to nothing by 1865.

When the war began, the Union was operating with an empty treasury and no national currency. Eventually the Lincoln administration financed the war by raising tariffs and excise taxes, by levying the nation's first income tax, and by selling war bonds to patriotic citizens. The Union finally issued $450 million of paper money, called greenbacks, which were legal tender but not redeemable in gold and silver. By making paper money legal tender, the government put badly needed money in the treasury, for the war was costing over $2 million a day. However, the value of the greenbacks gradually declined, contributing to a high rate of inflation.

As part of a general expansion of federal power, the Union government enacted a new National Bank Act in 1863, creating the National Banking System. All banks chartered under the act were required to invest one-third of their capital in federal bonds which were to be deposited with the United States Treasurer. Member banks were then authorized to receive national bank notes equal to 90 percent of the value of the bonds. In 1865 more than $200 million worth of these notes were in circulation. In addition, the banks were required to submit to regular federal inspection. The system enabled the administration to market its bonds more economically and to issue a unified national currency.

European Involvement

Although they proclaimed neutrality in the conflict, European powers looked favorably on the South's attempt to gain independence for several reasons. In England, the aristocracy was sympathetic toward the class-conscious, hierarchical South, and many British citizens would have been delighted to see a democracy fail. In addition, British merchants and industrialists looked forward to duty-free access to Southern cotton.

Nevertheless, Southern hopes of receiving active support from the European powers were doomed to disappointment. Many in Britain and France were morally opposed to slavery. In addition, Confederate leaders overestimated the importance of Southern cotton to the European economy. Britain had stockpiled surpluses of cotton in 1859 and 1860, so the Southern embargo on cotton shipments failed to have the desired effect. Then, when the stockpile ran low, Britain turned to India and Egypt for its supply. Besides, many English merchants were doing a brisk business with the North in arms and grain, which gave them strong economic reasons for urging neutrality. Finally, Europeans initially hesitated to interfere because they were confident that the South could win its independence on its own. By 1863, Northern victories had brought to an end any likelihood that Europeans would intervene on the side of the South.

The Trent Affair In 1861 there occurred one incident that brought England to the verge of war.

Jefferson Davis had sent two representatives, James Mason and John Slidell, to plead the Confederate cause in England and France. The men were sailing for Europe aboard the British steamer *Trent* when their ship was detained and boarded by Captain Charles Wilkes, commander of a warship in the Union blockade. Mason and Slidell were taken from the *Trent* and transported to the United States where they were imprisoned. Although Wilkes's action was very popular with the Northern public, it was denounced in London. The British foreign secretary sent a caustic note to the United States demanding release of the prisoners and a public apology.

Lincoln did not want a war with England, but neither did he wish to back down. To save face, Secretary of State Seward arranged for Mason's and Slidell's release on technical grounds, without ever admitting that the United States had been wrong to seize them.

British Sea Raiders Although the British did not intervene directly in the war, they considered mediating the conflict until the Union army began to win victories in the autumn of 1862. In the meantime, the British government irritated the North by allowing English shipyards to build sea raiders for the Confederacy. British law permitted the building of ships in England for belligerents, but it forbade these vessels from being "equipped, fitted out, or armed for fighting purposes." British shipbuilders got around these legal restrictions by allowing unarmed ships to leave England for an island port such as Nassau, where they were provided with British guns and ammunition. Lincoln, through Charles Francis Adams, the American minister to London, vigorously objected to this practice and threatened to unleash a "flood of privateers" against British sea trade. His objection went largely unheeded; several of these "brigands of the sea" plied the Atlantic, preying on Northern shipping. The most famous and successful of the raiders were the *Alabama* and the *Florida*, built for the Confederacy in Liverpool in 1862. The *Florida* was eventually captured and the *Alabama* sunk by the Union navy, but not before they had destroyed over $15 million worth of Northern commerce.

In 1863 Britain began construction on two Confederate warships equipped with iron rams and large-caliber guns. The United States threatened to attack neutral shipping if these armored vessels were used to break the Northern blockade. Under strong pressure from the American minister, the British government eventually seized the two heavy ironclads and added them to the Royal Navy. By this time the British recognized that the South was being defeated and did not want to be associated with the losing side.

Raising the Armies: North and South

The great disparity between the populations of the Union and the Confederacy was not at first reflected in the relative size of the two armies. Large areas of the North did not supply troops for the Union effort. Furthermore, some Union regiments had to be stationed in the West to regain control of the Indian territory from the Confederacy. Some Indian tribes, such as the Cherokee, were fighting alongside the Confederate army in the mistaken belief that a victorious South would protect their tribal lands.

Although the Union initially raised an army by calling for volunteers, it was ultimately forced to resort to financial enticements and the draft. States, cities, and counties sometimes paid additional bonuses to encourage enlistments. In time, Illinois volunteers were offered combined bonuses totaling $1056 each. Even so, the system had its drawbacks since men often picked up their bonuses and then deserted. Finding enlistments inadequate, the Union instituted conscription in March 1863. The new draft laws were widely resented because they discriminated in favor of the rich, who were either exempted or were able to pay someone to serve in their place. In New York City in 1863 the inequities of the draft, along with inflation and racial conflicts, led to four days of rioting which had to be put down by federal troops. Eventually three hundred thousand men out of a total of 1.9 million who served were drafted.

The Northern war effort was aided considerably by heavy immigration during the war years. Over eight hundred thousand newcomers arrived betweeen 1861 and 1865, a total which was greater than the total of war casualties. So many immigrants enlisted that eventually one-fifth of the Union forces were foreign-born.

The Confederacy, like the Union, first depended on volunteer enlistments to raise its army. However, after the first enthusiastic response, enlistments soon dropped, and by April 1862 the South, too, had to institute a draft. In the South, as in the North, the Conscription Act exempted certain professional and wealthy men, thus alienating many less privileged soldiers and contributing to widespread desertion. Moreover, states' rights sentiment was so strong among some state leaders that they refused to permit troops to join the Confederate army.

With resistance to volunteering and evasion of conscription on both sides, it was sometimes difficult to maintain military discipline. Although there are no reliable figures, estimates suggest that some two million men wore the Union blue and fewer than half that number wore the Confederate gray.

The North's numerical superiority would have been relatively unimportant in a short war, for the South had an initial advantage in its brilliant field

SOUTHERN VOLUNTEERS PUT ON A SHOW OF BRAVADO FOR A RICHMOND PHOTOGRAPHER. ONE YOUNG MAN IN THE UPPER LEFT FLOURISHES HIS BOWIE KNIFE FOR THE CAMERA.

THE SOUTH'S GREAT MILITARY GENIUS, ROBERT E. LEE.

GRANT'S HEAVY DRINKING AND UNKEMPT APPEARANCE MADE HIM A CONTROVERSIAL CHOICE AS LINCOLN'S COMMANDING GENERAL, BUT HE SOON PROVED HE KNEW HOW TO WIN BATTLES.

commanders. As the conflict persisted, however, and as Southern losses increased, the steady supply of fresh reinforcements to the Union army became an important psychological weapon which weakened the Confederacy's will to continue.

Commanders

For twenty years before the war, Southern officers had dominated the United States Army under the leadership of General Winfield Scott of Virginia.

Many Northern West Pointers found little opportunity for advancement under Scott and subsequently left the army. Southerners, on the other hand, moved up the ladder of command with relative ease. When the war broke out, these well-trained, senior officers embraced the Confederate cause.

Despite its superior generals, the South's only central military authority was Jefferson Davis, who insisted on formulating strategy himself. Until the Confederate Congress created the post of commander in chief during the closing months of the war, the most important Southern military post was that of Commander of the Army of Virginia, where much of the fighting took place. In June 1862 this position was given to Robert E. Lee.

Lee and Grant

Lee was the great military genius of the South. He had graduated from West Point with an outstanding record and served as Scott's right-hand man during the Mexican War. Although strongly opposed to both slavery and secession, Lee refused Lincoln's offer to command the Union army and instead dutifully returned to his native state of Virginia. During the war, he was often outnumbered and undersupplied in battle; nevertheless, Lee had the ability to build his army while he fought and was quick to take advantage of the enemy's mistakes. He was bold in forming and carrying out his plans and had a talent for forcing the enemy to strike on ground of his choosing, usually a position suitable for defense from which to send out flanking maneuvers. Lee's personal courage and imaginative concept of warfare were legendary; his humility and genuine concern for his troops earned him the complete devotion of his men.

Lee's strongest military assistance came from the tactical genius General Thomas Jonathan Jackson, nicknamed "Stonewall" for his unyielding stand at the first Battle of Bull Run. A grave and eccentric man, imbued with almost evangelical piety, Jackson soon proved himself a brilliant and aggressive strategist. He pushed himself as hard as he pushed his men and constantly harassed the enemy with crushing, lightning-quick strikes.

At the beginning of the war, the Union had no officers who could match the Confederate generals. General Winfield Scott was one of only two officers in service who had ever commanded troops sufficient in number to be called an army. As the war progressed, Lincoln desperately shifted his generals about, searching for a strong leader. Not until March 1864 did he find the general he was looking for—Ulysses S. Grant.

Unlike his Confederate counterparts, Grant did not come to his command with a long and distinguished military career behind him. After serving capably in the Mexican War, he had become bored by the inactivity of the peacetime army and had taken to drink. Eventually he was demoted and forced to resign. At the start of the Civil War, he was working in his family's leather store in Illinois and seemed destined to a life of mediocrity. But in June 1861 he joined a regiment of Illinois volunteers and was soon raised to the rank of brigadier general by the president. Stocky, unkempt, and shy, Grant was a controversial choice as Lincoln's commanding general. Yet he was confident and systematic in his understanding of military situations; he knew how to lead an army and how to win battles. While Southern tactics stressed careful maneuvering for position, Grant believed that a war of attrition was the way to win, and he struck ferociously at the South with all the resources at his disposal. Because of his zeal and fearlessness in battle, some of his contemporaries accused him of having a callous disregard for human life. However, his aggressiveness and determination fired the Union troops. Despite calls for Grant's dismissal after the terrible carnage at the Battle of Shiloh, Lincoln stood firm, claiming, "I can't spare this man—he fights."

The greatest of Grant's generals was William Tecumseh Sherman of Ohio. Sherman had a reputation for eccentricity; nevertheless, he was a tough, cool, quick-thinking fighter. The gaunt, red-whiskered general never displayed a strong ambition for power and, when asked to run for the presidency in 1884, he firmly declined. Nor did Sherman appear interested in the army's political intrigues. For him there was no glory in war—"It is all hell," he said.

Strategy and Conduct of the War

Most Northerners wanted to take the offensive and move quickly to put down the Southern rebellion. At the beginning of the war, General Scott offered Lincoln the Anaconda Plan, a scheme to blockade the South along its sea and land frontiers. Once the region had been cut off from outside resources, the Union could send in its powerful armies. This tactic of attrition—crushing the South gradually—resem-

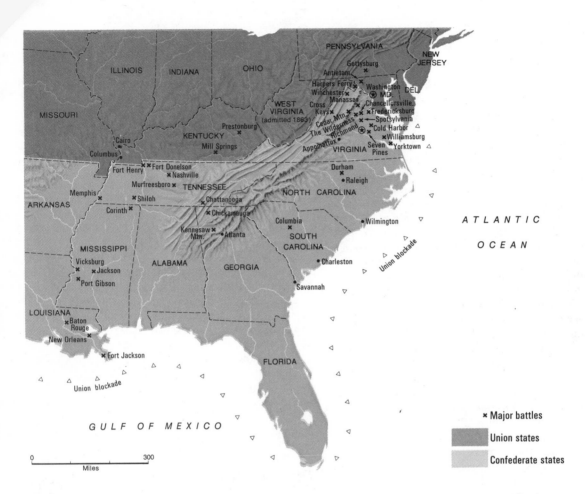

Major Battles of the Civil War

bled what finally did occur, but in the early months of the war it failed to meet the popular demand for a quick and decisive conclusion to the conflict.

When the war began, the South decided to pursue a defensive policy of holding its territory rather than using its initial military advantage to attack the North. This strategy backfired because it gave the North more time to prepare, and by the fall of 1862 a disciplined and confident Union army was taking shape.

The pattern of fighting was influenced largely by the Union's determination to take the Confeder-

ate capital of Richmond and by the geography of the Southern states. Because natural barriers prevented unified campaigns, unrelated skirmishes often occurred simultaneously in several locations. The fight for Richmond dominated the Eastern theater, from the Appalachian Mountains to the Atlantic Coast. Although Northern armies repeatedly battled their way toward the Southern capital, Richmond did not fall until the end of the war. The Western theater, from Tennessee to Mississippi, was dominated by the Union's efforts to hold Kentucky and Missouri and gain control of the Mississippi Valley.

From this area Northern generals hoped to strike the South with both land and naval forces via the Mississippi River and its system of strategic waterways.

Bull Run

The first major battle of the Civil War was fought for control of Richmond. In July 1861, Lincoln ordered General Irvin McDowell, commander of a motley collection of volunteers stationed in Washington, to advance on the Southern capital. General Patterson, a former militia commander, was to engage the Southern troops in the Shenandoah Valley. By detaining them he would leave McDowell free to attack the main Confederate force led by Brigadier General P. G. T. Beauregard. However, unknown to McDowell, the Confederates had evaded Patterson and were moving quickly by rail to reinforce Beauregard at his camp at Manassas Junction. On Sunday the inexperienced Union soldiers crossed the little stream called Bull Run, located only thirty miles from Washington, and met Beauregard's army of twenty-five thousand raw recruits.

At first a Union victory seemed certain. Then Stonewall Jackson arrived from Shenandoah, seized a key hill, and halted the Union advance. As Confederate pressure increased, the Northern lines faltered. Gradually rumors and panic spread through the Union regiments, and the retreat became a wild rout in which men threw away their weapons and fled blindly. The Confederates, who had also become disorganized, were unable to follow up their victory.

Bull Run was a terrible shock to Northern leaders. It convinced them that the war would not be won by calling out the militia for ninety days. Short-term regiments were sent home, and General George McClellan became commander of the new Army of the Potomac. McClellan was brilliant at organizing troops, but he took his time. While the administration chafed impatiently, he methodically whipped his demoralized regiments into a formidable professional army. On General Scott's retirement in the fall of 1861, McClellan was appointed general in chief of all the Union armies.

The Sea Blockade

In the fall of 1861, Lincoln ordered a land and sea expedition to seal off thirty-five hundred miles of Confederate coastline. Secretary of the Navy Gideon Welles impressed every vessel he could locate and approved designs for new warships, such as ironclads and steel gunboats. These forces took five Confederate forts during the winter, giving the Union a secure base for its blockading operations and forcing the Confederate government to divert some of its Richmond troops to guard against invasion from the sea.

Soon after the war began, the North managed to choke off almost 80 percent of Southern exports and imports. The encirclement of the South created serious supply problems and depressed Southern morale. Britain could have continued to trade legally with the South, for under international law enough ships had to be stationed outside a blockaded port to make entry clearly dangerous. Although this was not the case, the British chose to recognize the blockade, since in the future they might want the United States to do likewise.

The Battle for the Mississippi Valley

In 1862, while continuing to blockade the seacoast, the Union tried to divide the Confederacy by opening a path through the West. The goal was to gain control of the Mississippi Valley and then seal off the western half of the Confederacy beyond the Appalachian Mountains. The army under Grant's command had built a base at Cairo, Illinois. Subsequently, Union troops moved into northern Kentucky, while the Confederates held the southern part of the state. Jefferson Davis sent General Albert Sidney Johnston to defend the entire Mississippi area but neglected to give him enough soldiers. Johnston was outnumbered two to one.

Forts Henry and Donelson Early in February, Grant and his troops moved southwest along the Tennessee River toward Fort Henry on the Kentucky-Tennessee border. A flotilla of gunboats fired on the fort from the river while Grant's army attacked from the land. Fort Henry surrendered, thus destroying Johnston's access to the Tennessee River and forcing a retreat to nearby Fort Donelson. Although Fort Donelson resisted a gunboat bombardment, Grant, joined by General Henry W. Halleck and his men, successfully blocked all escape routes and called for an unconditional surrender. The fort was seized on February 16, and twelve thousand Confederates were taken prisoner. Union occupation of the two forts was a devastating blow to the South, for it destroyed Johnston's defensive line against invasion from the north and forced him to regroup his army farther south in northern Mississippi.

Shiloh The Confederates had been thrown off balance, and Lincoln was anxious to capitalize on the Union's advantage by moving Union troops into eastern Tennessee as soon as possible. Halleck, who was now the Union commander in the West, wanted to wait for more supplies, and his hesitancy cost the North precious time. When Halleck finally did send Grant after Johnston via the Tennessee River, the Confederates were revitalized and prepared. Grant established his forty thousand men at Pittsburg Landing and waited for reinforcements. While the Union forces were encamped, Johnston launched a heavy attack with forty-five thousand Confederate troops. On April 6 and 7, in the woodlands and pastures near a country meeting house known as Shiloh Church, the two armies engaged in the most extensive battle ever to have taken place on the North American continent.

The battle began in the rain on Sunday, and the action that day was brutal and confused. Grant was driven toward the river because his reinforcements had not arrived. The South lost the leadership of the courageous Johnston who bled to death from a minor leg wound, unattended during the heat of battle. Nevertheless, the Confederates came close to breaking the Union lines. Finally, during the night reinforcements reached the beleaguered Northerners, and on the following day Grant launched a bold counterattack. Overwhelmed by Union numbers, the Rebels were forced to retreat.

In a tactical sense, the Northern victory at Shiloh was very narrow, and both sides suffered heavy losses. There were more than ten thousand Confederate and thirteen thousand Union casualties. By Tuesday, it was still raining, and nine-tenths of the wounded lay where they had fallen. Many died from shock, exhaustion, and untreated wounds; some drowned in hollows filled by the downpour. Strategically, however, the North had gained a decisive advantage. Its forces now occupied much of Tennessee and Kentucky. The South had failed to prevent a concentration of federal troops within its territory, and its own forces were

in a vulnerable defensive position in the Mississippi Valley.

Farragut Takes New Orleans After the Battle of Shiloh, a powerful Union fleet under Flag Officer David Glasgow Farragut entered the Mississippi River from the Gulf of Mexico. Under heavy fire, Farragut managed to "run the forts" which protected New Orleans and took possession of the Confederacy's largest city and principal seaport. After Confederate troops were forced to withdraw, New Orleans was placed under the control of General Benjamin F. Butler. Butler's occupation was harsh and controversial. He issued an order stating that any female caught insulting a Union soldier would "be regarded and held liable to be treated as a woman of the town plying her trade." This act, which was considered an unforgivable insult by Southerners, inflamed the entire South.

Union Overconfidence By the spring of 1862 the Confederacy appeared near defeat. Most of the South's Atlantic coastline had been sealed off by the Union blockade. Halleck was in northern Mississippi, and Butler had moved up the river to seize Baton Rouge. In June the Union army took Memphis, paving the way for control of the Mississippi, and the Confederate army was also driven out of Corinth. In the Eastern theater, Lincoln was urging the cautious McClellan to advance against Richmond. In fact, the Lincoln administration was so confident that the war was about to end that it halted all further troop recruitments. This confidence proved premature, however, for a critical lack of military leadership resulted in uncoordinated actions in different theaters of the war. When McClellan began his drive on Richmond, just when a Union offensive in the West might have been decisive, that theater of the war became inactive.

McClellan's Peninsular Campaign

McClellan had spent months perfecting his army while the government and the public clamored for military action. Finally he convinced the impatient Lincoln to accept his plan to make a roundabout approach on Richmond from the southeast after floating a large army down the Chesapeake Bay to the tip of the Virginia peninsula. But McClellan's strategy was temporarily threatened by a new Confederate weapon—the ironclad warship.

Secretary of the Navy Welles had contracted to have built several gunboats armed with iron plates, and these little ironclads had been used by Grant in his campaigns on the Tennessee and Mississippi Rivers. In 1861 the Confederates salvaged a scuttled Union battleship, the *Merrimack*, which they rechristened the *C.S.S. Virginia*. This large vessel was reconditioned for naval warfare with a four-inch iron-plated citadel amidship, powerful guns behind, and an enormous iron ram at the bow. Although slow and clumsy, it was invulnerable to gunfire, and when it engaged Union vessels in March 1862, it caused a near panic and threatened the entire Union fleet around McClellan's forces.

The Union immediately countered with an ironclad warship of its own, the *Monitor*. For hours the ships battered one another until the *Merrimack* finally gave ground. Neither ship was sunk, but the *Monitor* ended Union fears that the *Merrimack* would take control of Chesapeake Bay.

A week after the duel between the ironclads, McClellan began moving troops and supplies to the peninsula. There he was met by the army of Joseph E. Johnston who, through a series of hit-and-retreat maneuvers, managed to considerably slow the Union land advance toward the Southern capital. When McClellan halted south of Richmond and demanded reinforcements, the South took the opportunity to place fifteen thousand soldiers, led by the wily Stonewall Jackson, in the Shenandoah Valley. This strip of land, northwest of Richmond, was of great strategic value, for it provided a natural avenue into both the North and the South. Jackson's goal was twofold: to keep reinforcements from joining McClellan and to deceive the Union into believing an attack on Washington was imminent.

Although his men were outnumbered three to one, Jackson convinced the Union army that his force was much larger through a daring series of

THE *MONITOR* (FOREGROUND) CLASHES WITH THE *MERRIMACK* AT CLOSE RANGE. THE BATTLE ENDED IN A STALEMATE WHEN THE REBEL VESSEL, UNABLE TO BRING ALL ITS GUNS TO BEAR, WITHDREW.

secret maneuvers, forced marches, and lightning attacks. Repeatedly, he checked the Northern army and seized valuable arms and supplies. As a result, Washington was reluctant to leave itself unprotected by sending reinforcements to McClellan. Instead the government diverted troops from the Richmond campaign to help drive out Jackson. Jackson left the Union army totally confused as to his strength, location, and plans. Finally, after eluding his pursuers, he dashed to assist Lee in the defense of Richmond.

Meanwhile, Confederate General Johnston, who held a defensive position at Yorktown, waited until McClellan was practically at the gates of the Confederate capital. During early summer the two armies clashed in a bloody and indecisive battle at Seven Pines. Heavy rains had turned the ground into a quagmire, when the Confederates launched an unsuccessful assault on McClellan's flank. Johnston was seriously wounded, and, as a result, President Davis appointed Robert E. Lee as Commander of the Army of Virginia.

The Seven Days' Campaign McClellan next settled down near the Chickahominy River to await reinforcements again and to prepare methodically for a

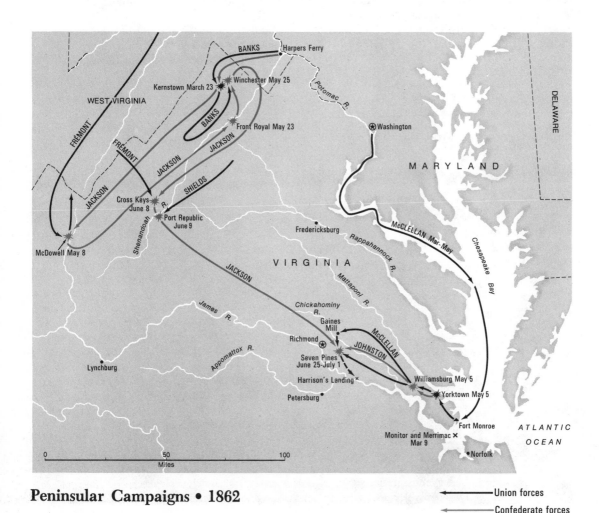

Peninsular Campaigns • 1862

Union forces
Confederate forces

seige from the north, a change in plans brought about by Jackson's confusing maneuvers. Lee, convinced that McClellan's spirit was weakened, decided to abandon the defensive strategy. By the last week in June, he had gathered an army of eighty thousand men. In a series of savage assaults, they forced McClellan to retreat and relentlessly pursued him in an attempt to destroy the Union army. By the end of the Seven Days' Campaign, Lee had clearly seized the initiative and thwarted the Union attempt to seize the Confederate capital.

Completely out of patience with McClellan's slowness and indecisive maneuvers, Lincoln brought Halleck back to Washington as general in chief in mid-1862. Halleck, however, proved incapable of directing all phases of the War. Lincoln at the same time put General John Pope in command of the remnants of the Union forces that had tried to destroy Jackson in the Shenandoah Valley.

Second Bull Run Pope was to move southward to join forces with McClellan, and together they would begin a new offensive against Richmond. Lee, unable to leave the peninsula while McClellan was present, boldly divided his forces and sent Jackson to halt Pope's advance. Several skirmishes ended late in August at the second Battle of Bull Run. There the Confederates held their ground until Lee's troops arrived and finally drove Pope back to Washington. Lincoln promptly fired him and recalled McClellan to defend the Union capital.

Aided by the genius of commanders such as Lee and Jackson, the Confederacy, which had been weakened in the spring of 1862, was on the offensive again by autumn.

Antietam In September 1862, a few weeks after the second Battle of Bull Run, Lee decided to strike the Union army in its own territory. In preparation for an invasion of Pennsylvania, he occupied Hagerstown, Maryland, and the South Mountain passes with half his men and sent the other half under Stonewall Jackson to take the federal arsenal at Harpers Ferry. Unfortunately for Lee, some Union soldiers found three cigars wrapped with Lee's orders and they turned them over to McClellan. Even after realizing that he was flanked by the two halves of Lee's army, McClellan moved slowly. By the time he had positioned himself for battle, Harpers Ferry had been successfully taken, and most of Jackson's men had returned to assist Lee.

McClellan and Lee finally clashed on September 17 above Antietam Creek near Sharpsburg, Maryland. Hoping to defeat Lee before help arrived from Harpers Ferry, McClellan massed three savage attacks in one day. Just in time, Confederate cavalry from the Ferry charged through the cornfields from the south, and the battle ended in a stalemate. It was perhaps the bloodiest single day's battle of the entire war: the North lost nearly thirteen thousand men and the South at least ten thousand. Although the fight was a draw tactically, strategically it was a Confederate defeat. Lee's plans to invade the North were shattered, and he was forced to withdraw into Virginia.

The Emancipation Proclamation

At the beginning of the war Lincoln believed his overriding purpose must be the preservation of the Union not the freeing of the slaves. Although he favored emancipation, he believed that it would be politically unwise to abolish slavery without ensuring compensation for slaveholders and without a plan to colonize freed blacks outside the United States. Lincoln never lost sight of the fact that the war was supported by two separate groups: Unionists (many of whom lived in the crucial border states), who believed blacks were inferior and who opposed abolition; and radical abolitionists, who viewed the war as a means of bringing about emancipation.

By early 1862, however, when the tide of battle seemed to be going against the North, Lincoln realized that the abolitionist demand for emancipation was gaining new support. Many people believed the South should be punished for using slaves to build fortifications and work the plantations while their masters went off to fight. As a result, the president subtly began to shift his position in the direction

GRAND SWEEPSTAKES FOR 1862, WON BY THE CELEBRATED HORSE EMANCIPATION.

of a declaration stating that the Union was fighting on behalf of human freedom. He feared that if he did not do so, military commanders in the field who favored emancipation might act on their own. He also was apprehensive that Congress might move to take control of the war and that European powers might throw their support on the side of the South.

Lincoln decided to maneuver cautiously until he felt secure that public sentiment would support his new policy. By April the Radicals in Congress had pushed through a bill abolishing slavery in the District of Columbia, and in June slavery was abolished in the territories. In July 1862 the president accepted the Second Confiscation Act which freed the slaves owned by persons serving in the Confederate Army. When Lincoln was finally convinced by newspaper reports that public opinion was becoming more favorable to emancipation he began working on his proposal. Secretary of State Seward urged him not to issue a public proclamation until the North had achieved a military victory, and he agreed to wait. His patience was finally rewarded by the success at Antietam. Subsequently, in Sep-

tember 1862, Lincoln issued a preliminary emancipation proclamation and announced that, unless the Confederacy surrendered, a final proclamation would be forthcoming in January. This final document declared that all seceded states that had not returned to the Union by January 1, 1863, were subject to the following decree:

I do order and declare that all persons held as slaves within said designated States and parts of states are, and henceforward shall be free; and that the Executive Government of the United States, including the military and naval authorities hereof, will recognize and maintain the freedom of said persons.

With these words the president asserted freedom for all slaves in areas that were in rebellion against the federal government. He said nothing, however, about emancipating slaves in the border states that remained in the Union, fearing that he would alienate them by declaring abolition there.

The proclamation was essentially a military measure aimed at confusing the Confederacy, and

Emancipation Proclamation Defended

"Thank God for what is already done, and let us all take heart as we go forward to uphold this great edict! For myself, I accept the Proclamation without note or comment. It is enough for me, that, in the exercise of the War Power, it strikes at the origin and mainspring of this Rebellion; for I have never concealed the conviction that it matters little where we strike Slavery, provided only that we strike sincerely and in earnest. So is it all connected, that the whole must suffer with every part. . . . "

Charles Sumner, U.S. Senator, 1863

Emancipation Proclamation Attacked

"The President has at last weakly yielded to the 'pressure' put upon him about which he has so bitterly complained, and issued his proclamation of negro emancipation . . . he has no constitutional power to issue this proclamation—none whatever. . . .

Nobody need argue with us that he has the power under military law. Military law does not destroy the fundamental civil law. In war, as in peace, the Constitution is 'the supreme law of the land.'

The government, then, by the act of the President, is in rebellion and the war is reduced to a contest for subjugation. . . . "

The Chicago *Times*, 1863

its immediate impact on the public was both controversial and divisive. It was popular with abolitionists but not with the majority of the Northern population. Although no slaves were actually freed, racial tension in some areas increased significantly. Following the preliminary proclamation, the Republican majority lost ground in the congressional elections of 1862. The Republican party was strongest in the border states where the army had stationed troops, but it lost important states such as Illinois, Pennsylvania, and New York to the Democrats. Yet, the proclamation pacified the Radical faction somewhat, and it won the admiration of the antislavery movement in England, despite the denunciations of some European diplomats and politicians.

Because the Union army needed additional recruits, Lincoln had begun enlisting blacks in 1862. Following the Emancipation Proclamation, the Union continued to enlist black volunteers with the president's encouragement. Of about half a million free blacks who had crossed over into Union territory, about two hundred thousand were working for the army. By the fall of 1864, there were over a hundred and fifty thousand black soldiers in the Union forces, most of them from the South. Many Southern blacks hesitated to join the army, since they were barred from becoming officers and were kept segregated. Others agreed with Frederick Douglass, who argued that wearing the American uniform was a step toward real citizenship. Black soldiers participated in some five hundred engagements and received twenty-two Congressional Medals of Honor. Thirty-eight thousand of them died fighting for the North.

Although blacks accounted for about 10 percent of the total enlistments in Union forces, the Confederacy could not bring itself to enlist slaves until a month before the end of the war. Instead, they impressed slaves into labor battalions in war-related industries.

1863–1865: The War Grinds to an End

After the Battle of Antietam and the Emancipation Proclamation, the South remained on the defensive and never again came close to victory. As long as reunification had been the primary issue, a negotiated peace had remained a possibility. After the Emancipation Proclamation, however, the South was determined to fight to a finish rather than negotiate the end of slavery.

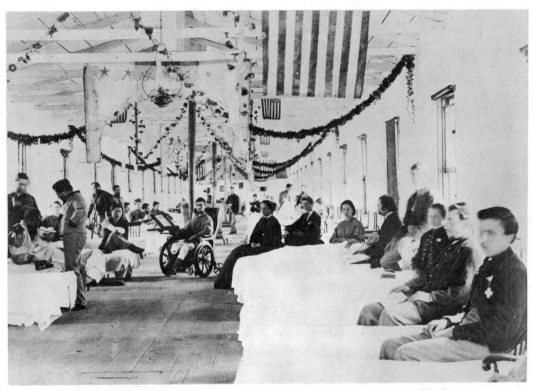

A WARD IN ARMORY SQUARE HOSPITAL, WASHINGTON, D. C. ON THE LEFT A BEARDED DOCTOR (STANDING) ATTENDS TO ONE OF THE PATIENTS.

As a first step toward the final defeat of the South, Lincoln again reshuffled his military commanders. After Antietam, he finally ran out of patience with McClellan's continued reluctance to strike against Lee and replaced him with General Ambrose E. Burnside. Ironically, Burnside had twice refused the position of Commander of the Army of the Potomac on the grounds that he was unqualified. General Buell, a friend of McClellan who shared his opposition to the Emancipation Proclamation, was replaced in the West by Major General William S. Rosecrans. Grant took charge of Union operations in northern Mississippi and western Tennessee.

Northern and Southern Offensives

In the Western theater in December 1862, Union forces under Rosecrans marched southeast of Nashville and engaged Confederate General Braxton Bragg's Army of Tennessee. Although the Confederates were eventually forced to retreat, three days of vicious fighting left the Union army so shattered that it did not resume the offensive for nearly six months. Meanwhile Grant was temporarily stymied in his attempt to capture Vicksburg, Mississippi.

In the East, Burnside had decided on an unprecedented winter campaign against Richmond. He intended to sneak around Lee's flank, cross the Rappahannock River at Fredericksburg, then march on to Richmond. But the Union army was delayed by hesitations and Burnside's insistence on building pontoon bridges, and by the time they crossed the Rappahannock, Lee was entrenched in an unassailable position atop the heights below Fredericksburg. In a series of hopeless assaults, Union soldiers rushed forward over their dead and dying in the face of concentrated Confederate artillery. Eventually, the incompetent Burnside, tears streaming down his face, ordered a retreat from Fredericksburg. Lincoln then replaced Burnside with "Fighting Joe" Hooker who began the long task of preparing the Army of the Potomac for a new spring offensive.

While Grant was organizing for another attempt to take Vicksburg in the West, Hooker began a giant pincer maneuver to trap and overpower Lee's depleted army. The Union offensive had very nearly succeeded, when Hooker suddenly lost his confidence and assumed a defensive position. In a desperate gamble, Lee and Jackson split their forces into three parts and launched a surprise attack. The resulting Battle of Chancellorsville (May 2–6), fought in dense woods and burning underbrush, ended in another spectacular victory for the South. Lee's greatest loss was the beloved Stonewall Jack-son who was shot accidentally by his own men while reconnoitering behind the lines during the night.

Heartened by the success at Chancellorsville, Davis and Lee decided to make one more attempt to invade the North. A victory in Pennsylvania would put the major cities of Philadelphia and Washington in direct peril, a threat which might tip the sentiments of war-weary Northerners toward peace. By June 28 Lee's entire army was in Pennsylvania. Hooker requested additional men and supplies, but Lincoln refused to send them, on the grounds that Hooker had shown at Chancellorsville that he did not know how to use his resources. The angry Hooker resigned and was replaced by General George Gordon Meade. On July 1, 1863, Lee and Meade joined combat at Gettysburg, Pennsylvania, in what was to be the most significant battle of the war.

Gettysburg Soon after detached Union and Confederate units clashed near Gettysburg, both armies rapidly converged on the town. The Union forces under Meade retreated to a strong position on Cemetery Ridge, protected from the north by Culp's Hill. Lee's men occupied Seminary Ridge about a mile distant across an open field. Against the advice of his second in command, Lee decided on a frontal attack. For three days wave after wave of Confederate soldiers, backed by heavy artillery fire, repeatedly attacked Cemetery Ridge only to be repulsed by valiant Union troops. In a final courageous assault, General George E. Pickett threw his Virginia division of fifteen thousand in a bold charge toward the ridge. Although ripped to shreds by Union fire, the Confederates actually reached the Union line. However, unable to hold their position, they were soon forced to retreat. Casualties on both sides were enormous; more than 25 percent of the combatants were killed. Finally Lee's offensive power was destroyed. He could only say, "All this has been my fault," and the following day the tattered Confederates returned to Virginia.

To Lincoln's dismay, Meade did not pursue Lee; however, the encounter proved that the South no longer had sufficient resources to mount an offensive campaign. The Confederates' final attempt to invade the North had failed. News of Lee's retreat reached the North at the same time as word of Grant's capture of Vicksburg, giving Union morale a tremendous boost.

Battles at Fredericksburg, Chancellorsville, Gettysburg

Grant Becomes Supreme Commander

The major event in the West during the late spring of 1862 was Grant's Vicksburg campaign. Located on a high bluff and manned with long-range guns, Vicksburg was unapproachable from the Mississippi River. Grant, however, engineered naval control of the river below Vicksburg, allowing him to proceed on a campaign across the state. Eventually Grant's men laid seige to Vicksburg by constructing miles of interlocking trenches and gun emplacements and by maintaining a constant bombardment from the river. For six weeks the defenders of Vicksburg lived underground, subsisting on mules, dogs, and rats. Help never came, and the fortress surrendered its hopeless position on July 4.

With the capture of Vicksburg, the federal government obtained a firm hold on the Mississippi River all the way to the Gulf Coast, and the Southern states west of the Mississippi River were detached from the rest of the Confederacy. Although the Union forces under Rosecrans were badly defeated by General Braxton Bragg at Chickamauga in northern Georgia (September 19–20), Grant forced Bragg out of Chattanooga and back into Georgia in November. By late November he had assumed control of Tennessee as well.

In March 1864, Lincoln appointed Grant to the post of General of the Armies. A politically popular choice, Grant had demonstrated at Vicksburg that the relentless application of Northern resources could wear down the South and lead to victory. Lincoln had found a general who would end the war within a year. Grant's next objective was to defeat the Confederacy's two major forces: Lee's army in Virginia and Johnston's force in Georgia. Grant planned to move on Richmond while Sherman drove toward Atlanta.

In Virginia, Grant and Lee fought for over a month near the Rapidan River. Their engagements, among the hardest fought in American history, included the Battle of Cold Harbor. Grant alone seemed convinced of the feasibility of a general assault against the Confederate line. His subordinates believed it was almost hopeless and before the battle quietly pinned scraps of paper bearing their names to their shirts. In less than ten minutes five thousand Union troops were dead; the wounded lay suffering for days until they died where they had fallen. In the North politicians and press alike assailed the commander as "Butcher Grant."

The War Ends

Once he had gained a foothold in Georgia, Sherman was ordered to march across the state, destroy Atlanta's resources, and cut off more of the West. After fighting off Johnston's delaying tactics during the summer, Sherman's troops occupied Atlanta on September 2, 1864. Sherman then moved his army across Georgia toward Savannah. During the march, he liberated Union soldiers from the shocking conditions of the prisoner of war camp at Andersonville and ordered his troops to devastate everything in their path. The desolation left by this "scorched earth" policy caused widespread suffering for civilians and contributed to the South's long-lasting hatred of the North. By February 1865 Sherman was moving across the Carolinas. Confederate resources were so low that General Johnston admitted, "I can do no more than annoy him." Subsequently, Union forces moved into North Carolina, and by the end of March they were in Goldsboro, 160 miles south of Richmond.

Grant's Vicksburg Campaign

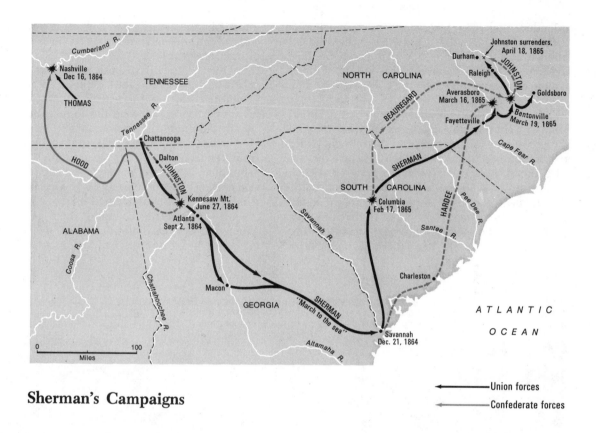

Sherman's Campaigns

Union forces
Confederate forces

In a desperate effort to break away and consolidate his forces with Johnston's, Lee attacked Grant. But in April 1865 Grant's troops fragmented Lee's right flank in a battle at Five Forks. At last Lee was forced to evacuate Richmond.

With the North's occupation of Richmond, most Southerners no longer had the will to continue the struggle. Loyalty to Robert E. Lee seemed to be the only unifying force left in the Confederacy. One of Lee's staff is said to have exclaimed, "Country be damned! There is no Country. There has been no Country, general, for a year or more. You are the Country for these men. They have fought for you. If you demand the sacrifice, there are still thousands of us who would die for you." Lee did not demand the sacrifice.

On April 9, in the McLean farmhouse at Appomattox Court House in southern Virginia, Lee surrendered his army to Grant. The two generals arranged the terms of surrender: Confederate soldiers were to be paroled and public property and war material surrendered. Officers would be allowed to keep their sidearms, and all men who owned a horse or a mule could "keep them to work their little farms."

Johnston surrendered to Sherman in North Carolina a few days later. By early June Jefferson Davis and a few Confederate officials had been arrested in Georgia and imprisoned in Fort Monroe. Gradually the remaining vestiges of Southern resistance were obliterated.

The Election of 1864

As the conflict was drawing to a close, Northern politics reflected the tensions that had been building during the war. On the one hand, Lincoln had offended moderates by issuing the Emancipation Proclamation. On the other hand, the Radicals blamed him for inefficiency and for Republican losses in the congressional elections of 1862. Finally, Union war casualties had upset everyone and increased the pressure for peace.

Yet the nation's economy was booming, stimulated by government purchases of war material. Crops were abundant and prices were high. Industrialization had begun in the North before the conflict and would probably have progressed without it. In fact, the intensified pace brought on by the war tended to disturb the normal flow of investments and to prevent innovations in industry. War profiteering and speculation were rampant, as they are in any war. Finally, labor shortages on the farms impeded agricultural growth, causing a rise in food costs which was not equaled by the increased wages of industrial workers.

Over protests from both moderates and Radicals, Lincoln won the 1864 Republican nomination primarily by his skillful control of patronage. With his supporters dominating the Republican convention in Baltimore, he was nominated unanimously. He further demonstrated his control by obtaining from the convention the nomination of Andrew Johnson of Tennessee, a member of the prowar faction of the Democratic party, as its vice-presidential candidate. The Republicans also wooed war Democrats by temporarily changing their name to the Union party. Their platform denounced slavery, declaring it a cause of the war, issued a call for

SHERMAN'S TROOPS LEFT A TRAIL OF DEVASTATION BEHIND THEM AS THEY MARCHED FROM ATLANTA TO THE SEA, DESTROYING ANYTHING THAT MIGHT BE USED BY THE REBELS TO CONTINUE THE FIGHT. THE RED-BEARDED GENERAL HAD NO ILLUSIONS ABOUT WAR: "IT IS ALL HELL," HE SAID.

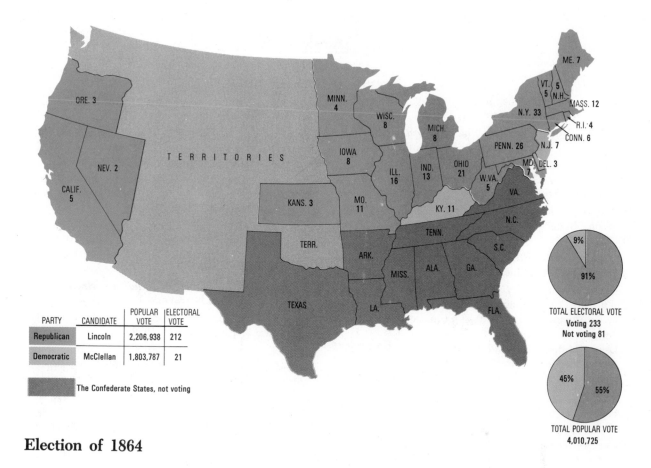

PARTY	CANDIDATE	POPULAR VOTE	ELECTORAL VOTE
Republican	Lincoln	2,206,938	212
Democratic	McClellan	1,803,787	21

The Confederate States, not voting

TOTAL ELECTORAL VOTE
Voting 233
Not voting 81

9%
91%

TOTAL POPULAR VOTE
4,010,725

45%
55%

Election of 1864

a united front in the prosecution of the war, promised protection for black soldiers, and encouraged immigration.

The Democrats, to please party regulars, gave their party's presidential nomination to General Mc-Clellan, the cautious but popular war hero. To appease the peace faction, the party platform condemned the war as a failure and called for an armistice that would permit peace negotiations based on a restored union of all the states. The Democratic platform excluded emancipation as a condition for peace. McClellan repudiated the platform, however, and ran as a war leader, attacking the Lincoln administration for inefficiency and for failing to prosecute the war successfully.

Lincoln Wins On August 23 Lincoln remarked: "This morning as for some days past, it seems probable that this administration will not be reelected." But with Sherman's occupation of Atlanta early in September, Northern spirits were raised, and the tide began to turn toward the Republicans. The Radicals then joined forces with the president to prevent a Democratic victory. Lincoln polled 55 percent of the popular vote of the dismembered Union and carried the electoral college, 212 votes to 21. Congress again went to the Republicans. Lincoln's reelection ensured that the war would not end until the Union had been restored and slavery had been abolished.

Readings

General Works

Beltz, Herman, *A New Birth of Freedom: The Republican Party and Freedmen's Rights, 1861 to 1866.* Westport, Conn.: Greenwood, 1976.

Catton, Bruce, *The Centennial History of the War,* Vols. I–III. Garden City, N.Y.: Doubleday, 1961–1963.

Cole, Arthur C., *The Irrepressible Conflict 1860–1865.* New York: Reprint House International, 1960.

Connelly, Thomas, *Army of the Heartland,* 2 Vols. Baton Rouge: Louisiana State University Press, 1967–1971.

Donald, David (Ed.), *Why the North Won the Civil War.* New York: Macmillan, 1960.

Eaton, Clement, *A History of the Southern Confederacy.* New York: Macmillan, 1954.

Foote, Shelby, *The Civil War,* 3 Vols. New York: Random House, 1958–1974.

Leech, Margaret, *Reveille in Washington, 1860–1865.* New York: Grosset & Dunlap, 1941.

Nevins, Allan, *The War for the Union,* Vols. I–III. New York: Scribner's, 1959–1970.

Parish, Peter J., *The American Civil War.* New York: Holmes & Meier, 1975.

Randall, James G., and David Donald, *The Civil War and Reconstruction.* Boston: Heath, 1961.

Vandiver, Frank E., *Their Tattered Flags: The Epic of the Confederacy.* New York: Harper Magazine Press, 1970.

Williams, Kenneth P., *Lincoln Finds a General: A Military History of the Civil War,* Vols. I–IV. New York: Macmillan, 1949–1952.

Special Studies

Andreano, Ralph (Ed.), *The Economic Impact of the American Civil War.* Cambridge, Mass.: Schenkman, 1967.

Catton, Bruce, *Grant Takes Command.* Boston: Little, Brown, 1969.

Cook, Adrian, *The Armies of the Streets.* Lexington: University of Kentucky Press, 1974.

Crook, D. P., *Diplomacy During the American Civil War.* New York: Wiley, 1975.

Current, Richard N., *The Lincoln Nobody Knows.* New York: McGraw-Hill, 1958.

Donald, David, *Lincoln Reconsidered.* New York: Random House, 1956.

Franklin, John H., *The Emancipation Proclamation.* Garden City, N.Y.: Doubleday, 1963.

Frederickson, George M., *The Inner Civil War: Northern Intellectuals and the Crisis of the Union.* New York: Harper & Row, 1965.

Hammond, Bray, *Sovereignty and an Empty Purse: Banks and Politics in the Civil War.* Princeton, N.J.: Princeton University Press, 1970.

McPherson, James M., *The Struggle for Equality: Abolitionists and the Negro in the Civil War and Reconstruction.* Princeton, N.J.: Princeton University Press, 1964.

Massey, Mary E., *Bonnet Brigades: American Women and the Civil War.* New York: Knopf, 1966.

Owsley, Frank L., *King Cotton Diplomacy.* Chicago: University of Chicago Press, 1959.

Randall, James G., *Constitutional Problems under Lincoln.* Urbana: University of Illinois Press, 1964.

Silbey, Joel H., *A Respectable Minority: The Democratic Party in the Civil War Era, 1860–1868.* New York: Norton, 1977.

Wiley, Bell I., *The Life of Billy Yank.* Indianapolis, Ind.: Bobbs-Merrill, 1952.

————, *The Life of Johnny Reb.* Indianapolis, Ind.: Bobbs-Merrill, 1943.

Williams, T. Harry, *Lincoln and the Radicals.* Madison: University of Wisconsin Press, 1941.

Primary Sources

Chestnut, Mary B., *A Diary from Dixie.* Boston: Houghton Mifflin, 1949.

Commager, Henry S. (Ed.), *The Blue and the Gray: The Story of the Civil War as Told by Participants,* Vols. I–II. Indianapolis, Ind.: Bobbs-Merrill, 1950.

Grant, Ulysses S., *The Personal Memoirs of U. S. Grant.* New York: Grossett & Dunlap, 1962.

McPherson, James M. (Ed.), *The Negro's Civil War.* New York: Pantheon, 1965.

Melville, Herman, *Battle-Pieces and Other Aspects of the War.* New York: T. Yoseloff, 1963.

Stephens, Alexander H., *Recollections.* New York: Doubleday, 1910.

Biographies

Connelly, Thomas L., *The Marble Man: Robert E. Lee and His Image in American Society*. New York: Knopf, 1977.

Dowdey, Clifford, *Lee*. Boston: Little, Brown, 1965.

Duberman, Martin, *Charles Francis Adams*. Boston: Houghton Mifflin, 1961.

Luthin, Reinhard H., *The Real Abraham Lincoln*. Englewood Cliffs, N.J.: Prentice-Hall, 1960.

Mitgang, Herbert, *The Fiery Trial: A Life of Lincoln*. New York: Viking Press, 1974.

Randall, James G., *Lincoln, the President: Springfield to Gettysburg*, Vols. I–IV. New York: Dodd, Mead, 1946–1955.

Sandburg, Carl, *Abraham Lincoln: The War Years*, Vols. I–IV. New York: Harcourt, Brace, 1939.

Strode, Hudson, *Jefferson Davis*, Vols. I–IV. New York: Harcourt, Brace, 1955–1966.

Van Deusen, Glyndon G., *William Henry Seward*. New York: Oxford University Press, 1967.

Fiction

Cable, George W., *Dr. Sevier*. Upper Saddle River, N.J.: Gregg, 1970.

Crane, Stephen, *The Red Badge of Courage*. New York: Macmillan, 1966. (Paper: Collier)

DeForest, John, *Miss Ravenal's Conversion*. New York: Holt, Rinehart & Winston, 1955.

Shaara, Michael, *The Killer Angels: A Novel About the Four Days at Gettysburg*. New York: McKay, 1974.

15 Reconstructing the Union

With malice toward none; with charity for all; with firmness in the right, as God gives us to see the right, let us strive on to finish the work we are in; to bind up the nation's wounds; to care for him who shall have borne the battle, and for his widow and his orphan—to do all which may achieve and cherish a just, and a lasting peace, among ourselves, and with all nations.

Abraham Lincoln, *Second Inaugural Address*
March 4, 1865

Significant Events

Lincoln's Proclamation of Amnesty and Reconstruction (Ten-Percent Plan) [December 1863]

Wade-Davis Bill [July 1864]

Thirteenth Amendment to the Constitution (ratified December 1865) [January 1865]

Freedmen's Bureau established [March 1865]

Lincoln dies [April 15, 1865]

Johnson's Proclamation of Amnesty and Pardon [May 1865]

Black Codes [1865 and 1866]

Civil Rights Act [April 1866]

Fourteenth Amendment (ratified July 1868) [June 1866]

Military Reconstruction Act [March 1867]

President Johnson impeached [February 1868]

Fifteenth Amendment (ratified February 1870) [February 1869]

Enforcement Acts [1870 and 1871]

Amnesty Act [1872]

Economic panic [1873]

Civil Rights Cases [1883]

Atlanta Compromise [1895]

Plessy v. *Ferguson* [1896]

Williams v. *Mississippi* [1898]

Guinn v. *United States* [1915]

RICHMOND, VIRGINIA, AFTER THE CIVIL WAR.

The Civil War preserved the republic and abolished slavery, but it left a nation bitter and divided. Of the tasks remaining to be accomplished, none was more critical than the need to restore the South to the Union without sacrificing the newly won freedom of the slaves.

In the North a great and stormy debate developed over the nature of the settlement to be imposed on the South. This debate, which largely determined the character of the postwar period, involved power struggles between the legislative and executive branches of government and between a triumphant Republican party and a resurgent Democratic party.

In the South the war and abolition left a society in disarray. During the Reconstruction period lingering Southern bitterness against the North was compounded by the efforts of many Northerners to prescribe the political and economic structure of the postwar South.

The options open to the North in reconstructing the defeated states of the Confederacy were circumscribed by the fact that the powers ascribed to the federal government under the Constitution were limited, and by the related awareness that any regulation of the social and economic life of the citizenry should be a state and local responsibility. The armies of both sides were disbanded and the men returned to civilian life with no further support than pensions for their services. In the South private companies financed by the states and foreign and Northern capital gradually rebuilt railroads and other facilities. Only in regard to the freedmen did the national government reluctantly become involved in a piecemeal approach to easing their transition to a new life.

Presidential Reconstruction Plans

The South at War's End

At the war's end the South was in disarray and its economy was in ruins. Charleston and Richmond had been almost completely leveled, and entire sections of Atlanta, Mobile, Vicksburg, and Galveston lay in ashes. Sherman's armies, following their commander's scorched-earth policy, devastated much of the Georgia and Carolina countryside on their march to Savannah. Transportation was a hopeless shambles. Roads were impassable, rivers were unnavigable, bridges were down, and wagons, horses, and steamboats had all but disappeared. The destruction of countless schools disrupted education; many teachers who had gone off to war would never return. Even more calamitous than the physical destruction was the huge loss of life. Out of an army of one million, some 260,000 Southerners died (Northern losses were no less consequential— 360,000 Northerners dead out of an army of 1.5 million).

The war also had severe economic effects on the South. Runaway inflation closed Southern banks and drove businesses into bankruptcy. Many large plantations were producing far below capacity, land values dropped dramatically, and little capital or credit was available for rebuilding or reinvesting.

The freeing of the slaves created an immediate labor shortage, since many freedmen were traveling from place to place in search of their families or moving into the towns in search of work. Plantation owners were alarmed by persistent rumors that the victorious North intended to carve up Southern plantations and distribute the land among the newly freed blacks. If all this were not enough, Southern whites looked upon the freedom of their slaves as a threat of unknown proportions to the future social and political order of the South.

Lincoln's Reconstruction Program

While the war was in progress President Lincoln began to lay the groundwork for rebuilding the nation. His primary goal for the immediate postwar period was to enable the Southern states to resume their rightful place in the Union while at the same time taking measures to ensure the "ultimate extinction" of slavery. On the question of the status of the South, Lincoln reasoned that because secession was an illegal act, the Confederate states had never really left the Union. All that was necessary was to remove the illegitimate rebel authorities and replace them with newly constituted, loyal state governments.

Lincoln believed there was some support for the republic in every Southern state, and he intended to make it as easy as possible for the former Confederate states to resume proper "practical relations" with the Union. Therefore, in December 1863 he issued his Proclamation of Amnesty and Reconstruction. Popularly known as the Ten-Percent Plan, the president's Reconstruction blueprint stipulated that all citizens of a Confederate state (with the exception of highly placed officials of the Confederacy) would be granted amnesty and would be returned all property lost in the war upon taking an oath of loyalty to the Constitution and to the laws and proclamations regarding slavery passed by Congress and the president during the war. When a number of voters in a state equal to 10 percent of those who had voted in the 1860 presidential election had taken this oath, those voters could write a new constitution creating a loyal government. The state could then resume its proper functions in the Union.

The loyalty oath was the only part of the plan that dealt with the abolition question. Lincoln made no provision for enforcing the oath, but instead called upon Southern leaders to bring about the permanent freedom of the slaves. Moreover, early in 1865 he stated publicly that he wished to see the suffrage extended at least to those blacks who were educated, who owned property, and "who serve our cause as soldiers." The federal government began almost immediately to carry out the provisions of the Ten-Percent Plan in the occupied states of Louisiana, Arkansas, and Tennessee. Lincoln installed military governors who began organizing the support of the loyal minority of citizens in preparation for establishing new state governments.

Many Republicans in Congress were willing to accept Lincoln's plan, but leading Radical Republicans considered it too lenient. Some Radicals did not share Lincoln's view that the Confederate states had not left the Union, and they wanted to punish the South by making the requirements for reentry more stringent. Radical Republicans also insisted that steps be taken to ensure that black people would be granted equality before the law and all the civil rights that entailed. Finally, all Republicans believed that as the representatives of the people it was their proper legislative function, and not the function of the president, to decide the terms on which the former states could be recreated.

The issues of which branch of government should have authority to formulate Reconstruction policy and what the nature of that policy should be became bound up in a struggle for power between the executive and the legislature. During the course of the war President Lincoln had strengthened the executive enormously at the expense of Congress. Now that the conflict was drawing to a close, Congress began to reassert its constitutional authority, using its legislative powers as the instrument.

In July 1864 Congress countered Lincoln's Ten-Percent Plan with the harsher Wade-Davis bill. The bill required that a majority of a state's voters, instead of just 10 percent, swear allegiance to the Union before being readmitted; it limited political participation to those who had been loyal to the Union during the war; and it required that the new state constitutions contain provisions repudiating all debts contracted by the Confederacy, abolishing slavery, and denying the vote to all ex-Confederate officials. Like Lincoln's plan, the Wade-Davis bill left to the states the determination of black civil rights. The bill was passed by Congress, but Lincoln, concerned that the Reconstruction process that was already well under way in Louisiana would be nullified by the bill and believing that the rights of freedmen could be better ensured by a constitutional amendment than by an act of Congress, let it die by pocket veto.

Radical Republicans, led by Thaddeus Stevens in the House and Charles Sumner in the Senate, were enraged. They responded with the Wade-Davis Manifesto, which censured the president and accused him of an "outrage on the legislative authority." Aware that he would have to make some concessions to the Radicals in order to proceed with Reconstruction, Lincoln began to formulate a new plan. But his efforts to devise a compromise with Congress were sidetracked by the resistance of conservative members of Congress to inclusion of a Radical proposal for universal black male suffrage. In January 1865, under pressure from Lincoln, Congress passed and later that year a majority of states ratified the Thirteenth Amendment to the Constitution prohibiting slavery or involuntary servitude in the United States. This was the first time the federal government had undertaken a nationwide reform in the area of domestic institutions, and it did so with a full awareness that the social consequences of freeing the slaves would still have to be worked out.

ONLOOKERS MOURN AS THE BODY OF PRESIDENT LINCOLN ARRIVES AT THE CITY HALL IN NEW YORK, 1865.

The Assassination of Lincoln

On April 9, 1865, with Lee's surrender to Grant at Appomattox Court House in Virginia, the restoration of the Union was no longer in doubt. But the North's triumph was shadowed by the tragedy that struck on Good Friday, April 14. That evening Lincoln and his wife drove to Ford's Theater in Washington to attend a play. Just after ten o'clock, John Wilkes Booth of Virginia, a young actor and pro-slavery fanatic, slipped unnoticed into the corridor behind the president's box while the one guard assigned to protect the president had stepped out for a drink. Through a hole he had bored earlier in the day Booth watched his victim, and at an amusing moment in the play, while the audience was laughing, he entered the box and shot the president in the head. Then, springing to the stage of the theater, he cried dramatically, "*Sic Semper Tyrannis!* The South is avenged!" and dashed through the wings to a waiting horse. The president, mortally wounded, was carried across the street to a private home. Early the next morning he died. Booth was hunted down and cornered in a barn in Virginia. The barn was set on fire and Booth was shot dead.

The news of Lincoln's death stunned the North. Grief-stricken mourners stood silently by the railroad tracks as his funeral train carried their leader home to Springfield. Lincoln's death suspended hopes for an early reconciliation between North and South. Whether the new president would be as compassionate to the defeated South remained to be seen.

Reconstruction under Andrew Johnson

The leadership of the divided nation now fell to Andrew Johnson. As a senator from Tennessee, Johnson had opposed secession and had continued to sit in Congress even after his state had withdrawn from the Union. For this action he became a hero to many Northerners, and his loyalty did not go unrewarded. When Tennessee fell to Union forces in 1862, Lincoln appointed Johnson military governor of the state. Two years later, Lincoln selected him as his running mate, and five months after the election Andrew Johnson was president.

Because Johnson detested the wealthy Southern aristocracy, the Radical Republicans at first thought they had an ally in the White House. Their optimism was short-lived, however. Johnson was no Radical, but a democrat who represented the interests of the small farmer. Moreover, his opposition to secession was a reflection of his reverence for the Constitution and the Union, not of a concern for racial justice.

It was Johnson's belief that the Constitution did not give to Congress the authority to dictate the terms by which the Confederate states could rejoin the Union. The new president therefore decided to direct the Reconstruction of each state himself, actively carrying out his policy "to restore said state to its constitutional relations to the Federal government" for seven months while Congress was not in session. He began by recognizing the new state governments of Louisiana, Arkansas, Virginia, and Tennessee that had been reorganized under Lincoln's Ten-Percent Plan. Next, in a Proclamation of Amnesty and Pardon, he set forth his own plan to be implemented in all Confederate states not already reorganized under the Ten-Percent Plan. Johnson's design was similar to Lincoln's in that it offered to pardon most ex-Confederates who would pledge their loyalty to the Union except that it excluded high-ranking Confederate officials and those owning property worth more than $20,000. These groups would be required to petition the president himself for pardon.

The plan provided for presidential appointment of a provisional governor in each state, election of delegates to state constitutional conventions, and the reorganization of the state governments. However, Johnson stipulated that before a state could be restored to the Union it must nullify its ordinance of secession, ratify the Thirteenth Amendment, and repudiate the Confederate debt.

Unfortunately, Johnson was not willing to move decisively to enforce the plan. Lincoln had believed that the Confederate South should not be given a strong voice in deciding on terms for resuming its role in the Union, but should be required to accept them as a consequence of defeat. As a Republican, Lincoln's goals had been similar to those of the congressional majority, and he had come to realize that the terms of Reconstruction had to be tough enough on the issue of the treatment of the freedmen to be acceptable to the people of the North. The North wanted to know that slavery was, indeed, dead and that the power of the former slaveholders was at an end. Johnson's enforcement of Reconstruction policy was not reassuring to Northerners. He did not attempt to enforce compliance with Northern demands, and in an attempt to create loyal regimes in the former Confederate states which would give him political support, he even implied that the South could ignore them. As a result, the South soon began to reassert its independence. Mississippi refused to ratify the Thirteenth Amendment, and Alabama refused to ratify part of it. South Carolina and Mississippi refused to repudiate their Confederate debts. Some states only "repealed" their secession ordinances, and some newly reorganized states actually sent as their representatives to Congress highly placed Confederate leaders and military men. As if this were not enough, the South moved to place restrictions on black people.

The Freedmen

The status of the freedmen in American life was the central issue in the aftermath of the Civil War. Although at the end of the war the Thirteenth Amendment was on its way to the states for ratification, the legal status of the freedmen as citizens had not yet been established. In Johnson's plans for Reconstruction, the welfare of the newly freed slaves had been subordinated to the reunification of the nation. Although only a few Radicals believed in absolute equality between the races, and although moderate Republicans were divided concerning the exact degree of suffrage that should be granted to blacks, in general the party thought blacks should be recognized as citizens with all the rights of free people. This view set them apart from the Democrats

TO DEAL WITH THE FOOD SHORTAGE THAT PLAGUED LOCAL AREAS AFTER THE WAR, STOREKEEPERS INSTITUTED A RATIONING SYSTEM. IN THIS PRINT GENTLEWOMEN, FREED BLACKS, AND POOR WHITE FARMERS HAVE GATHERED TO COLLECT THEIR ALLOTMENT.

and from President Johnson, and it laid the groundwork for a power struggle between Congress and the president, between the parties within Congress, and between the North and the South.

The Freedmen's Bureau and the Black Codes By the war's end homeless former slaves were crowding into shantytowns often built by the Union army, moving into Southern cities to find jobs, and migrating to the Texas frontier in search of land. So intolerable were conditions that in 1865 alone an estimated one hundred thousand blacks reportedly died from starvation and disease. In March 1865, while Lincoln was still president, the Union government passed a bill establishing the Freedmen's Bureau to provide relief to freed slaves and white refugees and to facilitate the transition from slavery to freedom. The bureau distributed food and helped blacks reestablish employment on the plantations on the basis of agreements with planters. It cooperated with private agencies and individuals in setting up schools and providing teachers for black people of all ages. Under its auspices, Atlanta University, Fisk University, and Howard University were established, and a Freedmen's Bureau study in 1866 found that black children in the South were attending school more regularly than were whites. In addition the Bureau performed thousands of marriage ceremonies legalizing black family life.

Meanwhile, in the absence of a unified Northern policy on the rights of the freedmen, the former

Confederate states began enacting measures designed to keep the ex-slaves in a position of economic, social, and political inferiority. Collectively called the Black Codes, these measures, passed in 1865 and 1866, reflected the widespread Southern view that blacks were innately inferior and must be kept in their appropriate subordinate position. At the same time that enactment of the codes granted the former slaves a legal status—including the right to make contracts, to sue and to be sued, and in some states to acquire property without restrictions—it limited their freedom of employment and generally prohibited them from voting, holding office, testifying against white people, serving on juries, or bearing arms. Of all the provisions of the Black Codes, the most repressive were vagrancy laws which authorized local authorities to arrest unemployed black people, fine them for vagrancy, and hire out those who could not pay the fine, their wages going to pay the fine. Some states even provided that black people who jumped their labor contracts could be dragged back by white "negro-catchers" who would be paid by the mile for their efforts.

President Johnson neither condemned nor condoned the Black Codes. He did suggest to Mississippi that Northern advocates of black suffrage would be disarmed if blacks who could read and write and owned property were enfranchised. But he did not object when this was not done, nor did he repeat the suggestion to other Southern states. Suffrage remained a privilege reserved for whites only, a situation that could be justified by pointing to the fact that outside of New England and New York blacks could not vote in Northern states either.

Agriculture: Sharecropping and Crop-Lien Systems

One of the provisions of the act establishing the Freedmen's Bureau involved the distribution of confiscated and abandoned Southern land to freedmen and poor white farmers. The land was to be rented for three years and then sold to the holder at its 1860 appraised value (although the law recognized that the government could not give a clear title under the wartime confiscation act). However, the black dream of "forty acres and a mule" was never realized. President Johnson quickly pardoned many previous owners and restored them to their land, thereby leaving very little land available for the freedmen. Moreover, the idea of confiscation was unpopular, since it ran counter to the firmly held American belief in the sanctity of private property and since it would impede the process of healing the bitter divisions between North and South. For a limited time Congress did open to former slaves some forty-six million acres of federal lands in the South, but most of the land was undesirable or difficult for black homesteaders to reach.

In the absence of a viable federal policy for providing the freedmen with land, the rural South began resolving the issue of the freedmen's role in the economy in its own way. With Southern agriculture in a state of total confusion at the end of the war, the planters had to change from being lords to being landlords, as historian James L. Roark has described it. Slowly, white landowners and black farm workers came to an accommodation. Impoverished plantation owners could not pay wages to their newly freed slaves, and freedmen wanted to escape from the gang labor and discipline of slavery. Through persuasion and sometimes under duress, many blacks signed annual labor contracts prepared by agents of the Freedmen's Bureau. Within a few years they generally became sharecroppers or in some cases sharetenants on small plots on the old plantations. Under the sharecropping system the plantation owner provided the sharecropper with land, shelter, seeds, tools, and animals and each agreed to share equally the profits of the forthcoming crop. The sharetenant owned his own mule and plow, and received a larger share of the crop.

Many plantation owners had been so devastated by the war that they could not even afford to advance to sharecroppers the food and other supplies they needed. In such instances owners often turned to local merchants for help, and as a result, both planters and sharecroppers became indebted to the merchants, who would demand that the most marketable crop—cotton or tobacco—be planted. The merchant's interest was secured by a lien on the crop. Although this crop-lien system revived Southern agriculture, it was inefficient and helped keep the Deep South a one-crop economy. With a limited supply of credit and an abundance of black labor that was increasingly subjected to legal restrictions, the introduction of technological advances in farming was retarded. Seventy-five percent of the black population endured submarginal economic conditions. Although some 20 percent of Southern black farmers owned their own land in 1880, like sharecroppers and tenant farmers, most were poor.

Nevertheless, the sharecropping system, which lasted into the twentieth century, did have some advantages for both the planter and the black farmer. At a time when there was a shortage of cash in the South, planters did not have to pay wages to the sharecroppers and could feel secure in retaining labor through the harvest. For their part, the sharecroppers had obtained the use of a plot of land in exchange for work. They had some freedom in deciding how much time to spend planting, cultivating, and harvesting the crop, and their return from the crop depended in part on their own effort. It has been estimated that the material income of a typical black family in 1879 was 39 percent greater than that received by slaves in 1859. Most important, blacks at last could live in family units in the privacy of their own cabins.

Congressional Reconstruction Plans

While efforts were under way to revive Southern agriculture, every former Confederate state except Texas had generally met the terms of either the Ten-

Percent Plan or Johnson's plan. Most had accepted the Thirteenth Amendment, and all had organized new state governments and elected new senators

and representatives. When Congress met in December 1865, the new Southern representatives arrived in Washington with the support of President Johnson. Congress, however, rebuffed them. The process of Reconstruction had gone ahead too fast, and the North did not find the terms of reconciliation acceptable.

Republican Views on Reconstruction

The Republicans were enraged by the Black Codes and by the reluctance of the Southern states to repudiate the ordinances of secession. They were further angered that Southern congressional delegations included many former top-ranking officers of the Confederacy, and that the delegations contained almost all Democrats, who would threaten the hard-won Republican majority in Congress. All Republicans were united in their belief that as the party that had saved the Union they must do everything possible to prevent the Democrats from gaining control of the government. Consequently, in what amounted to a rejection of presidential Reconstruction formulas, they flatly refused to seat the newly elected delegations and they immediately appointed their own Joint Committee on Reconstruction, which became a forum for many different points of view.

A few Radicals believed that the victorious North should change the entire power structure in the Southern states and force them to grant equal status to blacks. According to Thaddeus Stevens, black suffrage was the goal and far-reaching economic changes were the means. He proposed to confiscate the land of all former slaveholders, carve it up, distribute some of it to former slaves, and sell the rest. Charles Sumner was more interested in the political reconstruction of the South. He believed that the freedmen should become citizens and enjoy all the benefits of citizenship including the right to be heard in the courts and the rights to vote and to hold office. The suffrage, he reasoned, would protect their freedom and ensure economic opportunity. Sumner even went so far as to assert that blacks should participate in integrated public education.

The moderate Republican majority in Congress, however, did not share these strong views on the reorganization of Southern society. Even so, they disliked Johnson's Reconstruction program because it did not require a strong enough guarantee of Southern loyalty and gave no protection to black people. Although they did not believe in racial equality, they agreed with the Radicals that freedmen should be recognized as citizens. The future of the freedmen was not their sole concern, however. Well aware that if left to its own devices the South would rapidly become a Democratic stronghold, both moderate and Radical Republicans sought to ensure that their party would maintain a strong influence in the former Confederate states. Moderate Republicans began to fear that excluding blacks from the vote might result in a coalition of former rebels and Northern antiwar Democrats gaining control of the country. Thus, Republicans arrived at a commitment to black suffrage both in order to safeguard their own control of the national government and to give blacks the political power necessary to ensure racial justice in the South.

The Fourteenth Amendment

In 1866 Congress passed a bill to protect the rights of blacks by continuing and broadening the powers of the Freedmen's Bureau, which had originally been intended to operate for only one year. The Bureau was to continue its present activities and, in addition, was granted authority to protect blacks from discrimination by law or by custom and to inaugurate a modest land program. Johnson vetoed the bill and his veto was sustained. Some months later, however, a revised bill became law.

Next Congress passed a Civil Rights Act (over Johnson's veto) which guaranteed citizenship to blacks and prohibited discrimination against citizens on the grounds of race or color. Faced with a hostile president and a recalcitant South, Congress sought to give the new act constitutional protection by incorporating its provisions into an amendment to the Constitution. In taking this step, Congress was guarding against the annulment of the Civil Rights Act by a future Congress or by the Supreme Court.

The proposed Fourteenth Amendment was in effect a congressional plan for Reconstruction. Based on compromises between moderate and Radical Republicans, it was the final effort by the Congress to find a solution that would be acceptable to the South and that would at the same time guarantee the rights of the freedmen.

In an effort to prevent a state from denying political rights to any citizen, the amendment provided that anyone born in the United States was a citizen. This was the first time that American citizenship had been clearly defined. The amendment also stipulated that no state could deny any citizen the equal protection of the laws or deprive any citizen of life, liberty, or property without due process of law. Although not directly conferring suffrage on every citizen, the amendment declared that if a state denied the vote to any of its citizens, that state's representation in Congress and in the electoral college would be proportionately reduced. Finally, the Fourteenth Amendment disqualified from federal office all those who had at one time pledged loyalty to the Constitution and then had broken that oath to support the Confederacy. Such persons could hold office only if pardoned by two-thirds of the Congress.

From the congressional point of view, the Fourteenth Amendment was a fairly lenient proposal. The Southern states did not have to enfranchise the freedmen as long as they were willing to give up seats in Congress. Moreover, the amendment did not legislate the freedmen's economic independence at the expense of Southern whites. Yet it did affirm the constitutional rights of black people and it brought them under federal jurisdiction. It avoided the problem of black suffrage nationwide and at the same time kept former Confederates out of national office.

Had President Johnson been willing to accept the Fourteenth Amendment and to warn the South either to accept it or face harsher terms, the real difficulties of Reconstruction probably would have been over. But Johnson was no longer in touch with political reality. He believed that the Southern states were already reconstructed—that is, that they were valid states—and that a Congress operating without their participation was not a legitimate Congress. He overlooked the fact that the South had lost the Civil War and that the North was in a position to dictate its own terms. He advised the South to reject the amendment and to rely on a Republican defeat in the upcoming congressional elections.

The lines of opposition were clearly drawn, and the president decided to make the Fourteenth Amendment the major issue in the congressional elections of 1866. Laying his prestige on the line, Johnson embarked on a nationwide tour, campaigning hard for candidates who opposed the amendment. His two-fisted speaking style proved to be highly inflammatory in many parts of the country. When hecklers hurled insults at him, he responded in kind with his choicest homespun Tennessee epithets. The tour was a dismal failure. The mood of the North was against him. The election gave the Republicans a two-thirds majority in both houses of Congress, large enough to override any presidential veto. But even with the overwhelming Republican victory, ten of the eleven Southern states followed the president's advice and rejected the amendment. Furious at continuing Southern defiance, the new Congress was now in a position to enforce its will.

Radical Reconstruction

Although moderates wanted little more than to force the South to accept the Fourteenth Amendment, they united with Radical Republicans to dictate much harsher terms to the defeated states. The first Reconstruction Act, passed by Congress in March 1867 over Johnson's veto (and supplemented by three more Reconstruction Acts passed in 1867 and 1868), declared all existing state governments in the South to be illegal. This action enabled Congress to create new Southern state governments while avoiding the delicate constitutional issue of states' rights. Since no state governments legally existed, their rights could hardly be violated.

The Southern states (excluding Tennessee, which had ratified the Fourteenth Amendment and been readmitted to the Union in July 1866) were divided into five military districts under the control of the United States Army. A major general in each district was to supervise the registration of all male citizens without regard to color, except for those former public officeholders disfranchised by their participation in the rebellion. This new electorate would then choose delegates to state constitutional conventions and members of new state governments. The act further stipulated that each new state constitution be required to provide for male black suffrage and that each state be required to ratify the Fourteenth Amendment. After the states had met these conditions, and after the Fourteenth Amendment had become part of the federal Constitution, Congress would then readmit them to the Union and military occupation would end.

By July 1868 all the Confederate states except Mississippi, Texas, and Virginia had fulfilled these terms, the Fourteenth Amendment had become part of the Constitution, and Congress had seated the new delegations. Delays by the three recalcitrant states postponed their return to the Union until 1870, and Georgia, already readmitted, was removed for expelling black members from its legislature and not readmitted until 1870. In order to be readmitted these four states had to meet an additional requirement: they had to ratify the Fifteenth Amendment to the Constitution, which provided that "The right of citizens of the United States to vote shall not be denied or abridged by the United States or by any state on account of race, color, or previous condition of servitude."

Because the terms of the Military Reconstruction Act were a compromise between moderates and Radicals, they pleased no one completely. The Radicals were frustrated in their desire to provide land and education at federal expense to the freedmen and to end racial inequality. On the other hand, the president and the state governments already elected in the South were outraged by the provisions for military rule and black suffrage. Historians continue to disagree over the reasons behind the Republicans' interest in civil rights for black people. Some maintain that they were concerned with securing simple justice; others believe they were more concerned with securing votes for blacks in the expectation that blacks would vote Republican.

The Impeachment of Andrew Johnson

The Republicans were fully aware that military Reconstruction was abhorrent to Johnson, and they

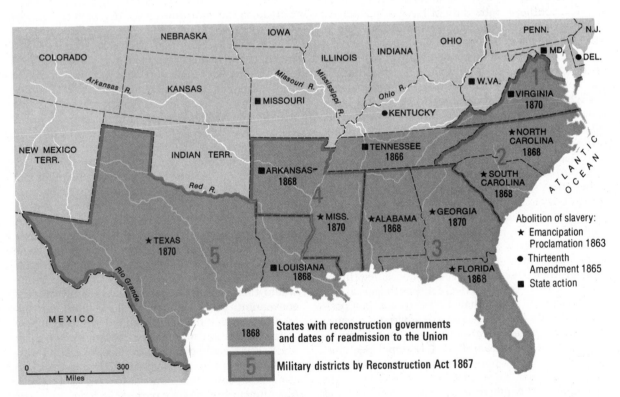

Reconstruction of the South • 1865 to 1877

THE SMELLING COMMITTEE, AN 1868 CARTOON, COMMENTS ON THE RADICAL REPUBLICANS' EFFORT TO IMPEACH PRESIDENT ANDREW JOHNSON.

feared that he would try to curb it. In their zeal to prevent presidential interference with the Reconstruction process, they began to overreach themselves. In 1867—over Johnson's veto—Congress passed two bills limiting the president's power. The Army Appropriations Act restricted his control of the army by preventing him from issuing military orders except through the general of the army who could not be removed without the consent of the Senate. The Tenure of Office Act prohibited him from removing federal officials, including his own cabinet members, without the consent of the Senate.

Believing the Tenure of Office Act to be unconstitutional, and confident that the Supreme Court would overturn it, Johnson decided in February 1868 to create a test case by removing without Senate consent the only Radical member of his cabinet, Secretary of War Edwin M. Stanton. The struggle between Congress and the president soon reached the point of no return. Radicals had been searching unsuccessfully for grounds which would

enable them to impeach the president, and his flouting of the Tenure of Office Act gave them the ammunition they needed. Within a few days the House of Representatives passed articles of impeachment against President Johnson for his deliberate violation of a federal law.

For the first time in American history, a president was tried in the United States Senate. The proceedings were heated and bitter, focusing on the question of what constituted an impeachable offense. Johnson's lawyers argued that the Constitution called for removal of a president only upon conviction of "high crimes and misdemeanors" and that none of the charges brought against Johnson could be so characterized. Clearly Johnson had not violated the Tenure of Office Act in removing Stanton, because Stanton was a Lincoln appointee who had served beyond Lincoln's term. The real issue was whether a president could be removed simply for being unacceptable to Congress. If the Senate voted to remove him, it would seriously undermine executive independence. The prosecution contended that officials could be removed for other than criminal offenses, such as actions or even intentions "against the public interest." Impeachment was the only way to get rid of an incompetent official. If the Senate had voted with the prosecution, it would have established a precedent for using impeachment as a means of expressing "no confidence" in an offcial. When the count was finally taken, the prosecution failed by only one vote to muster the two-thirds majority needed to remove Johnson from office.

Seven Republican senators joined the Democrats in voting to clear Johnson. They supported him because they considered the Tenure of Office Act unconstitutional and the president therefore innocent of the criminal offense they believed necessary for conviction. The outcome of the trial discouraged the future use of impeachment as a political weapon.

Although he completed his term, the beleaguered president was unable to secure the Democratic nomination in 1868. He returned to Tennessee where he failed in a number of attempts to be elected to local offices. Finally, in 1874 he was elected again to the United States Senate from Tennessee. He died the following year.

Thus the Radicals, at the height of their influence, impeached the president but they could not convict him. The effect of this case was to damage the Radicals' power irreparably. Thaddeus Stephens had died and Sumner never regained his former influence. The election of 1868 shifted congressional power into the hands of moderate Republicans who, along with the newly elected president, Ulysses S. Grant, were in disagreement with the harshness of Radical Reconstruction policy.

The South under Radical Reconstruction

For all the difficulties it produced, there were some solid achievements under Radical Reconstruction. The new constitutions produced by Southern constitutional conventions were distinct improvements over those they replaced. They provided for more equitable apportionment of representation; they further extended women's property rights and in some states provided divorce laws; they provided for penal-code reform; and they made many appointive offices elective. A system of state-supported educa-

tion was created throughout the South in an attempt to close the educational gap between the South and the rest of the nation. In addition, the reorganized governments encouraged the development of new industry.

From the perspective of most Southern whites, however, Radical Reconstruction had little to recommend it. For one thing, it upset the political balance by depriving large numbers of whites of the right to participate in the political process and hold public office. Although the number of disfranchised whites has often been exaggerated (it never exceeded 150,000), the fact remains that Northern Republicans played an inordinately large role in Southern politics during the Reconstruction era. In 1869 Northerners occupied four Southern governors' mansions, held ten Southern senate seats, and represented twenty Southern congressional districts. Opponents of Reconstruction called them "carpetbaggers," suggesting that they were moneyless opportunists who arrived with all their possessions in a carpetbag (a kind of valise) to plunder the South. Although some Northerners were indeed primarily interested in power and wealth, the majority were either idealistic reformers who went South to work for racial equality or Union veterans who had returned South hoping to build a future as planters or in business.

As bitterly as Southerners resented the presence of the Northern Republicans, they hated Southern Republicans even more. These "scalawags," as they were scornfully called, some of whom were small farmers or wealthy former Whigs, were held in contempt by their fellow Southerners who regarded them as unprincipled maneuverers who supported the enemy in order to advance their own interests. In fact, some among the wealthy Southern Republicans were men of previous political experience who had opposed secession; others were eager to control black voters in order to attain political office; still others were genuinely devoted to achieving equality for the freedmen. Among the small farmers, most were attracted to the Republican party because its program to improve internal transportation would help them get their crops to market.

Equally offensive to many Southerners was the part blacks began to play in the political process. Republican organizations called "Loyal Leagues" organized black voters, and in 1868 seven hundred thousand blacks voted for Grant, contributing heavily to his victory. Once the Republicans realized how important the black vote would be, they took steps to protect it by proposing the Fifteenth Amendment, which became part of the Constitution in March 1870.

Blacks also began to serve in public office. Between 1868 and 1875 two blacks served in the Senate and fifteen in the House of Representatives. A black man, Jonathan Jasper Wright, was appointed to the Supreme Court of South Carolina. Yet for the most part, black officeholders served at the state and local levels, and, considering the proportion of blacks living in the South, their participation in Southern politics must be considered extremely limited. They were a majority in only one state constitutional convention (South Carolina) and were never a majority in both houses of any state legislature. They never elected a state governor and seldom raised the issue of land confiscation.

Despite the achievements of Radical Reconstruction, some historians have alleged that it failed to create a new South because of the large-scale corruption, extravagance, and waste that characterized Reconstruction governments. In South Carolina, for example, the legislature voted to reimburse one of its members for $1000 he lost betting on the horses, and payments were made for at least three times as many militia as were actually serving in the state force. In Louisiana the annual cost of running the state government skyrocketed from $100,000 to $1 million under Reconstruction. Public funds were commonly squandered on furniture, homes, jewelry, and liquor for public officials, often plunging the states into debt.

It should be noted, however, that corruption in the South was due in part to the fact that many legislators lacked experience and lacked education. Moreover, political corruption existed in all parts of the country in the 1860s as a by-product of the lax moral climate following the war. In fact, the level of corruption in the Reconstruction governments was less than that in the national government.

The End of Reconstruction

From the very beginning of Reconstruction, Southerners bitterly resented the attempt to alter the political and social fabric of their region. Southerners' anger over the participation of blacks in the Radical governments was at the core of their efforts

THIS 1870 ENGRAVING DEPICTS THE PLIGHT OF THE BLACK PEOPLE AFTER THE CIVIL WAR.

to wrest leadership away from the reconstructed governments.

Former Southern political leaders were determined to "redeem" the South and restore themselves to power. In Virginia, Tennessee, and North Carolina, large white majorities were able to regain control of the governments through elections. Sensing a growing opposition in the North to Radical Reconstruction, President Grant made no move to prevent a peaceful return to white supremacy. In other states, however, white citizens resorted to terrorism. Thousands of white Southerners banded together in secret organizations such as the White Brotherhood, the Knights of the White Camelia, and the Ku Klux Klan. Best known of all the societies, the Klan was based mainly in the Deep South. Founded in 1866 as a social club, the Klan soon turned its attention to driving blacks out of Southern politics, depriving them of the franchise, and restoring white supremacy. Garbed in white hoods and long robes, Klansmen at first tried to intimidate blacks and so prevent them from voting by surrounding their cabins at night, making frightening noises, and firing guns in the air. Harassment quickly turned to violence, as black homes were burned, blacks were beaten or lynched, and both white and black Radical leaders were attacked. President Grant was deeply angered by the activities of the Klan, and Congress responded by passing the Force Acts of 1870 and 1871, which placed elections under federal jurisdiction, gave the President the right to impose martial law, and imposed fines and sentences on those convicted of interfering with any citizen's right to vote.

Despite these laws, white supremacists began to take more direct action to gain control of Southern governments. Although the president used his power under the Force Acts to institute martial law to quell rebellions in South Carolina, Louisiana, and Arkansas, paramilitary organizations such as the South Carolina Redshirts continued to terrorize blacks even more openly than the Klan had done. Other armed groups, such as the Rifle Clubs and the White Leagues, used coercion and even violence to ensure election victories. White men were faced with a choice of joining the Democratic party or being driven out of the community; black men were

deprived of the right to vote unless they voted Democratic. Those who persisted in their loyalty to the Republican party were denied employment or fired from the jobs they already had. Thus by means of violence and economic pressure blacks began to stay away from the polls and white supremacists welded the South into a solidly Democratic voting bloc.

While Southerners were growing more determined to restore their old political and social system, Northerners were losing interest in enforcing Reconstruction policies. They were growing less willing to bear the costs of defending the freedmen and of maintaining Republican regimes and an army in the South. The Northern business community wanted stability in the South so that normal cotton production and trade would be restored. The Republicans in the South could not accomplish this, but the white Southerners could.

Republican politicians also were beginning to realize that they could win national elections by

OF COURSE HE WANTS TO VOTE THE DEMOCRATIC TICKET COMMENTS ON THE POLITICAL PRESSURE BROUGHT TO BEAR ON BLACKS DURING RECONSTRUCTION. FIVE YEARS AFTER THE EMANCIPATION PROCLAMATION, EX-SLAVES HAD BECOME A SIGNIFICANT FORCE BACKING THE REPUBLICAN PARTY, AND WHITE SUPREMACISTS WERE DETERMINED TO RETURN POWER TO SOUTHERN DEMOCRATS.

INTERPRETING AMERICAN HISTORY

RECONSTRUCTION It was not until the 1890s that the first important historical perspectives on Reconstruction appeared. In *Reconstruction, Political and Economic*, William A. Dunning argued that Reconstruction had deprived Southern whites of their rightful control of Southern life and had given it instead to ignorant freedmen and unscrupulous carpetbaggers and scalawags. Central to Dunning's interpretation was his belief, much in vogue at that time, in the biological inferiority of blacks.

By the 1930s a new school of historians had emerged which rejected Dunning's perspective. Historians such as Francis B. Simkins, Robert Woody, and C. Vann Woodward contended that blacks had played a relatively minor role in Reconstruction politics. They argued, moreover, that the Radical Reconstruction governments in the South were set up mainly to ensure Republican control of the national government. But corruption under Radical Reconstruction regimes was no worse than in the North at the same time and was less prevalent in the Southern conservative regimes that followed. The real struggle of Reconstruction, these revisionist historians claimed, was the economic conflict between the business and financial interests of the North represented by the Radicals and the old agrarian interests of the South.

In the 1950s and 1960s a third historical interpretation of Reconstruction developed, attuned to the Civil Rights movement. This neorevisionist interpretation emphasized the moral issue of racial discrimination as the central theme of the Reconstruction struggle. Its proponents included R. P. Sharkey, Eric L. McKitrick, La Wanda and John Cox, and Kenneth M. Stampp. In general, these historians held that the Reconstruction era was a tragedy. McKitrick argued that Reconstruction was a failure because efforts to achieve racial equality created intense hostility in the white South. Stampp, on the other hand, maintained that if white Southerners had been forced to accept racial equality long enough, they ultimately would have acquiesced in it. The Coxes stressed that protection of the freedmen's civil rights was central to the conflict between Johnson and the Republicans.

In the 1970s historians continued to debate the impact of Reconstruction legislation. Some historians, such as Louis S. Gerteis and C. Peter Ripley, held that the Union Army and the Freedmen's Bureau tried to establish stability rather than to ensure real economic and political reform. In other words, their goal was to provide an orderly, cheap labor force of freedmen. Racism in the North was as strong as in the South and limited the effective enforcement of Radical Reconstruction. On the other hand, Herman Belz in *A New Birth of Freedom* (1976) has argued that before the war the definition of citizenship was determined by the individual states. The achievement of the war and the Republican party was to ensure through the Thirteenth, Fourteenth, and Fifteenth Amendments that citizenship and equal rights before the law would be uniform throughout the nation.

---

carrying the North and the West alone and that the Southern black vote was expendable. Reconstruction was now considered largely a failure, and as the 1872 presidential election drew near, Republicans wished to shed political liability. That year Congress passed an Amnesty Act which had the effect of restoring political participation to most white Southerners. As a result of an increased white vote, as well as infighting among Republicans who controlled the Reconstruction governments, these regimes began to topple. By the end of 1875 only Louisiana, Florida, and South Carolina still had Reconstruction governments. A year later, the disputed presidential election of 1876 was settled by a compromise that brought Reconstruction to an end. The last federal forces were withdrawn from the South in April 1877. The nation had been reunited but not reconciled.

As extreme as Radical Reconstruction seemed at the time, it did not change the basic structure of Southern life. Blacks were unable to achieve economic independence and so were unable to retain their political equality when Reconstruction ended. The machinery established to protect their right to vote proved inadequate. All that remained as a positive, enduring legacy of Reconstruction were the Fourteenth and Fifteenth Amendments to the Constitution.

Grant's Presidency

The Election of 1868

In 1868 the Republicans nominated General Ulysses S. Grant, an extremely popular war hero with few known political views, as their presidential candidate. The party continued to seek the support of Northern manufacturing interests by adopting a platform that supported a high tariff and encouraged cheap labor through a liberal immigration policy.

The Democratic nominee was Horatio Seymour, an opponent of Radical Reconstruction. Unlike the Republicans, the Democrats aimed their campaign at Western farmers and other indebted voters with a "cheap money" platform. During the war Congress had issued a large amount of paper money (greenbacks) that was not backed by gold. At the end of the war Congress gradually began withdrawing the greenbacks, against the wishes of debtors—Western bankers, farmers, and railroad pro-

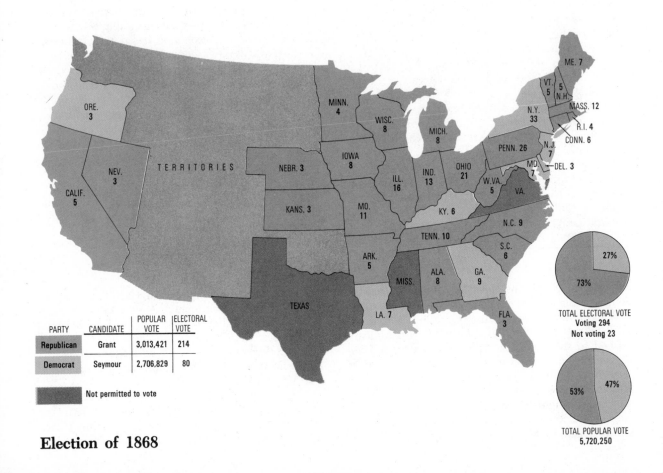

PARTY	CANDIDATE	POPULAR VOTE	ELECTORAL VOTE
Republican	Grant	3,013,421	214
Democrat	Seymour	2,706,829	80

Not permitted to vote

TOTAL ELECTORAL VOTE
Voting 294
Not voting 23

27%
73%

TOTAL POPULAR VOTE
5,720,250

53% 47%

Election of 1868

moters—who wanted to repay their debts with cheap money. Creditors—largely Eastern bankers and financiers—wanted to receive full value for the money they had lent and consequently favored withdrawing the greenbacks from circulation. The Democratic platform of 1868 supported the continued circulation of greenbacks.

Despite these clear economic differences between the parties, the decisive issue in the campaign proved to be the war that had ended three years earlier. The Republicans presented themselves as the party that had saved the Union and the Democrats as the party of rebellion. Grant's candidacy reinforced this view, and although the popular vote was close, the Republicans swept the electoral college 214 to 80.

Grant's Political Style

With his limited political experience, President Grant had no plans to initiate policies. He believed that the primary duty of the president was to execute the will of Congress. Those who hoped that he would be a firm and wise leader who would control the Radicals and raise the tone of public life were soon disappointed. Influenced by his military background, Grant ran the presidency along military lines, issuing commands and discouraging debate of the issues. At the same time, his lack of political experience and his receptivity to flattery made him an easy target of self-seeking politicians and business leaders. When he did act on his own initiative, as he did in choosing his advisors, the results were uneven. For example, his White House staff, which also controlled federal patronage appointments, was dominated by old army colleagues with no political experience; they dispensed jobs to friends, relatives, and those with the money to pay for their positions.

Economic Policies

One of the central domestic issues facing Grant was the need to formulate a policy on greenbacks. Grant wanted to please the Eastern financiers who had supported him, but feared that retiring the greenbacks would alienate those in debt. He finally settled on a compromise that would leave the greenbacks in circulation but make it possible to back them with gold in the future. Because the compromise was not especially popular with the large mass of voters, Grant supported the highly popular congressional measures aimed at eliminating the wartime income tax and excise duties.

Another economic issue was the high tariff Congress had enacted as an emergency wartime measure. When the war ended, manufacturing and industrial interests favored retaining the duties to keep out foreign competitive products. These interests had supported Grant in the election, and their lobbyists had little trouble convincing him that the high tariff should be retained. Some advisers claimed that high tariffs merely enriched Eastern industrialists at the expense of many consumers, especially Western farmers. But the president supported the protectionists in Congress, who raised duties on many products in 1870.

Corruption in Washington

The major issue of Grant's administration was misconduct in the federal government. During the eight years of his presidency, a number of those holding high political office used their power and influence to amass personal fortunes at the expense of the voters who had elected them. Other public officials were naive victims of businesspeople who exploited them and their offices. The result was a great loss of public confidence in government.

The corruption of the Grant years was largely the result of the relaxed moral climate in all segments of society following the Civil War. The growth of industrialization (to be described in Chapter 17) and of business enterprise related to the war effort encouraged the rise of a wealthy class of businesspeople and entrepreneurs. Americans worshipped wealth as never before, and the acquisition of material possessions became an obsession. A pattern of bribery and favoritism in government-business relations that had developed during the war years continued into the era of postwar politics.

Given this climate of corruption many politicians were unable to resist bribes for favors they could dispense freely. Others, including Grant himself, did not intentionally abuse their offices or gain personally from corruption, but were unwitting accomplices in scandal because of their naiveté and negligence. Infatuated by the startling successes of American business and possessing only a limited understanding of the complex postwar economic

THIS 1876 CARTOON ILLUSTRATES THE FOLLOWING "CON-
VERSATION" BETWEEN UNCLE SAM AND PRESIDENT GRANT.
UNCLE SAM: "THIS IS THE RESULT OF YOUR INEFFICIENCY.
CAPTAIN ROBINSON SAYS YOU HAVE KNOWN FOR FOUR
YEARS THAT THIS MAN HAS BEEN DEFRAUDING, YET YOU
HAVE KEPT HIM IN OFFICE." PRESIDENT GRANT: "HAVEN'T
I A RIGHT TO DO AS I PLEASE? DIDN'T I COME HERE TO
HAVE A GOOD TIME?" UNCLE SAM: "YES, IT APPEARS SO. IF I
DIDN'T KNOW HOW AVERSE YOU ARE TO RECEIVING PRES-
ENTS, I MIGHT HAVE SUSPECTED THAT THERE WAS A
LITTLE DIVVY SOMEWHERE."

situation, Grant allowed incompetence and corruption to invade his entire administration.

The boldest incident of corruption during
Grant's first term was the Fisk-Gould scandal. Jim
Fisk and Jay Gould, two speculators, conceived a
plan to corner the nation's gold supply. They would
buy up all the available gold, hold it until its price
soared, and then dump it on the market, reaping
enormous profits. Working through Grant's
brother-in-law, Gould managed to convince the
president to withhold the government's gold from
sale, a necessary part of the plan. The gigantic gamble came to a head on "Black Friday" (September
24, 1869), when a panic occurred at the New York
Stock Exchange because the price of gold had soared
too high. Finally realizing what was happening, the
president released $4 million in gold to stabilize the
market. But his action came too late to prevent serious damage to the business community.

That same year Grant was duped again, this
time by a group of American fortune hunters who
wished to exploit the economic potential of the
Dominican Republic. The speculators convinced

Grant that the island was of strategic importance to
the United States and should be annexed. Annexation, they argued, would lead to enormous business
profits. Only the opposition of the Senate, led by
Charles Sumner of Massachusetts, prevented the
annexation proposal from being accepted.

The Election of 1872: A New Party

Toward the end of Grant's first term, a group of disillusioned Republicans and Democrats formed the
Liberal Republican party. Angered by Radical
Reconstruction, scandal, and Grant's lack of interest
in civil service reform, the new party's members included an impressive number of reformers. Though
solidly united in their opposition to Grant, members
of the new party agreed on little else. Some favored
a low tariff; others were ardent protectionists. Some
wanted to circulate more greenbacks; others wanted
all greenbacks withdrawn. Some of the former
Democrats opposed military Reconstruction; others
wanted to avoid causing the party to be associated
with the Confederacy.

The candidate they nominated and the platform they formulated reflected the new party's internal conflicts. While the platform favored amnesty for all former Confederates and the withdrawal of troops from the South, it also approved Radical Reconstruction. On the tariff and greenback issues the Liberal Republicans were unable to reach agreement and took no stand at all. The platform did, however, voice strong support for civil service reform.

When the Liberal Republicans nominated Horace Greeley to oppose Grant in the 1872 election, they ensured their own defeat. Although well known as a newspaper editor and greatly respected for his years of crusading against slavery, Greeley was widely regarded as an eccentric. Nonetheless, the Democrats realized that their only hope of unseating Grant was to align themselves with the Liberal Republicans and endorse Greeley for president.

In contrast to the confusion surrounding the platforms of the Liberal Republican and Democratic parties, the regular Republican party stood on its record of high tariffs and Radical Reconstruction. Industrialists and bankers poured large sums of money into Grant's campaign. In the end, Grant won by a larger margin than he had before, and the Liberal Republican movement disintegrated.

The Crédit Mobilier Affair and the "Whiskey Ring" Scandal

During Grant's second term even worse scandals involving the government were exposed. There was corruption in the Bureau of Indian Affairs, and bribery of internal revenue officials was discovered. One of the worst scandals was the Crédit Mobilier affair, in which a construction company involved in building the transcontinental railroad bribed congressmen and other high government officials to prevent investigation of its fraudulent drain of profits from construction contracts. Grant's previous and current vice-presidents were both among the recipients.

Another scandal, the "Whiskey Ring" conspiracy, involved hundreds of distillers who bribed internal revenue officials to falsify reports that defrauded the government of millions of dollars in excise-tax revenue. When Grant's own private secretary, General Orville Babcock, was exposed as one

of the conspirators, Grant unquestioningly defended him and even sent a written character deposition to his trial. Babcock was acquitted and the president allowed him to resign quietly.

Corruption was not confined to the federal government. In large cities such as Chicago and Philadelphia politics was becoming dominated by political machines that maintained power by giving and taking bribes in return for favors. Perhaps the most notorious example was New York's Tweed Ring. Led by William Tweed, boss of the Democratic Tammany Hall machine, the ring, over a period of a few years, took some $200 million from the city through fraud and bribery, and gained control of the police and the courts. While he did work for improved urban services, "Boss" Tweed bribed the New York State legislature in 1869 into passing a new municipal charter which would have entrenched the machine in power. When the activities of the machine threatened to drive the city into bankruptcy, the ring finally was exposed by means of articles in the *New York Times* and through the political cartoons of Thomas Nast in *Harper's*

THE SCATHING CARTOONS OF THOMAS NAST EVENTUALLY LED TO THE DOWNFALL OF THE TWEED RING. ONE OF HIS MOST FAMOUS CARTOONS, *THE TAMMANY TIGER LOOSE—WHAT ARE YOU GOING TO DO ABOUT IT?* WAS PUBLISHED SEVERAL DAYS BEFORE THE CITY ELECTION OF 1871. IN RESPONSE THE VOTERS OUSTED THE RING'S OFFICIALS, AND TWEED WAS INDICTED FOR GRAND LARCENY.

Weekly. A committee led by Samuel J. Tilden secured Tweed's indictment, and in 1871 he was convicted and sent to prison.

The Panic of 1873

In addition to being plagued by scandal and corruption, the nation faced a disastrous economic decline culminating in the Panic of 1873. Since 1850 the economy of the North and West had grown steadily. Following the Civil War the growth rate had accelerated: thousands of new businesses were started, and railroads were built to link the various regions. By 1871, however, the new businesses and railroads had overexpanded and found themselves without the markets they needed to prosper. At the same time the nation's gold reserves were drained by a rapid increase of imports over exports. In Sep-

tember 1873 the foremost banking firm in America, Jay Cooke and Company, declared bankruptcy, triggering a chain reaction of over five thousand additional business failures. One-half million workers were soon out of jobs. The hard times that began in 1873 continued almost until the end of the decade.

The Compromise of 1877

The scandals of the Grant years had cost the Republicans control of the House of Representatives in the 1874 congressional elections. President Grant's popularity also had been badly eroded by corruption (now known as "Grantism") and the depression, but many Republicans still supported him for a third term in 1876. The president's supporters, known as the "Stalwarts," were opposed by the

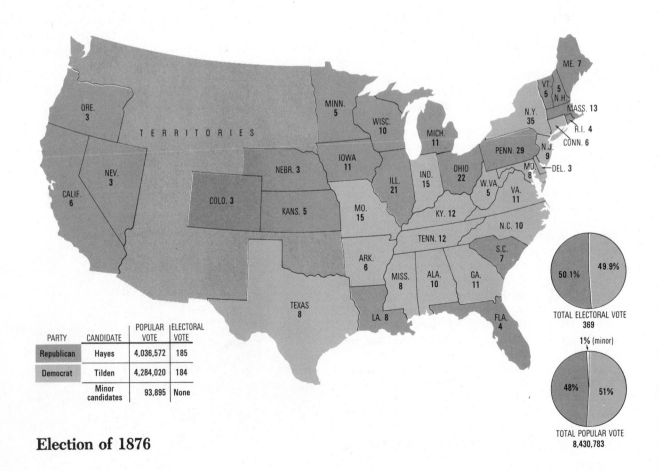

PARTY	CANDIDATE	POPULAR VOTE	ELECTORAL VOTE
Republican	Hayes	4,036,572	185
Democrat	Tilden	4,284,020	184
	Minor candidates	93,895	None

TOTAL ELECTORAL VOTE 369

50.1% 49.9%

TOTAL POPULAR VOTE 8,430,783

1% (minor) 48% 51%

Election of 1876

"Halfbreeds," Republicans who claimed to be reformers although they had remained loyal to the party in 1872. At the Republican convention the Halfbreeds supported the nomination of Speaker of the House James G. Blaine of Maine. Blaine, however, had been among those accused of dispensing favors to several railroads, and the Republicans finally decided to avoid all hint of scandal by nominating the untarnished Rutherford B. Hayes, three-time governor of Ohio.

The Democrats, also reacting against corruption in government, nominated Governor Samuel Tilden of New York, who had been instrumental in breaking up the Tweed Ring in 1871.

No clear issues divided the candidates. Both called for an end to Reconstruction, still in force in three Southern states. Both avoided taking a stand on the tariff issue. And both called for civil service reform to end corruption in government.

The vote was so close that on the morning after the election, the outcome was still undecided. Although Tilden had a popular majority and had carried many states, twenty electoral votes (the returns from Florida, South Carolina, Louisiana, and one electoral vote from Oregon) were in dispute. Nevertheless, Tilden had 184 of the 185 electoral votes he needed to win; if he could obtain only one of the twenty disputed electoral votes, a Democrat would occupy the White House for the first time since 1856.

Voters were surprised and concerned to learn that there was no means provided by the Constitution for determining the validity of disputed returns. On the question of the counting of electoral votes, the Constitution stated simply that "The President of the Senate shall, in the presence of the Senate and House of Representatives, open all the certificates and the votes shall then be counted." The problem was, who would do the counting? The Senate and its president were Republican, and the House was Democratic. Thus, no matter who did the counting, the process would not be impartial. To resolve the dilemma, Congress appointed a special commission to investigate the disputed returns and award them to the rightful winner. The commission was initially made up of five congressional Democrats, five congressional Republicans, and five Supreme Court justices (two Republicans, two Democrats, and an Independent). But at the last minute the Independent was disqualified (he was elected to the Senate and resigned his seat) and replaced by a staunch Republican. In a straight party vote the commission awarded all of the disputed electoral returns, and therefore the presidency, to Hayes. But it took further negotiation and compromise before Hayes could take office.

Although they had lost the battle for the disputed presidency, the Democrats still had a strong card left to play. Threatening a filibuster in the Senate to prevent the commission from reporting its findings, the Democrats in secret negotiations secured a Republican promise to (among other things) remove all remaining federal troops from the South. The Republicans knew that when the Reconstruction government fell, they could no longer count on the Southern black vote, and the South would be lost to the Democrats. They therefore abandoned the freedmen and tried to attract white Southerners to their camp by agreeing to end the military occupation of the South, to return control of federal patronage in the South to Southerners, to work for federal support for a projected transcontinental railroad (the Texas and Pacific), and to include at least one Southerner in Hayes's new cabinet. In return for these concessions, the Democrats agreed to support the election of a Republican Speaker of the House, even though they now controlled the chamber, and to uphold the rights of black people.

The compromise reached, Hayes moved into the White House without opposition, and the last federal troops were withdrawn from the South in April 1877. Hayes, however, reneged on his support for funds for the new Southern railroad, and the Democrats did not elect a Republican Speaker and did not uphold their promise to protect the rights of blacks. Thus in a quest for national reconciliation the political parties had worked out the Compromise of 1877 which brought a formal end to Reconstruction. Both parties left black Americans to fend for themselves.

Disfranchisement and Segregation of Blacks

With the end of Reconstruction, control of Southern politics was returned to the old planter aristocracy and the equally conservative new business class. This new ruling elite immediately took steps to ensure its continued political, social, and economic dominance.

Although the conservatives believed in white supremacy, they made no immediate attempt to disfranchise blacks. Having incited racist passions in order to regain control of their state governments, they now tried to quiet them. They were eager to gain the support of black voters for their efforts to industrialize the South, and they recognized the usefulness of the black vote in offsetting the opposition of poor whites to political dominance by the wealthy. Moreover, conservative Democrats tried to help blacks assert their influence in the Republican party against its white leadership. While often coerced to support conservative candidates, some 70 percent of black voters throughout the South continued to exercise their right to the franchise until the late 1880s.

By then, however, agricultural depression and unrest had changed conservative strategy. Poor white farmers always had objected to black suffrage because they understood that the black vote was being used against them to ensure economic dominance of the ruling wealthy elite. They therefore demanded that blacks be deprived of the franchise. The conservatives now complied, in part because they hoped to appease the poorer whites, and in part because they were aware that growing agrarian problems were causing white farmers to court the black vote. The idea of competition for the black vote was alarming to whites—rich and poor alike. Thus, in order to ensure white supremacy the wealthy conservatives formed a new coalition with poor farmers.

Now that the black vote was no longer useful, white Southerners moved to disfranchise their former slaves. Southern legislatures enacted a host of technical qualifications for voting. The new requirements were designed to prevent blacks from voting without violating the Fifteenth Amendment. Many states still used the poll tax, which had been instituted in the 1870s as a weapon against black voters, and several states enacted literacy requirements whereby voters had to demonstrate an ability to read and interpret the Constitution. Other states passed "grandfather laws" guaranteeing the right to vote only to those whose ancestors had voted in 1866. In addition to disfranchising black voters, this legislation reduced the overall turnout at election time and made the South a one-party region.

The resurgence of racist politics led to a more rigid segregation of the races in the South. Blacks had founded their own churches after the war, and black children attended separate public schools under the system established during Radical Reconstruction. Although transportation and some public services had not yet been segregated in the late nineteenth century, by 1900 legal measures to assure segregation, popularly called Jim Crow laws, had been enacted throughout the South. These statutes typically provided for separate railroad cars and in some states for segregated railroad stations, street cars, and other public services.

The efforts of Southern state governments to maintain white supremacy and then to bring about segregation of the races were aided by a number of decisions of the United States Supreme Court. In the *Civil Rights Cases* of 1883 the Supreme Court declared unconstitutional an 1875 Civil Rights Act which had guaranteed all citizens "full and equal enjoyment" of public places, ruling that Congress had no jurisdiction over discrimination by private individuals and private organizations. In *Plessy* v. *Ferguson* (1896) the Court further declared that it was not a violation of the Fourteenth Amendment, nor did it imply that black people were inferior, to

BLACK EDUCATOR BOOKER T. WASHINGTON.

Plessy v. Ferguson

"A statute which implies merely a legal distinction between the white and colored races . . . has no tendency to destroy the legal equality of the two races, or reestablish a state of involuntary servitude. . . .

Laws permitting, and even requiring, their separation in places where they are liable to be brought into contact do not necessarily imply the inferiority of either race to the other, and have been generally, if not universally, recognized as within the competency of the state legislatures in the exercise of their police power. The most common instance of this is connected with the establishment of separate schools for white and colored children, which has been held to be a valid exercise of the legislative power even by courts of states where the political rights of the colored race have been longest and most earnestly enforced. . . .

If the two races are to meet upon terms of social equality, it must be the result of natural affinities, a mutual appreciation of each other's merits and a voluntary consent of individuals. . . . If one race be inferior to the other socially, the Constitution of the United States cannot put them upon the same plane. . . ."

The United States Supreme Court, 1896

Plessy v. Ferguson: Dissenting Opinion

"Every one knows that the statute in question had its origin in the purpose, not so much to exclude white persons from railroad cars occupied by blacks, as to exclude colored people from coaches occupied by or assigned to white persons. . . . The fundamental objection, therefore, to the statute is that it interferes with the personal freedom of citizens. . . . If a white man and a black man choose to occupy the same public conveyance on a public highway, it is their right to do so, and no government, proceeding alone on grounds of race, can prevent it without infringing the personal liberty of each. . . .

In the view of the Constitution, in the eye of the law, there is in this country no superior, dominant, ruling class of citizens. There is no caste here. Our Constitution is color-blind, and neither knows nor tolerates classes among citizens. In respect of civil rights, all citizens are equal before the law. The humblest is the peer of the most powerful. The law regards man as man, and takes no account of his surroundings or of his color when his civil rights as guaranteed by the supreme law of the land are involved. . . ."

Justice John Marshall Harlan, 1896

---

enforce separate facilities for each race, so long as the facilities provided for blacks were "equal" to the facilities for whites. This decision provided the constitutional rationale for separating the races in many areas of life and particularly for maintaining the segregation of Southern schools for the next fifty years.

The Supreme Court upheld the literacy tests and poll taxes in *Williams* v. *Mississippi* (1898), declaring that since these laws did not "on their face discriminate between the races," they did not violate the Fifteenth Amendment. Sometime later, in *Guinn* v. *United States* (1915) the court invalidated the "grandfather laws," reasoning that their only possible purpose was to disfranchise black people and that they therefore violated the Fifteenth

Amendment. By this time, however, the discriminatory laws had already accomplished their purpose.

Many blacks at this time felt their best course of action was to accept their second-class status in exchange for the right to pursue economic security. In 1895 black educator Booker T. Washington called for an emphasis on self-help through manual labor, vocational education, and subsistence farming in a speech that became known as the Atlanta Compromise. "The wisest among my race," said Washington, "understand that the agitation of questions of social equality is the extremest folly. . . . It is important and right that all privileges of the law be ours, but it is vastly more important that we be prepared for the exercise of these privileges. The opportunity to earn a dollar in a factory just now is worth infinitely more than the opportunity to spend a dollar in an opera-house." Many white Southerners—recognizing in Washington's position support for the status quo—applauded the concepts embodied in the Atlanta Compromise. Some blacks, however, strongly opposed compromising their demands for the rights of full citizenship for possible economic advancement. In 1903 black intellectual W. E. B. DuBois asked, "Are we going to induce the best class of Negroes to take less and less interest in government, and to give up their daily right to take such an interest, without a protest? . . . Daily the Negro is coming more and more to look upon law and justice, not as protecting safeguards, but as sources of humiliation and oppression."

Conclusion

The Reconstruction of the nation lasted from 1863 to 1877. It began with the Emancipation Proclama-

tion and ended with the compromise that settled the disputed election of 1876. In the process blacks were freed from slavery, granted political equality, and then abandoned as the price paid for national reconciliation. Further, the antebellum domination of national politics by an agrarian South was replaced by a Northern-based political coalition closely attuned to the needs of an increasingly industrial economy, national in scope. Profound economic changes transformed American life by the end of the nineteenth century. Just as the course of Reconstruction had thwarted black hopes for economic opportunity, so the magnitude of the changes in the American economy would threaten the economic opportunity of countless other Americans. The varied responses to these economic developments ultimately transformed American politics as well.

Readings

General Works

Belz, Herman, *Reconstructing the Union*. Ithaca, N.Y.: Cornell University Press, 1969.

Buck, Paul H., *The Road to Reunion, 1865–1900*. Boston: Little, Brown, 1937.

Cash, Wilbur J., *The Mind of the South*. New York: Knopf, 1960.

Cruden, Robert, *The Negro in Reconstruction*. Englewood Cliffs, N.J.: Prentice-Hall, 1969.

Donald, David, *Liberty and Union*. Lexington, Mass.: D. C. Heath, 1978.

———, *The Politics of Reconstruction*. Baton Rouge: Louisiana State University Press, 1965.

Du Bois, William E. B., *Black Reconstruction in America, 1860–1880*. New York: Atheneum, 1969.

Fairman, Charles, *Reconstruction and Reunion, 1864–1888*. New York: Macmillan, 1971.

Franklin, John H., *Reconstruction After the Civil War*. Chicago: University of Chicago Press, 1961.

Gillette, William, *Retreat from Reconstruction, 1869–1879*. Baton Rouge: Louisiana State University Press, 1979.

Hyman, Harold M., *A More Perfect Union: The Impact of the Civil War and Reconstruction of the Constitution*. New York: Knopf, 1973.

Patrick, Rembert W., *The Reconstruction of the Nation*. New York: Oxford University Press, 1967.

Randall, James G., and David Donald, *The Civil War and Reconstruction*. Boston: D. C. Heath, 1961.

Stampp, Kenneth M., *The Era of Reconstruction 1865–1877*. New York: Knopf, 1965.

Trefousse, Hans L., *The Radical Republicans: Lincoln's Vanguard for Racial Justice*. New York: Knopf, 1969.

Wright, Gavin, *The Political Economy of the Cotton South*. New York: Norton, 1978.

Special Studies

Belz, Herman, *A New Birth of Freedom*. Westport, Conn.: Greenwood, 1976.

Benedict, Michael L., *A Compromise of Principle: Congressional Republicans and Reconstruction, 1863–1869*. New York: Norton, 1974.

Bentley, G. R., *A History of the Freedmen's Bureau*. New York: Octagon, 1970.

Cox, LaWanda, and John H. Cox, *Politics, Principle and Prejudice, 1865–66*. New York: Free Press, 1963.

Gerteis, Louis S., *From Contraband to Freedman*. Westport, Conn.: Greenwood, 1973.

Gillette, William, *The Right to Vote: Politics and the Passage of the Fifteenth Amendment*. Baltimore: Johns Hopkins Press, 1965.

James, Joseph B., *The Framing of the Fourteenth Amendment*. Urbana: University of Illinois Press, 1956.

Litwack, Leon F., *Been in the Storm So Long: The Aftermath of Slavery*. New York: Knopf, 1979.

Logan, Rayford W., *The Negro in American Life and Thought: The Nadir 1877–1901*. New York: Macmillan, 1965.

McCrary, Peyton, *Abraham Lincoln and Reconstruction*. Princeton, N.J.: Princeton University Press, 1978.

McKitrick, Eric L., *Andrew Johnson and Reconstruction*. Chicago: University of Chicago Press, 1960.

McPherson, James M., *The Abolitionist Legacy: From Reconstruction to the NAACP*. Princeton, N.J.: Princeton University Press, 1976.

_____, *The Struggle for Equality: Abolitionists and the Negro in the Civil War and Reconstruction*. Princeton, N.J.: Princeton University Press, 1964.

Meier, August, *Negro Thought in America, 1880–1915*. Ann Arbor: University of Michigan Press, 1963.

Nolen, Claude H., *The Negro's Image in the South: The Anatomy of White Supremacy*. Lexington: University Press of Kentucky, 1967. (Paper)

Roark, James L., *Master Without Slaves: Southern Planters in the Civil War and Reconstruction*. New York: Norton, 1977.

Trefousse, Hans L., *Impeachment of a President: Andrew Johnson, the Blacks & Reconstruction*. Knoxville: University of Tennessee Press, 1975.

Trelease, Allen W., *The White Terror: The Ku Klux Klan Conspiracy and Southern Reconstruction*, Kenneth B. Clark (Ed.). New York: Harper & Row, 1971.

Wharton, Vernon L., *The Negro in Mississippi, 1865–1869*. New York: Harper & Row, 1965.

Williamson, Joel, *After Slavery: The Negro in South Carolina During Reconstruction, 1861–1877*. Chapel Hill: University of North Carolina Press, 1965.

Woodward, C. Vann, *Reunion and Reaction: The Compromise of 1877 and the End of Reconstruction*. Boston: Little, Brown, 1966.

_____, *The Strange Career of Jim Crow*. New York: Oxford University Press, 1966.

Primary Sources

Cox, LaWanda, and John H. (Eds.), *Reconstruction, the Negro and the New South*. Columbia: University of South Carolina Press, 1973.

Current, Richard N. (Ed.), *Reconstruction, 1865–1877*. Englewood Cliffs, N.J.: Prentice-Hall, 1965.

Reid, Whitelaw, *After the War: A Tour of the Southern States, 1865–1866*. New York: Harper & Row, 1965.

Shenton, James P., *The Reconstruction, A Documentary History: 1865–1877*. New York: Putnam, 1963.

Washington, Booker T., *Up from Slavery*. New York: Bantam, 1970.

Biographies

Brodie, Fawn M., *Thaddeus Stevens: Scourge of the South*. New York: Norton, 1959.

Donald, David, *Charles Sumner and the Rights of Man*. New York: Knopf, 1970.

Hesseltine, William B., *Ulysses S. Grant: Politician*. New York: Ungar, 1957.

McFeely, William S., *Yankee Stepfather: General O. O. Howard and the Freedmen*. New Haven, Conn.: Yale University Press, 1968.

Van Deusen, Glyndon, *Horace Greeley: Nineteenth-Century Crusader*. Philadelphia: University of Pennsylvania Press, 1953.

Fiction

Faulkner, William, *Go Down, Moses*. New York: Random House, 1942.

_____, *The Hamlet*. New York: Random House, 1940.

The First Civil Rights Movement

RECONSTRUCTION AND EDUCATION

On a quiet morning in April 1865, a tall, dignified gentleman in a gray uniform handed his sword to a short, rumpled man in a blue uniform, and the shooting stopped in America's bloodiest war ever.

However, as one Civil War historian has pointed out:

The American Civil War did not end at Appomattox. Lee's surrender only marked the abandonment of armed resistance in a struggle that had been going on . . . for a generation or more. *

The next stage of that struggle was Reconstruction, a time when half the country ruled the other half as occupied territories, complete with military government and military supervision of the reconstruction process. Now the focus shifted from civil war to civil rights. The war confirmed that black

*Avery Craven, *Reconstruction: The Ending of the Civil War* (New York: Holt, Rinehart and Winston, Inc. 1969), p. 1.

people deserved the same freedoms as white people, but whether they deserved equality was another matter.

The issue of equality was felt strongly in the area of education. In fact, the structure of the present American educational system was set in place during the Reconstruction era.

After the war, millions of black people were thrown unprepared into a society whose rules and customs few of them understood, and many of them believed that education was their only hope. Most of the former slaves were illiterate, and their freedom was irrelevant if they could not read the wage contracts offered them by their new employers (who were, in many cases, their former owners).

Southern whites felt less pressure. Before the war, schooling and other matters of social welfare had been considered private affairs. Plantation owners had sufficient income to educate their children as they pleased, and poorer farmers generally distrusted education as an "upper class" extravagance. Immediately after the war, these attitudes were still widespread among people in the white community. Thus it was Southern blacks who took the lead in creating pressure for a

THE MISSES COOKE'S SCHOOL ROOM WAS A FREEDMEN'S BUREAU SCHOOL IN RICHMOND, VIRGINIA, 1866.

new approach to education in the South, leaving most whites to oppose or ignore their efforts.

The education of Southern blacks had already begun, even before the war had ended. In Louisiana, for example, fifteen thousand pupils attended 126 schools that had been set up by the military government before Lee's surrender at Appomattox. Northern philanthropic groups assisted the military effort, with the Freedmen's Aid Society taking the lead. By 1867 the society had enrolled eleven thousand pupils in schools throughout the South.

These early schools were open to all children, and were some of the first truly integrated schools in the United States. However, white resistance to the whole idea of black education can be measured by the fact that only 1 percent of all pupils were white. Many white Southerners were opposed to these schools, for not only were they mixed, but their Yankee teachers were also rumored to be preaching racial equality.

Over time, however, black enthusiasm for the new educational opportunities had a more positive impact on Southern whites. Edward Pollard, a South Carolinian who originally supported slavery, wrote a remarkable article about emancipation in an 1870 issue of *Harper's* magazine. Pollard declared that he had been wrong about black people and how they would use their new freedom. Among other reasons for his changed attitude, he noted, "I have witnessed the zeal with which the black people are availing themselves of the schools and means of education. . . ."

Other whites saw that a modern school system might benefit the South as a whole even though the idea was being urged primarily by blacks and Northern Reconstructionists. When new constitutions were written for the

THIS "EXTRACT FROM THE RECONSTRUCTED CONSTITUTION OF THE STATE OF LOUISIANA" CITES ARTICLE 135: "ALL CHILDREN OF THIS STATE SHALL BE ADMITTED TO THE PUBLIC SCHOOLS OR OTHER INSTITUTIONS OF LEARNING SUSTAINED OR ESTABLISHED BY THE STATE IN COMMON, WITHOUT DISTINCTION OF RACE, COLOR, OR PREVIOUS CONDITION. THERE SHALL BE NO SEPARATE SCHOOLS OR INSTITUTIONS OF LEARNING ESTABLISHED EXCLUSIVELY FOR ANY RACE BY THE STATE OF LOUISANA."

states of the old Confederacy, every one contained provisions for establishing a public school system. It was white support which ensured this.

The question of school integration was not raised at this time, and most of the new systems provided separate facilities for black and white children from the very beginning. But this was not really surprising. Even as late as the 1850s, most Northern states provided no public education for black children, and where they did, the schools were usually segregated.

In general, Northerners were as uncertain as Southerners about the notion of racial equality. The idea seemed especially threatening to laborers during the periods of economic decline in the decades after the Civil War. And, following a pattern that has persisted into modern times, Northerners were able to avoid the issue because so much of the nation's attention was focused on the more visible problems in the South.

Thus, perhaps it is not surprising that some Northern philanthropies, organized specifically to assist black educational development, refused to provide aid to integrated schools and colleges in the South. Integrated education, these charities believed, was a hopeless illusion, and would not be encouraged by their support.

Given this attitude in the North, Southern resistance to the idea could hardly be expected to decrease. In Louisiana, the only state where integration was practiced to any extent, the state school superintendent once remarked: "There is probably no other state in the Union where the work of popular education is conducted under the disadvantages which are encountered in Louisiana." The evidence indicates that the superintendent was not exaggerating. In 1874, for example, a mob attacked a mixed high school in New Orleans, and drove out all stu-

LOOKING TOWARD FREEDOM: TWO EMANCIPATED SLAVE CHILDREN, NAMED SIMPLY ISAAC AND ROSA, STAND DRESSED IN SPANKING NEW CLOTHES FOR THIS PICTURE TAKEN IN 1863, EMANCIPATION YEAR.

dents who were black or even suspected of having mixed blood.

Hostility to the public school systems was not limited to integrated schools, however. Even where facilities were segregated, white opposition sometimes flared into violence. In 1870, farmers in Mississippi were incensed over the high taxes they were paying to support public schools. They burned down a number of buildings, intimidated teachers, and forced schools to close in a number of counties.

As long as Reconstruction lasted, however, the new approach to education was never in any real danger. Blacks, sympathetic whites, and

Northerners controlled the state governments throughout the South, and this coalition was enough to keep the schools from being dismantled by their opponents.

In addition, opposition to the public schools lessened in the later phases of Reconstruction. As the South prepared to reenter the Union and began to build an economy less dominated by agriculture, the competitive advantages of a good education became more and more obvious.

Unfortunately, this late-blooming interest worked to the disadvantage of blacks, now that the school systems had been firmly established on a segregated basis. The South lagged behind the North economically and did not possess the resources to support separate schools that were truly equal.

As the Reconstruction period ended, politicians dedicated to retrenchment began taking over state governments throughout the South. Many of them were pledged to end the fiscal excesses which they claimed had been perpetrated by the Reconstruction governments. And "economy moves" were often aimed at the schools. Moreover, segregation made it possible to manipulate budgets so that cutbacks could fall most heavily on black schools. Over time, this practice would provide strong ammunition for opponents of segregation. It was also one of the factors leading to the Supreme Court's 1954 decision.

The school issue is a good example of how the country handled basic problems during the Reconstruction period. It also illustrates how decisions made in the past can affect the present. While Reconstruction fulfilled its goal of restoring the Union, it allowed slavery to be replaced by segregation. Just as slavery had generated a demand for black freedom which led to civil war, segregation produced a demand for equality which led to the civil rights movement.

Appendix

Appendix

Further Readings

Chapter 1

Beer, George L., *The Old Colonial System*, 2 volumes. Gloucester, Mass.: Peter Smith; Beer, George L., *The Origins of the British Colonial System*. Gloucester, Mass: Peter Smith; Bindoff, S. T., *Tudor England*. Baltimore, Md.: Penguin, 1950; Byrne, M. St. Clare, *Elizabethan Life in Town and Country*. New York: Barnes & Noble, 1961; Cheyney, E. P., *The Dawn of a New Era*. New York: Harper & Row, 1936 (Paper: Harper Torch Books, 1962); Enterline, James Robert, *Viking America: The Norse Crossings and their Legacy*. New York: Doubleday, 1972; Mattingly, Garrett, *The Armada*. Boston: Houghton Mifflin, 1959 (Paper: Sentry Edition, 1962); Notestein, Wallace, *The English People on the Eve of Colonization*. New York: Harper & Row Torchbooks, 1954; Parry, J. H., *The Spanish Seaborne Empire*. New York: Knopf, 1966; Reynolds, Robert L., *Europe Emerges: Transition Toward an Industrial World-Wide Society*. Madison: University of Wisconsin Press, 1961.

Contribution to the American Tradition. New York: Atheneum, 1962; Morgan, Edmund S., *Visible Saints*. New York: New York University Press, 1963 (Paper: Cornell University Press, 1970); Nettels, Curtis P., *The Roots of American Civilization*. New York: Appleton-Century-Crofts, 1963; Peare, Catherine O., *William Penn*. New York: Holt, Rinehart and Winston, 1957 (Paper: University of Michigan, Ann Arbor Books, 1966); Powell, Sumner C., *Puritan Village: The Formation of a New England Town*. Middletown, Conn.: Wesleyan University Press, 1963 (Paper); Rutman, Darrett B., *American Puritanism: Faith and Practice*. Philadelphia: Lippincott, 1970 (Paper); Rutman, Darrett B., *Winthrop's Boston: A Portrait of a Puritan Town, 1630–1649*. New York: Norton, 1965 (Paper); Smith, Bradford, *Captain John Smith*. Philadelphia: Lippincott, 1953; Wertenbaker, T. J., *The First Americans*. New York: Macmillan, 1927; Wildes, Harry E., *William Penn*, New York: Macmillan, 1974; Willison, George E., *Behold Virginia*. New York: Harcourt Brace Jovanovich, 1951.

Chapter 2

Adams, James T., *The Founding of New England*. Boston: Atlantic Monthly Press, 1921 (Paper: Atlantic Monthly–Little, Brown, 1965); Barbour, Philip, *Pocahontas and Her World*. Boston: Houghton Mifflin, 1970. Coleman, Kenneth, *Colonial Georgia: A History*. New York: KTO Press, 1976; Davis, Harold E., *The Fledgling Province: Social and Cultural Life in Colonial Georgia, 1733-1776*. Chapel Hill: University of North Carolina Press, 1976; Greven, Philip J., Jr., *Four Generations: Population, Land and Family in Colonial Andover, Massachusetts*. New York: Cornell University Press, 1970 (Paper); Lankgord, John (Ed.), *Captain John Smith's America: Selections from his Writings*. New York: Harper & Row, 1967; Leach, Douglas E., *Flintlock and Tomahawk: New England in King Philip's War*. New York: Norton, 1966 (Paper); Lockridge, Kenneth A., *New England Town: The First Hundred Years*. New York: Norton, 1970; Lucas, Paul R., *Valley of Discord: Church and Society Along the Connecticut River, 1636-1725*. Hanover, N.H.: University Press of New England, 1976; Middleton, Arthur Pierce, *Tobacco Coast: A Maritime History of Chesapeake Bay in the Colonial Era*. George Carrington Mason (Ed.), Newport News, Va.: Mariners' Museum, 1953; Miller, Perry, *Roger Williams: His*

Chapter 3

Bailyn, Bernard, *Education in the Forming of American Society: Needs and Opportunities for Study*. Chapel Hill: University of North Carolina Press, 1960 (Paper: Random House, 1962); Bonomi, Patricia U., *Factious People: Politics and Society in Colonial New York*. New York: Columbia University Press, 1971 (Paper); Bridenbaugh, Carl, *The Colonial Craftsman*. Chicago: University of Chicago Press, 1950; Bushman, Richard L., *From Puritan to Yankee: Character and Social Order in Connecticut, 1690-1765*. Cambridge, Mass.: Harvard University Press, 1967 (Paper: Norton, 1970); Cunliffe, Marcus, *The Literature of the United States*. Baltimore: Penguin, 1954; Curtin, Philip D., *Atlantic Slave Trade: A Census*. Madison: University of Wisconsin Press, 1969 (Paper); Davis, Richard Beale, *Intellectual Life in the Colonial South, 1585-1763*. Knoxville: The University of Tennessee Press, 1978; Franklin, John H., *From Slavery to Freedom: A History of Negro Americans*. New York: Random, 1969 (Paper); Hall, M. G., L. H. Leder, and M. G. Kammen (Eds.), *The Glorious Revolution in America: Documents on the Colonial Crisis of 1689*. Chapel Hill: University of North Carolina Press, 1964; Hindle, Brook, *The Pursuit of Science in Revolutionary America, 1735-1789*. Chapel Hill: University of North Carolina

Press, 1956; Meier, August, and Elliot Rudwick, *From Plantation to Ghetto*. New York: Hill & Wang, 1970 (Paper); Merritt, R. L., *Symbols of American Community, 1735–1775*. New Haven, Conn.: Yale University Press, 1966; Mullin, Gerald W., *Flight and Rebellion: Slave Resistance in Eighteenth Century Virginia*. New York: Oxford University Press, 1972 (Paper).

Chapter 4

Bowen, Catherine D., *John Adams and the American Revolution*. New York: Grosset & Dunlap, 1957 (Paper); Dickerson, Oliver M., *The Navigation Acts and the American Revolution*. New York: Octagon, 1974; Fithian, Philip V., *Journal and Letters of Philip V. Fithian, 1773–1774: A Plantation Tutor at the Old Dominion*. Charlottesville: University Press of Virginia, 1968; Ketchum, Richard M., and American Heritage Editors, *The World of George Washington*. New York: McGraw-Hill, 1974; Labaree, Leonard Woods, *Royal Government in America*. New Haven, Conn.: Yale University Press, 1930; Morison, Samuel E., *John Paul Jones: A Sailor's Biography*. Boston: Little, Brown, 1959; Namier, Lewis B., *England in the Age of the American Revolution*. New York: St. Martin's Press, 1961; Nash, Gary B., *Quakers and Politics: Pennsylvania, 1681–1726*. Princeton, N.J.: Princeton University Press, 1968; Trevelyan, George O., *The American Revolution*, Richard B. Morris (Ed.). New York: David McKay, 1964; Washington, George, *Journal of Major George Washington*, James R. Short and Thaddeus W. Tate, Jr. (Eds.). Charlottesville: University Press of Virginia, 1963.

Chapter 5

Alden, John R., *The American Revolution, 1775–1783*. New York: Harper & Row, 1954; Brown, Wallace, *The Good Americans*. New York, Morrow, 1969; Burnett, Edmund C., *The Continental Congress*. New York: Macmillan, 1941 (Paper: Norton, 1964); Chinard, Gilbert, *Thomas Jefferson: The Apostle of Americanism*. Ann Arbor: University of Michigan Press, 1957; Dodge, Ernest S., *New England and the South Seas*. Cambridge, Mass.: Harvard University Press, 1965; Ketchum, Richard M., *The Winter Soldiers*. Garden City, N.Y.: Doubleday, 1973; Kammen, Michael, *A Season of Youth: The American Revolution and the Historical Imagination*. New York: Knopf, 1978; Martin, J. Kirby, *Men in Rebellion: Higher Governmental Leaders and the Coming of the American Revolution*. New York: Free Press, 1976; McDonald, Forrest, *E Pluribus Unum: The Formation of the American Republic, 1776–1790*. Boston: Houghton Mifflin, 1965; Nelson, William H., *The American Tory*. New York: Oxford University Press, 1962 (Paper: Beacon Press, 1964); Nevins, Allan, *American States During and After the Revolution, 1775–1798*. Clifton, N.J.: Kelley; Norton, Mary Beth, *The Americans: The Loyalist Exiles in England, 1774–1789*. Boston: Little, Brown, 1972; Peckham, Howard H., *The War for Independence. A Military History*. Chicago: University of Chicago Press, 1958; Pocock, J. G. A., *The Machiavellian Moment: Florentine Political Thought and the Atlantic Republican Tradition*. Princeton, N.J.: Princeton University Press, 1975; Polishook, Irwin H., *Rhode Island and the Union, 1774–1795*. Evanston, Ill.: Northwestern University Press, 1969; Tyler, Moses C., *Patrick Henry*. Ithaca, N.Y.: Cornell University Press, 1962; Whitaker, Arthur P., *The Spanish-American Frontier: 1783–1795; The Westward Movement and the Spanish Retreat in the Mississippi Valley*. Boston: Houghton Mifflin, 1927 (Paper: University of Nebraska Press, 1969).

Chapter 6

Ammon, Harry, *The Genet Mission*. New York: Norton, 1973 (Paper); Beard, Charles A., *Economic Interpretation of the Constitution of the United States*. New York: Free Press, 1965 (Paper); Bemis, Samuel F., *Jay's Treaty*. New Haven, Conn.: Yale University Press, 1962; Bemis, Samuel F., *Pinckney's Treaty*. New Haven, Conn.: Yale University Press, 1960; Billias, George Athan, *Elbridge Gerry: Founding Father and Republican Statesman*. New York: McGraw-Hill, 1976; Boorstein, Daniel J., *Lost World of Thomas Jefferson*. Gloucester, Mass.: Peter Smith, 1960 (Paper); Bowers, Claude G., *Jefferson and Hamilton*. Boston: Houghton Mifflin, 1925; Boyd, Julian P., *Number Seven: Alexander Hamilton's Secret Attempts to Control American Foreign Policy*. Princeton, N.J.: Princeton University Press, 1964; Brown, Robert E., *Charles Beard and the Constitution*. New York: Norton, 1965 (Paper); Buel, Richard, *Securing the Revolution: Ideology in American Politics 1789–1815*. New York: Cornell University Press, 1972 (Paper); Clarfield, Gerald H., *Timothy Pickering and American Diplomacy, 1795–1800*. Columbia: University of Missouri Press, 1969; Cooke, Jacob E. (Ed.), *The Reports of Alexander Hamilton*. New York: Harper & Row, 1964; Farrand, Max, *Framing of the Constitution of the United States*. New Haven,

Conn.: Yale University Press, 1913 (Paper); Goebel, Julius, Jr., *History of the Supreme Court, Vol. I: Antecedents and Beginnings to 1800.* Roy Roberts (Ed.). New York: Macmillan, 1971; Hazen, Charles D., *Contemporary American Opinion of the French Revolution.* Baltimore: Johns Hopkins University Press, 1897; Hills, Peter P., *William Vans Murray, Federalist Diplomat: The Shaping of Peace with France.* New York: Syracuse University Press, 1971; Koch, Adrienne, *Philosophy of Thomas Jefferson.* New York: Quadrangle, 1964 (Paper); Kohn, Richard H., *Eagle and Sword: The Federalists and the Creation of the Military Establishment in America, 1783–1802.* New York: Free Press, 1975; Lycan, Gilbert L., *Alexander Hamilton and American Foreign Policy: A Design for Greatness.* Norman: University of Oklahoma Press, 1970. Lynd, Staughton (Ed.), *Class Conflict, Slavery and the United States Constitution: Ten Essays.* New York: Bobbs-Merrill, 1967 (Paper); Miller, John C., *Crisis in Freedom.* Boston: Little, Brown, 1964; Miller, John C., *The Federalist Era, 1789–1801.* New York: Harper & Row, 1960; McLaughlin, Andrew C., *Confederation and the Constitution 1783–1789.* Gloucester, Mass.: Peter Smith, 1905; Murphy, William, *The Triumph of Nationalism: State Sovereignty, the Founding Fathers, and the Making of the Constitution.* New York: Quadrangle, 1968; Rutland, Robert A., *Ordeal of the Constitution: The Antifederalists and the Ratification Struggle of 1787–1788.* Norman: University of Oklahoma Press, 1966; Schachner, Nathan, *The Founding Fathers.* New York: Putnam, 1954; Seed, Geoffrey, *James Wilson.* Millwood, N.Y.: KTO Press, 1978; Smith, Charles P., *James Wilson, Founding Father: 1742–1798.* Westport, Conn.: Greenwood, 1973; Stourzh, Gerald, *Alexander Hamilton and the Idea of Republican Government.* California: Stanford University Press, 1970; Walters, Raymond, Jr., *Albert Gallatin.* New York: Macmillan, 1957; Warren, C., *The Making of the Constitution.* Boston: Little, Brown, 1928; Whitaker, Arthur P., *The Mississippi Question, 1795–1803.* Gloucester, Mass.: Peter Smith, 1962; White, Leonard, *The Federalists: A Study in Administrative History.* New York: Macmillan, 1945; Wright, Benjamin F., *Consensus and Continuity, 1776–1787.* New York: Norton, 1967 (Paper).

Chapter 7

Adams, Henry, *History of the United States During the Administration of Jefferson and Madison.* Englewood Cliffs, N.J.: Prentice-Hall, 1963; Bowers, Claude G., *Jefferson in Power.* Boston: Houghton Mifflin, 1936; Brant, Irving, *The Fourth President: The Life of James Madison.* New York: Bobbs-Merrill; Brodie, Fawn M., *Thomas Jefferson: An Intimate History.* New York: Norton, 1974; Broussard, James H., *The Southern Federalists, 1800–1816.* Baton Rouge: Louisiana State University Press, 1978; Corwin, Edward, *John Marshall and the Constitution.* New Haven, Conn.: Yale University Press, 1919; Cunliffe, Marcus, *The Nation Takes Shape:*

1789–1837. Chicago: University of Chicago Press, 1959; DeConde, Alexander, *This Affair of Louisiana.* New York: Scribner, 1976; Engelman, F. L., *The Peace of Christmas Eve.* New York: Harcourt Brace Jovanovich, 1962; Kaplan, Lawrence S., *Jefferson and France: An Essay on Politics and Political Ideas.* New Haven, Conn.: Yale University Press, 1967; Kirk, Russell, *Randolph of Roanoke: A Study in Conservative Thought.* Chicago: University of Chicago Press, 1951; Rich, E. E., *The Fur Trade and the Northwest to 1857.* Buffalo, N.Y.: McClelland & Stewart, 1967; Schachner, Nathan, *Aaron Burr: A Biography.* Cranston, N.J.: Barnes, 1961; Schachner, Nathan, *Thomas Jefferson: A Biography,* Vols. I–II. New York: Appleton-Century-Crofts, 1951; Sheehan, Bernard W., *Seeds of Extinction: Jeffersonian Philanthropy and the American Indian.* Chapel Hill: University of North Carolina Press, 1973; VanEvery, Dale, *Ark of Empire, The American Frontier, 1784–1803.* New York: Morrow, 1963. Wiltse, Charles M., *The Jeffersonian Tradition in American Democracy.* Chapel Hill: University of North Carolina Press, 1935.

Chapter 8

Beveridge, Albert J., *The Life of John Marshall,* Vols. I–IV. Boston: Houghton Mifflin, 1916–1919; Brown, Norman D., *Daniel Webster and the Politics of Availability.* Athens: University of Georgia Press, 1969; Bruchey, Stuart, *The Roots of American Economic Growth, 1607–1861.* New York: Harper & Row, 1965; Burlingame, Roger, *The March of the Iron Men.* New York: Grosset & Dunlap, 1960; Current, Richard N., *Daniel Webster and the Rise of National Conservatism.* Boston: Little, Brown, 1955; Curti, Merle, *The Roots of American Loyalty.* New York: Columbia University Press, 1946; Green, Constance M. L., *Eli Whitney and the Birth of American Technology.* Boston: Little, Brown, 1956; Havighurst, Walter, *Voices on the River: The Story of the Mississippi Water Ways.* New York: Macmillan, 1964; Horwitz, Morton J., *The Transformation of American Law, 1780–1860.* Cambridge, Mass: Harvard University Press, 1977; Philbrick, F. S., *The Rise of the West, 1754–1830.* New York: Harper & Row, 1965; Shannon, Fred A., *America's Economic Growth.* New York: Macmillan, 1951; Warren, Charles, *The Supreme Court in United States History,* Vols. I–III. Boston: Little, Brown, 1923. Weisberger, Bernard A., *They Gathered at the River.* Boston: Little, Brown, 1958.

Chapter 9

Carter, Samuel, III, *Cherokee Sunset, A Nation Betrayed.* Garden City, N.Y.: Doubleday, 1976; Crenson, Matthew A., *The Federal Machine: Beginnings of Bureaucracy in Jacksonian America.* Baltimore: Johns Hopkins University Press, 1975; Dennison, George M., *The Dorr War: Republicanism on Trial, 1831–1861.* Lexington: University Press of Kentucky,

1976; Levine, Peter D., *The Behavior of State Legislative Parties in the Jacksonian Era: New Jersey, 1829–1844*. Cranbury, N.J.: Fairleigh Dickinson, 1977; Littlefield, Daniel F., Jr., *Africans and Seminoles: From Removal to Emancipation*. Westport, Conn.: Greenwood, 1977; McFaul, John M., *The Politics of Jacksonian Finance*. Ithaca, N.Y.: Cornell University Press, 1976; Pearce, Roy H., *The Savages of America*. Baltimore: Johns Hopkins University Press, 1965. Perdue, Theda, *Slavery and the Evolution of Cherokee Society, 1540–1866*. Knoxville: The University of Tennessee Press, 1979. Pessen, Edward, *Most Uncommon Jacksonians: The Radical Leaders of the Early Labor Movement*. Albany, New York: State University of New York Press, 1967; Pessen, Edward (Ed.), *New Perspectives on Jacksonian Parties and Politics*. Boston: Allyn & Bacon, 1969; Remini, Robert V., *Andrew Jackson*. Boston: Twayne, 1966. Shade, William G., *Banks or No Banks: The Money Question in Western Politics*. Detroit: Wayne State University Press, 1972; Swisher, Carl, *Roger B. Taney*. New York: Macmillan, 1935.

Chapter 10

Berlin, Ira, *Slaves Without Masters: The Free Negro in the Antebellum South*. New York: Pantheon, 1974; Billigmeier, Robert, *Americans From Germany: A Study in Cultural Diversity*. Belmont, Calif.: Wadsworth, 1974; Billington, Ray, *America's Frontier Heritage*. New York: Holt, Rinehart & Winston, 1966; Conrad, Alfred H., and John R. Meyer, *The Economics of Slavery and Other Studies in Econometric History*. Chicago: Aldine, 1964; Craven, Avery O., *Edmund Ruffin, Southerner*. New York: Appleton, 1932; Curti, Merle, *The Making of an American Community: A Case Study of Democracy in a Frontier County*. Stanford, Calif.: Stanford University Press, 1959 (Paper); Cooper, William J., Jr., *The South and the Politics of Slavery, 1828–1856*. Baton Rouge: Louisiana State University Press, 1978; Davis, James E., *Frontier America, 1800–1840: A Comparative Demographic Analysis of the Settlement Process*. Glendale, Calif.: Arthur H. Clark, 1977; Dick, Everett, *The Dixie Frontier*. New York: Knopf, 1948; Eaton, Clement, *The Growth of Southern Civilization*. New York: Harper & Row, 1961; Fishel, Leslie H., Jr., and Benjamin Quarles, *The Black American: A Documentary History*. Glenview, Ill.: Scott-Foresman, 1970 (Paper); Fishlow, Albert, *American Railroads and the Transformation of the Ante-Bellum Economy*. Cambridge, Mass.: Harvard University Press, 1965; Fogel, Robert W., *Railroads and American Economic Growth*. Baltimore: Johns Hopkins University Press, 1964; Fogel, Robert W., and Stanley Engerman, *Time on the Cross*. Boston: Little, Brown, 1974; Foner, Philip S. (Ed.), *The Factory Girls*. Urbana: University of Illinois Press, 1977; Gara, Larry, *The Liberty Line: The Legend of the Underground Railroad*. Lexington: University Press of Kentucky, 1967 (Paper); Goodrich, Carter (Ed.), *The Government and the Economy, 1783–1861*. Indianapolis: Bobbs-Merrill, 1966; Gray, Lewis C., *History of Agriculture in the Southern United States to 1860, Vols. I–II*. Washington, D.C.: Carnegie Institution, 1933; Handlin, Oscar, *Boston's Immigrants: A Study of Acculturation*. Cambridge, Mass.: Harvard University Press, 1959; Hareven, Tamara K., and Randolph Langenbach, *Amoskeag: Life and Work in an American Factory-City*. New York: Pantheon, 1978; Huggins, Nathan I., *Black Odyssey: The Afro-American Ordeal in Slavery*. New York: Random, 1979; Hirsch, Susan E., *Roots of the American Working Class: The Industrialization of Crafts in Newark, 1800–1860*. Philadelphia: University of Pennsylvania Press, 1978; Jordan, Winthrop, *The White Man's Burden*. New York: Oxford University Press, 1974 (Paper); Knights, Peter R., *The Plain People of Boston, 1830–1860: A Study in City Growth*. New York: Oxford University Press, 1973 (Paper); Lane, Ann J. (Ed.), *The Debate Over Slavery: Stanley Elkins and his Critics*. Urbana: University of Illinois Press, 1971 (Paper); Levine, Edward M., *Irish and Irish Politicians: A Study of Social and Cultural Alienation*. Notre Dame, Ind.: University of Notre Dame Press, 1966; Litwack, Leon F., *North of Slavery: The Negro in the Free States, 1790–1860*. Chicago: University of Chicago Press, 1961 (Paper); McCaffrey, Lawrence J., *Irish Diaspora in America*. Bloomington, Ind.: Indiana University Press, 1978; Rosenberg, Nathan (Ed.), *The American System of Manufactures*. Edinburgh: Edinburgh University Press, 1969; Peterson, Thomas V., *Ham and Japheth: The Mythic World of Whites in the Antebellum South*. Metuchen, N.J.: Scarecrow, 1978; Raboteau, Albert J., *Slave Religion: The "Invisible Institution" in the Antebellum South*. New York: Oxford University Press, 1978; Starobin, Robert, *Industrial Slavery in the Old South*. New York: Oxford University Press, 1970 (Paper); Wallace, Anthony F. C., *Rockdale: The Growth of an American Village in the Early Industrial Revolution*. New York: Knopf, 1978; Ware, Norman J., *The Industrial Worker, 1840–1860*. Boston: Houghton Mifflin, 1959; Weinstein, Allen, and Frank O. Gatell (Eds.), *American Negro Slavery: A Modern Reader*. New York: Oxford University Press, 1973.

Chapter 11

Brooks, Van Wyck, *The Flowering of New England*. Cleveland: World, 1936; Carwardine, Richard, *Trans-Atlantic Revivalism: Popular Evangelicalism in Britain and America*. Westport, Conn.: Greenwood, 1978; Chevigny, Bell Gale, *The Woman and the Myth: Margaret Fuller's Life and Writings*. New York: Feminist Press, 1976; Commager, Henry S., *The Age of Reform 1830–1860*. Princeton, N.J.: Van Nostrand, 1960; Conrad, Susan Phinney, *Perish the Thought: Intellectual Women in Romantic America, 1830–1860*. Secaucus, N.J.: Citadel Press, 1976; Cover, Robert, *Justice Accused: Anti-Slavery and the Judicial Process*. New Haven, Conn.: Yale University Press, 1975; Cromwell, Otelia, *Lucretia Mott*. New York: Russell & Russell, 1971; Filler, Louis, *The Crusade*

Against Slavery. New York: Harper, 1960; Foster, Charles I., *An Errand of Mercy: The Evangelical United Front.* Chapel Hill: University of North Carolina Press, 1960; Gusfield, Joseph R., *Symbolic Crusade: Status Politics and the American Temperance Movement.* Urbana: University of Illinois Press, 1966 (Paper); Howe, D. W., *The Unitarian Conscience: Harvard Moral Philosophy, 1805–1861.* Cambridge, Mass.: Harvard University Press, 1970; Katz, Michael B., *The Irony of Early School Reform: Education Innovation in Mid-Nineteenth Century Massachusetts.* Cambridge, Mass.: Harvard University Press, 1968 (Paper: Beacon Press, 1970); Kraditor, Aileen, *Means and Ends in American Abolitionism: Garrison and His Critics on Strategy and Tactics, 1834–1850.* New York: Pantheon, 1969; Lerner, Gerda, *The Grimke Sisters from South Carolina: Rebels Against Slavery.* Boston: Houghton Mifflin, 1967 (Paper); Levin, David, *History as Romantic Art.* Stanford, Calif.: Stanford University Press, 1959; Lumpkin, Katherine DuPre, *The Emancipation of Angelina Grimke.* Chapel Hill: University of North Carolina Press, 1974; Lutz, Alma, *Created Equal: A Biography of Elizabeth Cady Stanton.* New York: Octagon, 1973; Marshall, H. E., *Dorothea Dix: Forgotten Samaritan.* Chapel Hill: University of North Carolina Press, 1937; Matthiessen, F. O., *American Renaissance.* London: Oxford University Press, 1941; McLoughlin, William G., *Revivals, Awakenings, and Reform: An Essay on Religion and Social Change in America, 1607–1977.* Chicago: University of Chicago Press, 1978; Messerli, Jonathan, *Horace Mann, A Biography.* New York: Knopf, 1972; Miller, Perry (Ed.), *Margaret Fuller: American Romantic.* Garden City, N.Y.: Doubleday Anchor, 1963; Muncy, Raymond Lee, *Sex and Marriage in Utopian Communities: 19th Century America.* Bloomington: Indiana University Press, 1973 (Paper: Penguin, 1974); Nye, Russell B., *William Lloyd Garrison and the Humanitarian Reformers.* Boston: Little, Brown, 1955; O'Neill, William L., *Everyone Was Brave: The Rise and Fall of Feminism in America.* New York: Times Books, 1971; Osterweis, Rolin G., *Romanticism and Nationalism in the Old South.* Gloucester, Mass.: Peter Smith (Paper: Louisiana State University Press, 1967); Parrington, Vernon L., *Main Currents in American Thought,* Vols. I–III. New York: Harcourt, Brace, 1927–1930; Porte, Joel, *Representative Man: Ralph Waldo Emerson in His Time.* New York: Oxford University Press, 1978; Porter, David, *Emerson and Literary Change.* Cambridge, Mass.: Harvard University Press, 1978; Rudolph, Frederick, *The American College and University.* New York: Knopf, 1967; Scott, Anne F., *The Southern Lady: From Pedestal to Politics, 1830–1930.* Chicago: University of Chicago Press, 1970 (Paper); Sewell, Richard H., *Ballots for Freedom.* New York: Oxford University Press, 1976; Sorin, Gerald, *Abolitionism: A New Perspective.* New York: Praeger, 1972 (Paper); Stewart, James B., *Joshua R. Giddings and the Tactics of Radical Politics.* New York: University Press Book Service, 1970; Taylor, William B., *Cavalier and Yankee.* New York: Braziller, 1961; Thomas, Benjamin P., *Theodore Weld: Crusader for Freedom.* New Brunswick, N.J.: Rutgers University Press, 1950; Thomas, Robert David, *The Man Who Would Be Perfect: John Humphrey Noyes and the Utopian Impulse.* Philadelphia: University of Pennsylvania Press, 1977; Van Doren, Mark, *Nathaniel Hawthorne.* New York: William Sloane, 1949. Wacker, Peter F., *Moral Choices: Memory, Desire, and Imagination in Nineteenth-Century American Abolition.* Baton Rouge: Louisiana State University Press, 1978; Wallace, Anthony F. E., *Rockdale.* New York: Knopf, 1978; Wyatt-Brown, Bertram, *Lewis Tappan and the Evangelical War Against Slavery.* New York: Atheneum, 1969.

Chapter 12

Allen, Harry C., *Great Britain and the United States.* London: Odhams Press, 1954; Billington, Ray A., *The Far Western Frontier.* New York: Harper, 1965; Brack, Gene M., *Mexico Views Manifest Destiny, 1821–1846. An Essay on the Origins of the Mexican War.* Albuquerque: University of New Mexico Press, 1975; Cleland, Robert G., *This Reckless Breed of Men.* New York: Knopf, 1950; Connor, Seymour V., and Odie B. Faulk, *North America Divided: The Mexican War, 1846–1848.* New York: Oxford University Press, 1971; DeVoto, Bernard, *The Year of Decision: 1846.* Boston: Little, Brown, 1943; Fehrenbacher, Don E. (Ed.), *Manifest Destiny and the Coming of the Civil War, 1840–1861.* Arlington Heights, Ill.: AHM, 1970; Mantaigne, Sanford H., *Blood Over Texas: The Unpopular Truth About Mexico's War with the United States.* New Rochelle, N.Y.: Arlington House, 1976; Merk, Frederick, *The Oregon Question: Essays in Anglo-American Diplomacy and Politics.* Cambridge, Mass.: Harvard University Press, 1967; Merk, Frederick, *Slavery and the Annexation of Texas.* New York: Knopf, 1972; Morgan, Dale L., *Jedediah Smith and the Opening of the West.* Indianapolis: Bobbs-Merrill, 1929; Morgan, Robert J., *A Whig Embattled.* Lincoln: University of Nebraska Press, 1954; Price, Glenn W., *Origins of the War with Mexico: The Polk-Stockton Intrigue.* Austin: University of Texas Press, 1967; Rayback, Joseph G., *Free Soil: The Election of 1848.* Lexington: University Press of Kentucky, 1970; Unruh, John D., Jr., *The Plains Across: The Overland Emigrants and the Trans-Mississippi West, 1840–1860.* Urbana: University of Illinois Press, 1978.

Chapter 13

Baker, Jean H., *Ambivalent Americans: The Know-Nothing Party in Maryland.* Baltimore, Md.: Johns Hopkins University Press, 1977; Barney, William L., *The Secessionist Impulse: Alabama and Mississippi.* Princeton, N.J.: Princeton University Press, 1974; Blue, Frederick J., *The Free Soilers: Third Party Politics, 1848–54.* Urbana: University of Illinois Press, 1973; Boyer, Richard O., *The Legend of John Brown: A Biography and a History.* New York: Knopf, 1973; Campbell,

Stanley W., *Slave Catchers: Enforcement of the Fugitive Slave Law, 1850-1860*. Chapel Hill: University of North Carolina Press, 1970 (Paper: Norton, 1972); Capers, Gerald M., *Stephen A. Douglas, Defender of the Union*. Boston: Little, Brown, 1959; Channing, Steven A., *Crisis of Fear: Secession in South Carolina*. New York: Simon & Schuster, 1970; Cooper, William J., Jr., *The South and the Politics of Slavery, 1828-1856*. Baton Rouge: Louisiana State University Press, 1978; Davis, David B., *The Slave Power Conspiracy and the Paranoid Style*. Baton Rouge: Louisiana State University Press, 1970; Isely, Jeter A., *Horace Greeley and the Republican Party, 1853-1861*. New York: Octagon, 1965; Jaffa, Harry V., *Crisis of the House Divided: An Interpretation of the Issues in the Lincoln-Douglas Debates*. Garden City, N.Y.: Doubleday, 1959; Johnson, Michael P., *Toward a Patriarchal Republic: The Secession of Georgia*. Baton Rouge: Louisiana State University Press, 1977; Luebke, Frederick C. (Ed.), *Ethnic Voters and the Election of Lincoln*. Lincoln: University of Nebraska Press, 1971; Oates, Stephen B., *To Purge This Land with Blood: A Biography of John Brown*. New York: Harper & Row, 1972; Phillips, Ulrich B., *The Course of the South to Secession*. New York: Hill & Wang, 1964; Potter, David M., *Lincoln and His Party in the Secession Crisis*. New Haven, Conn.: Yale University Press, 1942; Pressly, Thomas J., *Americans Interpret Their Civil War*. New York: Free Press, 1965 (Paper); Quarles, Benjamin, *Allies for Freedom: Blacks and John Brown*. New York: Oxford University Press, 1974; Ruchames, Louis (Ed.), *John Brown: The Making of a Revolutionary*. New York: Grosset & Dunlap, 1969; Silbey, Joel, *The Shrine of Party: Congressional Voting Behavior 1841-1852*. Pittsburgh, Penn.: University of Pittsburgh Press, 1967; Swisher, Carl B., *Roger B. Taney*. New York: Macmillan, 1935; Thomas, Benjamin P., *Abraham Lincoln*. New York: Knopf, 1952.

Chapter 14

Andrews, J. Cutler, *The South Reports the Civil War*. Princeton, N.J.: Princeton University Press, 1970; Connelly, Thomas L., and Archer Jones, *The Politics of Command: Factions and Ideas in Confederate Strategy*. Baton Rouge: Louisiana State University Press, 1973; Cook, Adrian, *Armies of the Street: The New York City Draft Riots of 1863*. Lexington: University Press of Kentucky, 1974; Dowdey, Clifford, *Lee*. Boston: Little, Brown, 1965; Durden, Robert F., *The Gray and the Black: The Confederate Debate on Emancipation*. Baton Rouge: Louisiana State University Press, 1972; Ferris, Norman B., *The Trent Affair: A Diplomatic Crisis*. Knoxville: University of Tennessee Press, 1977; Foote, Shelby, *The Civil War* (3 Vols.). New York: Random House, 1958-1972; Gerteis, Louis S., *From Contraband to Freedman: Federal Policy Toward Southern Blacks, 1861-1865*. Westport, Conn.: Greenwood, 1973; Gilchrist, David T., and David Lewis (Eds.), *Economic Change in the Civil War Era*. Green-

ville, Del.: Eleutherian Mills-Hagley Foundation, 1965; Graebner, Norman A. (Ed.), *The Enduring Lincoln*. Urbana: University of Illinois Press, 1959; Kirwan, Albert D. (Ed.), *The Confederacy*. New York: Meridian, 1959; Leech, Margaret, *Reveille in Washington, 1860-1865*. New York: Grosset & Dunlap, 1941; Mitgang, Herbert, *The Fiery Trial: A Life of Lincoln*. New York: Viking, 1974; Myers, Robert M. (Ed.), *The Children of Pride: A True Story of Georgia and the Civil War*. New Haven, Conn.: Yale University Press, 1972; Nichols, Roy F., *The Stakes of Power*. New York: Hill & Wang, 1961; Niven, John, *Gideon Welles*. New York: Oxford University Press, 1973; Randall, James G., *Lincoln, the President: Springfield to Gettysburg*, Vols. I-IV. New York: Dodd, Mead, 1946-1955; Rawley, James A., *The Politics of Union*. Holt, Rinehart and Winston, 1974; Ripley, C. Peter, *Slaves and Freedmen in Civil War Louisiana*. Baton Rouge: Louisiana State University Press, 1976; Turner, Justin G., and Linda L. Turner (Eds.), *Mary Todd Lincoln: Her Life and Letters*. New York: Knopf, 1972; Williams, Kenneth P., *Lincoln Finds a General: A Military History of the Civil War*, Vols. I-IV. New York: Macmillan, 1949; Williams, T. Harry, *Lincoln and the Radicals*. Madison: University of Wisconsin Press, 1941; Wooster, Ralph A., *The Secession Conventions of the South*. Princeton, N.J.: Princeton University Press, 1962.

Chapter 15

Belz, Herman, *Emancipation and Equal Rights*. New York: Norton, 1978; Benedict, Michael L., *The Impeachment and Trial of Andrew Johnson*. New York: Norton, 1973; Brock, William R., *An American Crisis*. New York: St. Martin's, 1963; Buck, Paul H., *The Road to Reunion, 1865-1900*. Boston: Little, Brown, 1937; Carpenter, John A., *Sword and Olive Branch: Oliver Otis Howard*. Pittsburgh, Penn.: University of Pittsburgh Press, 1964; Current, Richard N., *Three Carpetbag Governors*. Baton Rouge: Louisiana State University Press, 1968; DuBois, William E. B., *Black Reconstruction in America, 1860-1880*. New York: Atheneum, 1969; Dunning, W. A., *Reconstruction, Political and Economic, 1865-1877*. New York: Harper & Row, 1968; Frederickson, George M., *The Black Image in the White Mind*. New York: Harper & Row, 1971; Gillette, William, *The Right to Vote: Politics and the Passage of the Fifteenth Amendment*. Baltimore: Johns Hopkins, 1965; Hershkowitz, Leo, *Tweed's New York—Another Look*. Garden City, N.Y.: Doubleday, 1977; Hesseltine, William B., *Lincoln's Plan of Reconstruction*. New York: Quadrangle, 1967 (Paper); Higgs, Robert, *Competition and Coercion: Blacks in the American Economy*. New York: Cambridge University Press, 1977; Holt, Thomas, *Black Over White: Negro Political Leadership in South Carolina During Reconstruction*. Urbana: University of Illinois Press, 1977; Hyman, Harold M. (Ed.), *New Frontiers of the American Reconstruction*. Urbana: University of Illinois Press, 1966; James, Joseph B., *The Framing of the Fourteenth Amend-*

ment. Urbana: University of Illinois Press, 1956; Kirwan, Albert D., *The Revolt of the Rednecks: Mississippi Politics, 1876–1925*. Gloucester, Mass.: Peter Smith, 1964; Kousser, J. Morgan, *The Shaping of Southern Politics: Suffrage Restriction and the Establishment of the One-Party South, 1880–1910*. New Haven, Conn.: Yale University Press, 1974; Mantell, Martin E., *Johnson, Grant, and the Politics of Reconstruction*. New York: Columbia University Press, 1973; McFeely, William S., *Yankee Stepfather: General O. O. Howard and the Freedmen*. New Haven, Conn.: Yale University Press, 1968; Mohr, James C. (Ed.), *Radical Republicans in the North: State Politics During Reconstruction*. Baltimore, Md.: Johns Hopkins University Press, 1976; Perman, Michael, *Reunion Without Compromise: The South and Reconstruction, 1865–1868*. New York: Cambridge University Press, 1973; Polakoff, Keith Ian, *The Politics of Inertia: The Election of 1876 and the End of Reconstruction*. Baton Rouge: Louisiana State University Press, 1973; Powell, Lawrence N., *New Masters: Northern Planters During the Civil War and Reconstruction*. New Haven: Yale University Press, 1980; Rabinowitz, Howard N., *Race Relations in the Urban South, 1865–1890*. New York: Oxford University Press, 1978; Ransom, Roger L., and Richard Sutch, *One Kind of Freedom: The Economic Consequences of Emancipation*. New York: Cambridge University Press, 1977; Rose, Willie Lee, *Rehearsal for Reconstruction: A Historical and Contemporary Reader*. New York: Random, 1964 (Paper); Simkins, Francis B., and Robert H. Woody, *South Carolina during Reconstruction*. Gloucester, Mass.: Peter Smith, 1932; Tindall, George B., *South Carolina Negroes, 1877–1900*. Columbia: University of South Carolina Press, 1970; Van Deusen, Glyndon, *Horace Greeley: Nineteenth-Century Crusader*. Philadelphia: University of Pennsylvania Press, 1953; Vaughn, William P., *Schools For All: The Blacks and Public School Education in the South*. Lexington: University Press of Kentucky, 1974; Wharton, Vernon L., *The Negro in Mississippi, 1865–1869*. New York: Harper & Row, 1965; Wiener, Jonathan M., *Social Origins of the New South*. Baton Rouge: Louisiana State University Press, 1978; Wiggins, Sarah Woolfolk, *The Scalawag in Alabama Politics, 1865–1881*. University: University of Alabama Press, 1977; Williamson, Joel, *After Slavery: The Negro in South Carolina During Reconstruction, 1861–1877*. Chapel Hill: University of North Carolina Press, 1965; Williamson, Joel R. (Ed.), *The Origins of Segregation*. Lexington, Mass.: Heath, 1968.

The Declaration of Independence

When in the Course of human events, it becomes necessary for one people to dissolve the political bands which have connected them with another, and to assume among the Powers of the earth, the separate and equal station to which the Laws of Nature and of Nature's God entitle them, a decent respect to the opinions of mankind requires that they should declare the causes which impel them to the separation.

We hold these truths to be self-evident, that all men are created equal, that they are endowed by their Creator with certain unalienable Rights, that among these are Life, Liberty and the pursuit of Happiness. That to secure these rights, Governments are instituted among Men, deriving their just powers from the consent of the governed, That whenever any Form of Government becomes destructive of these ends, it is the Right of the People to alter or to abolish it, and to institute new Government, laying its foundation on such principles and organizing its powers in such form, as to them shall seem most likely to effect their Safety and Happiness. Prudence, indeed, will dictate that Governments long established should not be changed for light and transient causes; and accordingly all experience hath shown, that mankind are more disposed to suffer, while evils are sufferable, than to right themselves by abolishing the forms to which they are accustomed. But when a long train of abuses and usurpations, pursuing invariably the same Object evinces a design to reduce them under absolute Despotism, it is their right, it is their duty, to throw off such Government, and to provide new Guards for their future security.—Such has been the patient sufferance of these Colonies; and such is now the necessity which constrains them to alter their former Systems of Government. The history of the present King of Great Britain is a history of repeated injuries and usurpations, all having in direct object the establishment of an absolute Tyranny over these States. To prove this, let Facts be submitted to a candid world.

He has refused his Assent to Laws, the most wholesome and necessary for the public good.

He has forbidden his Governors to pass Laws of immediate and pressing importance, unless suspended in their operation till his Assent should be obtained; and when so suspended, he has utterly neglected to attend to them.

He has refused to pass other Laws for the accommodation of large districts of people, unless those people would relinquish the right of Representation in the Legislature, a right inestimable to them and formidable to tyrants only.

He has called together legislative bodies at places unusual, uncomfortable, and distant from the depository of their public Records, for the sole purpose of fatiguing them into compliance with his measures.

He has dissolved Representative Houses repeatedly, for opposing with manly firmness his invasions on the rights of the people.

He has refused for a long time, after such dissolutions, to cause others to be elected; whereby the Legislative Powers, incapable of Annihilation, have returned to the People at large for their exercise; the State remaining in the mean time exposed to all the dangers of invasion from without, and convulsions within.

He has endeavoured to prevent the population of these States; for that purpose obstructing the Laws of Naturalization of Foreigners; refusing to pass others to encourage their migration hither, and raising the conditions of new Appropriations of Lands.

He has obstructed the Administration of Justice, by refusing his Assent to Laws for establishing Judiciary powers.

He has made Judges dependent on his Will alone, for the tenure of their offices, and the amount and payment of their salaries.

He has erected a multitude of New Offices, and sent hither swarms of Officers to harass our People, and eat out their substance.

He has kept among us in times of peace, Standing Armies without the Consent of our legislature.

He has affected to render the Military independent of and superior to the Civil power.

He has combined with others to subject us to a jurisdiction foreign to our constitution, and unacknowledged by our laws; giving his Assent to their acts of pretended Legislation:

For quartering large bodies of armed troops among us:

For protecting them, by a mock Trial, from punishment for any Murders which they should commit on the Inhabitants of these States:

For cutting off our Trade with all parts of the world:

For imposing taxes on us without our Consent:

For depriving us in many cases, of the benefits of Trial by Jury:

For transporting us beyond Seas to be tried for pretended offences:

For abolishing the free System of English Laws in a neighbouring Province, establishing therein an Arbitrary government, and enlarging its Boundaries so as to render it at once an example and fit instrument for introducing the same absolute rule into these Colonies:

For taking away our Charters, abolishing our most valuable Laws, and altering fundamentally the Forms of our Governments:

For suspending our own Legislature, and declaring themselves invested with Power to legislate for us in all cases whatsoever.

He has abdicated Government here, by declaring us out of his Protection and waging War against us.

He has plundered our seas, ravaged our Coasts, burnt our towns, and destroyed the lives of our people.

He is at this time transporting large Armies of foreign Mercenaries to compleat the works of death, desolation and tyranny, already begun with circumstances of Cruelty & perfidy scarcely paralleled in the most barbarous ages, and totally unworthy the Head of a civilized nation.

He has constrained our fellow Citizens taken Captive on the high Seas to bear Arms against their Country, to become the executioners of their friends and Brethren, or to fall themselves by their Hands.

He has excited domestic insurrections amongst us, and has endeavoured to bring on the inhabitants of our frontiers, the merciless Indian Savages, whose known rule of warfare, is an undistinguished destruction of all ages, sexes and conditions.

In every stage of these Oppressions We have Petitioned for Redress in the most humble terms: Our repeated Petitions have been answered only by repeated injury. A Prince, whose character is thus marked by every act which may define a Tyrant, is unfit to be the ruler of a free People.

Nor have We been wanting in attention to our British brethren. We have warned them from time to time of attempts by their legislature to extend an unwarrantable jurisdiction over us. We have reminded them of the circumstances of our emigration and settlement here. We have appealed to their native justice and magnanimity, and we have conjured them by the ties of our common kindred to disavow these usurpations, which, would inevitably interrupt our connections and correspondence. They too have been deaf to the voice of justice and of consanguinity. We must, therefore, acquiesce in the necessity, which denounces our Separation, and hold them, as we hold the rest of mankind, Enemies in War, in Peace Friends.

We, therefore, the Representatives of the united States of America, in General Congress, Assembled, appealing to the Supreme Judge of the world for the rectitude of our intentions, do, in the Name, and by Authority of the good People of these Colonies, solemnly publish and declare, That these United Colonies are, and of Right ought to be Free and Independent States; that they are Absolved from all Allegiance to the British Crown, and that all political connection between them and the State of Great Britain, is and ought to be totally dissolved; and that as Free and Independent States, they have full Power to levy War, conclude Peace, contract Alliances, establish Commerce, and to do all other Acts and Things which Independent States may of right do. And for the support of this Declaration, with a firm reliance on the protection of divine Providence, we mutually pledge to each other our Lives, our Fortunes and our sacred Honor.

The Constitution of the United States

We the people of the United States, in Order to form a more perfect Union, establish Justice, insure domestic Tranquility, provide for the common defence, promote the general Welfare, and secure the Blessings of Liberty to ourselves and our Posterity, do ordain and establish this CONSTITUTION for the United States of America.

Article 1

Section 1 All legislative Powers herein granted shall be vested in a Congress of the United States, which shall consist of a Senate and House of Representatives.

Section 2 The House of Representatives shall be composed of Members chosen every second Year by the People of the several States, and the Electors in each State shall have the Qualifications requisite for Electors of the most numerous Branch of the State Legislature.

No Person shall be a Representative who shall not have attained to the Age of twenty-five Years, and been seven Years a Citizen of the United States, and who shall not, when elected, be an Inhabitant of that State in which he shall be chosen.

Representatives and direct Taxes shall be apportioned among the several States which may be included within this Union, according to their respective Numbers, which shall be determined by adding to the whole Number of free Persons, including those bound to Service for a Term of Years, and excluding Indians not taxed, three-fifths of all other Persons. The actual Enumeration shall be made within three Years after the first Meeting of the Congress of the United States, and within every subsequent Term of ten Years, in such Manner as they shall by Law direct. The Number of Representatives shall not exceed one for every thirty Thousand, but each State shall have at Least one Representative; and until such enumeration shall be made, the State of New Hampshire shall be entitled to chuse three, Massachusetts eight, Rhode-Island and Providence Plantations one, Connecticut five, New-York six, New Jersey four, Pennsylvania eight, Delaware one, Maryland six, Virginia ten, North Carolina five, South Carolina five, and Georgia three.

When vacancies happen in the Representation from any State, the Executive Authority thereof shall issue Writs of Election to fill such Vacancies.

The House of Representatives shall chuse their Speaker and other Officers; and shall have the sole Power of Impeachment.

Section 3 The Senate of the United States shall be composed of two Senators from each State, chosen by the Legislature thereof, for six Years; and each Senator shall have one Vote.

Immediately after they shall be assembled in Consequence of the first Election, they shall be divided as equally as may be into three Classes. The Seats of the Senators of the first Class shall be vacated at the Expiration of the second Year, of the second Class at the Expiration of the fourth Year, and of the third Class at the Expiration of the sixth Year, so that one-third may be chosen every second Year; and if Vacancies happen by Resignation, or otherwise, during the Recess of the Legislature of any State, the Executive thereof may make temporary Appointments until the next Meeting of the Legislature, which shall then fill such Vacancies.

No Person shall be a Senator who shall not have attained to the Age of thirty Years, and been nine Years a Citizen of the United States, and who shall not, when elected, be an Inhabitant of that State in which he shall be chosen.

The Vice President of the United States shall be President of the Senate, but shall have no vote, unless they be equally divided.

The Senate shall chuse their other Officers, and also a President pro tempore, in the absence of the Vice President, or when he shall exercise the Office of the President of the United States.

The Senate shall have the sole Power to try all Impeachments. When sitting for that purpose, they shall be on Oath or Affirmation. When the President of the United States is tried, the Chief Justice shall preside: And no person shall be convicted without the Concurrence of two-thirds of the Members present.

Judgment in Cases of Impeachment shall not extend further than to removal from Office, and disqualification to hold and enjoy any Office of honor, Trust, or Profit under the United States: but the Party convicted shall nevertheless be liable and subject to Indictment, Trial, Judgment, and Punishment, according to Law.

Section 4 The Times, Places and Manner of holding Elections for Senators and Representatives, shall be prescribed in each state by the Legislature thereof; but the Congress may at any time by Law make or alter such Regulations, except as to the Places of Chusing Senators.

The Congress shall assemble at least once in every Year, and such Meeting shall be on the first Monday in December, unless they shall by Law appoint a different Day.

Section 5 Each House shall be the Judge of the Elections, Returns and Qualifications of its own Members, and a Majority of each shall constitute a Quorum to do Business; but a smaller number may adjourn from day to day, and may be authorized to compel the Attendance of absent Members, in such Manner, and under such Penalties, as each House may provide.

Each House may determine the Rules of its Proceedings, punish its Members for disorderly Behaviour, and, with the Concurrence of two-thirds, expel a Member.

Each House shall keep a Journal of its Proceedings, and from time to time publish the same, excepting such Parts as may in their Judgment require Secrecy; and the Yeas and Nays of the Members of either House on any question shall, at the Desire of one-fifth of those Present, be entered on the Journal.

Neither House, during the Session of Congress, shall, without the Consent of the other, adjourn for more than three days, nor to any other Place than that in which the two Houses shall be sitting.

Section 6   The Senators and Representatives shall receive a Compensation for their Services, to be ascertained by Law, and paid out of the Treasury of the United States. They shall in all Cases, except Treason, Felony, and Breach of the Peace, be privileged from Arrest during their Attendance at the Session of their respective Houses, and in going to and returning from the same; and for any speech or Debate in either House, they shall not be questioned in any other Place.

No Senator or Representative shall, during the Time for which he was elected, be appointed to any civil Office under the Authority of the United States, which shall have been created, or the Emoluments whereof shall have been increased, during such time; and no Person holding any Office under the United States shall be a Member of either House during his continuance in Office.

Section 7   All Bills for raising Revenue shall originate in the House of Representatives; but the Senate may propose or concur with Amendments as on other Bills.

Every Bill which shall have passed the House of Representatives and the Senate, shall, before it become a Law, be presented to the President of the United States; If he approve he shall sign it, but if not he shall return it, with his Objections, to that House in which it shall have originated, who shall enter the Objections at large on their Journal, and proceed to reconsider it. If after such Reconsideration two-thirds of that House shall agree to pass the Bill, it shall be sent, together with the Objections, to the other House, by which it shall likewise be reconsidered, and if approved by two-thirds of that House, it shall become a Law. But in all such Cases the Votes of both Houses shall be determined by Yeas and Nays, and the Names of the Persons voting for and against the Bill shall be entered on the Journal of each House respectively. If any Bill shall not be returned by the President within ten Days (Sundays excepted) after it shall have been presented to him, the Same shall be a Law, in like Manner as if he had signed it, unless the Congress by their Adjournment prevent its Return, in which case it shall not be a Law.

Every Order, Resolution, or Vote to which the Concurrence of the Senate and House of Representatives may be necessary (except on a question of Adjournment) shall be presented to the President of the United States; and before the Same shall take Effect, shall be approved by him, or being disapproved by him, shall be repassed by two-thirds of the Senate and House of Representatives, according to the Rules and Limitations prescribed in the Case of a Bill.

Section 8   The Congress shall have Power To lay and collect Taxes, Duties, Imposts and Excises, to pay the Debts and provide for the common Defence and general Welfare of the United States, but all Duties, Imposts and Excises shall be uniform throughout the United States;

To borrow money on the credit of the United States;

To regulate Commerce with foreign Nations, and among the several States, and with the Indian Tribes;

To establish an uniform Rule of Naturalization, and uniform Laws on the subject of Bankruptcies throughout the United States;

To coin Money, regulate the Value thereof, and of foreign Coin, and fix the Standard of Weights and Measures;

To provide for the Punishment of counterfeiting the Securities and current Coin of the United States;

To establish Post Offices and post Roads;

To promote the Progress of Science and useful Arts, by securing for limited Times to Authors and Inventors the exclusive Right to their respective Writings and Discoveries;

To constitute Tribunals inferior to the Supreme Court;

To define and punish Piracies and Felonies committed on the high Seas, and Offenses against the Law of Nations;

To declare War, grant Letters of Marque and Reprisal, and make Rules concerning Captures on Land and Water;

To raise and support Armies, but no Appropriation of Money to that Use shall be for a longer Term than two Years;

To provide and maintain a Navy;

To make Rules for the Government and Regulation of the land and naval forces;

To provide for calling forth the Militia to execute the Laws of the Union, suppress Insurrections and repel Invasions;

To provide for organizing, arming, and disciplining the Militia, and for governing such Part of them as may be employed in the Service of the United States, reserving to the States respectively, the Appointment of the Officers, and the Authority of training the Militia according to the discipline prescribed by Congress;

To exercise exclusive Legislation in all Cases whatsoever, over such District (not exceeding ten Miles square) as may, by Cession of particular States, and the acceptance of Congress, become the Seat of Government of the United States, and to exercise like Authority over all Places purchased by the Consent of the Legislature of the State in which the Same shall be, for the Erection of Forts, Magazines, Arsenals, dock-Yards, and other needful Buildings;—And

To make all Laws which shall be necessary and proper for carrying into Execution the foregoing Powers, and all other Powers vested by this Constitution in the Government of the United States, or in any Department or Officer thereof.

Section 9   The Migration or Importation of such Persons as any of the States now existing shall think proper to admit, shall not be prohibited by the Congress prior to the Year one thousand eight hundred and eight, but a tax or duty may be imposed on such Importation, not exceeding ten dollars for each Person.

The privilege of the Writ of Habeas Corpus shall not be suspended, unless when in Cases of Rebellion or Invasion the public Safety may require it.

No Bill of Attainder or ex post facto Law shall be passed.

No Capitation, or other direct, Tax shall be laid unless in Proportion to the Census or Enumeration herein before directed to be taken.

No Tax or Duty shall be laid on Articles exported from any State.

No Preference shall be given by any Regulation of Revenue to the Ports of one State over those of another: nor shall Vessels bound to, or from, one State, be obliged to enter, clear, or pay Duties in another.

No Money shall be drawn from the Treasury, but in Consequence of Appropriations made by Law; and a regular Statement and Account of the Receipts and Expenditures of all public Money shall be published from time to time.

No Title of Nobility shall be granted by the United States: And no Person holding any Office of Profit or Trust under them, shall, without the Consent of the Congress, accept of any present, Emolument, Office, or Title, of any kind whatever, from any King, Prince, or foreign State.

Section 10 No State shall enter into any Treaty, Alliance, or Confederation; grant Letters of Marque and Reprisal; coin Money; emit Bills of Credit; make any Thing but gold and silver Coin a Tender in Payment of Debts; pass any Bill of Attainder, ex post facto Law, or Law impairing the Obligation of Contracts, or grant any Title of Nobility.

No state shall, without the Consent of the Congress, lay any Imposts or Duties on Imports or Exports, except what may be absolutely necessary for executing its inspection Laws: and the net Produce of all Duties and Imposts, laid by any State on Imports or Exports, shall be for the Use of the Treasury of the United States; and all such Laws shall be subject to the Revision and Control of the Congress.

No State shall, without the Consent of Congress, lay any duty of Tonnage, keep Troops, or Ships of War in time of Peace, enter into any Agreement or Compact with another State, or with a foreign Power, or engage in War, unless actually invaded, or in such imminent Danger as will not admit of delay.

Article II

Section 1 The executive Power shall be vested in a President of the United States of America. He shall hold his Office during the Term of four Years, and, together with the Vice President, chosen for the same Term, be elected, as follows:

Each State shall appoint, in such Manner as the Legislature thereof may direct, a Number of Electors, equal to the whole Number of Senators and Representatives to which the State may be entitled in the Congress: but no Senator or Representative, or Person holding an Office of Trust or Profit under the United States, shall be appointed an Elector.

The Electors shall meet in their respective States, and vote by Ballot for two persons, of whom one at least shall not be an Inhabitant of the same State with themselves. And they shall make a List of all the Persons voted for, and of the Number of Votes for each; which List they shall sign and certify, and transmit sealed to the Seat of the Government of the United States, directed to the President of the Senate. The President of the Senate shall, in the Presence of the Senate and House of Representatives, open all the Certificates, and the Votes shall then be counted. The Person having the greatest Number of Votes shall be the President, if such Number be a Majority of the whole Number of Electors appointed; and if there be more than one who have such Majority, and have an equal Number of Votes, then the House of Representatives shall immediately chuse by Ballot one of them for President; and if no Person have a Majority, then from the five highest on the List the said House shall in like Manner chuse the President. But in chusing the President, the Votes shall be taken by States, the Representation from each State having one Vote; a quorum for this Purpose shall consist of a Member or Members from two-thirds of the States, and a Majority of all the States shall be necessary to a Choice. In every Case, after the Choice of the President, the Person having the greatest Number of Votes of the Electors shall be the Vice President. But if there should remain two or more who have equal votes, the Senate shall chuse from them by Ballot the Vice President.

The Congress may determine the Time of chusing the Electors, and the Day on which they shall give their Votes; which Day shall be the same throughout the United States.

No person except a natural-born Citizen, or a Citizen of the United States, at the time of the Adoption of this Constitution, shall be eligible to the Office of President; neither shall any Person be eligible to that Office who shall not have attained to the Age of thirty-five Years, and been fourteen Years a Resident within the United States.

In Case of the Removal of the President from Office, or of his Death, Resignation, or Inability to discharge the Powers and Duties of the said Office, the same shall devolve on the Vice President, and the Congress may by Law provide for the Case of Removal, Death, Resignation, or Inability, both of the President and Vice President, declaring what Officer shall then act as President, and such Officer shall act accordingly, until the Disability be removed, or a President shall be elected.

The President shall, at stated Times, receive for his Services a Compensation, which shall neither be increased nor diminished during the Period for which he shall have been elected, and he shall not receive within that Period any other Emolument from the United States, or any of them.

Before he enter on the Execution of his Office, he shall take the following Oath or Affirmation:—"I do solemnly swear (or affirm) that I will faithfully execute the Office of President of the United States, and will, to the best of my Ability, preserve, protect, and defend the Constitution of the United States."

Section 2 The President shall be Commander in Chief of the Army and Navy of the United States, and of the Militia of the several States, when called into the actual Service of the United States; he may require the Opinion, in writing, of the principal Officer in each of the executive Departments, upon any subject relating to the Duties of their respective Offices, and he shall have Power to Grant Reprieves and Pardons for Offences against the United States, except in Cases of Impeachment.

He shall have Power, by and with the Advice and Consent of the Senate, to make Treaties, provided two-thirds of the Senators present concur; and he shall nominate, and by and with the Advice and Consent of the Senate, shall appoint Ambassadors, other public Ministers and Consuls, Judges of the supreme Court, and all other Officers of the United States, whose Appointments are not herein otherwise provided for, and which shall be established by Law: but the Congress may by Law vest the Appointment of such inferior Officers, as they think proper, in the President alone, in the Courts of Law, or in the Heads of Departments.

The President shall have Power to fill up all Vacancies that may happen during the Recess of the Senate, by granting Commissions which shall expire at the End of their next Session.

Section 3 He shall from time to time give to the Congress Information of the State of the Union, and recommend to their Consideration such Measures as he shall judge necessary and expedient; he may, on extraordinary occasions, convene both Houses, or either of them, and in Case of Disagreement between them, with respect to the Time of Adjournment, he may adjourn them to such Time as he shall think proper; he shall receive Ambassadors and other public Ministers; he shall take Care that the Laws be faithfully executed, and shall Commission all the Officers of the United States.

Section 4 The President, Vice President and all civil Officers of the United States, shall be removed from Office on Impeachment for, and Conviction of, Treason, Bribery, or other high Crimes and Misdemeanors.

Article III

Section 1 The judicial Power of the United States, shall be vested in one supreme Court, and in such inferior Courts as the Congress may from time to time ordain and establish. The Judges, both of the supreme and inferior Courts, shall hold their Offices during good Behaviour, and shall, at stated Times, receive for their Services, a Compensation, which shall not be diminished during their Continuance in Office.

Section 2 The judicial Power shall extend to all Cases, in Law and Equity, arising under this Constitution, the Laws of the United States, and Treaties made, or which shall be made, under their Authority;—to all Cases affecting Ambassadors, other public Ministers and Consuls;—to all Cases of admiralty and maritime Jurisdiction;—to Controversies to which the United States shall be a Party;—to Controversies between two or more States;—between a State and Citizens of another State;—between Citizens of the same State claiming Lands under Grants of different States, and between a State, or the Citizens thereof, and foreign States, Citizens or Subjects.

In all Cases affecting Ambassadors, other public Ministers and Consuls, and those in which a State shall be Party, the supreme Court shall have original Jurisdiction. In all the other Cases before mentioned, the supreme Court shall have appellate Jurisdiction, both as to Law and Fact, with such Exceptions, and under such Regulations as the Congress shall make.

The trial of all Crimes, except in Cases of Impeachment, shall be by Jury; and such Trial shall be held in the State where the said Crimes shall have been committed; but when not committed within any State, the Trial shall be at such Place or Places as the Congress may by Law have directed.

Section 3 Treason against the United States, shall consist only in levying War against them, or in adhering to their Enemies, giving them Aid and Comfort. No Person shall be convicted of Treason unless on the Testimony of two Witnesses to the same overt Act, or on Confession in open Court.

The Congress shall have power to declare the Punishment of Treason, but no Attainder of Treason shall work Corruption of Blood, or Forfeiture except during the Life of the Person attainted.

Article IV

Section 1 Full Faith and Credit shall be given in each State to the public Acts, Records, and judicial Proceedings of every other State. And the Congress may by general Laws prescribe the Manner in which such Acts, Records and Proceedings shall be proved, and the Effect thereof.

Section 2 The Citizens of each State shall be entitled to all Privileges and Immunities of Citizens in the several States.

A Person charged in any State with Treason, Felony, or other Crime, who shall flee from Justice, and be found in another State, shall on demand of the executive Authority of the State from which he fled, be delivered up, to be removed to the State having Jurisdiction of the crime.

No Person held to Service or Labour in one State, under the Laws thereof, escaping into another, shall, in Consequence of any Law or Regulation therein, be discharged from such Service or Labour, but shall be delivered up on Claim of the Party to whom such Service or Labour may be due.

Section 3 New States may be admitted by the Congress into this Union; but no new State shall be formed or erected within the Jurisdiction of any other State; nor any State be formed by the Junction of two or more States, or parts of States, without the Consent of the Legislatures of the States concerned as well as of the Congress.

The Congress shall have Power to dispose of and make all needful Rules and Regulations respecting the Territory or other Property belonging to the United States; and nothing in this Constitution shall be so construed as to Prejudice any Claims of the United States, or of any particular State.

Section 4 The United States shall guarantee to every State in this Union a Republican Form of Government, and shall protect each of them against Invasion; and on Application of the Legislature, or of the Executive (when the Legislature cannot be convened) against domestic Violence.

Article V

The Congress, whenever two-thirds of both Houses shall deem it necessary, shall propose Amendments to this Constitution, or, on the Application of the Legislatures of two-thirds of the several States, shall call a Convention for proposing Amendments, which, in either Case, shall be valid to all Intents and Purposes, as part of this Constitution, when ratified by the Legislatures of three-fourths of the several States, or by Conventions in three-fourths thereof, as the one or the other Mode of Ratification may be proposed by the Congress; Provided that no Amendment which may be made prior to the Year One thousand eight hundred and eight shall in any Manner affect the first and fourth Clauses in the Ninth Section of the first Article; and that no State, without its Consent, shall be deprived of its equal Suffrage in the Senate.

Article VI

All Debts contracted and Engagements entered into, before the Adoption of this Constitution, shall be as valid against the United States under this Constitution, as under the Confederation.

This Constitution, and the Laws of the United States which shall be made in Pursuance thereof; and all Treaties made, or which shall be made, under the Authority of the United States, shall be the supreme Law of the Land; and the Judges in every State shall be bound thereby, any Thing in the Constitution or Laws of any State to the Contrary notwithstanding.

The Senators and Representatives before mentioned, and the Members of the several State Legislatures, and all executive and judicial Officers, both of the United States and of the several States, shall be bound by Oath or Affirmation to support this Constitution; but no religious Test shall ever be required as a qualification to any Office or public Trust under the United States.

Article VII

The Ratification of the Conventions of nine States shall be sufficient for the Establishment of this Constitution between the States so ratifying the same.

Done in Convention by the Unanimous Consent of the States present the Seventeenth Day of September in the Year of our Lord one thousand seven hundred and Eighty seven, and of the Independence of the United States of America the Twelfth. In Witness whereof We have hereunto subscribed our Names.

Articles in Addition to, and Amendment of, the Constitution of the United States of America, Proposed by Congress, and Ratified by the Legislatures of the Several States, Pursuant to the Fifth Article of the Original Constitution.

Amendment I [1791]

Congress shall make no law respecting an establishment of religion, or prohibiting the free exercise thereof; or abridging the freedom of speech, or of the press; or the right of the people peaceably to assemble, and to petition the Government for a redress of grievances.

Amendment II [1791]

A well regulated Militia, being necessary to the security of a free State, the right of the people to keep and bear Arms, shall not be infringed.

Amendment III [1791]

No Soldier shall, in time of peace, be quartered in any house, without the consent of the Owner, nor in time of war, but in a manner to be prescribed by law.

Amendment IV [1791]

The right of the people to be secure in their persons, houses, papers, and effects, againt unreasonable searches and seizures, shall not be violated, and no Warrants shall issue, but upon probable cause, supported by Oath or affirmation, and particularly describing the place to be searched, and the persons or things to be seized.

Amendment V [1791]

No person shall be held to answer for a capital or otherwise infamous crime, unless on a presentment or indictment of a Grand Jury, except in cases arising in the land or naval forces, or in the Militia, when in actual service in time of War or public danger; nor shall any person be subject for the same offence to be twice put in jeopardy of life or limb; nor shall be compelled in any criminal case to be a witness against himself, nor be deprived of life, liberty, or property, without due process of law; nor shall private property be taken for public use, without just compensation.

Amendment VI [1791]

In all criminal prosecutions, the accused shall enjoy the right to a speedy and public trial, by an impartial jury of the State and district wherein the crime shall have been committed, which district shall have been previously ascertained by law, and to be informed of the nature and cause of the accusation; to be confronted with the witnesses against him; to have compulsory process for obtaining witnesses in his favor, and to have the Assistance of Counsel for his defence.

Amendment VII [1791]

In Suits at common law, where the value in controversy shall exceed twenty dollars, the right of trial by jury shall be preserved, and no fact tried by a jury, shall be otherwise re-examined in any Court of the United States, than according to the rules of the common law.

Amendment VIII [1791]

Excessive bail shall not be required, nor excessive fines imposed, nor cruel and unusual punishments inflicted.

Amendment IX [1791]

The enumeration in the Constitution, of certain rights, shall not be construed to deny or disparage others retained by the people.

Amendment X [1791]

The powers not delegated to the United States by the Constitution, nor prohibited by it to the States, are reserved to the States respectively, or to the people.

Amendment XI [1798]

The Judicial power of the United States shall not be construed to extend to any suit in law or equity, commenced or prosecuted against one of the United States by Citizens of another State, or by Citizens or Subjects of any Foreign State.

Amendment XII [1804]

The Electors shall meet in their respective States and vote by ballot for President and Vice President, one of whom, at least,

shall not be an inhabitant of the same States with themselves; they shall name in their ballots the person voted for as President, and in distinct ballots the person voted for as Vice President, and they shall make distinct lists of all persons voted for as President, and of all persons voted for as Vice President, and of the number of votes for each, which lists they shall sign and certify, and transmit sealed to the seat of the government of the United States, directed to the President of the Senate; —The President of the Senate shall, in the presence of the Senate and House of Representatives, open all the certificates and the votes shall then be counted;—The person having the greatest number of votes for President, shall be the President, if such number be a majority of the whole number of Electors appointed; and if no person have such majority, then from the persons having the highest numbers not exceeding three on the list of those voted for as President, the House of Representatives shall choose immediately, by ballot, the President. But in choosing the President, the votes shall be taken by states, the representation from each state having one vote; a quorum for this purpose shall consist of a member or members from two-thirds of the states, and a majority of all the states shall be necessary to a choice. And if the House of Representatives shall not choose a President whenever the right of choice shall devolve upon them, before the fourth day of March next following, then the Vice President shall act as President, as in the case of the death or other constitutional disability of the President.—The person having the greatest number of votes as Vice President, shall be the Vice President, if such number be a majority of the whole number of Electors appointed, and if no person have a majority, then from the two highest numbers on the list, the Senate shall choose the Vice President; a quorum for the purpose shall consist of two-thirds of the whole number of Senators, and a majority of the whole number shall be necessary to a choice. But no person constitutionally ineligible to the office of President shall be eligible to that of Vice President of the United States.

Amendment XIII [1865]

Section 1 Neither slavery nor involuntary servitude, except as a punishment for crime whereof the party shall have been duly convicted, shall exist within the United States, or any place subject to their jurisdiction.

Section 2 Congress shall have power to enforce this article by appropriate legislation.

Amendment XIV [1868]

Section 1 All persons born or naturalized in the United States, and subject to the jurisdiction thereof, are citizens of the United States and of the State wherein they reside. No State shall make or enforce any law which shall abridge the privileges or immunities of citizens of the United States; nor shall any State deprive any person of life, liberty, or property, without due process of law; nor deny to any person within its jurisdiction the equal protection of the laws.

Section 2 Representatives shall be apportioned among the several States according to their respective numbers, counting the whole number of persons in each State, excluding Indians not taxed. But when the right to vote at any election for the choice of electors for President and Vice President of the United States, Representatives in Congress, the Executive and Judicial officers of a State, or the members of the Legislature thereof, is denied to any of the male inhabitants of such State, being twenty-one years of age, and citizens of the United States, or in any way abridged, except for participation in rebellion, or other crime, the basis of representation therein shall be reduced in the proportion which the number of such male citizens shall bear to the whole number of male citizens twenty-one years of age in such State.

Section 3 No person shall be a Senator or Representative in Congress, or elector of President and Vice President, or hold any office, civil or military, under the United States, or under any State, who, having previously taken an oath, as a member of Congress, or as an officer of the United States, or as a member of any State legislature, or as an executive or judicial officer of any State, to support the Constitution of the United States, shall have engaged in insurrection or rebellion against the same, or given aid or comfort to the enemies thereof. But Congress may by a vote of two-thirds of each House, remove such disability.

Section 4 The validity of the public debt of the United States, authorized by law, including debts incurred for payment of pensions and bounties for services in suppressing insurrection or rebellion, shall not be questioned. But neither the United States nor any State shall assume or pay any debt or obligation incurred in aid of insurrection or rebellion against the United States, or any claim for the loss or emancipation of any slave; but all such debts, obligations, and claims shall be held illegal and void.

Section 5 The Congress shall have the power to enforce, by appropriate legislation, the provisions of this article.

Amendment XV [1870]

Section 1 The right of citizens of the United States to vote shall not be denied or abridged by the United States or by any State on account of race, color, or previous condition of servitude—

Section 2 The Congress shall have power to enforce this article by appropriate legislation.

Amendment XVI [1913]

The Congress shall have power to lay and collect taxes on incomes, from whatever source derived, without apportionment among the several States, and without regard to any census or enumeration.

Amendment XVII [1913]

The Senate of the United States shall be composed of two Senators from each State, elected by the people thereof, for six years; and each Senator shall have one vote. The electors in each State shall have the qualifications requisite for electors of the most numerous branch of the State legislatures.

When vacancies happen in the representation of any State in the Senate, the executive authority of such State shall issue writs of election to fill such vacancies: *Provided*, That the legislature of any State may empower the executive thereof to make temporary appointments until the people fill the vacancies by election as the legislature may direct.

This amendment shall not be so construed as to affect the election or term of any Senator chosen before it becomes valid as part of the Constitution.

Amendment XVIII [1919]

Section 1 After one year from the ratification of this article the manufacture, sale, or transportation of intoxicating liquors within, the importation thereof into, or the exportation thereof from the United States and all territory subject to the jurisdiction thereof for beverage purposes is hereby prohibited.

Section 2 The Congress and the several States shall have concurrent power to enforce this article by appropriate legislation.

Section 3 This article shall be inoperative unless it shall have been ratified as an amendment to the Constitution by the legislatures of the several States, as provided in the Constitution, within seven years from the date of the submission hereof to the States by the Congress.

Amendment XIX [1920]

The right of citizens of the United States to vote shall not be denied or abridged by the United States or by any State on account of sex.

Congress shall have power to enforce this article by appropriate legislation.

Amendment XX [1933]

Section 1 The terms of the President and Vice President shall end at noon on the 20th day of January, and the terms of Senators and Representatives at noon on the 3d day of January, of the years in which such terms would have ended if this article had not been ratified; and the terms of their successors shall then begin.

Section 2 The Congress shall assemble at least once in every year, and such meeting shall begin at noon on the 3d day of January, unless they shall by law appoint a different day.

Section 3 If, at the time fixed for the beginning of the term of the President, the President elect shall have died, the Vice President elect shall become President. If a President shall not have been chosen before the time fixed for the beginning of his term, or if the President elect shall have failed to qualify, then the Vice President elect shall act as President until a President shall have qualified; and the Congress may by law provide for the case wherein neither a President elect nor a Vice President elect shall have qualified, declaring who shall then act as President, or the manner in which one who is to act shall be selected, and such person shall act accordingly until a President or Vice President shall have qualified.

Section 4 The Congress may by law provide for the case of the death of any of the persons from whom the House of Representatives may choose a President whenever the right of choice shall have devolved upon them, and for the case of the death of any of the persons from whom the Senate may choose a Vice President whenever the right of choice shall have devolved upon them.

Section 5 Sections 1 and 2 shall take effect on the 15th day of October following the ratification of this article.

Section 6 This article shall be inoperative unless it shall have been ratified as an amendment to the Constitution by the legislatures of three-fourths of the several States within seven years from the date of its submission.

Amendment XXI [1933]

Section 1 The eighteenth article of amendment to the Constitution of the United States is hereby repealed.

Section 2 The transportation or importation into any State, Territory, or possession of the United States for delivery or use therein of intoxicating liquors, in violation of the laws thereof, is hereby prohibited.

Section 3 This article shall be inoperative unless it shall have been ratified as an amendment to the Constitution by conventions in the several States, as provided in the Constitution, within seven years from the date of the submission hereof to the States by the Congress.

Amendment XXII [1951]

No person shall be elected to the office of the President more than twice, and no person who has held the office of President, or acted as President, for more than two years of a term to which some other person was elected President shall be elected to the office of the President more than once.

But this Article shall not apply to any person holding the office of President when this Article was proposed by the Congress, and shall not prevent any person who may be holding the office of President, or acting as President, during the term within which this Article becomes operative from holding the office of President or acting as President during the remainder of such term.

Amendment XXIII [1961]

Section 1 The District constituting the seat of Government of the United States shall appoint in such manner as the Congress may direct:

A number of electors of President and Vice President equal to the whole number of Senators and Representatives in Congress to which the District would be entitled if it were a State, but in no event more than the least populous State; they shall be in addition to those appointed by the States, but they shall be considered, for the purposes of the election of President and Vice President, to be electors appointed by a State; and they shall meet in the District and perform such duties as provided by the twelfth article of amendment.

Section 2 The Congress shall have power to enforce this article by appropriate legislation.

Amendment XXIV [1964]

Section 1 The right of citizens of the United States to vote in any primary or other election for President or Vice President, for electors for President or Vice President, or for Senator or Representative in Congress, shall not be denied or abridged by the United States or any State by reason of failure to pay any poll tax or other tax.

Section 2 The Congress shall have the power to enforce this article by appropriate legislation.

Amendment XXV [1967]

Section 1 In case of the removal of the President from office or his death or resignation, the Vice President shall become President.

Section 2 Whenever there is a vacancy in the office of the Vice President, the President shall nominate a Vice President who shall take the office upon confirmation by a majority vote of both houses of Congress.

Section 3 Whenever the President transmits to the President pro tempore of the Senate and the Speaker of the House of Representatives his written declaration that he is unable to discharge the powers and duties of his office, and until he transmits to them a written declaration to the contrary, such powers and duties shall be discharged by the Vice President as Acting President.

Section 4 Whenever the Vice President and a majority of either the principal officers of the executive departments, or of such other body as Congress may by law provide, transmit to the President pro tempore of the Senate and the Speaker of the House of Representatives their written declaration that the President is unable to discharge the powers and duties of his office, the Vice President shall immediately assume the powers and duties of the office as Acting President.

Thereafter, when the President transmits to the President pro tempore of the Senate and the Speaker of the House of Representatives his written declaration that no inability exists, he shall resume the powers and duties of his office unless the Vice President and a majority of either the principal officers of the executive departments, or of such other body as Congress may by law provide, transmit within four days to the President pro tempore of the Senate and the Speaker of the House of Representatives their written declaration that the President is unable to discharge the powers and duties of his office. Thereupon Congress shall decide the issue, assembling within forty-eight hours for that purpose if not in session. If the Congress, within twenty-one days after receipt of the latter written declaration, or, if Congress is not in session, within twenty-one days after Congress is required to assemble, determines by two-thirds vote of both houses that the President is unable to discharge the powers and duties of his office, the Vice President shall continue to discharge the same as Acting President; otherwise, the President shall resume the powers and duties of his office.

Amendment XXVI [1971]

Section 1 The right of citizens of the United States, who are eighteen years of age or older, to vote shall not be denied or abridged by the United States or any state on account of age.

Section 2 The Congress shall have the power to enforce this article by appropriate legislation.

Presidential Elections

Year	Candidates	Party	Popular vote	Electoral vote
1789	**George Washington**			69
	John Adams			34
	Others			35
1792	**George Washington**			132
	John Adams			77
	George Clinton			50
	Others			5
1796	**John Adams**	Federalist		71
	Thomas Jefferson	Democratic-Republican		68
	Thomas Pinckney	Federalist		59
	Aaron Burr	Democratic-Republican		30
	Others			48
1800	**Thomas Jefferson**	Democratic-Republican		73
	Aaron Burr	Democratic-Republican		73
	John Adams	Federalist		65
	Charles C. Pinckney	Federalist		64
1804	**Thomas Jefferson**	Democratic-Republican		162
	Charles C. Pinckney	Federalist		14
1808	**James Madison**	Democratic-Republican		122
	Charles C. Pinckney	Federalist		47
	George Clinton	Independent-Republican		6
1812	**James Madison**	Democratic-Republican		128
	DeWitt Clinton	Federalist		89
1816	**James Monroe**	Democratic-Republican		183
	Rufus King	Federalist		34
1820	**James Monroe**	Democratic-Republican		231
	John Quincy Adams	Independent-Republican		1
1824	**John Quincy Adams**	Democratic-Republican	108,740	84
	Andrew Jackson	Democratic-Republican	153,544	99
	Henry Clay	Democratic-Republican	47,136	37
	William H. Crawford	Democratic-Republican	46,618	41
1828	**Andrew Jackson**	Democratic	647,231	178
	John Quincy Adams	National Republican	509,097	83
1832	**Andrew Jackson**	Democratic	687,502	219
	Henry Clay	National Republican	530,189	49
	William Wirt	Anti-Masonic	33,108	7
	John Floyd	National Republican		11
1836	**Martin Van Buren**	Democratic	761,549	170
	William H. Harrison	Whig	549,567	73
	Hugh L. White	Whig	145,396	26
	Daniel Webster	Whig	41,287	14

Year	Candidates	Party	Popular vote	Electoral vote
1840	**William H. Harrison** (**John Tyler**, 1841)	Whig	1,275,017	234
	Martin Van Buren	Democratic	1,128,702	60
1844	**James K. Polk**	Democratic	1,337,243	170
	Henry Clay	Whig	1,299,068	105
	James G. Birney	Liberty	62,300	
1848	**Zachary Taylor** (**Millard Fillmore**, 1850)	Whig	1,360,101	163
	Lewis Cass	Democratic	1,220,544	127
	Martin Van Buren	Free Soil	291,263	
1852	**Franklin Pierce**	Democratic	1,601,474	254
	Winfield Scott	Whig	1,386,578	42
1856	**James Buchanan**	Democratic	1,838,169	174
	John C. Frémont	Republican	1,335,264	114
	Millard Fillmore	American	874,534	8
1860	**Abraham Lincoln**	Republican	1,865,593	180
	Stephen A. Douglas	Democratic	1,382,713	12
	John C. Breckinridge	Democratic	848,356	72
	John Bell	Constitutional Union	592,906	39
1864	**Abraham Lincoln** (**Andrew Johnson**, 1865)	Republican	2,206,938	212
	George B. McClellan	Democratic	1,803,787	21
1868	**Ulysses S. Grant**	Republican	3,013,421	214
	Horatio Seymour	Democratic	2,706,829	80
1872	**Ulysses S. Grant**	Republican	3,596,745	286
	Horace Greeley	Democratic	2,843,446	66
1876	**Rutherford B. Hayes**	Republican	4,036,572	185
	Samuel J. Tilden	Democratic	4,284,020	184
1880	**James A. Garfield** (**Chester A. Arthur**, 1881)	Republican	4,449,053	214
	Winfield S. Hancock	Democratic	4,442,035	155
	James B. Weaver	Greenback-Labor	308,578	
1884	**Grover Cleveland**	Democratic	4,874,986	219
	James G. Blaine	Republican	4,851,981	182
	Benjamin F. Butler	Greenback-Labor	175,370	
1888	**Benjamin Harrison**	Republican	5,444,337	233
	Grover Cleveland	Democratic	5,540,050	168
1892	**Grover Cleveland**	Democratic	5,554,414	277
	Benjamin Harrison	Republican	5,190,802	145
	James B. Weaver	People's	1,027,329	22

Year	Candidates	Party	Popular vote	Electoral vote
1896	**William McKinley**	Republican	7,035,638	271
	William J. Bryan	Democratic; Populist	6,467,946	176
1900	**William McKinley**	Republican	7,219,530	292
	(Theodore Roosevelt, 1901)			
	William J. Bryan	Democratic; Populist	6,356,734	155
1904	**Theodore Roosevelt**	Republican	7,628,834	336
	Alton B. Parker	Democratic	5,084,401	140
	Eugene V. Debs	Socialist	402,460	
1908	**William H. Taft**	Republican	7,679,006	321
	William J. Bryan	Democratic	6,409,106	162
	Eugene V. Debs	Socialist	420,820	
1912	**Woodrow Wilson**	Democratic	6,286,820	435
	Theodore Roosevelt	Progressive	4,126,020	88
	William H. Taft	Republican	3,483,922	8
	Eugene V. Debs	Socialist	897,011	
1916	**Woodrow Wilson**	Democratic	9,129,606	277
	Charles E. Hughes	Republican	8,538,221	254
1920	**Warren G. Harding**	Republican	16,152,200	404
	(Calvin Coolidge, 1923)			
	James M. Cox	Democratic	9,147,353	127
	Eugene V. Debs	Socialist	919,799	
1924	**Calvin Coolidge**	Republican	15,725,016	382
	John W. Davis	Democratic	8,385,586	136
	Robert M. LaFollette	Progressive	4,822,856	13
1928	**Herbert C. Hoover**	Republican	21,392,190	444
	Alfred E. Smith	Democratic	15,016,443	87
1932	**Franklin D. Roosevelt**	Democratic	22,809,638	472
	Herbert C. Hoover	Republican	15,758,901	59
	Norman Thomas	Socialist	881,951	
1936	**Franklin D. Roosevelt**	Democratic	27,751,612	523
	Alfred M. Landon	Republican	16,681,913	8
	William Lemke	Union	891,858	
1940	**Franklin D. Roosevelt**	Democratic	27,243,466	449
	Wendell L. Willkie	Republican	22,304,755	82
1944	**Franklin D. Roosevelt**	Democratic	25,602,505	432
	(Harry S Truman, 1945)			
	Thomas E. Dewey	Republican	22,006,278	99
1948	**Harry S Truman**	Democratic	24,105,812	303
	Thomas E. Dewey	Republican	21,970,065	189
	J. Strom Thurmond	States' Rights	1,169,063	39
	Henry A. Wallace	Progressive	1,157,172	

Year	Candidates	Party	Popular vote	Electoral vote
1952	**Dwight D. Eisenhower**	Republican	33,936,234	442
	Adlai E. Stevenson	Democratic	27,314,992	89
1956	**Dwight D. Eisenhower**	Republican	35,590,472	457
	Adlai E. Stevenson	Democratic	26,022,752	73
1960	**John F. Kennedy** (Lyndon B. Johnson, 1963)	Democratic	34,227,096	303
	Richard M. Nixon	Republican	34,108,546	219
1964	**Lyndon B. Johnson**	Democratic	43,126,233	486
	Barry M. Goldwater	Republican	27,174,989	52
1968	**Richard M. Nixon**	Republican	31,783,783	301
	Hubert H. Humphrey	Democratic	31,271,839	191
	George C. Wallace	Amer. Independent	9,899,557	46
1972	**Richard M. Nixon** (Gerald R. Ford, 1974)	Republican	47,169,911	521
	George S. McGovern	Democratic	29,170,383	17
1976	**James Earl Carter**	Democratic	40,827,394	297
	Gerald R. Ford	Republican	39,145,977	241

Date of Statehood

Delaware	December 7, 1787	Michigan	January 16, 1837
Pennsylvania	December 12, 1787	Florida	March 3, 1845
New Jersey	December 18, 1787	Texas	December 29, 1845
Georgia	January 2, 1788	Iowa	December 28, 1846
Connecticut	January 9, 1788	Wisconsin	May 29, 1848
Massachusetts	February 6, 1788	California	September 9, 1850
Maryland	April 28, 1788	Minnesota	May 11, 1858
South Carolina	May 23, 1788	Oregon	February 14, 1859
New Hampshire	June 21, 1788	Kansas	January 29, 1861
Virginia	June 25, 1788	West Virginia	June 19, 1863
New York	July 26, 1788	Nevada	October 31, 1864
North Carolina	November 21, 1789	Nebraska	March 1, 1867
Rhode Island	May 29, 1790	Colorado	August 1, 1876
Vermont	March 4, 1791	North Dakota	November 2, 1889
Kentucky	June 1, 1792	South Dakota	November 2, 1889
Tennessee	June 1, 1796	Montana	November 8, 1889
Ohio	March 1, 1803	Washington	November 11, 1889
Louisiana	April 30, 1812	Idaho	July 3, 1890
Indiana	December 11, 1816	Wyoming	July 10, 1890
Mississippi	December 10, 1817	Utah	January 4, 1896
Illinois	December 3, 1818	Oklahoma	November 16, 1907
Alabama	December 14, 1819	New Mexico	January 6, 1912
Maine	March 15, 1820	Arizona	February 14, 1912
Missouri	August 10, 1821	Alaska	January 3, 1959
Arkansas	June 15, 1836	Hawaii	August 21, 1959

Population of the United States

1790	3,929,214	1890	62,947,714
1800	5,308,483	1900	75,994,575
1810	7,239,881	1910	91,972,266
1820	9,638,453	1920	105,710,620
1830	12,860,692	1930	122,775,046
1840	17,063,353	1940	131,669,275
1850	23,191,876	1950	150,697,361
1860	31,443,321	1960	179,323,175
1870	38,558,371	1970	204,765,770
1880	50,155,783	1978	218,500,000 (approx.)

Chief Justices of the United States Supreme Court

John Jay, N.Y. 1789–1795	Salmon P. Chase, Ohio 1864–1873	Charles E. Hughes, N.Y. 1930–1941
John Rutledge, S.C. 1795	Morrison R. Waite, Ohio 1874–1888	Harlan F. Stone, N.Y. 1941–1946
Oliver Ellsworth, Conn. 1795–1799	Melville W. Fuller, Ill. 1888–1910	Fred M. Vinson, Ky. 1946–1953
John Marshall, Va. 1801–1835	Edward D. White, La. 1910–1921	Earl Warren, Calif. 1953–1969
Roger B. Taney, Md. 1836–1864	William H. Taft, Ohio 1921–1930	Warren E. Burger, Minn. 1969–

Presidents, Vice-Presidents, and Cabinet Members

President	Vice-President	Secretary of State	Secretary of Treasury	Secretary of War
1. **George Washington** 1789–1797 Federalist	John Adams 1789–1797	Thomas Jefferson 1789–1794 Edmund Randolph 1794–1795 Timothy Pickering 1795–1797	Alexander Hamilton 1789–1795 Oliver Wolcott 1795–1797	Henry Knox 1789–1795 Timothy Pickering 1795–1796 James McHenry 1796–1797
2. **John Adams** 1797–1801 Federalist	Thomas Jefferson 1797–1801	Timothy Pickering 1797–1800 John Marshall 1800–1801	Oliver Wolcott 1797–1801 Samuel Dexter 1801	James McHenry 1797–1800 Samuel Dexter 1800–1801
3. **Thomas Jefferson** 1801–1809 Republican	Aaron Burr 1801–1805 George Clinton 1805–1809	James Madison 1801–1809	Samuel Dexter 1801 Albert Gallatin 1801–1809	Henry Dearborn 1801–1809
4. **James Madison** 1809–1817 Republican	George Clinton 1809–1813 Elbridge Gerry 1813–1817	Robert Smith 1809–1811 James Monroe 1811–1817	Albert Gallatin 1809–1814 George Campbell 1814 Alexander Dallas 1814–1816 William Crawford 1816–1817	William Eustis 1809–1813 John Armstrong 1813–1814 James Monroe 1814–1815 William Crawford 1815–1817
5. **James Monroe** 1817–1825 Republican	Daniel D. Tompkins 1817–1825	John Quincy Adams 1817–1825	William Crawford 1817–1825	George Graham 1817 John C. Calhoun 1817–1825
6. **John Quincy Adams** 1825–1829 National Republican	John C. Calhoun 1825–1829	Henry Clay 1825–1829	Richard Rush 1825–1829	James Barbour 1825–1828 Peter B. Porter 1828–1829
7. **Andrew Jackson** 1829–1837 Democrat	John C. Calhoun 1829–1833 Martin Van Buren 1833–1837	Martin Van Buren 1829–1831 Edward Livingston 1831–1833 Louis McLane 1833–1834 John Forsyth 1834–1837	Samuel Ingham 1829–1831 Louis McLane 1831–1833 William Duane 1833 Roger B. Taney 1833–1834 Levi Woodbury 1834–1837	John H. Eaton 1829–1831 Lewis Cass 1831–1837 Benjamin Butler 1837

Secretary of Navy	Postmaster General	Attorney General
	Samuel Osgood 1789–1791 Timothy Pickering 1791–1795 Joseph Habersham 1795–1797	Edmund Randolph 1789–1794 William Bradford 1794–1795 Charles Lee 1795–1797
Benjamin Stoddert 1798–1801	Joseph Habersham 1797–1801	Charles Lee 1797–1801
Benjamin Stoddert 1801 Robert Smith 1801–1809	Joseph Habersham 1801 Gideon Granger 1801–1809	Levi Lincoln 1801–1805 John Breckinridge 1805–1807 Caesar Rodney 1807–1809
Paul Hamilton 1809–1813 William Jones 1813–1814 Benjamin Crowninshield 1814–1817	Gideon Granger 1809–1814 Return Meigs 1814–1817	Caesar Rodney 1809–1811 William Pinkney 1811–1814 Richard Rush 1814–1817
Benjamin Crowninshield 1817–1818 Smith Thompson 1818–1823 Samuel Southard 1823–1825	Return Meigs 1817–1823 John McLean 1823–1825	Richard Rush 1817 William Wirt 1817–1825
Samuel Southard 1825–1829	John McLean 1825–1829	William Wirt 1825–1829
John Branch 1829–1831 Levi Woodbury 1831–1834 Mahlon Dickerson 1834–1837	William Barry 1829–1835 Amos Kendall 1835–1837	John M. Berrien 1829–1831 Roger B. Taney 1831–1833 Benjamin Butler 1833–1837

Presidents, Vice-Presidents, and Cabinet Members

President	Vice-President	Secretary of State	Secretary of Treasury	Secretary of War
8. **Martin Van Buren** 1837–1841 Democrat	Richard M. Johnson 1837–1841	John Forsyth 1837–1841	Levi Woodbury 1837–1841	Joel R. Poinsett 1837–1841
9. **William H. Harrison** 1841 Whig	John Tyler 1841	Daniel Webster 1841	Thomas Ewing 1841	John Bell 1841
10. **John Tyler** 1841–1845 Whig and Democrat		Daniel Webster 1841–1843 Hugh S. Legaré 1843 Abel P. Upshur 1843–1844 John C. Calhoun 1844–1845	Thomas Ewing 1841 Walter Forward 1841–1843 John C. Spencer 1843–1844 George M. Bibb 1844–1845	John Bell 1841 John C. Spencer 1841–1843 James M. Porter 1843–1844 William Wilkins 1844–1845
11. **James K. Polk** 1845–1849 Democrat	George M. Dallas 1845–1849	James Buchanan 1845–1849	Robert J. Walker 1845–1849	William L. Marcy 1845–1849
12. **Zachary Taylor** 1849–1850 Whig	Millard Fillmore 1849–1850	John M. Clayton 1849–1850	William M. Meredith 1849–1850	George W. Crawford 1849–1850
13. **Millard Fillmore** 1850–1853 Whig		Daniel Webster 1850–1852 Edward Everett 1852–1853	Thomas Corwin 1850–1853	Charles M. Conrad 1850–1853
14. **Franklin Pierce** 1853–1857 Democrat	William R. King 1853–1857	William L. Marcy 1853–1857	James Guthrie 1853–1857	Jefferson Davis 1853–1857
15. **James Buchanan** 1857–1861 Democrat	John C. Breckinridge 1857–1861	Lewis Cass 1857–1860 Jeremiah S. Black 1860–1861	Howell Cobb 1857–1860 Philip F. Thomas 1860–1861 John A. Dix (1861)	John B. Floyd 1857–1861 Joseph Holt 1861
16. **Abraham Lincoln** 1861–1865 Republican	Hannibal Hamlin 1861–1865 Andrew Johnson 1865	William H. Seward 1861–1865	Salmon P. Chase 1861–1864 William P. Fessenden 1864–1865 Hugh McCulloch (1865)	Simon Cameron 1861–1862 Edwin M. Stanton 1862–1865

Secretary of Navy	Postmaster General	Attorney General	Secretary of Interior
Mahlon Dickerson 1837–1838 James K. Paulding 1838–1841	Amos Kendall 1837–1840 John M. Niles 1840–1841	Benjamin Butler 1837–1838 Felix Grundy 1838–1840 Henry D. Gilpin 1840–1841	
George E. Badger 1841	Francis Granger 1841	John J. Crittenden 1841	
George E. Badger 1841 Abel P. Upshur 1841–1843 David Henshaw 1843–1844 Thomas Gilmer 1844 John Y. Mason 1844–1845	Francis Granger 1841 Charles A. Wickliffe 1841–1845	John J. Crittenden 1841 Hugh S. Legaré 1841–1843 John Nelson 1843–1845	
George Bancroft 1845–1846 John Y. Mason 1846–1849	Cave Johnson 1845–1849	John Y. Mason 1845–1846 Nathan Clifford 1846–1848 Isaac Toucey 1848–1849	
William B. Preston 1849–1850	Jacob Collamer 1849–1850	Reverdy Johnson 1849–1850	Thomas Ewing 1849–1850
William A. Graham 1850–1852 John P. Kennedy 1852–1853	Nathan K. Hall 1850–1852 Sam D. Hubbard 1852–1853	John J. Crittenden 1850–1853	Thomas McKennan 1850 A. H. H. Stuart 1850–1853
James C. Dobbin 1853–1857	James Campbell 1853–1857	Caleb Cushing 1853–1857	Robert McClelland 1853–1857
Isaac Toucey 1857–1861	Aaron V. Brown 1857–1859 Joseph Holt 1859–1861 Horatio King (1861)	Jeremiah S. Black 1857–1860 Edwin M. Stanton 1860–1861	Jacob Thompson 1857–1861
Gideon Welles 1861–1865	Horatio King (1861) Montgomery Blair 1861–1864 William Dennison 1864–1865	Edward Bates 1861–1864 James Speed 1864–1865	Caleb B. Smith 1861–1863 John P. Usher 1863–1865

Presidents, Vice-Presidents, and Cabinet Members

President	Vice-President	Secretary of State	Secretary of Treasury	Secretary of War
17. **Andrew Johnson** 1865–1869 Unionist		William H. Seward 1865–1869	Hugh McCulloch 1865–1869	Edwin M. Stanton 1865–1867 Ulysses S. Grant 1867–1868 John M. Schofield 1868–1869
18. **Ulysses S. Grant** 1869–1877 Republican	Schuyler Colfax 1869–1873 Henry Wilson 1873–1877	Elihu B. Washburne 1869 Hamilton Fish 1869–1877	George S. Boutwell 1869–1873 William A. Richardson 1873–1874 Benjamin H. Bristow 1874–1876 Lot M. Morrill 1876–1877	John A. Rawlins 1869 William T. Sherman 1869 William W. Belknap 1869–1876 Alphonso Taft 1876 James D. Cameron 1876–1877
19. **Rutherford B. Hayes** 1877–1881 Republican	William A. Wheeler 1877–1881	William M. Evarts 1877–1881	John Sherman 1877–1881	George W. McCrary 1877–1879 Alexander Ramsey 1879–1881
20. **James A. Garfield** 1881 Republican	Chester A. Arthur 1881	James G. Blaine 1881	William Windom 1881	Robert T. Lincoln 1881
21. **Chester A. Arthur** 1881–1885 Republican		F. T. Frelinghuysen 1881–1885	Charles J. Folger 1881–1884 Walter Q. Gresham 1884 Hugh McCulloch 1884–1885	Robert T. Lincoln 1881–1885
22. **Grover Cleveland** 1885–1889 Democrat	T. A. Hendricks 1885	Thomas F. Bayard 1885–1889	Daniel Manning 1885–1887 Charles S. Fairchild 1887–1889	William C. Endicott 1885–1889
23. **Benjamin Harrison** 1889–1893 Republican	Levi P. Morton 1889–1893	James G. Blaine 1889–1892 John W. Foster 1892–1893	William Windom 1889–1891 Charles Foster 1891–1893	Redfield Procter 1889–1891 Stephen B. Elkins 1891–1893
24. **Grover Cleveland** 1893–1897 Democrat	Adlai E. Stevenson 1893–1897	Walter Q. Gresham 1893–1895 Richard Olney 1895–1897	John G. Carlisle 1893–1897	Daniel S. Lamont 1893–1897

Secretary of Navy	Postmaster General	Attorney General	Secretary of Interior	Secretary of Agriculture
Gideon Welles 1865–1869	William Dennison 1865–1866 Alexander Randall 1866–1869	James Speed 1865–1866 Henry Stanbery 1866–1868 William M. Evarts 1868–1869	John P. Usher 1865 James Harlan 1865–1866 O. H. Browning 1866–1869	
Adolph E Borie 1869 George M. Robeson 1869–1877	John A. J. Creswell 1869–1874 James W. Marshall 1874 Marshall Jewell 1874–1876 James N. Tyner 1876–1877	Ebenezer R. Hoar 1869–1870 Amos T. Akerman 1870–1871 G. H. Williams 1871–1875 Edwards Pierrepont 1875–1876 Alphonso Taft 1876–1877	Jacob D. Cox 1869–1870 Columbus Delano 1870–1875 Zachariah Chandler 1875–1877	
R. W. Thompson 1877–1881 Nathan Goff, Jr. 1881	David M. Key 1877–1880 Horace Maynard 1880–1881	Charles Devens 1877–1881	Carl Schurz 1877–1881	
William H. Hunt 1881	Thomas L. James 1881	Wayne MacVeagh 1881	S. J. Kirkwood 1881	
William E. Chandler 1881–1885	Thomas L. James 1881 Timothy O. Howe 1881–1883 Walter Q. Gresham 1883–1884 Frank Hatton 1884–1885	B. H. Brewster 1881–1885	Henry M. Teller 1881–1885	
William C. Whitney 1885–1889	William F. Vilas 1885–1888 Don M. Dickinson 1888–1889	A. H. Garland 1885–1889	L. Q. C. Lamar 1885–1888 William F. Vilas 1888–1889	Norman J. Colman 1889
Benjamin F. Tracy 1889–1893	John Wanamaker 1889–1893	W. H. H. Miller 1889–1893	John W. Noble 1889–1893	Jeremiah M. Rusk 1889–1893
Hilary A. Herbert 1893–1897	Wilson S. Bissel 1893–1895 William L. Wilson 1895–1897	Richard Olney 1893–1895 Judson Harmon 1895–1897	Hoke Smith 1893–1896 David R. Francis 1896–1897	J. Sterling Morton 1893–1897

Presidents, Vice-Presidents, and Cabinet Members

President	Vice-President	Secretary of State	Secretary of Treasury	Secretary of War*	Secretary of Navy*
25. **William McKinley** 1897–1901 Republican	Garret A. Hobart 1897–1901 Theodore Roosevelt 1901	John Sherman 1897–1898 William R. Day 1898 John Hay 1898–1901	Lyman J. Gage 1897–1901	Russell A. Alger 1897–1899 Elihu Root 1899–1901	John D. Long 1897–1901
26. **Theodore Roosevelt** 1901–1909 Republican	Charles Fairbanks 1905–1909	John Hay 1901–1905 Elihu Root 1905–1909 Robert Bacon 1909	Lyman J. Gage 1901–1902 Leslie M. Shaw 1902–1907 George B. Cortelyou 1907–1909	Elihu Root 1901–1904 William H. Taft 1904–1908 Luke E. Wright 1908–1909	John D. Long 1901–1902 William H. Moody 1902–1904 Paul Morton 1904–1905 Charles J. Bonaparte 1905–1906 Victor H. Metcalf 1906–1908 T. H. Newberry 1908–1909
27. **William H. Taft** 1909–1913 Republican	James S. Sherman 1909–1913	Philander C. Knox 1909–1913	Franklin MacVeagh 1909–1913	Jacob M. Dickinson 1909–1911 Henry L. Stimson 1911–1913	George von L. Meyer 1909–1913
28. **Woodrow Wilson** 1913–1921 Democrat	Thomas R. Marshall 1913–1921	William J. Bryan 1913–1915 Robert Lansing 1915–1920 Bainbridge Colby 1920–1921	William G. McAdoo 1913–1918 Carter Glass 1918–1920 David F. Houston 1920–1921	Lindley M. Garrison 1913–1916 Newton D. Baker 1916–1921	Josephus Daniels 1913–1921
29. **Warren G. Harding** 1921–1923 Republican	Calvin Coolidge 1921–1923	Charles E. Hughes 1921–1923	Andrew W. Mellon 1921–1923	John W. Weeks 1921–1923	Edwin Denby 1921–1923
30. **Calvin Coolidge** 1923–1929 Republican	Charles G. Dawes 1925–1929	Charles E. Hughes 1923–1925 Frank B. Kellogg 1925–1929	Andrew W. Mellon 1923–1929	John W. Weeks 1923–1925 Dwight F. Davis 1925–1929	Edwin Denby 1923–1924 Curtis D. Wilbur 1924–1929

*Lost cabinet status in 1947.

Postmaster General	Attorney General	Secretary of Interior	Secretary of Agriculture	Secretary of Commerce	Secretary of Labor
James A. Gary 1897–1898 Charles E. Smith 1898–1901	Joseph McKenna 1897–1898 John W. Griggs 1898–1901 Philander C. Knox 1901	Cornelius N. Bliss 1897–1898 E. A. Hitchcock 1898–1901	James Wilson 1897–1901		
Charles E. Smith 1901–1902 Henry C. Payne 1902–1904 Robert J. Wynne 1904–1905 George B. Cortelyou 1905–1907 George von L. Meyer 1907–1909	Philander C. Knox 1901–1904 William H. Moody 1904–1906 Charles J. Bonaparte 1906–1909	E. A. Hitchcock 1901–1907 James R. Garfield 1907–1909	James Wilson 1901–1909	George B. Cortelyou 1903–1904 Victor H. Metcalf 1904–1906 Oscar S. Straus 1906–1909	
Frank H. Hitchcock 1909–1913	G. W. Wickersham 1909–1913	R. A. Ballinger 1909–1911 Walter L. Fisher 1911–1913	James Wilson 1909–1913	Charles Nagel 1909–1913	
Albert S. Burleson 1913–1921	J. C. McReynolds 1913–1914 T. W. Gregory 1914–1919 A. Mitchell Palmer 1919–1921	Franklin K. Lane 1913–1920 John B. Payne 1920–1921	David F. Houston 1913–1920 E. T. Meredith 1920–1921	W. C. Redfield 1913–1919 J. W. Alexander 1919–1921	William B. Wilson 1913–1921
Will H. Hays 1921–1922 Hubert Work 1922–1923 Harry S. New 1923	H. M. Daugherty 1921–1923	Albert B. Fall 1921–1923 Hubert Work 1923	Henry C. Wallace 1921–1923	Herbert C. Hoover 1921–1923	James J. Davis 1921–1923
Harry S. New 1923–1929	H. M. Daugherty 1923–1924 Harlan F. Stone 1924–1925 John G. Sargent 1925–1929	Hubert Work 1923–1928 Roy O. West 1928–1929	Henry C. Wallace 1923–1924 Howard M. Gore 1924–1925 W. M. Jardine 1925–1929	Herbert C. Hoover 1923–1928 William F. Whiting 1928–1929	James J. Davis 1923–1929

Presidents, Vice-Presidents, and Cabinet Members

President	Vice-President	Secretary of State	Secretary of Treasury	Secretary of War*	Secretary of Navy*
31. **Herbert C. Hoover** 1929–1933 Republican	Charles Curtis 1929–1933	Henry L. Stimson 1929–1933	Andrew W. Mellon 1929–1932 Ogden L. Mills 1932–1933	James W. Good 1929 Patrick J. Hurley 1929–1933	Charles F. Adams 1929–1933
32. **Franklin Delano Roosevelt** 1933–1945 Democrat	John Nance Garner 1933–1941 Henry A. Wallace 1941–1945 Harry S Truman 1945	Cordell Hull 1933–1944 E. R. Stettinius, Jr. 1944–1945	William H. Woodin 1933–1934 Henry Morgenthau, Jr. 1934–1945	George H. Dern 1933–1936 Harry H. Woodring 1936–1940 Henry L. Stimson 1940–1945	Claude A. Swanson 1933–1940 Charles Edison 1940 Frank Knox 1940–1944 James V. Forrestal 1944–1945
33. **Harry S Truman** 1945–1953 Democrat	Alben W. Barkley 1949–1953	James F. Byrnes 1945–1947 George C. Marshall 1947–1949 Dean G. Acheson 1949–1953	Fred M. Vinson 1945–1946 John W. Snyder 1946–1953	Robert P. Patterson 1945–1947 Kenneth C. Royall 1947	James V. Forrestal 1945–1947
				Secretary of Defense James V. Forrestal 1947–1949 Louis A. Johnson 1949–1950 George C. Marshall 1950–1951 Robert A. Lovett 1951–1953	
34. **Dwight D. Eisenhower** 1953–1961 Republican	Richard M. Nixon 1953–1961	John Foster Dulles 1953–1959 Christian A. Herter 1959–1961	George M. Humphrey 1953–1957 Robert B. Anderson 1957–1961	Charles E. Wilson 1953–1957 Neil H. McElroy 1957–1961 Thomas S. Gates 1959–1961	
35. **John F. Kennedy** 1961–1963 Democrat	Lyndon B. Johnson 1961–1963	Dean Rusk 1961–1963	C. Douglas Dillon 1961–1963	Robert S. McNamara 1961–1963	

Postmaster General	Attorney General	Secretary of Interior	Secretary of Agriculture	Secretary of Commerce	Secretary of Labor	Secretary of Health, Education and Welfare
Walter F. Brown 1929–1933	J. D. Mitchell 1929–1933	Ray L. Wilbur 1933–1945	Arthur M. Hyde 1929–1933	Robert P. Lamont 1929–1932 Roy D. Chapin 1932–1933	James J. Davis 1929–1930 William N. Doak 1930–1933	
James A. Farley 1933–1940 Frank C. Walker 1940–1945	H. S. Cummings 1933–1939 Frank Murphy 1939–1940 Robert Jackson 1940–1941 Francis Biddle 1941–1945	Harold L. Ickes 1933–1945	Henry A. Wallace 1933–1940 Claude R. Wickard 1940–1945	Daniel C. Roper 1933–1939 Harry L. Hopkins 1939–1940 Jesse Jones 1940–1945 Henry A. Wallace 1945	Frances Perkins 1933–1945	
R. E. Hannegan 1945–1947 Jesse M. Donaldson 1947–1953	Tom C. Clark 1945–1949 J. H. McGrath 1949–1952 James P. McGranery 1952–1953	Harold L. Ickes 1945–1946 Julius A. Krug 1946–1949 Oscar L. Chapman 1949–1953	C. P. Anderson 1945–1948 C. F. Brannan 1948–1953	W. A. Harriman 1946–1948 Charles Sawyer 1948–1953	L. B. Schwellenbach 1945–1948 Maurice J. Tobin 1948–1953	
A. E. Summerfield 1953–1961	H. Brownell, Jr. 1953–1957 William P. Rogers 1957–1961	Douglas McKay 1953–1956 Fred Seaton 1956–1961	Ezra T. Benson 1953–1961	Sinclair Weeks 1953–1958 Lewis L. Strauss 1958–1961	Martin P. Durkin 1953 James P. Mitchell 1953–1961	Oveta Culp Hobby 1953–1955 Marion B. Folsom 1955–1958 Arthur S. Flemming 1958–1961
J. Edward Day 1961–1963 John A. Gronouski 1963	Robert F. Kennedy 1961–1963	Stewart L. Udall 1961–1963	Orville L. Freeman 1961–1963	Luther H. Hodges 1961–1963	Arthur J. Goldberg 1961–1962 W. Willard Wirtz 1962–1963	A. H. Ribicoff 1961–1962 Anthony J. Celebrezze 1962–1963

Presidents, Vice-Presidents, and Cabinet Members

President	Vice-President	Secretary of State	Secretary of Treasury	Secretary of Defense	Postmaster General*	Attorney General
36. **Lyndon B. Johnson** 1963–1969 Democrat	Hubert H. Humphrey 1965–1969	Dean Rusk 1963–1969	C. Douglas Dillon 1963–1965 Henry H. Fowler 1965–1968 Joseph W. Barr 1968–1969	Robert S. McNamara 1963–1968 Clark M. Clifford 1968–1969	John A. Gronouski 1963–1965 Lawrence F. O'Brien 1965–1968 W. Marvin Watson 1968–1969	Robert F. Kennedy 1963–1965 N. deB. Katzenbach 1965–1967 Ramsey Clark 1967–1969
37. **Richard M. Nixon** 1969–1974 Republican	Spiro T. Agnew 1969–1973 Gerald R. Ford 1973–1974	William P. Rogers 1969–1973 Henry A. Kissinger 1973–1974	David M. Kennedy 1969–1970 John B. Connally 1970–1972 George P. Shultz 1972–1974 William E. Simon 1974	Melvin R. Laird 1969–1973 Elliot L. Richardson 1973 James R. Schlesinger 1973–1974	Winton M. Blount 1969–1971	John M. Mitchell 1969–1972 Richard G. Kleindienst 1972–1973 Elliot L. Richardson 1973 William B. Saxbe 1974
38. **Gerald R. Ford** 1974–1977 Republican	Nelson A. Rockefeller 1974–1977	Henry A. Kissinger 1974–1977	William E. Simon 1974–1977	James R. Schlesinger 1974–1975 Donald H. Rumsfeld 1975–1977		William B. Saxbe 1974–1975 Edward H. Levi 1975–1977
39. **Jimmy Carter** 1977– Democrat	Walter F. Mondale 1977–	Cyrus R. Vance 1977–1980 Edmund S. Muskie 1980–	W. Michael Blumenthal 1977–1979 G. William Miller 1979–	Harold Brown 1977–		Griffin Bell 1977–1979 Benjamin R. Civiletti 1979–

*On July 1, 1971, the Post Office became an independent agency. After that date, the Postmaster General was no longer a member of the Cabinet.

Secretary of Interior	Secretary of Agriculture	Secretary of Commerce	Secretary of Labor	Secretary of Health, Education and Welfare*	Secretary of Housing and Urban Development	Secretary of Transportation
Stewart L. Udall 1963–1969	Orville L. Freeman 1963–1969	Luther H. Hodges 1963–1965 John T. Connor 1965–1967 Alexander B. Trowbridge 1967–1968 C. R. Smith 1968–1969	W. Willard Wirtz 1963–1969	Anthony J. Celebrezze 1963–1965 John W. Gardner 1965–1968 Wilbur J. Cohen 1968–1969	Robert C. Weaver 1966–1968 Robert C. Wood 1968–1969	Alan S. Boyd 1966–1969
Walter J. Hickel 1969–1971 Rogers C. B. Morton 1971–1974	Clifford M. Hardin 1969–1971 Earl L. Butz 1971–1974	Maurice H. Stans 1969–1972 Peter G. Peterson 1972 Frederick B. Dent 1972–1974	George P. Shultz 1969–1970 James D. Hodgson 1970–1973 Peter J. Brennan 1973–1974	Robert H. Finch 1969–1970 Elliot L. Richardson 1970–1973 Caspar W. Weinberger 1973–1974	George W. Romney 1969–1973 James T. Lynn 1973–1974	John A. Volpe 1969–1973 Claude S. Brinegar 1973–1974
Rogers C. B. Morton 1974–1975 Stanley K. Hathaway 1975 Thomas D. Kleppe 1975–1977	Earl L. Butz 1974–1976 John A. Knebel 1976–1977	Frederick B. Dent 1974–1975 Rogers C. B. Morton 1975 Elliot L. Richardson 1975–1977	Peter J. Brennan 1974–1975 John T. Dunlop 1975–1976 W. J. Usery 1976–1977	Caspar W. Weinberger 1974–1975 Forrest D. Mathews 1975–1977	James T. Lynn 1974–1975 Carla A. Hills 1975–1977	Claude S. Brinegar 1974–1975 William T. Coleman 1975–1977
Cecil D. Andrus 1977–	Robert S. Bergland 1977–	Juanita M. Kreps 1977–1979 Philip M. Klutznick 1979–	F. Ray Marshall 1977–	Joseph Califano 1977–1979 Patricia Roberts Harris 1979–	Patricia Roberts Harris 1977–1979 Moon Landrieu 1979–	Brock Adams 1977–1979 Neil E. Goldschmidt 1979–

				Secretary of Energy†	Secretary of Education‡	
				James R. Schlesinger 1977–1979 Charles W. Duncan, Jr. 1979–	Shirley M. Hufstedler 1979–	

*In 1979 HEW was renamed the Department of Health and Human Services. †Created in 1977. ‡Created in 1979.

Photo Credits

xii, Reproduced from the collections of the Library of Congress

2, Culver Pictures

4, Reproduced from the collections of the Library of Congress

12, The Bettmann Archive

15, The Peabody Museum of Salem

17, Courtesy of the American Museum of Natural History

20, The Bettmann Archive

27, The New York Public Library

29, The Bettmann Archive

36, Culver Pictures

38, The Peabody Museum of Salem

40, The Bettmann Archive

43, Reproduced from the collections of the Library of Congress

45, Culver Pictures

49, The Bettmann Archive

52, Brown Brothers

55, Historical Pictures Service, Inc., Chicago

60, Reproduced from the collections of the Library of Congress

63, The New York Public Library, I.N. Phelps Stokes Collection, Prints Division

67, Culver Pictures

71, The Bettmann Archive

74, The New York Public Library, I.N. Phelps Stokes Collection, Prints Division

76, The Bettmann Archive

81, Courtesy of Massachusetts Historical Society

83, Boston Museum of Fine Arts

86, The New York Public Library, I.N. Phelps Stokes Collection, Prints Division

91, The New Brunswick Museum, courtesy Webster Collection of Pictorial Canadiana

94, Reproduced from the collections of the Library of Congress

97, Brown Brothers

99, Brown Brothers

101, The Granger Collection

104, Culver Pictures

107, Connecticut Historical Society

110, Brown Brothers

115, The New York State Library, Albany

117, The New York State Library, Albany

118, Courtesy, The Henry Francis du Pont Winterthur Museum

122, American Antiquarian Society

126, The Old Print Shop, N.Y.C.

127, The Boston Public Library, Print Department

128, Culver Pictures

129, Reproduced from the collections of the Library of Congress

131, The Bettmann Archive

136, The Bettmann Archive

140, American Antiquarian Society

144, Culver Pictures

146, The Boston Public Library, Print Department

148, (left) Brown Brothers, (right) Historical Pictures Service, Inc., Chicago

150, The New York Public Library, I.N. Phelps Stokes Collection, Prints Division

153, Virginia Museum of Fine Arts

156, Brown Brothers

160, Culver Pictures

163, Yale University Art Gallery

165, The New York Public Library, I.N. Phelps Stokes Collection, Prints Division

167, The New York Historical Society

170, The Bettmann Archive

174, (top and bottom) The Bettmann Archive

176, Brown Brothers

183, White House collection

187, The Bettmann Archive

189, (a) The Bettmann Archive, (b) The New York Public Library, (c) Missouri Historical Society

191, The Bettmann Archive

193, The Bettmann Archive

194, The New York Historical Society

196, (left) The Bettmann Archive, (right) Culver Pictures

198, The Bettmann Archive

201, The Historical Society of Pennsylvania

204, Brown Brothers

208, Courtesy of the New York Historical Society, New York City

211, The Bettmann Archive

214, Culver Pictures

220, The New York Public Library, Astor, Lenox and Tilden Foundation

222, Reproduced from the collections of the Library of Congress

228, Boston Public Library, Print Department

236, Culver Pictures

239, The Bettmann Archive

241, The Bettmann Archive

248, Yale University Art Gallery

250, Culver Pictures

253, The Boston Public Library, Print Department

257, Harvard University, Houghton Library

261, The New York Historical Society

262, The Bettmann Archive

266, Reproduced from the collections of the Library of Congress

269, Culver Pictures

272, Reproduced from the collections of the Library of Congress

273, Engineering-Transportation Library, The University of Michigan at Ann Arbor

275, The Bettmann Archive

279, Culver Pictures

285, The Bettmann Archive

287, Culver Pictures

290, Historical Pictures Service, Inc., Chicago

292, General Research and Humanities Division, The New York Public Library, Astor, Lenox and Tilden Foundation

294, Museum of the City of New York

297, Courtesy, Kenneth M. Newman, The Old Print Shop

300, Brown Brothers

303, Brown Brothers

306, Courtesy of the Brooklyn Museum, Dick S. Ramsay Fund

310, The Bettmann Archive

312, Culver Pictures

314, Reproduced from the collections of the Library of Congress

316, The Bettmann Archive

320, Culver Pictures

322, Historical Pictures Service, Inc., Chicago

324, Thomas Gilcrease Institute of American History and Art, Tulsa, Oklahoma

328, The Boston Public Library, Print Department

331, Reproduced from the collections of the Library of Congress

334, (top) Denver Public Library, Western History Department, (bottom) Oregon Historical Society

338, The Bettmann Archive

339, The Boston Public Library, Print Department

343, Brown Brothers

345, The Boston Public Library, Print Department

347, Courtesy of the New York Historical Society, New York City

350, The New York Public Library, Rare Book Division

352, The New York Historical Society

355, The Boston Public Library, Print Department

358, Brown Brothers

359, Culver Pictures

361, Culver Pictures

364, Culver Pictures

365, Brown Brothers

372, The Boston Public Library, Print Department

374, Brown Brothers

378, Brown Brothers

380, Culver Pictures

382, The Boston Public Library, Print Department

385, Reproduced from the collections of the Library of Congress

386, Culver Pictures

389, The Boston Public Library, Print Department

391, Cook Collection, Valentine Museum, Richmond, Virginia

392, (left) Brown Brothers, (right) The Bettmann Archive

398, The Whaling Museum, New Bedford, Mass.

400, The Boston Public Library, Print Department

402, Reproduced from the collections of the Library of Congress

406, Courtesy, Kenneth M. Newman, Old Print Shop

410, Illinois State Historical Library, Springfield

Index

Index

A

Abenaki Indians, 90
Abernethy, T. P., 258
Abolitionist movement, 227, 314–318.
    See also Antislavery movement
    and "bleeding Kansas," 359
    and Mexican War, 341
    and Underground Railroad, 281
    in Whig Party, 260
Adams, Abigail Smith, 147, 148,
    149
Adams, Charles Francis, 390
Adams, John, 72, 102, 137, 184
    and Boston Massacre, 103
    conference with Gen. Howe, 123
    election as president, 173
    election as vice-president, 160,
    166
    at First Continental Congress, 106,
    107
    as minister to London, 138
    and Paris delegation, 132–133
    presidency of, 173–175
Adams, John Quincy, 175, 316, 321
    and election of 1824, 231–232
    and election of 1828, 240
    French mission of, 175
    and Monroe Doctrine, 217
    presidency of, 232–234
    as secretary of state, 215
    on slavery, 231
    and Treaty of Ghent, 205
Adams, Samuel, 137, 144
    at First Continental Congress, 106
    quoted, 100, 144
    and Sons of Liberty, 102
Adams-Onis Treaty (1819), 215–216,
    216(map)
Administration of Justice Act (1774),
    105
Admiralty courts, 99, 101

Africans. *See also* Blacks
    cultural heritage of, 61–62
    and introduction of slavery, 59
Agriculture
    of American Indians, 5
    and Civil War, 368, 388
    colonial, 41, 58–59, 63, 66
    in 1860, 276(map)
    expansion of, 275–276
    mechanization of farming,
    276–277
    and slavery, 277–283
    specialization in, 277
Aguinaldo, Emilio, 570, 571
Alabama (ship), 390
Alabama
    during Reconstruction, 415
    secession of, 371
    statehood, 227
Alamo, Battle of, 330, 331
Alaska, Russia in, 217
Albany, New York, 42, 70
Albany Congress, 93–94, 116
Albany Plan of Union, 117
Alcott, Bronson, 321
Aldrich, Anne, 149
Alexander VI (pope), 17
Algonquin Indians, 7–8, 90
Alien Act, 183
Alien and Sedition Acts (1798),
    176–177
Allan, Levi, 138
Allen, Ethan, 138
Allen, James, 368
Amendments to Constitution
    Bill of Rights, 162
    Twelfth, 232
    Thirteenth, 413
    Fourteenth, 418–419, 426
    Fifteenth, 423, 426
American Anti-Slavery Society,
    315

American Bible Society, 308
American Colonization Society, 317
American Peace Society, 312
American Slavery as It Is (Weld), 315
American Sunday School Union, 308
American System, 210–212, 232–233,
    260
American Temperance Union, 311
Amherst, Gen. Jeffrey, 94
Amnesty Act (1872), 425
Amsterdam, 19
Anaconda Plan, 393
Anderson, Robert, 373
Andrews, Charles M., 48, 108
Andros, Sir Edmund, 48–49
Anglican church, 13
    in colonies, 50, 76–77, 103
    after Revolution, 135
Annapolis Convention, 152
Anthony, Susan B., 314
Anti-Catholicism, 291. *See also*
    Catholic church
Antietam, Battle of, 399
Anti-Federalists. *See also* Federalists
    historical perspective on, 158–159
    policy of, 156–157
Anti-Masons, 254, 260
Antioch College, 314
Anti-Slavery Crusaders, 315
Antislavery movement. *See also*
    Abolitionist movement
    beginnings of, 134
    societies of, 316
    women in, 313
Apache Indians, 444
Appomattox Court House, 405
Architecture, pre–Civil War,
    307
Aristocracy, decline of, 135
Arkansas
    secession of, 387
    statehood, 331

Arkwright, Richard, 218
Army
    Continental, 121
    of the Potomac, 395
    of Virginia, 393
    and War of 1812, 200–201
Army Appropriations Act (1867), 421
Arnold, Benedict, 123, 127, 130
Art. *See also* Literature; Music
    of colonial period, 82–83
    Hudson River School, 305–306
Articles of Confederation, 136–137
Ashburton, Lord, 328
Assembly-line process, in munitions
    industry, 218
Assumption, 164
Atahualpa, 16
Atlanta, Union occupation of, 404
Atlanta University, 416
Attorney general, 161
Attucks, Crispus, 103
Austin, Stephen F., 330
Aztec Indians, 4, 16

B

Babcock, Gen. Orville, 429
Bacon, Nathaniel, 34
Bacon's Rebellion, 34
Bailyn, Bernard, 109
Balboa, Vasco Nuñez de, 16
Baltimore, Lord, 32, 50, 75
Baltimore and Ohio Railroad, 272
Bancroft, George, 48, 108
Banks
    and Panic of 1837, 257
    "pet," 256
Bank of the United States, First,
    164–165
Bank of the United States, Second,
    212
    collapse of, 255–257
    controversy over, 251–254
    McCulloch v. *Maryland*, 213, 254
    and Panic of 1819, 225–226
Banneker, Benjamin, 280
Baptist church, 135
    in colonial America, 76, 79, 80
    and Great Awakening, 298
    and reform movements, 308
Barbary pirates, 191–192

Barber of Seville, The
    (Beaumarchais), 128
Barbour, Philip P., 229
"Barnburners," 344
Barron, Comm. James, 193
Barton, Clara, 389
Bartram, John, 82
Beard, Charles A., 108, 158, 368
Beard, Mary, 149, 368
Beaumarchais, Pierre Augustin Caron
    de, 128
Beauregard, Gen. Pierre G. T., 375,
    395
Beckness, William, 337
Beer, George L., 48, 108
Bell, John, 367, 370
Belz, Herman, 425
Benjamin, Judah P., 385
Benson, Lee, 259
Benson, Mary Sumner, 147
    and Bank of the United States, 256
    and Jackson's candidacy, 240
    public land proposal, 247
    and tariff, 233
Berkeley, Lord, John, 42
Berkeley, William, 34
Berlin Decree (1806), 192
Bertie, Peregrine, 53
Bible
    and evangelical groups, 298
    Luther's translation of, 11–12
    Puritan interpretation of, 40–41
Biddle, Nicholas, 251, 252, 256
Bill of Rights, 162
Bingham, George Caleb, 306
Birney, James G., 316
Black Codes, 416, 418. *See also*
    Reconstruction
"Black Friday," 428–429
Black Hawk War, 246
Blacks. *See also* Africans; Civil rights
    movement
    in antebellum period, 288
    disfranchisement of, 431–432
    free, 280
    nineteenth-century attitudes
        toward, 369–370
    religion of, 298
    in Revolutionary War, 121
    and segregation, 433
    suffrage for, 238, 416–417
    in Union Army, 401

Blackwell, Elizabeth, 314
Blaine, James G., 431
Blair, Montgomery, 374
Blassingame, John, 281
Blow, Henry T., 360
Board of Trade, 48, 89
Boleyn, Anne, 13
Bolivar, Simon, 233–234
Boone, Daniel, 97
Boorstein, Daniel, 78, 109
Booth, John Wilkes, 414
Border states, 387
Boston
    early growth of, 68
    Irish immigrants in, 291
    and Plymouth Colony, 37
    population growth in, 284
Boston Associates, 286
Boston Coffee Party, 149
Boston Manufacturing Company,
    219
Boston Massacre, 103
Boston Newsletter, 83
Boston Tea Party, 104–105
Botany, 82
Bowdoin College, 303
Bowers, Claude, 258
Bowie, Jim, 330
Braddock, Gen. Edward, 93
Bradford, William, 36
    quoted, 30
Bradstreet, Anne, 82
Bragg, Gen. Braxton, 402, 404
Brandywine, Battle of, 126
Brattle Street Church, 77
Breckinridge, John C., 367, 370
Brent, Margaret, 72
Britain. *See* Allied Powers·
    England
Brook Farm, 309
Brooks, Preston, 359
Brown, Gen. Jacob, 203
Brown, John, 358, 366
Brown, Robert E., 109, 158
Brown University, founding of, 81
Bryant, William Cullen, 301
Buchanan, James M., 355
    election as president, 360
    and secession crisis, 368, 371
    and separatist movement, 372
    and slavery, 362
Buel, Jesse, 276

Buell, Gen. Don Carlos, 402
Bull Run
    first battle of, 395
    second battle of, 399
Bunker Hill, Battle of, 109, 120
Burgesses, House of, 31, 34
Burgoyne, Gen. John, 126, 127
Burnaby, Andrew, 64
Burnside, Gen. Ambrose E., 402
Burr, Aaron, 177
    duel with Hamilton, 190
    and election of 1804, 190
    trial for conspiracy, 191
Business. See Corporations
    during Civil War, 388
Butler, Sen. Andrew P., 359
Butler, Gen. Benjamin F., 396
Byrd, William, II, 83

C

Cabinet
    Confederate, 385
    Jackson's Kitchen, 242
    Washington's, 161
Cabot, John, 19
Cabot, Sebastian, 19
Calhoun, John C.
    and annexation of Texas, 332
    and Compromise of 1850, 346, 347
    and Jackson's candidacy, 240
    and protective tariff, 211, 248
    on slavery, 280, 317
    on transportation, 212
California
    congressional debate over, 345–346
    gold discovered in, 274, 345
    and Mexican War, 340, 341
    and Oregon controversy, 335
    settlement of, 337–339
    statehood, 347
Calvert, Cecil, 32
Calvert, George, 32
Calvert, Leonard, 32
Calvin, John, 12
Calvinism, in New England, 37. See
    also Puritanism
Canada
    ceded to England, 95
    Continental Army's invasion of,
        122–123

and Maine boundary dispute,
    327–329
and War of 1812, 201–202
Canals, 222–224, 223(map). See also
    Panama Canal
    Erie, 222, 224
    national program for
        improvements in, 212
Canning, George, 195, 196, 217
Cape Fear, North Carolina, 44
Capital
    move to Washington, D.C., 164
    New York City as, 160
    in Philadelphia, 164
Caribbean. See also specific islands
    British restriction of trade in,
        169–170
    and voyages of Columbus, 15–16
Carlyle, Thomas, 323
Carolina colonies, 44–45
    Fundamental Constitutions of,
        45
    settlement of, 44–45
Caroline (ship), 327, 328
"Carpetbaggers," 422
Carteret, Sir George, 42, 44–45
Cartier, Jacques, 18
Cartwright, Peter, 298
Cass, Sen. Lewis, 344
Castlereagh, Lord, 205
Catharine of Aragon (queen of
    England), 13
Catholic church
    and Irish immigrants, 288, 291
    school system of, 310
    in Texas, 330
Catlin, George, 307
Caucus system, 231, 232. See also
    Political parties
Cayuga Indians, 114
Censorship. See also Dissent;
    Propaganda
    proslavery, 318
Central America, 354–355
    canal project, 354–355
Champion, Deborah, 149
Champlain, Samuel de, 18
Chancellorsville, Battle of, 403
Channing, William Ellery, 308
Charles I (king of England), 19, 21,
    32, 37, 41
Charles II (king of England), 41, 42,

43–44, 47, 48
Charles River Bridge v. Warren
    Bridge, 263
Charleston, South Carolina
    British capture of, 130
    during colonial era, 63
    firing on Fort Sumter, 372–375
Charter of Liberties, 44
Chase, Samuel, 185
Chase, Sen. Salmon P., 317, 370,
    374
Cherokee Indians, 7, 74
    British treaty with, 97
    removal to Oklahoma, 243–246
Cherokee Nation v. Georgia, 245
Chesapeake (ship), 193, 194
Chesapeake Bay, colonies of, 33–34
Chicago, 277
    population growth in, 284
Chickamauga, Battle of, 404
Chickasay Indians, 5, 7
Children. See also Education; Family
    in frontier family, 70
    in textile industry, 286
China, trade with, 274
Choctaw Indians, 5, 7, 246
Church and State
    after American Revolution, 135
    separation of, 79
Cincinnati, Ohio, 277
Cities, early nineteenth-century, 285
Citizenship
    Fourteenth Amendment, 418–419,
        426
    residence requirement for, 183
Civil liberties, 191
    Federalist attack on, 176
Civil rights, during Civil War, 386
Civil Rights Act (1866), 418
Civil rights movement, 425
    first, 436–439
Civil service reform
    and election of 1876, 431
    during Grant presidency, 428
Civil War
    battles of, 394, 394(map)
    blockade of Southern ports, 388,
        390, 395
    border states in, 387
    causes of, 369–370, 375–376
    and Emancipation Proclamation,
        399–401

end of, 404–405
European involvement in, 390
financing of, 389–390
historical perspective on, 368
strategy and conduct of, 393–399
Clark, George Rogers, 130, 168, 188
Clark, William, 188, 189
Clay, Henry, 211, 215, 229, 246, 255
  and American System, 210
  and Bank of the United States,
    252–254
  and Compromise of 1850, 346, 347
  death of, 353
  and election of 1824, 232
  and election of 1828, 240
  and election of 1844, 332
  and Jacksonian presidency, 242
  land policy of, 247
  and nullification controversy, 251
  quoted, 197, 209
  slavery defended by, 228
  and Treaty of Ghent, 205
  and Tyler presidency, 327
Clayton-Bulwer treaty (1850), 354
Clermont (steamboat), 221
Clinton, Gov. De Witt, 159, 203
Clinton, Gen. Henry, 130
Clipper ships, 274
Cohens v. Virginia, 213
Cold Harbor, Battle of, 404
Cole, Thomas, 305–306
Colonies, American, 46(map)
  and Bacon's Rebellion, 34
  conflicts among, 72–75
  and Currency Act, 97–98
  education in, 80
  evolution of unity among, 106–112
  and Glorious Revolution, 49–50
  governments of, 88
  and Great Awakening, 77
  impact of religion on, 75–79
  and Indian warfare, 73–75
  Jamestown, 27–31
  Maryland, 31–33
  middle, 42–44, 63–66
  nationalities in, 65(map)
  and Navigation laws, 47–49
  life in, 33–34
  New England, 35–41, 66–70 (see
    also New England)
  overseas trade of, 69(map)
  Quartering Act and, 98

and question of authority, 89–90
royal governors in, 50
social stratification in, 58, 68
southern, 44–46, 58–63
and Stamp Act, 98
and Sugar Act, 98
women in, 70–72
Colonization. See also Expansion;
  Frontier
  early land grants, 28(map)
  economic and religious factors in,
    21–22
  French, 18–19
  role of merchants in, 9
Columbia College, founding of, 81
Columbia River Valley, 335
Columbus, Christopher, 3, 13–16
Committee system, 161. See also
  Congress
Committees of correspondence,
  103–104, 105, 110
Common Sense (Paine), 88, 110
Commonwealth v. Hunt, 287
Communication, telegraph, 273
Compromise of 1850, 347–348,
  348(map), 352, 356
Compromise of 1877, 430
Concord, Battle of, 108
Concurrent majority, Calhoun's
  doctrine of, 248–249
Confederate States of America
  army raised by, 391–392
  declaration of war by, 384
  formation of, 373
  government of, 384–385
  military commanders of, 392–393
  at outset of Civil War, 387
  resources of, 388
  at war's end, 412
Confederation period
  economic problems of, 142–143
  foreign affairs during, 137–139
  Shays's Rebellion during, 143–144
  western lands during, 139–149
Confederation of the United Colonies
  of New England, 39
Confessions of Nat Turner, The, 283
Confiscation Act (1862), 387
Congregational church, 76–77, 308
Congress, U.S.
  Constitutional provision for, 155
  first, 161–162

compared to Grand Council of the
  Iroquois League, 225
power limited by Articles of
  Confederation, 136–137
in Reconstruction, 417–422
President Washington and, 160–161
Connecticut
  colonial government of, 88–89, 90
  early settlement of, 41
Conquistadores, 5, 16, 17
Constitution, U.S.S., 202
Constitution, Confederate, 384
Constitution, U.S. See also
  Amendments
  Bill of Rights, 162
  Congress and, 155
  Hamilton's broad construction of,
    164–165
  Jackson's strict construction of,
    240–241
  Jefferson's strict construction of,
    164–165
  Marshall's interpretation of,
    213–214
  provisions of, 155
  ratification of, 156–160
  slavery and, 154–155
Constitutional Convention
  delegates to, 152
  Great Compromise, 154
  historical perspective on, 158–159
  Jersey Plan, 154
  Three-fifths Compromise, 154–155
  Virginia Plan, 153–154
Constitutional Union party, 367
Constitutions, state, 133–134
  Carolina's, 45
  Connecticut's, 41
Continental army, 121
  and British campaign against New
    York City, 123
  at Valley Forge, 129–130
Continental Association, 106–107
Continental Congress
  and Articles of Confederation, 136
  and Declaration of Independence,
    111
  First, 106–108
  and peace negotiations, 132–133
  Second, 108–110
  and state constitutions, 134
Coode, John, 50

Cooper, Sir Anthony Ashley, 44
Cooper, James Fenimore, 237, 301
Copley, John Singleton, 83
Copperheads, 386
Corn
  colonial cultivation of, 32, 63
  as predominant cash crop, 276
Corn belt, 276
Corn laws, British, 274
Cornplanter, Jesse, 115, 116
Cornwallis, Gen. Charles, 130, 131, 132
Coronado, Vásques de, 16
Corporations. *See also* Business; Industry
  rise of, 219
Cortes, Hernando, 16
Cotton
  dominance of, 219–220
  embargo on, 388, 390
  overproduction of, 225
  and slave labor, 278–279
Cotton gin, 220
  invention of, 219
  and slavery, 227
Council of the Indies, 18
County government, origins of, 66
Cowpens, Battle of, 130
Cox, John, 425
Cox, La Wanda, 425
Craven, Avery, 369
Crawford, William H., 212, 231, 249
Crédit Mobilier scandal, 429
Creek Indians, 57, 97, 161, 203
Crèvecoeur, St. John de, 57, 120
Crimean War, 363
Crittenden, John J., 371
Crittenden Compromise, 371
Crockett, Davy, 330
Cromwell, Oliver, 41
Crop-lien system, 417
Crusades, commercial effect of, 8
Cuba, attempted acquisition of, 352
Cuban-Americans, economic success of, 855–856. *See also* Hispanic-Americans
Cumberland Road, 212
Currency. *See also* Money
  during Confederation period, 142–143
  and long-distance trade, 8
Currency Act (1764), 97–98

Curtis, Benjamin R., 361
Cushing, Caleb, 274
Cuzco, 16

D

Dale, Thomas, 30, 31
Dana, Richard Henry, 321
Darrah, Lydia, 149
Dartmouth College v. *Woodward*, 214
Davenport, John, 41
Davis, David Brion, 369
Davis, Jefferson, 395, 405
  character of, 385
  and Fort Sumter attack, 373–375
  and military strategy, 392
  nomination as Confederate president, 384
Deane, Silas, 128
Dearborn, Gen. Henry, 201
Debates
  Lincoln-Douglas, 364–366
  Webster-Hayne, 249
Debt, national
  during Jefferson's two terms, 183
  after Revolutionary War, 163–164
  and War of 1812, 205
Decatur, Stephen, 202
Declaration of Causes of Taking-up Arms, 110
Declaration of Independence, 88, 105, 111–112, 119
Declaratory Act (1766), 100, 106
Deere, John, 277
Deerfield, Massachusetts, 90
de Soto, Hernando, 16
Deism, 80
Delaware
  and Civil War, 387
  colonial government of, 88–89
Democracy
  Jacksonian, 238, 258–259, 263
  Tocqueville on, 296
Democratic Clubs, 171
Democratic party
  and Bank of the United States, 255
  beginnings of, 240–241, 254–255
  Copperheads, 386
  and election of 1856, 360
  Irish-Americans in, 291

President Jackson in, 254–255
  and Kansas-Nebraska Act, 357
  northern and southern divisions, 360–367, 370
Democratic Republicans (Jacksonian coalition), 240–241, 254–255, 257, 258–260. *See also* Republicans, Democratic
Democrats, Southern, and election of 1860, 366–367
Demos, John, 77
Depression; *See also* Panic
  after Revolutionary War, 143
Dial, The, 300, 321
Dias, Batholomeu, 13
Dickerson, Oliver M., 48
Dickinson, Emily, 82
Dickinson, John, 102, 106, 154
Dinwiddie, Robert, 91, 92, 93
Disease. *See also* Standard of living
  and frontier life, 271
  and immigrant labor, 287
  and urban growth, 285
District of Columbia
  slave trade in, 316, 346
  slavery in, 400
Dix, Dorothea, 311, 389
Dominican Republic, attempt to annex, 428
Donelson, Fort, 395
Doolittle, Amos, 107
Douglas, Stephen A., 347, 386
  debates with Lincoln, 364–366
  and Dred Scott decision, 362
  and election of 1860, 366
  and Kansas-Nebraska Act, 356–357
  and popular sovereignty, 363
Douglass, Frederick, 314, 401
  on slavery, 281
  and Underground Railroad, 315
Dow, Neal, 312
Draft, during Civil War, 391
Drake, Sir Francis, 53
Draper, Mary, 149
Dred Scott decision, 360–362
DuBois, W. E. B., 434
Dunlop, William, 301
Dunkards, 66
Dunning, William A., 425
Durand, Asher, 305
Dutch West India Company, 42

E

Earl, Ralph, 107
East, and protective tariff, 227. *See also* Sectionalism
East India Company, British, 104, 105
Eaton, John H., 240, 249–250
Eaton, Theophilus, 41
Economic panic
  of 1819, 225–227, 238
  of 1837, 256–257, 261, 287
  of 1857, 363
  of 1873, 430
Economic Interpretation of the Constitution of the United States, An (Beard), 108, 158
Economy. *See also* Depression; Industry; Inflation; Panic
  during Civil War, 406
  dominance of cotton in, 219–220
  early industrialization, 217–219
  expansion and, 256
  laissez-faire policy, 261, 271
  New England's, 41
  post-Revolutionary War growth in, 165–166
  slave-dependent, 61, 278
  and transportation, 221–224
Education
  adult, 310–311
  in colonial era, 80–82
  influence of immigrants on, 293
  lyceum lectures, 294–296
  pre-Civil War reform in, 309–311
  and Reconstruction, 436–439
  in South, 422
Edwards, Jonathan, 78, 82
Edwards, Justin, 311
Elections, Constitutional provision for, 155
Elections, congressional
  of 1866, 419
Elections, presidential
  first, 160
  of 1792, 166
  of 1796, 173
  of 1800, 177, 182
  of 1804, 190
  of 1808, 195
  of 1816, 212–213
  of 1820, 224

  of 1824, 231–232, 231(map)
  of 1828, 240–241, 240(map)
  of 1832, 254–255, 255(map)
  of 1836, 260
  of 1840, 261–263
  of 1844, 332
  of 1848, 344
  of 1852, 353
  of 1856, 360
  of 1860, 366–371, 367(map)
  of 1864, 405–407, 407(map)
  of 1868, 426–427, 426(map)
  of 1872, 428
  of 1876, 430–431, 430(map)
Electoral college, Constitutional provision for, 155
Eliot, John, 40
Elizabeth I (queen of England), 13–19, 20
Elkins, Stanley, 159
Ellet, Elizabeth, 146–147
Emancipation Proclamation, 399–401
Embargo Act (1807), 194
Emerson, John, 360
Emerson, Ralph Waldo, 300–301, 312
Engerman, Stanley L., 281
England. *See also* Britain; Colonies
  and American Civil War, 390
  and American embargo, 192–195
  civil war of, 21
  colonization by, 19, 21–22
  Currency Act, 97–98
  and French and Indian War, 91–96
  Glorious Revolution in, 49
  and Jamestown settlement, 27–31
  mercantilism of, 47, 48
  monarchy of, 10
  and Plymouth colony, 35–37
  and Proclamation of 1763, 96–97
  Quartering Act, 98
  Reformation in, 13
  royal governors of, 88–89
  ships seized by, 168–169
  Stamp Act, 98
  Sugar Act, 98
  Townshend Acts, 101–102
  and Treaty of Paris, 95
  and War of 1812, 200–206
  wars with France, 90–91
English bill, 363

Enlightenment
  and American painting, 305
  and colonial America, 79–80
  and transcendentalism, 299
Era of Good Feelings, 212–217
Erie Canal, 222, 224
Erie Railroad, 471
Erskine, David M., 196
Essex (ship), 192
Essex Junto, 190
Ethnicity
  in American colonies, 65(map)
  in pre-Civil War America, 290–293
Europe
  competition for America, 18–22
  economic revolution of, 8–9
  and exploration of New World, 13–16
  Protestant Reformation in, 10–13
  and rise of national monarchies, 9–10
  and wealth from New World, 17
"Evacuation treaties," 245
Expansion. *See also* Frontier
  agricultural, 275–283
  and annexation of Texas, 329–333
  commercial, 274–275
  and Compromise of 1850, 348
  Gadsden Purchase, 355–356
  impact on Indians, 268
  industrial, 283–284
  and Maine boundary dispute, 327–329
  "manifest destiny," 326–327
  and Mexican War, 340–344
  and Oregon controversy, 333–335
  and Pierce presidency, 353–356
  and sectionalism, 344–348
  westward, 335–339, 336(map)

F

Factories. *See also* Industrialization
  development of, 218–219
  in early nineteenth century, 286
Fair Oaks, Battle at, 398
Farragut, David Glasgow, 396
Federalism, 114
Federalist Papers, The, 157–158, 159
Federalists
  accomplishments of, 177–178

composition of, 172–173
and conflict with France, 175
demise of, 224
at Hartford Convention, 203–204
historical perspective on, 158–159
policy of, 156–157
and Sedition Act, 176
and War of 1812, 198
and Whiskey Rebellion, 171
Fenno, John, 166
Ferdinand II of Aragon (king of
    Spain), 9, 15
Ferguson, Isabella, 146
Feudalism, in New World, 16
Few, William, 152
Fillmore, Millard, 360
    and Compromise of 1850, 347
    and election of 1856, 360
Finney, Charles G., 298, 315
Fisher, David, 178
Fisk, "Jubilee" Jim, 428
Fisk University, 416
Fitzhugh, George, 317
Five Forks, Battle of, 405
Five Nations Confederacy, 114
Flag
    American, 135, 136
    Bear, 339
Fletcher v. *Peck*, 214
Florida (ship), 390
Florida
    acquisition of, 214–215
    ceded to England, 95
    secession of, 371
Fogel, Robert W., 281
Foot Resolution, 247, 249
Force Act (1809), 195
Force Acts (1870 and 1871), 424
Foreign policy. *See also* Diplomacy
    of Jackson's presidency, 243
    Monroe Doctrine, 216–217
    after War of 1812, 214–216
Foster, Stephen, 307–308
Founding Fathers
    characteristics of, 152
    historical perspective on, 158–159
Fourier, Charles, 309
Fowler, Orin, 267
Fox, George, 43
Fox Indians, 246
Frame of Government,
    Pennsylvania's, 44

France, and American Civil War, 390
    and American embargo, 192–195
    and American Revolution, 127–129
    breaking of diplomatic relations
        with, 243
    colonial warfare of, 91–96
    exploration and colonization by,
        18–19
    and Louisiana Purchase, 185–188
    monarchy of, 10
    and Treaty of Paris, 95
    undeclared war against, 175–176,
        177
    wars with England, 90–91
Francis I (king of France), 18
Franco-American Alliance (1778),
    166–168, 175
Franklin, Benjamin, 70, 75, 82, 83,
    116, 137
    at Albany Congress, 94
    conference with General Howe, 123
    at Constitutional Convention,
        152–155
    and Declaration of Independence,
        111
    and French alliance, 128
    and peace negotiations, 132–133
    quoted, 96, 128, 155
    at Second Continental Congress,
        109
    on taxation of colonies, 101
Fredericksburg, Battle of, 402–403
Freedmen, 412. *See also* Blacks
    and Compromise of 1877, 431
    and education, 437
    during Reconstruction, 415–417
Freedmen's Aid Society, 437
Freedmen's Bureau, 416, 418
Freeholders, 32
Freeman, Thomas, 190
Freemasonry, and election of 1832,
    254
Freemen, 33–34
    in colonial era, 89
    pre-Civil War restrictions on, 317
"Freeport Doctrine," 365, 366
Free-Soilers, 354, 355
Free Soil party, 316–317, 344
    and *Dred Scott* decision, 362
    in Kansas, 358–359
Frelinghusen, Theodore, 77
Fremantle, Arthur J. L., 383

Frémont, John C., 339, 360
French and Indian War, 91–96,
    92(map)
    aftermath of, 94–96, 95(map)
    Albany Congress, 93–94
    campaigns of, 94
    Washington's mission, 91–93
Freneau, Philip, 166, 301
Frontier
    during colonial era, 69–70
    Lewis and Clark's exploration of,
        188–190
    life on, 271–272
    movement west and, 268–270,
        270(map)
    and railroads, 272–274
    and the Second Great Awakening,
        298
    settlement of, 270
    women on, 71–72
Fugitive Slave Act, and election of
    1856, 360
Fugitive slave law (1793), 345, 347,
    352, 371, 379
Fuller, Margaret, 300, 320–323
Fuller, Timothy, 320
Fulton, Robert, 221
Fundamental Constitutions, of
    Carolinia, 45
Fundamental Orders of Connecticut,
    41
Fur trade
    of Chesapeake Bay area, 34
    and French government, 19
    and Oregon controversy, 333, 335

G

Gadsden, Christopher, 102, 106
Gadsden, James, 355
Gadsden Purchase, 355–356
Gag Rule, 316
Gage, Gen. Thomas, 107, 109
Gallatin, Albert
    as secretary of treasury, 183, 200,
        212
    and Treaty of Ghent, 205
Galloway, Joseph, 106, 107
Gama, Vasco da, 13
Garden, Alexander, 82
Gardoqui, Don Diego de, 139

Garrison, William Lloyd, 315, 316
Gaspée (ship), 104
Gates, Gen. Horatio, 130
Gates, Sir Thomas, 30, 54
General Court, of Massachusetts Bay
    Colony, 39
Gênet, Edmond, 168
Geneva, Calvinism of, 12
Genovese, Eugene, 281
George II (king of England), 45
George III (king of England), 96,
    109–110, 111
Georgia
    Cherokee nation in, 244
    early settlement of, 45–46
    secession of, 371
German-Americans
    in Pennsylvania, 66
    in pre-Civil War America, 292–293
    spread of, 73
Germantown, Battle of, 126
Gerry, Elbridge, 175
Gerteis, Louis S., 425
Gettysburg, Battle of, 403
Ghana, kingdom of, 61
Ghent, Treaty of (1814), 205
Gibbons v. *Ogden*, 213
Giddings, Joshua R., 317
Gilbert, Sir Humphrey, 26
Gipson, Lawrence H., 108
Girondists, 167
Glorious Revolution, 49–50, 88, 96,
    98
Gold
    discovered in California, 274, 345
    mercantilist theory and, 47
    and sixteenth-century Spanish
        economy, 17
Goodman, Paul, 177
Goodyear, Charles, 283
Gosnold, Bartholomew, 53
Government Land Office, 268
"Grandfather laws," 432, 433
Grant, Ulysses S., 392, 393, 402
    and Battle for Mississippi Valley, 395
    at Battle of Shiloh, 396
    and corruption in Washington,
        D.C., 427–428
    economic policies of, 427
    and Lee's surrender, 405
    political style of, 427
    as presidential nominee, 426
    Vicksburg campaign of, 404

"Grantism," 430
Grasse, Comte de, 131, 132
Gray, Thomas R., 283
Great Awakening, 77–79, 111
Great Awakening, Second, 297–298
Great Compromise, 154
"Great Compromiser," 210
Great Fundamentals, 36
Great Migration, 37–39
Greeley, Horace, 322, 344, 384, 429
Greenbacks, 389–390. *See also* Money
Greene, Gen. Nathanael, 130, 219
Greene, Mrs. Catharine, 219
Green Mountain Boys, 127
Greenville, Treaty of (1795), 170
Grenville, George, 96, 98, 99
Grimké, Angelina, 313
Grimké, Sarah, 313
Guadalupe Hidalgo, Treaty of,
    (1848), 343
Guilford Courthouse, Battle of, 130
Guinn v. *United States*, 433
Gutman, Herbert G., 281

H

Hacker, Louis M., 48
Hakluyt, Richard, 26
"Halfbreeds" (Republican faction),
    431
Halfway Covenant, 76–77
Halleck, Gen. Henry W., 395, 396,
    399
Hamilton, Alexander, 156
    at Constitutional Convention, 152
    controversy with Jefferson, 166, 172
    death of, 190
    and election of 1796, 173
    and election of 1800, 177
    and *Federalist* papers, 157
    in first Congress, 161
    fiscal policy of, 162–166
    foreign policy of, 166
    quoted, 217
    in Washington's cabinet, 161
    on Whiskey Rebellion, 171
Hammond, Bray, 258
Hancock, John, 68, 109, 137
Harlan, John Marshall, 433
Harper, L. A., 48
Harpers Ferry, John Brown's raid on,
    366

Harper's Weekly, 429–430, 437
Harrison, Peter, 83
Harrison, William Henry, 198
    election as president, 260–261
    inauguration and death of, 327
    Tecumseh defeated by, 199–200
    and War of 1812, 202, 205
Hart, Nancy Morgan, 149
Hartford, Connecticut, 41
Hartford Convention, 203–204
Harvard College, 78, 80, 81
Hawthorne, Nathaniel, 76, 302,
    303–304
Hayes, Rutherford, B.,
        election as president, 431
Hayne, Robert, 249
Hays, Mary Ludwig, 148–149
Headright system, 31, 63
Henry, Fort, 395
Henry, Patrick, 102, 106, 137,
    158
Henry VIII (king of England), 13
Henry the Navigator (prince of
    Portugal), 13
Hessians, in American Revolution,
    110, 123, 126
Highways. *See also* Transportation
    Cumberland Road, 212
    Lancaster Turnpike, 221
Hildreth, Richard, 280
Hill, James J., 471
Hofstadter, Richard, 258
Holbrook, Josiah, 311
Holland. *See* Netherlands
Holmes, Oliver Wendell, 321
Holy Alliance, 217
Hooker, Gen. Joseph, 403
Hooker, Thomas, 41
Hopi Indians, 5
Horseshoe Bend, Battle of, 203, 239
Hortalez et Compagnie, 128, 129
House of Representatives. *See also*
    Congress
    constitutional provisions for,
        154, 155
House of Seven Gables, The
    (Hawthorne), 302
Houston, Sam, 330, 331
Howard University, 416
Howe, Adm. Richard, 123
Howe, Gen. William, 122, 123, 126,
    127, 130
Hudson, Henry, 19

Hudson River School, 305–306
Huguenots, 18, 64
Hull, Capt. Isaac, 202
Hull, William, 201
Hume, David, 80, 111
Huron Indians, 90
Hussey, Obed, 277
Hutchinson, Anne, 40–41, 72
Hutchinson, Thomas, 82, 99

I

Illinois, and frontier, 269
Illiteracy. See also Education
  in colonial America, 82
Immigrants. See also Ethnicity
  competition with free blacks, 280
  and Democratic party, 259
  in labor force, 287–288
  prejudice against, 288
Immigration
  colonial, 22, 37–39
  and ethnic diversity, 290–293
  and Know-Nothing party, 353
  Mexican, 330
  to middle colonies, 64–66
  and western lands, 269–270
Impeachment, of Andrew Johnson,
  420–422
Impressment, British policy of, 169,
  192–193
Incan Indians, 4–5, 16–17
Income distribution. See also Social
  stratification
  in early nineteenth century, 268
Indentured servitude, 31, 33–34
Independent Treasury Act (1840), 261
Indiana, and frontier, 269
Indians, American. See also specific
  tribes
  in The Book of Mormons, 298
  Catlin's paintings of, 307
  and early colonists, 8
  early migration of, 4
  impact of expansion on, 268
  Jackson's removal program for, 243
  and Jamestown settlement, 31
  during Jefferson's presidency, 199
  land cessions and migrations,
    244–246, 244(map)
  and League of Great Peace,
    114–117

northern, 5–8
origin of name, 16
Puritans' relations with, 39–40
and Quakers, 44
and settlement of New Mexico, 337
and War of 1812, 205
and warfare with colonists, 73
Industrialization, 195
  and American worker, 286
  and Civil War, 368, 388
  in early nineteenth century,
    217–218
  effects of, 308
  factory development, 218
  and labor movement, 286–288
  North vs. South, 352
  during pre-Civil War period,
    283–284
  rise of corporations, 219
  sectional aspects of, 284
  and urban growth, 284–286
Inflation. See also Economy
  during Civil War, 390, 412
  and frontier expansion, 271
  and Revolutionary War, 121
Ingersoll, Charles Jared, 301
Inman, Elizabeth, 72
"Intolerable Acts" (1774), 105
Iowa, University of, 314
Irish-Americans
  in labor force, 287–288
  in pre-Civil War America,
    290–293
Iron Act (1750), 48
Iron industry. See also Steel industry
  Mesabi Range, 329
Ironclads, 391, 395, 396–397
Iroquois Confederation, 7–8, 39, 74,
  114–117
  compared with congressional
    system, 225
  English alliance with, 90
  and French and Indian War, 93
Irving, Washington, 302
Isabella of Castile (queen of Spain), 9,
  15, 16

J

Jackson, Andrew, 203, 204, 205, 232
  and Bank of the United States,
    251–257

and Democratic coalition, 258–260
  election as president, 240
  and election of 1832, 254–255
  Florida invaded by, 215
  foreign policy of, 243
  historical perspective on,
    258–259
  Indian removal program of,
    243
  and internal improvements,
    246–247
  Kitchen Cabinet of, 242
  on national bank, 252
  and nullification controversy,
    250–251
  as people's candidate, 239–240
  as president-elect, 237
  and protective tariffs, 247–251
  and public lands, 247
  reelection of, 254–255
  spoils system of, 241–242
Jackson, Gen. Thomas Jonathan
  (Stonewall), 393, 395, 398,
  403
Jackson, Rachel, 241
Jacobins, 168
James I (king of England), 19, 21,
  26, 32
James II (king of England), 48,
  49
James, Marquis, 258
Jameson, J. Franklin, 108
Jamestown
  early years of, 29–30
  House of Burgesses, 31
  as Royal Colony, 31
  settlement of, 27–29
Japan, trade with, 274–275
Jarratt, Devereux, 64
Jay, John, 106, 129, 139
  British mission of, 169
  as chief justice, 162
  and Federalist papers, 157
  and Paris peace negotiations,
    132–133
  quoted, 137
Jay Cooke and Company, 430
Jay's Treaty (1794), 169–170, 175
Jefferson, Thomas, 72, 102, 105, 116,
  137
  on church and state, 135
  controversy with Hamilton, 166,
    172

and Declaration of Independence, 111
election as president, 177
fiscal policy of, 164–165
international problems of, 191–195
and judiciary, 184–185
and Louisiana Purchase, 185
as minister to Paris, 138
philosophy of, 182–183
political opponents of, 190
as presidential candidate, 173
quoted, 158, 181
reaction to Shays's Rebellion, 144
reelection of, 190
at Second Continental Congress, 109
as secretary of state, 166–167, 168, 183
and Sedition Act, 176
on slavery, 231
in Washington's cabinet, 161
on Whiskey Rebellion, 171
Jeffersonians. See Republicans, Democratic
Jenkins, Capt. Robert, 90
Jenkins's Ear, War of, 90–91
Jews, in colonies, 75
Jim Crow laws, 432
Johnson, Andrew, 406
impeachment of, 420–422
opposition to secession of, 415
and Reconstruction, 419
as vice-president, 406, 415
Johnson, Ludwell H., 368
Johnston, Gen. Albert Sidney, 395, 396, 398
Johnston, Joseph E., 397–398, 405
Joint-stock companies, 22, 26, 35, 37
Jordan, Winthrop, 369
Judicial review, 184, 213
Judiciary Act (1789), 162, 184, 185
Judiciary Act (1801), 184
Julian, George P., 317
Jumel, Betsy, 191

K

Kansas
crisis over, 362–363
and frontier, 269
settlement of, 358
statehood, 359, 363
Kansas-Nebraska Act (1854), 356–357, 356(map), 357–358, 360
Kearny, Col. Stephen W., 341
Kentucky
and Civil War, 387, 396
settlement of, 97
statehood, 170
Kentucky Resolutions, 177
Kenyon, Cecelia M., 159
King, Rufus, 197, 212
King George's War, 91
King Philip's War, 39–40
King William's War, 90
King's Mountain, Battle of, 130
Knights of the White Camelia, 423
Know-Nothing party, 353
and election of 1856, 360
and election of 1860, 367
Knox, Henry, 161
Ku Klux Klan, 423

L

Labor. See also Union Movement
colonial, 33
immigrant, 287
slave, 278–280, 314
Ladd, William, 312
Lafayette, Marquis de, 121, 130, 131
Laissez-faire economic policy, 261
and land speculation, 271
Lancaster Turnpike, 221
Land Act (1800), 226
Land Act (1820), 226
Land grants, early colonial, 28(map)
Land Ordinance (1785), 139
Land policy
frontier speculation, 271
graduation, 247
and Panic of 1819, 226
preemption, 247
and Specie Circular, 256
Larkin, Thomas, 339
Latin America. See Monroe Doctrine; specific countries
Latter-Day Saints, Church of Jesus Christ of, 298. See also Mormons
Lawgiver, 114
League of Great Peace, 8, 114–117
Leatherstocking Tales (Cooper), 301
Leather-tanning industry, 284
Leaves of Grass (Whitman), 302, 303
LeClerc, Gen. Charles V. E., 187, 188
Lecompton Constitution, 362–363
Lee, Arthur, 128
Lee, Mother Ann, 309
Lee, Richard Henry, 102, 106, 111
Lee, Gen. Robert E., 392, 393, 398, 405
Legislation
civil rights, 418
Legislature, colonial, 89, 98
Legree, Simon, 352
Leisler, Jacob, 49
Lemisch, Jesse, 109
Leopard (ship), 193, 194
Letters from an American Farmer (de Crèvecoeur), 57
Levine, Lawrence, 281
Lewis, Meriwether, 188, 189
Lexington, Battle of, 107–108
Liberal Republican party, 428
Liberator, The, 315
Liberia, 317
Liberty party, 316
Life-style. See also Standard of living
colonial, 33–34
on frontier, 271–272
of slaves, 317
Lima, Spanish viceroy in, 18
Lincoln, Abraham
assassination of, 414
background of, 363
character of, 364
debates with Douglas, 365–366
and election of 1864, 406
first inaugural address of, 373
on Mexican War, 340
nomination of, 367, 370
presidential campaign of, 370–371
reconstruction program of, 412–413
and secession crisis, 373–375
second inaugural address of, 411
on slavery, 351
as war leader, 385–386
Lindneux, Robert, 245
Literacy tests, 432
Supreme Court on, 433
Literature. See also specific works
colonial, 82

of late eighteenth century, 301
of pre-Civil War era, 302
Little Belt (ship), 197
Litwack, Leon, 369
Livingston, Robert, 111, 186–187,
  221
Locke, John, 45, 79–80, 111, 114,
  159, 300
Locofocoism, 259
London, Treaty of (1794), 169–170
London Company, 27, 31, 35
Lone Star Republic, 331
Lords of Trade, 48
Louis XVI (king of France), 128, 167
Louisbourg, Nova Scotia, 91
Louisiana
  ceded to Spain, 95
  secession of, 371
  statehood, 190, 227
Louisiana Purchase, 185–188,
  186(map), 206
Louisiana Territory, exploration of,
  188–190
L'Ouverture Toussaint, Pierre
  Dominique, 187, 188
Lovejoy, Rev. Elijah P., 315, 316
Lowell, Francis Cabot, 218–219
Lowell, Massachusetts, 219
  mills of, 286–287
Loyal Land Company, 91
"Loyal Leagues," 422
Lucus, Elizabeth, 72
Luther, Martin, 10–12
Lyceum movement, 311
Lyon, Mary, 314

M

McClellan, Gen. George B., 387
  peninsular campaign of, 396–399,
    397(map)
  as Democratic nominee, 407
McCormick, Cyrus, 277
McCormick, Richard P., 259
McCulloch v. *Maryland*, 213, 254
McDonald, Forrest, 158
McDowell, Gen. Irvin, 395
McHenry, James, 175
McKitrick, Eric L., 159, 425
Macon's Bill No. 2, 196–197
Madison, Dolley, 195, 196

Madison, James, 137, 152, 173
  and acquisition of Florida, 215
  at Constitutional Convention, 152,
    159
  and *Federalist* papers, 157
  in first Congress, 161
  and *Marbury* v. *Madison*, 184
  presidency of, 195–200
  and Sedition Act, 176
Magellan, Ferdinand, 16, 18
Magna Charta, 19, 21
Maier, Pauline, 109
Main, Jackson Turner, 158
Maine
  boundary dispute, 327–329
  Plymouth Company's settlement in,
    26–27
  statehood, 228, 229
Mali, kingdom of, 61
Manhattan Island, 42
"Manifest destiny," 326–327, 348. *See
  also* Expansion
Mann, Horace, 309–310
Manorialism, 8
Manufacturing. *See also* Factories;
    Industrialization
  in early nineteenth century, 218
  and Embargo Act, 195
  Hamilton's report on, 165–166
  inventions, 219, 467
  mass-production methods in,
    283–284
  North vs. South, 352
  and sectionalism, 284
  and tariff protection, 211
Marbury v. *Madison*, 184–185, 213
Marcy, William L., 354
Marlowe, Christopher, 52
Marriage of Figaro, The
    (Beaumarchais), 128
Marshall, John, 175
  appointment as chief justice, 184
  and Burr's trial, 191
  Cohens v. *Virginia*, 213
  Constitutional nationalism under,
    213–214
  Dartmouth College v. *Woodward*,
    214
  Gibbons v. *Ogden*, 213
  McCulloch v. *Maryland*, 213–214
  Marbury v. *Madison*, 184–185
  reactions to decisions, 214

Sturges v. *Crowninshield*, 214
Marx, Karl, 108
Marxist interpretations, of Civil War,
  368
Mary II (queen of England), 49, 98
Maryland
  and Civil War, 387
  colonial government of, 88–89
  colonization of, 31–32
  as feudal estate, 32
  religious toleration in, 33
  representative government in,
    32–33
  tobacco economy of, 33
Mason, George, 138
Mason, James, 390
Masons, and election of 1832, 254
Massachusetts. *See also* Boston
  Boston Massacre, 103
  colonial government of, 89
  committees of correspondence in,
    103–104
  education in, 80
  and Intolerable Acts, 105
  new charter for, 50
Massachusetts Bay Colony, 37–39,
  122
Massachusetts Government Act
  (1774), 105
Mass-production methods, 283–284.
  See also Industrialization
Mather, Cotton, 71, 82, 83
Matteson, Dorcas, 149
Matthews, Gen. George, 215
Mayflower Compact, 35
Maysville Road veto, 246
Mazzini, Giuseppe, 323
Meade, Gen. George Gordon, 403
Meat-packing industry, 277
  and sectionalism, 284
Melville, Herman, 302, 303, 304
Mennonites, 66
Mercantilism, 47
  historical perspective on, 108
Merchants, effect on colonization, 9.
  See also Trade
Merrimack (ship), 397, 398
Mesabi Range, 329
Methodist church, 79, 80, 135
  and Great Awakening, 297–298
  and Temperance movement, 311
Mexican War

beginning of, 340–341
conduct of, 341–342, 342(map)
legacy of, 343–344
peace settlement of, 342–343
Mexico
and annexation of Texas, 330
independence of, 338
Mexico City, Spanish viceroy in, 18
Meyers, Marvin, 259
Miami Indians, 169
Michigan, statehood, 331
Middle class, 296. See also Social
stratification
in colonial New England, 68
of Europe, 12
women in, 313
Middle colonies. See also Colonies
county government in, 66
immigration to, 64–66
landholding in, 63–64
slavery in, 59
Milan Decree (1807), 192
Military Reconstruction Act, 420
Miller, Douglas T., 259
Miller, William (clergyman), 298
Minorities. See Blacks; Ethnicity;
Women
Minstrel shows, 307
Mississippi
public school system in, 438
during Reconstruction, 415, 420
secession of, 371
Mississippi River
importance of, 138–139, 185
South's dependence on, 274
steamboat travel on, 222
Mississippi Valley, in Civil War,
395–396
Missouri
and Civil War, 387
constitution of, 229
statehood, 228, 229
Missouri Compromise, 227–231,
230(map), 362
Missouri Territory, 227
Mitchell, John (botanist), 82
Moby Dick (Melville), 302, 304
Mohawk Indians, 114
Monarchy
English, 10
Spanish, 9
Money. See also Currency; Gold;

Silver
greenbacks, 389–390, 426
Monitor (ship), 397, 398
Monmouth Court House, Battle of,
130, 148
Monroe, James, 173, 187, 193, 197,
224
and acquisition of Florida, 215
election as president, 212
Indian policy of, 243
presidency of, 213
Monroe Doctrine, 216–217
Polk corollary to, 340
Montcalm, Marquis de, 94
Monterey, California, 338, 339
Montesquieu, Baron de, 114, 135
Montezuma, 16
Montgomery, Gen. Richard, 122
Montreal, British capture of, 94
Moore's Creek Bridge, Battle of, 122
Moravians, 66
Morgan, Lewis Henry, 116, 117
Morgan, William, 254
Morison, Samuel Eliot, 78, 82
Mormons
early settlement of, 298–299
Utah settled by, 337, 338
Morris, Robert, 143
Mott, Lucretia, 313
Mount, William Sidney, 306
Mount Holyoke College, 314
Mount Vernon, 161

N

Napoleon, 175, 185
and American embargo, 197
Berlin Decree of, 192
and Louisiana Purchase, 187–188
Nast, Thomas, 429
Natchez Indians, 5
Natchez Trace, 221
Nathan, James, 322
National Bank Act (1863), 390
Nationalism, 263. See also Ethnicity
American, 79
after American Revolution, 135
American System, 210–212
Constitutional, 213–214
of John Quincy Adams, 234
Neo-Federalism, 210
National Republicans. See Whigs

National Road, 221, 226, 233. See
also Highways
Native Americans, 4. See also Indians
Naturalization Act (1798), 176
Navigation acts, 47–49, 95, 101
historical perspective on, 108
Navy, U.S.
ironclads in, 391, 395, 396–397
during Jefferson's presidency, 192,
193
and War of 1812, 200, 202
Nebraska Country, 356, 357
Neo-Federalism, 210
Netherlands
and American Revolution, 128–129
colonization of, 42
early exploration by, 19
New Amsterdam colony, 90
Neutrality, during Washington's
administration, 167
Neutrality Act (1794), 168
Nevins, Allan, 369
New Amsterdam, 42
New England
canal system in, 224
Dominion of, 48–49
family life in, 67
federalism in, 198
founding of, 35–41
in 1634, 38(map)
slavery in, 59
and War of 1812, 203
New England Anti-Slavery Society,
315
New England colonies. See also
Colonies
cities of, 68
Connecticut, 41
crafts in, 67–68
education in, 80
government of, 89
Massachusetts Bay, 37–39
New Hampshire, 41
Plymouth, 35–37
representative government in, 39
Rhode Island, 40–41
town-meeting government in,
66–67
triangular trade of, 68
New France, 18, 19
New Hampshire, as Royal Colony, 41
New Harmony, 308

New Haven, Connecticut, 41
New Jersey, and racial equality, 231
New Jersey Plan, 154
New Mexico
  and Mexican War, 341
  settlement of, 337
New Orleans, Louisiana, 170
  Battle of, 203, 204, 239
  importance of, 185, 187
  population growth in, 285
  Union capture of, 396
New World
  English presence in, 31
  European exploration of, 13–16
  first written constitution in, 41
  French in, 18–19
  joint-stock companies in, 22, 26,
    35, 37
  wealth from, 17–18
New York City
  British campaign against, 123
  Irish immigrants in, 291
  population growth of, 284
New York State
  canal system in, 224
  colonization of, 42
  constitution adopted by, 159
  landholding in, 63
  Progressive movement in, 581
New York *Times*, 429
Newfoundland
  ceded to England, 90
  fishing rights off, 95, 133, 205
Newport, Christopher, 54
Newport, Rhode Island, 69
  British capture of, 123
Newspapers
  black, 280
  colonial, 83
Newton, Sir Isaac, 79
Ninety-five Theses, 10–11
Nonintercourse Act (1809), 195
North. *See also* Sectionalism
  and Constitutional Convention,
    154
  economic interests of, 224–226
  industrialization in, 283, 284
  and Missouri Compromise, 227
  and protective tariff, 226
  reaction to Kansas-Nebraska Act
    in, 357
North, Lord Frederick, 103, 104–105,

122, 127, 132
North Carolina
  colonization of, 45
  Constitution ratified by, 160
  secession of, 387
Northwest Ordinance (1787),
    141–142, 141(map), 227
Northwest Passage, 18, 19
Nova Scotia, ceded to England, 90
Noyes, John Humphrey, 309
Nullification controversy, 210, 249,
    250–251

O

Oberlin College, 314
Oglethorpe, Gen. James, 45
Ohio, pioneering in, 141
Ohio Territory, 170
Ohio Valley, 96, 97, 106
Oil industry, early growth of, 283
Oklahoma
  and frontier, 269
  and Indian removal, 243
"Old Ironsides," 202
Olive Branch Petition, 109–110
Oneida Indians, 114
Onis, Luis de, 215
Onondaga Indians, 114
Opium War, 274
Orders in Council, British, 195, 196,
    200
Ordinance of Nullification, South
    Carolina's, 250–251
Oregon, settlement of, 333–334
Oregon Trail, 334
Oregon Treaty, 335
Osceola Indians, 246
Ossoli, Giovanni Angelo, 323
Ostend Manifesto, 354, 355
O'Sullivan, John L., 325, 326
Oswego, Fort, 126
Otis, James, 102, 103
Ottawa Indians, 96
Owen, Robert, 308
Owsley, Frank L., 369

P

Paine, Thomas, 87, 110, 111
Painting

genre painters, 306–307
Hudson River School, 305–306
neoclassicism in, 305
Pakenham, Sir Edward, 203
Palfrey, John Gorham, 78
Panama Railway Company, 354
Pan-American Congress (1825), 234
Panic. *See* Economic panic
Paper money, and election of 1868,
    426
Paris, Treaty of
  ending French and Indian War,
    94–95, 95(map)
  ending Revolutionary War, 133
Parishes, 62
Parliament, English, 10, 20
  and civil war, 41
  and colonization effort, 46–47
  and Glorious Revolution, 49
  and Massachusetts, 103
  relation with colonies, 99, 100
  struggles with king, 19–21
Parton, James, 258
Party platform, first, 255
Paterson, William, 154
Patriots, radical, 102, 106
Paxton expedition, 67, 74–75
Peabody, Elizabeth, 321
Peace Democrats. *See* Copperheads
Peacemaker, 114
Peace movement, 312
Penn, William, 42–44
Pennsylvania
  colonial government of, 88–89
  founding of, 43–44
  settlement of, 42–44
Pennsylvania, University of, 81
Pennsylvania Dutch, 66
Pensacola, 203
Pequot War, 39
Perfectionist settlement, 309
Perkins, Elizabeth Peck, 149
Perry, Comm. Matthew C., 274, 275
Perry, Capt. Oliver Hazard, 202, 205
"Personal liberty" laws, 346, 371
Pessen, Edward, 259
Peter Zenger case, 83
Petition of Right, 19–21
Philadelphia, 44
  and colonial trade, 63
  population growth in, 284
Philadelphia German Settlement

Society, 293
Philip II (king of Spain), 53
Philippines, trade with, 274
Philosophy
    democratic, 258
    of Enlightenment, 79
    transcendentalism, 299–301
Pickens, Francis W., 374
Pickering, John, 185
Pickering, Timothy, 175, 176, 190
Pickett, Gen. George E., 403
Pierce, Franklin
    election as president, 353
    foreign policy of, 353–356
Pietists, German, 73
Pike, Lt. Zebulon, 190
Pile, Howard, 237
Pilgrims, 22, 35, 36
Pinckney, C. C., 175, 176
Pinckney, Charles, 230
Pinckney, Thomas, 170, 173
Pinckney's treaty (1795), 170, 185
Pinkney, William, 193
Pioneering, views on, 140, 141
Pitcairn, Maj. John, 108
Pitcher, Molly, 148
Pitt, William, 94, 96
Pittsburgh, Pennsylvania, 226
Pizarro, Francisco, 16–17
Plains Indians, 5. See also Indians
Plantation system, 58–59, 278
Plessy v. Ferguson, 432, 433
Plymouth Colony, 35–37
Plymouth Company, 26
Pocahontas, 29, 30, 54
Pocket veto, 242
Poe, Edgar Allan, 303, 304–305, 322
Political convention, first national,
    254–255
Political parties. See also specific
        parties
    beginnings of, 172–178
    third, 344
Politics
    "dark-horse" candidates, 332
    democratization of, 238–239, 263
    Jacksonian, 241–246
    "petticoat," 249–250
    racist, 432
    spoils system, 241–242
Polk, James Knox, 353
    domestic policy of, 333

election as president, 332
    on Mexican War, 340
    and Oregon controversy, 333
Polk corollary, to Monroe Doctrine,
    340
Pollard, Edward, 437
Poll tax, 432, 433
Ponce de León, Juan, 16
Pontiac, Chief, 96
Poor Richard's Almanack, 83
Pope, Gen. John, 399
Population growth, in American
        colonies, 58
Port Royal, Nova Scotia, 90
Portsmouth, Rhode Island, 41, 68
Portugal
    early exploration by, 13
    and Treaty of Tordesillas, 17
Postmaster general, 161
Potter, David M., 370
Powers, Hiram, 307
Powhatan, 54
Powhatan Indians, 29, 31
Preble, Comm. Edward, 192
Predestination, doctrine of, 12
Preemption Act (1841), 271
Presbyterian church, 73
    in colonial America, 75
    and reform movements, 308
Presidency
    Congress and, 415–416
    constitutional provision for, 155
President (ship), 197
Presidios, 337
Prevost, Sir George, 203
Primogeniture, 135
Princeton, Battle of, 123
Princeton University, 81
Printing press, invention of, 13
Prison system, reform in, 311
Proclamation of Amnesty and
        Reconstruction, 413, 415
Proclamation of 1763, 96–97
Protestantism. See also specific
        churches
    Reformation, 10–13
    spread of, 12–13
Public school system. See also
        Education
    in South, 438
Pueblo Indians, 5
Puget Sound area, 335

Pulaski, Casimir, 121
Puritanism
    challenges to, 76–77
    historical perspective on, 78
    and Unitarianism, 299
Puritans, 13
    and Dominion of New England, 49
    early settlement of, 37–39
    government of, 39
    in New World, 22
    Quakers persecuted by, 43–44
    witchcraft trials, 77

Q

Quakers, 43–44, 80, 312
    and American Indians, 75
    in Philadelphia, 64
    women among, 72
Quartering Act (1765), 98, 102
Quebec, 18
    British capture of, 94
Quebec Act (1774), 105–106
Queen Anne's War, 90
Quids, 191
Quitrent, 31

R

Racism
    and Emancipation Proclamation,
        401
    and free blacks, 280
    and public school system, 438
    and Reconstruction, 425
Railroads
    and Civil War, 388
    early, 272–274
    and Gadsden Purchase, 355
Raleigh, Sir Walter, 26
Randall, James G., 369
Randolph, Edmund, 153, 159, 161
Randolph, Edward, 48
Randolph, John, 190
Randolph, Peyton, 106
Readers, McGuffey's, 309, 310
Reconstruction, 420(map)
    Congress and presidency during,
        417–422
    Congressional plans for, 417–426
    and education, 436–439
    end of, 423–426, 431

freedmen during, 415–417
historical perspective on, 425
under Andrew Johnson, 415
Lincoln's plan for, 412–413
radical, 419–423
Republican views on, 418
Reconstruction Acts (1867, 1868),
419, 420
Reed, Esther, 149
Reeder, Andrew H., 358
Reform. *See also* Social reform
Tocqueville on, 296
Reform movements
abolitionist, 314–318
educational, 309
model communities, 308–309
peace, 312
prisons and mental hospitals, 311
temperance, 311–312
women's, 312–314
Regulators, 73
Relief Act (1821), 226
Religion. *See also specific
denominations*
and art, 305
in colonial America, 75–79
and colonization, 22, 26
and Enlightenment, 80
in Maryland, 33
in New England, 35
of North American Indians, 5
Quakerism, 44
in Rhode Island, 40
Second Great Awakening, 297–298
in sixteenth-century Europe, 11
Tocqueville on, 296–297
Renaissance, 13
Republican party
and election of 1856, 360
origins of, 357
Republicans, Democratic
(Jeffersonian party), 172
composition of, 173
dissolution of, 232
and election of 1824, 231
increase in popularity of, 177
Republicans, radical. *See also*
Reconstruction
and Lincoln's reconstruction
program, 413
and Union military policy, 386–387
Revere, Paul, 83, 108

Revivalism
of antebellum period, 297–298
of colonial era, 79
Revolution, American
historical perspective on, 108–109
social reform of, 134–135
women in, 146–149
Revolution, French, American
reaction to, 166–167
Revolutionary War, 120–133
campaigns of, 122–127,
124–125(map)
causes of, 102–112
French alliance, 127–129
military and financial problems,
120–121
peace negotiations, 132–133
strategic advantages of colonies,
121–122
Treaty of Paris, 133
Rhee, Syngman, 759
Rhode Island
colonial government of, 88–89, 90
during Confederation period, 143
Constitution ratified by, 160
founding of, 40
Rhodes, James Ford, 368
Rice, Rev. David, 297
Richmond, Virginia, 394, 405,
410–411
fight for, 394
North's occupation of, 405
Rifle Clubs, 424
Rimini, Robert V., 259
Ripley, C. Peter, 425
Ripley, George, 309
Roanoke Island, 26
Roark, James L., 417
Roman Catholic church, and
Protestant Reformation, 10. *See
also* Catholic church
Rosecrans, Major Gen. William S.,
402, 404
Rousseau, Jean Jacques, 114
Rubber industry, 283
Rule of 1756, 168
Rush, Richard, 217
Rush-Bagot agreement (1817), 205
Russworm, John, 280
Rutgers College, 81
Rutledge, Edward, 123
Rutman, Darrett B., 78

S

Sac Indians, 246
Sacajawea, 188
Sacramento Valley, 339
St. Augustine, Florida, fort at, 18
St. Clair, Arthur, 169
St. Leger, Col. Barry, 126
Salem, Massachusetts
settlement of, 37
witchcraft trials in, 77
Samson, Deborah, 147–148
San Diego, 338
San Francisco, 338, 339, 345
population growth in, 285
Sandys, Sir Edwin, 31
Sanford, John A., 361
Sanitation, and urban growth, 285
Santa Anna, Gen. Antonio Lopez de,
330, 340, 341, 342
Santa Barbara, 338
Santa Fe, 337, 341
Santo Domingo, 187
Saratoga, Battle of, 127, 128
Savannah, Georgia, British capture
of, 130
"Scalawags," 422
Scarlet Letter, The (Hawthorne),
302, 304
Schlesinger, Arthur M., Jr., 258, 369
Schools. *See also* Education
influence of immigrants on, 293
public, 310 (*see also* Public school
system)
Schumacher, Ferdinand, 293
Science. *See also* Technology
during colonial era, 82
Scorched-earth policy, of Civil War,
404, 406
Scotch-Irish
immigration to middle colonies of,
66
spread of, 73
Scott, Dred, 360–361
Scott, Gen. Winfield
and election of 1852, 353
and Civil War, 374, 392, 393, 395
and Mexican War, 341–342
and War of 1812, 203
Sculpture, pre-Civil War, 307. *See
also* Art
Second Confiscation Act (1862), 400

Sectionalism. *See also* Frontier; North; South
  after 1812, 224–225
  and election of 1848, 344
  and industrialization, 284
  during Jackson's presidency, 246–251
  and Kansas-Nebraska Act, 357
  and protective tariff, 211
Sedition Act (1798), 176, 183
Segregation. *See also* Desegregation
  Plessy v. *Ferguson* decision, 432, 433
  in public school system, 438–439
Seminole Indians, 246
Senate, U.S.
  constitutional provision for, 154
  and Johnson impeachment trial, 421–422
Seneca Falls, Women's Rights Conventions, 313, 586
Seneca Indians, 114
Separation of powers, principle of, 153–154, 155
Separatists, and Anglican church, 13, 25. *See also* Puritans
Serra, Father Junipero, 337
Seven Days' Campaign, 398–399
Seventh-Day Adventist church, 298
Seward, William H.
  as abolitionist, 317
  and Clay Compromise, 346
  and election of 1832, 254
  and election of 1860, 367
  and Emancipation Proclamation, 400
Sewing machine, invention of, 284
Seymour, Horatio, 386, 426
Shakers, 309
Shakespeare, William, 13
Shannon, William, 358
Sharecropping system, 417
Sharkey, R. P., 425
Shays, Capt. Daniel, 144
Shays's Rebellion, 143–144
Sheffield, Lord, 138
Shelburne, Lord, 132
Sherman, Gen. Tecumseh, 393, 404, 405, 406
Sherman, Roger, 111
Shiloh, Battle of, 396
Shipbuilding industry, 9, 142
Siam, trade with, 274

Simkins, Francis B., 425
Simms, William Gilmore, 301
Singer, Isaac, 284
Sioux Indians, 7–8
Slater, Samuel, 218
Slave trade
  abolition of, 277
  in Chesapeake Bay area colonies, 33
  Continental Congress's abolishment of, 134
  in District of Columbia, 346
  of Spanish colonies, 18
Slavery
  and annexation of Texas, 331, 332
  black response to, 281–283
  and compromise of 1850, 348, 352
  and Constitutional Convention, 154
  and election of 1824, 231–232
  and election of 1860, 366
  and Emancipation Proclamation, 399–401
  growth of, 277–283
  historical perspective on, 369–370
  inhumanity of, 280–281
  introduction of, 58–61
  and Mexican War, 344
  and Missouri Compromise, 227–231
  vs. segregation, 439
  Southern defense of, 317–318
  Nat Turner's rebellion, 281–282
  and Underground Railroad, 281–282, 282(map)
Slaves
  organization of, 278
  revolts of, 230, 281–282
Slidell, John, 341, 390
Slums, 285. *See also* Housing
Smelling Committee, 421
Smith, Adam, 80
Smith, Capt. John, 27
  leader of Jamestown settlement, 29–30, 52–55
  quoted, 26, 30
Smith, Joseph, 298, 337
Smith, Sydney, 301
Social reform, after Revolutionary War, 134–135
Social stratification
  of colonial society, 58, 68
  and plantation system, 278

Society of Friends. *See* Quakers
Songhai, kingdom of, 61
Sons of Liberty, 99, 100, 102, 103
Soulé, Pierre, 354
South. *See also* Sectionalism
  agriculture in, 277
  and attempted acquisition of Cuba, 354
  class structure in, 277–278
  and Constitutional Convention, 154
  cotton economy of, 219–220
  economic interests of, 224–226
  economic recovery of, 417
  industrialization in, 283, 284
  and Missouri Compromise, 228
  and protective tariff, 226, 247
  under Radical Reconstruction, 422–423
  railroad building in, 274
  Reconstruction of, 420(map)
  revivalism in, 298
  ruling elite in, 431
  secession of, 346, 371–373
  and tariffs, 233
  white supremacists in, 423, 424
South Carolina
  British capture of, 130
  colonization of, 44–45
  economic depression in, 247, 248
  and protective tariff, 250
  during Reconstruction, 415
  secession of, 350–351, 371
South Carolina Redshirts, 424
Southern colonies
  aristocracy of, 62–63
  education in, 81
  introduction of slavery in, 59
  plantation system of, 58–59
Southern Pacific Railroad, 469, 470
Spain
  and American Revolution, 128–129, 139
  cession of Florida to U.S., 214–215
  colonial government of, 18
  early exploration by, 13–16
  Mississippi River controlled by, 138–139
  monarchy of, 9
  overseas settlements of, 16–17
  Pinckney's treaty with, 170, 185
  and Treaty of Paris, 95
  and Treaty of Tordesillas, 17

and wealth from New World, 17–18
Spanish Armada, 13
Specie Circular, 256
Spice trade, Portugal's control of, 13
Spoils system
    of Jackson's administration, 241–242
Spreckels, Claus, 293
Squanto, 35
Squatters' rights, 271
"Stalwarts" (Republican faction), 430
Stamp Act (1765), 98, 100–101
Stamp Act Congress, 99–101
Stampp, Kenneth, 281, 369, 425
Standard of living
    on frontier, 271–272
    of Southern slaves, 281
Standish, Capt. Miles, 35
Stanton, Edwin M., 421
Stanton, Elizabeth Cady, 313
State Department, 161. See also Foreign policy
States
    post–Revolutionary War debts, 164–166
    ratifying conventions of, 156, 157–160
    and Virginia and Kentucky Resolutions, 177
    western territorial claims of, 137
States' rights
    and Articles of Confederation, 136
    and Confederacy, 384, 385
    and draft, 391
    and Jackson's bank veto, 254
    and Jackson's presidency, 249
    during Reconstruction, 419
    and Supreme Court, 263
    and "War Hawks," 197
State of the Union speech, first, 161
Stay laws, 143
Steamboats, 221–222
Stearns, J. B., 153
Steel industry, early growth of, 283
Stephens, Alexander H., 384, 385
Steuben, Baron Friedrich von, 121, 131
Stevens, Thaddeus, 254, 386, 413, 418, 422
Stowe, Harriet Beecher, 314, 352
Strikes. See also Union movement
    of Lowell girls, 287

Lynn shoemakers', 287
Sturges v. Crowninshield, 214
Stuyvesant, Peter, 42
Suffolk Resolves, 106
Suffrage
    black, 280, 416–417, 418, 424
    liberalization of, 238
Sugar Act (1764), 98
Sumner, Charles, 428
    as abolitionist, 317
    Brooks-Sumner affair, 359
    declining influence of, 422
    quoted, 401
    as Radical Republican leader, 413
    Reconstruction views of, 418
Sumner, William Graham, 258
Sumter, Fort, attack on, 372–375
Supreme Court
    Charles River Bridge v. Warren Bridge, 263
    Cherokee Nation v. Georgia, 245
    Cohens v. Virginia, 213
    Commonwealth v. Hunt, 287
    constitutional provision for, 155
    Dartmouth College v. Woodward, 214
    Dred Scott v. Sanford, 361
    establishment of, 162
    Fletcher v. Peck, 214
    Gibbons v. Ogden, 213
    Guinn v. United States, 433
    McCulloch v. Maryland, 213, 254
    Marbury v. Madison, 184–185, 213
    on national bank, 256
    Plessy v. Ferguson, 432, 433
    Sturges v. Crowninshield, 214
    Williams v. Mississippi, 433
    Worcester v. Georgia, 245
Symposium Club, 321

T

Talleyrand-Perigord, Prince de, 175, 176
Tallmadge, James, Jr., 228, 229
Tammany Hall, 291, 429

Taney, Roger B., 255, 263, 361
Tariff. See also Economy
    in Civil War, 389
    during Grant administration, 427
    during Jackson administration, 247
    nullification controversy, 250–251
    and Panic of 1819, 226
    sectionalism and, 211, 224–225, 226–227
    southern support of, 226
    Walker, 333
Tariff Act (1792), 166
Tariff of 1816, 226
Tariff of 1828 (Tariff of Abominations), 233, 240
Tariff of 1842, 327
Tariff of 1857, 363
Taxation, without representation, 98
Taylor, Edward, 82
Taylor, Zachary, 341, 343
    and Compromise of 1850, 347
    election as president, 344
Tea Act (1773), 105
Tea tax, 103
Tecumseh, 198, 200, 201, 202, 205
Telegraph lines, and railroad expansion, 273
Temperance movement, 311–312
Tender laws, 143
Tennant, Gilbert, 78
Tennessee
    during Civil War, 396
    secession of, 387
    settlement of, 97
    statehood, 170
Tenochtitlán, 4
Ten-Percent Plan, 413, 415, 417
Tenskwatawa, 200
Tenure of Office Act (1867), 421, 422
Texas
    annexation of, 329–333
    independence of, 330–332
    during Reconstruction, 417, 420
    secession of, 371
    settlement of, 329–330
    statehood, 332–333
Textile industry
    industrialization of, 218–219
    labor in, 286
    and wool growers, 226
Thames, Battle of, 202
Thirty-nine Articles (1571), 13
Thomas, Jane, 149

Thoreau, Henry David, 302–303
Tilden, Samuel J., 430, 431
Timberlake, Peggy O'Neale, 249–250
Tippecanoe, Battle of, 200
Tobacco industry
  and colonial trade, 31
  labor in, 33
  overproduction in, 98
  after revolution, 143
  in southern colonies, 59
Tocqueville, Alexis de, 246, 296
Toleration Act (1649), 33, 49
Tordesillas, Treaty of, 17
Tories, 120
  at Kings Mountain, 130
  in South, 130
Town meeting, 39, 66
Towns. See also Cities
  New England, 37
Townshend, Charles, 101
Townshend Acts (1767), 101–102, 103
Trade
  during Confederation period,
    142–143
  effect on colonization, 9
  and Embargo Act, 195
  expansion of foreign, 274–275
  growth of domestic, 275
  and Navigation Acts, 48
  and Panic of 1837, 256–257
  and protective tariffs, 211
  spice, 13
  West Indian, 234
Trade unions, pre-Civil War, 287.
  See also Union movement
Trail of Tears, 245–246
Transatlantic cable, 274
Transcendentalism, 299–301, 308,
  309, 321
Transcontinental Treaty (1819),
  215–216, 216(map)
Transportation. See also Highways
  and agricultural expansion, 277
  canal system, 222–224, 223(map)
  clipper ships, 274
  in colonial era, 70
  and domestic trade, 275
  early railroads, 272–274 (see also
    Railroads)
  national program for
    improvements in, 212
  steamboats, 221–222
  turnpikes, 221, 223(map)

and urban growth, 284–286
Transylvania Company, 97
Travis, Col. W. B., 330
Treaty of Fort Greenville (1795),
  170
Treaty of Ghent (1814), 205
Treaty of Guadalupe Hidalgo (1848),
  343
Treaty of London (Jay's treaty)
  (1794), 169–170, 175
Treaty of Paris (1763), 94–95,
  95(map)
Treaty of Paris (1783), 133
Treaty of Tordesillas (1494), 17
Trent (ship), 390
Trenton, Battle of, 123, 126
Trist, Nicholas, 342–343
Tubman, Harriet, 315, 378–381
Turner, Frederick Jackson, 70, 258
Turner, Nat, 281, 283
Turnpikes, 221. See also Highways
Turnverein, 293
Tweed, William, 429
Two-party system, origins of,
  257–263
Tyler, John, 261, 327
Tyler, Royall, 301
Type foundry, 285

U

Uncle Tom's Cabin (Stowe), 314, 352
"Underground Railroad," 281,
  282(map), 315, 379–380
Union. See also Civil War; North
  army raised by, 391–392
  military commanders of, 393
  at outset of Civil War, 387
  resources of, 388
Union party, 406
Unitarianism, 299, 308
United States
  on eve of Civil War, 375(map)
  1854, 270(map)
Universities
  in colonial period, 80–81, 82
  opened to women, 314, 321
Upshur, Abel P., 332
Utah
  Mormons in, 337
  statehood, 337
Utopian experiments, 308–309

V

Vallandigham, C. L., 386
Valley Forge, Continental Army at,
  129–130
Van Buren, Martin, 233, 240, 317
  campaign of, 261, 262
  election of, 260
  and election of 1848, 344, 345
  and "petticoat politics," 249–250
  presidency of, 261
Vancouver Island, 335
Vanderbilt, "Commodore" Cornelius,
  354
Van Deusen, Glyndon, 259
Vergennes, Comte de, 128, 132, 133
Vermont
  admission to Union, 138
  during American Revolution, 127
  "personal liberty law" of, 352
Verranzano, Giovanni da, 18
Vesey, Denmark, 230
Vespucci, Amerigo, 16
Vetoes, presidential
  Jackson's bank, 254
  pocket, 242, 413
Vicksburg, siege of, 404
Virginia. See also Jamestown
  committees of correspondence in,
    104
  constitution adopted by, 159
  House of Burgesses, 34
  overproduction of tobacco in, 34
  during Reconstruction, 420
  secession of, 387
  tobacco economy of, 33
Virginia Company, 26
Virginia Plan, 153
Virginia Resolutions, 176–177
Voltaire, Francois Marie Arouet de,
  114
Voting. See also Suffrage
  Black Codes and, 416–417
  "grandfather laws" and, 432, 433
  Jacksonian liberalization of,
    238–239
  in state constitutions, 134

W

Wabash and Erie canals, 224
Wade-Davis bill, 413

Walden (Thoreau), 302
Walker, Robert J., 362
Walker, William, 354
Walker Tariff (1846), 333
Wampanoag Indians, 39
Wanghia, Treaty of, 274
Ward, John, 259
War of 1812
  British attack, 202–203
  and Canada campaign, 201–202
  declaration of, 200
  effects of, 205
  and Hartford Convention, 203
  naval war, 202
  northern campaigns of, 199(map)
  postwar diplomacy, 204
  "War Hawks," 197–198, 210
Warr, Lord de La, 54
Warre, Henry, 334
Warren, Mercy Otis, 147, 148
Washington, Booker T., 432, 433
Washington, D.C.
  burning of, 203
  capital established in, 164
Washington, George
  as commander in chief, 109, 121
  Congress and, 160–161
  at Constitutional Convention, 152, 153
  Farewell Address, 173
  at First Continental Congress, 106, 107
  in French and Indian Wars, 92–93
  and Jay's treaty, 170
  neutrality policy of, 168
  presidency of, 160–161
  quoted, 97, 139
  reaction to Shays's Rebellion, 144
  at Valley Forge, 129–130
  at Yorktown, 131, 132
Washington Post, 838
Wayne, Gen. "Mad" Anthony, 169
Webster, Daniel, 233, 248, 249, 353
  and compromise of 1850, 346, 347
  election of 1836, 260
  and Jacksonian presidency, 242
  and Maine boundary dispute, 328–329
  on national bank, 252
Webster, Noah, 178
Webster-Ashburton treaty, 327–329, 329(map)
Weld, Theodore Dwight, 315

Welles, Gideon, 397
West, *See also* Frontier; Sectionalism
  economic interests of, 225
  industrialization in, 283, 284
  and protective tariff, 227
  and railroads, 272–274
  revivalism in, 298
  settlement in, 268–272
West Indian trade, during Jacksons' presidency, 243
West Virginia
  and Civil War, 387
  statehood, 387
Whaling, 274
Wheat production, 276
Wheatley, Phyllis, 301
Whigs, and election of 1836, 260
  and election of 1852, 353
  and Mexican War, 341, 343
  origins of, 257
  Rockingham, 96, 100
  and Tyler presidency, 327
Whiskey Rebellion, 170–171
"Whiskey Ring" scandal, 429
Whiskey tax, 183
White, Hugh Lawson, 260
White Brotherhood, 423
White Leagues, 424
Whitefield, George, 78
Whitman, Walt, 296, 302, 303
Whitney, Eli, 218, 219, 220
Wigglesworth, Michael, 82
Wilburn, Jean A., 259
Wilde, Oscar, 285
Wilderness Road, 221
Wilkes, Capt. Charles, 390
Wilkinson, Gen. James, 139, 191
Willamette Valley, 334
William III (King of England), 49, 98
William and Mary College, 81
Williams, Roger, 40, 76
Williams v. *Mississippi*, 433
Wilmot, David, 344
Wilmot Proviso, 344, 345, 346
Wilson, Charles E., 772
Wiltse, Charles M., 258
Winthrop, John, 37, 39, 78, 80
Wirt, William, 254
Wise, John, 82
Witchcraft trials, 77
Wolcott, Oliver, 175
Wolfe, Gen. James, 94

Woman in the Nineteenth Century (Fuller), 321–322
Women
  in American Revolution, 146–149
  in antebellum period, 288
  and Civil War, 388–389
  in colonial America, 31, 70–72
  and education, 310, 314, 321
  in Iroquois political system, 114–115
  in labor force, 467, 493, 494–495
  right to divorce of, 134–135
  suffrage for, 238
  in textile industry, 286
Women's Medical College of Pennsylvania, 314
Women's movement, pre-Civil War, 312–314
Wood, Gordon S., 159
Woodbury, Levi, 233
Woodward, C. Vann, 425
Woody, Robert, 425
Worcester v. *Georgia*, 245
Workers. *See also* Labor union movement
  in early nineteenth century, 286
Workingmen's party, 255
Wren, Christopher, 83
Wright, Jonathan Jasper, 423

X

XYZ Affair, 175–176

Y

Yale College, 81
Yellow fever, 285, 572. *See also* Disease
Yemassee, The (Simms), 301
York, 188
York, Duke of, 42. *See also* James II
Yorktown, Battle of, 130–132
Young, Brigham, 337, 338
Young, Owen D., 713

Z

Zenger, Peter, 83
Zoology, 82
Zuni Indians, 5